CAMBRIDGE]

Books o,

MW01139159

Religion

For centuries, scripture and theology were the focus of prodigious amounts of
scholarship and publishing, dominated in the English-speaking world by the work
of Protestant Christians. Enlightenment philosophy and science, anthropology,
ethnology and the colonial experience all brought new perspectives, lively debates
and heated controversies to the study of religion and its role in the world, many
of which continue to this day. This series explores the editing and interpretation
of religious texts, the history of religious ideas and institutions, and not least the
encounter between religion and science.

Adversus Judaeos

A. Lukyn Williams (1853–1943) presents here a wide range of examples of Christian
apologetic writings about Judaism. Taking material from the earliest years of the
Christian Church until the Renaissance, the book investigates sources with Syriac,
Greek, Spanish, and Latin origins. It includes observations on lost or possible books
such as the first 'Book of Testimonies' posited by J. Rendel Harris (with whom
Williams did not fully agree) which pre-dated the Biblical Gospels; incomplete
early treatises; and scriptural extracts. Concerned more with historical detail than
with exegesis, Williams' study provides extensive scholarly commentaries on all the
texts included and covers possible dates of origin, sources, intended audience, and
biographical information about the authors. First published in 1935 with the aim of
offering source material in an area often neglected by scholars, the book remains a
useful resource for students and scholars of Christian–Jewish relations.

Cambridge University Press has long been a pioneer in the reissuing of out-of-print titles from its own backlist, producing digital reprints of books that are still sought after by scholars and students but could not be reprinted economically using traditional technology. The Cambridge Library Collection extends this activity to a wider range of books which are still of importance to researchers and professionals, either for the source material they contain, or as landmarks in the history of their academic discipline.

Drawing from the world-renowned collections in the Cambridge University Library and other partner libraries, and guided by the advice of experts in each subject area, Cambridge University Press is using state-of-the-art scanning machines in its own Printing House to capture the content of each book selected for inclusion. The files are processed to give a consistently clear, crisp image, and the books finished to the high quality standard for which the Press is recognised around the world. The latest print-on-demand technology ensures that the books will remain available indefinitely, and that orders for single or multiple copies can quickly be supplied.

The Cambridge Library Collection brings back to life books of enduring scholarly value (including out-of-copyright works originally issued by other publishers) across a wide range of disciplines in the humanities and social sciences and in science and technology.

Adversus Judaeos

*A Bird's-Eye View of Christian
Apologiae Until the Renaissance*

A. LUKYN WILLIAMS

CAMBRIDGE
UNIVERSITY PRESS

CAMBRIDGE UNIVERSITY PRESS

Cambridge, New York, Melbourne, Madrid, Cape Town,
Singapore, São Paolo, Delhi, Mexico City

Published in the United States of America by Cambridge University Press, New York

www.cambridge.org
Information on this title: www.cambridge.org/9781108039680

© in this compilation Cambridge University Press 2012

This edition first published 1935
This digitally printed version 2012

ISBN 978-1-108-03968-0 Paperback

ADVERSUS JUDAEOS

The statues of the Church and Synagogue at Strasbourg, the former standing upright with cross in one hand and chalice in the other, and the latter in a dejected attitude with bandaged eyes, broken staff and the tables of the law falling from her left hand.

From P. Weber, *Geistliches Schauspiel und Kirchliche Kunst*, by permission of Paul Neff Verlag.

ADVERSUS JUDAEOS

A BIRD'S-EYE VIEW OF CHRISTIAN *APOLOGIAE* UNTIL THE RENAISSANCE

by

A. LUKYN WILLIAMS, D.D.

HON. CANON OF ELY

CAMBRIDGE
AT THE UNIVERSITY PRESS
1935

LONDON
Cambridge University Press
FETTER LANE

NEW YORK · TORONTO
BOMBAY · CALCUTTA · MADRAS
Macmillan

TOKYO
Maruzen Company Ltd

PRINTED IN GREAT BRITAIN

IN MEMORIAM
FRANCISCI CRAWFORD BURKITT, D.D.
IN UNIVERSITATE CANTABRIGIENSI
PROFESSORIS NORRISIANI
RELIGIOSI ERUDITI
AMICI MAECENATIS
MEDIO IN LABORE ABREPTI
AD MAIOREM DEI GLORIAM

CONTENTS

* = of special interest; H = the author knew Hebrew; J = the author knew Judaism; [ ] = but only slightly.

BOOK II. *THE SYRIAC WRITERS*

ADVERSUS JUDAEOS

I regret that although I originally intended to include some remarks on the following Treatises I inadvertently failed to do so.

A.L.W.

March 1936

GREEK

Euthymius Zigabenus, monk at Constantinople, † after 1118. *Panoplia*, ch. viii. Migne, *P.G.* cxxx. 258–306. Academic. Quotations from earlier Fathers.

LATIN

Fulbert, Bp of Chartres, † 1028. *Tractatus C. Judaeos. P.L.* cxli. 306–318. Slight; on Gen. xlix. 10. Some Jews suppose it to refer to the authority of Jewish householders.

William of Champeaux, Bp of Châlons-sur-Marne, † 1121. *Dialogus sive Altercatio cujusdam Christiani cum Judaeo de fide Catholica. P.L.* clxiii. 1045–1072 (in *opuscula dubia*). Interesting (e.g. the Nut, coll. 1048D).

Guibert of Nogent, † not later than 1124. *Tractatus de Incarnatione adversus Judaeos. P.L.* clvi. 490–527. Academic.

Odo, Bp of Cambrai, † 1135. *Disputatio c. Judaeum Leonem nomine de adventu Christi filii Dei. P.L.* clx. 1103–1112. About the Atonement, and a little about the Virginity of B.V.M. Interesting, probably based on a real discussion.

Rupert of Deutz, † 1135. *Annulus sive Dialogus inter Christianum et Judaeum. P.L.* clxx. 561–610. (3rd Book.) Apparently only academic.

Richard of St Victor, † 1173. *De Emmanuele libri duo. P.L.* cxcvi. 601–666. On Isa. vii. 14 only.

Walter de Meula de Castellione, † c. 1200. *Tractatus sive Dialogus magistri Gualteri Turnacensis et Balduini Valentianensis c. Judaeos. P.L.* ccix. 423–458.

Alanus de Insulis, † 1203. *Contra haereticos libri quattuor. Liber tertius c. Judaeos. P.L.* ccx. 399–422.

PREFACE

I thank my many friends and acquaintances who have suffered my importunity in seeking information from them: in particular Mr Herbert Loewe, Reader in Rabbinics in the University of Cambridge; Dr E. J. Thomas, of the University Library; and my old friend and pupil, the Rev. L. Zeckhausen, of the Church Missions to Jews.

I am also most grateful to the Managers of the Hort Fund, to the University Press, and especially to Dr F. C. Burkitt (whose loss is deplored by the whole University), for substantial assistance in the publication of this book, and to the Editors of the *Church Quarterly Review* and the *Churchman* for permission to use three or four papers published in their journals.

Since my manuscript was completed Dr James Parkes has published the first volume of his comprehensive survey of *The Conflict of the Church and the Synagogue: a study in the origins of antisemitism* (1934). At first I was afraid that he would have made my own work superfluous. But our aims are so different that this is not the case. He has attempted "to present all, not a selection, of the known facts of Jewish-Christian relations", laying special stress on the legislation affecting the Jews in the first eight or nine centuries of our era. My study is very limited, and is concerned solely with the endeavours of certain Churchmen to win Jews to Christ by their writings, or, at least, to protect Christians against the arguments of their Jewish neighbours. The two books are complementary. Dr Parkes concludes that Anti-Semitism is almost entirely the fault of the Church. I am concerned to show that she did take an intellectual, and often a devout, interest in the spiritual welfare of the Jews around her. After reading his book I have added a few references in the notes. I am also deeply indebted to him for calling my attention to an unpublished manuscript of Jacob of Serug, and for permitting me to use the information he gives about it.

A. L. W.

September 1935

INTRODUCTION

We Christians, who believe that our religion is the One Religion for Jews, Mohammedans and all the world, wonder sometimes what means our forefathers in the Faith used to present it to non-Christian peoples. The ordinary histories, no doubt, tell us of the courage and devotion with which they offered themselves for personal work in foreign lands, and of the marvellous success which was often granted to them. But of their literary efforts to further their cause we are told comparatively little.

Nowhere is this more true than in work among the Jews. Every one knows that Justin Martyr wrote in the middle of the second century a *Dialogue with Trypho*, a document purporting to give an account of his discussion with a Jew whom he met at Ephesus, and, in fact, showing first-hand knowledge of the difficulties felt by Jews in accepting Christianity. But most readers stop there, and many even suppose that Christians did little more by their writings to convince Jews of the truth until the beginning of the nineteenth century. The fact, of course, is that innumerable treatises were composed throughout the whole interval.

The present volume is an attempt to indicate briefly the nature of some of these treatises, as well as the circumstances which called them forth. For it is unfitting that the learning and zeal of the authors of such books should be forgotten. Another reason indeed might be suggested, that the study of these documents will not only recall to the minds of readers their duty to the Jewish nation, but also supply arguments likely to be of assistance in their presentation of the Faith. But, to speak candidly, these writings are not of as much practical help as might have been expected. The arguments too often resemble the armour of mediaeval knights to be of any use to twentieth-century protagonists. Here and there, no doubt, a weapon may be found, which, though blunted by long and unskilful usage, may, when sharpened in its edge or modified in its form, prove of some value. But, in general, the missionary of to-day will find little in these old writers which he can still dare to use. Modern weapons in our spiritual warfare are not only different, but, for our own day, incomparably better.

The origin of this book lies in some lectures given many years ago to a class of young men preparing for Christian work among the Jews. For it was desirable that they should know something of what others had done before them, and both learn the mistakes of their predecessors, and also perhaps find some hints as to the best method of approach to those whom they desired to serve. But I was appointed to another sphere of work, and my lectures had perforce to cease, and although I kept an eye open for allusions to the subject, it was only long afterwards that I had leisure and opportunity to return seriously to it.

What then has been written with the object either of winning Jews to Christ, or, at least, of enabling Christians both to understand and to withstand the attacks of Jews upon the Christian Faith? For Jews have never been backward in attack. It will be self-understood that it was not possible to include in our study of the subject such casual expositions of Old Testament passages as are to be found in commentaries or in sermons, even though many of the commentators and preachers have had Jews expressly in mind. It has therefore been necessary to confine the study to whole treatises directly or indirectly concerned with Jews and Judaism.

Yet even here there have been further limitations.

For I have been unable either to see the many manuscripts preserved in various libraries, whether published or not, or to obtain photographs of them. This book therefore deals only with such treatises as were written from the first century of our era to the beginning of the Renaissance, and are available in print. It is also probable that I have not been able to trace even some of these, particularly if they have been published in languages of which I have no knowledge.

It will also be understood that it is not proposed to discuss the right or wrong use of the specific passages quoted by any author from the Old Testament. That is the task of the Bible commentator. Yet the relation of their use in general to the modern methods of interpretation will be apparent on almost every page.

It must be confessed that the subject appeals at first sight only to students of the Bible; or, rather, only to that small section of these which takes an interest in the historical development of Biblical exegesis, and again, and more particularly, to those very few students who desire to apply their knowledge of the Bible to the Christian's task of winning all nations (including the Jewish nation) to faith in Christ.

Yet the subject may well appeal to a much wider class of readers. For example, the present writer, at least, has wished again and again that he had a good knowledge of Roman Law, and also of the gradual development of the Latin tongue into the Romance languages; and, again, that he had mastered the geographical and ethnological peculiarities of Syria and Mesopotamia; also, that he understood more of the relations of the Syrian Church to that of Southern Egypt during the fourth to the seventh century; and, again, that he was well acquainted with the history of early mediaeval "France", and the character of its society; and even that he knew more of the origins of the Drama in Northern Europe; and, further, that he had an intimate acquaintance with the history of the latter years of the Eastern Empire.

Besides such details there has continuously been before him the question of the Bible text used by the Christian writers, whether this were of the precise form of the Greek version of the Old Testament which they used, or that of the Syriac version of the New Testament, or even that of the Latin versions, Old Latin or Vulgate. Philosophy, also, as it developed for better or for worse, has had its claims, and, naturally, the growth of Jewish, and especially of Jewish Antichristian, interpretation of the Scriptures. All these subjects have had to be considered by the author, and his attempts to study them have, at least, shown him his own ignorance of "what every schoolboy knows". Yet as he himself has experienced their absorbing interest, so he hopes that some of this may be shared by his readers. In every case he has tried to indicate where fuller information may be found.

It is not improbable that the reader may at first receive an impression of sameness as he studies the various treatises considered in this volume, but further examination will show him that there is not one among them which has not something peculiar to itself, something different from all its predecessors and successors. The writers are, in fact, no mere copyists of other men's productions. Indeed, it is very seldom that we are able to trace any copying at all. Whether this was due to distance, or to difference in language, or of moral environment, or, as is probable, to two or three of these causes together, is not clear. But such is the fact. Of course there is often a great similarity in the interpretation of Biblical passages, which has given rise to the rather careless assumption on the part of modern writers that the later author used the earlier; but in reality, as is often pointed out in the following pages, this affords little or no evidence of literary connexion, but only of the permanence of the same methods of interpreting Scripture which had prevailed in the Church almost, or quite, from the very first.

BOOK I

THE ANTE-NICENE FATHERS

CHAPTER I

THE EARLIEST BOOKS OF TESTIMONIES[1]
? c. A.D. 45

Dr Edwin Hatch appears to have been the first in modern times[2] to suggest—in 1889, the year of his death—that composite quotations from the Old Testament were derived from earlier collections of Bible passages. Speaking of the Jews he says: "It may naturally be supposed that a race which laid stress on moral progress, whose religious services had variable elements of both prayer and praise, and which was carrying on an active propaganda, would have, among other books, manuals of morals, of devotion, and of controversy. It may also be supposed, if we take into consideration the contemporary habit of making collections of *excerpta*, and the special authority which the Jews attached to their sacred books, that some of these manuals would consist of extracts from the Old Testament."[3]

In this, however, he is thinking solely of collections of extracts from the Old Testament made by Jews for Jewish edification and propaganda. It is curious that the next step, which seems so natural to us after it has been pointed out, was never in his mind, viz. Collections of "Extracts from the Old Testament" drawn up by Jewish Christians for controversy with Jews.[4]

Sanday and Headlam in 1895 developed the suggestion, when they thought that "the habit had probably arisen of quoting

---

[1] Parts of this paper were read at a meeting of the Victoria Institute in 1929, and are printed in the *Transactions*. I should like to say here, once for all, that, although I cannot accept Dr Rendel Harris' theory of *one* Book of Testimonies only, I gladly acknowledge my debt to his learning and research. I have used both parts of his *Testimonies* (1916 and 1920) very freely.

[2] Harnack says (*Hist. of Chr. Dogma*, edition 3, E.T. i. 175), "Hatch has taken up the hypothesis of earlier scholars." Perhaps he means Credner, *Beiträge zur Einl.* ii. 318–328. Cf. Moffatt, *Introd. to Lit. of N.T.* edition 3, 1918, pp. 23–25.

[3] *Essays in Biblical Greek*, 1889, p. 203.

[4] Harnack (*loc. cit.*) does not seem to go beyond Hatch. Sanday, however, as early as 1876, nearly came to this when he said: "We know that types and prophecies were eagerly sought out by the early Christians, and were soon collected in a kind of common stock from which every one drew at his pleasure" (*The Gospels in the Second Century*, p. 272).

passages to prove the calling of the Gentiles (evidently therefore
'the habit had arisen' among Jews who were Christians); and
these would become commonplaces, which at a not much later
date might be collected together in writing".[1]

Sanday and Headlam became more definite a few pages further
on, where, in considering the close relationship between St Paul's
and St Peter's quotations of Isa. xxviii. 16 (the Stone), they say:
"This may have arisen from St Peter's acquaintance with the
Romans; but another hypothesis may be suggested (observe that
this plainly is considered an original suggestion on their part),
which will perhaps account for the facts more naturally. We know
that to prove from the Scriptures that Jesus was the Christ was the
constant practice of the early Christians. Is it not possible that
even as early as this there may have been collections of Old
Testament texts used for controversial purposes arranged according
to their subjects, as were the latter *Testimonia* of Cyprian?"[2]

These words come so very close to the theory as it is expounded
by Dr Rendel Harris that we may assume that the suggestion was
at once accepted by him, and indeed marks the point from which
he started, whether he was aware of this or not.[3] His theory is
this: A Collection of texts from the Old Testament which bore
testimony to Christ and Christian teaching—hence called the *Book
of Testimonies*—was drawn up in very early times, indeed before
the composition of our present Gospels. It antedates "the four
Gospels, since it is earlier than the earliest of the four".[4] It pre-
cedes even St Paul's Epistles. It was "an Apostolic work, which
passed into obscurity."[5] "It was a *vade-mecum* for teachers, and
indeed for all who wished to answer objections made by Jews, and
to win them to the true faith."[6] "Apollos might come to Ephesus
with a minimum of luggage, and still be able to convince the Jews
publicly concerning Jesus Christ; but, without minishing the
scholarship of the great rival and colleague of St Paul, we may be

[1] On Rom. ix. 26, p. 264.   [2] On Rom. ix. 33, p. 282.
[3] Rendel Harris does not refer to Sanday and Headlam in *Test.* i. 3, but
passes from Hatch and Harnack to Dr Drummond (*Fourth Gospel*, 1903, p. 365),
who says: "It is conceivable that there may have grown up, whether in writing
or not, an anthology of passages useful in controversy, and that this affords
a possible explanation of the phenomena of the Johannine quotations."
[4] *Test.* i. 23. Box (*Centenary Bible, St Matthew*, 1922, p. 24) has a clear account
of this early "Messianic *florilegium*".
[5] *Test.* i. Introduction.
[6] It was "the propaganda material of a new religion" (*Test.* ii. 94).

sure that the average Christian man and woman had a slender
Biblical collection, and depended for the most part on the hand-
book, which was published under the name and authority of
St Matthew."[1]

Further, Dr Rendel Harris thinks, although the *Book of Testimonies* became gradually expanded and modified, it yet remained
essentially the same book, continuing in existence throughout the
first, second, third, and indeed many centuries, at least as late as
the twelfth, and perhaps to a time even later than the invention
of printing.[2]

The germs of the Christian appeal to the Old Testament are to
be found in our Lord's own teaching. He said, for example, that
Isaiah's words described the attitude of the Jewish Traditionalists
towards Him: *This people honoureth Me with their lips, but their heart
is far from Me.*[3] He also quoted Genesis as confirming His attitude
to the question of divorce.[4] Then, again, He quotes Ps. cxviii to
illustrate the treatment that He was already receiving, and was
about to receive, from the Jews, with the assurance of the ultimate
triumph that the psalm foretold of Him: *The Stone which the
builders rejected*, etc.[5] Further, He appeals to Ps. cx as a witness that
He held, after all, a higher relation towards David than might be
gathered from His earthly descent from him: *The LORD said unto
my Lord, Sit Thou on My right hand.*[6] It will have been noticed that
all these passages have been taken from the Gospel according to
St Mark, because that is certainly the earliest of the Four, and not
likely to contain references to Old Testament texts which were
adduced only by Apostolic or Evangelistic preachers, and, though
placed in our Lord's mouth, were not really spoken by Him. That

[1] *Test.* ii. 108.
[2] *Test.* i. 101. Two side-issues connected with this *Book of Testimonies* may
be mentioned, although to discuss them would take us too far from our main
objective.

A. J. H. A. Hart suggested in the *Expositor*, July, 1906, that the *Logia* of
Papias were such a Collection of Old Testament texts.

B. There is some slight evidence for attributing the *Book of Testimonies* to
St Matthew in the fact that a *Book of Testimonies* exists under the name of Matthew
the Monk. Although this, as it stands, belongs perhaps to the beginning of the
fourteenth century, there are some reasons for believing that the work underlying it was composed in quite early times. It is divided into five books like
Papias' Commentaries.

[3] Mark vii. 6 (see Isa. xxix. 13).   [4] Mark x. 7 (see Gen. ii. 24).
[5] Mark xii. 10 (see Ps. cxviii. 22 *sq.*).
[6] Mark xii. 36.

question, however, though of extreme importance and interest, is not before us.

But the real starting-point for us lies in the last chapter of St Luke. We are told there that on the walk to Emmaus and again shortly afterwards, our Lord showed to His disciples *from Moses and all the Prophets*, and again, *from the Law of Moses, and the Prophets, and the Psalms, the things concerning Himself.* He gave the testimony of *the Scriptures* to His sufferings, to His rising from the dead on the third day, and to the preaching of repentance and remission of sins to the Gentiles as well as to the Jews. From this passage it would appear that although our Lord had occasionally referred to the Old Testament in confirmation of His actions or teaching, and had indeed also, as we learn from other Gospels than St Mark's, especially indicated to His disciples some confirmation from the Old Testament of the fact that He should die and rise again, yet He had never put the whole case so fully and systematically before them as in that walk to Emmaus and at His subsequent appearance to the eleven. It was, for example, no part of the equipment of the twelve or the seventy when they were sent out through Galilee.

Rendel Harris is right when he says: "It is not possible to reduce this statement to a lower meaning than that the early Church believed that they had supreme authority for their method in dealing with the Old Testament, and that this authority thus given to the method must have covered, in part, the matter and the arrangement."[1] In any case, would not the passages adduced by our Lord be so stored up in their minds, and the method be so brought home to them by Divine influence after Pentecost, that they would hand it on to others, who, in their turn, were coming into contact with other Jews, and be required to bring before them the evidence of the Old Testament Scriptures?

There is, however, no direct evidence for the existence of one such *Book of Testimonies par excellence*. It has indeed been supposed that Pseudo-Gregory of Nyssa in the latter part of the fourth century quotes it by name,[2] but this is an error. The title of his work is *Selections of Testimonies to Jews (taken) from the Old Testament* ('Εκλογαὶ μαρτυριῶν πρὸς 'Ιουδαίους ἀπὸ τῆς παλαιᾶς), and he nowhere hints that he has used any collection of excerpts, much less that he used any one famous book. A similar mistake has been made about Dionysius bar Salibi, in the twelfth century, in his

---

[1] *Test.* ii. 97. Cf. also pp. 70, 95.
[2] Rendel Harris, *Test.* i. 35.

treatise *Against the Jews.*[1] After giving many quotations from the Old Testament he says in v. 17: "All these testimonies give information about the Three Persons", etc. Then in sec. 18 he adds: "For after we have shown from the Scriptures", etc. The Syrian Father is referring to the Scriptures only, and uses an ordinary word[2] for their testimonies in its ordinary sense.[3]

For, in fact, there is every probability that there was not only one *Book of Testimonies*, but several. It is not likely that at first the Old Testament passages were even written down at all, for they would be but few, and very easily remembered. But as time went on, and the multitude of the believers increased, and their unconverted friends asked them the reason of the Faith that was in them, many would begin to make written memoranda of the chief texts for their own use. It is not probable that such notes would always be alike. To one Evangelist certain texts would appeal, to other Evangelists others. There would thus be many little *Books of Testimonies*, as we may call them.[4] But in process of time there would arise someone who felt called upon to produce, perhaps for the purpose of teaching the teachers, something more elaborate and more complete. He would never, indeed, get anything quite complete, but he would do his best. One such writer would enlarge, but another would trim away such texts as he himself did not find relevant. But there would inevitably be a large measure of matter that was common to all such books. And, in fact, several of such little books have survived to our own time.

Not that any lists of actually Apostolic, or even sub-Apostolic, days have survived. They have not. How devoutly we wish they had! We have nothing really definite even of the second century, though the little tract called *Jason and Papiscus*, written not later than the middle of that century, was criticised severely by Celsus about A.D. 178, and not very favourably by Origen about A.D. 248. But with the exception of its general character, and of one or two quotations, it is completely unknown to us. Tertullian, however, at the end of the second century gives us such a list in his treatise *Against the Jews*, and so especially does Cyprian nearly fifty years later in

---

[1] Edition Zwaan, Leiden, 1906.   [2] ܣܗܕܘܬܐ   [3] *Test.* i. p. 58.
[4] So, we are told, "Among the Waldensians [in the twelfth century] the minister or teacher carried his little book in his hand, containing various portions of the Bible, sometimes the whole of the New Testament, with chosen selections from the Old" (L. Isr. Newman, *Jewish Influence on Christian Reform*, 1925, p. 226).

the first two books of his *Testimonies*. Soon after that they begin to increase in number, the more noticeable being Pseudo-Gregory of Nyssa's *Selections* of such Testimonies in the latter part of the fourth century. Perhaps the most complete of all such lists is Isidore of Seville's treatise *Against the Jews* in the very end of the sixth century. There are also *The Teaching of Jacob* (*James*) in the seventh century, the five-chaptered treatise of Matthew the Monk (but perhaps even as late as cent. xiv), and so on till Dionysius bar Salibi's treatise *Against the Jews* in the twelfth century. But similar lists have never ceased to be drawn up, and hardly a year passes in which some devout and worthy soul does not compile such a collection of proof-passages for Jewish readers, under the naïve assumption that it has never been done so well before.[1]

Now are there traces of the existence and use of such little *Books of Testimonies* in the New Testament itself? Have we any evidence that the Evangelists, for example, used such compilations?

How can we know? What tests can we apply to finding out whether the New Testament writers used such books? In the first place would not the passages selected be arranged under subjects, or, at least, some passages be placed under other passages, without much consideration of the Biblical books from which the individual verses were taken? For example: Isaiah is a big book, and its name is more easily remembered than that of most books; passages from it would be so numerous, and often so important, that texts from other lesser books might well be found in a list containing passages taken chiefly from it. A text from Malachi, for instance, might easily be put in a list made up chiefly of passages from Isaiah. If so, it would be very easy for a writer to attribute a passage to Isaiah which really occurs only in Malachi. This seems a reasonable explanation of what has happened in Mark i. 2. The Evangelist says: *Even as it is written in Isaiah the Prophet*, and promptly quotes not Isaiah but Malachi, adding a passage from Isaiah immediately afterwards. He may well have been using a *Book of Testimonies* in which Malachi is quoted under the general heading of Isaiah.[2] It is worth noticing that Justin, in the middle of the second century, makes the same kind of mistake when he affirms

---

[1] So M. J. Brierre-Narbonne, *Les Prophéties Messianiques de l'Ancien Testament dans la Littérature Juive*, Paris, 1933. Also his *Exégèse talmudique des prophéties messianiques*, Part i. 1934, ii. 1935.

[2] Yet Q did not use a *Book of Testimonies*. For he quotes Mal. iii. 1 alone (see Matt. xi. 10; Luke vii. 27), while both Matt. iii. 2 and Luke iii. 4 only copy Isa. xl. 3 from Mark.

that Isaiah says: *A Star shall arise out of Jacob* (Num. xxiv. 17), and only afterwards adds, *And a Flower shall come up from the root of Jesse* (Isa. xi. 1).[1]

So also in Pseudo-Gregory of Nyssa "Isaiah" is said to write: *Did I ever command in the day that I brought them out of the land of Egypt* etc. (Jer. vii. 22), followed by *To what purpose is the multitude of your sacrifices*, etc. (Isa. i. 11).[2] So too Irenaeus quotes Isa. liii. 8, then Lam. iv. 20, as Jeremiah's (this was natural enough), and then goes on to say that "the same Prophet" said Isa. lvii. 1, 2.[3]

Closely akin to this, though not quite identical, is the case where a single text, one alone and not connected with a second as in our last examples, is wrongly attributed to a certain author. For some reason or other such wrongly attributed texts are often found in the name of Jeremiah. In the New Testament the famous example is Matt. xxvii. 9: *Then was fulfilled that which was spoken by Jeremiah the prophet*, but the words given are those of Zech. xi. 13, with perhaps some reminiscences of the language of Jer. xviii. 2 and xix. 1, 2. It may perhaps be mentioned here that in Matt. xiii. 35 the Sinaitic MS. reads (with some lesser authorities): *That there may be fulfilled that which was spoken by the prophet Isaiah saying, I will open My mouth in parables: I will utter things hidden from the foundation of the world*, though the words really are found only in Ps. lxxviii.

Justin, it may be added, does the same sort of thing when he says that those Christians who are of Gentile origin are greater in number and truer than those who are of Jewish or Samaritan origin, and (a little further on) proves this by saying: We will report what has been said by Isaiah the prophet. For he said thus: *Israel is uncircumcised in heart, but the Gentiles in the uncircumcision* (of their flesh), a saying which occurs only in Jer. ix. 26.[4]

The combination of two or more passages of the Old Testament recurring in two or more authors, without any error of nomenclature such as we have already seen, also suggests the use of a *Book of Testimonies*. For example, parts of Ps. cx, either *Sit Thou*

---

[1] 1 *Apol.* xxxii. 12. Justin's reference in *Trypho*, cvi. 4, is right.
[2] *Test.* xii (Zacagni, p. 315); R. H. *Test.* i. 35. The two passages occur, but separately and without any names, as early as *Barnabas*, ii. 5, 7, but only Isa. i. 11 in Cyprian, *Test.* i. 16.
[3] *Preaching*, §§ 70–72; R. H. *Test.* i. 69 *sq.* Observe that Justin Martyr (1 *Apol.* xlviii. 4) also quotes Isa. lvii. 1, 2, but with no reference to "Jeremiah".
[4] 1 *Apol.* liii. 3, 10, 11. It may be noticed that although Lactantius is following Cyprian in his recension of texts, and although Cyprian attributes Jer. iv. 3 *sq.* to its proper author, Lactantius himself says it is by "Isaiah" (*Instit.* iv. 17). See R. H. *Test.* i. 79.

on *My right hand*, or *Until I put Thy enemies under Thy feet*, are combined with Ps. viii. 6, *Thou hast put all things under His feet*, by
St Paul, both in 1 Cor. xv. 25 *sq.* and in Eph. i. 20, 22, and also
by the writer to the Hebrews in i. 13; ii. 6–8. It is possible, of
course, that the writer to the Hebrews knew St Paul's Epistles,
but it is at least as probable that both he and St Paul were
using a common source, part of such a book as those we have in
mind.[1]

There is, again, a passage in Acts xxvi. 22 *sq.* to which an even more
striking interpretation has been given. The Greek is difficult, but the
R.V. represents it fairly when it reads: *I stand unto this day, testifying
both to small and great, saying nothing but what the prophets and Moses
did say should come; how that the Christ must suffer, and how that he first
by the resurrection of the dead should proclaim light both to the people and
to the Gentiles.* The wording from the first *how* onwards so closely
resembles that of the titles to chapters in Cyprian's collection of
Testimonies and elsewhere, that the suggestion has been made that
we have here in fact the actual titles, or two titles, of sections in the
Book of Testimonies which lay before St Luke when he compiled
the Acts, one showing that Christ was to suffer, and the other that
He was to rise again. It is not impossible.[2]

We can, I think, hardly be wrong in considering that the writers
of the New Testament had at their disposal collections of what we
call proof-texts from the Old Testament.

We must, however, be on our guard against assuming that

---

[1] Similarly, Justin (*Trypho*, lxxvi. 7; xlv. 4) combines Ps. cx. 3 and Ps. lxxii.
5, 17; and so also does Pseudo-Gregory of Nyssa (*Test.* i. 292); and also Dionysius bar Salibi, v. 9 (p. 28). In Irenaeus' *Preaching*, § 43, they are also combined,
under the name of "Jeremiah". So Lactantius *Inst.* iv. 8 quotes Jeremiah (i. 5)
and then attributes to him a form of Ps. lxxii. 17. Again, *Barnabas* (xii. 10 *sq.*)
combines Ps. cx. 1 with Isa. xlv. 1. Cyprian quotes (*Test.* i. 21) Isa. xlv. 1 alone.
But Pseudo-Gregory of Nyssa (*Test.* xvi. 324) combines them, adding: "Isaiah
says more clearly (than David) *The Lord saith to my Christ Cyrus*, explaining that
this cannot refer to Cyrus the Persian, for Cyrus was killed by the Massagetae,
and his skin made into a bottle." Not dissimilar is the curious interpretation
that *Presents to king Jareb* (*Jarim*, LXX) in Hos. x. 6 refers to the sending of Jesus
by Pilate to Herod! This is found in Justin (*Trypho*, ciii. 4), Irenaeus (*Preaching*,
§ 77), Tertullian (*c. Marc.* iv. 42), Cyril of Jerusalem (*Cat.* xiii. 14), and elsewhere (see R. H. *Test.* i. 66 *sq.*).

[2] R. H. *Test.* i. 19 *sq.*, 59. Zwaan in Foakes-Jackson and Lake's *Beginnings
of Christianity*, ii. 49 *sq.*, says that "headlines" from the *Book of Testimonies* are
"quoted", and adds that "the interruption of Festus shows that Paul had been
pouring out a stream of such 'proof-texts' (xxvi. 24), referring to Gospel history
(xxvi. 26) as their fulfilment".

because two writers agree in their application of an Old Testament text, especially if that interpretation is strange in our eyes, one of them must have been dependent on the other. For it may well be that they have both used the same method of interpretation quite independently, or even followed an application of it already found in Christian circles. In other words, it is not the literary lists of Old Testament passages that are of primary importance, but the current method of interpretation.

Now the witness of the Old Testament to doctrine and to life was everything to the Jews. And, further, Jews and Christians were agreed about the quality and extent of the inspiration of the Old Testament Scriptures. This was considered to be so full that Jewish teachers could say—at least in the sixth century, and perhaps even in the third—that although the word of a mere man has only one true meaning *God spoke one thing, but two things did I hear* (Ps. lxii. 11); "for this power belongeth unto God; one utterance issues in many meanings. So we read in Jeremiah: *And as a hammer when it smiteth the rock* (Jer. xxiii. 29); as this hammer divides itself into many sparks [or, perhaps, into many shivers], so one utterance issues in many meanings."[1]

Besides, Jews were wont to learn by the experience of new facts to see ever fresh meanings in Scripture, as Klausner has shown.[2] This principle was taken over gladly by such Jews as became Christians, who allowed the new facts about the Christ as seen in Jesus of Nazareth to throw light on the sense of the Scriptures. Toy was quite right when he said in 1884: "The New Testament writers handle the Old according to a Talmudic manner *plus* their Messianic hope."[3] They would naturally see at once the Christian interpretation of a few great passages such as Isa. liii (the Passion), and Isa. xxviii. 16, Dan. ii. 34, and Ps. cxviii. 22 (the Stone), and the method would be continued from year to year and from decade to decade, with ever enlarging scope of Christian exegesis. In this way there gradually arose a *corpus* of traditional explanation of the Old Testament.[4] Whether this was ever written down as fully as any one person could write it, or whether only certain parts of it

[1] T. B. *Sanhed.* 34 a; cf. *Mechilta* on Ex. xv. 11 (Horowitz edition, p. 143, l. 4).
[2] *Die Messianische Vorstellungen des jüdischen Volkes im Zeitalter der Tannaim,* 1904, p. 88. Cf. my *Hebrew-Christian Messiah,* 1916, p. 12.
[3] *Quotations in the New Testament,* 1884, p. 21. See Vacher Burch in R. H. *Test.* ii. 34.
[4] For an example of development in such a use of the Old Testament, see Cyprian's *Test.* ii. 16 (the Stone); 19 (the Bridegroom); 20 (the Cross).

were written down, was more or less accidental. It depended on whether the need arose.

We know that sometimes the need did arise. Cyprian's "filius", Quirinus, i.e. probably a layman in his diocese, asked his "father" Cyprian, and Isidore's sister Florentina asked her brother, for such a summary of Old Testament texts which they could use for the furtherance of their own faith, or for direct controversy with Jews. At other times, as with *The Teaching of Jacob* in the seventh century, a manual was desired for instructing Jews who, alas, had been baptised by force. But in no case is there any mention of a standard book from which compilers could draw. There was only the traditional teaching which Christian teachers had received. It was the *method* which continued, not the *book*.

It will be noticed that, doubtless, so long as the same method of curious verbal interpretation of Scripture lasted, so long would common matter be likely to continue. Thus we cannot be surprised that the use of common matter remained as late as Dionysius bar Salibi in the twelfth century, for the method of interpretation lasted until then.

One rather asks whether we have any reason to think that it ceased at that date. True that in one particular there has been a change, and it is so great as to veil the continuance of the one method. It is this. The current Greek version of the time and district was in early days the standard used for quotations from the Old Testament. Jerome's work at the end of the fourth century, in some degree, and the renaissance of Hebrew scholarship in the sixteenth century, in a greater degree, changed that standard from the Greek to the Hebrew. But the method remained the same. And tracts have ever since appeared, using the very same texts, and the very same interpretations, because the method of interpretation is the same.

To sum up. The *Book of Testimonies*, considered as one book, is a myth. But the proper meaning of "myth", we have often been told, is the pictorial representation of a spiritual truth. In this case the truth denotes the permanence of a certain method which produced catena after catena of texts from the Old Testament which were regarded as *Testimonies* to Christ and Christianity. Words were everything; grammatical meaning and historical reference were of little account.

A final word on the mentality of those who pursued this method in the first few centuries. Originally they were but simple folk,

Galilean fishermen, and afterwards Gentile converts, who were, for the most part, of humble training. If one of the early believers had had Rabbinic teaching like St Paul, he would continue to use the same method of interpretation.

But when philosophers began to accept Christ there came a slight reaction. Perhaps even the Fourth Gospel represents the better side of that reaction, as Vacher Burch suggests.[1] Similarly, Justin Martyr's *Dialogue with Trypho* may well be the attempt of a Christian philosopher to put the arguments for Christ in a way which would appeal to Jews of education more than the common method. But it almost perished, its text now resting in reality on only one manuscript, and it had little, if any, influence on writers after the time of Irenaeus and Tertullian. It is not by accident, on the other hand, that though the simple tract *Jason and Papiscus* was ridiculed by Celsus, and not defended in its form by Origen, it had an enormous number of imitators. For, as we all know, the simpler the method the more easily is it grasped and followed, especially in ages when learning tends to diminish rather than to increase. For indeed scholarly attempts to grapple with the Old Testament as such did not come to their own much before our own time, and, until they did, so long was the Old Testament treated as little more than an arsenal of separate weapons for Christian warfare.

Attention may be called to the fact that in the *Books of Testimonies* there is very little reference to the Holy Communion, although Mal. i. 11 is adduced in evidence that it was foretold. Did the early Christians not attach the same importance to that Sacrament which it holds to-day?

In any case, the great lesson of the *Books* is the antiquity, and indeed the priority, of the orthodox idea of Christ. In other words, the more the facts about the *Books of Testimonies* are studied the earlier and the more definite does the orthodox belief in Christ appear. The compilers of the *Books*, even in those earliest forms which preceded the Gospels, knew of no stage of belief in Christ as only a man. On the contrary, they regarded Jesus from the very first as having been born of a Virgin, and indeed as Very God who had come down from heaven.

And it was these simple-minded Christians, with their crude and naïve use of the Old Testament, who conquered the world, because they were filled with zeal for Jesus the Christ, Son of God, Son of man, Redeemer, and Saviour, and Judge.

[1] R. H. *Test.* ii. 71.

CHAPTER II

THE EPISTLE OF BARNABAS[1]

BEFORE A.D. 100

Although this Epistle is not an attempt to win the Jews to Christ, yet it contains so much about Judaism, and is so greatly concerned with rebutting the objections brought by Jews against Christianity, and is, again, so early a document as to be included in all collections of "The Apostolic Fathers", that it must be briefly considered here.

When, however, was it written? The earlier its date, the greater its interest and importance. What evidence do we possess for determining its date?[2]

The external evidence will not detain us long. There is no sure evidence that the Epistle was used, much less that it was attributed to a certain author, before about A.D. 190, when Clement of Alexandria quotes it again and again (in all its parts) in his *Stromateis*. In II. vi. 31 he writes: "rightly therefore the Apostle Barnabas says: 'From the portion I have received I have been eager to write briefly to you', quoting from *Barn.* i. 5; ii. 2, 3."[3] References have been found also in Justin Martyr, Hermas, and Irenaeus, but in no case is there certainty. On the other hand we may assume that Dr Muilenburg in particular, and in some degree Dr Armitage Robinson and Dom Connolly, have proved that the author of the *Didaché* was dependent on *Barnabas* in the sections dealing with the Two Ways. But there is at the present moment no agreement about the date of the *Didaché*. Some place it at the

---

[1] The most satisfactory edition for serious work is that of F. X. Funk, in his *Patres Apostolici*, 1901, i, pp. xx–xxxii, 38–97; Introduction, Text, Latin Translation and brief Notes. Funk's small edition of the same year is convenient, as is also Lightfoot and Harmer's *The Apostolic Fathers*, 1891, a translation only. H. Windisch, *Der Barnabasbrief*, 1920, provides no Text, but a Translation and excellent and full notes. See also in *J. Th. St.* April, 1934, xxxv. 113–146, "a revision and amplification" by J. Armitage Robinson of the first chapter of his *Barnabas, Hermas and the Didache* (1920).

[2] See my detailed examination of the date in *J. Th. St.* October, 1933, xxxiv. 337–346.

[3] Muilenburg gives a long list of Clement's parallels to *Barnabas* (p. 25).

end of the first, but others (including the three scholars just named) at the end of the second century.

We may now turn to the internal evidence as to its date. What we can gather from the Epistle itself may be summed up under three headings: what it does not say; what it does say in general terms; and what definite marks of time it seems to contain.

1. *What it does not say.*

In all writings, particularly those of a controversial kind, and especially when an author has in view the object of guarding those committed to him in doctrine and practice, we may expect to find allusions to definitely erroneous modes of teaching or morals.

Strangely enough our author makes no reference to Church organisation. The attitude of Ignatius is unknown to him. Even the fears and the earnest warnings of Clement of Rome find no parallel. Nor are St Paul's Pastoral Letters applied. *Barnabas* thinks no more of organisation than does the Epistle of James, perhaps not even as much, for St James at least mentions "the elders of the Church", who are to be summoned to pray over a sick man after using the usual remedies (Jas. v. 14). Of more importance is *Barnabas*' absolute silence with regard to the heresies. There is no trace of Gnosticism in the technical sense, e.g. of the teaching of Valentinus, whose date seems now to be placed about A.D. 120. Nor is there a word about Marcion (also about 120, it appears), or Marcionism, for *Barnabas*' attitude towards the Old Testament is wholly different. Nor is there even a suggestion that the author knew of Cerinthus and the heresy associated with his name.

For all that we have learned so far, the *Epistle of Barnabas* might have been written at any time after, say, A.D. 40.

2. *But what does the Epistle say in general terms?*

Does it show any knowledge of the New Testament books? This is more than doubtful, as may be seen in the classical discussion of the subject in Dr J. V. Bartlet's paper vouched for by a Committee of the Oxford Society of Historical Theology in its *The New Testament in the Apostolic Fathers*, 1905. For although our author quotes, ὡς γέγραπται, a saying which is almost exactly that which is found in Matt. xxii. 14: "Many are called but few are chosen", yet, as it is not uncommon for the Fathers to quote as Scripture words which we cannot find in our canonical books, so this saying need not be from Matthew. Cf. *Barnabas* itself, vii. 4: "What then saith He in the Prophet, And let them eat, etc.?" These words existed, presumably, in some book, but we do not know which. So, "Many are called", etc. may be quoted from a document earlier or later than Matthew. Cf. even 2 (4) Esdras viii. 3: "Many have been created, but few shall be saved." Dr Bartlet thinks Barnabas used the Epistle to the Romans (iv. 3, 10 *sq.* (17), see *Barn.* xiii. 7; Rom. ix. 7–13, see *Barn.* xiii. 2, 3). Other allusions in *Barnabas* to New Testament books have been supposed.[1] But none are certain. For myself I become increasingly convinced that Patristic authors used earlier writings much less than has been thought, and that phrases and interpretations commonly supposed to indicate literary dependence are due really to phraseology and interpretation spread over the whole Church. Such phrases and interpretations form, that is to say, extremely doubtful evidence that one writer took them from another.

The characteristic mark that we do find in the *Epistle of Barnabas* is the author's continual use of Jewish methods of interpreting Scripture. I say Jewish, and not Alexandrian-Jewish, for it is a vulgar error to suppose that such methods—strange as they appear to us—either originated in Alexandria or were the peculiar mark of Alexandrian Jews. The mistake arose, no doubt, from the fact that our earlier scholars who dealt with the subject could read Philo easily enough, but had no knowledge of Talmud or Rabbinic. The point, I may add, is not unimportant, for Barnabas' use of such methods does not in reality throw any light on the place where he wrote. Neither, I may add, does the fact that he wrote in Greek and used the Greek version of the Old Testament point to Alexandria. Indeed it may be suspected that the differences in *Barnabas* from the Vatican or Alexandrian MSS. indicate rather a different locality.[2] But almost nothing is known as yet about either the LXX itself or its relation to the various forms of its text. Further, very little weight can be attached to the fact that Clement of Alexandria is the first to mention the Epistle, for Origen of Alexandria is the first to mention the *True Word* of Celsus, and this, he expressly tells us, was sent there from Rome.

Be that as it may, our author's Jewish methods of interpretation

[1] J. A. R. finds several indications of Barnabas' knowledge of *Ephesians* (*loc. cit.* e.g. p. 135 *sq.*).

[2] Preliminary studies of the subject may be found in Hatch, *Essays*, 1889, pp. 180–186; Swete, *Introduction*, 1900, pp. 411–413.

recur again and again. Does their recurrence throw any light upon the date of the Epistle? I cannot think that it does. For, after all, Christian Jews only carried on the methods of Biblical interpretation which they had used before their conversion, and Gentile Christians naturally followed suit. In themselves, that is, these quotations throw little light even upon the question whether our author was of Jewish or of Gentile origin, and none at all upon that of his date.

So far the Epistle might still have been written at any time after, say, A.D. 40 or, if we are to accept the supposition that the author was acquainted with books of the New Testament, at any time after, say, A.D. 80.

3. There are, however, two passages in the Epistle which have been thought to provide very clear indications of its date.

One is in xvi. 3, 4, where Harnack and others suppose that Barnabas is referring to the building of a temple by the Jews, either actually begun or only proposed, during the rebellion of Barcochba (say, A.D. 131), or even to that of the heathen temple built by Hadrian after 135. But even J.A.R. became convinced of the futility of this interpretation, for he says: "It is reasonably certain that Barnabas refers to the spiritual Temple, 'which is being gloriously builded in the name of the Lord'."[1]

The second passage is much more definite, though even here the interpretations of the exact point of time indicated differ by some twenty years.

It is iv. 4, 5. The author has spoken of the near approach of the Coming of the Lord, and adds: "And the prophet also says thus: *Ten kingdoms shall reign upon the earth, and after them shall rise up a little king, who shall subdue three of the kings under one.*" (So Dr Lowther Clarke's translation, but ὑφ' ἕν, not ὑφ' ἕνα, can hardly mean here anything but "at once".) The passage is taken from Dan. vii. 24. Barnabas goes on to say: "Similarly Daniel says concerning the same: *And I beheld the fourth beast, wicked and powerful and fiercer than all the beasts of the sea,*[2] and how that *ten horns arose from it, and out of these a little excrescent horn,* and how that *it subdues under one* (or "at once", but here the neuter may refer to κέρας) *three of the great horns*" (cf. Dan. vii. 7 *sq.*, 19 *sq.*).

The author means, it would seem, that already the Roman Empire has had ten horns (i.e. ten Emperors), and even three

---

[1] *Op. cit.* p. 129. *Cf. infra,* p. 406.
[2] So the Constantinopolitan MS. and the Latin version.

more who are soon to be, or have already been, subdued by a little horn.

What then was the exact date when the author was writing?

Bishop Lightfoot regarded Vespasian as the tenth Roman Emperor (counting from Julius Caesar), and the "three" as Vespasian and his two sons (Titus and Domitian) associated with him in the supreme power. The destroyer would then be Antichrist, who may have been identified with Nero, supposed at that time to be still alive and about to return. If so, the Epistle will have been written between A.D. 75 and 79 when Vespasian died.[1]

Another opinion is that the little horn is Nerva, who was elected Emperor by the Senate after the murder of Domitian, the last of the three Flavian Emperors, and reigned from A.D. 96 (Sept.) to 98 (Jan.). The Epistle will then have been written between these two dates. On the whole this chronology is perhaps simpler, and the date more probable.[2]

It will thus be seen that in any case the Epistle must have been written before A.D. 100.

Who then was the author? Clement of Alexandria, as we have seen, says that he was the Apostle.[3] No doubt this is just within the bounds of possibility,[4] for in A.D. 75 or thereabouts he might be still alive, though he seems to have been older than St Paul (Acts xiv. 12). But the writer of our Epistle implies that he was not of the first generation of believers, for he speaks of the Lord choosing His own Apostles although they were godless in the extreme (v. 9).[5] Besides, the Epistle is certainly inferior to what we should have expected of the Apostle in both style and matter. For the writer is but a simple-minded man.

If then he was not the Apostle, was he a Jewish or a Gentile Christian? It is not easy to say, for while his reference to himself

---

[1] Ramsay (*The Church in the Roman Empire*, 1893, p. 308) agrees with the date, but arrives at it in a different way. He omits Otho and Vitellius from the list of Emperors (for "in the time of the Flavian Emperors" to include them "would have been treason"), and reckons Vespasian as the eighth, Titus as the ninth, and Domitian as the tenth, who were all to perish at the hands of the returning Nero.   [2] This date is preferred by Funk, 1901, p. xxv.

[3] So also Jerome (*De Vir. Ill.* vi). But Origen and Eusebius do *not* say so expressly.

[4] Unless the statement be true (first found in "Mark's" *Acta et Passio Barnabae* (perhaps cent. v), in Tischendorf, *Acta Ap. Apoc.* 1851, § 23) that he was martyred at Salamis in Cyprus on June 11, A.D. 53 or 64.

[5] ὄντας ὑπὲρ πᾶσαν ἁμαρτίαν ἀνομωτέρους. Celsus said the same, and Origen suggests that Celsus had read Barnabas' "Catholic Epistle" (*c. Celsum*, i. 63).

and his readers[1] as "novices" (ἐπήλυτοι), or perhaps even as "proselytes" (προσήλυτοι, Const. MS. and Latin), suggests the latter, his literary methods suggest the former. We must especially guard against adducing the apparent inaccuracies in his presentation of details of Jewish rites as confirmation of this Gentile authorship, for they rather suggest intimate knowledge of traditional practice.[2]

What then were the aim and purpose of the writer? Plainly his object was not, as with writers of a hundred years later, to establish certain doctrines of the Faith, or to oppose the views of certain heretics. His aim is at once wider and simpler than that. He has in his mind the twin dangers of Judaism and Antinomianism. He fears the influence of the Jews and the laxity of the heathen, and, from the very first, he has before his eyes both these rivals to true Christianity, although the former is more prominent in chapters i–xvii, and the latter in chapters xviii–xxi.

Yet it should be observed that with regard to the former he never shows bitterness against the Jews or Judaism.[3] He may write contemptuously, but he never writes bitterly.

Yet with regard to the ceremonies and rites of the Old Testament, although he is no Marcionite in his doctrine of God, he approaches Marcion in his view of these. For he goes far beyond Philo, who accepted, in general, the legal obligation of performing the rites ordered, though insisting that they had spiritual meanings also. Barnabas accepts the latter only, and taught that God never intended the former. Speaking of the dietary laws he says: "So then it is not a commandment of God that they (the Jews) should not bite with their teeth, but Moses spake it in spirit."[4] But an evil angel persuaded the people to understand them literally.[5] As Lightfoot says: "He accuses the Jews of misunderstanding them (the Lawgiver and the Prophets) from beginning to end, and intimates that the ordinances of circumcision, of the sabbath, of the distinctions of meats clean and unclean, were never intended to be literally observed, but had throughout a spiritual and mystical significance."[6]

---

[1] iii. 6. See also xiv. 5; xvi. 7.   [2] *Vide infra*, pp. 22–25.

[3] "After reading the Epistle again and again I find no trace of animosity against the Jews" (J. A. R. *op. cit.* p. 145). Contrast W. J. Ferrar, *The early Christian Books*, 1919, p. 38.

[4] Lightfoot's translation: ἄρα οὖν οὐκ ἔστιν ἐντολὴ θεοῦ τὸ μὴ τρώγειν, Μωϋσῆς δὲ ἐν πνεύματι ἐλάλησεν (x. 2).   [5] ix. 4.

[6] *The Apostolic Fathers*, p. 239. Cf. also the *Epistle to Diognetus*, iii and iv.

Yet, after all, it is with the true Christian life that he is most concerned. It is into this that he puts his strength, and fairly lets himself go. For in the last four chapters of his Letter he crowds into a small space example after example of what believers ought to do and to avoid. To be sure, these chapters are concerned with, as he says, the Two Ways. But we must beware of thinking that because the *Didaché* also describes the Two Ways these chapters are a mere mechanical addition to our Epistle, perhaps even an addition by a copyist. For certainly the thought of the Two Ways was present to our author's mind from the first.[1] Further, we are assured that the chapters are earlier than the *Didaché*, the author of which has used them, and also that they are identical in style with the preceding chapters, and that they were probably composed by the writer of our Epistle himself.[2] The verdict of so able a critic as the late Dean of Wells must needs weigh heavily. One only wonders whether a simple-minded writer like the author of our Epistle would have been able to compose, either out of his own head or from a Jewish document already known to him, a description of the Two Ways of life and death which was so greatly appreciated as to be used by later writers. There is no certain usage of the earlier part of the Epistle, for apparent references to that, with the exception of those made by Clement of Alexandria,[3] are due to other causes, as we have already seen. Barnabas belongs in reality to the school of the compilers of the little *Books of Testimonies*, although he insists on the ethical side of our religion far more strongly than they. Perhaps, however, this difference is more apparent than real in the case of the earlier compilers of those books, for the evidence for their contents lies chiefly in such peculiarities of their use of Old Testament prophecies as can be easily recognised. Christian ethics are less dependent than Christian doctrine upon proofs from the Old Testament.

So we may come to the Epistle itself. After a charming Introduction (ch. i), in which the author speaks of his affection for his "sons and daughters",[4] writing, as he says, "not as a teacher, but as one of you", and bids them live a very godly life, he shows in

---

[1] i. 4, "the Lord journeyed with me on the way of righteousness"; iv. 10, "the works of the evil way"; v. 4, "the way of righteousness...the way of darkness". See further J. A. R. *op. cit.* p. 130 *sq.*

[2] *Vide supra*, p. 14.   [3] *Vide supra*, p. 14.

[4] On this salutation see E. J. Goodspeed, *Journ. Bibl. Lit.* 1915, p. 162 *sq.* Muilenburg (p. 59) has a full analysis of the Epistle

ii–iv that external ritual is worthless as a means to this, whether it be sacrifices or fasts, for God never intended their literal observance (Isa. i. 11, 13; Jer. vii. 22 *sq.*). Indeed the observance of these is compatible with evil living. But Christ came to purify us (v. 1).[1] The author then shows that the Old Testament led us to expect this. For it foretells in prophecies His suffering and His incarnation (v, vi), and in ritual (the goats and the Red Heifer) His sufferings and their effect (vii, viii). Having shown that Christ and His work were thus foretold, Barnabas proves next that the ordinances observed by Christians were foretold also (ix–xii). For circumcision (ix) and dietary laws (x) had always a spiritual and not a literal meaning (in God's intention), and the Prophets directly foretold Baptism and the fact of Christ's cross (xi, xii). He then proves that Christians, not unbelieving Jews, are the true heirs of salvation, as was understood by the Patriarchs (xiii), Moses, and the Prophets (xiv), Christians thus possessing the true Sabbath (xv), and being themselves the true Temple (xvi). He concludes this portion of his Epistle by saying that he has done his best to write plainly of such things as are profitable to salvation, but has not touched on the future (whether immediate or distant) because these things are expressed in parables (presumably still in the Old Testament) which his readers will not understand (xvii). So he passes on to another lesson, that of the Two Ways (xviii), the Way of light (xix) and the Way of the Black One (xx), each of which he describes in detail. In his final chapter (xxi) he entreats his readers to live for God, and he again reveals his own devout and earnest character.

It remains for us to consider very briefly a few of the more noteworthy passages. Dr M. R. James[2] points out that an obscure quotation in ii. 10 is said in the Constantinople manuscript to come from the *Apocalypse of Adam*, and that there is no reason to doubt the truth of the statement.[3] Again, Barnabas has no doubt about the existence of "the Evil One". "We ought to learn

---

[1] "The deeper meaning of the past, which has only come to light through Christ—that is the *gnosis* which he has to offer them" (J. A. R. *op. cit.* p. 124).

[2] *The Lost Apocrypha of the O.T.* 1920, p. 1.

[3] "To us then He says thus, *A sacrifice to the Lord is a troubled spirit; a savour of sweetness to the Lord is a heart glorifying Him that hath formed it.*" The Constantinople MS. has in its margin, "Ps. l and in the *Apocalypse of Adam*". In any case the second clause (though it has affinities with Ps. l. 23 and Zech. xii. 1) is not Biblical in its entirety. It occurs also in Irenaeus, *Heresies*, IV. xxix. 3 (xvii. 2), and in Clem. Alex. *Paed.* iii. 12.

accurately, Brethren, about our salvation, lest the Evil One cause error to enter into us secretly, and cast us, as with a sling, away from our life."[1] He is "the Black One".[2]

The author gives us a typical midrash on Ex. xxxiii. 1, 3 in vi. 8–19. Moses says: *Behold, these things saith the Lord God; enter into the good land which the Lord sware unto Abraham, Isaac, and Jacob, and inherit it, a land flowing with milk and honey.* What is *the land*? It is Jesus. "For man is earth suffering ($\gamma\tilde{\eta}\ \pi\acute{\alpha}\sigma\chi\text{ou}\sigma\alpha$)." Barnabas seems to know —or to have heard from a Jew—that *'adam* (man) is connected with *'adamah* (earth). And into Jesus we must enter. For He is *a land flowing with milk and honey*, i.e. He gives us "wisdom and understanding of His secret things". For, again, the verse implies a re-creation of us, "so that we should have the soul of children".[3] For at Creation God spoke with reference to the Son, *Increase and multiply*, and later with reference to us, for He made a second creation, *Behold I make the last things as the first.*[4] We then are brought into the good land, and are kept alive (as children) first by *honey* (faith in the promise) and then by *milk* (the word).[5] And so we shall live to become lords of the earth,[6] if not fully now, at least hereafter.

It is, however, when our author comes to speak of the foreshadowing of Christ in the ritual observances of the Old Testament that questions of special interest arise.[7] For he refers to certain details as being mentioned in Scripture, and yet the evidence which he gives for his statements is obscure. For example, he tells us: "*What then saith He in the prophet?*[8] *And, let them eat of the goat that is offered at the Fast for all their sins.* Attend carefully; *And let all the*

---

[1] ii. 10.

[2] iv. 10, "lest the Black one ($\dot{o}\ \mu\acute{\epsilon}\lambda\alpha\varsigma$) gain a secret entrance"; xx. 1, "the way of the Black one is crooked". Cf. 2 Enoch vii. 2: The evil angels "were gloomy in appearance, more than the darkness of the earth". Cf. *Acts of Thomas,* 55; Syriac *Acts of Philip* (M. R. James, *Apocr. N.T.* 1924, p. 451); T. B. *Qidd.* 30 b, "if this ugly one (מנוול, i.e. the evil principle) meets thee, draw him to the house of learning", i.e. overcome him by study. For "black" as a figure for evil see *Apoc.* vi. 5 (punishment), and Hermas, *Sim.* ix. 8 (sin).

[3] Barnabas does not here mention Isa. vii. 21, but evidently has it also in mind.

[4] vi. 13: λέγει δὲ κύριος, Ἰδού, ποιῶ τὰ ἔσχατα ὡς τὰ πρῶτα. If κύριος referred to Jesus we might take the quotation as a paraphrase of Matt. xix. 30; xx. 16, but it has surely the same reference as in § 12 (Gen. i. 28, God). The words may be based on Isa. xliii. 18 *sq.*; xlvi. 10.

[5] Cf. 1 Pet. ii. 2.   [6] Gen. i. 28.   [7] vii, viii.

[8] Moses, as in vi. 8, 10, 13; xiv. 2.

priests alone eat the entrails inwashed with vinegar."[1] In the first place, no such clear and definite statements exist in Holy Scripture. In the second place, Barnabas ignores the fact that of the two goats appointed as a sin-offering[2] on the Day of Atonement, one was let go into the wilderness, and the other was not eaten at all.[3] There was, however, a third goat which was offered the same day, after, as it seems, the more formal offering, *One he-goat for a sin offering, beside the sin-offering of atonement,*[4] and Barnabas seems to have confused this with the other. But it is curious that both Philo and the Mishna appear to have made the same mistake.[5]

Barnabas also combined with his statement about the goats of the Day of Atonement the charge given to Aaron and his sons to eat *those things wherewith atonement was made...but a stranger shall not eat thereof.*[6] And again he seems to combine an inaccurate reminiscence of the words *its inwards and its legs shall he* (the priest) *wash with water.*[7] Perhaps he may be thinking of the order that the Passover lamb was not to be *sodden at all with water.*[8]

Other matters of interest in connexion with the goat which was taken out into the wilderness are that the people were all to spit upon it,[9] that scarlet wool was to be put about its head,[10] that "he that takes the goat leadeth it into the wilderness, and takes off the wool and puts it on the shrub which is called Raché (bramble),[11] the shoots of which we are accustomed to eat when we find them in the country. Of this bramble alone is the fruit thus sweet....The accursed one is crowned. For they shall see Him in that day wearing the long scarlet robe about His flesh, and shall

---

[1] vii. 4. [2] Lev. xvi. 3.

[3] Although it was not a whole burnt-offering as was the ram (Lev. xvi. 3), but a sin-offering, and the flesh of sin-offerings was ordinarily eaten by the priests (Lev. vi. 26), yet there was a specific exception to this rule, that *no sin-offering, whereof any of the blood is brought into the tent of meeting to make atonement in the holy place, shall be eaten: it shall be burnt with fire* (Lev. vi. 30).

[4] Num. xxix. 11. Cf. Josephus, *Antt.* III. x. 3 *sq.*, § 240 *sq.*

[5] Philo, *Spec. leg. (de Victimis)*, I. 3, § 190, p. 240: ταῖς δ' ὁλοκαύτοις καθ' ἑκάστην ἡμέραν ἑορτῆς (New Year) παρέπεται χίμαρος, ὃς καλεῖται μὲν περὶ ἁμαρτίας, καταθύεται δὲ εἰς ἁμαρτημάτων ἄφεσιν, οὗ τὸ κρέα τοῖς ἱερεῦσιν εἰς ἐδωδὴν ἀπονέμεται. So *Menachoth*, xi. 7 (10): "If the Day of Atonement falls on a Friday the goat of the Day of Atonement is eaten in the evening. The Babylonians eat it raw, because they like it so."

[6] vii. 4 (see Windisch); Ex. xxix. 32 *sq.* [7] Lev. i. 9. [8] Ex. xii. 9.

[9] vii. 8. See Tertullian, *Adv. Jud.* xiv.

[10] *Ibid.* And so *Yoma*, iv. 2; vi. (8).

[11] "*Rubus fruticosus*, as common in many parts of Palestine as in England" (Tristram, *Nat. Hist. of the Bible*, 1889, p. 430).

say, Is not this He whom once we crucified, and spat upon, and set at nought? Of a truth this was He who then said He was the Son of God."[1] The wool in the thorns "is a type of Jesus set forth for the Church. For whoever wishes to take the scarlet wool must suffer much, because the thorn is severe."[2]

In chapter viii our author expounds the type of the Red Heifer, but with curious differences from the Bible account.[3] Men "who have sins that have come to maturity"[4] are to kill it, and boys[5] are to take the ashes, place them in baskets, and put round them the scarlet wool on wood ("here again is the type of the cross, and the scarlet wool"), and the hyssop, "and so the boys are to sprinkle the people one by one, that they may be purified from their sins".[6] A further explanation follows: the "calf" is Jesus; the men are sinners who brought Him to the slaughter ("so no longer are they men [who offer]; no longer have sinners glory").[7] The boys are they who preached to us the Gospel, twelve for the twelve tribes of Israel. "But why are the boys who sprinkle three in number? For a testimony unto Abraham, Isaac, and Jacob.[8]...But why wool and hyssop together? Because in His kingdom shall be evil and foul days, in which we shall be saved, as he who has pain in his flesh is healed by the foulness of the hyssop."[9]

The most famous example of Barnabas' trust in the Jewish method of finding hidden meanings in plain statements of Scripture occurs in ix. 7–9, where he tells us that Abraham "looked forward in the spirit unto Jesus, when he circumcised (Isaac, etc.) after having received the ordinances of three letters". He explains this last clause by showing that, when we are told that *Abraham circumcised of his household eighteen males and three hundred* (Gen. xvii. 23, 27 with xiv. 14), the 318 may be written in three letters, the first two of which are *iota* and *eta* (IH), which equal 18, and are the beginning of the word ΙΗΣΟΥΣ (Jesus). The third letter is Τ (300), which is a cross.[10] "He therefore shows (us) Jesus in the two letters,

---

[1] *Ibid.* Cf. Matt. xxvi. 63 *sq.* with xxvii. 29 *sq.*   [2] vii. 11.

[3] Num. xix.   [4] ἐν οἷς εἰσιν ἁμαρτίαι τέλειαι.   [5] παιδία and (§ 4) παῖδες.

[6] There is nothing of this in the Bible or the Mishna.

[7] viii. 2: εἶτα οὐκέτι ἄνδρες, οὐκέτι ἁμαρτωλῶν ἡ δόξα. The words are very obscure, but seem to contrast the children with the men.

[8] Barnabas gives both numbers (12 and 3) in order to add midrash to midrash.

[9] viii. 6.

[10] Our writer evidently knew no Hebrew, but depended entirely on Greek. But the *order* is not that of our present LXX text (A) but of another form of it which corresponded to the order of the Hebrew, and is found in several MSS.

and the cross in one." Barnabas adds: "He who set within us the innate gift of His teaching[1] knoweth (the truth of what I say). No one ever learned from me a more genuine word, but I know that ye are worthy."

A strange addition to the Biblical dietary laws occurs in x. 7, where Barnabas tells us, *Neither shalt thou eat the hyaena*, which, he says, means, "Thou shalt not be an adulterer, etc. for this animal changes its sex every year". So the common people believed, says Pliny, though, he adds, Aristotle denied it.[2] But where did Barnabas find the words in Scripture?

When Barnabas turns to the Old Testament predictions of Christian rites he still finds more than the Bible really contains. He naturally contrasts the true fountain of life with the pit of death.[3] He adds, rather curiously, "Is my holy mountain a desert rock (i.e. with no living water flowing from it)? For ye shall be as young birds fluttering when deprived of their nest."[4] He finds both the cross and baptism mentioned in Ps. i. 3, *And he that doeth these things shall be like the tree[5] which is planted at the water-partings*, which means, "Blessed are they who having placed their hope on the Cross went down into the water".[6] "And again another prophet says, *The land of Israel was praised above all the earth*, meaning that He will glorify the vessel of the Spirit." The last words seem to mean that He would glorify both Jesus[7] and those who are baptised as He was.[8]

One of the quotations adduced to show that the Cross of Jesus was predicted of old has given rise to much discussion. He tells us: "Likewise again He defineth concerning the cross in another prophet, who says, *And when shall these things be accomplished, saith the Lord? When a tree is bent down and rises up, and when blood flows*

In the Chester-Beatty papyrus (P 45) ΙΗ is the regular abbreviation for Ἰησοῦς. For the circumcision of the 318 cf. the note on Tertullian, *Adv. Jud.* iii (*infra*, p. 46).

[1] διδαχῆς, Vatican MS. and the Latin version.

[2] *Hist. Nat.* viii. 30 (44). See also Tertullian, *de Pallio*, 3. Clem. Alex. discusses the question in *Paed.* ii. 10.

[3] xi. 2. See Jer. ii. 12 *sq.*

[4] xi. 3. Based on Isa. xvi. 1 *sq.*

[5] τὸ ξύλον, i.e. the Cross, Gal. iii. 13. Cf. the *Dialogue with Trypho*, lxxxvi. 4–6.

[6] xi. 6 and 8.

[7] In vii. 3 the human body of Jesus is called "the vessel of the Spirit"; here, it seems, His mystical Body.

[8] xi. 9. The quotation is a paraphrase of Zeph. iii. 19.

from the tree."[1] Pseudo-Gregory of Nyssa says in very similar language: "And again, *And then shall these things be accomplished, saith
the Lord, when the Tree of trees lies down, and rises up, and when blood
shall trickle from the Tree.*"[2] So also Pseudo-Jerome in a homiletic
exposition of Mark xv. 33 says: "Here blood trickled from the
Tree."[3] All three quotations, though perhaps not independent,
may well be Christian adaptations of the purely Jewish passages
in 2(4) Esdras, where the Seer asks in iv. 33: "How long and when
shall these things (come to pass)?" and in v. 5: *And blood shall
trickle from a tree* (or *from wood*).[4]

Again, we all know that when we desire to express in very few
words our own exposition of a passage of Scripture we find it
convenient only to interpolate a phrase into the original, thereby
giving to it the sense that we feel is there. Barnabas does so also.
For this is the easiest explanation of his quoting the words spoken
by Moses to Joshua on sending him out as a spy: *Take a book in
thine hands and write what the Lord says, because the Son of God will cut
off by the roots all the house of Amalek in the last days.*[5] This is not a
formal quotation, but only Barnabas' Christian interpretation of
Ex. xvii. 14, when the Lord bids Moses: *Write this down for remembrance in a book, and speak this in the ears of Joshua, for I will utterly
blot out the remembrance of Amalek from under heaven.*

It is interesting to find that the Greek version of Isa. xlv. 1 had
already become so altered as to give a Christian interpretation. For
the quotation runs: *The Lord said unto my Christ the Lord* (Κυρίῳ),

---

[1] xii. 1: ὅταν ξύλον κλιθῇ καὶ ἀναστῇ, καὶ ὅταν ἐκ ξύλου αἷμα στάξῃ.

[2] *Selected Testimonies against the Jews*, vii (= Migne, *P.G.* xlvi. 213): καὶ πάλιν,
καὶ τότε ταῦτα συντελεσθήσεται, λέγει κύριος, ὅταν ξύλον ξύλων (*var. lect.* ξύλῳ)
κλιθῇ, καὶ ἀναστῇ, καὶ ὅταν ἐκ ξύλου αἷμα στάξει.

[3] "Hic stillavit sanguis de ligno" (Valesius, xi. 2nd App. 126).

[4] "Et respondi et dixi: usquequo et quando haec?...de signis autem...et
de ligno sanguis stillabit, et lapis dabit vocem suam." See further in Bensly-
James, *The Fourth Book of Ezra*, 1895, pp. xxviii *sq.*, and James' *Lost Apocrypha
of the O.T.* 1920, pp. 89, 101, where he quotes a similar phrase from the Slavonic
Ladder of Jacob. He, however, does not think the words are due to the passage
in Esdras. See also *The Rest of the Words of Baruch*, 1889, ix. 14 *sq.* and Rendel
Harris' remarks. J. A. R. in *J. Th. S.* April, 1934, xxxv. 128, finds an allusion
to our passage in Irenaeus v. ii. 3: "The tree (ξύλον) of the Vine having been
bended to the earth bore fruit." But while Barnabas refers to the Cross, Irenaeus
refers to a vine-shoot bent into the ground (εἰς τὴν γῆν) and in due course
bearing fruit, and so providing wine for the Eucharist. He can hardly have had
Barnabas itself in mind, though the form of the expression may be due to the
Christian adaptation of Esdras.

[5] xii. 9.

where the LXX is: *to my anointed, Cyrus* (Κύρῳ), nearly following the Hebrew.[1]

Last of all may be mentioned a passage in which Barnabas has probably been misunderstood, as though he intended to deny the Davidic ancestry of our Lord.[2] For referring to Ps. cx. 1 he writes: "Since then they will say that Christ is son of David, David himself prophesies, fearing and understanding the error of sinners, *The Lord saith*, etc." But there does not appear to be any early Patristic evidence for this interpretation,[3] and the context is quite consistent with the usual explanation of our Lord's words that He desired only to call attention to the fact that He was more than the Messianic hero expected by the Jews as the son of David.[4]

[1] xii. 11. The same error is to be found in Tertullian, *Adv. Jud.* vii; Cyprian, *Test.* i. 21, and elsewhere.

[2] xii. 10. See Rendel Harris, *Test.* i. 37; Vacher Burch, *Jesus Christ and His Revelation*, p. 94.

[3] Though "Marinus", who represents the unorthodox, urges it against Adamantius (Adamantius, *Dialogue*, iv. 858 (v. 12)).

[4] In xv. 4 Barnabas says that a "day" means 1000 years, but his language is more like 2 Pet. iii. 8 and *Trypho*, lxxxi. 3 than Ps. xc. 4.

CHAPTER III

THE DIALOGUE OF JASON AND PAPISCUS[1]

? BETWEEN A.D. 135 AND 178

All that we know about this famous treatise may be stated very briefly. It was written in Greek, and was read by Celsus the heathen philosopher of Rome, who used it in his *True Account* (*c.* A.D. 178), where he described it as "fitted to excite pity and hatred instead of laughter". For "the fallacy of it and of other works of the same kind was manifest to all". Origen, however (*c.* A.D. 248), though considering it one of the least important of the many treatises containing allegorical explanations and interpretations, useful to the simple-minded, but not to the more intelligent, speaks of it as a work in which a Christian (i.e. Jason) is described as conversing with a Jew (i.e. Papiscus) on the subject of the Jewish Scriptures, and proving to him that "the predictions concerning Christ fitly apply to Jesus". He adds that the Jew maintains his cause in no ignoble or unseemly manner, "not unbecoming the character of a Jew".[2] A later author, Celsus the African, so called to distinguish him from his earlier namesake, translated the *Dialogue* into Latin, and tells us that Jason was a Hebrew Christian and Papiscus an Alexandrian Jew, and that Papiscus was won over by Jason and was baptised. He even speaks of the treatise as "that famous and noteworthy and splendid work".[3]

Further, it was attributed to Ariston of Pella (*c.* A.D. 140) by one Maximus (? cent. vii), who adds, very strangely, that Clement

---

[1] *Altercatio Jasonis et Papisci*. The materials for the study of this are collected in Routh, *Reliquiae Sacrae*, 1846, i. 95–109; Migne, *P.G.* v. 1277–1286; and especially in Harnack, *Texte u. Unters.* 1883, I. i. 115–130 (*Die Überlieferung d. griech. Apol.*), and his *Altchristl. Lit.* 1893, i. 92–95. See also Bardenhewer, *Gesch. d. altkirchl. Lit.* 1913, i. 202–206; Juster, *Les Juifs dans l'Empire Romain*, 1914, i. 54 *sq.*

[2] For these references to Celsus and Origen see the latter, *c. Celsum*, iv. 52 (*vide infra*, p. 90).

[3] See Celsus' Letter, sending his translation to one Bishop Vigilius, contained in Cyprian's works (Hartel, iii. 119–132). Harnack formerly thought that this was Vigilius of Thapsus, and that this Celsus wrote in the fifth century. But he has come to the much more probable opinion that he wrote in the end of the third (*Gesch. d. altchr. Lit., Die Chronologie*, II. ii. 390–393).

of Alexandria said in the sixth book of his (lost) Hypotyposes that it was written by St Luke.[1] Further, if the quotation of Ariston of Pella's reference to Hadrian's decree forbidding the Jews to visit Jerusalem (A.D. 135) was taken by Eusebius from our *Dialogue*, it must have been written between 135 and 178, the date of the *True Account*, and probably nearer the former than the latter date.[2]

Of the contents of the *Dialogue*, besides this rather doubtful item in Eusebius, we know only that (1) it interpreted the phrase "In the beginning" (Gen. i. 1) as "In the Son";[3] (2) it spoke of "seven heavens";[4] (3) it contained the words Λοιδορία θεοῦ ὁ κρεμάμενος, i.e. as Jerome says,[5] "Maledictio Dei qui appensus est", which resembles Aquila's version of Deut. xxi. 23 more closely than any other, but is not actually Aquila's, and cannot therefore be adduced with any confidence as evidence that the *Dialogue* was written after Aquila (? 130).

That is all we know about the *Dialogue of Jason and Papiscus*. But the very meagreness of our materials has left free play for imagination. It has therefore been seriously argued that authors who interpret Gen. i. 1 in the same way that the *Dialogue* does, as we have seen, used the *Dialogue* itself, and this has served as a basis for supposing that the rest of any document in which such an interpretation is found is derived in greater or less measure from our *Dialogue*.[6] But our present materials are altogether too small to

---

[1] Migne, *P.G.* iv. 421. Cf. Routh, *op. cit.* p. 96.

[2] *Ch. Hist.* IV. vi. 3. See also Tertullian, *Adv. Jud.* xiii, with which Eusebius has verbal coincidences. For the decree compare Justin, *Trypho*, xvi. 2 (*infra*, p. 34).

[3] See Harnack's note on Gen. i. 1 in his "Evagrius' *Altercatio Simonis et Judaei et Theophili Christiani*" (*Texte u. Unters.* 1883, I. iii. 130–134); Jerome, *Quaest. Heb. in Gen.* i. 1 (Vallarsi, iii. 305): "*In principio fecit Deus caelum et terram. Plerique existimant, sicut in Altercatione Jasonis et Papisci scriptum est,...in Hebraeo haberi, in Filio fecit Deus caelum et terram.*" So Tertullian, *c. Prax.* § 5; and Hilary on Ps. ii, § 2. Harnack thinks the interpretation goes back to Prov. viii. 22, by which the Arian Bishop Maximinus illustrates it (ch. x, *vide infra*, p. 307). It occurs also in the *Consultationes of Zacch. and Apollon.* II. iii (*vide infra*, p. 297), and in the anonymous *Tractatus contra Judaeos* (A.D. 1166), § 2 (*vide infra*, p. 395). So also in *Tim.-Aq.* Fol. 78 r⁰ (*infra*, p. 73).

[4] In Maximus' Scholia on the *Mystical Theology*, i. 3, attributed to Dionysius the Areopagite, therefore later than the end of the fifth century (Routh, *op. cit.*).

[5] On Gal. iii. 13 (Vallarsi, vii. 456). Tertullian, *Adv. Jud.* x, treats of this quotation from Deut. xxi. 23 at length (*vide infra*, p. 49). See also Justin, *Trypho*, lxxxix, xcvi. 1 (*infra*, p. 39); Evagrius, *Alt. Sim.* § 22.

[6] For example, Harnack formerly argued that the *Altercatio Simonis et Judaei et Theophili Christiani* by Evagrius (of whom nothing is known save that he must

warrant any such comparison and deduction. It is at least as probable that the explanation of Gen. i. 1 which seems so strange to us, but was completely in accordance with Rabbinic methods (as every tyro who has read Rashi on the passage knows), formed a part of that common traditional teaching of the Church which has been elucidated in our chapter about the *Book of Testimonies*. The *Dialogue of Jason and Papiscus* has perished—though it may still be hidden in some library—and whether it influenced later writers (other than those already mentioned as definitely using it) we have no means of knowing.

have lived in the west, probably Gaul) is substantially our *Dialogue* worked up to date (? cent. v). But he has rightly given up this theory (*Altchristl. Lit.* 1893, i. 95). F. C. Conybeare, again, thought that the *Dialogue of Athanasius and Zacchaeus* (which he attributed to the second century!) reproduced large portions of it.

CHAPTER IV
JUSTIN MARTYR
THE DIALOGUE WITH TRYPHO[1]
BETWEEN A.D. 155 AND 161

A Jewish gentleman, cultured and courteous but not very learned in his own religion, was walking one day with some friends in the Colonnade at Ephesus, about the year 136, and met there a man wearing a kind of cape which proclaimed him scholar and philosopher. The Jewish gentleman greeted him politely, and expressed a desire for some profitable intercourse. The philosopher was Justin; the Jew Trypho—at least that is the name which is recorded, but was perhaps only given to him later by Justin, in allusion to his famous and very learned contemporary, R. Tarphon. They conversed on Christianity at some length and for two days, and afterwards Justin wrote out a full account of their discussion.[2]

His narrative unfortunately has not come down to us either complete, or in finally polished form. It has lacunae—one very serious[3]—and in the latter part has much repetition. In fact, the last sixty-eight chapters (lxxv–cxlii) probably represent only rough drafts of the previous portion, together with some new matter. But as there is practically only one manuscript it is impossible to test subjective impressions by "external" evidence.

We are compelled therefore to limit ourselves to the more salient parts of the treatise, which, however, indicate quite clearly Justin's methods and arguments.

[1] Τοῦ ἁγίου Ἰουστίνου φιλοσόφου καὶ μάρτυρος πρὸς Τρύφωνα Ἰουδαῖον Διάλογος. Such is the title found in the only manuscript, viz. C, No. 450 in the National Library at Paris. For the MS. Ch., which is now (1935) at Cheltenham, is a slightly inaccurate copy of that. Unfortunately even C cannot be wholly trusted, for it is demonstrably careless in the other treatises that it contains. The best edition is by E. J. Goodspeed, *Die ältesten Apologeten*, 1914 (Trypho, pp. 90–265). The standard text is in J. C. T. Otto, *S. Justini Philosophi et Martyris Opera*, 3rd edition, 1877. I venture to refer readers of this chapter also to my *Justin Martyr, The Dialogue with Trypho*, Translation, Introduction and Notes (S.P.C.K. 1930), for fuller information on nearly all the points on which I touch here. Justin's treatise was dedicated to a friend named Marcus Pompeius (cxli. 5; cf. viii. 3), of whom nothing is known.

[2] In cxx. 6 he says "I addressed myself to Caesar in writing", with direct reference to 1 *Apol.* i. Thus the *Trypho* was written after the First *Apology*, and probably between A.D. 155 and 161, at Rome.   [3] lxxiv. 3.

He begins with the meeting in the Colonnade told from Justin's standpoint. Then, taking advantage of Trypho's statement that he had been spending time in Greece and Corinth, with its implication that he had been studying philosophy, Justin asks him why he should expect to find more advantage in philosophy than in the teaching of his own Lawgiver and Prophets. Trypho was astounded at such a question from him, but Justin went on to explain the strength and weakness of philosophy as such. For he himself had studied it in all its Schools, including the Platonic. With this indeed he had once been satisfied, until he met by chance a venerable and elderly person who showed him in Socratic dialogue its inability to teach the highest of all wisdom, the knowledge of Truth. For this was to be found only in the Prophets, who "both glorified the Maker of all things as God and Father, and proclaimed the Christ sent from Him, as His Son".[1] "If therefore you have any regard for yourself, and are in earnest after salvation, and are trusting on God, you may, forasmuch as you are no stranger to the subject, know the Christ of God, and be initiated (i.e. be baptised), and then lead a prosperous and happy life."[2]

At this Trypho's companions laughed aloud, and even Trypho himself smiled. And he tells Justin that he had better have kept to philosophy: "For while you remained in that mode of philosophy and lived a blameless life, a hope was left you of a better fate, but when you have forsaken God, and placed your hope on a man, what kind of salvation yet remains for you? If therefore you are willing to listen also to me (for I already reckon you as a friend), first be circumcised, then (as is commanded in the Law) keep the Sabbath and the Feasts and God's New Moons, and, in short, do all the things that are written in the Law, and then perchance you will find mercy from God. But Messiah, if indeed He has ever been and now exists anywhere, is unknown, and does not even know Himself at all, nor has any power, until Elijah shall have come and anointed Him, and shall have made Him manifest to all. But you people, by receiving a worthless rumour, shape a kind of Messiah for yourselves, and for His sake are now blindly perishing."[3]

Justin replies quite courteously that Christians have not been led astray, and adds: "For if you will attend I will show you that we did not believe empty fables, or words that cannot be proved,

---

[1] vii. 3.

[2] viii. 2. For the value and character of Baptism, see xiv. 1 *sq.*

[3] viii. 3, 4. The reference to the coming of Elijah recurs in xlix, *passim.*

but such as are full of the Divine Spirit, gushing forth with power, and teeming with grace."[1]

But at this Trypho's friends again rudely laughed out loud, so Justin began to leave them, but on Trypho's entreaty consented to discuss the question if his companions would either be quiet or withdraw.

After Trypho had expressed his agreement with Justin as to the absurdity of the popular tales about the Thyestaean banquets of the Christians, he adds: "I know too that the commands given you in what is called the Gospel are so admirable and great that I suspect that no one can keep them. For I took some trouble to read them. But we are especially at a loss about this, that you, saying you worship God, and thinking yourselves superior to other people, separate from them in no respect, and do not make your life different from the heathen, in that you keep neither the feasts nor the sabbaths, nor have circumcision, and, moreover, though you set your hopes on a man that was crucified, you yet hope to obtain some good from God, though you do not keep His commandments. Now have you not read: *That soul shall be cut off from his people* (Gen. xvii. 14) which shall not be circumcised on the eighth day? The charge refers alike to strangers and to purchased slaves. It follows that when you have directly despised this covenant you neglect the commands that come afterwards, and as persons who know God you attempt to persuade us, though you practise none of these things which they who fear God do. If therefore you have any defence to make with regard to these points, and can show us how you have any hope at all, even though you do not keep the Law, we would very gladly hear from you. Afterwards let us examine the other points in the same way."[2]

Then Justin begins his argument, in which the order is not as remarkable as the number of his digressions.

Two or three of these may be mentioned at once.

Justin insists that the Jews had falsified their Scriptures, evidently, as he implies, to prevent the Christians finding in them passages which should confirm their faith. Neither he nor Trypho knew Hebrew, so that both had to be content with the current form of the Septuagint. For general statements see lxxi. 2 and lxxiii. 5 *sq.* and for a specific instance lxxii. 2 *sq.*, where Jer. xi. 19 (*the lamb . . . let us cast wood into His bread*)[3] is said to have been recently excised,

---

[1] ix. 1. [2] x. 2–4.
[3] See my note on Isidore, *Contra Judaeos*, xxxv, *infra*, p. 287.

though it is found to-day in all copies of the Greek and the Hebrew. Another case is lxxiii. 1, where he says that *from the Tree* has been excised from Ps. xcvi. 10 in *The Lord reigned from the Tree*.[1] In lxxii. 4 he claims an evidently Christian passage which speaks of the Descent into Hades as having been in "Jeremiah", and in lxxii. 1 another equally strong Christian passage, which tells of the Crucifixion and the ensuing punishment of the Jews, as having been in "Esdras".

That quotations from the Old Testament are sometimes assigned to wrong authors is explicable in days when books were comparatively clumsy and inconvenient.[2]

Again, we have the interesting piece of information that after the futile revolt of Barkokba Hadrian forbade all Jews to enter Jerusalem, a prohibition which seems to have lasted till the fourth century.[3]

Perhaps it may be convenient to mention here Justin's strange list of Jewish sects which orthodox Jews would not acknowledge. These (in Justin's order) are Sadducees, Genistae, Meristae, Galileans, Hellenians, Pharisees, and Baptists. Of these nothing is known about the Genistae and Meristae, or the Hellenians unless we emend the word to Hillelites. Perhaps the Galileans are the reputed followers of Judas of Galilee, and the Baptists are presumably a branch of the Essenes.[4]

Justin also complains several times that the Jews curse in their synagogues those who believe in Christ. Probably this curse was originally directed against Jewish-Christians only, but even so Justin's mistake is quite natural and perhaps even logical.[5]

Akin to this is Justin's accusation of the Jews for sending out selected men from Jerusalem into all the earth "saying that a

[1] See Isidore, *ibid.*

[2] In xiv. 8 "Hosea" is a mistake for Zechariah (xii. 10), and in xxix. 2; xlix. 2 "Zechariah" is put for Malachi.

[3] xvi. 2; xcii. 2. Cf. 1 *Apol.* xlvii. 6; Tert. *Adv. Jud.* iii; Euseb. *Ch. Hist.* IV. vi. 3.

[4] lxxx. 4. Cf. Epiphanius, *Adv. Haeres.* I. xiv; Dionysius bar Salibi, *Against the Jews*, I. 4–11 (*infra*, p. 109).

[5] xvi. 4; xcvi. 2. The Palestinian or older form of the Twelfth Benediction in the Eighteen Prayers (*Shemônê Esreh*) of the Jewish Prayer Book runs: "To the apostates let there be no hope, and the kingdom of pride do Thou quickly root out in our days. And let the Christians (*nôtzrim*) and the heretics (*mînim*) perish as in a moment. Let them be wiped out of the book of life, and with the righteous let them not be written. Blessed art Thou, O LORD, who subduest the proud." This was said at Jabneh (*c.* A.D. 100) by Samuel the Small, and apparently composed by him (T. B. *Berakoth*, 29 a).

godless sect, namely, of Christians, had appeared, and recounting what all who know us not are wont to say against us".[1] Although there is no confirmation of this from Jewish sources, it is probably correct, for Jewish representatives were sent from Palestine to all the centres of the Diaspora taking information about the Calendar, and it may be inferred that they carried also such legal decisions as would affect the community at large.

If we disregard Justin's digressions, and even the order in which he deals with his various subjects, his argument may be stated thus:

I. The Old Testament itself looks forward to the Law being superseded. To this is added a more detailed study of the various ordinances of the Law.

II. The Old Testament itself looks forward to the Coming of the Messiah and even predicts details about Him, which are in fact fulfilled in Jesus. It tells us also of His two Advents (not only of one); of His pre-existence and His Divine nature; and His life on earth. In connexion with this Justin deals particularly with the Coming of Elijah; the Virgin Birth, which, as he rightly insists, has nothing in common with heathen myths; the Holy Spirit descending on Him at His Baptism; His humiliation in general; His Crucifixion and His Resurrection.

III. Justin informs us of certain interesting facts about Christians, and mentions some of their beliefs. He himself "and all other entirely orthodox Christians" believe in the Millennium "in a Jerusalem built up and adorned and enlarged, as the prophets Ezekiel and Isaiah and all the rest acknowledge".[2] Again, he tells us of false Christians;[3] the observance of the Law by some Christians;[4] and Evil Angels.[5]

IV. He also dwells at some length on the Call of the Gentiles,[6] and God's present relation to the Jews, with their behaviour towards Him.[7]

A common argument with Christians has always been that Jewish kings lasted until the birth of our Lord, and then came to an end, for this was the meaning of Gen. xlix. 10, *The sceptre shall*

---

[1] xvii. 1. Parkes (p. 80) gives a possible reconstruction of the letter which they carried, based on Justin, Eusebius and Jerome.

[2] lxxx. 5; also lxxxi. Cf. *Barn.* xv. 4 (*supra*, p. 27, note 3).

[3] xxxv; lxxx. 3; lxxxii. [4] xlvii.

[5] lxxix. [6] cix–cxi; cxv–cxxv; cxxx.

[7] xvi; xvii; cxii–cxiv; cxxxi–cxxxvi.

not depart from Judah, nor the ruler's staff from between his feet, until Shiloh come. But the Jews countered this by saying that Herod the Great (and therefore, of course, his son) was not really a Jew. For Antipater, Herod the Great's father, was an Ascalonite, carried off by Edom in a raid. Justin refers to this, but adds that in any case a High Priest survived, and now the Jews had neither him nor their own kings.[1]

Justin is careful to point out that Jeremiah contemplates a change in the Law, for he speaks of a new Disposition. *Behold the days come, saith the Lord, that I will make a new Disposition,* etc. (Jer. xxxi. [xxxviii.] 31 *sq.*). For Christ "is the new Law, and the new Disposition, and the Expectation of those from among all the nations, who await the good things that come to them at the hands of God. For we are the true and spiritual Israelitish nation."[2]

No longer do Prophets exist among the Jews, but we Christians have still the gifts of prophecy, for they have been transferred to us.[3]

He has, as is to be expected, a good deal to say about Circumcision,[4] the Sabbath,[5] and the Dietary Laws.[6]

To Whom does the common Old Testament phrase *The Angel of the LORD* really refer? The question can hardly be said to be settled even in our own day. Justin, indeed, is not as clear and explicit in his *Trypho* as he is in 1 *Apol.* lxiii, but even here it is fairly plain that he means us to understand that the Angel who spoke to Moses at the burning bush, and is afterwards called God, is not the Supreme God as such, but One who was truly God yet in some sense also His Messenger. "We shall not understand the God who conversed with Moses from the bush to have been the Maker of the universe, but Him who was proved to have appeared to Abraham [and Isaac] and Jacob, who is also called an Angel of the God who was the Maker of the universe."[7]

In lxxxvi. 2 Justin urges that when Jacob saw One standing on the ladder (Gen. xxviii. 12 *sq.*) this was not God the Father, as, he adds, he has already shown. But where? It may be a vague reference to lx. 2 *sq.*, but, more probably, to a passage which has not come down to us.

[1] lii. 3. In chapters lii–liv he discusses Gen. xlix. 9–12.   [2] xi. 3–5.
[3] lii. 4; lxxxii. 1; lxxxvii. 5. Cf. Tertullian, *c. Jud.* viii (*vide infra,* p. 48).
[4] xxiii. 3–5. Cf. x. 3 (*supra,* p. 33).
[5] xxiii. 3: "Nature does not idle nor keep Sabbath....Before Moses there was no need of keeping Sabbath."   [6] xx.
[7] lx. 3. The sentence is attributed to Trypho in the MSS., but this is evidently a mistake, for it is the Christian and not the Jewish interpretation.

Of even more interest is Justin's use of Prov. viii. 22–36. For after saying that "God has begotten as a Beginning (Prov. viii. 22) before all His creatures a kind of Reasonable Power from Himself, which is also called by the Holy Spirit the Glory of the Lord, and sometimes Son, and sometimes Wisdom, and sometimes Angel, and sometimes God, and sometimes Lord and Word" he compares the case with ourselves. "For when we put forth any word, we beget a word, not putting it forth by scission, as though the word within us was diminished." He then adds: "The Word of wisdom will act as witness for me, being Himself this God begotten of the Father of the universe, and being all the time the Word and Wisdom and Power and Glory of Him who begat and spake as follows by Solomon." He then quotes the passage in Proverbs at length.[1]

He confirms this from Gen. i. 26, repudiating the Jewish suggestion that God merely said *Let us make* to Himself, and also the opinion which, according to the present text of Justin, was regarded as heretical by Jews though it is now almost the accepted one among them, that the words were addressed to the angels. He continues: "But this Offspring, which in reality was put forth from the Father before all His works, was with the Father, and with Him the Father conversed, as the word shows us plainly by means of Solomon, that this Itself which is called Wisdom by Solomon was begotten by God as (the) Beginning before all the works, and as (His) Offspring."[2]

The reader will have noticed that in the last two quotations (both referring to Prov. viii. 22) Justin speaks of Christ as "the Beginning". It is not unreasonable to suppose that Justin was acquainted, like his predecessor the author of *Jason and Papiscus*,[3] with the Midrashic interpretation of Gen. i. 1, and saw there the truth that Christ Himself was that glorious "Beginning" in whom all things were made.[4]

With regard to the Messiah Justin strongly insists that Ps. cx cannot refer to Hezekiah, as he says the Jews interpreted it,[5] but only to Christ.

So too he discusses at some length the meaning of Isa. vii. 14:

[1] lxi. [2] lxii.

[3] *Vide supra*, p. 29, with the note.

[4] In lxv. 5 Justin quotes Isa. xlii. 10: *His Beginning is from the end of the earth*, where the LXX has read *tehillāthô* ("His praise") as *techillāthô*.

[5] xxxii. 6–xxxiii. 2; lxxxiii. There seems to be no corroborative evidence that the psalm was interpreted of Hezekiah, at least before the third century. See my note on *Trypho*, lxxxiii. 1 (*op. cit.*).

The Virgin shall conceive. Whether or not Aquila's translation was actually in his hands, he knows of the rendering *the young woman*, but rejects it as offering no solution of the strange sign to Ahaz. The point of the prophecy, he says, lies in its extraordinary character, and there is nothing remarkable about a young woman having a child.[1]

While it is not possible to give the arguments of Justin in detail within the limits of this chapter, a few points of deep interest may be mentioned.

Not unnaturally he tilts against the worship of Mithra which was gaining so many recruits at that time, and says that his asserted birth from a Rock, a rock being also the place for the initiation of his worshippers, was, in reality, due to an imitation of the prophecy in Dan. ii. 34 *sq.*, the *Stone cut out without hands*.[2] He also finds that this passage in Daniel is a clear statement that this "is not a human work, but of the will of God, the Father of the universe, who brought it forward".[3] Justin learns from the passage, that is to say, that the Messiah was not to be of human but of Divine origin.

When, however, Justin thinks of our Lord as the Stone he does not limit himself to the image as such, but insists again and again that circumcision by knives of Stone (Josh. v. 2) suggests the same thing. True circumcision of the heart is brought about only by the true Stone, the Lord Jesus Christ. No doubt this is a pretty conceit, and allowable if the Rabbinic standard of Midrash be accepted, but Justin, it is to be feared, meant much more than that. To him it was "proof" in almost our meaning of the word—that the Old Testament does definitely predict Christ and all that appertains to His work.[4]

---

[1] lxvii. 1; lxxxiv. After all, whatever the real interpretation may be, Aquila gives only the etymological meaning of the word, but the LXX its meaning in the context, for the point is that the damsel was not married when Isaiah uttered the prophecy.

[2] lxx. 1. He says more exactly that the followers of Mithra are initiated "in a place to which they give the designation of a cave", this being in imitation of our Lord's birth in a cave (lxxviii. 5 *sq.*). See the *Protevangelium of St James*, §§ 18, 19, 21.   [3] lxxvi. 1.

[4] "Jesus Christ circumcises all them who will, with knives of stone" (xxiv. 2). In cxiii. 6 *sq.* the knives of stone are more precisely defined as "the words of our Lord Jesus". In any case the phrase points to a spiritual circumcision, for "Joshua even circumcised them who entered into that holy land with a second circumcision". Similarly, Justin points out that Isaiah (i. 16) does not refer to a bath, but to the laver of salvation, ch. xiii. 1. Cf. Cyprian, *Test.* i. 24 (*infra*, p. 60).

The difficulty that Jews have always felt, that Crucifixion implies a curse, according to Deut. xxi. 23, is discussed by Justin. "We doubt", says Trypho, "whether the Christ was crucified with such dishonour, for he that is crucified is said in the Law to be accursed."[1] And again: "We know that He suffers, and is to be brought as a sheep. But prove to us whether He must even be crucified, and die in so disgraceful a fashion, by the death that in the Law is accursed."[2] Justin replies: "Every race of men will be found to be under the curse according to the Law of Moses.... If, therefore, the Father of the universe purposed that His own Christ should receive on Himself the curses of all, on behalf of men of every race, knowing that He would raise Him up after being crucified and dying, why do you speak of Him who endured the suffering of these things in accordance with the purpose of the Father as though He was accursed, and do not rather lament for yourselves?"[3] And again: "Further, what is said in the Law, *Cursed is every one which hangeth on a tree*, strengthens our hope in its dependence on the crucified Christ, not because He who has been crucified is accursed of God, but because God foretold what would be done by all of you and such as you, when ye did not know that this is He who was before all things and the eternal priest of God, and King, and Christ."[4]

Justin, indeed, is so intent on the salvation won for us by the cross of Christ that he sometimes finds symbols of the Cross in verses of the Old Testament where we can hardly see them. The Brazen Serpent on the pole indeed does not come into this category, for we have been trained by the Fourth Gospel to find the Cross there.[5] But to find it in God's blessing of Joseph recorded in Deut. xxxiii. 13–17, *His horns are the horns of an unicorn*, is a different thing: "For no one could say or prove that the horns of a unicorn are of any other matter or form than of the figure which represents a cross. For the one piece of wood stands upright, from which the upper part is raised up into a horn, when the other piece of wood is fitted on, and the ends seem like horns joined to that one horn. And the piece fixed in the middle itself on which they that are crucified are upborne also projects like a horn, and itself looks like a horn, when fashioned together and fixed in with the other horns."[6]

Another example is the Paschal lamb. "That sheep which was commanded to be roasted whole was a figure of the suffering of

---

[1] lxxxix. 2.   [2] xc. 1.   [3] xcv. 1 *sq.*   [4] xcvi. 1.
[5] xci. 4; xciv. 1–3; cxxxi. 4.   [6] xci. 1 *sq.*

the cross, by which Christ was to suffer. For when the sheep is being roasted it is roasted arranged in fashion like the fashion of the cross, for one spit is pierced straight from the lower parts to the head, and one again at the back, to which also the paws of the sheep are fastened."[1]

Again, a very common prediction of the Cross is found in the attitude of Moses when he prayed at the battle with the Amalekites. "Moses himself prayed to God, stretching out his hands on either side. But Hur and Aaron supported them the whole day long, lest he should be weary and they should fall down. For if any of this figure that imitated the form of a cross had given way the people, as is written in the writings of Moses, were defeated. But if he remained in this position, so long was Amalek overcome, and as he prevailed he prevailed by the cross. Not because Moses prayed thus was the people therefore superior, but because the name of Jesus (Joshua) being at the head of the battle, he (Moses) was making the figure of the cross."[2]

Akin to the figures of the Cross is Justin's interpretation of the Two Goats offered at the Fast, of which one was sacrificed to the LORD, and the other sent away as a Scapegoat, the latter being an announcement of the first Advent, when the elders and the priests laid their hands on Jesus, putting Him to death, and thus sending Him off. The former represented His second Advent because in the same place of Jerusalem He will be recognised. Justin's exposition, but not his language, recalls *Barnabas* (vii. 6–11).[3]

Even Noah's Ark is pressed into the cause. "For Christ, being the First-born of every creature, has also become again the head of another race, which was begotten anew of Him by water and faith and wood, which held the mystery of the cross, even as Noah also was saved in wood, when he was borne upon the waters with his family."[4] In one chapter (lxxxvi) Justin combines many types of Christ and His cross.

Here perhaps should be mentioned Justin's curious use of "Flower" (ἄνθος), taken from the Septuagint of Isa. xi. 1, a thought which is enlarged in Irenaeus, *Preaching*, § 59: "And by Flower he (the Prophet) means His flesh, for from spirit it budded

---

[1] xl. 3.

[2] xc. 4 *sq.* See also xci. 3; cxi. 1; cxii. 2. In lxxv. 2 Justin asks "Who was it that led your fathers into the land?" He answers in effect, He on whom is My Name (Ex. xxiii. 20 *sq.*), i.e. Joshua (Jesus) who was formerly called only Oshea. See also cxxxi. 4 *sq.*   [3] xl. 4 *sq.*   [4] cxxxviii. 2.

forth." Cf. the *Discussion of Zacchaeus and Apollonius* (II. iii): "in odore floris et gratia signatus est Christus."[1] And in Evagrius, *Discussion between Simon and Theophilus* (§ 15): "Christ the Flower of the Patriarchs according to the flesh." For other references see Rendel Harris, *Test.* ii. p. 62.[2]

That Isa. viii. 4, *The riches of Damascus and the spoil of Samaria shall be carried away before the king of Assyria*, was fulfilled by the coming of the Wise men from the East, to acknowledge Christ, is a very common interpretation among Church writers, but is found, as it seems, for the first time in the *Trypho*. "We cannot grant you," says Justin to Trypho, "as you desire to expound it, that Hezekiah made war on the men in Damascus, or in Samaria, in the presence of the king of Assyria.... And you cannot prove that this has ever happened to anyone among the Jews, but we can prove that it took place in the case of our Christ. For at the very time that He was born wise men came from Arabia and worshipped Him, after they had first been to Herod who was king at that time in your land, whom the word calls the king of Assyria because of his godless and wicked mind."[3] And again: "That saying, also of Isaiah, *He shall take the power of Damascus and the spoils of Samaria*, meant that the power of the devil, who dwelt in Damascus, should be overcome by Christ at His very birth. And this is proved to have taken place. For the Wise Men, who had been carried off as spoils for all kinds of evil actions, which were wrought in them by that demon, by coming and worshipping Christ are shown to have departed from that power which had taken them as spoil, which (power) the word signified to us in a mystery as dwelling in Damascus."[4]

Justin continues: "And that selfsame power, as being sinful and wicked, he rightly calls Samaria in parable. Now that Damascus did and does belong to the land of Arabia, even though it is now allotted to that which is called Syrophoenicia,[5] not even any of you can deny. So that it would be well, Gentlemen, if you were to learn the things that you do not understand from them who have received grace from God, even us Christians, and not to be always striving to prop up your own doctrines, and do despite to those of God."[6]

[1] In *Zacch. and Apoll.* II, ix the Blessed Virgin is the Shoot, and Christ the Flower.
[2] cxxvi. 1.
[3] lxxvii.   [4] lxxviii. 9.
[5] This clause is an addition by a copyist, for the "allotment" was made by Septimius Severus in A.D. 194.   [6] lxxviii. 10.

The Epilogue is worth quoting in full for its evidence of the kindly spirit of the disputants. "Now Trypho paused somewhat, and then said: You see that it was not by design that we fell into a discussion over these matters. And I acknowledge that I have been extraordinarily charmed with our intercourse, and I think that these are of like opinion with myself. For we have found more than we expected, or than it was even possible for us to expect. And if we could do this more frequently we should receive more benefit, while we examine the very words (of Scripture) for ourselves. But since, he added, you are putting off to sea, and expect to begin your voyage every day, do not scruple to think of us as your friends when you take your departure.

"As regards myself, I replied, I could wish, if I remained here, that such a discussion should take place every day. But as I am expecting to embark at once, if God permit and help me, I urge you to enter on this greatest of all contests for your own salvation, and to endeavour to prefer to your own teachers the Christ of Almighty God.

"After which they departed, finally praying for my deliverance from the dangers of the sea, and from all ill.

"And I prayed also for them, saying: I can make no greater prayer for you, Gentlemen, than this, that having come to know that happiness is given to every man through this Way, you may do in all respects the same as we, acknowledging that the object of our worship is the Christ of God."[1]

One hopes that Justin's prayer was granted. For the discussion was conducted in a seemly way, and the impression that we receive from it is far more favourable than that which we get from the majority of our treatises. Justin, no doubt, was the more learned of the two in Jewish matters, but Trypho was perhaps the more polished man of the world. Both were earnest and sincere, and neither shows any sign of desiring a merely verbal victory. While some others of the *Antijudaica* are more elaborate, and some more deeply steeped in Jewish lore and acquaintance with Judaism in general (notably Ramon Martini's *Pugio Fidei* of the fourteenth century, and Paul of Burgos' *Scrutinium Scripturarum* of the fifteenth), there is no Dialogue as such which is conducted on quite so high a level of courteousness and fairness until Gilbert Crispin's at Westminster in the end of the eleventh century.

[1] cxlii.

CHAPTER V

TERTULLIAN

IN ANSWER TO THE JEWS[1]

c. A.D. 200

It is said that when the future Emperor Caracalla was about seven years old, in A.D. 195 or 196, a fellow playmate, presumably slightly older, became inclined to Judaism and was so severely chastised by the Emperor Severus and his own father, that the young prince took this punishment deeply to heart.[2]

Be that as it may—and we can hardly take Noeldechen's suggestion seriously that this event in Rome moved Tertullian in Carthage to write our treatise—there is no doubt that a few Christians did apostatise to Judaism, while, on the other hand, many were desirous of winning Jews to Christianity. Also a large number of Jews lived in North Africa, as the big Jewish cemetery at Carthage still testifies.[3] There was therefore sufficient reason for the *Adversus Judaeos* to be composed, both as a protection to Christians, and as a means of winning Jews.

Directly, however, we examine it we are struck by its twofold character. The first eight chapters are crisp and polished—if such words may be used of Tertullian's harsh and rugged style—the last six chapters are drawn out, and altogether more loosely strung together. It is no wonder therefore that their relation to the first part has caused much controversy, at least from the time of Semler, who was frankly sceptical about many of the works attributed to Tertullian.[4] Neander thought that only chh. i–viii were Ter-

[1] *Adversus Judaeos*, Oehler's edition, 1853, is still the best. The treatise is translated by Thelwall in the Ante-Nicene Library, 1870.

[2] "Septennis puer, cum conlusorem suum puerum ob Judaicam religionem gravius verberatum audisset, neque patrem suum neque patrem pueri velut auctores verberum diu respexit." Spartianus (*c.* 285), *Ant. Caracalla*, i, in the *Scriptores Hist. Aug.* Teubner, 1927, i. 183. See Noeldechen (*vide infra*, p. 44), 1894, pp. 87–89.

[3] See Monceaux, *Hist. Littéraire de l'Afrique Chrétienne*, 1901, pp. 9, 294; *Jew. Enc.* iii. 594, 617.

[4] Semler denied the genuineness of the whole treatise. His criticism was published in his edition of Tertullian (1770–1773), and may be found more conveniently in Oehler, vol. iii, where, further, the parts of our treatise that resemble *Adv. Marc.* are set forth in parallel columns (pp. 639–657).

tullian's, and chh. ix–xiv were compiled by an unknown author from *Adversus Marcionem*, iii,[1] and this is still the opinion of many critics. But Noeldechen,[2] by comparing the *Adv. Jud.* with Tertullian's other writings in general[3] as well as with *Adv. Marc.* iii, comes to the conclusion that our chh. ix–xiv are a rough draft made by Tertullian, and chh. i–viii a more finished sketch, while the whole tract was afterwards used freely by Tertullian for the third book of his *Adv. Marc.* (*c.* A.D. 210). Noeldechen thinks that the *Adv. Jud.* was written in A.D. 195–6.[4]

Harnack is equally sure that chh. ix–xiv contain nothing contradictory to Tertullian's authorship,[5] but has a theory of his own that Tertullian wrote chh. i–viii after the first edition of his *Adv. Marc.*, which already contained the amplifications (*Ausführungen*) that we now find in *Adv. Marc.* iii (third edition), and then added chh. ix–xiv out of the first. For, having the contents of those chapters there already, he naturally would not use the *Adv. Jud.*

Neither theory is very attractive, but the important point is that both scholars agree that chh. ix–xiv were written by Tertullian himself.

Both, however, wrote before serious notice had been paid to the suggestion that the Church possessed catenae of Old Testament passages thought to bear upon the truth of Christianity. And though recent writers have exaggerated this fact, and, going beyond all probabilities, have tried to prove the existence of one such *Book of Testimonies* only, which continued, somewhere or other, down to the twelfth century—though not quoted by name[6] and visible only by identity of Old Testament quotations—there is this much truth in the theory, that such catenae existed, differing greatly in

---

[1] *Antignostikus*, 1825 (Bohn's translation, ii. 530). So also J. M. Fuller in *Dict. Chr. Biog.* 1887, iv. 827.

[2] In his two treatises *Die Abfassungszeit der Schriften Tertullians, Texte u. Unters.* v. 2, 1889; *Tertullians Gegen die Juden, T. u. U.* xii. 2, 1895.

[3] E.g. in phraseology (1895, pp. 35–46).

[4] Monceaux strongly prefers A.D. 200–206. He thinks the second edition of the Anti-Marcion refers to it (iii. 7): "Discat nunc haereticus ex abundanti *cum ipso* licebit *Judaeo* rationem quoque errorum." "Tertullien indique clairement ici qu'il va faire un emprunt à son traité *Contre les Juifs* et reproduire son raisonnement sur les causes d'erreur, parce que Marcion lui-même reproduisait une objection des Juifs" (*op. cit.* i. p. 205; cf. p. 295). In any case it was written before he became a Montanist (A.D. 207), for it contains no trace of the heresy. Harnack's theory requires the late date.

[5] "Weder in Stil, noch in den Anschauungen findet sich m. E. irgend etwas Untertullianisches" (*Altchristl. Lit.* 1904, ii. 2, p. 290).

[6] For Pseudo-Gregory's words do not bear out that explanation. See above on *The Books of Testimonies*, p. 6.

details, and yet necessarily containing much common matter. These would therefore lie ready at hand for Tertullian to incorporate. It seems not unlikely therefore that he used such a catena for the *Adv. Jud.*, and using it again, or perhaps only what he had already incorporated from it, revised and polished and adapted the passages to suit his rather different objective in the more important treatise against Marcion.

It is not necessary, however, to spend more time over this controversy, for in any case the question of the unity and even the authorship of the tract *In Answer to the Jews* is of little more than academic interest for our purpose. Every one is agreed that the third book against Marcion was written by Tertullian, and there is hardly a quotation from the Old Testament, or any interpretation of a quotation, in the *Adv. Jud.* which is not to be found there.

It will be sufficient therefore to consider the tract itself, and that as a whole.[1]

Tertullian tells us that he found a Jewish proselyte—a man of Gentile stock, but whether he had ever been a Christian or had been only a heathen he does not say, but apparently the latter—arguing with a Christian in favour of Judaism; and that Tertullian thought it well to state the evidence for the true faith more clearly in writing than was possible in the rather misty verbal discussion.

I. Beginning, it would seem, with the assumption that the Gentile had some warrant for accepting the chief truths of Judaism, and that by admitting him the Jews acknowledged that their religion was not for Jews only, Tertullian discusses the true nature of the Law, and shows its temporary character (chh. i–v).

If Gentiles are admissible to God's Law, the Jew need not despise them. In fact God's promise to Rebecca, "two peoples and two nations" (Gen. xxv. 23), refers to both Jewish and Gentile believers, and hints that whereas the younger son was to be greater than the elder, so there were to be more Gentile believers than Jewish (ch. i).[2]

---

[1] For convenience' sake, and without prejudice to further examination, I shall speak of the author of chh. ix–xiv as "Tertullian". He knew no Hebrew.

[2] In this chapter Tertullian pictures to us "the calf-like head" of the Golden Calf coming out from the melted gold first: "Cum...aurum fuisset igne conflatum et processisset eis bubulum caput" (Ex. xxxii. 24). If this supposition was current among the Jews it may have given rise to the later belief that the Calf came out alive and skipping (Midr. *Tanchuma, Ki Tissa*, § 19, edition 1902, p. 103 a; not in Buber's edition); see *Jew. Enc.* iii. 509.

Again, the Old Testament itself suggests that the Law of Moses
was not intended to last for ever. There was a Law before that
Law, which would have been sufficient, if it had been kept. Its
essence indeed is for all, but not its totality. That former Law was
long before Moses; it existed even in Eden. Noah, Abraham, and
others were found righteous by the observance of this natural Law,
under which Melchizedek was even a priest. Adam knew nothing
of Sabbath or Circumcision. Had circumcision been so important,
why was not Adam circumcised (ch. ii)?

What then was the use of Circumcision? It was given to
Abraham[1] and to Moses (see what is said about Zipporah) as a
sign by which Israelites were to be distinguished, that thus they
should not be able to enter Jerusalem—in accordance with
Hadrian's decree.[2] But Jeremiah announces a new Law,[3] from
which we may learn that bodily circumcision was to come to an
end. No doubt therefore we Gentile believers are the people of
whom Isa. ii. 2 *sq.* speaks (ch. iii).

It is the same with the Sabbath. Its observance was to be but
for a time, even as it was unknown to the Patriarchs. Observe too
that the Prophets themselves distinguish between Jewish sabbaths
and eternal and spiritual sabbaths, for Isaiah speaks of *your
sabbaths*,[4] and "Isaiah" of *My sabbaths*.[5] Isaiah refers to the eternal
sabbath when he says that all flesh shall come to worship in
Jerusalem.[6] "And this we must understand was fulfilled in the
time of Christ, when all flesh, i.e. every nation, came to worship
in Jerusalem God the Father through Jesus Christ His Son, as was
foretold by the Prophet, *Behold, the proselytes shall go unto Thee
through Me*."[7] Tertullian points out further that after Moses' time
even the observance of the sabbath did not consist in cessation

---

[1] Tertullian curiously puts the circumcision of Abraham (Gen. xvii. 10) *before*
he received the bread and wine at the hands of the uncircumcised Melchizedek
(Gen. xiv. 18). There may be some connexion between this and *Barnabas*' statement (ix. 8) that Abraham circumcised his 318 trained men whom he took with
him to pursue the four kings (Gen. xiv. 14); for circumcision may be a midrashic
expansion of "trained", "initiated".

[2] Cf. *Trypho*, xvi. 2 (*supra*, p. 34). See also *infra*, ch. xiii.

[3] Jer. xxxi. 31 *sq.* Cf. *Trypho* often, e.g. xi. 3–5 (*supra*, p. 36).

[4] Isa. i. 13.

[5] Ezek. xxii. 8. Tertullian says "Isaiah". For similar errors see *Trypho*, xiv.
8 (*supra*, p. 34).

[6] Isa. lxvi. 23.

[7] "Ecce proselyti per me ad te ibunt" (Isa. liv. 15 LXX).

from work, for the people went round Jericho for seven days, and the Maccabees fought on a sabbath (ch. iv).[1]

So again with Sacrifices. Both earthly and spiritual were alike foretold, and in fact even from the beginning the former were fore-shown in the offerings of the elder son, Cain, who represented Israel, and the latter in those of Abel the younger son, representing us Christians. The latter alone were accepted, for true offering to God must be made by spiritual sacrifices, as the Psalmist says.[2] Further, Tertullian notes, the former sacrifices were to be offered in a place in the Holy Land alone, "both for sins and for persons",[3] and nowhere else than in the Holy Land. Whereas of spiritual sacrifices God says that they shall be offered in every place (ch. v).[4]

II. Now that Tertullian has shown that the Old Testament contemplates a cessation of the Law of Moses with its component earthly parts, he turns to ask whether He who was to give the new spiritual Law has come or not. The answer is that He has come indeed, and that He is Jesus (chh. vi–xiv). For the ancient Law and the Prophets could not have ceased unless He were come (ch. vi).

We see that the prophecies that the nations should hear Him are already being fulfilled,[5] even to the very ends of the earth, including "the parts of Britain unreached by Rome" (ch. vii).[6]

But is the time itself in agreement with that which is foretold in Scripture? Tertullian answers this question by examining in detail the prophecy of Dan. ix. 20–27, proving (according to his methods)[7] that these verses refer to the period from the Birth (and consequent Death) of Christ to the destruction of Jerusalem, for "the seventy

[1] Josh. vi. 4; 1 Macc. ii. 41.   [2] Ps. li. 17.
[3] "Tam pro peccatis quam pro animabus", i.e. to atone for sins and also to consecrate persons, etc.   [4] Mal. i. 11.
[5] Isa. xlv. 1 is quoted as "Christo meo Domino", reading Κύρῳ (Cyrus) as Κυρίῳ, as in *Barnabas*, xii. 11 (*vide supra*, p. 26), though neither language nor context suggests any literary dependence.
[6] "Britannorum inaccessa Romanis loca." Tertullian is quite eloquent here.
[7] These are so far from clear, and are based on such a mistaken system of chronology, that they need not detain us. "But the principles of the calculation are, that the commencement of the Seventy Weeks is to be dated from the first year of Darius, in which Daniel states that he saw the vision—that sixty-two weeks and half a week were completed in the forty-first year of the reign of Augustus when Christ was born—and that the remaining seven weeks and half a week were completed in the first year of Vespasian, when the Jews were reduced beneath the Roman yoke" (Bishop Kaye, *Collected Works*, 1888, viii. 355 *sq.*). Peter Damian refers to Tertullian's argument (*vide infra*, p. 370).

hebdomads" were completed in the first year of Vespasian, when
Jerusalem was taken. Further, Dan. ix. 24 says that "vision and
prophecy were sealed",[1] which is true, "inasmuch as He is the
signet (*signaculum*) of all the prophets, fulfilling all things which
they had previously foretold. For after the (first) Advent of Christ
...there is no longer vision or prophet to announce Him as yet
to come." Jews indeed can bring forward no prophets or miracles
since that time, for, on Christ being baptised, "the whole quantity
of former spiritual gifts ceased in Christ" (ch. viii).[2]

Here, as has already been said, ends the unique portion of our
book. The following chapters have much that is verbally identical
with passages in the third book against Marcion. But there is not
sufficient evidence (as has been seen) for denying their proper place
here also in the original form of our treatise. They do in fact
continue the argument, though, as it seems, in a rougher, more
detailed, and less polished form, being, perhaps, taken with little
alteration from some *Book of Testimonies*.

The author turns now to consider prophecies about our Lord's
birth, showing that they have been fulfilled. He naturally begins
with the words of Isaiah,[3] stating the Jewish objection that the
name Emmanuel was never used of our Lord, and answering it by
appealing to the meaning of the term. Further, he insists that the
actions predicated of the Child must be understood figuratively
only.[4] It may perhaps be urged that the Old Testament knows
nothing of the word "Jesus" as the name of the Messiah. Not so,
replies Tertullian, it is indicated plainly by the change from
"Oshea" to "Joshua" as the name of him who was to lead Israel
into the promised land.[5] So again Joshua is called "Angel",[6] just
as John the Baptist was,[7] and it may be noted that He who spoke
to Moses was not the Father, but the Son.[8] Again, we learn in

[1] "Signari visionem et prophetiam dicebat."
[2] "Omnis plenitudo spiritualium retro charismatum in Christo cesserunt."
Cf. Justin's *Trypho*, lxxxii. 1 (*vide supra*, p. 36).
[3] Isa. vii. 14. Cf. *Trypho* often, e.g. lxxxiv (*supra*, p. 38).
[4] For His conquest of Samaria, Damascus, and the Assyrians (Isa. viii. 4)
being fulfilled in the coming of the Magi, see *Trypho*, lxxvii (*supra*, p. 41).
[5] Cf. *Trypho*, lxxv. 2 (*supra*, p. 40). For Tertullian's identification of Christ
here with the flint knives of Josh. v. 2, see *Trypho*, cxiii. 6 (*supra*, p. 38).
[6] Ex. xxiii. 20. The *Trypho* does not say that Joshua was called "Angel",
though it applies the term to Christ, lix. 1–lx. 4 (*supra*, p. 36).
[7] Mal. iii. 1.
[8] "Nam qui ad Moysen loquebatur, ipse erat dei filius, qui et semper
videbatur."

Isa. xi. 1 that the Messiah was to be of the line of David, and, further, the word *virga* ("shoot") there suggests *Virgo*, the Virgin Mary herself.[1] Not only so, but we see predictions of the character, the preaching, and even the miracles, which were all satisfied in Jesus (ch. ix).

Tertullian then refers to the predictions of the Passion and Death, and it is in ch. x, perhaps, that the suggestion that he used a list of proof-passages is the most convincing. He begins by stating the objection felt by Jews to the death upon the cross, for it is said, *Cursed is every one that has hung on a tree*.[2] He replies that an examination of the facts removes the difficulty. For Moses was not dealing with hanging on a tree in general, but with the specific case of a malefactor, a man punished in this way because he deserved it. Christ had not deserved punishment, and therefore the objection does not apply to Him. He was crucified only to fulfil other Scriptures.[3] At this point Tertullian makes an interesting remark when he meets the argument that the predictions about our Lord ought to have been much clearer.[4] For he says that the balder the statement of the suffering to be endured by the Messiah had been, the greater would have been the stumbling-block to Jews. And, on the other hand, the more magnificent the promises of the Messiah's greatness, the less clearly must they be fore-shadowed, in order that the difficulty of understanding them might not be merely intellectual, but dependent on the grace of God.

The wood borne by Isaac hinted at the Cross. Joseph was sold by his brethren, and in connexion with this Tertullian recalls his blessing by Jacob. For Jacob speaks of him as a bull, and a bull has horns which in themselves suggest the Cross.[5] Besides, Christ,

[1] "Fuit enim de patria Bethlehem et de domo David, sicut apud Romanos in censu descripta est Maria." Tertullian omits this sentence in his *Adv. Marc.* iii. 17, perhaps because he himself was thinking of Luke iii. 31, and his readers might suppose him to be referring to independent evidence of the Roman courts, which, so far as he knew, was non-existent.

[2] Deut. xxi. 23. Cf. Gal. iii. 13; *Trypho*, lxxxix. 2. The *text* is adduced also in *Jason and Papiscus* (p. 29); *Tim.-Aq.* Fol. 100 v° (*infra*, p. 74); "Anastasius", Second Add. (p. 179); Alvaro (p. 225). On the subject cf. Dalman, *Jesus-Jeschua*, 1922, p. 168, E.T. p. 186. I cannot find any trace of the *argument* Tertullian uses. [3] E.g. Ps. xxii. 17.

[4] See Gregentius, First Day (p. 143); *Troph. Dam.* iii (p. 165); *Papiscus and Philo*, § 11 (p. 173); "Anastasius", ii (p. 179); Gennadius (pp. 192 *sq.*).

[5] Cf. *Trypho*, xci. 1 *sq.* (*supra*, p. 39). Oehler's text is "nam et benedicitur a patre in haec verba Joseph" and Deut. xxxiii. 17 is quoted (i.e. Moses' words). But he warns us "a patre *om. cd.*" *Adv. Marc.* iii. 18 has the same mistake.

as a bull, tosses nations by *faith* from earth to heaven,[1] and will toss them, through His *Judgment* of them, from heaven to earth. Similarly, when Simeon and Levi hamstrung a bull,[2] this meant that the Scribes and Pharisees were not only to slay Christ, but in their fury to fix His tendons with nails.[3] Again, the cross is prefigured by Moses' session in Joshua's fight with Amalek,[4] and his setting up the Brazen Serpent.[5] It is spoken of also in Ps. xcvi. 10,[6] and was to be borne on Messiah's shoulder.[7] And Jeremiah speaks of wood being put into His bread.[8]

The twenty-second psalm is full of references to our subject, and Isa. liii says that the Messiah's reward is given Him because of His death. Amos viii. 9 *sq.* foretells even the darkness of the day of the Passion, which proved to be the beginning of the Jews' captivity and dispersion. Lastly, Tertullian goes so far as to say that Moses refers in so many words to the Passion of Christ, when he writes, not *the passover of* God, as such, but *the passover of the Lord*, i.e. of Christ (ch. x).[9]

But, besides these varied predictions and hints of the Lord's death, the Old Testament foretells that after this has been brought about the ruin of the Jewish nation will be at hand. See Ezek. viii. 12–ix. 6, where the Prophet says also that those who have on their foreheads the sign of a Tau[10] shall be kept safe. Further, Moses foretells the dispersion and misery of the nation, when, as he says, *thy very Life* (i.e. Christ) *shall be hanging on the Tree before thine eyes.*[11] Thus again all vision and prophecy were sealed in Christ, as is said also in ch. viii and ch. xiv, end (ch. xi).

The very short ch. xii gives us only a summary of the argument of ch. vii.

Then comes a chapter which, like the first eight, is not to be found in the Anti-Marcion. But it is thoroughly Tertullianic. For

---

[1] Cf. *Trypho*, xci. 3.

[2] Gen. xlix. 6.

[3] Not in *Trypho*.

[4] *Trypho*, xc. 4 (*supra*, p. 40).

[5] *Trypho*, xciv. 2 (*supra*, p. 39).

[6] *a ligno*; see *Trypho* (*supra*, p. 34).

[7] Isa. ix. 6.

[8] Jer. xi. 19 LXX. Cf. *Trypho*, lxxii. 2 (*supra*, p. 33).

[9] Ex. xii. 11, 27.

[10] The last letter of the Hebrew alphabet, in Ezekiel's time in the form of a St Andrew's cross.

[11] "Et erit vita tua pendens in ligno ante oculos tuos" (Deut. xxviii. 65 *sq.*). See also ch. xiii, "lignum passionis Christi, unde vita pendens a vobis credita non est". The same passage is quoted in Cyprian, *Test.* ii. 20 (p. 62); *Ath.-Zacch.* §§ 36 *sq.* (p. 123); *Zacch.-Apoll.* ii. vi (p. 297); *Ps.-Greg. Nyssa*, vii (p. 127); "Anastasius", iii (p. 177) (cf. *Tim.-Aq.* Fol. 133 r°).

with reference to the time of which Daniel spoke, the author brings forward a demurrer[1] to the effect that when it is said that Christ shall come from Bethlehem in the future, it is no longer possible for Him to do so. No Israelite is there, or indeed is allowed to go there.[2] Again, how shall Messiah be anointed in the future, for the chrism cannot be made in captivity?[3] And indeed Daniel says that anointing shall be exterminated.[4]

Then many texts are quoted, most of which have been adduced already in these pages. The chapter ends with a challenge to restore Judaea to the condition in which it was when Jesus came, for the predictions of the Old Testament were in fact fulfilled in that condition, and the effects of the Dispersion, etc., were dependent on it (ch. xiii).

Last of all, Tertullian gives us "the clue" (*ducatum*) to the error of the Jews. They do not see that the Old Testament speaks of two Advents of the Messiah, one in suffering and death, of which proofs have already been given, and the other in glory and judgment. The Jews ought to have recognised this second advent as being a second (without prejudice to the first) in Dan. vii. 13; Ps. xlv; viii. 5 *sq.*; Zech. xii. 10; iii. 3, 5.[5] The chapter and the treatise end with a renewed appeal on the basis of Christ's present work. You Jews, our author writes, cannot urge that "what you can see already is to take place in the future. Either you must deny that what you see with your own eyes was foretold in prophecy, or (at least) the prophecies (when you hear them read) have actually been fulfilled, or, if you accept both statements they will have been fulfilled in Him of Whom they were prophesied" (ch. xiv).[6]

---

[1] "Praescribamus." Cf. Tertullian's *De Praescriptione.*

[2] By Hadrian's decree. Cf. c. iii, and *vide supra*, p. 34.

[3] Ex. xxx. 20–33. There is no reason to accuse Tertullian of forgetting that our Lord was not anointed with visible chrism. He is but meeting the Jews on their own ground, when they say that the true Messiah of the future must be so anointed.   [4] Dan. ix. 26 LXX (not Theod. Hebr. or Vulg.).

[5] In Zech. iii. 3, 5, the sordid attire of Jeshua (the very name of Jesus is foretold!) indicates the first Advent in the flesh with its trials, and the change to glorious raiment the second Advent. Tertullian adduces also the two goats of Lev. xvi, one of which was girt with scarlet and subjected to spitting ("circumdatus coccino...consputatus"), though the latter point is not stated in Scripture, nor, as it seems, in the written traditions of Judaism, but is mentioned in *Barn.* vii. 8 (*supra*, p. 23). *Trypho*, xl. 4 (*supra*, p. 40), also uses the account of the two goats for the same general purpose.

[6] "Non potes futurum contendere quod vides fieri. Haec aut prophetata nega, cum coram videntur, aut adimpleta, cum leguntur, aut si non negas utrumque, in eo erunt adimpleta in quem sunt prophetata."

So the treatise ends. The author has been short and sensible throughout, according to the knowledge and methods of his day, and has sufficient acquaintance with the popular objections adduced by Jews to justify his writing. But he is very inferior to Justin Martyr in any personal knowledge of his opponents and their religion.

It may be asked whether he made use of Justin's *Trypho*. It is commonly asserted that this was the case, on the ground that he employs many of the Old Testament passages found in Justin, and these in the same way, however strange it may appear to us. But the similarity lies only on the surface, and was perhaps inseparable from both the Jewish and the Christian manner of exegesis at the time. The texts are seldom, if ever, quoted in the same order or connexion,[1] and the common treatment of the Old Testament is better explained by the existence of a traditional method of exposition, and by the probability that catenae of Old Testament proof-texts were in the possession of both writers.

---

[1] The twofold explanation of the Bull and its Horns (xiv; *supra*, pp. 49 *sq.*) is hardly a case in point. For it is all one passage.

CHAPTER VI

HIPPOLYTUS

A DEMONSTRATION AGAINST THE JEWS[1]

BEFORE A.D. 238

This Fragment need not detain us long. For it is of no special interest or importance in itself, but derives both only from the learning and character and position of its reputed author. Neither is it necessary to enter into the many questions connected with Hippolytus. They may be found discussed in Lightfoot's classical investigation.[2] It is sufficient to say here that he was Bishop of Portus, near Ostia, and the port of Rome, and died between A.D. 235 and 238. He appears also to have been the last writer closely connected with the Church at Rome who used Greek as his medium for expressing his thoughts. His contemporary Callistus and the succeeding Popes seem always to have written in Latin.

The beginning of the treatise appears to be lost, for the Fragment starts off brusquely with:

(1) "Now then (οὐκοῦν), incline thine ear to me, and hear my words, and give heed, thou Jew." You boast of having killed Jesus, but let us consider whether perchance this is not the means of your being in your present troubles.

(2) Let him then be introduced before us who speaketh by the Holy Spirit, and saith truth—David the son of Jesse. The author then turns to what is virtually an exposition of the sixty-ninth Psalm from the Christian point of view. *Save me, O God...for I am sunk in the mire of the abyss*, i.e. in the corruption of Hades, by the transgression in Paradise.

[1] *Demonstratio c. Judaeos* ('Αποδεικτικὴ πρὸς 'Ιουδαίους). The Fragment is published in Migne, *P.G.* x. 787–794. An English translation by S. F. D. Salmond is contained in Clark's *Ante-Nicene Library, Hippolytus*, ii. 41–45 (1871).

[2] *Apostolic Fathers, Clement of Rome*, ii. 317–477. Lightfoot points out (p. 395) that the Pseudo-Cyprianic *Adv. Jud.* (*vide infra*, p. 65) has also been attributed, though quite arbitrarily, to Hippolytus. Probably Hippolytus did write a treatise against the Jews, for the mutilated inscription on his statue is best so filled up. But whether our treatise is really his, as the one MS. affirms, may be questioned. Harnack's conclusion, at the end of a very cursory examination, is that it is by Hippolytus, but in its present form has been worked over by a Monophysite (*Chronologie*, 1904, ii. 218 *sq.*).

(3) *Then I restored,* says Christ, *that which I took not away,* because I endured the death which was not Mine by sinning. And again, *Let not them be ashamed who want to see* My resurrection on the third day, to wit the Apostles.

(4) Christ prayed all this "economically" (οἰκονομικῶς) as man, being, however, very God.[1]

(5) *Let their table become a snare and retribution.* Of what retribution does he speak? Manifestly, of the misery which has now got hold of thee.

(6) Further, *And their back do Thou bend always*; that means, in order that they may be slaves to the nations, not four hundred and thirty years as in Egypt, nor seventy as in Babylon, but *bend* them to servitude, He says, *always.*

(7) But why, O prophet, tell us, and for what reason was the Temple made desolate? Was it for the calf of long ago, the idolatry, or for the blood of the Prophets? Or for the adultery of Israel? No! For in all these they always found pardon open to them. "It was because they killed the Son of their Benefactor (τοῦ Εὐεργέτου), for He is co-eternal with the Father."[2] Wherefore the Psalm continues: *Let them be blotted out of the book of the living, and not be written with the righteous,* i.e. with their holy fathers and patriarchs.

(8) What sayest thou to this, O Jew? It is neither Matthew nor Paul that saith these things, but David, thine anointed, who awards and requites these terrible sentences on account of Christ. And like the great Job, addressing you who speak against the righteous and true, he says: *Thou didst sell the Christ like a slave, thou camest unto Him like a robber in the garden.*[3]

(9) "I now set before you also the prophecy of Solomon, which speaks of Christ, and announces clearly and perspicuously things concerning the Jews; and those which not only are befalling them at the present time, but those, too, which shall befall them in the future age, on account of the contumacy and audacity which they

---

[1] Harnack (*loc. cit.*) says the same formula occurs in a quotation from Hippolytus given by Photius.

[2] συναΐδιος. Harnack thinks this is Monophysite (*loc. cit.*).

[3] καὶ ὡς ὁ μέγας ᾽Ιώβ, ἐρῶν πρὸς ὑμᾶς τῷ δικαίῳ καὶ ἀψευδεῖ λέγοντας, οὕτως· ᾽Ηγόρασας τὸν Χριστὸν δουλοπρεπῶς, ἦλθες πρὸς αὐτὸν ληστρικῶς ἐν τῷ κήπῳ. "Et tanquam ille magnus Job, ad vos contra justum et verum loquentes ita effatur: Emisti Christum tanquam servum; venisti ad eum tanquam ad latronem in hortum" (Turrian in Migne). Theodotion's version of Job xl. 25 (=xl. 30 [Heb.]; A.V. xli. 6) has ἀγοράσουσιν αὐτόν, but that seems to be the only clue in Job.

exhibited toward the Prince of Life; for the Prophet says...*Let us lie in wait for the righteous...because He calleth Himself the Child of God*....Listen to this, O Jew! None of the righteous or prophets called himself the Son of God. Solomon therefore is speaking of Christ. *Let us see, then, if His words be true...for if the just man be the Son of God, He will help him, and deliver him from the hand of his enemies. Let us condemn him to a shameful death, for he shall be visited according to his words.*"[1]

(10) After quoting Ps. ii. 5: *He* (namely Christ) *shall...vex them in His sore displeasure*, the author turns again to Wisdom (v. 1–9), where the Jews are described as lamenting their folly, and confessing their ignorance—and the Fragment comes to an untimely end!

[1] Wisd. ii. 12–20.

CHAPTER VII

CYPRIAN

AD QUIRINUM (LIBER TESTIMONIORUM)[1]
A.D. 246–248

Between A.D. 246 and 248,[2] or a few months later, Quirinus, a wealthy layman, wrote to his friend and Bishop, Cyprian, asking for a short résumé[3] of the Divine lessons which the Lord had given us in Holy Scripture. The Bishop gladly acceded to the request of his "beloved son" (*fili carissime*), and sent him the first two books of our treatise, and later, as it seems, the third book. Cyprian tells us that he had compiled the Books himself, "as much as my very ordinary memory suggested, with selected headings appended, thus providing material for fuller explanation rather than having given it".[4] And this is an accurate description of the work. For it is little more than a collection of Bible passages without any such discussion as may be found, for example, in Justin's *Dialogue with Trypho*. The work is, in fact, drawn up on the lines of the simple summaries of the early little *Books of Testimonies*, the *Dialogue of Jason and Papiscus*, and such like.

It should, however, be noticed that neither in Quirinus' request nor in Cyprian's reply is there any mention of the Jews. It has

---

[1] The standard edition is still Hartel's, Vienna, 1868, but Dr C. H. Turner has shown that the MS. preferred by Hartel (A, cent. vii) is inferior to L (cent. ix), whose evidence is relegated to the notes (*Journ. of Theol. Studies*, 1905, vi. 246–270; 1908, ix. 62–87; 1928, xxix. 113–136; 1930, xxxi. 225–246). Hence in the following pages the readings of L have been accepted. The original title seems to have been either simply *Ad Quirinum* (Jerome, *Dial. c. Pelag.* i. 32, Vallarsi, ii. 729) or possibly *Liber Testimoniorum* (Augustine, *c. duas Epist. Pelag.* iv. 21, Migne, x. 623). Dr Turner limits himself to discussing the relation of Cyprian's text to other forms of the Old Latin. Intensely interesting and important though this question is, it does not fall within our purview (see the note *infra*, p. 63). Again, the subject of Book III is so confined to the duties and privileges of Christians that it does not concern us.

[2] Bardenhewer, *Gesch. d. altkirchl. Lit.* 1914, ii. 473. Certainly before the outbreak of the Decian persecution in A.D. 250. Cf. C. H. Turner, *J. Th. St.* 1930, xxxi, 229 *sq.*

[3] If, at least, we may accept as genuine the Prologue to Book III of the *Testimonies*, resembling though it does a later summary of Quirinus' less definite words in the Prologue to Books I and II, together with the effect produced by a perusal of the books themselves.

[4] Book I, Prologue.

therefore been seriously doubted whether either Quirinus or Cyprian had them expressly in mind. If they had not, the justification for including the work in this volume may also be doubted. But the justification is evident. For even if its primary aim was to strengthen the faith of Gentile believers who already had some acquaintance with the Old Testament, yet they must have had many Jewish friends and acquaintances to whom a defence of their faith was necessary. Hence it is not surprising that the first two books deal almost exclusively with the evidence to Christianity which is to be found in the Old Testament,[1] while the third book is entirely for convinced Christians, bringing out their privileges and duties as described in the pages of the New.

Cyprian's own account of the first two books is as follows. In the first "We have endeavoured to show that the Jews in accordance with the predictions have gone back (*recessisse*) from God, and have lost the favour of God, which had been given long ago, and promised for the future. Further, that there have come into their place Christians, who win their position by their faith in the Lord (*fide Domini promerentes*), and come from all the Gentiles and even the whole world. The second book contains the mystery of Christ (*Christi sacramentum*), that He who was announced according to the Scriptures has Himself come, and has done and has accomplished every single thing by which it was foretold He could be understood and recognised. All this is likely to be of help to the readers to draw the first outlines of the Faith." But, he continues, you will gain more strength and heartfelt understanding by the study of the sacred books themselves.[2]

In accordance with Cyprian's description the contents of Book I are exclusively devoted to Jewish subjects. Gentile Christians would, in fact, take but little interest in this book unless they were confronted with practical difficulties in defending their faith against Jews. For Jews were active opponents, as Celsus' *True Discourse* shows us, with its abundant use of their objections.

Book I has twenty-four formal headings, which may be grouped as follows.

A. §§ 1–7. *The Jews themselves*; their sins, and their spiritual blindness, though the Scriptures were to be understood when Christ came. The consequent loss of Jerusalem and of the Light of the Lord.

---

[1] There is, however, no trace of any direct discussion with Jews, or indeed of any real knowledge of the difficulties felt by them.
[2] Book I, Prologue.

B. §§ 8–18. *Their Ceremonies and Institutions*; Circumcision; the old
and the new Law and "Disposition" (*Dispositio*); the old and the new
Baptism, Yoke, Shepherds, Temple, Sacrifice, Priesthood. Further, a
Prophet like Moses was to come who should give a new Covenant
(*Testamentum*).

C. §§ 19–23. *The New People and its greater privileges.* A new people;
the Church to have more children than the Synagogue; Jews to lose
the bread and cup of Christ and all His grace, but we to accept them;
the new name of Christians is to be blessed in the earth; more Gentiles
than Jews come to the Kingdom of Heaven.

D. § 24. *Jews can be pardoned for their sins only by washing in the blood
of Jesus by Baptism*, and thus passing over into the Church, and obeying
His commands.

Book II contains a logical arrangement of prophecies of the
Incarnation and work of Christ.

A. §§ 1–7. In general, Christ is the First-born and the Wisdom of
God, by whom all things were made; the Fulfilment of Prov. ix. 1–6;
the Word of God; the Hand and Arm of God; Angel; God; further,
Christ our God was to come as Illuminator and Saviour of the human
race.

B. §§ 8–15. *The Incarnation and Life and Death of Christ.* Though He
was Son of God from the beginning, He was to be begotten according
to the flesh, the sign being that He was to be born of a virgin; thus to
be both man and God, compounded of each nature (*ex utroque genere
concretus*), that He might be able to be the Mediator between us and
His Father. He was to be born of the seed of David according to the
flesh, in Bethlehem, and of low estate in His first Advent. He was that
Just One whom the Jews were to kill, the Sheep and the Lamb, who
had to be killed. Further, concerning the mystery of His Passion.

C. §§ 16–19. *The effect of His work in general.* He was to be the Stone,
which was to become a mountain and fill the whole earth, the mountain
which was to be manifested in the last times, to which the Gentiles
should come, and the just ascend. He was also to be the Bridegroom,
with His bride the Church, from which many spiritual sons should be
born.

D. §§ 20–23. *His Death.* The Jews were to crucify Him, but in His
Passion of the Cross and its sign is all virtue and power. For in that sign
of the Cross is salvation for all who are marked on their forehead. There
was to be darkness at midday.

E. §§ 24–30. *His conquest of death, His Resurrection, and the result.* He
was not to be overcome by death, or remain in Hades, but to rise on
the third day, and receive all power from the Father for ever. One
cannot come to God the Father save through Him. He is to come as
Judge, and He is King, to reign for ever, being both Judge and
King.

A few illustrations of Cyprian's method will be useful.

The heading of I, § 4 is, That the Jews would not understand the sacred Scriptures, but they were to be understood (*intellegi haberent*) in the last times, after Christ had come. In proof of this he adduces Isa. xxix. 11, 18, the man who has a sealed book given him to read, *but in that day the deaf shall hear the words of the book, and as for those who are in darkness and a cloud, the eyes of the blind shall see.* So also Jer. xxiii. 20, *In the last days ye shall know them.* Dan. xii. 4, 7 also says, *Seal the book to the time of the end, until many learn and know-ledge be filled. For when there is the dispersion they shall know all these things.* These prophecies are confirmed by three sayings in the New Testament, 1 Cor. x. 1; 2 Cor. iii. 14 *sq.*; Luke xxiv. 44 *sq.*

So in the next section, that Jews can understand nothing of the Scriptures unless they have first believed in Christ, among other proofs Cyprian gives Hab. ii. 4, *Now the just lives from faith in Me* (Justus autem ex fide mea vivit).

In § 7, that the Jews were to lose the light of the Lord is proved from Isa. ii. 5 *sq.*, *Come ye and let us walk in the Light of the Lord, for He abandoned* (dimisit) *His people the house of Israel.* On the subject (§ 8) of the first circumcision in the flesh being made void, and a second in the spirit being promised instead (*repromissa*), he quotes the favourite passage, *And the Lord said to Joshua* (ad Jesum), *Make thee knives of stone* (Josh. v. 2), which, no doubt, Cyprian interpreted with many of the Fathers as indicating Christ's work on men's hearts by means of His spiritual precepts.[1] Compare also his quotation in § 9 from Isa. viii. 16 *sq.*, *Then shall they be manifest, who sign the Law* (apparently by circumcision), *that they may not learn. And one will say, I wait for God, who hideth His face from the house of Jacob, and I will be trusting on Him.*[2]

For the subject of § 15, that Christ would be the house and temple of God, and the old temple would cease and a new one begin, Cyprian rather strangely quotes 2 Sam. vii. 4, 5, 12–14, 16: *...I will raise up thy seed after thee...He shall build Me a house...and I will raise up his throne, and I will be to him for Father, and He shall be to me for Son, and His house shall obtain faith* (et fidem consequetur domus ejus),[3] *and His kingdom be for ever in My sight.*

When Cyprian is showing in § 20 that the Church is to have

[1] E.g. *The Dialogue with Trypho*, xxiv. 2; cxiii. 6 *sq.* (*supra*, p. 38).
[2] "Tunc manifesti erunt qui signant legem, ne discant, et dicet, expecto Deum, qui avertit faciem a domo Jacob, et fidens ero in illum."
[3] Cf. a var. lect. of LXX, πιστευθήσεται (Large Cambridge edition).

more children than the Synagogue he quotes 1 Sam. ii. 5, *The barren hath borne seven,* and he adds that these are the seven Churches. Hence St Paul wrote to seven Churches, and there are seven in the Apocalypse, that the number seven may be kept, just as there were seven days in which God made the world; and there are seven angels who stand and live before the face of God, as the angel Raphael says in Tobit (xii. 15); and the seven-formed lamp for the Tabernacle of Witness; and the seven eyes of the Lord which watch the world; and the stone with seven eyes, as Zechariah (iii. 9) says; and the seven spirits and the seven candlesticks in the Apocalypse; and the seven columns on which Wisdom builds her house, as Solomon tells us (Prov. ix. 1).

Among the many proof-passages which Cyprian quotes in support of his thesis that the Gentiles would have more faith in Christ than the Jews (*Quod Gentes magis in Christum crediturae essent,* § 21) is Num. xxiii. 24, *Behold a people shall rise up as a pride of lions* (quasi populus leoninus). Then follows Deut. xxviii. 44, *You Gentiles shall be for the head, but an unbelieving people for the tail.* Then comes Jer. vi. 17 *sq.* under the name of "Ezekiel".[1]

On § 22, That the Jews were to lose the bread and cup of Christ, is quoted Isa. iii. 1, (The Lord) *shall take away the potency of bread and the potency of water* (valentiam panis et valentiam aquae).

Lastly, in § 24, for washing sins away in the blood of Christ by Baptism Cyprian quotes Isa. i. 14–20, to which Justin Martyr seems to refer in his *Dialogue.*[2]

In the second book, on the Incarnation and its implications, it is but natural that Cyprian should make much of the description of Wisdom in the Book of Proverbs. The first text adduced to show that Christ is the First-born, etc., is Prov. viii. 22–31, *The Lord established Me as the Beginning of His ways for His works, before the ages He founded Me,* etc. So also Ecclus. xxiv. 3–6, 19 (Vulg. 5–11, 25 *sq.*), *I came forth from the mouth of the Most High before every creature;* and Ps. lxxxix. 27, *I also will make Him My First-born, and the Most High among the kings of the earth.* Similarly in § 2, referring to His Passion and the cup and the altar, Cyprian quotes Prov. ix. 1, *Wisdom... has slain her victim* (hostiam), *has mixed her wine in the cup, and has prepared her table, and sent out her servants* (the Apostles).

For Christ being the Word of God (§ 3) Cyprian gives us Ps. xxxiii. 6, *By the Word of God were the heavens made firm* (solidati), and

---

[1] On quotations under wrong titles, see *Dialogue with Trypho,* xiv. 8 (*supra,* p. 34).   [2] xiii. 1 (*supra,* p. 38).

Ps. cvii. 20, *He sent His Word* (Sermonem) *and healed them.* That He was to be the Hand and the Arm of God (§ 4) he finds in Isa. lix. 1, *Has the Hand of God no potency*, and in Isa. liii. 1, *To whom has the Arm of God been revealed?* In § 6, that Christ was to be God is proved from Gen. xxxv. 1, *Bethel...make an altar there to that God who appeared to thee* (illi Deo, qui tibi apparuit). Among other passages he quotes Isa. xlv. 15, *For Thou art God, and we knew it not, O God of Israel, the Saviour.* He adds the famous passage in "Jeremiah" (Baruch iii. 35–37);[1] also Ps. lxviii. 4, *Sing unto God, sing praises to His name; make a way for Him who ascends in the west, God is His name.*[2] He also quotes Ps. lxxxii. 1, 6, *God stood in the congregation of God, judging gods in the midst....I said, Ye are Gods, and all sons of the Most High*, and he explains it, and quotes John x. 34 to confirm his explanation. Lastly, he quotes the Gospel *cata Matthaeum* (Matt. i. 23), *And ye shall call His name Emmanuel, which is interpreted, God with us.*

In § 7, to prove that Christ would come as God, the Illuminator and Saviour of the human race, Cyprian quotes, among other passages, Isa. lxiii. 9, *Not an elder nor an angel but the Lord Himself shall set them free.*[3] Though He was Son of God "from the beginning" (§ 8) yet He had to be begotten again according to the flesh, as Ps. ii. 7 shows, and as Paul says, "ad Thessalonicenses II" but really Gal. iv. 4, *But when the fulness of time came, God sent His Son, born of a woman.* So in § 9 Cyprian says, "This seed God had foretold would come forth from a woman, to crush the devil's head," as Gen. iii. 14 *sq.* tells us.

In § 10 Cyprian proves that Christ was to be both man and God, compounded (*concretus*) of two natures, from Jer. xvii. 9, *And He is man, and who will know Him*, a curious misinterpretation of the Hebrew, derived from the LXX and also perhaps from Symmachus (see Field). Jerome, on the passage, jeers at this argument against the Jews, "bono quidem voto, sed non secundum scientiam" (Vallarsi, iv. 960).

To show that Christ is that Just One whom the Jews were to kill (§ 14) Cyprian quotes Wisd. ii. 12–17, 19–22, *Let us lay hold of the Just One, because He is displeasing to us*, etc. He adds Ex. xxiii. 7, *The innocent and Just One thou shalt not slay.*

[1] See Index.
[2] "Iter facite ei qui ascendit in occasu, Deus nomen illi."
[3] Cf. Moffatt: "It was no envoy and no angel, 'twas his own Presence saved them."

Cyprian gives many references to the Stone as a title of the Christ (§ 16); see the *Dialogue with Trypho*, lxxvi. 1 (*supra*, p. 38). Cyprian mentions the stone on which Moses sat (Ex. xvii. 12)[1] and the stone with which David slew Goliath (1 Sam. xvii. 49). This last passage teaches us that "the devil and his servants are laid low, being conquered on that part of the head which they had not sealed. But by this sign we are at once ever safe and live".

The same Stone was to become a mountain and fill the whole earth (§ 17); see Dan. ii. 31–35. And to this the Gentiles were to come; see Isa. ii. 2–4.

In § 19 Christ is to be the Bridegroom. After quoting five texts Cyprian adds: "The mystery of this matter was shown in the case of Joshua the son of Naue when he was bid put off his shoes (Josh. v. 15), for he himself was not the Bridegroom. For it was written in the Law[2] that whoever refused marriage should lay aside his footgear, but he who was to be the bridegroom should wear it."

Under the heading, That the Jews were to fasten Him to the Cross (§ 20), Cyprian includes Deut. xxviii. 66, *And thy Life shall be hanging before thine eyes*; Ps. cxix. 120, *Fasten My flesh with nails from fear of Thee*; and even Num. xxiii. 19, *Not as a man is God hung, nor as a son of man does He suffer threats*.[3]

Yet "in the suffering of the Cross and the sign of it is all virtue and power" (§ 21). For "by this sign of the Cross Amalek also was conquered by Joshua through Moses", see Ex. xvii. 9–16. There was to be darkness at midday in His Passion, see Jer. xv. 9, *Her sun is gone down, while it was yet day.* That He was to receive all power from the Father (§ 26) is proved from Dan. vii. 13 *sq.*, with a strange mixture of the texts of the Septuagint and Theodotion.[4]

There are two other questions of no little interest, and strictly germane to our subject, viz. What sources did Cyprian use for this collection of Biblical passages? and What use was made of his *Testimonia* by later writers?

The first question is closely connected with the subject of the *Books of Testimonies*, which has been already discussed.[5] For, no

[1] "By the mystery of the stone and the steadfastness of his session Amalek was overcome." At the sight of this stone God is to be blessed, T. B. *Berakoth*, 54 a, b. See my note on the *Dialogue with Trypho*, cxi. 1 (1930, p. 228).

[2] Deut. xxv. 9. Cf. Ruth iv. 7.

[3] Field gives much information about this strange rendering (*Hexapla, in loco*).

[4] Cf. Swete, *Introd. to O.T. in Greek*, 1900, pp. 421 *sqq.*

[5] *Vide supra*, pp. 3–13 and *infra*, p. 126.

doubt, some such collections were available for Cyprian's use, preserved perhaps in a library belonging to the principal church in his diocese, and he would not hesitate to avail himself of them. He had also, as we know, the writings of Tertullian in constant use, and whether "Tertullian's" *Adversus Judaeos* is actually his or not, it is almost contemporary with Tertullian, and presumably was at Cyprian's disposal. In any case Tertullian's treatise against Marcion contains much in common with that collection of texts.

The second question, What use was made of Cyprian's *Testimonia* by later writers?, is less in the air. But one has to exercise care in framing the answer. For it has been too readily assumed that because a later writer quotes the same passage as Cyprian, and gives the same explanation as he, the later writer used the earlier. But if, as we have seen reason to believe, the traditional method of quoting the Old Testament and explaining it was very widely spread, there is no reason why the later writer should not have been quite independent of the earlier.

The soundest test is that of peculiarities of similar language in the quotations, though even this test is not infallible. For if both writers belonged, say, to North Africa, we should expect them to show the same peculiarities of Biblical phraseology.

But allowing for this, we can say with some confidence that Cyprian's *Testimonia* were used at least by Maximinus and the author of *Zechariah and Apollonius*.[1]

Lastly, it will be seen from these few specimens out of the numerous passages incorporated in Cyprian's *Testimonia*[2] that the early Church was not in the least concerned with what is to us the first question of all when we read the Bible—What meaning did the writer intend to convey to his contemporaries? Cyprian and the Fathers in general were quite content with the method of their Jewish predecessors, seeing in the Bible anything which could by any possibility be seen there. But they improved on the Jews, for their Bible was not the Hebrew Bible, but the Greek version of it in some form or other, or even a secondary translation such as the

---

[1] On the subject generally consult H. A. A. Kennedy on the Old Latin Versions in Hastings, *D.B.* iii. 54; Burkitt, *The Rules of Tyconius*, 1894, p. cxix. It must be remembered that the question is that of the use only of Books I and II of the *Testimonia*. Dr Burkitt pointed out to me that to interpret Num. xxiii. 19 of the Crucifixion is possible only in the Latin, for the Hebrew is "repent", and the Greek διαρτηθῆναι, "is kept in suspense". Hence probably Maximinus knew his Cyprian, as also did the author of *Zechariah and Apollonius*.

[2] There are said to be 700, including Book III.

Latin. It is an attitude of mind which is altogether different from our own, and indeed seems to us dishonouring to God. For there is no evidence (but rather the reverse) that He gave His message in a form free from human errors even at the first, much less that He has brought it down to our own day free from copyists' mistakes, and even less that He gave translators any inspiration at all in the usual meaning of the word. Nearly all the Fathers, however, held that the Bible was inspired word for word and letter for letter, and this even in translations. Thus, if a passage of Scripture was at all patient of a meaning, however far-fetched, that meaning was quite legitimately to be accepted, and this not by Christians only, but also by opponents. Hence it could be used to show to Jews the all-embracing fact that the doctrine of the New Testament was already existing in the Old, and indeed lay almost on its surface, to be seen by those whose eyes were not plastered over by unbelief.

Cyprian shared this simple-minded doctrine, and had therefore no hesitation in compiling his "proofs" of Christianity from the Old Testament. For he was not a scholar trained in the study of Holy Scripture, and it never occurred to him to attempt to defend his use of this passage or of that. His strength lay in religious practice and ecclesiastical organisation, and if, for moral and spiritual purposes, the latter is inferior, the former is far superior to mere accuracy in Biblical scholarship.

APPENDIX

A few lines must be added about some of the documents entitled *Spuria* in Hartel's edition of Cyprian's works.

I

The Letter of Celsus ("Afer"), *Ad Vigilium episcopum de Judaica Incredulitate*.[1] See what has been said about the date of this (probably the end of thet hird century) in the chapter on *The Dialogue of Jason and Papiscus*.[2] Nothing is known either of the writer or of the recipient of the Letter. For this Bishop Vigilius can hardly be the Bishop of Thapsus who was alive in A.D. 484. The Letter is almost certainly earlier than that. For the identification of Christ and the Holy Spirit, if it does not point to an Arian writer,[3] cannot well be later than the end of the third century.

Its contents are: (§ 1) Jews are blamed for showing more blindness and obstinacy than Gentiles. Yet (§ 2) God invites them to "return",

[1] Hartel, iii. 119–132. [2] *Vide supra*, p. 28.
[3] Cf. the essay on Maximinus.

i.e. to believe on Christ. For (§ 3) the Light of Salvation has arisen, as the Magi told them, and (§ 4) as the Prophets had clearly stated would be the case. They (§ 5) were the forerunners who prepared the camp (*metatores*) for the coming of the Lord, speaking of Him as the Stone for the corner,[1] and the Day in which we should walk.[2] For (§ 6) He is the Sun of righteousness.[3] Further, there is (§ 7) the example of Abraham, who believed God, etc.[4] At this point (§ 8) comes the reference to *The Dialogue of Jason and Papiscus*, which has been mentioned. Celsus then passes (§§ 9, 10) to express his hope to see the glad day when Vigilius shall be martyred, for martyrdom is a sign of Christ's friendship, and he believes that the merits of Vigilius' righteous life will purge himself (Celsus) from his sins, appealing to the effect of Job's prayer for his friends. So mayest thou, "most holy Saint, have me thy servant Celsus in mind".

It is quite an interesting little letter, but, except for its use of a few texts, throws no light on the form of the Christian argument as addressed to Jews.

II

The *Adversus Judaeos*,[5] by an author of whom we know nothing at all, though Harnack would attribute it to Novatian at Rome, "the convenient residuary legatee of any works whose authorship is unknown".[6] Its date is probably of the third century. It is an emotional sermon with very little in it. It blames the Jews who were rightly cast out. A new Law has been given to the Gentiles, but individual Jews can be restored on repentance.[7]

III

De Montibus Sina et Sion.[8] This is an interesting little tract—a homily or part of one—containing quaint interpretations of words such as Sina, Sion, and Adam, based in part on the numerical values of the letters. Its aim is to show that Sina has to do with the Law, and belongs to earth, but Sion with heaven, and to the Gospel.[9] Among its not very numerous quotations may be mentioned Wisd. ii. 19–22;[10] also Cant.

---

[1] Ps. cxviii. 22.

[2] Perhaps a reference to Ps. cxviii. 24, and certainly to Rom. xiii. 13: "Sicut in die honeste ambulemus, id est in Christo et mandatis ejus, cujus lumine ac monitis luminati," etc.

[3] Mal. iv. 2.   [4] Gal. iii. 6.

[5] Hartel, iii. 133–144; arbitrarily attributed to Hippolytus by De Magistris, 1795. See Lightfoot, *Clement of Rome*, 1890, ii. 395. Cf. Migne, *P.G.* x. 787–794.

[6] "Bénéficiaire commode des ouvrages sans maître" (Labriolle, *Histoire de la Littérature Latine Chrétienne*, 1924, p. 223, E.T. 1924, p. 166).

[7] Parkes has a long quotation giving a bitter résumé of Jewish history in the Old Testament (*Conflict of Church and Synagogue*, 1934, pp. 105 *sq.*).

[8] Hartel, iii. 104–119. Juster, i. 58, dates it between A.D. 210 and 240 in Africa, and refers (among others) to Turner in *J. Th. St.* 1906, vol. vii, pp. 597–600, and to Corssen, *Z.N.T.W.* 1911, pp. 1–36.

[9] § 11.   [10] § 7; *vide supra*, p. 55.

i. 6, *They made me as a guard of an orchard*, "because in a garden He hung between two robbers fastened on a tree", the two robbers being the Gentiles and the Jews.[1] Further, Moses went up to Mt Sinai to receive the Law for the Jews, but Christ is a mountain, the holy Tree of His Kingdom. "For the Law of Christians is the holy cross of Christ the Son of the living God, as the prophet also says, Thy Law is in the midst of my belly." For there was He struck, and from His side blood and water flowed out....*For from Sion shall the Law go forth*, viz. from the royal Tree, *and the word of the Lord from Jerusalem*, which is the Church.[2]

There is, however, nothing to show that the treatise was intended for Jewish readers.

[1] § 7.   [2] § 9.

CHAPTER VIII

THE DIALOGUE OF TIMOTHY AND AQUILA[1]

c. A.D. 200

We turn now to a rather strange and very interesting document, which has been too much neglected, a writing which, according to the Title in the Vatican MS., records a discussion "that took place in Alexandria in the days of Cyril the most holy Archbishop of Alexandria", and, if we may believe its Epilogue, was held in the presence of "the King and his Angelic Excellency the King's bishop".[2]

This would place the treatise between A.D. 412 and 444, though what a "King" was doing in Alexandria at that time it is hard to say. The probability, however, is that both the Title and the Epilogue belong to a later time than the bulk of the treatise, and, in fact, may have been added in almost any period by a zealous and imaginative copyist.[3] That, however, some sort of a Dialogue between a Christian and a Jew did take place, upon which this treatise was founded, is clear from the statement that the bystanders broke out once into laughter when the Jew was cornered and was obliged to confess that in one point the Christian was right.[4]

[1] Published by F. C. Conybeare in *Anecdota Oxoniensia, The Dialogues of Athanasius and Zacchaeus and of Timothy and Aquila*, 1898. Unfortunately Conybeare prints only the text of *Timothy and Aquila*, with references to Bible passages, but without numbering the paragraphs, or even indicating accurately the limits of each Folium. He has prefixed a valuable Introduction to the two Dialogues. His text of *Timothy and Aquila* is taken from one manuscript only, now in the Vatican (cent. xii), but E. J. Goodspeed has published collations of the beginning of the treatise from a MS. in the Escorial (cent. xv), and the whole from a MS. at Paris (cent. xiii) in the *Journal of Biblical Literature*, 1905, pp. 58–78. The Paris MS. seems generally to represent an earlier form of the text, but has serious lacunae. As the Folia of the Vatican MS. are given by Conybeare, and are much shorter than his printed pages, it is convenient to refer always to them.

[2] τὸν βασιλέα, καὶ τὸν ἰσάγγελον αὐτοῦ ἐπίσκοπον (Fol. 138 r°). The Paris MS. unfortunately has a long lacuna here.

[3] The Title in the Escorial MS. is only *A Discussion of a Christian named Timothy with a Hebrew philosopher named Aquila*; Ἀμφιβολία χριστιανοῦ ὀνόματι τιμοθέου μετὰ ἑβραίου φιλοσόφου ὀνόματι ἀκύλα.

[4] Fol. 100 r°. Those present were, it would seem, chiefly Jews (Fol. 76 v°; cf. 78 r°), but there was "a great audience" (Fol. 76 v°).

Apart from the Title and Epilogue, what can be learned of the date of composition? One cannot appeal to external evidence, for the treatise is never quoted, or, apparently, ever used, by other writers, save (as it seems) by the author of the *Dialogue of Athanasius and Zacchaeus*, the date of which itself requires investigation.[1]

The internal evidence, on the other hand, is fairly decisive. There is, for example, the very interesting list of the canonical books of the New Testament,[2] given to satisfy the Jew that the Christian will use in the discussion no other books. The list runs: "The first book is the Gospel, then the Acts of the Holy Apostles and again their Epistles, and the fourteen Epistles of Paul. These we hold; but all the rest are apocryphal."[3] It will be observed, first, that the classification of the Catholic Epistles with the Acts, so common in the manuscripts themselves, is here mentioned by an independent writer; secondly, that the Apostles are called "Holy" ("the Acts of the Holy Apostles"), an addition generally late, but found in the Memphitic version (? cent. ii). It must be remembered, however, that the word "holy" is just such an addition as would slip in later, whether the copyist made the addition intentionally or otherwise.[4] Thirdly, St Paul's Epistles are fourteen, this inclusion of the Epistle to the Hebrews being evidence of Eastern as contrasted with Roman provenance; and, fourthly, the absence of all reference to the Revelation of St John, which suggests that our author lived in a place where, and at a time when, its canonicity was denied. On the whole, therefore, the list points to the Eastern or, probably, the Egyptian Church rather than the Western, and a time not later than the end of the second century. For Clement of Alexandria (*c.* A.D. 200) fully accepted the canonicity of the Book of the Revelation.[5]

While, however, the author professes to use only the books enumerated in the above list, some of his quotations differ strongly from the contents of our four canonical Gospels. In fact he evidently lived in a period (and a locality) when accounts of our Lord's life were circulating, and received as authoritative, which we should repudiate to-day.

[1] For the relation of *Ath.-Zacch.* to *Tim.-Aq.*, *vide infra*, pp. 117, 122 *sq.*
[2] On the list of the canonical books of the Old Testament, *vide infra*, p. 72.
[3] Foll. 77 v°; 78 r°: πρώτη βίβλος ἐστὶ τὸ εὐαγγέλιον, εἶτα αἱ πράξεις τῶν ἁγίων ἀποστόλων· καὶ πάλιν αἱ ἐπιστολαὶ αὐτῶν, καὶ αἱ ἀπὸ παύλου ΙΔ ἐπιστολαί· ταύτας ἔχομεν ἡμεῖς· τὰ δὲ λοιπὰ πάντα ἀπόκρυφά εἰσιν.
[4] Contrast Fol. 132 r°, where "holy" is absent.
[5] Clement quotes it repeatedly, e.g. *Paed.* i. 6; ii. 11.

For example, we find the Jew saying, "About this Jesus, as his Memoirs contain, in those which you call Gospels,[1] *We find whence he is, and his parents with him, and how is this man God?*"[2] As the quotation stands it appears to be based on a combination of John vii. 27 and vi. 42, but it is probably taken direct from some Gospel narrative which has not come down to us. If it comes from a Harmony, it is not from Tatian's, so far as we possess this as Tatian left it.

Again, much stress is laid upon the fact that the evil spirits call our Lord Son of David,[3] but our present Gospels give no example of this.

Again, we find ten or eleven lines of a quotation saying that the mountains were shaken when the veil of the Temple was rent, and the rocks were burst, the tombs were opened, and the bodies of many that slept arose, and were addressed by those who saw them: "Art not thou such an one?" together with their answers, that Christ had broken the gates of Hades, and binding him (Hades personified) had released them and raised them with Himself.[4] This treatment of "the Harrowing of Hell", as though it were so much part of Scripture (in accordance with the Christian's promise to use no other authority) that it could be used in evidence, points to a date before the Church had quite decided which Gospel narratives were canonical and which were not.

Again, we find the Christian saying, *When the Jews saw all these things accomplished, they lamented with a great lamentation,*[5] as it is written by Zechariah the prophet, with a full quotation of Zech. xii. 10–14. It has been suggested that the writer is using the *Gospel of Peter*.[6] But the similarity is not at all close, and even if he were using it the *Gospel of Peter* is not one of our Four. Once more, that is to say, he is writing before the distinction between canonical and uncanonical Scriptures was fully made.

---

[1] Fol. 80 r⁰. Reading with Conybeare's emendation, καθὼς τὰ ὑπομνήματα αὐτοῦ περιέχουσιν ἐν τοῖς λέγετε εὐαγγελίοις.

[2] Εὑρίσκωμεν (v.l. ομεν) πόθεν ἐστίν, καὶ τοὺς γονεῖς αὐτοῦ σὺν αὐτῷ, καὶ πῶς θς ἐστιν οὗτος.   [3] Fol. 112 r⁰.

[4] Fol. 133 v⁰. This is not in the *Gospel of Peter*, nor at all identical with the *Acta Pilati (Gospel of Nicodemus)* as given in M. R. James, *Apocryphal N.T.*, or in Tischendorf, *Evangelia Apocrypha*, 1876.

[5] Fol. 135 r⁰: ταῦτα πάντα ἑωρακότες τελεσθέντα οἱ Ἰουδαῖοι, ἐκόψαντο κοπετὸν μέγα.

[6] Τότε οἱ Ἰουδαῖοι καὶ οἱ πρεσβύτεροι καὶ οἱ ἱερεῖς ἰδόντες οἷον κακὸν ἑαυτοῖς ἐποίησαν, ἤρξαντο κόπτεσθαι καὶ λέγειν, οὐαὶ ταῖς ἁμαρτίαις ἡμῶν, vii. 25.

Besides, however, the evidence of our author's Canon of the New Testament, and of his use of forms of Gospel narratives which are not identical with our own, he had a text of New Testament writings which was current in wide circles during the second century, but not long afterwards.

The first example is the passage where the Jew says that "in the Gospel according to Matthew (i. 16) there is contained: *Jacob begat Joseph, the husband of Mary, of whom was born Jesus who is called Christ, and Joseph begat the Jesus who is called Christ,* about whom we are now speaking; he says that *he begat him* from Mary".[1] Probably the text is conflate (*of whom was born Jesus who is called Christ* being an orthodox interpolation), and the Jew found in his authority the statement that Joseph was the father of Jesus, as is read by the Sinaitic MS. of the Old Syriac, which repeats the word *Joseph,* making it the subject to *begat Jesus.*[2] In any case it was only in quite early centuries (save in very narrow circles) that this kind of text was current.

That the author was influenced by "Western" readings may be seen also in his reference to Acts xi. 26: "Even as it is written in the Acts of the Apostles, that *they were termed first in Antioch...for the disciples to be called Christians.*"[3]

---

[1] Fol. 93 rº: καὶ ἐν τῇ νέᾳ δέ ἐστιν ἐν τῷ κατὰ ματθαία (*sic*), οὕτως δὲ περιέχει· ὅτι Ἰακὼβ ἐγέννησεν τὸν Ἰωσήφ, τὸν ἄνδρα μαρίας· ἐξ ἧς ἐγεννήθη ι̅σ̅ ὁ λεγόμενος χ̅σ̅, καὶ Ἰωσὴφ ἐγέννησεν τὸν ι̅υ̅ τὸν λεγόμενον χ̅υ̅, περὶ οὗ νῦν ὁ λόγος, φησὶν ἐγέννησεν ἐκ τῆς μαρίας.

[2] On the other hand, in the Ferrar Group and the Koridethi text probably ἐγέννησεν is used of the mother, as occasionally elsewhere (Luke i. 13, 57; John xvi. 21), the passage being then understood: "Jacob begat Joseph, to whom the Virgin Mary was betrothed and bare Jesus who is called Christ." Ἰακὼβ δὲ ἐγέννησεν τὸν Ἰωσήφ, ᾧ μνηστευθεῖσα Μαριὰμ ἐγέννησεν Ἰησοῦν τὸν λεγόμενον χριστόν. In Foll. 93 vº and 113 rº the text is orthodox, though still rather "Western".

[3] Fol. 132 rº: καθὼς γέγραπται ἐν ταῖς πράξεσιν τῶν ἀποστόλων, ὅτι ἐχρημάτισαν πρῶτον ἐν Ἀντιοχείᾳ καλεῖσθαι τοὺς μαθητὰς χριστιανούς. The words are corrupt, but at least recall the reading of Cod. Bezae, τότε πρῶτον ἐχρημάτισεν (*sic*) ἐν Ἀντιοχείᾳ οἱ μαθηταὶ χρειστιανοί (*sic*). The same influence, but of a later type, may be seen in the Epilogue, where, in answer to the Jew's question what he should do to be saved, the Christian replies: *If thou believest with all thy heart, and with all thy power, and with all thy might, and with all thy understanding, arise, and be baptised and wash away thy sins, calling on the name of the Lord Jesus* (Fol. 138 rº). The latter part, from *arise* onwards, is from Acts xxii. 16. But *If thou believest with all thy heart* points to a MS. containing the reading of E and 69, with Cyprian and the Latins. The remainder seems to be peculiar to our author, but illustrates the natural tendency to develop a suggestion.

Further, besides the Canon and the use both of uncanonical writings and of a strange text, the trouble taken by our author to depreciate in the eyes of the Jew and the attendant audience the famous translation of Aquila suggests that this had not been very long before the world. Perhaps even the name Aquila was given to the Jew of the Discussion (Fol. 76 r⁰) because Aquila and his version represented the Jewish mind so accurately. However that may be, our author is at pains to show that the translator was not a man to be trusted or respected (Foll. 117 v⁰–119 r⁰). He had been a heathen; then a Christian; then, because he could not get his own way, a Jew; and then he used his recently acquired knowledge of Hebrew to mutilate the Scriptures, partly by wrong translation, partly by omission of passages that were in favour of the Christian faith. Though proof is lacking it is a reasonable supposition that Aquila's version had become known to the majority of Jews only comparatively few years before our treatise was composed, and had been seized upon by them in their endeavour to confute the Christian argument.

The evidence therefore tends to show that the treatise was composed about the end of the second century of our era, probably not in Alexandria itself, but in some less important place in Egypt. The Title and the Epilogue (though not necessarily by the same hand) were added perhaps in the end of the fifth century, probably in Egypt, though, again, not in Alexandria.

But is the Christological Doctrine of the treatise in accordance with so early a date as the end of the second century?[1] Yes, it seems to be, save for one sentence. For with that one exception there does not appear to be any indication of controversies belonging to the third or later centuries. The Christian's faith, as depicted in the Dialogue, is simple, accepting indeed the full Divinity of our Lord, but not defining this, or mentioning differences of opinion with regard to His relation to the Father. There is, however, as has been said, one exception to this. For we find the Christian saying: "Know, therefore, O Jew, that the divine Scriptures did not conceal the one Essence (τὴν ὁμοουσιότητα) of the Father and the Son and the Holy Ghost."[2] It is very improbable that an orthodox writer would have used this term before the Council of Nicaea in A.D. 325. Yet the sentence is so unique

[1] The famous passage about the Incarnation (Fol. 93 r⁰) has been already mentioned, p. 70.

[2] Fol. 107 r⁰.

in this treatise, and comes in so abruptly, even so unnecessarily for the meaning of its context, that we are justified in regarding it as a later addition, made perhaps by the same editor who added the Title and the Epilogue.[1]

It is never very easy to give a summary of the contents of such treatises as this, for they almost always digress from the subject which they are more immediately considering. But, bearing this in mind, we may say that the writer of this Dialogue has planned out his work in the following manner. After an Introduction (Foll. 75 v°–79 v°) in which he narrates the historical (?) occasion of the Discussion, and defines the Scriptural sources to which appeal may be made by either side, he considers, I, *The Trinity and the Incarnation* (Foll. 79 v°–113 v°); then II, *The Rejection of the Jews in favour of the Gentiles* (Foll. 113 v°–132 v°); then III, *The Passion and Resurrection of Christ, and the future Judgment by Him* (Foll. 132 v°–138 r°); and he adds an Epilogue, in which are described the conversion and baptism of the Jew, the Christian becoming ordained for the purpose of baptising him (Foll. 138 r°– 138 v°).

The Introduction tells us the occasion of the Dialogue. A certain Jew, one Aquila, was going about the synagogues and even the streets arguing against the Faith, for the Christ was still to come, there being, according to the Scriptures, but one God, and Jesus being only a man. But a certain Christian, one Timothy—a layman, as appears in the Epilogue—hearing him speak, made the sign of the Cross, and said, Shall we sit down together and discuss the matter out of the Divine Scriptures? So on the morrow they sat "in a place called the Cloister",[2] and with a great audience standing by they began the Discussion, the Jew enquiring what Scriptures the Christians desired to use. A list of the Old Testament books is given first, noticeable for saying that "the Fifth book is Deuteronomy, not dictated by the mouth of God [but deutero-nomied, 'second-lawed', by means of Moses]; therefore it was not put into the *aron*, that is, the ark of the Covenant".[3]

---

[1] The doctrine of the Perpetual Virginity of the Blessed Virgin (Fol. 94 r°) is found as early as Clement of Alexandria (*Strom.* vii. 16). The sign of the Cross (Foll. 76 v°; 78 r°) is mentioned by Tertullian as being employed on all occasions (*De Cor. Mil.* § 3). *The Testament of Solomon* (Fol. 83 r°) probably dates from the middle of the second century.

[2] ἐν τόπῳ καλουμένῳ δρόμῳ.

[3] Fol. 77 r°: Ε δὲ βίβλος ἐστὶ το δευτερονόμιον, οὐ διὰ στόματος θεοῦ ὑπαγορευθέντα [ἀλλὰ διὰ μωυσέως δευτερονομιθέντα (*sic*), Escorial MS.]. For a

Last in the list come the books of Judith and Esther, "for Tobit, and the Wisdom of Solomon, and the Wisdom of Jesus the son of Sirach, the Seventy-two interpreters set in the Apocrypha".[1] The New Testament list has been already mentioned.[2]

I. The first subject of discussion is *The Trinity, with the Incarnation.* Has God a Son? Is He Jesus? Is the Cross prefigured in the Old Testament? Is the Trinity mentioned? As to the Sonship, the author begins with Gen. i. 1, *In the beginning God created the heaven and the earth,* "and the Christian rose up, bowed his head, making the sign of the Cross towards the east, and wept when he said the words; and his hearers did the same, being pricked in their hearts, and all said with one voice, One God". The allusion and interpretation are not clear, but it seems not unlikely that the author intended his readers to infer the meaning found as early as *Jason and Papiscus,* viz. that *In the beginning* refers to the Logos.[3] After other passages he quotes Prov. viii. 27–30 to show that God had a Counsellor,[4] whom, however, the Jew claims as God's own wisdom, not this Jesus.[5] But the Christian urges that when God said *Let us make* (Gen. i. 26), He was addressing not His own wisdom, nor angels, but "the marvellous Counsellor who was in the beginning"; and he quotes Micah v. 2; Isa. liii. 8; and, as so often, Baruch iii. 37, 38; Christ the Lord who *hath found out all the way of knowledge, and hath given it unto Jacob His servant, and to Israel that is beloved of Him, and afterwards appeared on the earth, and was conversant with men.*[6] *Jacob* and *Israel,* it will be observed, seem to be used as titles of Christ, as in Justin's *Dialogue with Trypho.*[7]

The Jew, however, desires proof that the Counsellor is Jesus, and the Christian begins a list of many texts in the Old Testament

further explanation of Deuteronomy see Maximinus, cap. 1 (*infra,* p. 307). I can find no parallel to this extraordinary statement, and can only conjecture that the similarity of the meaning of the Greek word δευτέρωσις to that of the Hebrew word Mishna (which may mean "repetition") is responsible for some confusion of thought. The *Didascalia Apostolorum* in cap. xxvi (Lagarde, p. 107; Connolly, p. 216) has much to say of the *Deuterosis,* i.e. God's second legislation (in contrast to the Decalogue and the Judgments) insisting on sacrifices and ceremonies, but that is an entirely different matter.

[1] εἰς τὰ ἀπόκρυφα παρέδωκαν ἡμῖν οἱ ο̄β̄ ἑρμηνευταί.
[2] *Supra,* p. 68 *sq.*
[3] Fol. 78 r°. See the note on *Jason and Papiscus, supra,* p. 29.
[4] σύμβουλος, Fol. 79 v°.
[5] This subject is treated more fully in the *Dialogue of Athanasius and Zacchaeus,* §§ 13, 21, *vide infra,* pp. 119–121.
[6] Fol. 81 r°.   [7] §§ c. 4; cxxv. 5.

predicting our Lord's life, even to minute details, such as even
Pilate's act of washing his hands. The author's strange ignorance
of Hebrew, by the by, is shown here in his explanation of *Emmanuel*,
"the half of which (we are told) is Syriac, for *Emma* means *with us*,
and the other half is Hebrew, for *nuel* means *God*".[1] And there
immediately follows: "And further in the second Psalm David
says thus, *The Lord said unto me, Thou art My Son, to-day have I
begotten Thee.*" This the Jew interprets of Solomon, and continues
"or dost thou not know that before he was born God said of him,
I will be to him Father, and he shall be to Me son. Therefore also when
he was born he said *Didich*—my interpreter."[2] The text is corrupt,
but if Conybeare's emendation is right the explanation is probably
that *Didich* represents *Jedidiah*, for so Aquila ("my interpreter",
according to the Jew in our Dialogue) renders 2 Sam. xii. 25, *And
he called his name Jedidiah* (ἰεδιδία) *because of the Lord*, the ἰε having
been merged in εἶπεν and the final α having been read as χ.[3]

Naturally the question of the death of Jesus holds a large place
in the objections raised by Jews against His Messiahship. Hence
the Christian is concerned with showing that it was foretold, and,
in particular, that there is much in the Old Testament about the
Cross. Was not the Ladder (Gen. xxviii. 12) seen by Jacob fixed
on earth but reaching unto heaven?[4] Did not Moses stretch out
his hands in prayer when fighting against Amalek (Ex. xvii. 12),
who is Antichrist?[5] Does not Deut. xxi. 23 say: *Cursed is every one
who hangeth on a tree*? which means (against the Jew's objection) not
that Jesus was accursed Himself, but that He bore away the curse
on men, destroying the curse written in the Law.[6]

Yet does the Old Testament indicate that God is a Trinity?
Assuredly, for the threefold *Holy* in Isa. vi. 1–3 means nothing less.[7]

[1] Fol. 82 vᵒ.

[2] Fol. 83 rᵒ: εἶπεν διδίχ (*sic*) ὁ ἑρμηνεὺς ἐμός. So Conybeare, but his MS. has
ὁ ἑρμηνεῦ ἐμός (*sic*), and the Paris MS. has διδίχ ὁ ἑρμηνεύεται ἐμός.

[3] I owe part of this explanation to Prof. F. C. Burkitt. In any case it may
be noticed that Qimchi (A.D. 1160–1235) on 2 Sam. xii. 25 connects this verse
with the promise in 2 Sam. vii. 14, as our author's Jew does. The Paris MS.,
on the other hand, suggests that a word has fallen out between ἑρμηνεύεται
and ἐμός (Query, ἀγαπητός. Cf. the title of Ps. xlv), but then the force of the
last syllable (*yedîd-jah*) is neglected.

[4] Fol. 98 vᵒ. Cf. *Trypho*, lxxxvi (*supra*, p. 36).

[5] Fol. 99 vᵒ. Cf. *Trypho*, xc. 4 (*supra*, p. 40). Our author hints that the
Stones (*sic*) set under Moses were also a type of the true Stone; cf. Cyprian,
Test. ii. 16 (*supra*, p. 62).

[6] Fol. 100 vᵒ. Cf. *Trypho*, lxxxix. 2 (*supra*, p. 39). [7] Fol. 101 rᵒ *sq*.

And then the author breaks off to tell us that the Pearl is a picture of the Incarnation. For when the oysters are open that they may feed, the lightning flashes down, and the creature enclosing it receives something of water (so the Paris MS.), of brilliancy[1] (so the Vatican MS.) within itself, and thus out of light and lightning and water the pearl is born. So was Christ born of the Virgin according to the flesh by the Holy Spirit; as Isaiah said: *The Virgin shall conceive and bear a son* (Isa. vii. 14) and his Mother shall not know a man.[2]

When the Jew argues that, although there are many references to the various forms of the Spirit's work, he awaits further information about this Son, the author relates the visit of the Three men to Abraham in Gen. xviii. But can it be Jesus who then appeared? asks the Jew.[3] And when the reply is given that the Scriptures do not conceal the oneness of essence of the Father, the Son and the Holy Spirit,[4] the Jew states that if all that the Scriptures say of these things really refers to Jesus, then he is persuaded. So the author shows that the blessings promised at first sight to Jacob and Judah could not be really intended for them, but for their great descendant. For Jacob suffered from famine and feared Esau (Gen. xxxii. 11); the sweet smell of Esau's garments (Gen. xxvii. 27) meant the myrrh upon the head, of which David speaks (Ps. cxxxiii. 2). And Judah's blessing (Gen. xlix. 9) could not have been for Judah. For the words (in the Septuagint) are *From the shoot, my son, art thou gone up,*[5] and *the Shoot* refers to Jesus (Isa. xi. 1), Jacob himself affirming by this that He to whom the blessing refers is not of ordinary descent from him.[6]

II. Our author then (Fol. 113 v°) turns to the second great subject of his theme, the rejection of the Jews and the choice of the Gentiles. We rejected! cries the Jew; did not God make a Covenant with us in blood at Horeb, and you say He abolishes it! Yes, replies the Christian, for He promises a new Covenant (Jer. xxxi. 31–33); and Hosea speaks plainly of your rejection and the choice

---

[1] τοῦ νοεροῦ, "the intellectual". But this gives no sense: I suggest that it may be a Syriasm.

[2] Fol. 102 r°. The last clause reads as though it were part of the prophecy, but probably the author only intends to give his own summary of the meaning.

[3] Foll. 106 r°; 107 r°.   [4] *Vide supra*, p. 71.

[5] Gen. xlix. 9: ἐκ βλαστοῦ, where the Hebrew is *from the prey* (*tereph*). But *taraph* is used of a fresh-plucked leaf (Gen. viii. 11). *Nezer* (*shoot*) is translated βλαστός in Isa. lx. 21 by Symmachus and Theodotion.

[6] Fol. 113 r°: διὰ τὸ χωρὶς συνουσίας μου προελθεῖν αὐτὸν ἐκ παρθένου ἁγίας.

of the Gentiles (Hos. i and ii); and Moses himself foretells both your punishment and the turning of the Gentiles to God (Deut. xxxi. 16; xxxii. 37, 43). True, that God gave you the Land of Israel, but He calls you despisers of Him (Hab. i. 5 LXX). When the Jew urges (not unfairly, judging by our modern interpretation) that Christians wrest the Scriptures, Timothy retorts with a violent attack on Aquila (the namesake of his Jewish antagonist) and on his version.[1] We must therefore, according to Timothy, accept in preference to Aquila's version that of the Seventy-two, which was evidently inspired by the Holy Spirit, for the translators, dwelling in separate huts, were found to agree word for word.

No doubt, to us who live in the twentieth century this seems absurd, but it must not be forgotten that it was the accepted doctrine of the Church at least as late as the end of the sixteenth century. Both the Septuagint and the Vulgate were credited then with the inspiration of every letter, as may be seen in the quotations from Leon de Castro and others in the writings of Luis de Leon (†1591). Luis de Leon himself, on the other hand, "offended many by bringing philology to bear on the Scriptures, and others by insisting on their historical meaning, denying, for instance, that every part of every Psalm must be referred to Christ".[2] Can we wonder that a writer in an Egyptian backwater in the end of the second century knew no better?

Yet, argues the Jew, Jesus said nothing of this judgment of the Jews when He stood before Pilate! No, answers the Christian, but He had recently spoken the parable of the Unjust Husbandmen.[3] When the Jew argues that after Isaiah's condemnation of them in the earlier part of his first chapter he says later in *v.* 26: *Afterward she shall be called the city of righteousness*, the answer is that between the affliction of the Jews and their ultimate restoration the Gentiles shall be accepted.[4] For the Law is to go forth, not from Jerusalem, or from the children of Israel and the Jews, but from *Sion*,[5] of which Solomon spoke in Cant. ii. 13, 14: *Arise, my love, my fair one, and come away, O my dove, that art in the clefts of the rock, in the covert of the*

---

[1] *Vide supra*, p. 71.

[2] Luis de Leon was very "modern". He regarded the Jews as blind, but still loved by God, capable of great services as missionaries. He pointed out also that our Lord Himself was a Jew. See A. F. C. Bell, *Luis de Leon*, 1925, pp. 147–149.

[3] Fol. 121 v°.

[4] Cf. *Barn.* xvi. 3–10. Cf. *supra*, p. 17.

[5] Isa. ii. 3.

steep place.[1] And we to-day see these warnings and promises all being fulfilled.

The Jews condemned the Judge of all to death. How so? asks the Jew. How can you reconcile His willingness to die with His being the Judge of all?[2] I will do so presently, replies the Christian; but His death was foretold in the Old Testament, and even details in connexion with it, as, *e.g.* the darkness (Isa. xiii. 10) and the descent to hell (Ps. lxviii. 6 [LXX]). He suffered willingly, as Jeremiah foretold (xi. 19; Ps. xciv. 8–11; Isa. l. 6). For such passages do refer to Jesus. See also Ps. xxii. Also that He was to be Judge is taught in Daniel, *one coming like the Son of man*, etc. (Dan. vii. 13).

Then follows the Epilogue. "But the Jew remained speechless about an hour.... He said, Of a truth you have persuaded me from all sides of your argument that He is God of gods and Lord of lords, and King of kings, and that our fathers sinned grievously in laying hands upon Him. Now, therefore, O man of God, tell me what I must do to be saved." The multitude cried: "The Faith of the Christian is victorious, and the King assented, and his Angelic Excellency the King's bishop."[3]

"And the Jew rose up and fell at the Christian's feet, and lifted up his voice in lamentation, and said to him, The Lord will require my soul at thy hands if thou make me not a Christian. And the Christian raised him up saying that he should remain there, and went in to the most holy Bishop, [who said,] Child, the husband-man that laboureth must be the first to be partaker of the fruits. Thou hast laboured, take thou his fruit first. But when he said, I am not among the clergy, the Bishop went quickly into the church. And he said, Peace be to thee, and ordains him Deacon. And then he said again, Peace be to thee, and makes him Presbyter, and gives to him other Presbyters and Deacons for the ministration of the Sacrament. And they give him a roll on which were written the invocations and prayers of the Office. And he who was hence-forward the most holy presbyter Timothy went off together with the other priests and deacons to the place where Aquila was expecting him, and he took him and led him into the church. And they performed the Office, and baptised him into the name of the Father and the Son and the Holy Ghost, changing his name to Theognostos.[4] And when he had received the undefiled Mysteries

---

[1] Fol. 130 r°.   [2] Fol. 133 r°.   [3] Fol. 138 r°. *Vide supra*, p. 67.
[4] Theognostos was the name of a writer and priest of Alexandria in cent. iii, and of a priest there in cent. iv. See *Dict. Chr. Biog.* iv. 989 *sq.*

he became the receptacle of the Holy Ghost—he who was once a Jew, but now a Christian by [the grace of (Paris MS.)] God; he who was once a wolf, but now had become Christ's sheep. And Timothy the Presbyter received him in his own house, and they were continually praising together Father, Son, and Holy Ghost; to whom be all Glory, Honour, Might and Adoration, now and always and for ever and ever, Amen."

CHAPTER IX

CELSUS AND ORIGEN

c. A.D. 178 AND *c.* A.D. 248

In the last quarter of the second century of our era the rapid spread of Christianity was disturbing the equanimity of Roman philosophers. It seemed too disgraceful in its origin, too unpatriotic towards its Jewish ancestry, and too contrary to the demands and prospects of the Empire, to deserve consideration—yet it was growing. True that most of its adherents were of the poorer classes, mere scum of Orontes in Roman eyes, but there were others, some educated, some even of noble birth. Emperors indeed had already tried to extirpate it, and would yet try. But it was also the duty of scholars to warn the upper classes against its insidious advance.

This, as it would seem, was the motive that moved Celsus to write his *True Account*. We know very little of him, nothing indeed for certain, save what his treatise tells us. He was evidently a learned man, a fervid admirer of Plato, and well acquainted with other philosophical authors, as, for example, Heracleitus, and with Greek literature in general. He was, as it seems, a Roman lawyer, and wrote in A.D. 178, or thereabouts.[1]

His treatise has come down to us only in the form of quotations direct and indirect, but these probably represent almost seven-eighths of the whole, so that we can form a very good notion of what it really was.[2]

Its subject was wide, nothing less than the defence of heathen polytheism, and Celsus' method of persuading his readers was to show that Christianity was contemptible even when compared with Judaism, and, again, that what was common to the two was incredible and ridiculous, in a word, unworthy of the consideration of a worshipper of the Gods.[3]

[1] There is no direct evidence that Celsus lived in Rome, but various indications in his work make this almost certain. See Patrick, p. 9 (*vide infra*, p. 80).

[2] A critical edition of it (so far as it can be recovered) has been published by O. Glockner, 1924, in Lietzmann's series.

[3] The *True Account* may be divided as follows. Celsus begins by attacking Christianity from the Roman standpoint as encouraging "secret associations", and as depending on Judaism, which itself was barbarous (Origen, i. 1–27). He then, Part I, brings forward a Jew, whom he represents, first, as disputing

The latter part of his argument falls outside our subject. The former does not. For Celsus professedly draws his arguments against Christianity when compared with Judaism from statements made against it by the Jews.

That indeed Celsus ever came into contact with Jews of great learning may well be doubted.[1] The objections to Christianity which he quotes are quite ordinary, such as any Jew might have adduced. But he puts them so well, and gives so many, that his treatise may well have served as a storehouse from which the rank and file of educated, though not learned, Jews, drew argument against Christians. It must also have been known rather widely for copies of it to have reached Alexandria.

It does not appear, indeed, that Origen had come across it before his wealthy patron Ambrose expressed a wish that he should answer it, to which, however, Origen did not much care to accede. For not only does he seem to have had but a poor opinion of the worth of Celsus' writing, but he also insists that argument as such plays a very small part in the defence of the Gospel compared with the personal experience of Christ by the believer.[2]

But he yields, and writes a long and able book in reply.[3] The greater part of it indeed hardly concerns us, for Origen, like Celsus, has polytheism chiefly in mind, yet, in following the *True Account* paragraph by paragraph, he deals with Jewish objections as they occur, and in so doing provides material which he hopes may strengthen wavering Christians, and also lead non-Christians to consider the claims of the Faith.[4]

Of Origen's fitness to discuss the relative claims of polytheism and Christianity—whether the former was that of the populace or

with Jesus and often refuting Him (i. 28–71), and then as arguing with Jewish Christians (ii). The remainder of the treatise, Part II, consists of objections made by Celsus in his own person about the Incarnation and cognate questions (iii–v. 65), the contrast between Christianity and Philosophy (v. 65–vii. 61), and, lastly, a defence of philosophical polytheism (vii. 62–viii). See the summary in J. Patrick's careful study, *The Apology of Origen in reply to Celsus*, 1892, pp. 18–83. Consult also Dr J. S. Whale's excellent article in the *Expository Times*, 1930–31, pp. 119–124.

[1] R. Simeon ben Jochai, however, was at Rome soon after A.D. 156, pleading against a decree issued then, so it is just within the bounds of possibility that Celsus, as a lawyer, met him.

[2] See his Preface, § 3 *sq.*

[3] "The best and the most comprehensive defence of the Christian faith which has come down to us from the days of the Fathers" (Hort, *Six Lectures on the Ante-Nicene Fathers*, 1895, p. 131).　　　　[4] Preface, § 6.

of the philosophers—there can be no doubt. Though the son of Christian parents he was steeped in classical and philosophical lore from his youth. But was he qualified to understand and to meet the objections to Christianity raised by the Jews? On the whole we are probably justified in saying that he was. His mother indeed has been thought to have been of Jewish origin,[1] but Krauss goes beyond the evidence in thinking that she taught him Hebrew.[2] He had, however, several Jewish teachers, and refers sometimes to the general methods of Hebrew scholars, relating many of their allegorical expositions (Hagadoth).[3] He expressly mentions "the Patriarch Huillus", i.e. Hillel, the son of the Patriarch Gamaliel III;[4] and, at Caesarea or its neighbourhood, where he stayed for twenty-five years, he may well have come into contact with the famous R. Hoshaia, "a pupil of the patriarch Jehuda I and one of the compilers of the Tosephta",[5] who, after being at Sepphoris, lived many years at Caesarea. Be this as it may, Origen often refers to his discussions with Jews,[6] and he certainly shows himself able to discuss such Jewish objections as he finds in the *True Account*, and to meet them satisfactorily.[7]

The first assertion which Celsus quotes from his Jew is that Jesus invented the tale of His birth from a virgin, though He was really

[1] As Westcott suggests, *Dict. Chr. Biog.* iv. 97.

[2] See Krauss' essay, "The Jews in the works of the Church Fathers" in the *Jew. Qu. Rev.* October, 1892, v. 139. He quotes Jerome, *Ep.* xxxix. 1, *Ad Paulam*, where, however, the reference is not directly to Origen, but to Paula's deceased daughter, who rivalled Origen in her knowledge of Hebrew. For after a few days she emulated her mother's zeal in learning and singing the Psalms.

[3] Krauss, *op. cit.* pp. 139–157.

[4] So *Jew. Enc.* vi. 401. See Origen, *Selecta in Psalmos*, Introd.: ἀνακινουμενος περί τινων λογίων θεοῦ ᾿Ιούλλῳ (Migne's Lat. *Jullo*) τῷ πατριάρχῃ. G. F. Moore thinks this "a scribal error for ᾿Ιούδας (Judah II)", *Judaism*, 1927, i. 165, i.e. the brother of this Hillel. (Lomm. x. 352; Migne, *P.G.* xii. 1056.) Cf. Jerome, *Adv. Ruf.* i. 13.

[5] See Bacher on "The Church Father Origen and Rabbi Hoshaya" in *Jew. Qu. Rev.* 1891, iii. 357–363; also Eisenstein in *Jew. Enc.* vi. 475 *sq.* Cf. my note 2 on Justin's *Trypho*, xxiii. 4.

[6] i. 45, 55, 56; ii. 31 (*vide infra*, p. 83).

[7] On the other hand, his words "as they say" (ὡς φασι) in i. 34 of a term in the Hebrew text—and his information is wrong—suggests either that his Hebrew was slight, or that he had not the means at hand of verifying his quotations (see p. 82). The standard edition of Origen's *C. Celsum* is that by Koetschau, 1899, in the Leipzig *Corpus*. See also Migne, *P.G.* xi. 637–1632. The English translation by Crombie (books VII, VIII by Cairns) in Clark's *Ante-Nicene Library* (1871) seems to be excellent, save where the text used is inaccurate.

the son of a soldier named Panthera and of a poor woman who gained her livelihood by spinning, and was dismissed by her husband as an adulteress.[1] Origen replies to the effect that while the Jews had made up this story to overthrow the belief in the miraculous conception by the Holy Spirit, it "preserves the fact that it was not by Joseph that the Virgin conceived Jesus". He further asks whether it is suitable and probable that a soul which has conferred such benefits on the world should have had an illegitimate body.[2] He appeals also to Isa. vii. 14, but wrongly endeavours to support the virginity of Isaiah's 'almah from Deut. xxii. 23 *sq.*, where, "as they say", 'almah also occurs. This, however, is not the case. Two words are in the Hebrew, but neither is 'almah.[3]

Celsus goes on to affirm that because of His poverty Jesus went down to Egypt, hired Himself out as a servant, had experience there of certain miraculous powers on which Egyptians pride themselves, and then returned to Palestine, giving Himself airs with these powers, and because of them proclaimed Himself as God.[4] Origen's reply to this is much what our own would be, viz. that the moral teaching of Jesus, insisting, as it does, on our responsibility to God, does not fit in with His being a mere charlatan.[5] For "He showed Himself not merely to His true disciples, but also to all others, as the pattern of the perfect life".[6]

In answer to Celsus' objection to the incident of the dove at Christ's baptism as being uncorroborated, Origen points out that no Jew would have made such an objection. For, as he had already said to other Jews when disputing with them, they were inconsistent in accepting the miracles of Moses while they denied those of Jesus.[7] Here Origen digresses for a moment, that he may show that Moses and the Prophets were truly prophets sent by God, and also prophesied about Jesus. The coming of the Holy Ghost was foretold by them, and its reality has been seen in the miracles of Jesus and of His disciples, down to Origen's own day.[8] Origen

---

[1] i. 28, 32. The Jewish sources are given by Strack, *Jesus, die Häretiker und die Christen*, 1910, §§ 3 a, 9 a.   [2] § 32 *sq.*

[3] § 34 *sq.* *Naar(ah)* and *bethûlah* come in Deut. xxii. 23 *sq.*, but 'almah in Isa. vii. 14. Compare Chrysostom's ignorance introduced by "as they say" in his commentary on Isa. vii. 18 (*vide infra*, p. 133).

[4] i. 28. Cf. §§ 6, 26.   [5] i. 28, 38.

[6] i. 68: παράδειγμα ἀρίστου βίου.

[7] i. 45. Cf. Gennadius, *Refutation*, p. 134 v (*infra*, p. 192).

[8] i. 46; Isa. xlviii. 16.

here again recalls his discussions with other Jews. These, for example, understood Isa. liii to refer to the whole people of Israel regarded as one individual, who are in dispersion and in suffering, in order to gain proselytes. But Origen "pressed" his opponents "hardest with the expression", "Because of the iniquities of My people was He led away to death". For if the people, as the Jews say, are the subject of the prophecy, how is the man said to be led away to death "because of them", unless he be a different person from that people of God?[1]

On another occasion he discussed the forty-fifth psalm, when "the Jew, who was deemed a learned man",[2] being very perplexed, answered that *v.* 6 ("Thy throne, O God") refers to God, and *v.* 7 ("Thou hast loved righteousness") to the Messiah.[3]

Celsus' Jew, however, asserts that "countless individuals" claim that the predictions alleged to refer to Jesus refer really to themselves, to which Origen replies that history has no knowledge of such "countless individuals", save Theudas, Judas a Galilean, and Dositheus and Simon the two Samaritans.[4]

Then comes the subject of the Magi and the massacre of the children—for, as Origen complains, Celsus does not keep to historical sequence. Here Origen twits Celsus with calling the Magi "Chaldaeans"—"the blunder of one who cannot distinguish between Magi and Chaldaeans"—and he wonders why he has omitted to mention the star as the occasion of their coming. For the Magi, "beholding a divine sign in the heaven, desired to learn its significance": it had, in fact, been foretold by Balaam.[5]

More important is the Jew's argument here that though professedly Herod was anxious to kill the child who might become King, yet Jesus did not become King, but wandered about.[6]

Further, adds Celsus, He went about with ten or eleven of the wickedest of tax-gatherers and sailors. Your figures are inexact, says Origen, for they were twelve, and only one was a tax-gatherer, unless we include Lebes according to one copy of Mark, and others were fishermen rather than sailors. Besides, does not His choice

[1] i. 55. [2] *Vide supra*, p. 81.
[3] i. 56. On this Psalm see my *Christian Evidences*, §§ 564–569.
[4] i. 57.
[5] i. 58–60; Num. xxiv. 17 (LXX): ἀνατελεῖ ἄστρον ἐξ Ἰακώβ, καὶ ἀναστήσεται ἄνθρωπος ἐξ Ἰσραήλ.
[6] i. 61. The argument that Jesus was never King became a very favourite one with later Jews. See, for example, R. Isaac of Troki's *Chizzuk Emunah* in my *Christian Evidences*, §§ 15, 27, 79.

of unlikely instruments prevent suspicion of artifice? And does not the success of their work justify His choice? And, again, why should He be blamed for choosing "the wickedest" of men if it makes them holy?[1]

But Jesus hid Himself, just as He had done in Egypt! But what harm is there, replies Origen, in using means to escape? Did not Aristotle do as much? God might have preserved Him from Herod by a miracle, but there was a "moral fitness that ways and means should be made use of to ensure the safety of Jesus". Again, a merely miraculous preservation of Him would not have shown (as He wished it to be shown) that within the external form of Jesus there was some higher element of Divinity.[2]

Yet when Jesus was challenged in the Temple to perform a miracle, why did He refuse (Matt. xii. 38 *sq.*)? Rather, why should He accept the challenge? replies Origen. For now "the whole inhabited world contains the work of Jesus". Consider the fact of the many Churches founded by those who have been converted from innumerable sins.[3] For indeed the miracles of Jesus and His disciples create a presumption in favour of His teaching, backed up as it was by the excellency of His life.[4] The moral argument is never far from Origen's thoughts.[5]

In any case, says Celsus, the body of Jesus could not have belonged to God, for it suffered. Origen points out that such a body was necessary if Christ was to be in all respects like men (though He had no sin). For He was a great wrestler with temptation.[6] In other words, Origen here, as continually, seizes on the vital point of the Incarnation, the perfect humanity of the Logos. Origen would have had nothing to do with the phrase beloved of modern Jewish writers "half man and half God". Jesus, he would have said, was wholly man, with all human weaknesses save those due to sin, and yet was God.

Celsus' Jew, however, does not restrict himself to direct attacks on Jesus; he also addresses converts from Judaism to Christianity, though in doing so he naturally often attacks our Lord indirectly.

Why, he asks, have you forsaken the Law of your fathers? Origen replies: "Those from among the Jews who believe in Jesus have not forsaken the Law of their fathers." For they live in accordance with it, and are called Ebionites ("poor"), in accord-

---

[1] i. 62 *sq.*
[2] i. 65 *sq.*
[3] i. 67.
[4] i. 68 (*vide supra*, p. 84).
[5] E.g. iii. 51. See also *infra*, pp. 87 *sq.*, 90.
[6] μέγας ἀγωνιστής (i. 69).

ance with its poverty. And the Apostles who preached to the Jews observed it also.[1] He further says that Christians do not treat the things written in the Law with disrespect, for they show the depth of wisdom that they contain. In fact they give them more honour than do the Jews, who treat them superficially, and hold them as in some degree even fabulous.[2]

When the Jew objects that Jesus taught nothing new about the Resurrection and the Judgment, Origen replies that He at least told them the kingdom of God would be taken from them, for not observing in their life the teaching of the Prophets. Also he points out that the present doctrines of the Jews are mere trifles and fables, while those of Christ elevate the soul. Further, that although Jesus Himself kept the Law, and even its sacrifices, this does not prevent our recognising Him as the Son of God, the Son of Him who gave the Law and the Prophets. And, he says again, we Christians do not transgress them, but keep them in a higher sense than do the Jews.[3]

Jews sometimes call Jesus arrogant and a liar, but they bring no proof of their assertions. They say too He was an impostor, but what other impostor has introduced doctrines that convert men from wickedness? They argue too, How could we Jews who made it known that One was to come from God have rejected Him when He came? That, replies Origen, is a silly argument;[4] as though men were never inconsistent! Besides, Isaiah long since said that this would be the case.[5] Celsus' Jew may object to it, but the fact remains that their rejection of Jesus has caused their present state of calamity and exile.[6]

But can Jesus be God, cries the Jew, when He fled and tried to escape, and was betrayed! Yes, argues Origen at some length. For we must not regard either the body or the soul of Jesus as Divine;[7] it was the Logos-God, the Son of the God of the universe,[8] who spoke in Jesus "I am the Way, and the Truth, and the Life", and "I am the Door", etc. The Jews should study the witness of the Prophets that He was to be a Great Power, and God "next to the God and Father of the universe".[9] For to whom else did God

[1] ii. 1.   [2] ii. 4.   [3] ii. 5 *sq.*
[4] πάνυ εὔηθες.   [5] Isa. vi. 9.   [6] ii. 7 *sq.*
[7] Origen seems to mean that they belonged to the perfect humanity of Jesus (cf. *De Princip.* ii. 6).
[8] ὁ λόγος Θεός, καὶ Θεοῦ τῶν ὅλων υἱός (ii. 9).
[9] μεμαρτυρημένον ὡς μεγάλην ὄντα δύναμιν καὶ Θεὸν κατὰ τὸν τῶν ὅλων Θεὸν καὶ πατέρα (ii. 9). Migne has a note defending this interpretation of the Greek.

speak, "Let there be light", etc., and "Let us make man according to our image and likeness", and who else save the Logos could have done as He was bid? Besides, we can see from the Gospels themselves that Jesus' divinity was not limited to His body and soul, for the Baptist's words imply that though Jesus was visible to all, yet *There is standing One among you, whom ye know not.*[1] Yet, adds Origen, we do not separate the Son of God from Jesus, for after the Dispensation[2] the soul and the body of Jesus have become one with the Logos of God. For if St Paul can say of the believer that he is one spirit with the Lord,[3] how much more divinely and in greater measure is the unity of That which was united with the Logos of God! He showed Himself as the power of God, by His miracles.[4] In any case, the endurance and resolution shown by His disciples is a very evident proof to all candid minds that they at least were persuaded of the truth of what they wrote,[5] even though He was betrayed by one, as other leaders have been.[6]

Among the many falsehoods said to have been made up by the disciples are Christ's predictions. Yet, says Origen, they have come true! For who else than Christians are brought before kings and rulers for their opinions?[7] Besides, the disciples would hardly have made up fictions to their own discredit, e.g. the Denial of Christ by Peter.[8] Again, it is said to be a mere fiction that He died and rose again, for how could He be immortal if He died? Origen replies to the effect that as a compound being Jesus was not immortal; His immortality began after He had died.[9] Again, there is the case of the traitor. Would he continue to act after he had been pointed out as such? But this continuance in ill-doing is not uncommon.[10] Yet did he not betray Jesus by God's decree, and how then can he be blamed? Origen rightly shows that according to Jewish and to Greek teaching foreknowledge is not the same as necessity. One might as well argue against taking medicine, on the ground that if one is fated to get well one will do so whether it be taken or not.[11]

---

[1] John i. 26.

[2] μετὰ τὴν οἰκονομίαν, referring to the Incarnation.

[3] 1 Cor. vi. 17.

[4] ii. 9. This section is hard, but representative of the Christian philosophy, with which Origen is always trying to arrive at a fundamental agreement.

[5] ii. 10. The foundation of Paley's famous argument.

[6] ii. 11.   [7] ii. 13.   [8] ii. 15.

[9] ii. 16.   [10] ii. 18.   [11] ii. 19 *sq.*

Yet why did Jesus wail and pray for escape, saying, *O Father, if it be possible, let this cup pass from me?* Origen answers, first, that Celsus quotes only half the saying, and omits *Nevertheless not as I will, but as Thou wilt*, words which show the cheerful obedience of Jesus to the will of His Father. He answers, secondly, that it was out of love for His people that Jesus thus prayed, for He foresaw the misery which their crime of killing Him would bring upon them, and He would spare them this if it were possible to do so.[1]

Then Celsus attacks the credibility of the Christian records from another side. They have been corrupted and even remodelled! Origen replies that he knows of none who have made alterations, save "the followers of Marcion, and of Valentinus, and I think also those of Lucian". And, in any case, it is no real charge against true Christianity.[2]

Again, Celsus' Jew argues that the prophecies may be applied to ten thousand things more credibly than to Jesus. Yet Celsus has taken no trouble to prove his statement in detail, though he is here attacking this extremely important argument of Christians. Besides, no Jew would really have made such an objection; he would only have tried to show that this or that prophecy did not refer to Jesus.[3]

But the prophets foretell the coming of a mighty potentate. This difficulty has been met already by the truth of the Second Coming. But when the Jew adds, "and not such a pestilence as Jesus", this indeed is thoroughly Jewish in its expression of hatred. Yet does "a pestilence" convert men from an evil life to one which is "according to nature, marked by self-restraint and the other virtues"?[4]

Still, His divinity should have been as self-evident as the sun! So it was! For in His days righteousness has arisen, and the teaching of peace, "which does not permit men to resist their enemies".[5]

Origen then quotes some slight and superficial objections connected with what Celsus' Jew had supposed Jesus ought to have done if He were divine, but they need not be mentioned here, for Origen rightly accuses Celsus of showing a very unphilosophical spirit in such matters.[6] But in reply to the Jew's taunt that Jesus gained over no one during His life, he asks him how he would explain the envy of the High Priests that multitudes were following Him, and the tears of St Peter after his denial of Him.[7]

Far more serious is the charge that Jesus "did not show Himself

[1] ii. 24 *sq.*   [2] ii. 27.   [3] ii. 28.   [4] ii. 29.
[5] ii. 30.   [6] ii. 31–40.   [7] ii. 39.

to be pure from all evils",[1] but as no evidence is adduced for such a statement Origen rightly ignores it for the moment.[2] Later, however, when the complaint is made that Jesus "makes use of threats, and reviles men on light grounds, when He says Woe unto you", Origen rightly answers that God Himself had used expressions of no less severity in the Prophets.[3]

§§ 43–53 contain objections which either are of little importance or have been discussed already.

The question of the Resurrection of Christ was seen by Celsus and his Jew to be all important, and naturally receives much attention. It was like the heathen tales of Pythagoras, says the Jew, or of Rhampsinitus who played at dice with Demeter in Hades, and returned to the upper world with a golden napkin received from her as a gift. Who then saw Jesus after He rose? A half-frantic woman, or some one who dreamed or imagined it as he desired, or who wished to make other impostors like himself! Origen reminds the Jews that heathen unbelievers may throw back such arguments against the Jews' own belief in Moses and his miracles. At any rate Jesus' death was public, and the disciples would not have taught His Resurrection with such courage had they themselves invented it.[4]

But perhaps the wounds of Jesus were not really severe! Yes, the evidence shows they were. And a marvellous Resurrection was, after all, in accordance with the prophecy of Ps. xvi. 10 *sq.* His appearances in fact were on a different level from those of the heathen fable.[5]

The objection, however, is urged that "if Jesus desired to show that His power was really divine, He ought to have appeared to those who had ill-treated Him, and to him who had condemned Him, and to all men universally".[6] This is a common argument of the poorly educated even to-day, and probably we should answer that nothing is more alien to the Christian religion than faith produced by portents, and lacking any moral quality. The Christianity of the New Testament is nothing at all if it is not ethical. In other words, opponents of God are not in a position

[1] μὴ δείξαντι ἑαυτὸν πάντων δὴ κακῶν καθαρεύοντα.
[2] ii. 41 *sq.* The charge was hardly revived before our time, when the two learned Jewish writers, Mr Joseph Jacobs (*Jew. Enc.* vii. 164) and Mr Claude Montefiore (*The Teaching of Jesus*, 1910, p. 54) accuse our Lord of injustice and inconsistency much as Celsus does. But *vide infra*, p. 414. See, further, Origen's argument, *supra*, p. 85.
[3] ii. 76.   [4] ii. 54–60.   [5] ii. 61 *sq.*   [6] ii. 63.

to receive external evidences of Him and His work. Christ who refused to give a sign from heaven would have stultified Himself if He had granted even a stronger sign from which there was no escape.

Origen's reply is essentially on these lines. For he insists that Jesus appeared "according to their several ability to receive Him". For indeed He did not seem to be the same to those who were brought to Him in the lower part of the mountain of the Beatitudes "as to those who were able by reason of their strength to go up the mountain along with Him". In other words, how could the enemies of Jesus see Him after the Resurrection when their eyes were darkened by reason of that enmity? The argument seems to be perfectly sound.

Similarly, to Celsus' assertion that Jesus "had no longer occasion to fear any man after His death, being, as you say, a God, nor was He sent into the world at all for the purpose of being hid", Origen rightly retorts that "He was sent into the world not only to become known, but also to be hid".[1] Jesus in fact could, and can, be seen only where there is spiritual affinity.

Yet why did Jesus die at all? Why did He not disappear from the Cross? Origen's reply is to the effect that besides the value to us of the symbolism of "dying with Christ", "the Cross of Christ", and so on, it was appropriate that He should go through all the processes of human nature, and die and be buried as we are.[2]

But where is He, says the Jew, that we may see and believe Him? We answer: "Where is He now who spoke in the prophecies, and who wrought miracles?...Are *you* to be allowed to meet the objection, that God does not perpetually show Himself to the Hebrew nation, while *we* are not permitted the same defence with regard to Jesus?"[3]

Yet, adds the Jew, "Did Jesus come into the world for this purpose, that we (Jews) should not believe Him?" Not with this purpose, is the answer, but with this result, as the Prophets foretold, together with the call of the Gentiles.[4]

Origen's second Book ends with the Jew's conclusion that Jesus is only a man, and with Origen's reply that no mere man could have accomplished what Jesus did and is doing, converting so vast a multitude from sin and cowardice to godliness and courage.[5]

With the rest of Origen's treatise we have, as has already been said, little to do. But we may notice that he points out that the

[1] ii. 63–68.　　[2] ii. 69.　　[3] ii. 77.　　[4] ii. 78.　　[5] ii. 79.

national expectation of a Messiah is a striking phenomenon in religious history, and demands serious study irrespective of the claims of Jesus.[1] Again, Origen, like most of the Fathers, asserts with confidence that the Jews are never to be restored to their former condition.[2] He also refers to the little treatise *Jason and Papiscus*.[3]

More important is his argument that while Judaism is essentially a national religion, Christianity is one that is universal, not superior to that of the Jews only, but overcoming the religions of the Gentile world.[4]

After all, our readers may say, these arguments used by Origen are not made with the view of winning the Jews to Christ, but with that of rebutting objections made by them, and made by them not directly but only through the medium of a Gentile. This is true, but it is impossible to exclude the study of Origen from our survey of works intended to win the Jews to Christ. For his treatise is of value in levelling the road along which the Christ may come to human hearts, breaking down some of the barriers that prevent His entry.

And, further, in the places where Origen lived and worked the Jews were so intermingled with Christians that the latter required to be fortified with arguments, if they were to fulfil their duty of presenting Christ to those of their fellow townsmen who still accepted Moses only, and rejected Him of whom he wrote.[5]

Besides, of all the early writers on the relations of Judaism and Christianity Origen is the one who approaches most nearly to our own times in his sense of values. True, that he uses certain prophecies in a way forbidden to us, but he seizes on moral aspects both in the case of our Lord and that of believers as few writers do. He rises above the level of the majority of apologists, whose primary conception is the purely intellectual argument of the congruity of the New Testament record of Jesus with Old Testament prophecy, and he tends to make us fall in love with Jesus Himself. He might, no doubt, have said far more about the perfection of Jesus in His character, and ought to have done so, but he at least says something of the kind, and draws our attention to Him far more than does any other controversial writer until comparatively modern times.

---

[1] iii. 2. Cf. Patrick, *op. cit.* p. 199.

[2] θαρροῦντες δ' ἐροῦμεν, ὅτι οὐδ' ἀποκατασταθήσονται (iv. 22). Spencer has a long note on this subject (*Annott.* pp. 50 *sq.*).

[3] iv. 52 (*vide supra*, p. 28).   [4] iv. 22, 32.   [5] John v. 46.

BOOK II
THE SYRIAC WRITERS

INTRODUCTION

THE JEWS: CHRISTIAN APOLOGISTS IN THE SYRIAC-SPEAKING CHURCH

By the "Syriac-speaking Church" is meant that portion of the Eastern Church which used the Syriac language in its public worship and its ordinary literature, whether it was Catholic, Nestorian, or Jacobite.

The Aramaic language prevailed at different times over a very large range of country, extending from Palestine, not to say Egypt, in the west to Persia in the east. And it has at least half a dozen dialects of greater importance, with others of less. We, however, are concerned with but one. For the only dialect of Aramaic in which Christian writings on the subject of Judaism are found is that which is known as Syriac, and was current in Northern Mesopotamia. Other dialects written in Syriac character contain nothing for our purpose, and almost everything of Aramaic in Hebrew character is of Jewish authorship.

Now it might have been supposed that in view of the large number of Jews in Mesopotamia the Syriac Fathers would have much to say about them. This is not the case. The fact is that by far the greater number of the Jews were in the south, in the Babylonia of the narrowest meaning of the word, which extended from Nehardea some seventy miles southwards to Sura. This was a comparatively small district, in which lay the two great seats of Jewish learning, Pumbeditha and Sura.[1] It was always under the rule of the Sassanid kings till the Mohammedan conquest of A.D. 651. Probably only a few Christians ever lived there, and these either did not make books, or had not the good fortune to attract the notice of the copyists who have preserved for us the writings of their northern co-religionists.

For the Syriac-speaking Christians, as we know them, lived in the North. Their great centre was Edessa, which after A.D. 216 was almost continually within the limits of the Roman Empire, and shared the advantages, and sometimes the disadvantages, of that connexion. Nisibis, on the other hand, about a hundred and

[1] See Graetz, *Geschichte*, 1866, iv. 271 *sq.* (E.T. ii. 509); *Jew. Enc.* i. 145; ix. 208.

thirty miles nearly due east, was held by Rome until A.D. 363, and, after that, remained under the Sassanids.

It is difficult to arrive at a satisfactory conclusion about the number of the Jews in Edessa and Nisibis. On the one hand, "the Christianity of Mesopotamia came probably from Edessa, and the original missionaries, and their northern converts as well, were of the Jewish people".[1] On the other hand, there appear to have been comparatively few Jews in Edessa after the fourth century, though there were presumably still many at Nisibis.[2] At Mosul (Nineveh), less than a hundred miles east by south of it, there were probably more.

[1] Frank Gavin, p. 112 (*Aphraates and the Jews*, published originally in the *Journal of the Society of Oriental Research*, October 1923, vii. 96–166). Mr Gavin's paper is important, not only for Aphraates but also for its discussion of the Church and Jewish affairs in the East generally. The legend of Abgar, King of Edessa, may have some foundation of truth. Addai on his arrival at Edessa took up his residence in the house of Tobias, son of Tobias the Jew, who was of Palestine (*Doctrine of Addai*, ed. Phillips, p. 5 *sq.*). The Peshitta version of the O.T. was made by Jews or Jewish Christians. Cf. Duval, *Lit. Syr.* 1907, p. 30 *sq.*; and his *Histoire, politique, religieuse et littéraire d'Édesse*, 1892, pp. 108–110.

[2] For the existence of a Jewish School of teachers at Nisibis see Gavin, pp. 112–114; Paul Kahle, *Masoreten des Westens*, 1927, pp. 51–55.

CHAPTER X

APHRAHAT

A.D. 336–345

The two earliest writers in the Syriac language whose books (of any size) have come down to us, excluding the unknown translators of the Scriptures, and also Tatian the framer of the Harmony of the Gospels called the *Diatessaron*, are Aphrahat and Ephraim. Apart from the fact that they were contemporaries, they have very little in common. Ephraim, as will be seen, is a versifier, delighting in artificiality of form and superabundance of verbiage, and is concerned chiefly with the intellectual claims of orthodox Christianity, in contrast to the pretensions of heretics. Aphrahat is simplicity itself, with a nervous, direct style of prose, doing his best to warn his congregation against the sins to which they are tempted, errors of life even more than of mind. He is therefore incomparably the more attractive of the two to the modern reader.

Not much is known of the life of Aphrahat. He was born of heathen parents (*Hom.* ii. 20; xvii. 8, 10), perhaps as early as A.D. 290, and died about 350, after being for some years Bishop and Abbot of the Monastery of Mar Mathai on the eastern, i.e. the Persian, side of the Tigris, a few miles ("four hours ride") northeast of Mosul. It is perched "near the summit of Jebel Makloob", and still exists under the name of Sheikh Matta. When Dr Badger visited it in 1844 and 1850 he found the Jacobite Metropolitan (*matran*) living there with two monks only (1850), five villages, numbering some 350 families in all, forming his diocese.[1]

Aphrahat's twenty-three Homilies were all written, as he himself tells us, in A.D. 336–345, the first ten in 336, 337, the next twelve in 344. They are not, however, a casual collection of addresses, but "a full and ordered exposition of the Christian faith in answer to a request for information from an inquirer".[2]

[1] G. P. Badger, *The Nestorians and their Rituals*, 1852, i. 95–98. He gives a picture of the Monastery and a plan of its church.

[2] F. C. Burkitt, *Early Eastern Christianity*, 1904, p. 82. The enquirer was evidently the Head of a Monastery of some kind. Aphrahat's writings with a translation, and notes, in Latin by Parisat are published in the first volume (parts i and ii) of the *Patrologia Syriaca*, 1894. The dates are given in *Hom.* xxii. 25. Parkes, pp. 276–279 (*vide supra*, p. xiii) should also be consulted.

Most of them are very helpful spiritually, owing to the simple faith they exhibit, and they have a good deal of interest for our present purpose. For Aphrahat not only always feels the necessity of strengthening the faith of Christians against the arguments of the Jews,[1] but also occasionally appeals to the Jews directly.[2]

There is not much for our purpose in Homilies i–iv, though in i. 19 he bids each of his readers abstain from observing "hours, sabbaths, new moons and annual festivals", kept presumably by their Jewish neighbours. This is fully in accordance with the fiery words of Chrysostom,[3] and, as will be seen, with those of a later poem falsely attributed to Ephraim.

In Homily v (*de Bellis*) Aphrahat argues that Daniel's expression "the saints of the Most High shall receive the Kingdom"[4] cannot refer to Israel. For is Israel to come on the clouds! Jeremiah rightly calls the Jews "reprobate silver", because the LORD rejected them.[5] They did not receive the Son of man. But the Kingdom is for the Romans, and the sons of Esau keep the Kingdom for Him who gave it, "until He comes whose it is".[6]

The eleventh Homily (*de Circumcisione*) contains more. It deals with the whole question of circumcision, starting from the promise to Abraham that he was to be father of many nations, and not of one only. To be sons and heirs of Abraham depends on moral behaviour; wrongdoing makes the Jews but men of Sodom and Gomorrah. Faith is more important than circumcision, which is only the seal of faith (§§ 1, 2). Again, a change of covenant is nothing new. God's covenant with Adam was that he should not eat of the tree. With Noah it was the Bow in the cloud; with Abraham, already chosen because of his faith, circumcision as a seal and a mark for his descendants; and with Moses the Passover lamb. And as the Jews did not keep the Law, God made it useless, and said He would give a new one that was quite different. For the new covenant is, "They shall all know me",[7] etc. And now those who are already circumcised in heart live, and are circumcised again over the true Jordan, which is the baptism of the remission of sins (§ 11). This reference to Joshua suggests to

---

[1] Cf. xii. 11. The following pages (96–102) deal strictly with Aphrahat's arguments for Christianity as contrasted with Judaism. For his whole attitude towards Jewish thought see Gavin's detailed investigation, *op. cit.* pp. 127–166.

[2] xii. 7; xvii. 1, 10; xxi. 1–7.

[3] E.g. *c. Judaeos*, i and ii.

[4] Dan. vii. 18.

[5] Jer. vi. 30.

[6] Gen. xlix. 10; §§ 21–24.

[7] Jer. xxxi. 31, 34.

Aphrahat the many ways in which Joshua's actions foreshadowed those of his great Namesake, and Aphrahat's phrases remind us of Justin's in his *Dialogue with Trypho*, § cxiii.[1] Only two need be mentioned. As Joshua circumcised the Jews with a knife of stone (Josh. v. 2; Aphrahat hovers round the same references to Christ the true Stone that Justin gives without actually repeating them; but cf. *Hom.* i. 6–9) so Jesus circumcises in baptism by the sword which is the word.[2] Joshua raised stones for a testimony in Israel; Jesus called Simon a firm stone, and set him up as a faithful witness among the Gentiles. Joshua was the Saviour of the people; Jesus of the nations. Blessed therefore are they who are circumcised in heart, and are born again of the waters of the second circumcision. They shall receive the inheritance with Abraham the faithful leader and the father of all nations. For faith was reckoned to him for righteousness (§ 12).

The twelfth Homily (*de Paschate*) also touches on a common point of dispute between Jews and Christians, the due observance of Passover. For Aphrahat insists that it can be kept only in Jerusalem, though the Jews still think they can keep it in their dispersion. They even dare to make an ark, though they had been told in Jer. iii. 16 that *they shall not remember it, and it shall not be made again* (§ 3). Aphrahat had evidently heard of the "ark" in which the sacred rolls were kept in the synagogue,[3] but misunderstood its object. Similarly he says in § 11, "they make a chest and an ark of the covenant". He adds a strange interpretation of Jer. xii. 9, "a painted bird has become an inheritance for Me" For this is the Gentile Church, "painted" because it is of many tongues and of distant peoples (§ 4).[4]

His thirteenth Homily (*De Sabbato*) also takes up a subject of common discussion between Christians and Jews. The Jews boast that they live by the sabbath, because they keep both it and tradition, and for this reason Aphrahat ventures to discuss it (§ 1). He says that the sabbath was not given to distinguish between life and death, righteousness and sin. It was not intended, that is to say, to be the great test of obedience to God, but was given for rest—he evidently means physical rest—just as other precepts are also given, the observance of which is necessary for continuance

---

[1] *Vide supra*, p. 40.
[2] Heb. iv. 12. See on Isidore's *c. Judaeos*, II. xvi (*vide infra*, p. 291).
[3] See also Chrysostom, *Adv. Jud.* vi. 7 (*infra*, p. 135).
[4] See the Appendix on Isidore, II. ix (*infra*, p. 290).

in this life.[1] Therefore is it enjoined also upon the domestic animals
that toil.[2] But those parts of creation which do not toil, as, for
example, the sun, and birds, etc., do not require such a command
(§§ 2, 3). Had it been necessary for righteousness it would have
been given to Adam and the Patriarchs (§§ 4–8). Yet if God rested,
how much more should we (§ 11)! Proper rest on the sabbath is
to choose God's way, and because the Jews did not so keep it they
were scattered abroad (§ 13).

The fourteenth Homily is only an exhortation to Bishops, and
contains nothing for our purpose. But the fifteenth deals with that
very common subject of discussion, the distinction of foods. In
reality no foods are "clean" or "unclean". Food as such does not
commend us to God,[3] and the laws that God gave the Israelites
concerning it were only to keep them from the religion and crimes
of Egypt (§§ 1–3). Observe that the food which the ravens brought
to Elijah came from Jerusalem, given them by the priests at God's
command. So it was clean for Elijah though brought by unclean
birds (§ 5). You, O obstinate scribe of the Law, Teacher of the
people, should be assured that after the sin of the Golden Calf God
gave, as Ezekiel said, "precepts that were not good",[4] and among
these the rules about foods, because of your sins. And Israel is not
clean for a single day,[5] and no one is justified by the Law (§§ 7, 8).
Aphrahat closes this Homily by saying that he has now dealt with
the three things of which the Jews boast, Circumcision, Sabbath,
and Foods.

Aphrahat has already touched on the great question of the call
of the Gentile Church, but considers it more directly in the sixteenth
Homily. The Gentiles were called *before* Israel,[6] and, later on, when
Israel did not hear the Prophets, these turned to the Gentiles. So
that God has really left Israel. "Jacob" sometimes means Gentile
believers who walk in the light of the Lord,[7] and sometimes the
Jews who are rejected.[8] They "seek the word of the Lord but do
not find it",[9] because He has taken it from them (§§ 1–5). He
then gives examples of Gentiles who, having pleased the Lord, were
more justified than Israel, as for instance Jethro, and his seed "who

[1] Lev. xviii. 5.   [2] Ex. xx. 10; xxiii. 12.
[3] 1 Cor. viii. 8.   [4] Ezek. xx. 25 *sq.*
[5] Lev. xv. 5 *sqq.*
[6] Gen. xvii. 5. Cf. Bar Salibi, ii (*infra*, p. 110): Isidore's *c. Judaeos*, II. iv
(*infra*, p. 290).
[7] Isa. ii. 5.   [8] Isa. ii. 6.
[9] Amos viii. 11 *sq.*

set their nest in a Rock",[1] and the Gibeonites. So "the stranger in your midst shall be above and you below",[2] because of the good deeds of the Gentiles (§ 6). The Saviour shall be for a covenant of the people (Israel), and a light to the Gentiles;[3] "and the Glory of the Lord shall be revealed, and all flesh shall see the life (*sic*) of God".[4] It is therefore useless to boast of being children of Abraham (§§ 7, 8).

The seventeenth Homily, "*Of the Messiah, that He is the Son of God*", however, is the one which is generally supposed to be directed especially against the Jews. For it begins (at least in the form in which it has come down to us) with the words: "A reply against the Jews who revile the people of God." They say: "You worship and serve a man who was begotten, and a human being who was crucified. You call a human being God, and, though God has not a son, you say of this Jesus who was crucified that He is the Son of God." The whole Homily is devoted to a reply to this attack by the Jews on the central truths of our Faith.[5]

Aphrahat begins by claiming that we are right to call Jesus God, as well as many other names, for Moses was so called (Ex. vii. 1). Also He is rightly called Son of God, since even Israel had this appellation.[6] Shall not we then call Him Son of God, by whom we have come to know God? Besides, it is used of Solomon.[7] Again, Israel is called both "gods" and "sons of the Most High", though, as they did not repent, he said they should "die as men and fall like one of the princes".[8] See §§ 2–4.

Further, God gives the honoured name of Divinity to whom He wills, and has many titles, e.g. Almighty, Lord of Hosts, etc. (§ 5). He calls even Nebuchadnezzar King of kings, and He lets princes receive honour. He dwells in men,[9] and says they are the temple of God.[10] When man knows his Creator God is formed in his mind; but He is not formed in those sons of Adam who know Him not (§§ 6, 7). If then we honour wicked men how much more should we honour Jesus, who turns us from sin and did so much for us (§ 8).

---

[1] Num. xxiv. 21.   [2] Deut. xxviii. 43.   [3] Isa. xlii. 6.
[4] Isa. xl. 5. "Life" is a common Syriac rendering of "salvation", which the LXX reads.
[5] It is one of the eight Homilies translated by Dr Gwynn in the *Nicene and Post-Nicene Fathers*, vol. xiii. F. C. Burkitt gives a full summary of it (*Early Eastern Christianity*, 1904, pp. 90–93).
[6] Ex. iv. 22 *sq.*   [7] 2 Sam. vii. 14.
[8] Ps. lxxxii. 6 *sq.*   [9] Lev. xxvi. 12.
[10] Jer. vii. 4 *sq.*

Observe the trend of Aphrahat's argument. He is not arguing on *a priori* grounds, or on the mere statements of tradition, nor even on the mere words of Scripture. He is trying to go to the root of the matter—that Jesus by His life and actions reveals to us God so fully that He may be called God Himself, with much fuller right than any to whom the name, or any almost equivalent title, is given in the Old Testament. Perhaps the argument does not go as far as we should like, and leaves room for the supposition that Jesus is not, after all, the Incarnation of the very and eternal Deity. But it forms a sound foundation on which to build this higher truth.

Then Aphrahat shows that Jesus was promised by the Prophets, and that He was called by them the Son of God, and he adduces the usual texts, Pss. ii. 7; cx. 3; Isa. ix. 6 *sq.*; vii. 14, with Matt. i. 23 (§ 9).

But, he continues, thou perhaps wilt say that Christ has not yet come! Granting for the moment that He has not, yet it says, "the peoples will expect him",[1] and I, Aphrahat, from "the peoples", have heard He is coming, and have believed on Him, and by Him adore the God of Israel. Will He blame me? But, in fact, your objection is invalid. The Prophets do not permit you to say He has not come. See Dan. ix. 26 *sq.*, which says that when Christ comes and is killed, then Jerusalem is to be destroyed and not to be rebuilt. So there is no use in your hoping that it will be. Also the Prophets tell us of the suffering and death of Christ.[2] So § 10.

In the last section (§ 11) he gives a string of the various titles of Christ, which, with § 2, recalls to us the lists in Justin's *Dialogue with Trypho*.[3]

The eighteenth Homily deals with the objections raised by Jews to the Christian teaching about virginity and chastity. Monasticism was spreading fast, and, not unnaturally, the Jews pointed out that it was not the ideal of true religion, in spite of the fact that Jeremiah was expressly told to remain single.[4] Aphrahat is very eloquent here, but says nothing that is of special value for our purpose. He grants at the end that not all can receive his teaching.[5]

---

[1] Gen. xlix. 10.

[2] E.g. Ps. xxii. 17–19; Isa. lii. 13–15; liii. 2, 5.

[3] c. 4; cxxvi. 1; *vide supra*, pp. 40 *sq.*

[4] Jer. xvi. 2.　　　　　　　　　　[5] Matt. xix. 11; 1 Cor. vii. 26.

In the nineteenth Homily Aphrahat returns to the question to which he had alluded in xvii. 10, viz. the restoration of the Jews to Palestine. He argues that their hope is utterly mistaken, based on a wrong interpretation of Scripture. He argues in particular, and at some length, from Dan. ix. 23–27, paying special attention to the chronology there implied. But we to-day know more of chronology than Aphrahat, and more also of the providential care of the Jews for near two thousand years, and especially of the wonderful way in which they are now beginning to return to Palestine.

The twentieth Homily, on supporting the poor, contains nothing of interest for our purpose. In Aphrahat's exposition of the parable of Dives and Lazarus he says that Lazarus typifies our Saviour, and the dogs us Gentiles, who lick His wounds when we take His body and set it before our eyes (§ 8). Again, "The Lord God shall kill thee (the rich man, the Jews), and shall call His servants by another name", i.e. Christians.[1]

The twenty-first Homily, on Persecution, is interesting as showing that Aphrahat did sometimes come into direct contact with Jews. For he tells us that a Jew who was called a wise man said to him with reference to Matt. xvii. 19; xxi. 21 (Faith can remove mountains): "You plainly have no wise man whose prayer is heard, or you would no longer be persecuted." Aphrahat answers fairly enough, Do you think that God is with you, though you are scattered abroad? Certainly, he replied, because of Lev. xxvi. 44. Well then, I said, appealing to Isa. xliii. 2, 3, have you no wise man among you who can walk safe in the sea or in fire? Any explanation you can give convinces me as little as my explanation convinces you (§§ 1, 2).

The Jew went on to argue from Ezek. xvi. 55 that Sodom should be restored and be in slavery to Israel, Jerusalem being in her former glory. I, says Aphrahat, thought his argument contemptible, and asked, Is part of the prophet's saying in anger and part in kindness? No, said the Jew, all of it is said in anger. Very well, said I, you are right. All is said in anger, and Jerusalem is reckoned as worse than Sodom. Aphrahat then argues at length that as Sodom is not yet restored Jerusalem cannot be, and that Sodom, Tyre, Babylon, Jerusalem are all addressed in the same language. Besides, if you Jews reproach us for not being released from persecution, why are you not? The answer is that you are

[1] Isa. lxv. 15.

still condemned for your sins (§§ 3–7). Aphrahat then shows by examples from Scripture the spiritual advantage of being persecuted. Joseph, for instance, was persecuted by his brethren. This leads him to say that Joseph was a type of Christ. As Joseph was given his many-coloured robe, so was Jesus given by His Father His body from the Virgin (§§ 8, 9). So also Moses and Joshua were persecuted, each being a type of Christ, and many another saint until Mordecai. Jesus Himself was the greatest of all martyrs. As Diocletian persecuted our brothers in the West, so we now, for our sins, are enduring persecution, that Christ's words may be fulfilled (§ 23).

The twenty-second Homily on Death and the latter times is excellent of its kind, but has nothing for our purpose. It gives the dates of all Aphrahat's Homilies (§ 25).

The supplementary Homily, the twenty-third, of the grape in the cluster,[1] shows that as the cluster is not destroyed because of the good grape in it, so is the world preserved because of the righteous. Aphrahat traces down the blessing in the grape from Adam to Christ, when the grape was taken away from the cluster and the whole vine overthrown, the blessing of God then flowing from Jesus to the Gentiles.

If we consider the work of Aphrahat as a whole we see that although he makes little direct reference to the Judaism of his time—as we find this recorded in the Jewish books which were either already written or were in process of formation—he yet knew a good deal about the Jews and their doctrines, doubtless from coming into close contact with them. Also he seems to have felt very strongly that some of his people were exposed to the danger of being led astray by Jewish practices and even Jewish arguments. This fear indeed seems always to have been at the back of his Homilies, even when his primary thought was the edification of his readers. His writings, that is to say, indicate only occasionally direct endeavour to present Christ to the Jews, but always show a desire to equip His people with arguments likely to be useful in controversy with them.

[1] Isa. lxv. 8.

CHAPTER XI

PSEUDO-EPHRAIM, ETC.

Cent. iv, v, vi

Ephraim is very different from Aphrahat, especially in his poems, not only in the obscurity of his style due to conceits of versifying, and in his pathetic attempts at bearing down heretics by ponderous intellectualism, but also by his lack of interest in our immediate subject. His genuine works contain no one treatise solely or even mainly concerned with the Jews.

Doubtless, as has been already said, there were comparatively few Jews at Nisibis, but one would have supposed he would have come across some, during the sixty years or so that he lived there. Perhaps he did, and perhaps while he was there he wrote something about them. But all that we have of his—and there is much— seems to date from his arrival in Edessa A.D. 364. He died in A.D. 373, or possibly 378.

His commentaries, in prose, on books of the Bible occasionally touch on the subject, e.g. at Gen. xlix. 10, and somewhat at Isa. vii. 15. There seems to be also nothing in his poem against heretics, Jews, and Julian, printed in the opening pages of Overbeck (1865).[1]

In writings, however, that are falsely attributed to Ephraim there is something of interest to us. Dr F. C. Burkitt had occasion to investigate the dates of two in his study of Ephraim's *Quotations from the Gospel*,[2] the *De Magis* and the *De Fine et Admonitione*, and says that they were both composed at Antioch after the time of Chrysostom († A.D. 407), i.e. some forty or fifty years later than Ephraim's death.

In the *De Magis*[3] we read: "He that eateth with the magicians shall not eat the body of our Lord, and he that drinketh with the enchanters shall not drink the blood of the Messiah, and he that

---

[1] S. Krauss has an important section on Ephraim in his "The Jews in the Church Fathers" (*Jew. Qu. Rev.* Oct. 1893, vi. 88–99). He complains bitterly of Ephraim's hatred of the Jews, but shows he knew Hebrew, and at least something of Judaism. But he accepts Pseudo-Ephraim as well as what is genuinely Ephraim's.

[2] *Texts and Studies*, 1901, vii. 2, p. 81.

[3] Lamy, *S. Ephraem Syri Hymni et Sermones*, ii. 399.

eateth with the Jews shall not inherit life eternal." And again: "Everyone that hath eaten and drunken and mingled with the Jews entereth thither into the accusation that he hath become the comrade of the crucifiers."[1]

It seems that much the same is said in *De Fine et Admonitione* in Lamy, iii. 137, 165.

The writer appears to be warning his readers against taking part either in the practices of sorcerers, or in the festivals of the Jews. The warnings of Aphrahat (*supra*, p. 96) and even of St Paul[2] had not sufficed.[3]

Another Pseudo-Ephraimitic writing is of much more interest to us, and one would like to think that it was by Ephraim himself, the *Rhythm against the Jews delivered upon Palm Sunday*.[4] In it the poet—for the author does occasionally rise almost to poetry—begins by appealing to Christians, who are bid come with joy and keep the festival, to Nature in sky and earth, and even to Jerusalem, as it were, for Messiah comes upon Palm Sunday. Alas, that to-day the Vine of Israel is broken, but in its place is Christ the true Vine that grew among the nations. Israel is desolate. But Christ makes His entry into Zion, the Prophets leading the way with their trumpets, proclaiming Him in their sayings. A long string of the chief Messianic passages is then given, prophecy after prophecy. The Gentile Church worships, but the Jews are indignant. For they have rejected the King. As the Father was exchanged for a calf, so was the Son for a thief and murderer. They vexed the Holy Spirit, though they once possessed a knowledge of the Trinity, and they honoured heathen gods. Therefore they are rightly punished. Yet Israel expects to be restored! But the promises to Israel are, in reality, fulfilled in the Church. The Jews fail to see that the types of Christ in the Old Testament were shown to be true in Him. If He did not perform them[5] then let it not be believed on the earth that He is king for ever! But if He did, let

---

[1] Lamy, ii. 411.   [2] Gal. iv. 9 *sq.*

[3] See Chrysostom's invective against incantations, *c. Judaeos*, viii. 7 (also *vide infra*, p. 135). Chrysostom also speaks of the use of amulets with the names of demons engraved on them, in much the same way as Pseudo-Ephraim conjoins Judaism and sorcery. See Aphrahat, i. 19.

[4] Assemani, iii. 209. Dr F. C. Burkitt told me that this is a liturgical piece much later than Ephraim. It is not contained in the early MSS. of Ephraim, and the festival of Palm Sunday was not held regularly at Edessa till about A.D. 500. An English translation is given by J. B. Morris in the Oxford *Library of the Fathers*, 1847, pp. 61–83.   [5] E.g. Zech. ix. 9.

the Jews be ashamed. He is the true Stone foretold by Isaiah,[1] Amos,[2] and David.[3] Therefore let us exult with the children, as the colt, like the cherubim, bears up His glory! The Synagogue asks with contempt, Who is this? But blessed be He who caused the haughty one that did not receive Him to be trodden down, and chose the Church—Lo! she praiseth Him with Hosannas. The poem closes much as it began, with appeals to the Prophets and David to look at Christ's entry into Jerusalem and to praise; to Jerusalem to see that Zech. ix. 9 *sq.* is fulfilled; to aged Jacob, for Gen. xlix. 10 is satisfied; and lastly bids thee, thou Holy Church, give praise upon the Feast Day of our Redeemer, who hath come and delivered thee from error.

It is all very pleasing and likely to move the hearts of a Christian audience, for whom it was no doubt intended. Even so it fails, by omitting to say a single word about the attractiveness of Jesus. Though it was not a direct attempt to present Christ to the Jews, it yet served the important purpose of moving Christians to value Him more, and fit them the better to witness to Him.

Another Rhythm attributed to Ephraim, numbered Forty-four in Eighty Rhythms upon the Faith,[4] does seem to indicate more personal acquaintance with Judaism. For § 3 refers to the Jewish use of many names of God, though they reject the one Name. They were rooted out, because they did not believe in the Son. In § 5 Jewish objections are adduced: "Who is this? whose son is He? And how came He, or will He come? And they thought it impossible for a Virgin to bring forth, and the elders and the scribes blasphemed Him, because they had begotten a Christ for themselves which was no Christ.... The Jews are looking for the dream of their own intellect."

Jacob of Serug (*c.* A.D. 450–521) wrote three *Homilies against the Jews* which have been edited, translated and annotated by the Rev. I. K. Cosgrove (D.D. Lond.), now Minister of the Garnethill Synagogue, Glasgow, from a manuscript in the British Museum. Dr Parkes says of it: "He appears to be dealing with real difficulties raised in the minds of his congregation by their Jewish neighbours. He avoids the conventional abuse directed against the crucifiers of Christ, and reproaches them rather for not subsequently recognising the fulfilment of prophecy in Him. His strong point is that a prophecy cannot be fulfilled twice, and that therefore there is

---

[1] xxviii. 16. [2] vii. 7. [3] Ps. cxviii. 22.
[4] Assemani, iii. 1; J. B. Morris, *op. cit.* p. 247.

nothing left for which the Jews can wait. 'Our Lord when He came grasped the totality of prophecy', and therefore gave no opportunity for another to come."[1]

A few bare titles of works of the fifth and sixth centuries have survived. Marootha, Bishop of Meiparket, who died before A.D. 420, wrote a *Book of Evidences*.[2]

Mana (not the earlier of the same name), who lived A.D. 457–484, wrote *Against the Jews*.[3]

One John, a Nestorian of the sixth century, wrote a treatise against the Jews.[4] He is presumably the same as Johanan of Beit Raban, a Nestorian who wrote *On the customs of the Jews*.[5]

---

[1] P. 279. It is much to be wished that the necessary funds to publish Dr Cosgrove's important book were forthcoming.

[2] Baumstark, *Geschichte der syrischen Literatur*, 1922, p. 105.

[3] *Ibid.* See also *Dict. Chr. Biog.* iii. 859.

[4] Mentioned in Mingana, *Narsai*, i. 36. See Duval, *La Littérature Syriaque*, 1907, p. 346.

[5] Given in the list by Mar Abd Isho' (Ebed Jesu). See Badger, *Nestorians*, ii. 368. See also *Dict. Chr. Biog.* iii. 405. It was composed after A.D. 1315–6 (Baumstark, p. 325).

CHAPTER XII

DIONYSIUS BAR SALIBI

COMMENTARIES; AGAINST THE JEWS

Cent. XII

Our next and last author is Jacob, who took the name of Dionysius at his consecration, Bar Salibi. He was the Jacobite metropolitan of Amid (Diabekr), high up on the Tigris, about one hundred miles north-east of Edessa. He died in November, A.D. 1171. He was a man of much learning, and, while he had little originality, was very diligent in his use of the writings of his predecessors, in particular Ephraim, Chrysostom, and Cyril, and exercised a sound judgment in the results at which he arrived.[1] His commentary on the Gospels, of which only St Matthew has appeared as yet,[2] is sensible and to the point, and gives him occasion sometimes to meet the objections of the Jews. For example, these[3] urge that Moses said in Deut. iv. 2, Do not add to the Law or diminish from it, and the Gospel is an addition. Bar Salibi replies that the Jews themselves added the Prophets and the Sapiential books.

They also say that the Gospel contains self-contradictory statements. He replies that this is the case with the Law as well, for though Gen. ii. 17 says, "in the day thou eatest thereof thou shalt surely die", Adam lived for 930 years after.

Later on[4] the Jews are represented as saying that Jesus was not in fact called Emmanuel, and therefore cannot be He to whom the prophet refers.[5] He replies, Was Isaiah ever called Maher-shalal-hash-baz,[6] or Jerusalem named City of righteousness and Faithful city?[7] More to the point is his explanation that such titles

---

[1] His works are slowly being published in the *Scriptores Syri*, with a Latin translation.

[2] *Scriptores Syri*, vol. xcviii, Rome, 1906 and 1915. One of the MSS. was written as early as A.D. 1174, only three years after Bar Salibi's death.

[3] P. 17. The pagination of the Syriac is followed.

[4] P. 81 *sq.*, on Matt. i. 22.

[5] Isa. vii. 14. This difficulty is often raised by ignorant Jews at the present day.

[6] Isa. viii. 1, 3. Bar Salibi forgets that the name was that of his son.

[7] Isa. i. 26.

are not names, but representations of the facts. Jesus was called Emmanuel because He, being God, lived with us bodily and openly. He adds the remark that He was not merely joined to a man, i.e. as a help to him, as the Nestorians impiously affirm.

Again,[1] the Jews explain Micah v. 2 of Zerubbabel, but Bar Salibi replies that he was not born in Bethlehem, but in Babylon, as his name shows.

A little later[2] he discusses the Jewish objection that the prophecies "He shall be called a Nazarene" and "out of Egypt have I called my son" are not found in the Old Testament. Without mentioning Hos. xi. 1, as he might well have done in the case of the second phrase, he answers, first, that they deal with the humiliation of Christ, for Nazareth suggests contempt[3] and Egypt His flight. Secondly, that it is not surprising if some passages of Holy Writ were handed down until the Evangelist's time by tradition only, for the Jews were very careless about their Scriptures. The Old Testament itself refers to lost writings, as, for example, the Book of the Wars of the Lord,[4] the Book of Jashar,[5] the prophecy of Jonah,[6] the promise "Thou hast said, the world shall be built up in goodness",[7] and in Isaiah we read: "This is the word which the LORD spake against Moab (in time past)."[8] Thirdly, he points out that the Hebrew of "branch" in Isa. xi. 1 is *nezer*, and that the Gospel interprets Old Testament sayings by events of later days.[9]

He also[10] mentions the Jewish objection that the quotation of "three days and three nights" was not the same as rising on "the third day". Bar Salibi replies that the meaning is identical, and in accordance with the common usage of speech. Jesus rose within the period suggested by the phrase used of Jonah.

The only other volume of Biblical commentaries by Bar Salibi yet published is one containing his exposition of the Revelation of St John, the Acts, and the seven Catholic Epistles. It does not seem to have anything directly for our purpose, but we may notice that on Acts vi. 11 he gives an admirable summary of the aim of St Stephen's speech, and then says: "After he has shown that the

---

[1] P. 102, on Matt. ii. 6.   [2] Pp. 123–125, on Matt. ii. 23.
[3] John i. 46.   [4] Num. xxi. 14.
[5] 2 Sam. i. 18.   [6] 2 Kings xiv. 25.
[7] Ps. lxxxix. 2 in the Syriac.   [8] Isa. xvi. 13.
[9] This was also the Jewish method. See Lukyn Williams, *The Hebrew Christian Messiah*, 1916, p. 12 *sq.*; Klausner, *Die Messianischen Vorstellungen*, u.s.w., 1904, p. 88.
[10] Pp. 329–331, on Matt. xii. 40.

temple and the place (Jerusalem) are not necessary, and that the Law is much more recent (than the revelation to the patriarchs), he points out that they are useless, and that the ancients were victorious apart from Temple and Law."

While these quotations are sufficient to show that Bar Salibi bore the Jews in mind when writing for Christian people, another writing of his proves that he felt himself called upon to deal with them directly. For he composed a long treatise entitled *Against the Jews*.[1] It does not indeed display any great knowledge of Judaism, in its customs and doctrines, but Bar Salibi did, apparently, come into contact with Jews, for the objections to this or that part of the Christian argument which he puts into the mouth of Jews are such as they may well have brought forward. Like almost all Eastern writers he seldom finishes off his arguments, but drops a subject and takes it up again. Possibly, however, in his case this points to separate conversations with Jews, on which he had made notes which were afterwards rearranged, not, alas, as lucidly as they might have been.

The treatise is divided into nine chapters, and De Zwaan (as it appears) has subdivided these into sections for convenient reference.

In chapter I, after giving the meaning of "Israel" and "Jew", and a description of the various divisions of the Jews much after the manner of Epiphanius,[2] he says that they were dispersed because they worshipped idols and crucified their Lord. If they object that the destruction of Jerusalem was by men and not by God, he asks, Who then held back the fire that fell on the sacrifices? Who fashioned the Voice that was heard? Who annulled the power that was used to heat the oil in the horn? Who prevented the power in the stones on the priest's breast? He implies that though man destroyed, God showed His approval by His own acts. This dispersion too has proved to be permanent.

In chapter II he reminds the Jews that they cannot keep the Feasts and the Sacrifices, for they were to be observed in Jerusalem only. He touches on circumcision, reminding them that Abraham

---

[1] Edited by J. De Zwaan, Leiden, 1906, from a manuscript now in the Rylands Library, Manchester. An English translation with notes, etc., was promised by Rendel Harris, but has not yet (1934) appeared. Neither is the treatise so far included in the *Scriptores Syri*.

[2] *Adv. Haeres.* I. xiv, *P.G.* xli. 239. Cf. *Dialogue with Trypho*, lxxx. 4 (*supra*, p. 34).

and his predecessors lived as Christians without circumcision and sabbath; and that, like Melchizedek, the uncircumcised may be greater than the circumcised. He also touches on the doctrine of the Trinity,[1] and the Sabbath. God can give rules and also take them away if people have grown out of them. The Gentiles of old, in the time of Noah and Melchizedek and Job, had "a chosen lip",[2] but it was taken away from them because of idolatry. So now through Messiah God has "turned" it back to them. And further, as a sorcerer will hand a colt over to the bites of a snake, in the presence of many, and will heal it by his antidote[3]—not for the honour of the colt, but that he may exhibit the power of his drugs, and draw the people to them—so, by performing miracles to restore the Jews to health, did God attract the Gentiles.

"Chapter III refers to the worship of Messiah." So Bar Salibi says, but he is discursive as usual. For he here definitely quotes and answers various objections raised by Jews, e.g. Why do not *all* the Gentiles worship Christ? Where does the Old Testament speak of Christ's suffering and rising? We have crucified your God, and He could not help Himself! David's throne was to be on earth, and Christ's is in heaven! The Messiah would not have been crucified, for it is written of Him that He remains. After answering these difficulties, as a rule quite briefly, he quotes at greater length additional prophecies of the abolition of the sacrifices and feasts.

Chapter IV also takes up a whole series of questions raised by Jews: Whence is it known that the Messiah has come? Was not circumcision given to us Jews? Must not the Law be observed under the penalty of a curse? Are not we really the children of Abraham? Then follow many objections dealing with the relation of Christ to God the Father, and then, How can bread be the body of God? To which Bar Salibi replies that in the figure of bread we eat the body of our God, even everlasting life.

After briefly mentioning the prophecies of the two Advents of Christ, he adduces more questions brought forward by the Jews, e.g. How do we know that the Messiah is the Word of God? Answer, "He sent His Word and healed them."[4] The chapter ends by Bar Salibi saying that the doctrine of the Trinity is like the sun, for the sun and its brightness and its heat are one. So also

[1] E.g. Gen. i. 26.
[2] Zeph. iii. 9. Cf. Aphrahat, xvi. 1 (*supra*, p. 98).
[3] θηριακή.   [4] Ps. cvii. 20.

God revealed His threefold Personality to Abraham[1] and to Moses.[2]

Chapter v deals in more detail with the doctrine of the Trinity, adducing more Jewish questions, especially with regard to the Incarnation.

Chapter vi shows that many of the details of the Passion were foretold in the Old Testament. There are added other questions by the Jews about the coming of Elijah, the abrogation of the ceremonial Law, the reason why Christ was circumcised. The answer to the last is, Lest He should be thought to be transgressing the Law. But He ordained Baptism for the Apostles. He is the Prophet of Deut. xviii. 18, and, as Isa. ii. 3 says, the new Law was to go out from Mount Zion, i.e. at the Ascension.

Chapter vii purports to treat of the Resurrection of Christ, but after giving the Old Testament evidence for His Burial, Resurrection, and Ascension,[3] it discusses Jewish enquiries about the rejection of Israel and the choice of the Gentiles. It inserts among these the Jewish opinion that the Servant in Isa. liii refers to Hezekiah, adding their objection that if it refers to Messiah, "then your Messiah is a servant and the Word is not God". Bar Salibi says that the title "Servant" is metaphorical. For "as a servant sweeps the house, so did He sweep the world seeking the coin which He had lost; and as servants fill water so He gave water to the Samaritan woman, and washed the disciples",[4] but points out that it was only one of many titles which refer to the Messiah, e.g. Lion's cub, Star, Sun, Child, Councillor, etc., etc. Jonah fled from going to the Gentiles because he saw that the grace of prophecy was passing away from the Jews to them.

Chapter viii returns to the question by the Jews as to what the prophecies say about Baptism, and then to a difficulty which could not have arisen in the early centuries, that Christians worship the Cross and the bones of saints, in view of Ex. xxxiv. 14 and similar texts. The Christian apologist replies, First, God forbid that we should worship graven things. You Jews honour the ark, the tables of the Law, etc. We worship Him who was crucified on the wood, and "whenever we see the Cross it is as though we saw the Messiah who was crucified upon it". Secondly, as to our honour of the martyrs. As Abraham worshipped before the sons of Hamor, and all worship before kings, "so we worship the martyrs in order that

[1] Gen. xviii. [2] Ex. vi.
[3] Ps. xlvii. 5. [4] vii. 14.

we may be helped by their prayers". Bar Salibi's reply is not as satisfactory as in the first case.

But you Jews rejected your own prophets, and also the Son, who came at the time foretold in Dan. ix. 25. Even if, as the Jews assert, the number of Daniel's "weeks" should be doubled, the time is now very far exceeded. They would have to be trebled, and yet the Jews still reject the truth that the Messiah has come.

In chapter ix the Jews boast that they alone are the children of Abraham, and our author points out that Abraham was to be father to the peoples, not to the Jews only. Also they say to us, Keep the Law. But no one can do so, and therefore was it that Christ came. You must "kiss the Son".[1] But, say the Jews, you have learned the Scriptures from us! Yes, but, unlike you, we have seen the interpretation of them. But now "the young birds have flown, and the senseless still sit on the nest". The chapter ends with a full discussion of Daniel's prophecy which had been touched upon in viii. 6 *sq.*

The whole treatise closes with an appeal to the Jews to turn to God while there is yet time.

Regarding Bar Salibi's work as a whole it is plain that he covers a great deal of ground, and shows no little acquaintance with the kind of objections that Jews have made in all ages. But, as a rule, his arguments are not such as scholars can use to-day in addressing Jews. We rather bring before them such parts of the evidence as the gradualness of the revelation of God, the attractiveness of the Lord Jesus, His truthfulness, and the greatness of His claims.

For the New Testament is not wholly unknown to most Jews to-day, and we can therefore appeal to it as a trustworthy presentation of Jesus, asking them to co-ordinate the facts related there with what they already know of God. This was impossible in the time of Dionysius bar Salibi, and even till quite recently in our own time. We do not however forget that there are still very many Jews who know nothing whatever of the New Testament, and therefore can only be reached first of all by the Old. For even that records the manifestation of God who reveals Himself at last in Christ, "the effulgence of His glory, and the very expression of His being".[2]

[1] Ps. ii. 12.
[2] Heb. i. 3.

CONCLUDING REMARKS

This very short review of the Apologetic Literature (as regards the Jews) of the Syriac-speaking Church shows us that it cannot hold comparison with that of Spain (for example), either in extent and scholastic learning, or in continuance of tradition. Between Aphrahat in the fourth century and Bar Salibi in the twelfth there is almost a blank, and neither of these has the systematisation of an Isidore, the learning of a Raymund Martini, or the forcefulness of a Paul of Burgos. Bar Salibi has indeed many interesting points, but is distinctly second-rate.

Aphrahat, however, stands on a different level. His piety and sweet reasonableness, together with his patent knowledge of his subject, places his writings among the most attractive in the whole of Christian polemical literature for the Jews. Naturally he is not modern, but we may well pray to resemble him more both in knowledge and in Christian spirit. Workers among the Jews to-day might do much worse than make a prayerful study of the Homilies of Aphrahat.

How was it then that, so far as we know, the Syriac-speaking Church had so little effect on the Jews of Mesopotamia? One can only guess. Was it that it was itself exposed to persecution? Yet this would, at any rate, be better than the effect of persecuting Jews, as in Spain. Was it that its leaders and writers cooped themselves up in monasteries, shutting themselves off, more and more, from intercourse with their Jewish neighbours? Or was it that it lost little by little its sense of missionary duty—at least towards the Jews, for towards the Gentiles it was quite otherwise, at least in its Nestorian branch? We can only say that the reason is obscure. In any case, the failure of the Syriac-speaking Church to do its uttermost to win Jews to Christ prevented the influx of Jewish energy into its ranks, and may thus have contributed to the spiritual torpor into which it gradually fell. For if our own life is to be at its best, it must have given itself for others.

BOOK III

GREEK WRITERS

A.D. 325–1455

CHAPTER XIII

THE DIALOGUE OF ATHANASIUS AND ZACCHAEUS[1]

c. A.D. 325

This is much less interesting than the *Dialogue of Timothy and Aquila*, with which it is associated in both ancient and modern times, but it is more thoughtful. In the earlier part of the treatise the writer seems to have used *Timothy and Aquila*, yet not slavishly, and indeed his omission of some of Timothy-Aquila's arguments is strange. One would have expected, for example, that the interpretation of *In the beginning* as referring to the Logos, which is at least suggested in *Timothy and Aquila*, Fol. 78 r⁰, would have appealed to him. But he makes no allusion to it. Perhaps the early interpretation had passed out of sight by the time he wrote.[2]

For as a whole *Ath.-Zacch.* seems to be later than *Tim.-Aq.*, chiefly because it is an attempt to combine Christian thought, and even philosophy of a kind, with arguments drawn directly from separate texts. It tries, that is to say, to bring into a focus the passages relative to the Wisdom of God, and to show that this Wisdom, by which, as is granted, God created all things, was, in reality, no mere attribute (as is a man's wisdom) but a permanent Being, essentially one with the Father, yet not the Father. This, in

---

[1] Edited from a single MS. at Vienna (which is not later than the twelfth century) with introduction and notes (especially illustrating similar passages in early Christian literature) by F. C. Conybeare in *Anecdota Oxoniensia*, 1898. He has added the text (only) of the *Dialogue of Timothy and Aquila* (*vide supra*, p. 67). An Armenian version of our Dialogue (not later than the first half of the fifth century) is translated by Conybeare in the *Expositor*, 1897, v. 300–320, 443–463. It defines the Athanasius as "Bishop of Alexandria". For some details illustrating the connexion between the two documents see the Appendix at the end of this chapter.

[2] See the Appendix to this chapter. One shrinks from multiplying sources, but the conditions of the problem would be satisfied by postulating a little *Book of Testimonies* which contained texts common to *Ath.-Zacch.* §§ 1–21 and *Tim.-Aq.*, especially Foll. 76–81. Or possibly *Ath.-Zacch.* used a draft of our *Tim.-Aq.* which was earlier than that which has come down to us. But to identify this with any form of the *Dialogue of Jason and Papiscus*, as Conybeare tries to do, is to follow an *ignis fatuus*, *vide infra*, p. 118.

fact, is the characteristic of the tract, distinguishing it from perhaps all other writings of the same kind.[1]

But if our Dialogue is later than *Tim.-Aq.*, the original form of which, as has been seen, is to be placed about A.D. 200, how much later is it? The absence of any reference to Islam does not indeed absolutely preclude a date as late as the seventh century, but makes it very improbable. And further, the absence of any of the technical terms of the controversies in the second half of the fourth century suggests that it was written earlier than that. On the other hand, Jerusalem is described as a Christian city, with monks living there, the Church of the Resurrection already built, and all the kings bringing in their glory.[2] The wise also, the rhetoricians, and the poets are offering the wealth of their words to Christ, and abjuring idolatry.[3] All this points to a date not earlier than about A.D. 325.[4]

The outline of the contents of our treatise, so far as it is possible to give an outline, when the author (as usual) has not a very systematic mind, may be given as follows. After a Prologue, describing the circumstances in which the discussion arose (§§ 1, 2), the author deals with the following subjects: I. The Old Testament speaks of Wisdom as with God at the Creation, and as a fellow-Counsellor with Him, having a Being other than the Father's, though not another God (§§ 3–20). II. The Incarnation, and particularly the Cross and Death (§§ 21–45). III. Jesus is the Anointed (i.e. the Christ), because His is the anointing by the Spirit (§§ 46–56). IV. A consideration of what is intended by the New Name which it is said God will give, and, in connexion with this, of the Rejection of the Jews and the Choice of the Gentiles (§§ 57–71;[5] cf. *infra*, §§ 90, 91). V. A consideration of several details: i. Miracles (§§ 72–75). ii. The Massacre of the Innocents (§§ 76–80). iii. Psalm cx and Solomon (§§ 81–89). iv. The Call of the Heathen (§§ 90, 91). v. Circumcision (§§ 92–

[1] The identification of the Logos with Wisdom is in itself as early as Justin's *Trypho*, lxii. 4 (*supra*, p. 37).

[2] § 70.   [3] § 71.

[4] The use of ἀπαράλλακτος in § 98 suggests the same date. It is impossible to accept Conybeare's suggestion (§ 125) that the Dialogue was written before Justin's *Trypho* (between A.D. 155 and 161).

[5] In § 61, when the Christian has argued in all seriousness that the present misery of the Jews is a proof of their present rejection, the Jew replies: "No one insults another by way of argument." The Christian answers: "I do not insult thee; far be it from me to do so."

113 and 122–127). vi. Daniel vii (§§ 114–121). vii. Sacrifices (§§ 128, 129). Epilogue, The Conversion of Zacchaeus (§ 130).

It is worth while tracing out how our author treats of the Divine Wisdom, as he proves from the Old Testament the existence of what we now call a second Personality in the Divine Unity. He has asked, Who was addressed by God in the words *Let us make man in our image and likeness* (Gen. i. 26)?[1] It cannot, he says, be the Speaker Himself, because of the plural. Nor can it be the Angels, for one would not call them God's fellow-workers. God in fact made all things *in Wisdom*.[2] And to Him,[3] it is plain, He said *Let us make*, etc. We are right also in identifying Wisdom with Christ, for again the prophet says: *By the Word (Logos) of the Lord were the heavens made*.[4] There is thus in the Deity an Image of God the archetype, and after this Image man was made,[5] the word *our* pointing to the common Being (ὑπόστασις) of the Archetype and the Image, all this indicating not that there is a second God, but that the Wisdom of God is the "effulgence" of the Divine Light.[6] It cannot, however, be argued that because the word "Wisdom" (σοφία) is feminine therefore Christ must be feminine also, any more than that because "soul" (ψυχή) is feminine a man's soul must be feminine. This is a matter of mere linguistics.[7] Nor again, when Scripture says the heavens were made by the word of the Lord *and all the host ("power") of them by the breath of His mouth*,[8] can the reference be to vocal organs and respiration.[9] The Jew here catches at the word "power", and asks if "the Power" is also God, and the Christian replies that it was by that "power" that God says: *Behold Adam has become as one of Us*,[10] and goes on to explain that there is a kind of "power" by which God commonly converses.[11] For it says, *When He was preparing the heaven I was with Him, and I was by Him arranging (all things)*, and *I was that in which He was delighting*.[12] When the Jew objects that the passage does not say

[1] § 5.　　　　　　　　　　　[2] § 6. See Ps. civ. 24.
[3] "Wisdom is spoken of in the masculine gender by reason of her identification with Christ" (Conybeare).
[4] § 7. See Ps. xxxiii. 6.
[5] See Conybeare, with his quotation from Tertullian, *Adv. Prax.* 12.
[6] § 9. See Wisd. vii. 26; Heb. i. 3.
[7] § 10.　　　　　　　　　　　[8] Ps. xxxiii. 6.
[9] § 11.　　　　　　　　　　　[10] § 12. See Gen. iii. 22.
[11] Our author appears to mean that "Power" is a synonym of "Word" and thus refers to Christ, but it is possible that, consciously or unconsciously, he is influenced by the thought of a Third "Person" in the Trinity, the Holy Spirit.
[12] Prov. viii. 27, 30.

"I was God", the Christian tells him that he too (like Christ) may *advance in stature and wisdom*, but must be content to go slowly.[1]

The Jew then acknowledges that there is a certain "Power" in which God delighted, but asks for proof that it was God. The reply is that the visit to Abraham related in Gen. xviii. 17–26 suggests the question, Who spoke to Abraham, God Himself, or His Power? When the Jew answers, God Himself,[2] the Christian raises the old difficulty. The words are: *The Lord God rained upon Sodom and Gomorrah brimstone and fire from the Lord out of heaven*; from what Lord then did the Lord God so act? The Jew objects, It does not say *the Lord God rained*, but *the Lord rained*, to which the Christian replies gently enough, Most copies add *God*, but it is unimportant, for it is clear that He who rained is He who said to Lot that He would not destroy Zoar.[3] When Zacchaeus the Jew then objects that it was an angel who *rained from the Lord God*, Athanasius the Christian retorts, So you call the angel of the Lord, Lord, but will not call His Power Lord! The Jew's answer is that he is using a term applied in Scripture to the former which is not to be found applied to the latter.[4] Athanasius replies that he has already quoted the words *He made all things in Wisdom*, a phrase which includes this "raining"—and this does not mean that the Lord God rained from the Lord of Wisdom, but that Wisdom Himself, being both Lord and God, *rained from the Lord God*.

When the Jew points out that *God* is here a false reading, and therefore Athanasius implies that Wisdom is called *the Lord God* and God Himself is called only *the Lord*,[5] the reply is that there was no need to add the term *God* to the Creator of all, but that it was advisable to add it when speaking of Wisdom, for He knew the disobedience of some.[6]

So there are two Gods! the God and Father of all, and God who is Wisdom! God forbid! cries the Christian, for there is one nature, will, and harmony. Would you say that a king and his image are two kings? True, that in human things an image is by imitation, but in the case of God by natural Being.[7] Yet surely, says the Jew, it does mean two Gods? You would be right, no doubt, is the reply, if the Original and the Image had two wills, but you are wrong when there is the same will, knowledge, opinion, and nature. There is, in fact, but one God, because His Being is unchangeable.[8]

[1] § 13.   [2] § 14.   [3] § 15.   [4] § 16.
[5] § 17.   [6] § 18.   [7] § 19.
[8] ἀπαράλλακτος. *Vide supra*, p. 118.

In Moses' writings there are two illustrations of this. According
to Moses a man and his wife are unchangeable in opinion, will,
and being, for he says they are *one flesh*.[1] And again in his Song at
the Red Sea he says, *horse and rider He cast into the sea*, because of the
sameness of their nature. If he applied a term in the singular
number to horses and riders, although they are corporeal, how
much more would he have used the plural for the incorporeal God
and His Word who is God, if they had more than One![2]

The author goes on to show that the Incarnation of Wisdom was
foretold, quoting, as usual, the famous description of Baruch iii.
37, which says that when men were *perishing* Wisdom *appeared
on earth and was conversant with men*.[3] Blasphemy! cries Zacchaeus,
the Wisdom of God cannot enter into a human womb! Don't be
excited, replies Athanasius, Wisdom frames every man in the
temple of his mother's womb; see Jer. i. 5. It is on a par with the
Divine method generally, even as the sun is not injured by falling
on dead bodies and corruption, but purifies them. So does the
great Artificer sanctify the womb, open the gates of the flesh, order
everything and preserve it, and at last bring it to complete perfection.[4] Then the passage in Baruch is treated in more detail, our
author using the appellation "the Wisdom of God" in preference
to any other.[5]

With regard to other points very few out of the many details
found in this treatise have not already been considered elsewhere
in this volume, but two or three may be mentioned here.

In § 24 *sq.* the Christian defends his naming Jeremiah as the
author of Baruch iii. 35–37 by saying that "Jeremiah with Baruch
and Lamentations and the Epistle are written in one book, and
these four as one book are called 'Jeremiah'".

In § 33 *sq.* the Magi are said to be the *Damascus* and the *Samaria*
which it was foretold in Isa. viii. 4 the Child should conquer. For
"they who are likeminded with the Egyptians are called in
Scripture Egyptians; and with the Canaanites, Canaanites; and
with the Amorites, Amorites (Ezek. xvi. 3). And so them who
were likeminded with the Damascenes [and Samaritans], it called
[Damascenes] and Samaritans."[6]

In § 45 the phrase born "of the Holy Spirit and Mary the Virgin"

[1] Gen. ii. 24.   [2] § 20.
[3] § 21. Cf. *Tim.-Aq.* Fol. 81 r° *sq.* (*supra*, p. 73).
[4] §§ 22, 23.   [5] *Vide supra*, p. 118.
[6] Cf. *Trypho*, lxxviii. 9 (*supra*, p. 41).

is in verbal agreement with the original text of the Roman Creed quoted by Marcellus of Ancyra in his letter to the Bishop of Rome, *c.* A.D. 337.[1]

In § 65 *sq.* Isa. lxi. 9, *and their seed shall be known among the Gentiles*, is quoted and perhaps explained as meaning that the Apostles and the physical descendants of Jews (ἔκγονα) were recognised as Jews, the promise of Isa. lxi. 1–11 being thus fulfilled.[2] But, more probably, he is thinking only, or at least chiefly, of spiritual descent. See, in particular, Augustine, *Adv. Judaeos*, vii. 9 (*infra*, p. 315).

AN APPENDIX

Showing in some detail the relation of Ath.-Zacch. to Tim.-Aq.

The §§ refer to Ath.-Zacch.; the Foll. to Tim.-Aq.

§ 1 = Fol. 76 r⁰. Both treatises begin, quite naturally, with the statement that there is but one God. Observe that the phrase "Christ is God" comes early in Ath.-Zacch. but late in Tim.-Aq. Both include the *Shma'* and Isa. xliv. 6. But Ath.-Zacch. alone has Ps. lxxxi. 8–10.

§ 3 = Fol. 78 r⁰. Both say, Let us start from the first book of the Old Testament and take the others in order. Only Tim.-Aq. refers to Gen. i. 1 (*vide supra*, p. 73).

§ 3 = Fol. 78 v⁰. Ath.-Zacch. at once discusses Gen. i. 26, but in Tim.-Aq. this is adduced only after passages which, though rather similar to Gen. i. 26, are not addressed to any one.

§ 4 = Fol. 79 v⁰; cf. Fol. 80 v⁰. Ath.-Zacch.: Did Christ exist at Creation, when He was born in the time of Augustus! Tim.-Aq. has only the same general argument.

§§ 5, 6 = Foll. 78 v⁰ *bis*; 79 r⁰ *bis*. Ath.-Zacch. renews the discussion of Gen. i. 26, which has been continuous in Tim.-Aq. Both show that the words were not addressed to angels.

§ 7. In Ath.-Zacch. it was Wisdom to whom God spoke. Tim.-Aq. in Fol. 79 v⁰ quotes Prov. viii. 27–30 for the thought of a σύμβουλος at the Creation, identifying Him with the σύμβουλος of Isa. ix. 6, and in Fol. 81 v⁰ applying the term σύμβουλος to Gen. i. 26, and expressly identifying Him with Wisdom. Cf. § 13, *infra*.

§ 8 = Fol. 79 r⁰. Both quote Ps. xxxiii. 6 in connexion with Gen. i. 26.

§ 13 = Fol. 81 v⁰. Both quote Prov. viii. 27 *sqq.* of Wisdom; Tim.-Aq. in connexion with σύμβουλος.

§ 13 (*cont.*) = Fol. 79 v⁰. In both the Christian tells the Jew that he must learn the Alphabet, and in much the same context.

---

[1] See Hahn, *Symbolik*, 1897, p. 22 *sq.*
[2] See Conybeare, *Proleg.* pp. xxxix–xlii.

§ 15 = Foll. 81 v°; 105 v°. Both refer to Gen. xix. 24, but Ath.-Zacch. is clearer and fuller. N.B. In Tim.-Aq. Fol. 105 v° is clearer than Fol. 81 v°.

§ 21 = Fol. 81 v° *sq.* Both raise the question of the Incarnation. Ath.-Zacch. says the Logos is God and Wisdom. Tim.-Aq. says that God has a σύμβουλος.

§§ 30–32 = Foll. 94 v°; 111 r°. Both discuss Isa. vii. 14, but in different contexts. Ath.-Zacch. asks what sign is there in a νεᾶνις having a son? Tim.-Aq. argues that νεᾶνις and παρθένος are one, i.e. synonymous, at least in usage.

§§ 36, 37 = Fol. 133 r°. Both quote Deut. xxviii. 66 as referring to the Crucifixion and the Darkness. But while the matter is the same, the order of its parts is different.

§ 43 = Fol. 76 v°. In both the Jew says that he knows all about the origin of Jesus, but there is no verbal resemblance.

§ 57 = Fol. 92 v°. Ath.-Zacch. says, When you are converted you shall know the meaning of the New Name. Tim.-Aq. says you shall then know the meaning of *the sacrifice of praise* (Ps. l. 14). The two accounts seem to be independent.

§ 61 = Foll. 100 v°; 134 v°. Ath.-Zacch. (Armenian): Insults are not argument. Tim.-Aq.: Insult is unbecoming in the case of a fellow-enquirer.

§ 62 = Fol. 88 v°. Ath.-Zacch. (Armenian): The Blessings promised to the Jews are to be fulfilled in the future. Tim.-Aq.: All the prophecies about the Jews and the Messiah, etc. refer to the future.

§ 66 = Fol. 126 r°. Ath.-Zacch.: The promise about the seed of Abraham being known among the Gentiles refers to the Apostles. Tim.-Aq.: It refers to Jesus and believers.

§§ 103, 105 = Fol. 125 v°. Both discuss Ps. lxxii. 6–19. Ath.-Zacch. deals only with the question of the permanence of Solomon, and the foreknowledge of the name of Christ. Tim.-Aq. asks, Can you show me Solomon's seat, i.e. his ivory throne and his kingdom?

§§ 108, 120 = Fol. 91 r°. Both say that if Messiah were to come He would find that all the prophecies about Him had already been fulfilled. Tim.-Aq. refers to the tribe of Dan as a Judge, but not Ath.-Zacch.

CHAPTER XIV

PSEUDO-GREGORY OF NYSSA

SELECTED TESTIMONIES FROM THE OLD TESTAMENT AGAINST THE JEWS

c. A.D. 400

No one believes that the treatise entitled *Selected Testimonies from the Old Testament against the Jews*[1] was written by Gregory of Nyssa, although it is attributed to him at the head of the treatise, and, indeed, belongs approximately to his time.[2] As Gregory died in A.D. 394–5, and it is hardly likely that his writings were imitated directly they were written, we shall not be far out if we place this document about A.D. 400.

Whoever wrote it was not a man of outstanding ability, much less of originality of thought. To most readers perhaps its chief interest lies in the character of the Greek version of the Psalms and Prophets which he uses. For this often differs much from the Vatican text.[3]

For our purpose, however, its interest is of another kind. For it is one of the most typical of the *Books of Testimonies*, the Collections, that is to say, of passages which seemed to the early Church to bear witness to Christ. It is in the succession of Cyprian, Isidore, and Dionysius bar Salibi, to mention only such treatises as are strictly confined to "testimonies". It is, in other words, one of the more notable examples of the crystallisation into fixed forms of that

---

[1] τοῦ ἐν ἁγίοις Γρηγορίου ἐπισκόπου Νήσσης Ἐκλογαὶ μαρτυρίων πρὸς Ἰουδαίους ἀπὸ τῆς παλαιᾶς, μετά τινος ἐπεξεργασίας περὶ τῆς ἁγίας Τριάδος· ὅτι Λόγον καὶ Πνεῦμα ἔχει ὁ Θεός, κατὰ τὰς γραφάς· Λόγον ἐνυπόστατον, καὶ ζῶντα, καὶ Πνεῦμα ὡσαύτως. "The blessed Bishop Gregory of Nyssa's Selected Testimonies against the Jews from the Old Testament, together with a somewhat full investigation about the Holy Trinity, that God has Word and Spirit, according to the Scriptures, Word self-subsistent and living, and Spirit likewise." The treatise is in Migne, *P.G.* xlvi. 194–234; first published by Zacagni, *Collectanea Monumentorum*, 1698, pp. 288–329.

[2] See Bardenhewer, *Gesch. d. altkirchl. Lit.* 1912, iii. 202.

[3] I cannot find that it has been the subject of any special study in this respect. And until the Cambridge Larger Edition of the LXX has reached the Psalms and the Prophets (in several years' time), it is almost impossible for a non-specialist to make any profitable study of the various readings that the *Selections* exhibit.

homiletical treatment of Old Testament passages which lends itself to the demonstration from Scripture of God's preparation for our Lord Jesus Christ, as seen in predictions of His coming, and all that His coming involved.

This will be seen from an enumeration of the headings of the chapters of the work.

i. There is no separate title, but it deals with the doctrine of the Holy Trinity.

ii. Other proofs of the same kind, concerning the Coming of the Lord in the flesh.

iii. Concerning His birth from a Virgin.

iv. Concerning the marvels which the Lord was about to do when He had become man.

v. Concerning the Betrayal.

vi. Concerning the Passion.

vii. Concerning the Cross and the Darkness that took place.

viii. Concerning the Resurrection of Christ.

ix. Concerning the Ascension.

x. Concerning the glory of the Church.

xi. Concerning Circumcision.

xii. Concerning Sacrifices.

xiii. Concerning observance of the Sabbath.

xiv. Concerning being Sealed.

xv. Concerning the Gospel.

xvi. Concerning the unbelief of the Jews, and concerning the Church of the Gentiles.

xvii. That Elijah will come before the Second Coming of the Lord.

xviii. That we shall be called Christians.

xix.[1] That Herod shall be troubled, and all who are with him.

xx. Concerning the Baptism (of Jesus).

xxi. Concerning the going down of the Lord into Egypt.

xxii. Concerning the Holy Spirit.

The full title of the treatise includes, as will have been seen, "a somewhat full investigation about the Holy Trinity, that God has Word and Spirit, according to the Scriptures, Word subsistent and living, and Spirit likewise".

Therefore without any Introduction—and the absence of this is quite an unusual feature of our books—the author plunges *in medias res* with his proofs for the Trinity. Ps. xxxiii. 6 is the starting-point, for it speaks of both Word and Spirit; "By the Word of the

---

[1] Chh. xix–xxii are absent from one of the MSS., and are said to contain references to Chrysostom's writings, and certainly do not fall under the plan of chh. i–xviii. They have probably been added by a copyist.

Lord were the heavens made, and all the host of them by the Spirit of His mouth." "Word", it is argued, cannot here mean merely striking the air by the organs of the voice, nor can "Spirit" refer to breath. For the Word was with God, and was God,[1] and it was the Spirit of truth that proceedeth from the Father.[2] Ps. cxlvii. 18 makes all clear: "He shall send His word",[3] and a word that is not self-subsistent cannot be sent.[4] Similarly in Ps. civ. 30 the Lord says, "Thou wilt send out Thy Spirit", and this is followed by, "Who stood as the support of the Lord, and saw His Word?"[5] But a man's word is seen.

The writer then adds a large number of the usual Old Testament texts, occasionally explaining them by one from the New Testament. But none calls for special notice.[6]

The second chapter is entitled "Others of the same kind concerning the Coming of the Lord in the flesh",[7] and contains more than forty proof-passages, including Baruch iii. 36, 37.[8]

The third chapter is "Concerning His birth from a Virgin". After combining Isa. vii. 14 with viii. 4, i.e. the prophecy of Emmanuel with the prediction, "He shall take the power of Damascus and devour the spoils of Samaria",[9] he quotes Wisdom viii. 20, "Being good I came into an undefiled body", and asks triumphantly, "Who then was good before His birth? And who came into an undefiled body?"[10]

Then comes an interesting passage. For after quoting Isa. ix. 5 *sq.* our author adds, "And again, 'Behold the heifer has borne, and she has not borne'. Now this indicates the Virgin."[11] He

---

[1] John i. 1.   [2] John xv. 26.   [3] ἀποστελεῖ τὸν λόγον αὐτοῦ.

[4] Λόγος δὲ ἀνυπόστατος οὐκ ἀποστέλλεται.

[5] τίς ἔστη ἐν ὑποστηρίγματι κυρίου, καὶ εἶδε τὸν λόγον αὐτοῦ; From Jer. xxiii. 18 (LXX ὑποστήματι, "base"). In either case *sôd* ("council") seems to have been read as *ysôd* ("foundation"). Theodotion in Ezek. xii. 14; xxxviii. 6 uses ὑποστήριγμα of the bands or hordes *supporting* a general.

[6] Rendel Harris makes much of many of these texts, to prove his theory that "Nyssen" (as he calls this Pseudo-Gregory of Nyssa) was using the Book of Testimonies. See "Gregory of Nyssa" in the Indices to his *Book of Testimonies*, vols. i and ii.

[7] τοῦ αὐτοῦ ἕτερα περὶ τῆς ἐνσάρκου τοῦ κυρίου παρουσίας.

[8] See the note in Index.

[9] See *Trypho*, lxxviii. 9 (*supra*, p. 41).

[10] The author of *Wisdom* probably refers to the soul of Solomon in whose name he writes.

[11] καὶ πάλιν, Ἰδοὺ ἡ δάμαλις τέτοκε, καὶ οὐ τέτοκε· τοῦτο δὲ δηλοῖ τὴν παρθένον. Tertullian, *de Carne Christi*, xxiii, quotes this as from Ezekiel. See M. R. James, *Lost Apocrypha of the O.T.* 1920, p. 67.

seems to have thought the words were in Isaiah, for he continues, "And again, 'Butter and honey shall He eat'."[1] On this he makes the curious comment, "He was fed on this when His Mother went down from the enrolment. For afterwards she had a full flow of milk."[2] Other proof-texts in this chapter that may be mentioned are Ezek. xliv. 1 *sq.*, "This gate shall be shut", referring to the perpetual Virginity![3] Also the Stone in Dan. ii. 34, which, as being "cut out without hands", also points to the Virgin Birth. Also Isa. viii. 1, the "roll of new large papyrus", on which the comment is, "The papyrus is new, clean, not having been written on; so also the Virgin is holy, with no carnal knowledge of a man".

In ch. iv Isa. xlix. 6, 8 is quoted as having been said by "Jeremiah", and appeal is made to Baruch iii. 35, "This is our God, no other shall be reckoned with Him", to prove that "Jeremiah" is speaking of One who was no mere man.

There is nothing in ch. v that calls for special remark, but in ch. vi the author argues against the Jewish interpretation of Isa. liii, which finds there only a reference to the nation of the Jews in Babylon. He asks, How can a people be led to death for the sins of the people? And, For whose sins did it suffer? The common application of Jer. xi. 19 to Christ (the lamb and the wood into His bread) is also given.[4]

In ch. vii Deut. xxviii. 66, "your life hanging", makes its appearance again as a prophecy of the Crucifixion.[5] Then, after quoting Isa. lxv. 2, the outstretched hands, and Isa. lxii. 10, "Raise up a standard (i.e. the Cross) for the nations", he continues, "And again, And then shall these things be accomplished, saith the Lord, when the Tree of trees lies down, and rises up, and when blood shall trickle from the Tree."[6]

Among the proof-texts predicting Christ's Resurrection in ch. viii is cited Isa. xxxiii. 10, "Now I will arise, saith the Lord, now I shall

---

[1] Isa. vii. 15.

[2] τούτῳ γὰρ ἐτρέφετο κατιούσης τῆς μητρὸς αὐτοῦ ἀπὸ τῆς ἀπογραφῆς· ὕστερον γὰρ εὐπόρησιν γάλακτος. Gregory of Nyssa in his genuine Oration on 1 Cor. xv. 28 (Migne, *P.G.* xliv. 1307) refers to His eating butter and milk, but that is all.

[3] See Rufinus, *On the Creed* (c. A.D. 390), § 9.

[4] *Trypho*, lxxii. 2 (*supra*, p. 33).

[5] See Tertullian, *Adv. Jud.* xi (*supra*, p. 50).

[6] καὶ πάλιν, καὶ τότε ταῦτα συντελεσθήσεται, λέγει Κύριος, ὅταν ξύλον ξύλων κλιθῇ, καὶ ἀναστῇ, καὶ ὅταν ἐκ ξύλου αἷμα στάξει. Cf. *Barn.* xii. 1 (*supra*, p. 25). The variant reading ξύλῳ for ξύλων is improbable.

be glorified, now I shall be exalted, now ye shall see, now ye shall
be saved", where the last two clauses are not represented in the
Hebrew, and the last not even in the ordinary text of the LXX,
but in our document only.

Ps. lxxxviii. 4 comes also, "Free among the dead"—"But who
is free from death save God?"[1]

Chh. ix and x have nothing of interest, but in ch. xi the author
pleads that Circumcision was not from the beginning, but was
instituted at a certain time that it might also have an end at a
certain time.[2] He then quotes Jer. xxxi. 31 and ix. 26, and adds,
"And again, 'circumcise your heart, and not your uncircumcised
flesh'"—plainly a translation from a Semitic original, but not to
be found in the Old Testament.[3] So again, after quoting Jer. iv. 4,
he adds, "And Jeremiah, *And circumcise to God the uncircumcision of
your heart*", which may be taken from Aquila's version of Deut. x.
16, *And circumcise the uncircumcision of your heart.*[4] Our author then
argues rather interestingly that uncircumcision is compatible with
godliness, but that circumcision was given to keep Abraham and
his seed pure until Christ should come, that the Law as a kind of
party wall[5] might separate them from others. But when He for
whom this was arranged was born, all these things were abolished,
as being no longer necessary.

Ch. xii has a curious repetition. For, after quoting Jer. vii. 22
about sacrifices, he adds, and 'Isaiah', but gives us the same
passage from Jeremiah over again in other words, neither of the
passages agreeing with the LXX or with the Hebrew.[6] He then
turns again to Isa. i. 11, 14.

His argument about the Sabbath (ch. xiii) is suggestive. The
Sabbath, he says, was given to stop the desire for money. For when

[1] ἐν νεκροῖς ἐλεύθερος· τίς δὲ ἐλεύθερος θανάτου εἰ μὴ ὁ θεός;
[2] Cf. Andronicus, lviii (*infra*, p. 187).
[3] καὶ πάλιν, περιτέμνεσθε τὴν καρδίαν ὑμῶν καὶ μὴ τὴν σάρκα τῆς ἀκροβυστίας
ὑμῶν. Cf. Jer. iv. 4; ix. 25 sq.
[4] (καὶ περιτεμεῖσθε) (τὴν) ἀκροβυστίαν καρδίας (ὑμῶν).
[5] ὥσπερ τι διάφραγμα.
[6] Probably this is merely an error of a copyist, who found a secondary version
of Jer. vii. 22 in the margin, and by accident placed it in the text *after* the word
"Isaiah", which was intended to refer only to Isa. i. 11, 14. Rendel Harris
(*Testimonies*, i. 35 sq.) discusses this in relation to *Barn.* ix and Cyprian, *Test.* i. 8,
and, of course, finds in it evidence for his Book of Testimonies. But when he
says that "Nyssen" is "ostensibly quoting Testimonies", he has mistaken the
meaning of the word, which refers to the Scriptures as such, and not to a
collection of excerpts (*vide supra*, p. 6).

the people came out from Egypt, and had nothing save what they had received from the Egyptians, they were eager to make money by continuous toil. Therefore their labour was limited to six days only.

"On the Seal" (ch. xiv)—apparently the Cross in Baptism—the passages *The light of Thy countenance was set as a sign upon us*,[1] and *Establish with me a sign for good*,[2] and *Thou hast given a sign to them that fear Thee*,[3] are followed by a strange adaptation of Ezek. ix. 4, where God says *O Son of man*(!), *pass through... and set the sign*.[4] He adds that sacrifices were ordered in support of the Levites, who had no land, for God did not wish priests to be supported by their own toil or business, not to say huckstering.[5]

In ch. xv, "Concerning the Gospel", i.e. preaching it, he quotes Ps. lxviii. 11, *The Lord shall give* (His) *word to them* (men) *that preach the gospel with great power*.[6] And he then quotes Isa. lii. 7 in the form found in Rom. x. 15, which he doubtless knew better than the earlier version.

It is not surprising that Pseudo-Gregory gives a large number of predictions of the unbelief of the Jews and the resultant Church of the Gentiles (ch. xvi). Most are not of special interest, but on Jer. i. 9, 10 (*Behold, I have put My words in thy mouth: see, I have this day set thee over nations and kingdoms, to root up, and to pull down, and to destroy, and to build up, and to plant*) our author asks, What kingdoms did Jeremiah set up, or what nations did he destroy? No doubt the words are spoken of the Lord, who rooted out from every soul that believes Him the kingdom of the adversary; who pulls down the buildings of wickedness, and instead of those toilsome rules and regulations implants those that are better.[7]

It is worth noticing that also in this chapter[8] the author quotes Matt. xxi. 43 as though it were part of the Old Testament.

On our author's use of Isa. xlv. 1, "The Lord saith to my Christ Cyrus", and his argument that it is ridiculous to think that this refers to Cyrus, see *Barn.* xii. 11 (*supra*, p. 26).

[1] Ps. iv. 6: ἐσημειώθη ἐφ' ἡμᾶς τὸ φῶς τοῦ προσώπου σου.
[2] Ps. lxxxvi. 17.   [3] Ps. lx. 4.
[4] Υἱὲ ἀνθρώπου, διέλθε...καὶ δὸς τὸ (so AQ) σημεῖον.
[5] ἠγοῦν καπηλείας.
[6] κύριος δώσει ῥῆμα τοῖς εὐαγγελιζομένοις δυνάμει πολλῇ.
[7] καὶ τῶν μοχθηρῶν δογμάτων καταφυτεύσας τὰ κρείττονα. For δόγματα see Col. ii. 14, with my note there (*C.G.T.* p. 98).
[8] ὅτι ἀρθήσεται ἀπὸ τῶν 'Ιουδαιῶν ἡ βασιλεία τοῦ θεοῦ, καὶ δοθήσεται ἔθνει ποιοῦντι τοὺς καρποὺς αὐτῆς.

There is nothing of interest in ch. xvii, but when proofs for the New Name of Christians are brought forward in ch. xviii the author claims as Hosea's the utterance, *And in the last time His name shall be manifest in all the earth, and many peoples shall be called by His name, and walking according to His ways shall live in them.*[1] This seems to be due to a mixture of Mal. i. 14 and Isa. ii. 2 *sq.*

The last four chapters (xix–xxii) are no part of the original work, as has been said already, but a patchwork from other writers. According to ch. xix the trouble of Herod the Great, and of those who were with him, is predicted in Jer. iv. 9.[2]

Ch. xx tells us that the Baptism of our Lord (especially, but also of others) is foreshown in Ezek. xlvii. 8: *This water which goeth forth into Galilee shall sanctify the waters, and it shall be that to every soul on which this water cometh, it shall live and be healed.*[3] And, again, there is Jer. xlix. 19 = xxix. 20: *Behold, as a lion shall He come up from the midst of the Jordan.*

For our Lord's visit to Egypt (ch. xxi) we have the usual texts, Isa. xix. 1, 21—regardless of the fact that no record has been given to us of the direct effect of that visit upon the Egyptians. Ch. xxii contains many predictions about the Holy Spirit, e.g. Job xvii. 3. It may be noticed also that Num. xi. 16 is attributed to "Exodus", and Hagg. ii. 6 to "Zechariah". The last text quoted is to show that the Resurrection is brought about by the Spirit, for David says: *Thou wilt take away their breath (spirit), and they shall fail, and shall return to their dust. Thou shalt send forth Thy Spirit, and they shall be created; and Thou shalt renew the face of the earth.*[4]

With these words the treatise ends, or rather the copyist's additions end, and it cannot be said that these have increased the value of the treatise as a whole. For nowhere does it rise beyond the naïve interpretations of the ordinary believer in the end of the fourth century, never attempting independent reasoning, or suggesting any line of argument which appeals to us to-day. It is hard,

---

[1] καὶ ἔσται ἐπ' ἐσχάτου τὸ ὄνομα αὐτοῦ ἐπιφανὲς ἐν πάσῃ τῇ γῇ, καὶ τῷ ὀνόματι αὐτοῦ ἐπικληθήσονται λαοὶ πολλοί, καὶ κατὰ τὰς ὁδοὺς αὐτοῦ πορευθέντες, ζήσονται ἐν αὐταῖς.

[2] Matt. ii. 3.

[3] τὸ ὕδωρ τοῦτο τὸ ἐκπορευόμενον εἰς τὴν Γαλιλαίαν, ἁγιάσει τὰ ὕδατα· καὶ ἔσται, πάσῃ ψυχῇ, ἐφ' ἣν ἂν ἐπέλθῃ τὸ ὕδωρ τοῦτο, ζήσεται καὶ ἰαθήσεται.

For εἰς τὴν Γαλιλαίαν the Hebrew is *'el haglîlah haqadmônah*; the LXX, εἰς τὴν Γαλειλαίαν τὴν πρὸς ἀνατολάς. But our author omits the latter clause. The rest of the quotation is peculiar also.

[4] Ps. civ. 29 *sq.*

in fact, to think that it could ever have been of use for practical controversy with Jews, of whom the author seems to have no personal knowledge.

It was fitted only to increase the devotional love of convinced Christians for their Bible, foretelling, as it seemed to them to do, the life and work of their Saviour in full detail.

CHAPTER XV

CHRYSOSTOM

A.D. 347–407

Chrysostom's *Homilies against the Jews*[1] are glorious reading for those who love eloquence—and zeal untempered by knowledge. The Golden-mouthed knew little of Judaism, but he was shocked that his Christian people were frequenting Jewish synagogues,[2] and were attracted to the synagogal Fasts and Feasts, sometimes by the claims to superior sanctity made by the followers of the earlier religion, so that an oath taken in a synagogue was more binding than in a church,[3] and sometimes by the offer of charms and amulets in which Jews of the lower class dealt freely. We cannot blame Chrysostom therefore for doing his utmost to prevent apostasy, partial or complete, and we cannot but praise him for the straightness of his speech, and his passionate desire that every one of his hearers should not only refrain from religious intercourse with Jews, but also do his utmost to keep his brethren in the same Christian path.[4] Sometimes also there are direct appeals to Jews to turn to the true faith.[5]

[1] Paris reprint of Montfaucon's Benedictine edition, 1834, i. 712–843; Migne, *P.G.* xlviii. 843–942. The Homilies were delivered at Antioch soon after the beginning of his presbyterate, A.D. 386. Usener (1889, quoted in Juster, *Les Juifs dans l'empire Romain*, 1914, i. 62) gives the exact date of each, ranging from August 387 to September 389. Bishop Chase's early work, *Chrysostom, a study in the history of Biblical interpretation*, 1887, is still very valuable, but chiefly for the saint's exegesis of the New Testament.

[2] The tendency of professing Christians to frequent synagogues is not peculiar to Chrysostom's time and place. M. Isidore Loeb in his illuminating essay on *La Controverse religieuse entre les Juifs au moyen âge en France et en Espagne* tells us that in the Middle Ages the semi-Christianised peoples found it difficult to distinguish between Judaism and Christianity, or, at least, to see where one left off and the other began. They knew that Christianity had its roots in Judaism, and that the weekly day of rest, Easter, and Pentecost, were taken from the Jews, and the mother religion had fascination for them. At Lyons they used to go to the synagogue, pretending that the sermons were better than those of the Christian priests. In 1290 in Provence and the neighbouring countries Christians made offerings in the synagogue, and paid solemn respect to the roll of the Law (*Revue de l'histoire des religions*, 1888, xvii. 324 *sq.*).

[3] i. 3.

[4] This is the key-note of each of the Homilies.

[5] E.g. v. 12.

But that is all that can be said. Chrysostom's sermons were intended almost entirely for his Christian listeners, and only exceptionally for Jews. How could it be otherwise? We gather from these Homilies that the Jews were a great social, and even a great religious, power in Antioch, but that Chrysostom himself had had no direct intercourse with them worth mentioning, and knew nothing of their real reasons for refusing to become Christians.[1] Far more serious still than his ignorance is his lack of a real evangelistic spirit in his relation to them. There is no sign that he felt the slightest sympathy with them, much less a burning love for the people of whom His Saviour came in the flesh, or, indeed, that he regarded them in any other way than as having been rightly and permanently punished for their treatment of Christ, and as still being emissaries of Satan in their temptation of Christians. But that is not the way to present Christ to the Jews, or even to speak of them when preaching to Christians.[2]

It is, therefore, not worth our while to give a summary of the Homilies. It will be sufficient to indicate some of Chrysostom's remarks.

The first Homily was evidently preached in the early part of September, for he begins by saying that many feasts of the wretched Jews are at hand—Trumpets (i.e. the New Year), Tabernacles, Fasts[3]—and he must therefore preach at once. The Jews have rejected God's Light, as the Prophets foretold. They serve demons, and yet Christians will go to be healed by them![4] His second Homily was but five days before the Fast, say in the very beginning of October, and he warns his people again. Shall Christians practise

[1] It is asserted that he knew Hebrew because he says in his Homily on Heb. vii. 2 that *Sedech* is rightly interpreted "righteousness", and *Melchi*, "king". But any educated priest of Chrysostom's time would have known that much, without any personal knowledge of the language. His ignorance is shown plainly in his exposition of Isa. vii. 18, where, speaking of the LXX, "and to the bee", he adds: "The Syriac and the Hebrew, as they say, do not speak of bees but of wasps"—Ὁ Σύρος καὶ ὁ Ἑβραῖος, ὥς φασιν, οὐ λέγουσι, μελίσσας, ἀλλὰ σφῆκας (Montfaucon, vi. 99; Migne, *P.G.* lvi. 86). But the Hebrew has *D^eborah*, "bee", and it is followed by both the Targum and the Peshitta, though it is true that in the Peshitta the word may mean "wasp" as well as "bee". Chrysostom's informants were wrong, and he could not correct them. Cf. the remarks on Origen, *supra*, p. 82.

[2] Chrysostom's hatred of the Jews is not confined to these eight Homilies, as may be seen from the countless references to them scattered throughout his works, covering more than seven columns in Montfaucon's Index.

[3] In 1935 on Sept. 28, Oct. 12, and Oct. 7 respectively.

[4] i. 7.

the Law? Shall a bird that is caught in a trap by only one foot be able to escape? The third Homily was delivered near Passover, which Jews still pretend to keep, though now they have no real unleavened bread or passover, for they are no longer in Jerusalem.[1]

The Jews say that they hope to see their city restored! No, they are mistaken. The Temple will never rise again, nor the Jews return to their former polity. Jesus Himself says this in Luke xxi. 24. The Jew, no doubt, rejects this saying, for, says he, "He who speaks thus is mine enemy. I crucified Him, and how shall I receive His testimony?" "Yet, O Jew," replies Chrysostom, "herein lies the wonder, that He whom you crucified did afterwards pull down your city, scatter your people, and disperse your nation throughout the whole world"—and not even so do you recognise Him as God and Master![2]

At this point[3] Chrysostom says he will consider Christ's character and manner of life, and the reader begins to hope for something answering to our modern treatment of the attractiveness of Jesus. But in vain. Chrysostom speaks only of the truthfulness of His prophecies, even when He foretold the honour to be paid to the woman with the alabaster phial of ointment, poor and unknown though she was. He speaks also of the difference between Christ and other teachers (e.g. Zeno, Plato, Socrates, Diagoras,[4] Pythagoras, Apollonius of Tyana), for, while they tried to make polities, Christ alone succeeded. Christ then was no deceiver, and you Jews ought to believe Him.

Again, consider the difference of this captivity from those in Egypt and in Babylon. A limit of years was promised to those, but none has been foretold of this. Your three attempts to restore your state have all been failures, under Hadrian, under Constantine ("as is known to your old men"), and, as even your young people know, twenty years since, under that wicked Emperor Julian. For you then tried even to rebuild the Temple, and so offer sacrifices on the altar. But fire prevented your work. You can still see the foundations lying bare.[5] Will not you Jews believe even yet? Must

---

[1] iii. 3; iv. 3; vii. 1 *sq.* Cf. Deut. xvi. 5 *sq.* See also below, p. 139. Andronicus, *Dial.* ch. liv, has the same argument (*vide infra*, p. 187).

[2] v. 1.   [3] v. 2.

[4] In Athens, 424 B.C. (*Dict. Greek and Roman Biography*).

[5] v. 11. *Vide infra*, p. 139; *vide supra*, p. 17, on *Barn.* xvi. 3. F. C. Conybeare has an important discussion about the ultimate source of Chrysostom's information in his *Timothy and Aquila*, pp. xxv–xxxiii. Cf. also Gennadius, Fol. 131 r. (*infra*, p. 191).

I remind you of other prophecies, predicting that your affairs were to come to an end, and ours flourish with another form of sacrifices? Malachi, who came after, and not before, the Captivity in Babylon, foretells our Eucharist, "every where" in place, "pure" in character, and for the "Gentiles".[1]

You cannot understand how it is that this present Captivity is lasting so long, because you sin less than of old! The reason for its length is that you slew the Christ.[2] If He had been the deceiver and transgressor you say He was, you ought to have been praised for your action, as Phinehas was for his; but you are in disgrace.[3]

Do not tell me that a synagogue is holy because the Law is lying there, and the books of the Prophets! That is not enough to make a place holy. Did the Ark make the temple of Dagon holy?[4] Which is better, for books to lie there, or to utter what the books contain? And, further, you need to have in your hearts what they contain. For the devil himself may utter holy words, and yet remain the devil! Demons could bear true witness,[5] but we do not put them into the order of the Apostles for all that!

Neither words nor books suffice. Therefore I hate the synagogue, and I hate it all the more that it has the Law and the Prophets, because they are used as traps for the simple-minded. Now the Jews boast of believing the Prophets and yet insult Him of whom the Prophets tell![6] The "ark" which the Jews have in their synagogue is no better to my mind than the little "arks" (or "boxes") I can buy in the market—yea, it is much worse, for those at any rate can do no harm.[7]

The rest of the *Homilies against the Jews* either repeat what has been already said, or contain nothing worthy of our notice.

It was right to begin our study of Chrysostom with his eight *Homilies against the Jews*, for they present him to us in his most typical attitude. But he wrote another treatise, more akin to the ordinary dissertations on the Jews. It is entitled *A Demonstration to Jews and Greeks that Christ is God, from the sayings concerning Him everywhere in the Prophets.*[8] It is probably incomplete, for it ends

[1] v. 12; Mal. i. 11.
[2] vi. 2. For the Jewish argument, *vide infra*, p. 137.   [3] vi. 3.
[4] vi. 7. Cf. i. 6, where Chrysostom says that although the Septuagint is still in the temple of Serapis it has not made that temple holy.
[5] Acts xvi. 17.   [6] vi. 6.
[7] vi. 7. Aphrahat (Hom. xii. 4) also ridicules the idea that the Jews still have an ark (*vide supra*, p. 97).
[8] Migne, *P.G.* xlviii. 813–838; Montfaucon, 1834, i. 681–712.

abruptly, and Chrysostom's promise[1] to speak more fully about
the Jews is not fulfilled. It is impossible that in saying this he can
have been looking forward to his *Homilies*, for his *Demonstration*
breathes an utterly different spirit from theirs, showing no trace
of their rancour. Yet there can be no suspicion of the genuineness
of the *Demonstration*, for the eloquence of parts is unmatched in any
other writer. Probably it was written before Chrysostom had any
assured position in Antioch, at the beginning of his diaconate
(A.D. 381), rather than of his priesthood (386), if it was not even
an earlier production still, composed for the benefit of his fellow
monks.[2]

He begins with addressing the Greeks, and it is doubtful whether
he ever ceases having them chiefly in mind, even though he refers
very often to the Jews and their sacred Scriptures. He is careful
to start from a point with which he and his audience will agree,
namely that it was Christ who founded the race of Christians, and
their Churches. From the Scriptures he will show Christ's power,
and indeed His Divinity, for no mere man could have done what
He has done and that in so short a time, winning over to a new life
men of all nations who are corrupt of heart, and that by means,
at the first, of eleven very ordinary persons.[3] Christ has done this
in spite of the fact that He died by the shameful death of crucifixion. And though He is still opposed, yet martyrs still die for
Him, even among the Persians.[4]

The argument has no little validity at the present day.

At this stage[5] Chrysostom says that he must bring the books of
the Jews into the midst and go through their testimony.[6] For the
Prophets foretold that Christ was to come as man, as, for example,
in the words of Baruch: *This is our God, no other shall be reckoned with
Him. He found out all the way of knowledge, and gave it to Jacob His
servant, and to Israel that is beloved of Him. Afterward did He appear
upon earth, and lived along with men.*[7] So before His incarnation He
was already ordering all things.

Chrysostom then quotes many of the ordinary Messianic texts.
Among these is *the Prince of Peace*.[8] For men's peace indeed is easily

[1] Cap. xvii.
[2] Bardenhewer, however, places it "etwa aus dem Jahre 387" (iii. 348).
[3] See more fully in cap. xii.   [4] Cap. i.   [5] Cap. ii.
[6] Cf. the note on Augustine, *infra*, p. 313. See also *Papiscus and Philo*, § 7 (*infra*, p. 172).
[7] Baruch iii. 35–37. See Cyprian, *Test.* ii. 6 (*supra*, p. 61).
[8] Cap. ii; Isa. ix. 6.

broken, but not the peace which He gives in the heart. Another less usual text is *He shall inherit many*,[1] as implying the Descent into Hades and the rescue of many thence. Another is *Thou shalt make them rulers over all the earth*,[2] as referring to St Peter and St Paul being greater than kings.[3] Another, *a wolf shall pasture with a lamb*,[4] foretells the peaceful union of various nations under the one yoke of Christ.

Again, the character of the Jews themselves has been improved by their emulation of us. Besides, although the Old Testament in general pays no honour to Virgins, David does foretell the glories of ours,[5] and our Bishops are also mentioned.[6]

Further, the Scriptures foretell a day of reckoning for the Jews for their many sins,[7] when God shall come and take away their sacrifices, etc., etc., and their kings. Contrast the present glory of the Cross. "Kings put off their crowns, and take up the Cross, the symbol of Christ's death. The Cross is on their robes of state, and on their crowns. It is at their prayers, and on their weapons; and upon the Holy Table stands the Cross. Everywhere throughout the world the Cross shines out, beyond the brightness of the sun. For *His rest shall be glorious*."[8] The glory of men dies with them, but not so Christ's.[9] "Kings and Generals and Rulers and Consuls, slaves and free, private persons, wise and foolish, barbarians, and all the varied races of mankind, and whatsoever land the sun o'erlooks—throughout this vast extent His name is spread, and His worship; that you may learn the meaning of that prophecy, *And His rest shall be glorious*. The very tomb of His slain body, small and narrow though it be, is more revered than the countless palaces of kings, more honoured than the kings themselves." Chrysostom goes on to say that Christ's honour has even spread to His disciples, for even kings become door-keepers of the fishermen. He who once

---

[1] Cap. v; Isa. liii. 12 LXX. Cf. the complaint of Death in the Harrowings of Hell, in *Testamentum Domini Nostri Jesu Christi*, i, § 28 (Rahmani, 1899, p. 64).

[2] Cap. vi; Ps. xlv. 16.   [3] He dwells on this again in cap. ix.

[4] Isa. xi. 6.   [5] Cap. vii; Ps. xlv. 14.

[6] Isa. lx. 17 LXX.

[7] Cap. viii. J. H. Weiss, on the other hand, says that the Jews themselves attributed the destruction of Jerusalem to Christianity, the great apostasy from the principles of Judaism, quoting the Midrash on Lamentations (*Echa Rabbathi*), "Israel did not go into captivity until they denied the Only One, circumcision, the Ten Commandments, and the Pentateuch" (*Dor dor wdorshaw*, iii. 129). I cannot find the quotation in *Echa Rabbathi*. Does Weiss intend to give only the general sense of the beginning of the Introduction?

[8] Isa. xi. 10 (cf. *infra*, p. 404).   [9] Cap. ix.

hung upon the Cross, execrated and accursed, the type of all punishment, has now become the object of desire and affection.

Yet[1] why is it that the Cross is thus honoured? It was the symbol of horrible death, and, as such, held in abhorrence. What is the reason for the change? Because it has become the subject of benediction,[2] the bridle of demons, a muzzle for the power of the adversaries. It has destroyed death, broken hell's gates of brass, and crushed its iron bars, rescuing the whole world lying under condemnation, and curing the heaven-sent plague of our maddened human nature. What the miracles and mercies of Old Testament times could not do, the Cross has done; as Jeremiah foretold: *This shall be My Covenant for them, when I take away their iniquities and remember their sins no more.*[3]

Again,[4] although there have always been many Jews who have believed on Christ, it is not strange that all have not, for even in Old Testament times they often did not rise to their opportunities. Yet Christ's own predictions show His power. These are of two kinds,[5] of things that take place in this life, and of such as are to be in the distant future and after this life. He spoke of the Church before it existed,[6] and also stated that it should never be overcome. Consider how it has spread throughout the world in this short time. After an eloquent passage Chrysostom continues, Yes, "and beyond our civilised world.[7] For even the British Isles, which lie outside this sea of ours, in the very ocean itself, have felt the power of the word. For even there Churches exist, and altars have been set up...." "And by whose persuasion? By eleven men, unlearned, untrained, no speakers, unknown, poor", etc., mere "fishermen and tentmakers, men of foreign tongue", using the Hebrew language only.

This success too was won in the face of difficulties of all kinds,[8] for the preaching of the Gospel brought division and war into every house, until all its inmates were led one after another to the faith. But the more the difficulties and the persecutions, the more the disciples rejoiced, that they were worthy to suffer for His sake.

Christ predicted more glories still for the distant future.[9] For what He built none could pull down; what He pulled down, none

---

[1] Cap. x.
[2] εὐλογίας ὑπόθεσις.
[3] Cf. Jer. xxxi. 34.
[4] Cap. xi.
[5] Cap. xii.
[6] Matt. xvi. 18.
[7] ὑπὲρ τὴν οἰκουμένην τὴν καθ' ἡμᾶς.
[8] Cap. xiii.
[9] Cap. xvi.

could build up. In our own generation that king who surpassed all others in iniquity gave his sanction and assistance to rebuilding the Temple. A beginning was made, but no progress at all, for fire sprang forth from the foundations and drove the Jews away.[1] Nor is there any hope of the Temple ever being rebuilt, in spite of the abundance of Jews, and of it being illegal for them to offer sacrifices elsewhere.[2] But all this, together with Daniel's prophecy, I shall expound more plainly and explicitly when I come to speak of the Jews.[3]

You Gentiles do not believe the story of Christ's miracles, and you do believe that of His crucifixion, although they are narrated by the same persons! And history shows the trustworthiness of Christ's teaching. For the Jews failed utterly to rebuild the Temple.

Here the treatise suddenly breaks off, and we are left wondering whether it was ever completed. Certainly the present form of the second half of cap. xvii is compatible with it being only rough notes.

PSEUDO-CHRYSOSTOM

It is convenient to mention in this place two documents falsely attributed to Chrysostom, which are to be found as *Spuria* in the editions of his works.

The title of the first is *Against Jews and Greeks* (i.e. *Heathen*) *and Heretics; and with reference to the words "Jesus was called unto a Marriage"*.[4] It is a poor little tract quite unworthy of Chrysostom, and was directed in the first place against some persons who asserted that marriage was a spiritual hindrance. The author knows that in itself it is not. Nor is celibacy, nor wealth, nor poverty, nor royalty, nor slavery. He also attacks a Jewishly inclined Heretic who has unworthy and gross thoughts about the Divine Fatherhood of the Son. Even Aaron's calf that came up out of the fire should have suggested better thoughts than that.[5] Moved probably by

---

[1] Cf. Hom. v. 11 (*vide supra*, p. 134).
[2] *Vide supra*, p. 134.   [3] Cap. xvii (*vide supra*, p. 134).
[4] Πρὸς 'Ιουδαίους καὶ ῞Ελληνας καὶ αἱρετικούς· καὶ εἰς τὸ, 'Εκλήθη 'Ιησοῦς εἰς γάμον. Montfaucon, i. 1008–1015; Migne, *P.G.* xlviii. 1075–1080. There is nothing in the matter to indicate the date, but an examination of some of the strange words might be helpful. "Stylus sagaci viro indignus, argumenta ut plurima levia et futilia" (Benedictine editor).
[5] Montfaucon, col. 1013. This Jewish objection is not uncommon.

this the author places between those two chief subjects an attack
on the Jews in general. For they have been ungrateful from the
beginning. The destroying angel in Egypt spared only those houses
on which the blood was sprinkled. And, mark you, the blood was
not sprinkled on the wall, but on the wooden lintel. For salvation
comes by the Tree, the Cross of Christ.[1]

The second tract among the *Spuria* which professedly bears upon
our subject is one entitled, *Against Jews, with reference to the Brazen
Serpent*, etc.[2] It is an address intended for Christian people only,
but has a good many verbal references to Jews. The only point of
interest for us seems to be the remark: "As the word could bring
water out of a rock, yet until the rock saw the type of the cross, it
did not obey; so here also it could put the serpents to flight, but
until the serpents saw the image of the cross, which deadens the
bites of the demons, they were not blunted."[3]

[1] Montfaucon, col. 1012.

[2] Κατὰ ᾽Ιουδαίων εἰς τὸν ὄφιν τὸν χαλκοῦν κ.τ.λ. Montfaucon, x. 1027–1039;
Migne, *P.G.* lxi. 793–802. It has been wrongly attributed to Severian, Bishop
of Gabala A.D. 400 (Bardenhewer, iii. 364). A sermon with a somewhat similar
title is really his.

[3] 855 A. The type of the cross is Moses' rod. Cf. *Trypho*, lxxxvi and cxxxviii. 2.

CHAPTER XVI

THE DISCUSSION OF
ARCHBISHOP GREGENTIUS
WITH THE JEW HERBAN[1]

c. A.D. 480

We can picture the scene, the crowded assembly under the open sky, the King upon his throne, with Gregentius the Archbishop at his side, "Scribes and Pharisees" with other learned Jews from all the cities crowding round in support of Herban their spokesman, and, seated near by, the secretary Palladius taking down the speeches. We can hear the Archbishop demanding a statement of the difficulties which the Jew feels in becoming a Christian, and note his readiness in debate. For he had an intimate acquaintance, not indeed with Jews or Judaism (knowing nothing of either), but with the approved and traditional method of meeting Jewish objections. We can feel the contempt of the cultivated Greek and highly placed ecclesiastic for a mere Jew, and can appreciate the good temper with which the latter states his case, free from all servility.

Naturally this Discussion has nothing distinctively original in the general treatment of its subject. The difficulties professed by Jews in accepting Christianity have always been the same; while the deeper reason, the natural dislike of that humiliation of spirit which is necessary for the reception of the Cross of Christ, has remained unnoticed by them, and but dimly perceived by Christians. There are the usual questions, as, for example, why Christians disregard the Law and its ordinances, just noticed here but not dwelt upon; whether the seed of Abraham stands for Jews or Christians; how the doctrine of the Trinity can be true; or that of the Incarnation of the Son of God; and these questions are stated and discussed in the ordinary manner, with appeals to well-worn texts.

And yet this treatise has its distinctive points and its own interest.

[1] τοῦ ἐν ἁγίοις Γρηγορεντίου 'Αρχιεπισκόπου γενομένου Τέφρων Διάλεξις μετὰ 'Ιουδαίου 'Ερβὰν τοὔνομα. Migne, *P.G.* lxxxvi. 621–784. Cf. Krumbacher, *Byz. Lit.* 1897, p. 59.

These lie in the personality of the disputants—for if Gregentius is commonplace, Herban is not; in the historical setting—this is the earliest record of a public controversy in presence of royalty; in the special order in which the controversy takes its course; in the striking events which mark its close; and lastly, as we now know, in the reaction which followed them.

Nothing is known of Herban save what may be gathered from this document, and little more of his opponent. Gregentius is said to have lived for many years as an anchoret in Egypt, and then to have been sent with his secretary Palladius by Proterius, Patriarch of Alexandria (who died in A.D. 487), to be Bishop of Tephra (Ẓafār), the capital city of the Himyarites (or Homerites, as they are called in patristic writings) in South Arabia.[1] A book exists entitled *The Laws of the Homerites,* which is attributed to him.

The Discussion of Gregentius with Herban the Jew professes to be the record of a four-day public controversy between them, taken down by the Palladius above-mentioned. We may reasonably suppose that some years elapsed from Gregentius' appointment as Bishop before he would be able to persuade the King to arrange such a Discussion, which therefore can hardly have taken place much earlier than A.D. 490. The end of the document implies that some years had elapsed since the controversy itself. But it contains nothing that points definitely to a later age, and there does not appear to be any valid reason to doubt that the narrative, essentially as we have it, belongs to the beginning of the sixth century. It may be dated, with some confidence, between A.D. 510 and 520.

When we turn to consider the substance of the Discussion we find that, as with the majority of these polemical tracts, it is very diffuse, and goes from point to point without much method. One wishes in vain that their writers had been as orderly as Isidore of Seville. It must be sufficient therefore to indicate what seem to be the primary objects of discussion on each of the four days, selecting from each anything that is of special interest.

The general subject of the First Day seems to be the Divinity of Christ. The Archbishop asks why Herban resists the light of the Sun of righteousness, and the latter retorts by saying that Christians resist God even more by following other customs than those He has ordained. For Gentiles are inferior to Jews, whom God protected in coming forth from Egypt. Gregentius replies that rather the Jews were like the Egyptians, for they perished in the wilderness.

---

[1] Ẓafār was about 50 miles N.N.W. of Aden.

At this Herban expresses his regret that the Scriptures had ever been translated into Greek! The subject of the Trinity is then discussed, the Archbishop pleading that it is not he but David who teaches it. But, says the Jew, how can a crucified Nazarene, a malefactor, be the Son of God? Deut. xxviii. 66 *sq.*, replies Gregentius, points to Jesus on the cross; you are to *see* the life hanging there. Consider also Gen. xlix. 10. Ah well, says Herban, when He comes we shall believe on Him. Fool, retorts his Eminence, it says, He that cometh is the expectation of the Gentiles, and we Gentiles have believed on Him. So He has already come. *Israel the beloved* and *Jacob the servant* in Baruch iii. 36 *sq.* mean Jesus. You conjecture that Jesus is God, replies the Jew, when the preceding words in that same passage are *This is our God, and there shall none other be accounted of in comparison of Him!* I make no conjecture, says Gregentius, for *v.* 37 says that He *did appear upon earth, and was conversant with men.*

Prophecies and types of the Cross are then advanced.[1] Herban asks why the prophets did not speak more plainly, and is told that they use parables because they are not tied by the ignorance of those to whom they spoke.[2] Ps. lxxii is discussed, and the reference to Jesus is upheld. When the Jew urges that when Solomon "humbled the false accuser" (*v.* 4, LXX), it was not only one but all the tyrant demons, the Archbishop grants that Solomon did indeed "keep the demons in jars, and sealed them down, and covered them with earth", but adds that he was overcome by them, and showed no sign of repentance. No one blesses the name of Solomon. Yet your Christ, replies the Jew, could not even save Himself! What then of Ps. xvi. 10? says the Archbishop. On the Jew asserting that this cannot refer to the Son of God, but to a servant who is entreating, Gregentius replies that He is there speaking as Man, for the form of a servant was necessary in fighting against the adversary. "I'm in a maze," cries Herban, "the son of Joseph the carpenter and of Mary his wife is the Son of God who comes into the world!" Ps. ii. 7 and cx. 1 are adduced as proofs.

But evening had now come, and the Jews rejoiced that Herban had had enough independence to stand up to the Archbishop in

[1] Cf. Justin, *Dialogue with Trypho,* xl. 3; xc. 4 *sq.* (*supra,* pp. 39 *sq.*).
[2] Cf. Andronicus, *c. Jud.* iii (*infra,* p. 182). Observe that there is no mention of the argument which is to be found in tracts of the seventh century onwards, that if they had spoken plainly of Jesus their writings would have been destroyed by the Jews.

discussion, and they eagerly covered him with kisses. He said, let us rather pray that the God of the Law may help us; because, as you see, the Archbishop is very skilful in the Scriptures, and no little strength is needed to persuade him. He knows the subject, and how to bring arguments against us. So they encouraged him not to be afraid.

The prominent matters of discussion on the Second Day are the meaning of the Law, the nature of Israel, and the Restoration to the Land.

The King is present as before, and the Archbishop, after commanding silence, informs the Jew that Christians do not, as he supposes, worship idols or any other than the One God. To this Herban replies that they blaspheme in saying that the Crucified is at the right hand of the power of God. But, Gregentius retorts, Ps. cx. 2 says even more, for *the Lord shall send forth the rod*, and this suggests the cross. Then he should have said so, answers the Jew. Besides, when it adds *out of Sion* the implication is that it had come first from Mount Sinai, and the wood from which the Cross was cut cannot be shown to have come from there.[1] Gregentius points out that a rod has no power in itself, but the Cross needed power from the heavenly Sion. The Logos took the Rod, and smote all His enemies with it.

Shall Joseph's son judge the world? asks the Jew. But He is not Joseph's son, replies the Christian. Consider Ps. cx. 3, *Before the morning-star I begat Thee*, and His human nature was born of the Holy Spirit through the Virgin, who remained inviolate. For in Isa. xxix. 11 *sq.* the sealed book is the Virgin; the man is Joseph; the man knows letters, i.e. Joseph had had another wife; the man could not read the divine letter, i.e. Joseph could not have carnal intercourse with Mary. As the fire did not consume the bush, so she remained Virgin even after the Birth. Then, retorts Herban, He was born only in semblance and appearance! Nay, for remember how Habakkuk visited Daniel in the sealed den.[2] Further, though He died a violent death, this also was foretold in Isa. liii.

Herban was silent for a full hour, and the other Jews were confounded; while the Christians praised the High Priest, and the King rejoiced, for he had never heard the truth so clearly before. And once more the Jew says "I'm in a maze"—for Moses bids us

---

[1] This appears to be the meaning of a difficult passage (col. 653 B).
[2] Bel and the Dragon, *v.* 36.

serve God alone (Deut. vi. 4), and yet David and Isaiah say this of Him who is reckoned Christ!

That, says the Archbishop, answers to Isaiah's words, *Who hath believed?* If your fathers disbelieved when they saw Christ's miracles how can you—you *offspring of vipers*—believe when you only hear of them?

Yet, says Herban, our Law is the greater, for it was given before yours. See too Ps. xix. 7, *restoring the soul.* That, replies Gregentius, speaks of a future Law, and my Christ is *the Law of the Lord*, who has turned thousands and tens of thousands to Him, for my Christ is sinless. Hab. iii. 3 is then discussed at some length with curious interpretations. *Paran*, for example, "the darkshaded mountain" of the LXX, means that Messiah was hidden in the Virgin. "God" and "the Holy One" are both mentioned. When the Jew affirms that they are two names for one object he is asked which is the greater, and, on his replying "God", the Archbishop triumphantly cries, "So there is a greater and a less Name in God!" It means, he adds, that He shall come, but in a body. And indeed the preceding verse *between the two living creatures* (LXX) refers to His two natures, human and Divine.

Yet, says Herban, the old wine is better than the new. No doubt, is the reply, your Law is wine, but it has gone bad.

Then follow many passages dealing with the relation of God to Israel, and again others referring to the Restoration to the Land. But is not, asks the Archbishop, Jerusalem now filled with Churches of the Crucified Christ? Further, the name Israel, "The Mind seeing God",[1] no longer is yours, for you have willingly shut your eyes, and it has been given to the Gentiles. *And I will charge the clouds to pour no rain* upon the vineyard (Isa. v. 6), where the *clouds* mean the prophecies and the books of the Law, and the *rain* is the words and thoughts, because you cannot understand what the Scripture says. Neither is it of any use for Herban to appeal to passages indicating God's blessing upon the Jews, for the Archbishop invariably answers that they all refer to the Church.

Yet, after all, retorts the Jew, Moses charged us in Deut. iv. 26 not to believe in another God. But Christ is not "another God", replied Gregentius, and adds, with some attempt at philosophising,

[1] Νοῦς ὁρῶν τὸν θεόν. Cf. Philo, *De Praemiis et Poenis*, § 7; Mangey, ii. 415. So Jerome on Isa. i. 3 (Israel, id est, mens videns Deum), but rejected in his *Quaest. Hebr. Gen.* xxxii. 28.

this νεώτερος θεός (to use your phrase) is necessary, for without Him God the Father works nothing, even as a King needs speech to issue his edicts. God works by His Word (Ps. xxxiii. 6). But if you do not believe God, you will not believe me, no, not if you live as long as Methuselah! You must be baptised, Isa. i. 16. No, retorts Herban, the verse refers to ceremonial washing in the Temple laver, after sin has been committed.

At the end of this second day the Jews once more rejoiced over Herban, and the Christians over "the blessed Gregentius, because the grace of the Spirit was with him".

The account of the Third Day begins by the Archbishop taking up Herban's last argument, and replying that Isa. i. 16 cannot refer to legal washing, for the whole chapter shows that God does not want the Jews to appear in the Temple before Him. He could not therefore bid them use legal washing. But, replies Herban, why did He say (Isa. i. 25 *sq.*), *I will purge thee by fire that thou mayest be clean?* He refers, is the answer, to the effect of the Babylonian captivity. Yet does not, Herban asks, Isa. x. 17–20 tell of our final salvation and of the destruction of the Gentiles? Certainly not, Gregentius replies, it means that when Israel is under Rome Christ will come, and be rejected by the Jews, and will ascend to heaven, and send out His disciples, and turn all the Gentiles to the knowledge of Himself. Isa. xlix is discussed, the Archbishop urging that the Judaea which shall be inhabited for ever is "the Judaea above, the country of the Word of God who took human flesh of the line of Judah". So too Ps. xlvii must refer to the Ascension of Christ with His rule over *all the nations*. When Herban adduces Ps. lxxvii. 14 *sq.* the Archbishop says that the hour is too late to discuss it then. And the King rose up and the silence was broken.

But as the Jews encouraged Herban, he answered, When I consider the man and his intelligence I shall never be able to convince him. In fact we shall be worsted by him. For I saw this night Moses and Jesus standing on a pinnacle of some temple and disputing. And I saw Moses worshipping Him, and binding his hands to Him, as to the Lord God, and standing by Him in fear. I cried, "Lord Moses, it is a fine thing that you are doing!" He turned and rebuked me, "Cease, I make no mistake. I am not on your side. I recognise my Maker and Lord. What then have you to do with the just Archbishop, whom you trouble in vain? Still, you shall see to-morrow and next day that you will be badly defeated, and will, as I, worship Him, my Jesus and Lord." These things have I seen, Brethren, and know not what they mean. Still, I will do my best.

Next day, the Fourth Day, when the assembly had been prepared the King came with the Archbishop. And Herban too stood with the priests and the teachers of the Law, who accompanied him.

Tell me, said the Archbishop, who is the Holy One in whom is God's way? Israel, said Herban boldly, for it is said in our Law, which is higher than yours, *I said ye are gods* (Ps. lxxxii. 6). Liar! retorted the Archbishop, you holy, who slew in body the God of heaven and earth! You forget the rest of the verse, *you shall die.* The Holy One is Christ. Perhaps, said the Jew, you want to enlarge on Ps. xcvi. 5, *the gods of the Gentiles are demons?* From the day, replied Gregentius, that the Lord Jesus was crucified all the gods went away like smoke. If you do not believe me bring me some demoniacs, and I will call on the Lord Jesus, and the demons will be seized with terror and depart. Yes, says Herban, I have heard that the prophets of the Christians in these days, and especially those who have forsaken all, and live in the deserts, do great miracles. No doubt you can injure me, but persuade me first with words, and then act if you are allowed to do so.

They then discuss Ps. xcvii. 1; xcix. 1, *the Lord reigneth,* and then the Jew returns to his old difficulty that he cannot understand how the Christ could suffer and die. The Archbishop explains that as all had sinned, even the Jews, and the Demon was rejoicing thereat, God nevertheless did not wish to act tyrannically or unjustly even to him by seizing man out of his hands, but sent His Logos, who is united with a man in the Virgin's womb (the Archbishop comes very near heresy), and defeats the demons, dies, and rescues men from Hades, and afterwards ascends, and sends out His disciples, to the Jews first and then to all the Gentiles. If Christ had appeared in all this as God, the devil might have had some excuse for thinking he had not been treated fairly.

But Jesus broke the sabbath, and this was the reason why our fathers crucified Him! What then, replies Gregentius, is there against the Law in His raising the dead and working other miracles of kindness? Yes, says Herban, how does He say, *I go to my Father and your Father, to my God and your God* (John xx. 17), if He was the true Son of God? For I often read your Gospels, saying to a Christian friend, Hand me one of your books, that I may gain profit from them, and become a Christian. Small blame to you

for this! says the Archbishop. But when Jesus said *Father* and *God*
He had His human nature in His mind.

Herban sees Palladius, "whom the Archbishop had brought
with him from Alexandria as his secretary", writing down the
whole discussion, and remarks that what has been said will be
made clear (δηλωθήσονται) to others. Yes, replies Gregentius, for
the opening (δήλωσις) *of Thy words giveth light, and giveth understanding
unto the simple* (Ps. cxix. 130). But, cries Herban, who are *the simple?*
You Hebrews, replies Gregentius, who had the imperfect law.
Imperfect! when Moses and Elijah had their sight perfected by it!
Yes, "imperfect", not ineffectual, for even they were not made
perfect. It was only Jesus who was sinless, and took on Himself the
sin of the whole world, and deifying the lower nature took it to
heaven and made it sit down with God the Father. This is true
perfecting.

Why waste time! cries Herban, I'll end the controversy.[1] Show
me Jesus and I'll be a Christian! Then the Jews shouted, Don't be
deceived! Play the man! For nothing is stronger than the God
of our fathers. But Herban said, You talk nonsense. If he persuades
me that Jesus indeed is He about whom the Prophets spoke so
much, I shall be an alien from the God of our fathers if I do not
believe on Him, free from all doubt.

But how, said Gregentius, do you wish me to convince you?
Pray your Master, replied Herban, if He is in heaven, as you say,
to come down to me, that I may behold Him and speak with Him,
and be baptised.

Yes, shouted the Jews, let us see if your talk is justified by deeds.
Show us your Christ, and we will believe. But privately they said,
Do you wish him to show us this? Alas, we shall become Christians!
But how can He appear, when His bones are in the tomb?

The Archbishop goes away a little distance to pray, bending
three times to the very pavement, and when the King and that
part of the multitude which believed saw him praying, and had said
Amen, then there was a great earthquake, and a thunderstorm
arising in the east. All were terrified and fell to the ground. The
heavens opened, a bright cloud unfolded itself from the gate of
heaven, and came towards them, and behold! the Lord Jesus, who
cried aloud, "At the entreaty of the Archbishop I appear before
you, I who was crucified of your fathers." The eyes of the Jews
were blinded, like Paul's, and Christ withdrew in the cloud.

---

[1] Ἐγὼ παραλύσω τὴν δίκην.

Herban is led by the hand to the Archbishop, complaining that Christ has rendered evil for evil. Nay, is the reply, seeing the Lord with unworthy eyes you were blinded. If then our eyes are opened, says Herban, we will be baptised. Not so, but if you like I will baptise you and then you will recover your sight. But suppose you baptise us and our eyes are not opened! I will baptise one of you as a test.

So one Jew was baptised, and he saw, and he cried aloud, "Jesus Christ is very God, and I believe on Him". The rest were then baptised, and recovered their sight. Herban confessed his faith, and his reverence for Gregentius. Now the King was his sponsor, and gave him the name of Leo, and made him a member of his Council. Innumerable[1] Jews were baptised with him, and at the command of the King and Archbishop "the whole congregation of the Jews which dwelt in all the cities of the kingdom" were also baptised. At the Archbishop's suggestion the King forbade them living any more together, but dispersed them among the Christians, marriages with unbaptised Hebrews being strictly prohibited. "So the whole Jewish nation became mingled with the Christian, and kneaded together in the course of time completely forgot its ancestry."

The document ends with a description of the blessed effect of this illumination of the whole kingdom of the Homerites (τῶν Ὁμηριτῶν)—joy, peace, divine services, almsgiving, the rescinding of all unjust laws, though offenders against God's law were put to death. And the King obeyed Gregentius until his death some thirty years later, when he was buried in Tephar the royal city of the Homerites, Serdidus his son succeeding him, and being like his father in all things. Gregentius dies soon, and is buried in the cemetery of the great church, with grievous lamentation.

What does it all mean? Is it not in reality an idealised description of a sincere attempt to win the Jews by methods which seemed right at the time? The Archbishop appears to have done his best—with very inadequate knowledge of the real difficulties felt by Jews—to persuade them of the truth of Christianity. But the closing pages raise the suspicion that there was more than moral suasion at work. The velvet glove covered, one fears, the iron hand.

If so, the reaction was terrible. For after the death, presumably,

---

[1] ὡσεὶ πεντακισχιλίων πεντακοσίων χιλιάδων.

of the successor of Gregentius' patron, there was persecution, and almost the extermination, of the Christians by a Jewish ruler.

We are not indeed yet in a position fully to co-ordinate the events recorded in the newly discovered fragments of the *Book of the Himyarites*[1] with such other information as we possess about the Himyarite kingdom. But it seems that in A.D. 523 a Jew named Masrūq,[2] only indirectly connected with the reigning house, usurped the throne, and, with the help of "Jewish priests who were from Tiberias", and of some who were "Christians in name", seized the capital Ẓafār (Tephar), and offered to all the Christians in the kingdom the choice of Judaism or death.[3] There was a very large number of martyrs, male and female, some being killed with the utmost cruelty. Many were in the Church at Ẓafār when it was burnt after the siege. It is consoling to know that the triumph of Masrūq and his followers was but shortlived. For during the persecution a Christian fled to the Emperor Justin (A.D. 518–527), at Byzantium, who sent him, with recommendations, to the King of Abyssinia. The latter, "the Christ-loving king Kāleb", came with a great army, defeated and slew Masrūq, and told the priests to grant absolution to those remaining Christians who had apostatised out of fear, and now repented. But even the success of the Abyssinian Christians did not last more than half a century. For about A.D. 570 they were displaced by "a small band of Persian adventurers"[5] who in their turn had to give way to the enthusiastic followers of Mohammed early in the seventh century.

[1] They were found in 1920 in the cloth-covered boards of a Syriac liturgy written in A.D. 1469–1470. They have been edited, with a Translation and Introduction in English, by A. Moberg, Lund, 1924.

[2] His name is written upside down in the MS., as a form of execration.

[3] Syriac text, p. 7 a, ll. 2 *sq.*, 7 *sq.*

[4] See Parkes (*supra*, p. xiii), p. 258 note, for references to articles upon this subject.

[5] *Enc. Brit.* ed. 11, s.v. *Sabaeans*, xxiii. 956.

CHAPTER XVII

THE TEACHING OF JACOB

(SARGIS D'ABERGA)

A.D. 634

How was it that the Emperor Heraclius (A.D. 610–641) took such strong measures against the Jews? It is true that the assertion that even in his treaty with Sisebut, King of the Visigoths, in 612 he insisted that the latter should have all Jews baptised, or driven out of his kingdom, cannot be proved, but the tale itself witnesses to the opinion men had of him. What moved him so decisively? For this Roman nobleman from Africa was a great man, perhaps, with Theodosius, the greatest between Constantine and Constantine Palaeologus (in whose reign Constantinople was captured by the Turks, and the Empire destroyed for ever), and he was not likely to be moved by sudden impulse or unreasoning dislike.

More than one answer has been given. He was but continuing the policy of his predecessor Phocas, the rough centurion who murdered Maurice, seized the Empire, and ruled it ignorantly and savagely. The Jews had revolted, notably in Antioch, and had been put down with barbarity. Heraclius perhaps thought they would soon rebel again. But a truer reason lies in his very greatness. Just as in earlier centuries it was the better Emperors of Rome who persecuted the Christian faith, so was it with Heraclius. As their aim was to develop the Empire, or at least to restore the old-time energy of its citizens, so his was to save it from the decay with which it was threatened, and to preserve it from enemies without and within. As, again, Diocletian found a body of persons who were unwilling to be merged in the religious unity of the Empire, or acknowledge even their human ruler as in some sense divine, Heraclius found one also. That they were Christians in the one case and Jews in the other does not affect the principle. To heathen and Christian Emperor alike it seemed monstrous that there should be any subjects to whom his will was secondary. Unity of heart alone produces the union of perfect service. Compulsion or banishment seemed to be the only alternatives.[1]

[1] "The greatest complaint against him (Louis XV) is the persecution of the Jansenists, to whom he is a bitter enemy; not, however, out of love to the Jesuits, but because it is a maxim of his policy not to suffer any difference of

We see plainly enough that Diocletian was wrong in his opinion of the ultimate effects of Christianity on politics. Heraclius, it is probable, was equally wrong in his opinion of the ultimate effects of Judaism. But he had many excuses. The Jews of his day had commercial colonies in every town on the Mediterranean coasts, and in the frontier cities of Mesopotamia, where the Roman and the Persian Empires met.[1] They also, thanks to the bigotry of so-called Christians, felt more at home with Persian than with Roman rulers, and had shown from time to time a desire to assist the former. An angular rocky mass not fitting into the structure of the State, and yet providing a foothold for those who wished to pull that structure down, challenged the architect to endeavour to dislodge it from his building. We can sympathise with Heraclius.

The consequence of his severity was that a large number of Jews were baptised during his reign, not voluntarily in the true meaning of the word, but from fear, or even by direct physical compulsion. Naturally they were but poor converts, in most cases still firmly attached to Judaism, and knowing very little of the doctrines of Christianity. The Church, however, did not feel that it had met its responsibility as soon as they were baptised. It endeavoured to show them by argument after baptism what it ought to have convinced them of before, and drew up treatises to instruct them suitably to their needs.

One of these, written in A.D. 634, has come down to us under the title of *The Teaching of Jacob* in the Greek,[2] and of *Sargis d'Aberga* in the Ethiopic. The translator into Ethiopic modified it not a little by shortening its arguments and omitting some topical allusions which his readers would not understand, but retained its general sense.[3]

opinions, but to oblige everybody to hold one faith, that he may the easier keep them under one master" (George Lyttelton, writing at Lyons, Oct. 16, 1729. See Maud Wyndham, *Chronicles of the eighteenth century*, 1924, i. 24).

[1] R. P. J. Pargoire, *L'Église Byzantine de 527 à 847*, 1905, p. 173.

[2] Διδασκαλία 'Ιακώβου.

[3] It was translated also into Syriac, Arabic, and Slavonic. It was critically edited in Greek by Bonwetsch in the *Abhandlungen der kön. Gesellschaft der Wissenschaften zu Göttingen. Phil.-histor. Klasse, Neue Folge*, Bd. xii. 3, Berlin, 1910. The Ethiopic with a French translation was edited by Nau in *Patr. Orient.* iii. 4 (1909) and xiii. 1 (1919). Nau has also published the Greek text of part i used by the Ethiopic translator in *Patr. Orient.* viii. 5 (1912). M. Périer gives some account of an Arabic version in *Patr. Orient.* xiii. 1, Appendix (19); see also Nau, 1912, pp. 7–9. S. Krauss has a study of it in the Hebrew review, *Zion*, 1927, pp. 28–37, paying special attention to information about the topography and history of Palestine in the seventh century.

The title in Ethiopic, *Sargis d'Aberga*, represents the title in the original, George the Eparch, or Governor, and suggests the narrative form in which the treatise is composed. Sergius, or George, the Governor,[1] had had all the Jews of Carthage[2] brought before him, asking them if they were the servants of the Emperor (Heraclius). When they replied that they were, he told them that their master wished them to be baptised. On their demurring, very naturally, he abused them, and had the ceremony performed by force. The treatise then centres round two of them, Joseph the narrator, and Jacob. The latter has had visions encouraging him to study the Scriptures, and he then teaches Joseph and other Jews who had been baptised like himself, that, after all, the Christian doctrine is true. When they recall the evil and Anti-christian bitterness of Jacob's own past life, he acknowledges it all, stating that he had sided first with the Green faction (mostly imperial), and afterwards with the Blue (generally anti-imperial), according as he had found opportunities of injuring Christians, and that he had helped in the murder of Bonosus, the imperial general who had avenged the Jewish riots in Antioch, dragging his corpse through the streets of Constantinople. Further, he had come from the capital pretending to be a Christian, but had betrayed himself by a hasty exclamation, and had been baptised by force. But now, he says, he has become a different man altogether. Indeed, the picture given of him throughout the tract is that of a very devout and humble saint, who loves to be alone that he may pray, and search the Scriptures more thoroughly.

A third prominent actor is soon brought in, one Justus, an unbaptised Jew, who has come to Africa from Palestine, and is strongly opposed to the truth. He is a learned man, son of a learned man, Samuel. Jacob himself had been Samuel's disciple. Most of the latter part of the tract is taken up with discussions between Jacob and Justus, in one of which Justus loses his temper and tries to strangle Jacob with his turban. The result, however, is that Justus acknowledges the strength of Jacob's arguments, and accepts Christ. Joseph is not prominent, but narrates what is said. It should, however, be noticed that great emphasis is laid on secrecy. The Jews are represented as fearing lest the Christians

[1] There were several Governors of this name over Africa, e.g. under Justinian about A.D. 543, and one mentioned by St Maximus in the seventh century. See Nau, *op. cit.* p. 6.

[2] Or possibly Carthagena in Spain.

come to hear that they have been raising objections against Christianity, and all the Jews in the story take an oath not to set down anything in writing. But Joseph breaks his oath by putting his son Simon behind the door, and bidding him record all that is said.

The substance of the argument[1] is expressed in the sub-title, "that one must not keep sabbath now that Christ has appeared, and that He is indeed the Christ who has come, and not another". In other words, the Law with its requirements has passed away, and the Son of Mary is the true Messiah. The Law and the Prophets could not set men free from heathenism and the power of the demons, and lead us to the knowledge of God (i. 5). The Sun of righteousness therefore arose, the Logos who appeared in the flesh, whom humanity now worships as a Brother (i. 8). He brought in the new and perfect Law (i. 10 *sqq.*), so that Baptism takes the place of Circumcision, and the Festival of the Resurrection[2] that of the Sabbath. We must therefore no longer Judaise and be Christians as well. When the Sun has arisen there is no more need of moon and stars.

Christ is indeed the Messiah, as is proved by the time fixed for His coming, and the prophecies of His sufferings (i. 23), death, and resurrection (i. 24–27). When the body of Christ had been buried, the Word of God who dwelt in it took as His spoil all the power of the Devil, and freed all humanity, which had been held down by him. For "He sent His Word and healed them".[3] Isa. liii cannot refer, as our teachers say, to Josiah, for he was not crucified with ungodly robbers, nor did the Gentiles place their hope on him. He was to be betrayed and crucified (i. 31 *sqq.*, even His cross may be honoured, though not really worshipped), and was to ascend to heaven (i. 35 *sqq.*). The old Law is abrogated. Another has been proclaimed, that of Christ. We have the holy Gospels of the New Covenant, the sevenfold light spoken of in the Prophets (i. 29).[4] The Word took our flesh in the end of the days, because men could not endure to look on His bare Divinity (i. 36).[5] The Church

---

[1] The admirable summary in Bonwetsch (*op. cit.* p. viii *sq.*) has been taken as the basis of this and the next two paragraphs. For many details in the argument see below, pp. 155 *sqq.*

[2] I.e. Sunday.　　　　　　　　　　　　[3] Ps. cvii. 20.

[4] Cf. Isa. xxx. 26. The treatise quotes the passage directly of Christ elsewhere (i. 28; ii. 2).

[5] Cf. "Anastasius", 2nd Addition, *infra*, p. 179.

takes the place of the Synagogue (i. 37 *sqq.*). Further, Mary (not merely Joseph) was herself of the tribe of Judah (i. 49 *sq.*), thus obviating the common Jewish objection to the ancestry of Christ.

With this the First Discussion ends. Four others follow at intervals of a few days. The Law and the Prophets tell of Christ the Son of God, and the blessed Trinity (ii. 1–5). They also foretell the Incarnation (ii. 6 *sqq.*), and the substitution of the Gentiles, in the place of Israel (iii. 5 *sqq.*). The writer then considers again, and at greater length, the statements of Daniel about the time at which the Messiah was to come, and what is to be expected after His coming (iii. 8 *sqq.*; iv. 3), namely the coming of Antichrist (v. 1), the end of the world and the Second Advent (v. 4 *sqq.*). He closes with mentioning many of the types of Christ's Passion.

While this very short summary of the argument is perhaps sufficient, there are some details of interest which should not be overlooked. "We wish both to keep Sabbath and also to believe Christ" (i. 12 [14]).[1] Herod the Great was an Ascalonite (i. 22 [23]).[2] Josephus is quoted in the same section as saying that when Christ was crucified voices were heard, "Let us go forth, and no longer remain."[3] Jacob asserts that Annas and Caiaphas were of the tribe of Levi, and the Scribes of that of Simeon, so that the prophecy of Gen. xlix. 5–7 was fulfilled in them in the time of our Lord (i. 26 [31]). There is also the statement, "As those before the Law of Moses were under the law of Nature (ὑπὸ τὸν φυσικὸν νόμον), and it was not necessary for them to keep the Sabbath, but when the Law came he who would not do so was accursed, so again it is not necessary to keep the Sabbath now that Christ the true light has come" (i. 28 [35]). "Esdras" ("Sirach" in v. 15) shows that the crucified Christ was God, for he says, *Blessed be the Lord who spread out His hands and saved Jerusalem* (i. 33 [42]).[4] "God sent me a certain Jew in Ptolemais, and he expounded the genealogy of Mary. I said to him mockingly, 'She of Judah!' Now that Jew was a great teacher of the Law, of Tiberias. And he said, Why do the Christians magnify Mary? She is the daughter of David and not *Theotokos* (i.e. born of God), for Mary is a woman, daughter

---

[1] So the Greek, but the Ethiopic, "We can keep the Sabbath, and we do not believe in Christ", which gives no sense, unless with a note of exclamation. The references to the Ethiopic are always in square brackets.

[2] See Justin's *Dialogue with Trypho*, lii. 3 (*supra*, p. 36), and in greater detail, Dionysius bar Salibi on Matt. ii. 22 (*Scriptores Syri*, xcviii).

[3] *Wars*, VI. v. 3, § 299.

[4] This may be some form of Ecclus. li. 19 (26).

of Joakim, and her mother was Anna. Now Joakim is son of Panther, and Panther was brother of Melchi, as the tradition of us Jews in Tiberias has it, of the seed of Nathan, the son of David, of the seed of Judah.... Do not let the Christians suppose then that Mary is from heaven (ἐκ τῶν οὐρανῶν ἐστίν). As the Jew said this in disparagement (ἐξευτελίζων), I glorified God who made the hidden things plain. And our Gospel is true, when it says that Mary is the kinswoman of Elisabeth, for the tribes of Judah and of Levi were mingled" (i. 42 [54]).[1]

Again, the priesthood of us Jews was taken away by God, because we transgressed His commands, see 1 Sam. ii. 27–34 (ii. 2 [57]). And Jacob says, with painful sarcasm, We must not write (*vide supra*) "lest any tell the Christians, for they keep their belief in orthodox dogmas, and say that the Son is *homoousios* with the Father, and also the Holy Spirit, etc., which we do not receive. They will perhaps curse us as heretics. We have not yet learned the syllables of the faith of Christ, for Christians have anathematised Bishops, etc." (ii. 5 [59]). Justus tries to strangle Jacob with his turban, but is rebuked by other Jews (iii. 4 [68]). To Jacob's enquiry, Is the Roman Empire (ἡ Ῥωμανία) suffering diminution, Justus answers, It if be diminished a little we hope that it will rise again, for the Messiah must come while it is still standing (iii. 8 [77]). To Justus' enquiry whether the Fourth Beast in Daniel had much power afterwards, Jacob replies, Assuredly, "From the Ocean, i.e. Scotland, and Britain, and Spain, and France, and Italy, and Greece, and Thrace, as far as Antioch, Syria, Persia, and all the East and South, and Egypt, and Africa, and Upper (ἄνωθεν) Africa are the boundaries of the Romans until this very day, and the pillars (στῆλαι) of their kings are seen in brass and marble" (iii. 8 [80]). "Yet now Rome is humbled."

Jacob fasted much to have his mind sober for the Divine Scriptures (iii. 8 [8]). Justus objects to the use of Wisd. v. 3, 6, as being an apocryphal book (iv. 6). Ps. li. 2, 7 refers to Baptism (iv. 7 [89]). "You do well", says Justus, "to write down the Divine wisdom that gushes forth from the mouth of Jacob" (v. 3). Jacob says that when the Jews set the church at Ptolemais on fire, and the Christian houses, he was helping, and he entered into the Bishop's house, "and found there an old and a new covenant. And we took up the books of the Law and the Prophets, and rent asunder those of Christ. And I took up wonderful parchments of Bishops (μεμβράϊνα

---

[1] See also Andronicus' *Dialogue*, xxxviii (*infra*, p. 185).

θαυμαστὰ ἐπισκόπων), having the names of Basil, Gregory, Epiphanius, Ambrose, Ephraim and Antiochus,[1] and read them, mocking and laughing at them." He read them to Leontius (a cleric who on the threat of being killed had become a Jew, iv. 7 [90]), who told him that the Catholic Church said that Christ was *homoousios* with God. Jacob now sees that he was right (v. 12 [109]). Jacob says that some Jews say that the skull of Adam lies at Golgotha (v. 13 [111]).[2]

Again, we get an interesting glimpse of the attitude of the Jews in the early part of the seventh century toward Mohammed. Justus says that his brother Abraham of Caesarea had written to tell him that a false prophet had appeared among the Saracens. When Sergius Candidatus was killed by them Abraham was at Caesarea, but then went by boat to Sycamin.[3] There he found the Jews glad at Candidatus' death, and saying that a great Prophet had appeared among the Saracens. But a very old Jew groaned and said, "He is a deceiver; do Prophets come with sword and blood? I fear lest the Christ whom the Christians worship was He who was sent by God, and that instead of Him we shall receive Hermolaos" (i.e. Antichrist). He bids therefore Abraham go and learn more about him. So, adds Abraham, I went, but found nothing but bloodshed. "For he says he has the keys of Paradise, which is incredible" (v. 16 [117]).

Lastly, Jacob invites Justus to come home with him, "and let us observe the agape" (Ethiopic). So he set the table before Justus and said, "Say the blessing, my brother." Justus replied, "It is your part to say the blessing." Jacob said, "May Christ give His blessing!" Justus said, "Amen", but added that he knew Jacob wished by the invitation to test the reality of his conversion (v. 17 [119]). Justus puts off his baptism until he has won his wife and near relations to the faith, hoping to be baptised with them (*ibid.*). Jacob teaches him the Creed and the Lord's Prayer (v. 18 [120]).

Taking the treatise as a whole, it is a very human document, and not unattractive, even to us. It portrays the experience of Jews who had been baptised by force, with the natural abhorrence of Christianity felt by most of them, and also the desire of some of

---

[1] Probably the Bishop of Ptolemais, *c.* A.D. 401, who afterwards went to Constantinople, where he died, A.D. 408.
[2] Cf. *Quaest. ad Antiochum*, xlvii (Migne, *P.G.* xxviii) (*vide infra*, p. 160).
[3] Between Ptolemais (Acre) and Caesarea.

them to understand it. Perhaps the author looked with too rosy a pair of spectacles on the result of the efforts of those who were truly converted to win their brethren, but this is excusable. The treatise represents a side of religious life which is not often brought forward, and had it not been preserved we should have lost a vivid picture of the past.

CHAPTER XVIII

SOME MONKISH THESES OF THE NEARER EAST IN THE SEVENTH TO THE ELEVENTH CENTURIES

We doubtless underrate the activity of the *Scriptorium* of an ancient monastery. We are, indeed, well aware that the present existence of most of such Classical and Patristic authors as have survived is due to the learning of the mediaeval monks, whose dwellings were generally held inviolate by foes, so long as these were themselves of the Christian faith. But we are apt to forget that Monasticism began before the Middle Ages, and that from the first the men who drew aside from the world were often of studious habits, and desirous of consecrating their gifts of thought and expression to the service of their Saviour.

We know, again, that such theological study formed an important part of the daily duty in the monasteries founded by St Honorat and Cassian off the coast of the Riviera and in Marseilles, at the beginning of the fifth century, and that Benedict insisted upon it in Italy in the sixth.[1] But the life of the West was hardly so different from that of the East as many suppose. We think of the greater writers of the Eastern Church, men who became noted also for their ecclesiastical work, and we forget that often they had been trained in monasteries, and must have acquired from their teachers there, and from the materials for study placed at their disposal, their own erudition and dialectic skill. The monasteries of the East, in fact, were, speaking generally, centres of theological learning, and provided opportunities for discussion of theological subjects between their inmates.

It is in such circles that we ought probably to find the origin of not a few documents entitled *Ad Judaeos*, which give the impression of being written by those who had indeed Jews around them, and therefore feared the influence of Jews on others if not on themselves, yet never came into any close intellectual contact with Jews. They

---

[1] "Otiositas inimica est animae: et ideo certis temporibus occupari debent fratres in labore manuum, certis iterum horis in lectione divina" (Rule, § 48).

wrote in the hope that their words would provide weapons for
their brethren who did meet them, and would also answer difficulties about the relation of the New Testament and the Church
to the Old Testament and the Synagogue.[1] The former reason
must not be eliminated, or even unduly minimised, although the
latter was more successful in the results attained.

I. QUESTIONS ADDRESSED TO ANTIOCHUS THE DUX

Among such documents is a simple little tract now to be found as
the last (cxxxvii) of the *Questions addressed to Antiochus the Dux*
(i.e. a military Governor of a Province, presumably of Egypt, in
this case), falsely attributed to Athanasius.[2] Many of the preceding
Questions are of some interest, but most do not touch upon our
subject,[3] and some are on very trivial matters.[4] But Question
cxxxvii is of quite a different kind, and contains not merely a
short enquiry and answer, but fills some eight columns of the
Greek of Migne's bilingual edition. We may guess that originally
it had no connexion with the *Questions* proper, and has been added
to them only because it began with a question.

The date of the tract is uncertain but it is certainly earlier than
the seventh century, for it has no reference to the Image controversy. Its editor in Migne, indeed, says that it is "not unworthy
of Athanasius". But there is no reason to place it as early as his
time, and the terms used of the Blessed Virgin[5] are at least as late
as the fifth century. The way in which it is used by writers of the
seventh century suggests that it may date from the sixth.[6]

[1] *Vide infra*, p. 161.
[2] *Quaestiones ad Antiochum ducem.* Migne, *P.G.* xxviii. 589–700. On the *Dux*
see A. Robertson in his volume on *Athanasius* in the *Nicene and Post-Nicene Fathers*,
1892, p. xci. The name Antiochus is not included in the list of *Duces* of Athanasius' lifetime.
[3] But Q.xxxvii is, Why do we Christians turn to the East and Jews to the
South? Q.xxxviii, If Christ was circumcised, why are not we? Q.xxxix, Our
"worship" of the Cross is like Jacob honouring Joseph's staff, and the Jews the
Tables of the Law. Q.xli, If we separate the two bits of a cross they become
merely common wood (cf. *infra*, p. 162). Q.xlii, How can we be sure that
Christianity is really superior to other faiths? Answer, Think of the persecution
it endured at first. No Christian Emperor has ever been killed by barbarians.
Nor could they destroy his image with the cross on the coinage. Q.xlvii, Adam
lies at Calvary (see *Dict. de Théologie Catholique*, 1923, i. 381–384).
[4] Q.lvii, How did Cain learn to kill Abel? for no one had been killed before?
Answer, The devil taught him in a dream.
[5] *Vide infra*, p. 161.   [6] *Vide infra*, p. 162.

"Since Christians and Jews acknowledge Christ," it begins, "and the Jews doubt about His advent, asserting that He has not come, but say that He will come, how should we persuade them that Christ is God, and also is true and not a deceiver, as they suppose?"

The first three of the fourteen answers which follow this question deal with the difficulties specifically enumerated here, proving from the Old Testament (1) that Christ is God (e.g. Baruch iii. 37), (2) that He has already come (e.g. Dan. ix. 24, 26), and (3) from History, that He is true and no impostor, because His own predictions have been fulfilled.[1] With the fourth answer the author begins to deal with the subject more widely: "But that we may completely condemn the blindness of the Jews, and, further, that we who believe may be stronger in our faith in Christ, we will bring the testimonies (μαρτυρίας) from the Old Testament about the whole dispensation of Christ and the defence of the Gospel. For this will be useful to all who wish to consider it."

The word "testimonies" is interesting as carrying us back in thought to the *Testimonia* of the early centuries, for the subject-matter of the present tract has much in common with them, although there seems to be no literary dependence. For if the desire was to prove that the Old Testament contemplated the life and work of Christ, and proclaimed His pre-existence, etc., etc., the teaching would necessarily run upon the same general lines. Here the author quotes texts showing the pre-existence of Christ, His incarnation (including the bringing in of the Gentiles), His birth in Bethlehem and His actions, His aim in coming (i.e. to subdue the devil), His bonds, crucifixion, resurrection, and Ascension. Many details are included throughout. The testimonies end with the quotation of Dan. vii. 9–11, whence, the author says, it is clear that the beast mentioned is Antichrist. The conclusion is that the Son "for our salvation in the last days became man of our all-holy undefiled Lady, the Mother of God and ever-virgin Mary".[2]

If we must give a verdict upon Question cxxxvii as a whole, we must confess that in itself it is neither of importance nor of interest. It smacks of midnight oil, not the busy market or the court of the synagogue. But it does not stand alone. It was certainly used by

[1] See *Trophies* (*infra*, p. 163); "Anastasius" (p. 176).
[2] Cf. *Papiscus and Philo* (*infra*, p. 172).

the author of the *Dialogue of Papiscus and Philo*[1] and perhaps by others.[2]

II. THE TROPHIES OF DAMASCUS

Our next document indeed is more than a mere thesis, for it has a certain amount of facts behind it. It was written in A.D. 681,[3] and is known by the name of *The Trophies of Damascus*, but its title is rather, "Trophies framed against Jews in Damascus".[4] This means, as it appears, "Monuments of victories over Jews in Damascus set forth in some order". For the writing is not an account of the conversion of individual Jews, but of controversial discussions with them, in which victory goes to the Christians.

Damascus[5] seems a strange place for such discussions, especially as it was in the possession of the Mohammedans at that time, but the author was a monk, who doubtless lived in one of the monas-

[1] *Vide infra*, pp. 169–174.

[2] For completeness it may be added that Migne prints immediately after this another document of thirty-six more Questions and Answers (cc. 699–708), similar in form to the earlier hundred and thirty-six, and of even less interest. And he adds a Fragment (c. 709 *sq.*) relative to the worship of Images. In this the argument is, If the wood of a cross is divided it is no longer adored (see Q. xli, *supra*, p. 160; Leontius, *infra*, p. 166). We adore an image not for itself but only because it tells us of Christ. Further, some words in *Athan. c. Arios*, iii. 5 (Migne, *P.G.* xxvi. 331 B) are applied to images. An image, after seeing the King, might say, "I and the King are one. I then am in him and he in me. And what thou beholdest in me, this thou beholdest in him, and what thou hast seen in him, this thou seest in me. He therefore who worships the image worships in it the King. For the image is his form and likeness."
This last passage belongs clearly enough to the end of the seventh century or later, and it is worth quoting only for comparison with similar thoughts in late documents to be mentioned soon.

[3] The date is "the twenty-first year of Constantine the upheld of God, our King after Constantine, in the month of August, of the ninth Indiction". An Indiction was the period of fifteen years for which the taxes were fixed, and this is the ninth year. The dates of the beginning of the Indictions are known, and 681 is the only year that suits. Constantine IV (Pogonatus) seems to have reigned for some time conjointly with his father Constans (officially called "Constantine") before the latter's death in 668.

[4] πεπραγμένα τρόπαια κατὰ 'Ιουδαίων ἐν Δαμασκῷ. G. Bardy has published the Greek text with a French translation, Introduction, and notes in *Patr. Orient.* xv. 2 (1920). For the meanings of the word *Trophy* see Athanasius, *De Incarnatione*, §§ 24, 29, 32.

[5] It is possible, however, that the traditional interpretation of *the power of Damascus* (Isa. viii. 4 LXX) as the power of Satan, which was overcome by Christ, may have had something to do with the choice of the name. Cf. Justin's *Trypho*, lxxviii. 9 (*supra*, p. 41).

teries in the neighbourhood, and desired the conversion of the Jews, just as in another writing contained in the same manuscript from which the Trophies was printed he desired the restoration of the Monophysite heretics to the true faith.

He was, as has been said, a monk (Prol. 3; IV. vii. 1), who had travelled to Sinai and elsewhere (III. vii. 11), and was loyal to the Empire (Title; II. iii. 2). He lived in times when Christians had been taken prisoners (II. iii. 1), and fifty years after the beginning of great wars (II. iii. 2), for some fifty years had elapsed since the Mohammedans first attacked Palestine. His defence of the worship of Images (III. vi. 1) suggests that the Iconoclastic controversy had formally begun (A.D. 680), but Leontius of Neapolis of Cyprus had written in a similar way not later than the beginning of the century.[1]

The treatise gives an account of four discussions, held on different days, the First being the best worked out, and dealing especially with the witness of the Old Testament to the Divinity of the Messiah. It is characteristic of the author that he allows his Jewish opponents to argue quite sensibly against the Christian interpretation of some of his proof-texts. Naturally, however, he is sometimes very horrified at what they say. They are represented as Jews who had some anxiety lest Christianity should be true, and had mentioned this to a boy, who told them of the learned monk who would resolve their difficulties while concealing their secret.

The Second discussion deals especially with the fall of the Jewish polity and the triumph of Christianity, but also treats of Isa. liii and the suggestions of the Cross which are to be found in the Old Testament, especially in the case of the Brazen Serpent. The Third claims that "Christian" is indeed a new name, as promised in Isa. lxv. 15, and defends the worship of the Cross and Images. For the Jews themselves would adore the Ark and the Cherubim if these still existed, and they do in fact pay similar honour to their Book of the Law.[2] The Fourth discussion treats in particular of the date of Messiah's coming, as determined in the Book of Daniel, and also shows that as Christ's own prophecies of events have been fulfilled so also credence should be given to His doctrinal teaching.[3]

---

[1] If the Fragments attributed to him are really his (*vide infra*, p. 166).
[2] Cf. *Quaestio* xxxix (*supra*, p. 160); Leontius (*infra*, p. 166); Stephen of Bostra (*infra*, p. 167); Jerome of Jerusalem (p. 169); *Papiscus and Philo* (p. 171); "Anastasius" (p. 177); Andronicus (p. 185); Paul of Burgos (*infra*, p. 272).
[3] See also *Quaestio* cxxxvii (*supra*, p. 161).

There are many details in the treatise which are of some interest.
The author has a theory of the Redemption which recalls the far
more elaborate system of Anselm. Christ paid no redemption
money to the devil, but offered Himself to the Father for us,
enduring the death which we owed (I. i. 3). The Christian explains
the reason why the doctrine of the Trinity was not revealed in the
Old Testament more clearly. It was from fear of the influence of
Egyptian polytheism, "these be thy gods, O Israel".[1] For the
same reason nothing is said about the help given by the angels in
the creation of the world. Sacrifices, again, were just a concession
to the moral weakness of Israel (I. iii. 2). Gen. iii. 22, "the man is
become as one of us", means that one of Us will become man
according to the flesh (I. iii. 3 *sq.*). Adam was made two days after
the stars, and yet (it is implied) Messiah was born before the
Morning Star (I. iv. 2–5).[2] A miracle is "a strange action which
takes place contrary to usage" (I. v. 2).[3] In Ps. cxviii. 27 it is quite
unimportant whether we translate "hath shined" or "will shine";
the striking thing is that David calls the Coming One God and
Lord (I. vi. 2).[4] Hab. iii. 2–5 is expounded interestingly in I. vii.
2–6. On the second day the Jews bring certain chosen and eloquent
(λογίους) men who know the Scripture minutely, yet have no real
understanding of it (εἰς ἄκρον γινώσκοντας τὴν γραφήν, καὶ μηδὲν
ἐπιγινώσκοντας, I. viii. 4). The Christian at first shirks the dilemma
of answering the question whether Christians spring from Esau or
from Jacob (II. i. 2), though he answers it in III. ii. The author even
rises to eloquence when recounting the many parts of the world
which Christians now possess (II. ii. 1 *sq.*).[5] Among the answers to
the objection that Christ has not fulfilled the promise that Messiah
should bring peace, one is that Jews themselves say that the *horn*
in Dan. vii. 7 *sq.* refers to the Messiah, and yet wars are prophesied
in the immediately following verses (II. iii. 5). The Jew protests
against explaining the Scriptures otherwise than literally, and
refuses to ἑρμηνεῦσαι τὴν γραφήν!! To this the Christian replies,
"Pray tell me then, since you know that the Old Testament is to
be understood literally, how you explain, 'Cursed is he who has

---

[1] Cf. "Anastasius", Addition (*infra*, p. 179).

[2] The argument is stated more clearly in *Papiscus and Philo* (*infra*, p. 172).

[3] Cf. Jerome on Isa. vii. 14; Augustine, Serm. 147, *De Tempore* and Serm. 44,
De verbis Domini. See further J. B. Frey, "La révélation d'après les conceptions
juives au temps de J.-C." in *Revue Biblique*, 1916, pp. 477–480 (from Bardy).

[4] Cf. *Papiscus and Philo* (*infra*, p. 172).

[5] Cf. *Papiscus and Philo* (*infra*, p. 173).

no seed in Israel',[1] when Elijah and others were unmarried" (II. iv. 1 *sq.*). As a glass filled with water in sunlight causes fire, and yet neither glass nor water nor sun is polluted, so did Christ remain uninjured though born of the Virgin; "for the bare Godhead could not appear to man, nor suffer on our behalf" (II. v. 3). Some Gentile philosophers recognised God, and spoke of Him more than your legalists (III. iii. 3). We Christians eat pork, because He who freed me from circumcision freed me also from abstinence from pork. God forbade it, not because it was unclean in itself, but because it was the one flesh-food in Egypt, where beef and mutton were not allowed (III. vi. 5).[2] Adam, when driven forth from Eden, was placed opposite to it, so that he should see it and desire it (III. vii. 3). You ask why we pray to the East, but why do you Jews (in Damascus) pray to the South? I myself, says the writer, have seen the place where Moses received the Law, and it shows that he was then standing facing the East. Further, the mark of Moses' loins is impressed upon the rock (III. vii. 11). In answer to the enquiry why the Prophet did not say clearly all about Christ, and, in consequence, Christians now take a bit of prophecy from here and another from there, the Christian says that as the Jews rejected Christ so they would certainly have rejected and killed any prophet who had spoken thus clearly. So that, for safety's sake, God was obliged to let the prophets each say only a little bit about Him (III. viii. 3).[3] The Gospels disagree with each other, cry the Jews. Yes, says the Christian, for if they had agreed in details it would have been said there was collusion. Besides, even the Prophets sometimes disagree verbally (III. x. 1 *sq.*).

In IV. iv a long list of Persian, Greek, and Egyptian rulers is given, to show the Chronology indicated in the Book of Daniel. From the graves of some of the Martyrs myrrh gushes forth like fountains (IV. v. 6).

The treatise closes with a vivid description of the varied effect of the discussions—"They all went away, some silent, some murmuring, others groaning, and others saying, 'By the Lord, the father has got the better of us.' Others shook their heads, and said to each other, 'By the Law I think we are wrong.' Some who were

---

[1] Is the reference to Hos. ix. 14?

[2] On pork, see the end of this treatise, *infra*, p. 166; "Anastasius", Addition (p. 179).

[3] Cf. *Papiscus and Philo* (*infra*, p. 173); "Anastasius" (p. 179); Gennadius (*infra*, pp. 192 *sq.*).

older said in jest, 'O dear, how many bits of pork we might have had!' Some at once become friends to Christians instead of enemies; others watch and wait for the opportunity of baptism. Of these those are specially dear to me who have come to the Church wholeheartedly and in truth, and, having received the seal of baptism, speak against the Jews without experiencing defeat, fighting for us, before us, and with us, belonging to the Father and the Son and the Holy Spirit, to whom be glory and might for ever and ever, Amen."

This ending of the treatise is in accordance with the spirit of it as a whole. For it is very human, and its arguments are not infrequently such as can be used even to-day. It appears to have influenced the author of the *Dialogue between Papiscus and Philo*,[1] but only indirectly, for while many of the thoughts are common to the two treatises the language differs.

III. LEONTIUS

Leontius, Bishop of Nicomedia in Cyprus, lived A.D. 590–668, and wrote five books against the Jews. Whether, however, the fragments attributed to him[2] are really his is another matter. He hardly lived late enough to be so decided an advocate of the use of images as the fragments reveal. For this is the cause of their preservation, that in his arguments against the Jews he pleads that Christians do not really worship the wood of the Cross. On the contrary, so long as the two pieces of wood are so placed as to form a Cross, a Christian worships it as a "type", and a reminder of what was done for us on the Cross, but if they are separated they are burned.[3] So when we kiss the king's seal it is not the clay or the parchment that we reverence, but the symbol of the king. If, in the absence of a father, his children will kiss with tears his staff or his cloak, shall we not so kiss the Cross as Christ's staff, the manger and stall at Bethlehem as His home, and reverence Nazareth as his country, and Jordan as His holy laver? After all, you Jews show similar respect to the Book of the Law; yet you do not worship its leather and its ink, but the words of God written in it.[4]

[1] *Vide infra*, p. 169.
[2] See Migne, *P.G.* xciii. 1597–1612, from Mansi, *Conc.* xiii. 43 *sqq.* Consult also Krumbacher, *Byz. Lit.* 1897, p. 191.
[3] Cf. *Quaest.* cxxxvii. Appendix (*supra*, p. 160).
[4] Col. 1599 B. See *Trophies* (*supra*, p. 163).

IV. STEPHEN OF BOSTRA

Stephen of Bostra, of whom we know almost nothing save that he wrote *Against the Jews*, is quoted by John of Damascus[1] to the same effect as Leontius. You Jews, he says, made the Ark and the Cherubim, etc., reverencing but not worshipping them, and we too make images of the saints for remembrance. For "an image is the name and likeness of the things that are written in it".[2]

V. ST JOHN OF DAMASCUS

John of Damascus himself (died perhaps Dec. 4, 749)[3] has a short chapter upon our subject, entitled *Against the Jews, concerning the Sabbath*.[4] After showing that the Law about the Sabbath was some-times broken in Old Testament times, without fault being found (e.g. Elijah and Daniel *fasted* on the sabbath, and the Israelites circumcised on the eighth day even if it was a sabbath), he points out that the sabbath was made for rest and worship. But now that Christ has come, all, and no longer part, of our time is to be spent for God. We should always have a desire for God, always anger against His enemies. And that poor beast of burden, our body, should have rest from the slavery of sin, and be made to serve the commands of God. We therefore celebrate the perfect rest of human nature, namely the day of the Resurrection. In the same way, circumcision is no longer necessary; there must be the putting off of bodily pleasure. Now the number "seven" refers to all the present time, yet Eccles. xi. 2 says, "Give a portion to seven, yea, even unto eight", and "the eighth" in Pss. vi and xii (titles) refers to the future resurrection. Thus the Law looked forward beyond the Sabbath to the Rest of the true Israel.

VI. JEROME OF JERUSALEM

The little treatise attributed to *Jerome of Jerusalem* demands rather more attention. Who he was we do not know, but John of Damascus refers to him as πρεσβύτερος Ἱεροσολύμων,[5] and he is called

[1] *De Imaginibus*, iii (Migne, *P.G.* xciv. 1375 B–D). See note[5] *infra*.
[2] See *Trophies* (*supra*, p. 163, with note).
[3] Tixeront, *Patrologie*, 1918, p. 416.
[4] *De Fide Orthodoxa*, iv. 23 (Migne, *P.G.* xciv. 1201–1206).
[5] Migne, *P.G.* xl. 846. The authenticity, however, of this third book of John of Damascus on Images is very doubtful, and the reference occurs only in the Appendix to that (see Batiffol, *Revue des Questions Historiques*, xxxix [1886], 248–255).

Theologus Graecus to distinguish him from other Jeromes.[1] His date is quite uncertain, but is now generally placed in the eighth century.

The title of the treatise is *A Dialogue of the blessed Jerome concerning the Holy Trinity, the discussion of a Jew with the Christian*.[2] The Jew begins by asking how in view of Deut. xxxii. 39, "there is no god with Me", Christians can adore the Father, Son and Holy Spirit; they are like idolators. The Believer (ὁ πιστός) allows that it is a great mystery, and argues that in view of the Jew's own inability to understand God it is unreasonable for him to expect the explanation of the generation of the Son. Further, which suits the idea of the immortal God better, the belief that He has a Son immortal and perfect like Himself, or that He should be the Father of a foolish "son", Israel?

Yet, the Jew presses, If God has a Son, tell me how and when He begat Him. The Believer replies that he cannot but acknowledge that God has a Son in view of Ps. cx. 3; ii. 7; and that there is also the Holy Spirit, in view of Joel ii. 23; Isa. xliv. 3. When, further, the Jew admits that this Spirit is Uncreated, Without beginning, Incomprehensible,[3] like God, the Believer replies that his opponent is convicted out of his own mouth of worshipping a Duad, namely, God and the Spirit of God. Just as the Jew does not really acknowledge two Gods but only One, so also is it with the Christian. Many illustrations are adduced, e.g. the soul, the word or reason (λόγος), the body, yet one man; or the gold, the image, the inscription, yet one coin. So is it with the all-holy Trinity, "the Unity is without confusion in one tri-personal Being and Godhead".[4]

The Jew continues, If I call Christ God, I dare not call Him of one essence (ὁμοούσιος) with the Father.[5] To this the Believer replies, If you wholly confess Him to be God, you must. For we do not mean that there are three persons like Abraham, Isaac, and Jacob. But how can you expect to understand God when you are ignorant of things on earth? Tell me, What is the nature of the flea? And what is its ψυχή? What are its habits? And who taught it to hide in the seams and folds of dresses?

---

[1] *Dict. Chr. Biog.* iii. 28.

[2] Migne, *P.G.* xl. 847–860: Διάλογος περὶ τῆς Ἁγίας Τριάδος, ἐρώτησις Ἰουδαίου πρὸς τὸν Χριστιανον.   [3] ἄκτιστον, ἄναρχον, ἀκατάληπτον.

[4] ἀσύγχυτος ἡ ἕνωσις ἐν τρισυποστάτῳ μιᾷ οὐσίᾳ καὶ θεότητι.

[5] Compare *Trophies*, 1. ii. 3.

The Jew harks back. But where are we taught the doctrine of the Trinity in the Old Testament? The Believer quotes the stock passages—and the Fragment ends!

Migne adds a second short treatise of seven columns upon Baptism attributed to the same Jerome; I was baptised as an infant, and know the effect it had upon me. And he adds a third small fragment, the piece quoted by John of Damascus, defending the use of images on the ground that the Jews made the Ark, etc.;[1] and saying, "we do not worship the Cross as God".

The Second Fragment is negligible for our purpose, and the Third is only interesting to us because its argument occurs in other documents connected with our subject. But the First shows that Jerome of Jerusalem probably had had, at some time or other, personal controversy with Jews. Anyhow, he puts his case more vividly than do many others who write either nominally or actually against them. After all, the Christian Church was even in the eighth century exposed to danger from Jewish influence, and felt bound to argue with Jews according to its opportunities and knowledge.

VII. THE DIALOGUE OF PAPISCUS AND PHILO

Our next document is the *Dialogue of Papiscus and Philo*.[2] This may well have been its original title, the name Papiscus, the Jew, being taken from the ancient *Dialogue of Papiscus and Jason*,[3] and Philo being a common name among Christians. But as time went on some copyist thought rather of Philo the great Jewish writer of the first century, and gradually the title became altered and enlarged to the form found in the MSS., "The Dialogue of Papiscus and Philo, Jews, who were wise men (σοφῶν = *Chakamim*) among the

---

[1] See *Trophies* (*supra*, p. 163, with the note).

[2] Edited carefully by A. C. McGiffert, Marburg, 1889, from such MSS. as he was acquainted with. He prefixed a valuable introduction, containing a list and very brief summary of thirty-one "Anti-Jewish" works in Greek and twenty-nine in Latin. It is greatly to be regretted that Dr McGiffert, formerly President of the Union Theological Seminary, New York, did not continue his early studies in the direction of our subject. In particular, he does not seem ever to have published the *Contra Judaeos* of Thaddaeus Pelusiota (A.D. 1265), which he transcribed from three MSS. in Paris (*Dialogue*, p. 18), for this appears to be of no little interest. E. J. Goodspeed considers a Dresden MS. of *Papiscus and Philo* in the *American Journal of Theology*, 1900, pp. 796–802.

[3] There seems to be no connexion in subject-matter between the two Dialogues.

Hebrews, with a certain monk (one MS. adds 'Anastasius'), concerning the Faith of the Christians and the Law of the Hebrews, held in the presence of an assembly of Christians (two MSS. add 'and Arabs') and Jews."[1]

McGiffert had only two MSS., P (i.e. Paris Gr. 1111, of cent. xi or xii) and V (i.e. Venice Gr. 505, about cent. xiv), with a collation of the first three chapters from M (i.e. a MS. at Moscow, Gr. $\frac{314}{\text{ccci}}$ of cent. xv). But Bardy[2] mentions others at Paris, especially Gr. 1788 of the year A.D. 1440. The important thing is that V, though the later MS., gives a shorter and earlier text than P, and so does Paris 1788, with, says Bardy, a still better text.

It is necessary to say something about the two recensions of our Dialogue. There is first the question of the date of the treatise, and secondly that of the nature of the additions in the Longer Form. As for the dates, the shorter form (V) says that Christ spoke 600 years ago,[3] and that the Jews have been scattered for 600 years,[4] thus suggesting that it was written in the end of the seventh century. It says also, strangely, that they have had no altar or ark, etc. for 670 years, which may be due to an intermediate recension.[5] In this last passage the longer recension (P) reads expressly 1000 years, which brings the date to the end of the eleventh century.[6]

The additions in the Longer Recension are of two kinds, a good many short sentences and short paragraphs in the body of the treatise, amplifying points of interest, and two very long paragraphs towards the end. One of these embodies many prophecies of details in our Lord's life,[7] and the other deals chiefly with prophecies from Daniel foretelling the destruction of Jerusalem, the Dispersion of the Jews, and the Coming of the Messiah.[8]

---

[1] Ἀντιβολὴ Παπίσκου καὶ Φίλωνος Ἰουδαίων τῶν παρ' Ἑβραίοις σοφῶν πρὸς μοναχόν τινα περὶ πίστεως χριστιανῶν καὶ νόμου Ἑβραίων κροτήθεισα ἐπὶ δήμου χριστιανῶν καὶ Ἰουδαίων.

[2] *Les Trophées de Damas*, 1920, p. 186 (*vide supra*, p. 162).

[3] § 10, near end. P here has vaguely "many years".

[4] § 16, near beginning. P omits.

[5] § 16, eight lines lower down.

[6] In § 10, beginning, P contains the assertion that Christians have been persecuted for twenty years, and McGiffert connects this with the persecution in Egypt which was begun at Alexandria in 1058 A.D. But it is very doubtful whether the Dialogue had anything to do with Egypt.

[7] Nearly all § 12 (McGiffert, pp. 66–73).

[8] All §§ 17, 18 (McGiffert, pp. 80–83).

It is of still greater interest that in this Dialogue we are able to get behind, as it were, the methods of mediaeval writers, and to see them at work. We know some of the sources which the author of this Dialogue used, and the way in which his work was used in its turn. Among the sources he used are the *Trophies*,[1] and, in particular, the *Quaestio ad Antiochum Ducem*, cxxxvii.[2] Several references to the *Trophies* are given in the following pages, but the curious may consult Bardy's edition, p. 186. A study of this will, however, lead to the conclusion that the agreement extends so rarely to the words (as compared with the thoughts) that probably the author of the Dialogue had only an indirect knowledge of the *Trophies*.[3] And on p. 173 *infra* will be found a case where the Dialogue differs so much from the *Trophies* that the author can hardly have known this.

With regard to the *Quaestio* it is very different. The author of the Longer Recension has copied whole passages from it word for word, and incorporated them, of course without acknowledgment.[4]

On the other hand the Dialogue has itself been used very largely by the author of the next treatise to be mentioned, the *Dissertation against the Jews* by one Anastasius, falsely accredited to Anastasius of Sinai.[5] The relationship is discussed at length by McGiffert,[6] who concludes that "Anastasius" used the Shorter Recension directly, but not the Longer, and that on the contrary the Longer used "Anastasius". But this seems very doubtful in view of the use of *Quaestio* cxxxvii by the author of the Longer Recension. The authors of the Longer Recension and "Anastasius" were probably contemporary.

The *Dialogue of Papiscus and Philo* begins with an objection raised by the Jew to the use of images, and the answer is much in the style of the *Trophies* and Leontius, that as Jacob did not worship

---

[1] *Vide supra*, pp. 162–166.   [2] *Vide supra*, pp. 160–162.
[3] The ending, however, of the Dialogue in the MS. Paris 1788 recalls very distinctly that of the *Trophies* as quoted *supra*, p. 166. See Bardy, p. 186, note.
[4] McGiffert does not mention this, but the fact is self-evident.
    Quaest. §§ 6, 7 = Dial. § 2, McGiffert, pp. 66, l. 33–68, l. 9.
    Quaest. §§ 8–12 = Dial. § 12, McGiffert, pp. 69, l. 3–73, l. 32.
    Quaest. §§ 12, 13 = Dial. §§ 17, 18, McGiffert, pp. 82, l. 25–83, l. 8, the
    end of the treatise.
[5] *Vide infra*, p. 175.
[6] *Op. cit.* pp. 35–37. The relationship of the Longer Recension to *Quaest.* cxxxvii.

Joseph's staff, but only honoured him who held it, and that as the
Jews themselves in bowing before the Cherubim and Ark only
honoured God who ordered them,[1] so was it with the Christians,
who indeed burn the images when they become old or the painting
rubbed off. The fact that no more is said of image worship until
near the end of the tract (where a different argument is adduced)
suggests that it may be an addition to the original document.[2]

The real subject of the Discussion is then stated. For the Jew
asks (§ 2), Why do you blaspheme, saying that God has a Son? The
Christian replies, It is not we who say this but your own Scripture,
and quotes Ps. ii, which cannot refer to Solomon, for he never
ruled over the ends of the earth. When the Jew urges (§ 3) the
objection that a Son will not "ask" like a servant, the Christian
reminds him that a father will often bid his son "ask". "I have
begotten thee" refers to the begetting in the flesh, "for by the good
pleasure of the Father He was born of the holy Mother of God and
Ever-Virgin Mary"[3]—titles which show that the tract is not earlier
than the fifth century at least.

But, says the Jew (§ 4), was He begotten before the world, and
was He God? Who, asks the Christian (§ 5), was David's Lord
and Master in Ps. cx? *Jew*, He had none save God. *Christian*,
Quite so, therefore, since he says that Christ is his Lord and Master,
Christ was born before the worlds. The words are expressly "before
the morning star" (LXX), while Adam came into existence two
days after the stars.[4] He is "after the order of Melchizedek",
i.e. priest of the Gentiles, as was Melchizedek. Like Melchizedek,
again, Christ bids us offer a bloodless sacrifice to God.

After referring to Prov. viii and Ps. lxxii the Christian asks the
Jew (§ 6) what sort of Messiah he expects, and on being told,
A man like one of the prophets and not God, he appeals to the
multitude to note what has been said, and has the books of the
prophets brought from the synagogue to be the final test (§ 7).[5]

Many passages are then adduced. Among them we may notice
(§ 8) Ps. cxviii. 27, "God is the Lord and He has (already) shined
upon us." Not so, cries the Jew, but "shine Thou upon us",
referring to the future. One may smile at the literalness of both

[1] See *Trophies* (*supra*, p. 163, with note).   [2] § 15, McGiffert, p. 15.
[3] Cf. *Quaest. ad Ant.* (*supra*, p. 161). At this point the later author adds a
reference to Prov. viii. 24 *sq.*
[4] See *Trophies* (*supra*, p. 164); "Anastasius" (*infra*, p. 176).
[5] Cf. Chrysostom (*supra*, p. 136).

Christian and Jew, but the latter evidently knew no Hebrew, which is here almost unambiguous, but only the Aramaic of the Targum, which in itself may be either the past or the imperative. Anyhow, is the reply, it refers to one who is God, and He is plainly our Christ, not yours, for you Jews expect only a man, not God.[1] But He is God who "comes from Teman" (Hab. iii. 3), and "Jeremiah" (really Baruch iii. 35–37) is very definite.[2]

The author then (§ 9) shows that Christ was to come to reign over the Gentiles, and to take the place of Moses. Further, the sacred sites of the Jews have become Christian sanctuaries,[3] and (far and wide, even to the very isles of Britain) Judaism and heathenism are silent, and the message of Christ is proclaimed and honoured. We Christians were indeed once persecuted, but the true faith still stands; it has not been wiped out. You cannot explain this (§ 10) unless God was for us. The very coinage displays the Cross,[4] which Cross reigns everywhere, is current everywhere. For six hundred years have we been preserved.[5]

But (§ 11), say the Jews,[6] If the Prophets said all this about the Christian Christ, why did they not tell the Jews plainly that the Christ would come, and bring both the Law and its sacrifices to an end? The Christian replies quite rightly, that they would have been stoned, and their books burned, which would have been an injury to us, for now we can convince the Jews from their own prophets.[7]

§ 12 is quite short—less than half a page—in the earlier but eight pages in the later form of the Dialogue. It gave originally only five quotations from the Old Testament, concerning the chief events of our Lord's life.

§ 13 deals more in detail with the argument that History confirms the Divinity of Christ, for He has destroyed the temples of the heathen, Memphis and the Nile in Egypt, and Cyzicus and Ephesus.[8] And yet the Jews call us idolators, though they them-

---

[1] See *Trophies* (*supra*, p. 164 *sq.*). Observe that the author does not follow *Trophies* in regarding the sense as unimportant.

[2] For Hab. iii. 3, *vide supra*, p. 164. Baruch iii. 37 is quoted also in *Quaest.* cxxxvii. 1 (*vide supra*, p. 160).

[3] Cf. *Trophies* (*supra*, p. 164).   [4] Cf. "Anastasius" (*infra*, p. 176).

[5] *Vide infra*, p. 174.

[6] The only place where the plural is used, apart from the title (see McGiffert's note, p. 89).

[7] See *Trophies* (*supra*, p. 165).

[8] Cf. *Trophies*, II. ii. 1. Other places are mentioned in the Longer Recension.

selves say Glory to thee, Nebuchadnezzar![1] I honour the Cross only as the type of Christ. Nor, though persecuted, do I deny my God. If some Christians have denied, yet not so many as you Jews, who have not been exposed to persecutions and death.[2]

§ 14. If you Jews ask why the prophets did not foretell the coming of our Christ I ask why they did not tell you that you must not believe the mere man Jesus.[3]

§ 15 returns to image-worship, with the retort that in Babylon the Jews worshipped the image of Nebuchadnezzar.[4] In fact you committed all sorts of sins in spite of God's having done so much for you. Moses said Deut. xxxii. 20.

§ 16. Formerly God had mercy on you in your captivity and brought you back from Babylon. But now He has scattered you for six hundred years. Six hundred and seventy years[5] indeed you have had no altar, ark, prophet, or place, nor have you been able to keep the Passover, which was not to be observed outside Jerusalem. What is the sin that has caused all this? It is your treatment of Christ. "But we Gentiles were called by Christ, and serve Him, and glorify Him, together with the Father and the Holy Spirit, for ever and ever, Amen."

The earlier form of the Dialogue ends thus, and suitably. The second chapter of Anastasius has a similar ending.

The Longer Recension adds two more sections, the first (§ 17) expounding Dan. ix. 23–27 and vii. 13 *sq.*, making use, as it seems, of *Quaestio* cxxxvii. 12, but not quoting it verbally until quite the end of the section. The quotation is carried on throughout § 18, which states the reason for the whole discussion, "to rebuke the Jewish hardness of heart and craziness", when Christ has already come for our Salvation in accordance with prophecy.

It cannot be said that the document in itself is particularly interesting. The author does not appear to have had direct knowledge of Judaism, nor to describe a real discussion. He has studied his subject in his library, and the result is comparable to a prize essay.

[1] "Anastasius" (*infra*, p. 177).   [2] See further § 15.
[3] "Anastasius" (*infra*, p. 177).
[4] "Anastasius" (*infra*, p. 177).   [5] *Supra*, p. 170, with note.

VIII. "ANASTASIUS"

Among the works attributed to Anastasius of Sinai (cent. vii) is a *Dissertation against the Jews*.[1] He did indeed write a tract of the same character, but not this one, for its contents differ from what he tells us,[2] and it also speaks of more than eight hundred years as having elapsed since the destruction of Jerusalem,[3] and indeed mentions "these barbarians, the Turks" as holding Persia, which they took in 1038.[4] This tract therefore cannot in its present form have been written before the eleventh century.

The tract is in three parts, besides the additional matter affixed to it.

I. How should one begin argument with a Jew? By asking him the meaning of names in the Old Testament, and showing him their true meaning with reference to Christ. Then tell him that even his own Scriptures say the same as Christians. For to whom was Gen. i. 26 addressed? To angels! Are they then equal with God? The phrase "Let us make" teaches the Jew, as "He made" excludes the polytheism of the Heathen. Again, Gen. ii. 7 refers to the work of the Holy Spirit, of whom the Prophets speak, e.g. Isa. lxi. 1; Joel ii. 28. Even the "Hear, O Israel", etc. tells of the Trinity. Consider the second Psalm, where *v.* 8 implies a wider reign than ever Solomon enjoyed, and *v.* 9 was fulfilled when the Roman Empire was given to Christ. Besides, the overthrow of the Jewish kingdom was foretold. Christ was to be of David's seed, and this is true, for "the Mother of God, the Ever-Virgin Mother of Christ our God" was of the race of David. And David's kingdom was taken away, but Christ's endures for ever (Dan. vii. 13 *sq.*). Perhaps the Jew may argue that this prophecy refers to the future;

---

[1] Διάθεσις κατά 'Ιουδαίων. Migne, *P.G.* lxxxix. 1203–1272, with two additions, coll. 1272–1282. A Latin translation made by a Jesuit father, Francis Turrian, was published in 1603 (without the Greek) in Canisius' *Antiquae Lectiones*, iii. 55 *sqq.*, 123–186. This, however, lacks the beginning of Migne's text, and has some minor differences, but has the same mutilation at the end. It has the same additions, and also a compendium of arguments taken mostly from Chrysostom's *Homilies against the Jews*. On its relation to the *Dialogue of Papiscus and Philo, vide supra*, p. 171. I have noted a very few of the points common to the two documents, or to "Anastasius" and the *Trophies*.

[2] In his *Hexaemeron*, vi (Migne, *P.G.* lxxxix. 933 B). His reference to matter which he has said "in secundo libro adversus Judaeos" is hardly consistent with our col. 1205 B, C.

[3] Contrast *Papiscus and Philo, supra*, p. 170.

[4] Col. 1212 A: τῶν βαρβάρων τούτων τῶν τουρκῶν.

when the Jewish nation will be restored. What! Will God again renew that which He has abolished? Impossible! It is nowhere said that a restoration of the Jews is to be expected after the end of the present course of this world. Or perhaps you Jews expect Elijah to be your Christ (c. 1213 A)? Nay, they cannot be identical. Besides, history as described in Dan. ii. 44 *sq*. shows that Christ must have come.

In c. 1216 B the argument passes to the question of the Divinity of the Christ. He was before the world was created; for David, who was no polytheist, said Ps. cx. 1, and in *v*. 3 He was born before the morning star, which itself was created two days before Adam.[1] But what does it say about the Anointed One whom you Jews expect?[2] Tell me, is he God or mere man like David? The Jew replied, He is to be man, not God, for there is only one God, not two, as the Christians say. Yet, answers the Christian, the Prophets call Him God, and this is the decisive test of our two faiths. See Ps. cxviii. 26 *sq*.; Isa. lxiii. 9; Gen. xlix. 10, and other passages.

Again (c. 1220 D), Christ's own prophecies have been fulfilled,[3] and He is received everywhere, even in Britain. Christians have been persecuted, but the Church has not failed. The sign on the coinage of our Kings is the very sign of Christ Himself.[4] Where are the persecutors, Diocletian and Nero, Vespasian, Herod, and Maximian, and all who slew the martyrs? Christ's promise has held true, "I am with you all the days" (c. 1225 B).

II. The second Discussion (c. 1228 A) begins with the Jewish question, Why did not the Prophets speak clearly about Christ? and the answer is, Because you would have stoned them.[5] But consider Baruch iii. 35–37; Isa. lxiii. 9. Was not Christ's Baptism foretold in Ps. xxix. 3, "on many waters", and His actions and Passion in numbers of texts?

Besides (c. 1233 A), the present condition of heathen worship proves the truth and power of Christ.[6] Are not you Jews ashamed when you call us Christians idolators? If you had your way you would not let one of us live. While you ask, Why did not the

---

[1] Cf. *Troph. Dam.* (*supra*, p. 164); *Papiscus and Philo* (*supra*, p. 172).
[2] Cf. *Trophies*, i. iv. 1.
[3] See *Quaest. ad Ant.* (*supra*, p. 161) and especially *Trophies* (*supra*, p. 163).
[4] *Papiscus and Philo* (*supra*, p. 173).
[5] See *infra*, p. 179: and Tertullian, *Adv. Jud.* x (*supra*, p. 49).
[6] *Papiscus and Philo* (*supra*, p. 173).

Prophets speak plainly about Christ, we may ask in turn, Why did they not warn you against Jesus, if He was really a deceiver?[1]

Then (c. 1233 c) the Jew asks, Why do you Christians make crosses and worship them? The answer is, Why do you Jews worship the Book of the Law, and Jacob Joseph's staff? If you Jews say, We do but worship the power of the words, as Jacob only Joseph who held the staff, so also do we reply in the same sense. We worship the images of Christ and Saints only in the same way that you worship the Cherubim and the Ark.[2]

Again (c. 1235 B), some Christians indeed have denied the Faith, but not so many as you Jews, who worshipped the image of Nebuchadnezzar.[3] You were ungrateful, making the Calf, etc. Yet since you returned from Babylon you have worshipped no idols; what sin then is it which has caused your present state? It is more than eight hundred years since God scattered you throughout all the earth, and brought Titus and Vespasian from Rome against you, who slaughtered you, as Josephus says. So that you have no altar, ark, or place for Passover. The sole reason is that you killed Christ. Hence you are cast out for ever.

III. In the third Discussion (c. 1240 A) the controversy is still hotter. You Jews expect as Messiah a Jew, the Son of David, bringing about the restoration of the Law, the sacrifices, and your race. But the prophecy of Daniel makes it clear that the Christ must have come. For when He comes sacrifice and offering shall be taken away (Dan. ix. 24–27). Besides, Jer. xxxi. 31 *sq.* prophesies a new covenant.

The Jew says (c. 1241 A): You Christians place your hope on a criminal hung on a gibbet! The Christian replies, But you Jews worshipped a brazen serpent! You slew Christ, on the ground that He was a transgressor, and had annulled both the Law and the Sabbath. Yet the Prophets foretold that One should be sold and killed—did they refer to your Christ or to ours? Consider Isa. liii. He (c. 1244 c) was prefigured in the Rock from which the water flowed.[4] As the senseless rock was smitten, so from His dead body flowed blood and water for them that believe on Him, unto eternal life. The Passion (Deut. xxviii. 66)[5] and the earthquake (Ps. xcvii. 4) are foretold.

[1] *Papiscus and Philo (supra,* p. 174).
[2] *Trophies (supra,* p. 163, with note).
[3] *Papiscus and Philo (supra,* p. 174).
[4] *Vide infra,* p. 179.　　　　[5] See Index.

Then (cc. 1245 D, 1248 A) follows a curious passage of uncertain meaning. You Jews have already in your Memoirs[1] what we are now about to say. "For your Fathers wished to change their defeat into victory, and ordered that no Jew should have in writing the acts of Christ or enquire about them or read them, lest this toil should give information to many." But we Christians say this to you who know (the facts), even though you are compelled to hide the truth, in accordance with your custom.

Did not the Magi, he continues, cause witness to be borne to Christ's birth at Bethlehem? Did not John the Baptist witness to Him? And other witnesses were "Nicodemus your ruler, and Nathanael, and Joseph of Arimathaea, and Bizes and Alexander, who also ate with Him at the marriage of Simon the Galilean, whereat He changed the water into wine".[2]

The testimony of Josephus to Jesus is then quoted. But, the author adds, you always did reject God. See Acts vii. 51 *sq*. Read also Ps. xcv. 8–11, speaking of another keeping of the Sabbath, which is the result of faith in Christ. Then follows a long series of quotations from the New Testament. After quoting much of Heb. ii. the author continues (c. 1264 D): "All this is said after the manner

---

[1] ἐν ὑπομνήμασιν, "in commentariis", Turrian, Migne. The meaning of ὑπόμνημα is very doubtful. In *Ex. R.* § 28 the plural is transliterated, with the meaning "public records", "acts" (see Jastrow, p. 31 b). But Turrian seems to have thought of the Midrashim. If the former interpretation be accepted, the passage implies that the Jews possessed official documents describing the life and trial of our Lord. If the latter it is an adumbration of the Dominican appeal in the thirteenth century to the Talmudic writings as confirming Christian doctrine.

[2] "Anastasius", Migne, *P.G.* lxxxix. 1248 B: Λοιπὸν Νικόδημος ὁ ἄρχων ὑμῶν, καὶ Ναθαναήλ, καὶ Ἰωσὴφ ὁ ἀπ' Ἀριμαθίας, καὶ Βιζῆς καὶ ὁ Ἀλέξανδρος, οἱ καὶ συνέφαγον αὐτῷ ἐν τῷ γάμῳ Σίμωνος τοῦ Γαλιλαίου, ἐν ᾧ καὶ τὸ ὕδωρ εἰς οἶνον μετέβαλεν. Βιζῆς. In Canisius, p. 141, *Bizas*. The word is possibly a corruption of ῾Ροῦφος, for there is some tradition that Rufus and his brother Alexander were among the earliest disciples of our Lord (see M. R. James, *The Apocryphal New Testament*, 1924, pp. 194, 458). But the order of the two names is against this (Mark xv. 21), and palaeographists think the change from *Rufus* into *Bizes* very unnatural. Dr R. P. Casey and Dr B. F. C. Atkinson suggest that it is a Thracian word, such as lies at the root of Byzantium. A monk, Maximus, was interned at Bizya in Thrace (Duchesne, *L'Église au VIème siècle*, 1925, p. 456). Βύζας is the name of a Thracian king (Migne, *P.G.* xcii, 649 P). Chrysostom addresses his Ep. lvi to ῾Ρομύλῳ καὶ Βύζῳ, where a number of MSS. read Βίζῳ. In the Paris supplement to the Vatican MS. of the Gelasian sacramentary there is "Thomas qui interpretatur...abysus [i.e. T⁰hôm] didimus" (*J. Th. St.* July, 1926, p. 369). It is doubtless only a curious coincidence that the Aram. *Biza* (ביזא) means a female breast, and thus suggests Thaddaeus.

of men, for He is not our High Priest as God, but as Man; nor did He suffer as God, but as Man. Nor did He learn our affairs by experience, but knows everything clearly as God and the Maker of the world."

In c. 1268 A the author expounds 1 Cor. x. 1–4 in the sense that the sea is Baptism, the cloud is the grace of the Holy Spirit, Moses is the priest, the Rod is the Cross, the passage of Israel means that men are being baptised, the Egyptians are the demons, and Pharaoh is the devil. The rock is the side of Christ.[1] The rock did not really follow, but the grace of Christ did, which made the rock to flow.

After considering Acts xiii, and saying that Israel has not attained righteousness because it sought it by the Law and not by faith (Rom. xi. 8), the treatise comes to a sudden end with Rom. xi. 9 *sq.* The absence of the usual ascription makes it clear that something is missing.

Perhaps it is the consciousness of this that has led to two Additions in the MS. used by Mai, and copied by Migne, of which the first (cc. 1272 D–1274 C) is entitled *A little Dialogue with Jews.*[2] It begins with the question of a Jew, Why do you Christians eat pork? The answer explains the Christian position with regard to foods. God made all things for good use.[3]

The second Addition ("Ετερα 'Ερώτησις) is longer (cc. 1274 D–1282), and is more on the lines of the first Discussion. If a Hebrew says to you, How are you a child of Abraham? say to him, By Faith (Gen. xvii. 5), but you Jews are Amorites by nature (Ezek. xvi. 3). If the Hebrew argues, How can you believe in one who was crucified (Deut. xxi. 23)? ask him, How can you believe in the Brazen Serpent? If he says that Deut. xviii. 15 shows that Messiah is man and not God, reply that Christ's body was like Moses' veil, hiding the Godhead. Remind him that God could not speak clearly about Christ, for the Jews would have burnt the books recording this.[4] In fact, they almost stoned Moses.

Why should you Jews doubt about the Godhead in three Persons in view of Gen. xviii. 3?[5] If you say that the doctrine of the Trinity ought to have been revealed more clearly to Israel, remember the danger of polytheism at that time.[6]

---

[1] *Vide supra*, p. 177.
[2] Διάλογος μικρὸς πρὸς 'Ιουδαίους.
[3] On pork see *Trophies* (*supra*, p. 165).
[4] Cf. *supra*, p. 176.
[5] See Index.
[6] See *Trophies* (*supra*, p. 164).

Again, you say (c. 1280 A) that Christ called Himself man, not God. But if so why did you crucify Him? Do you answer, Because He broke the Law and the Sabbath? Did He? Would you save a beast on the Sabbath, and not a man? You yourselves circumcise a child on a sabbath.

Again, Jeremiah promised a New Covenant, one issuing from Sion. Abraham was justified by faith alone, not by circumcision, and as long as Israel did not mingle with other nations there was no circumcision, but, when they came into Palestine, then we read (Josh. v. 2): "Take knives of stone, and sit down and circumcise the children of Israel."

Here the Fragment ends abruptly.

As a whole, it must be confessed, the treatise is not of much value, but it at least shows that the tradition of composing Dissertations against the Jews was maintained, and that there still remained in the Church a desire to win over to the true faith those who were attached to the Synagogue. If the zeal of Christians then was greater than their knowledge, it was zeal, and if it was zeal for others tempered with the desire to strengthen their own faith it was still worthy of all praise. At the very least, the Monks of old reprove us of to-day who are too often satisfied with a dim perception of the claims of Christianity upon ourselves, and neglect the duty of preaching it to those of our neighbours who are still ignorant of it.

CHAPTER XIX

ANDRONICUS OF CONSTANTINOPLE

A DIALOGUE AGAINST THE JEWS

? A.D. 1310

Our next treatise[1] is sometimes attributed to an Emperor, Andronicus I Comnenus, who reigned at Constantinople A.D. 1183–1185, but, unless a later copyist has adapted the original calculation to his own time, it was composed much later, in A.D. 1310.[2] In any case, a note at the head of the treatise runs: "The doctrinal grace of these discourses,[3] refuting the error of the Hebrews, shows to the faithful the ways of piety. Now I Andronicus wrote it, moved by love, being a nephew of the Roman Emperor of the race of Comnenus, born of my father Sebastocrator to see the sweet light."[4]

The object of the work is thus primarily for Christians, and only indirectly for Jews. Yet Andronicus himself tells us in his Preface that it arose out of discussions about the religion of the Jews, which he had held with certain sophists and students of the [Jewish] Law whom he met at Constantinople, and in Macedonia, and Thessaly.

It is possible that these semi-learned Jews (for he implies that

---

[1] The *Dialogue of Andronicus of Constantinople against the Jews*, Migne, *P.G.* cxxxiii. 791–924, in a Latin translation only. The Greek has never been printed, but exists in at least three MSS., at Vienna, Munich, and Paris. See F. Nau, "La Didascalie de Jacob", in *Patr. Orient.* viii. 737–740 (1912); and K. Krumbacher, *Byz. Lit.* 1897, p. 91.

[2] Ch. xli. *Vide infra*, p. 185.

[3] Ἡ δογματικὴ τῶνδε τῶν λόγων χάρις (*vide* next note). The sense of this appears to be: The theological statements that follow are due to the grace of God given me, and have the effect of grace upon their readers.

[4]
        Ἡ δογματικὴ τῶνδε τῶν λόγων χάρις,
        Τὴν Ἑβραϊκὴν ἐξελέγχουσα πλάνην,
        Τὰς εὐσεβεῖς δείκνυσι τοῖς πιστοῖς τρίβους.
        Ἔγραψα δὲ αὐτὴν Ἀνδρόνικος ἐκ πόθου,
        Ἀδελφόπαις ἄνακτος, Αὐσόνων γένους
        Κομνηνοφυοῦς, ἐκ Σεβαστοκράτορος
        Εἰς γῆν προαχθείς, καὶ γλυκὺ βλέψας φαός.

they were Jews) raised objections which he himself could not easily answer, and that therefore he felt the more moved to study and then to help his brethren. If so, it is to be regretted that he did not take his task more seriously, and learn something about Jewish ways of thinking. For Andronicus shows little acquaintance with Judaism.[1]

The Introduction tells us that certain Jews asked Andronicus to give them information about Christianity, and to tell them his reasons for despising the Jewish religion. He replies that so far from despising it he finds it to be the shadow and figure of salvation, and, on being pressed further, he blames the Jews for two things: first, for breaking the Law and murdering the Prophets, and, secondly, for rejecting the true Light,[2] and even slaying Him. The Jews then urge Andronicus to begin with the first, but to prove it only from their own prophets. "If I prove it," he answers, "will you confess that you are wrong?" "Certainly," they say, "but first remove one objection, How is it that three Gods are honoured by you Christians in view of Ex. xx. 5, 'I am the Lord your God, a jealous God'?"

At this point the first chapter begins. Andronicus urges reverence in speaking about God, for no one has ever seen or known Him as He is, nor even seen His glory. But he adds a summary of the Christian doctrine of the Trinity in the form of a Creed, saying afterwards that all people and Nature herself, and the Law, the mistress of Nature,[3] agree about God the Father who was without beginning, and must have made this universe, just as from hearing a harp we infer the existence of a harpist.

He then meets objections to God having a son, adducing the passages of Scripture ordinarily quoted, being careful to point out, with some attempt at philosophy, that God's revelation does not reveal Him in His true nature, but only in His activity. So the Prophets did not describe the true being of the Holy Trinity, but each as he grasped the truth.[4]

---

[1] On the other hand he is a kindly man and well educated. He has made good use of the *De Pascha* of Gregory of Nazianzum, to whose writings the Editors give many references.

[2] "Meus amor Jesus (for this phrase compare chh. xxi, xxviii) in Evangelio ait, Ego sum Lux et Veritas et Via."

[3] "Ac naturae magistra lex."

[4] "Vates, non puras SS. Trinitatis apparitiones, sed pro suo quisque captu conscripserunt." Chh. iv, v. In ch. iii he had explained why the Old Testament had not spoken more clearly. Cf. *supra*, p. 143.

After the Fall God did not speak directly with men, but suffered them to be raised to the knowledge of Himself by the beauty of His works. You Jews, however, are blinder than your fathers, for you have falsified what is written.[1]

The Jews cry out, "By Moses, who divided the Red Sea with his right hand! All you state is true!" But tell us, who of our Prophets speaks of God begetting God, or of God as begotten?[2] He quotes, in answer, the usual texts, and reminds them that corruption is not necessary to Divine generation. It is like "a word from a mind, or the light from the sun". Then they cry, Thanks be to God; you have proved everything beautifully as regards the Son. Tell us now about the Holy Spirit.[3]

He does so, and then proceeds to give his evidence of hints in Scripture about the Three Persons of the Trinity.[4] For instance, the proposed three days' journey into the wilderness,[5] the three rods peeled by Jacob,[6] the three days of Jonah,[7] Elijah's threefold drenching the sacrifice,[8] and Daniel's prayer three times a day,[9] are all such hints. The passage is interesting for the light it throws on the development of the devout Christian interpretation of the Scriptures, but assuredly the texts are useless for the purpose for which they are introduced. Yet, "True," cry the Jews, "our Fathers busied themselves with the bare letter in vain, and fell into error".

Yet why did God reject us Jews? Because, is the answer, He acts as men deserve,[10] and you could not expect Him to act otherwise with you. For you rejected Him when He became incarnate, as the Prophets foretold.[11] But, say the Jews, prove this from Moses in Genesis or Exodus! Nay, if you do not believe the clearer passages in the Prophets, how will you believe the obscurer in Moses? And if you ask, Why did He not tell us more plainly, I answer that the time had not yet come, and you would have been in danger of spiritual adultery if He had done so.[12]

But, indeed, Scripture is full of references to Christ. See the

---

[1] See Justin's *Trypho*, lxxi. 2 (*supra*, p. 33).
[2] Ch. v, end.   [3] Ch. viii.
[4] Ch. x.
[5] Ex. iii. 18: "Ea, inquam, res Trinitatem innuere mihi videtur!"
[6] Gen. xxx. 37: Poplar, almond, and plane.
[7] Jonah iii. 3.   [8] 1 Kings xviii. 34.   [9] Dan. vi. 10.
[10] Ch. x.
[11] Ch. xi. See Baruch iii. 36 *sq.*; Isa. vii. 14; Prov. i. 24 *sq.*
[12] Ch. xii. Cf. ch. iv.

history of Abraham,[1] of Jacob,[2] of Joseph,[3] Moses and Joshua. "So my dear Jesus, taking the constitution of Adam, led those that trust Him into the heavenly Jerusalem, that is everlasting."[4]

You have answered us, say the Jews, wonderfully well (our writers are always so very pleased with their own efforts!), but what is the reason why the Son of God became man? Andronicus replies, not unfairly and with deeper thought than usual: If you will explain why God created the hosts of heaven, and man, you will also easily know with certainty the reason for the Incarnation. They answer, The former was out of God's kindness. Quite so, replies the Christian, and how much more should He preserve what He had made![5] But why did He not conquer the devil as God? Why need He be man? Because it is more glorious for God to conquer by flesh, than to put forth His power as such. Turn then to Him before it is too late.[6]

When the question is raised, Why did Christ desire to be born of a Virgin? and some texts have been adduced in reply, the Jews answer, It does not seem to us unnatural (*insolens*) that one who is anointed should be called by the Prophets the Servant and the Son of God. For of us Isaiah (really Jer. xxxi. 9) speaks, "Ephraim is My first-born".[7]

More interesting than Andronicus' succeeding quotations of common texts to show the expectation of the Messiah in the Old Testament is his answer to the Jewish question how a Christian can show that the Virgin Mary was of the family of David. For confessedly both the genealogies are Joseph's. Andronicus says that he will prove it not from Christian writings, but from a Jewish

[1] For example, the two servants in the sacrifice of Isaac are Pilate and Herod; the third day is the day of the Resurrection; the wood on Isaac is the cross carried by our Lord; the knife is the soldier's spear; "and they went both of them together", i.e. both Natures in the One Person of Christ (ch. xvi).

[2] The Stone on which Jacob laid his head is Christ (ch. xx), as also is the Stone which covered the well's mouth (ch. xxi). Again (ch. xxi) the Ladder is a type of the Blessed Virgin by whom we are raised from earth to heaven. With reference to Jacob's rolling away the stone, and feeding the flock, Andronicus says: "All this too did my dear Jesus do (atque haec quidem meus amor Jesus)" (Col. 826 D).

[3] Ch. xxiv. The camels with spices, etc. of Gen. xxxvii. 25 hint at Annas and Caiaphas when clothed with their high priestly robes. And, further, camels, which remember injuries more than all other animals, stand here for hatred of the truth.

[4] "Meus amor Jesus, assumpto Adami temperamento, sibi credentes in coelestem et perennem Hierosolymam perduxit" (ch. xxviii).

[5] Ch. xxix. [6] Ch. xxx. [7] Ch. xxxi.

book which he met with in Macedonia at the house of a Jew named Elijah, a scholar in the Law. "Raging against the Virgin Mary, the book asks, Why do Christians extol Mary so highly, calling her nobler than the Cherubim, incomparably greater than the Seraphim, raised above the heavens, purer than the very rays of the sun? For she was a woman of the race of David, daughter of Anna and Joachim who was son of Panther. Now Panther and Melchi were brothers, sons of Levi, of the stock of Matthan, whose father was David of the tribe of Judah." It goes on to speak about the brothers Jacob and Eli in the two genealogies, and about various relations.[1]

Naturally the question of the date of the appearing of Messiah is discussed, and as usual, Gen. xlix. 10 and Dan. ix. 24–27 are considered. The latter passage gives occasion for a remark which incidentally fixes the date of the treatise. "So the desolation of Jerusalem happened in the year of creation 5563; but up to the present time, 6818, the Jews have been in exile all these 1255 years without a kingdom."[2]

Andronicus then turns to the consideration of certain Christian practices. You Jews indeed suppose that our worship of images is idolatry, but you are wrong. After all, "God is marvellous in His saints".[3] Two examples of the awful effect of Jewish irreverence are then given. At Beyrout a Christian left in his house by accident a painting of Christ upon the Cross, and when the house was taken over by a Jew, the picture was put on the ground, spat upon, nailed, and pierced in the Saviour's side, whereon blood and water flowed out. The Jews present were so horrified that they were baptised. The other was in St Sophia at Constantinople. For there is a well there the cover of which was that of the well where the Saviour invited the Samaritan woman to come to Him. Crowds therefore used to come to see it, and to see also the picture of Christ

[1] Chh. xxxvii, xxxviii. Observe that the same passage occurs in *The Teaching of Jacob* (*supra*, p. 156), but the words are not so identical as to make it probable that Andronicus used that treatise. Cf. Nau, p. 738.

[2] Ch. xli. The era of Constantinople is used, according to which the creation of the world was in 5508 B.C. Thus here $5563-5508=55$, and $6818-5508$ $=$A.D. 1310. So also $1255+55=$A.D. 1310. "Igitur accidit Hierosolymae vastitas anno ab orbe condito quinquies millesimo, quingentesimo tertio et sexagesimo: usque ad praesentem vero, sexies millesimum octingentesimum, octavum et decimum: Judaei totis mille ducentis quinque et quinquaginta sine regno exsulant."

[3] Ch. xliii; Ps. lxviii. 35. The Hebrew must mean "holy places". The LXX is ambiguous, but either meaning suits Andronicus' argument.

painted above the east door. But one day a Jew struck the picture
with a knife, and blood flowed out. He threw the picture into the
well with the knife still in it. But it was taken up, and restored to
its proper place with hymns and songs. The Jew and his family
were baptised. The Jews in the Dialogue now confess that the
Christian worship of images is lawful, and compare their own
Cherubims of gold. For "our ancestors, they say, did not worship
the gold but Cherubim, whom they fashioned in order to keep
the Holy of Holies more holy".[1]

Again, Baptism is as necessary for the Christian as crossing the
Red Sea was for the Jews, if these were to be fed with the bread
of Angels.[2]

Again, the Jews ask whether a man is allowed both to believe
in Christ and also to keep the Jewish Law. Christ, is the reply,
said that no one can serve two masters, and, further, "a certain
Philosopher affirms that the Good is not good if you do not perform
it in a good way".[3]

After Andronicus has brought texts forward to show that the
Law must pass away,[4] the Jews ask why Moses should say Lev.
xviii. 5, *Keep My statutes*, etc. The Christian replies: The Law no
doubt is good, but when the Sun of righteousness has arisen, all
the lesser lights are extinguished.[5] But it is said of the Gospel,
*This is the book of the commandments of God, and the Law that endureth
for ever.*[6]

Further, David himself speaks of the spread of the Gospel, when
he says: *In the Churches bless ye God the Lord.*[7] For in the Law of
Moses there was no priest outside the Temple at Jerusalem. "But
now from the rising and the setting of the sun, has the Church been
established. For everywhere are temples, Patriarchs, High Priests,
Priests, and Levites in their multitude; in all villages and towns
alike you may see the unbloody sacrifice ever being offered, and

---

[1] Ch. xliv: "Haud equidem aurum coluerunt, sed Cherubinos, quos ut
sanctius sacrarium cingerent, finxerunt." For this reference to the Cherubim
see *Trophies* (*supra*, p. 163).

[2] Ch. xlv.

[3] Ch. xlvii, end: "Nam et Philosophus quidam bonum censet non esse
bonum, si eo bene non fungare." Who? In Western writers of the twelfth
century *the philosopher* is Plato, but later Aristotle (*Legacy of Israel*, p. 246).

[4] E.g. Jer. xxxi. 31 *sq.*; and Isa. xlii. 9, as it seems, though in the peculiar
form, "vetera fluxerunt, nova quoque ego annuncio" (ch. xlix).

[5] Ch. xlix.   [6] Ch. l; Baruch iv. 1.

[7] Ps. lxviii. 26: "In Ecclesiis benedicite Deo Domino."

the Name of God being praised and honoured throughout the whole wide world."[1]

But where is your Jewish temple to-day? And, if Uzziah was condemned for his profanation, how much more will they be who dare to observe Passover and Feasts outside the Temple at Jerusalem, boasting that they are keeping the Law?[2] The Jews answer, Possibly the keepers of the Law are deceiving us, lest their own privileges be touched.[3]

A curious argument is deduced from Zech. viii. 23, *ten* (Gentile) *men shall take hold*. For these refer to the Apostles. But why only ten instead of twelve? Because Isaiah[4] did not include the two who came from Benjamin and Dan, the former being St Paul, the latter Judas, whose treachery was predicted in Gen. xlix. 17.[5]

Curious also is the argument against the permanence of Circumcision based on the absence of the words *for ever* in Gen xvii. 9, and the use instead of *in their generations*, i.e. as long as you please Me.[6]

The treatise concludes in a nice spirit. We cannot set forth the virtues of God as we ought, for even the angels scarcely do this— see Gregory of Nazianzum in his treatise on the Passover.[7] But we have done what we could. As the poor widow brought her two mites, so have we consecrated to God our study of the truth.[8]

---

[1] Ch. liii.

[2] Ch. liv. Cf. Chrysostom, *Hom. in Jud.* iii. 3, iv. 4 and 6 (*vide supra*, p. 134).

[3] "Et omnino fortasse est, ut nos legis custodes decipiant, ne prerogativa honoris deturbentur" (Col. 894 B).

[4] *Sic*, though Zechariah has been quoted. Similarly in ch. xxxi, Jer. xxxi. 9 is quoted as Isaiah's.

[5] Ch. lv. In ch. lvi the common interpretation of Jer. xi. 19 is given, that the tree refers to Christ's cross, and the bread to Christ Himself, as He says in John vi. 48 sq., *I am the bread which came down out of heaven*.

[6] Ch. lviii. Cf. ch. xiii; "Pseudo-Gregory of Nyssa", xi (*supra*, p. 128).

[7] *Vide supra*, p. 182.

[8] "Nos quidem certe (illius clementia perspecta) veritatis studium, quasi vidua illa duos teruncios, sanctum et sacrum jussimus."

CHAPTER XX

GENNADIUS

c. A.D. 1455

A REFUTATION OF THE ERROR OF THE JEWS FROM SCRIPTURE AND FROM HISTORY, AND A COMPARISON WITH THE TRUTH OF CHRISTIANITY, IN THE FORM OF A DIALOGUE.[1]

Constantinople had fallen (May 29, 1453), the city had been sacked, the Sultan had ridden in victoriously, but no Patriarch had come to do him homage, though he desired to see him and discuss with him questions of religion. He summoned the ecclesiastics and asked the reason. The answer was that the former Patriarch had resigned some months before, and none had been appointed in his room. He gave orders that an election should be made at once, and the unanimous choice fell on Georgius Scholarius, who took the name of Gennadius. The Sultan received him with the ritual that was usually paid to a Patriarch, and sent him with guards of honour to the palace allotted to his use. But Gennadius soon moved to the monastery of the Blessed Virgin (Panmakista). After five years he resigned his Patriarchate, and withdrew to a monastery in Serrae in Macedonia, where he lived till his death, about 1468.

He was a learned man, who had been on the Greek commission at the Council of Florence (A.D. 1439) and had taken part in the controversy with the Bishop of Rome, and had written several theological works. He had also long since taken some interest in the controversy with Jews, for he had not only composed a summary of the doctrines and laws of the Christian faith to be found in

---

[1] Ἔλεγχος τῆς Ἰουδαϊκῆς [πλάνης ἔκ τε τῆς γραφῆς] καὶ ἐκ τῶν πραγμάτων [καὶ πρὸς τὴν χριστιανικὴν ἀλήθειαν παράθεσις] ἐν σχήματι διαλόγου. The only text published is the edition by A. Jahn (Leipzig, 1893) with introduction and notes. He tells us (p. xiv sq.) that he had some correspondence with Migne about its being included in *Patrologia Graeca*, but that although many of Gennadius' writings may be found there (vol. clx) Jahn's offer was not accepted. Apparently Migne drew the line very strictly at the year 1453. The title is barely legible in the MS. chiefly followed by Jahn, but the words in brackets, though supplied from elsewhere, are undoubtedly genuine. Unfortunately Jahn made no division into sections, so that one can refer only to the folios of the MS., which are much shorter than Jahn's pages.

the New Testament, but had also compiled a list of the chief passages in the Old Testament which foretold the coming of Christ and proved the truth of the Christian religion. Now, however, while he was still at Constantinople,[1] or possibly during one of his compulsory later visits there (Jahn, p. vii *sq.*)—for he tried in vain to lay his hands on a book that had been lost in the sack of the city[2] though he had been able to save his own writings—he issued in more thorough and deliberate form a treatise which should at once strengthen wavering Christians against the arguments of Jews,[3] and enable them even to carry the war into the enemies' camp and win them to Christ.

The present treatise (*c.* A.D. 1455) is the result of his efforts, and is, as it would seem, the last of the Greek *Apologiae* which have come down to us. It considers the question with some degree of originality, and is not without some value for us to-day. For Gennadius is not here concerned with the usual "Messianic" passages of Scripture as such—his earlier compilation had dealt sufficiently with them, and he now only adds it as an Appendix— but endeavours conscientiously to show the mistaken position of the Jews and to meet the difficulties they feel.

To be sure, he shows no knowledge of Judaism in the strictest sense of the word. Nor was this likely. For he was a monk until he was Patriarch, and could have had but little first-hand acquaint- ance with Jews, and during his short Patriarchate it is quite unlikely that he would come in contact with the more learned of them—who were generally not blessed with worldly goods—but only with the more prosperous, such as merchants and semi-political leaders. Gentlemanly and courteous and orthodox they might be, and evidently were, but quite ignorant of Rabbinic learning. Similarly Justin Martyr presents to us only a Trypho, though Justin knew enough to have discussed Jewish matters with R. Tarphon. Gennadius had no such knowledge, and does not pretend to ascribe it to either of his puppets, the Jew or the Christian.

Gennadius then is no mere collector of "proof-passages". If a few occur in his treatise it is because they can hardly be avoided. For his purpose is quite different. This is to show, first, that the Jews of his time are not true Jews, for they act not in accordance with, but contrary to, the teaching of Moses, and, secondly, that the facts of history make it plain that God is still displeased with them, the only valid reason for this displeasure being their con-

[1] *Infra*, p. 197.   [2] *Infra*, p. 195.   [3] *Infra*, p. 202.

tinued rejection of the Lord Jesus Christ. The Epilogue says, as is to be expected, that the Jew is convinced by the arguments of the Christian, and, after study of the further documents which he is to receive from the author, evidently hopes to be baptised.

Shall we discuss our differences, says the Christian?[1] Certainly, replies the Jew, but in a simple way, for we have no leisure for mere reasoning. But we need somewhat full statements, not so much of doctrines as of facts. You are right, says the Christian. Now, are you a Jew? Of course, is the reply. No, you are not! Even though Jerusalem and its neighbourhood were formerly called Judaea, it is not called so now, and you do not come from there. You may be a Bithynian, an Ephesian, a Byzantine, or a Thessalian.

That makes no difference, retorts the Jew; I am a Jew by race, religion, and language. Never mind language, replies the Christian. I know Latin, but am not therefore a Latin. Nor would I call myself even a Greek, because my opinions are not such as the Greeks once held. I prefer to be named from my chief glory, and if any ask me what I am, I shall answer, I am a Christian. But you mean that you call yourself a Jew because you follow Moses? "Certainly." But, replies the Christian, you do not follow Moses; you are against him, and therefore you are not a Jew. On the Jew's emphatic insistence that he is, for he believes and obeys Moses, the Christian proceeds to defend his assertion.

He points out[2] that *the Lord said unto Moses, I will raise them up a prophet from among their brethren, like unto thee; and I will put My word in his mouth, and he shall speak to them according to what I command him* (Deut. xviii. 18). And he adds[3] that Moses declared (ἐξεῖπε) to the people of the Jews: *The Lord God will raise up a prophet from among our brethren like me, and every soul that will not hear that prophet shall be destroyed* (Deut. xviii. 15, 19). Yet you disbelieve Him whom Moses foretold, and therefore you disobey Moses.

You argue, however, continues the Christian, that that Prophet has not yet come, but will come later. The former is unreasonable, the latter impossible. He surely has come already, because, in the first place, He was expected to come soon (and not at the end of the world), as Deut. xxxiv. 10 (written after Moses' death) suggests to us: *There hath not arisen as yet in Jerusalem one like Moses, whom the Lord knew face to face.* And, in the second place,[4] Jews who did not believe Him were to be destroyed, so that He certainly came before

---

[1] f. 125 r.   [2] f. 126 r.
[3] f. 126 v.   [4] f. 127 v.

they were destroyed at the Fall of Jerusalem. I do not say[1] the Jews crucified Jesus, but disregarded Him, as Moses said. Not even Pilate wished to crucify Him, but the people were persuaded by the High Priests and Pharisees, because Jesus always seemed burdensome to them. For He would have led them away from sin, and the whole Jewish people by their means, and the rest of the nations from demon worship and polytheism, leading them to the one God. But they refused to accept the Divine message. So the Jews perished, but the whole world was saved spiritually, turning from error, true "philosophy" thus winning the day.

Further, it is impossible that the Prophet of whom Moses spoke can come hereafter. For the Jews cannot be gathered to Jerusalem again,[2] not merely because of the arrangements (θέσεις) of us Christians, but because although the length of former captivities and the release from them were clearly foretold, in the present case the severity was foretold, but no limit was fixed.[3] See Dan. ix. 27.[4] This was confirmed by the failure of the attempts made by Jews to restore the city and to rebuild the Temple, in the time of Hadrian, Constantine the Great, and Julian. It was God who was at the back of all human opposition to it, and even though Julian helped the Jews,[5] yet he was powerless against God.

To-day two religions divide the world, Christianity and Mohammedanism, and as long as the latter rules Egypt and Palestine your hope is powerless. And[6] if ever Christians gain possession of Jerusalem—which seems unlikely—the Jews will be no better off, and certainly will not be able to conquer both Mohammedans and Christians. You cannot therefore expect the coming of Messiah. So that,[7] unless the word of God has failed, Moses must refer to Jesus, and therefore do I say to you that you are opposing Moses, and are not even a Jew. But I will give you other proofs.[8]

Yet, argues the Jew, are you yourself satisfied with this interpretation of Moses' words? Yes, indeed! No, you are not, continues the Jew, for Moses said *a Prophet*, and you Christians call him not a Prophet, but "Son of God" and "God", and there is much difference between "God" and "Prophet", between "Servant" and "Master". We Jews therefore are right.[9]

---

[1] f. 128 v.   [2] f. 129 v.
[3] Cf. Chrysostom, *Hom. c. Jud.* v. 1 and 11 (*supra*, p. 135).
[4] f. 130 r.
[5] f. 131 r. Cf. Chrysostom, *Hom. c. Jud.* v. 11 (*supra*, p. 134).
[6] f. 131 v.   [7] f. 132 r.   [8] f. 132 v.   [9] f. 133 r.

We grant the goodness of your disposition, says the Christian, and I have good hope that this discussion will be for your profit, for you are not prejudiced as too many Jews are. But[1] examine the case of our Jesus. It is not a question of what a man's claims may be, or of what people think about him, but whether his course of action, his message, and life fit Moses' words. We[2] ourselves should have believed Jesus for His deeds only, but to those who reject Him we add Moses' testimony. Jesus, at any rate, has, even as Prophet, turned the whole earth from demon-worship, so that[3] if you only acknowledge Him as Prophet you, as a wise man, will receive what He tells us of His relation to God the Father. For it is not possible that He, being such as He was, should tell lies about Himself.

We grant also,[4] adds the Christian, that Moses was a very great man. Every one honours him, for the Law he gave, the wisdom he brought from the Egyptians, and the miracles that he wrought. Diodorus a Greek says that he was called "God" among the Jews.[5] Pharaoh[6] and the Egyptians treated Moses as a god (Ex. vii. 1), even as Nebuchadnezzar worshipped Daniel (Dan. ii. 46); so easily did polytheists make men gods. For this reason Moses thought it enough to show the majesty and divinity of Him who was to come by calling Him a Prophet. At the same time he hinted that He should be greater than the ordinary prophets, for He was to be a Lawgiver like Moses himself, namely to improve men's doctrines and ethics and "speak" to men from God, and thus be greater than Moses.[7] Further, Moses' Law could not conquer human hindrances, but the Law to be given by the One to come would be able to do so, being a guide to the Divine will, not to the Jews only, but to all others. Further,[8] while it was necessary that Moses should not be altogether ignorant of such a new dispensation, it was also necessary that he should not know it in detail. And,[9] even if he had thus known it, it would not have been suitable that he should portray it thoroughly. For this was unnecessary, and, besides, the Jews would not have received it. Suppose Moses had

---

[1] f. 133 v.
[2] f. 134 v. Cf. Origen, *c. Celsum,* i. 45 (*supra,* p. 82).
[3] f. 135 r.   [4] f. 136 r.
[5] Gennadius had a corrupt text of Diodorus, who, speaking of the reverence paid to Mneva (not Moses) by the Egyptians, also said that Moses called upon Jaho ('Ιαώ) as God (Diod. Sic. i. 94).
[6] f. 136 v.   [7] f. 137 r.
[8] f. 138 r.   [9] f. 139 v.

written details of the Incarnation (the Humanity and yet the full
Deity of Christ), His life and crucifixion and resurrection, and the
consequent punishment of the Jews, would they not only have
revolted against Moses and slain him, as one trying to deceive
them and their descendants?[1] Besides,[2] if everything about Christ
had been so clearly and definitely stated by Moses this would have
been equivalent to moral compulsion to believe in Christ. He did
not, therefore,[3] call Him God, but only Prophet, for this was
sufficient for those who were willing to fit the events with the
prophecies—those events and Jesus' life being far more wonderful
than the things of Moses.

The later Prophets,[4] however, did speak of various details about
Christ, which we will set before you if you like. Or does what I
have said seem to you improbable?

I do not say that, replies the Jew, but I cannot agree with your
statements right away.[5] But I should be glad if you would fulfil
your promise of showing me by other arguments that I was acting
in contradiction to the Law of Moses.

Certainly, and I can do so quite briefly. For Moses so attached
the ritual details to the Temple that to try to perform them elsewhere is to sin. The Exiles in Babylon recognised this, looking
forward to the promised Return. But[6] as there is no prophecy of
Return from the present Exile, and as there is no room left for
fresh prophets—for of their three duties, guidance in keeping the
Law, insistence on Repentance to remove punishment, and the
proclamation of God's care for the whole human race, the first
two are out of date, and the last has been accomplished by Christ.
Thus John the Baptist was the last prophet, and he proclaimed
that the Promised One had come. With this[7] a calculation of dates
from Dan. ix. 24–27 agrees. Yet[8] to-day the Jews dare to transgress
the Law by singing, and pretending to sacrifice (ὑποθύοντες), and
praying, though they are in a foreign land.

Besides,[9] what use is Circumcision? Abraham was guided by
God to use it, but only as a temporary drug (ὥσπερ τι φάρμακον
πρόσκαιρον), and a sign to differentiate Jews from Gentiles.
Circumcision of the heart ought to have been sufficient, but now

---

[1] Cf. *Trophies* III. viii. 3 (*supra*, p. 165).
[2] f. 141 v. [3] f. 142 r. [4] f. 142 v.
[5] f. 143 r. [6] f. 144 v.
[7] f. 145 v. Gennadius here refers to Philo and Josephus (cf. *infra*, p. 203).
[8] f. 146 r. [9] f. 147 r.

Jews are worse than Gentiles. It is not circumcision that now prevents the fullest intercourse between Jews and Christians, much less between Jews and Mohammedans. If Moses and the Prophets could rise, they would say, Children?[1] is it not even as we said? In the hardness of your hearts you think only about your synagogues and your actions and words there, though the time for these is gone. Have you any objections to make?

The Jew answers, You seem to me not far from the mark, but I do not understand God's former special goodwill towards us, and our present misery. So I ask, First, Can God change, as men's legislation changes? Secondly,[2] Is it in accordance with His equity (ἐπιείκεια) to repel those who follow His lesser laws when they are not in a position to keep the greater?

To this the Christian replies: What I have already said ought to have removed your difficulty, but I will repeat myself. The Deity does not change, but original sin had weakened human nature, so that it could not keep the original law of God. God therefore[3] renewed this Law by preparation for it through Moses, and by the perfecting through Jesus, or, as we may say, by Himself and not a man. The Law of Jesus therefore does not overthrow the Mosaic Law, but rather perfects it, kindling in us afresh the spark of the Natural Law, as is clear from the Gospel teaching, and from the lives of the Disciples and their successors. Men crucify the flesh, living in wildernesses to purge themselves from temptations and to arrive at the love of God. Jesus[4] prayed for those who sinned in ignorance, and during the forty years before the prophecies of the destruction of Jerusalem were fulfilled His power was magnified, and He drew the whole world towards Him. But[5] the present unbelieving Jews are more to blame than ever.

What say you, O Jew, for I will still call you by this name, because you seem to me to show yourself a true Jew, not ignorant of the pearls that lie in the Book of Moses and of the other Prophets?

The Jew. If your argument is sound God has indeed acted wisely and with forethought, but you will confer a great favour on me if you will tell me three things: first, making the order of the laws plainer, and the way of salvation; secondly, setting forth plainly the Law of Jesus which you call the Evangelical Law, for though we have met with your Gospels there is very little of such a Law there, put out strictly, for it is difficult to be summarised, being interrupted

---

[1] f. 150 r.   [2] f. 151 r.   [3] f. 152.
[4] f. 153 v.   [5] f. 154 v.

by so much narrative; thirdly, setting forth in order the prophecies about Christ.

Yet all this can be referred to another meeting, if it please you to grant us one. But I would now ask, Why have you Christians suffered not less than we, and almost all your sacred things have perished (i.e. in the sack of Constantinople)?

The Christian.[1] I thank God you do not contradict what I have said. As to your first two questions, I long since made a compilation of the Evangelical laws and wrote an account of the one way of man's salvation.[2] These I will send you to-morrow together with the answer to your third question, a collection of the sayings of the Prophets about Christ, which we have drawn up with a view both to our own confirmation in the faith, and to the confutation or persuasion of the Jews.[3]

I am grieved[4] that though I have made much search (f. 159 r) I cannot send you also a book that has been lost in the sack of the city containing the forecasts (προαγορεύσεις) about Christ spoken by the Sibyls and the Oracles in Delphi and Daphne, which were all collected in one volume written out from very old books. For I wish you to know that there have been many wise prophetesses, the Erythraean, the Cumaean, and others, nine in all, called Sibyls, "and Sibyl means the counsel of God" (θεοβούλη). For they spoke especially about the mystery of Jesus. There are also oracles of the Greeks, given (though inspired by demons) that the Greeks might have witness from their own country, and be more ready to accept the truth. They were the means of the conversion of the great king Constantine (together with the miraculous signs vouchsafed to him), and of the wiser of those who were in Greece. For when the Apostles came there the signs at the Passion had prepared all the wise men in Greece, and some who were still alive were baptised, and showed their faith by their writings, e.g. Hierotheus[5] and Dionysius, both leaders in the Areopagus.

But[6] I must pass on to your question about the present sufferings of us Christians.[7]

---

[1] f. 156 r.

[2] The titles of these are, *Concerning the worship of God, or The Evangelical Law in Epitome,* and, *Concerning the only way towards man's salvation* (see Jahn's note *in loco*).

[3] This is the *Delectus Prophetiarum de Christo,* which Jahn has printed immediately after the *Refutation* (*vide infra,* p. 202).   [4] f. 157 r.

[5] See F. S. Marsh, *The Book of the Holy Hierotheus,* 1927, p. 234 *sq.*

[6] f. 159 r.   [7] *Vide supra.*

Notice, however, first that the Jews also expect the conversion of the world, though they differ from us as regards the time of this. Greeks also long for it, but not those of to-day. For some follow the silly talk of Pletho[1] and try to revive heathenism. But the older Greeks believe this to be the seventh and last millennium, in which the world will be destroyed by a flood of fire from the sky. Daniel (ix. 24–27), John[2] the Divine (Apoc. vi. 12 *sq.*), and Paul,[3] the blessed Disciples of Christ, and Christ's own sayings (Matt. xxiv. 3, 29 *sqq.*) confirm this. We know not the exact time, but wickedness is to increase, with persecution.

As to our present sufferings, they are but partial, and most Christians are free from them. So that Jews can find no argument in this. And again, Christians may suffer because they sin against the laws of Jesus, and in any case they willingly bear all things for Christ. Jews[4] indeed toil in business and have but earthly aims, losing the gain, but the hope of Christians is sure. The contest of our faith now being carried out in us Christians is not due to the fact that we are worse than other Christians, but to the fact that we are better, i.e. more exact in our opinions. For such are they who belong to the Eastern Churches by common consent; for even those who differ from us in doctrine do not think we break away from them through evil motives, but because we do not wish to communicate with those who overstep the mark in some section of the common faith. God will reward the more particular and persevering, and will judge those who by their actions darken the gifts of the faith, some more lightly[5] because of the greatness of their trials on behalf of the faith, or because of their lack of opportunity of learning. For Providence always acts reasonably.

Then Gennadius turns to glorify the Eastern Church. For it was in Asia that the Preparation by Moses was first given, and there also the utterly perfect Law was sown and rooted, and after much toil burst into flower. There too was the blood of the martyrs first shed, there the army of the faith was tested, and the soldiers of Christ gained their victory and garlands. It was there that the assaults of heretics came, and the conquests over them were won. There, too, after these had ceased, were the wars voluntarily under-

[1] Georgius Pletho, a Byzantine writer, *c.* 1400.
[2] f. 160 v.
[3] Perhaps a mistake for Peter, Acts ii. 19 *sq.*
[4] f. 162 r.
[5] f. 162 v.

taken against demons and passions in the mountains by those who could not bear to live outside the warfare for Christ, and, for this reason, chose a voluntary crucifixion in their flesh and its lusts (as we said before),[1] and entered on the philosophy according to Christ, living in it continuously until their holy departure from the body. But[2] I count this city (Constantinople)[3] and its neighbourhood as belonging to Asia, not only because the sea that separates is so narrow, but also because it shares in its former warfare and victory, and stands out first not only of Asia but of all the earth. In this land therefore was it necessary that the last trials and conquests should take place before the Second Coming of Christ. So then we have confidence, and hope of the victors' crown. For in us is the freedom of the spiritual Law, which binds us not with songs and places and carnal and temporary sacrifices. For our worship needs no priests, or incense, or slaughter of beasts, or blood, or smoke, but our souls' approach to God in broken heart and humble spirit. Of this worship, whether of our fathers in the deserts, or of those who live apart (ἰδιάζοντες) in the cities, the violence of our masters (i.e. the Mohammedan conquerors) cannot deprive us.[4]

But the Jews[5] oppose all Scripture and all else that would lead them to fuller light, and slander the Saviour, adducing impossible arguments that what Moses foretold has not taken place, and still more impossible dreams that this will take place in the future. And they renew the old disobedience of their common fathers in their own persons with this great addition, that they not only flee from His rule and hide themselves from it even as they did, but with still more daring shame exile themselves from both the material paradise,[6] together with those their common fathers, and also from the spiritual and mystical paradise, together with the leaders of the second and worse transgression of the soldiers of Christ.[7] And thus they deprive themselves of the Divine Love, and shall be deprived for ever.

---

[1] *Vide supra*, p. 194.   [2] f. 163 r.
[3] Observe where Gennadius is writing; *supra*, p. 189.
[4] Gennadius himself had obtained the concession of Christian worship from the Sultan Mohammed II (Jahn, p. xv).   [5] f. 164 v.
[6] Gennadius refers to such sensuous descriptions of Paradise (*Gan Eden*) current among mediaeval Jews as may be found in the *Jew. Enc.* ix. 516 *sq.* Whether, however, these were intended to be understood literally is doubtful. Cf. Omar Khayyám and even Rev. xxi *sq.*
[7] Presumably Christian heretics.

If[1] you believe the Gospel and gladly receive the symbol of this faith, and enter the holy shrine, then the Mother of the faithful, the Church, will nourish and feed you, and you will then be a real disciple of Moses and the Prophets, as we are, numbered with the choir of those that sing with them.

But I would first ask you some questions arising out of our conversation.

The Jew. Pray ask them.

The Christian. Do they who believe one who says he has come from God as a Lawgiver, and promise to obey his legislation, and then transgress it, one in one detail and one in another, commit sin against God?

The Jew. Yes, and Jews acknowledge God, and when they know they commit sin are eager to make satisfaction and repentance.

The Christian. And it is agreed that when any have received a Law as from God, they all either regard it[2] alike or are alike careful in keeping it?

The Jew. No. For, in order that the sayings of the Law may be comprehended, expositors and teachers are appointed in the nation, to elucidate to the simpler minded the aim of the Law, and to destroy the errors of those who regard it differently, by the vote and common consent of the wiser in the nation, and punishments are set for transgressors according to their transgression.

The Christian. I congratulate you on your excellent reply.

The Jew. But would it be possible for God to compel all in the nation to the knowledge of the Law and the fulfilment of it?

The Christian. Possible, no doubt, if He would. But He cannot wish it, for this is impossible for human nature, so long as it is human nature, possessing free will. And is not this even more true in the case of many greater nations which are given a Law than in that of one, and with regard to a Law that is more difficult to apprehend and more difficult to be observed?[3]

This will account for the differences of opinion among Christians about our Jesus, because of the greatness of the mystery concerning Him, and because of human weakness, or even in some persons the mere love of contention, especially in the early days of our faith. And traces of these still remain, yet all Christians are ready to die for Christ. But such differences of opinion and failure in

---

[1] f. 165 r. [2] f. 165 v.

[3] f. 166 r. He seems to mean that it would be worse to compel the many nations than only the one (Israel).

obedience cannot be attributed to the faith concerning Jesus, and to His laws. For it cannot be otherwise so long as men have free will. Not that the mind willingly gives place to falsehood, but it is deceived by the will, which is itself deceived by what has the appearance of truth, or grasps it by sensation only and not by reason, or accepts it through the high estimation in which it holds its teachers.

But now let us consider point by point the work of Jesus, both what He Himself achieved by placing men in a proper faith concerning God, and what is still being achieved in those who believe His Law to be divine.

I ask you therefore:[1] Is it not true that while the whole world was ungodly and polytheistic the Jewish nation alone was truly religious, small though it was? And in this chaos of the human race could God have proposed anything greater or more worthy of Himself than to draw the whole world unto true religion, and unto Himself their Creator and Master, and to open to them the door of eternal life, though it had been rightly shut, but now able to be opened only by His uttermost love for man, as indeed it will be?

Yes, answers the Jew, and such a re-creation would in some ways be greater than the first.

The Christian. Moses failed,[2] but through the proclamation of Jesus the world, orthodox and unorthodox, and even false believers (i.e. Mohammedans), believe in one God, and polytheism and idolatry are gone, while the doctrine of the Incarnation together with all it implies bears fruit in all the earth. Is all this true?

The Jew. Yes, as regards the cessation of polytheism and the belief in the unity of God.

The Christian. Now could all this be expected from a mere man, however good he might be? Was[3] the conversion of the world a merely human work? If Moses was believed on by Jews for the comparatively little that he accomplished, how much more should Jesus be? For Moses prepared for Him. Is not His Divinity shown by the Prophets? Was He not to be the expectation of the Gentiles (Gen. xlix. 10), the King who would reign for ever (Zech. ix. 9)?

Yet some say[4] that Jesus never called Himself the Son of God. But that statement is easily disproved from the sayings in the Gospels. And again, that He only called Himself son of God by *Grace*, as all who live according to God may be called sons of God.

[1] f. 167 r.   [2] f. 168 r.   [3] f. 169 r.   [4] f. 170 r.

If He snatched (ἥρπαζεν) such glory to Himself, when it did not belong to Him, would it have been possible for Him to have been so much loved by God, and accounted worthy of so much glory, and to have accomplished so much, and all of it in accordance with the Divine will and the Divine honour, etc.?[1]

What think you of all this?[2] We have said nothing about His miracles, but bring our defence of Him solely from the results of the work of His disciples and later followers.

The Jew. I have no reply to make as a Jew, but I would ask you—

The Christian. Nay, wait a moment. Is it right[3] for a good and wise master not to exceed the measure of the sins when he is punishing them? Assuredly, says *the Jew*. Or, adds *the Christian*, to punish his servants, or children, furiously when they are obeying him?

The Jew. God forbid!

The Christian.[4] Did not your Fathers think they were doing right when they crucified Jesus, and do not you agree with them, and believe you are showing great piety in sharing that piety of your Fathers?

The Jew. Jews certainly think so.

The Christian. Where then is the Divine righteousness? For God punished the Jews when they committed idolatry, etc., and yet forgave them—but when they performed the greatest possible act of piety (as they supposed) God smote them. And their (supposed) piety and their punishment continue still! Where are God's wisdom, goodness, and righteousness? The Jews still exhibit the same "piety" towards the followers of Jesus. And,[5] besides, the Jews are more particular than ever in respect of ethics, not quarrelling, but acting honestly, caring for their widows and orphans, loyal to the State, etc. Yet they receive this bitter and toilsome life from God, and not for three years (as in the time of Elijah), nor seventy (as in Babylon), nor four hundred (as in Egypt), but for more than fourteen hundred years, being scattered throughout the world! This must surely be for some great act of impiety that they have committed, or (as in fact it is) for what the Jews thought and still think to be an act of piety, their treatment[6] of the Saviour.

But this shall be the end of our discussion with the Jews, and the completion of my present argument with you.

[1] Gennadius almost rises here to eloquence.   [2] f. 171 r.
[3] f. 171 v.   [4] f. 172 r.   [5] f. 173 r.   [6] f. 174 r.

The Jew. I thank you indeed, and, as I said at first,[1] when I expressed the hope that it was not without God that this good fortune happened to us, I have now in fact learned that it is so. When therefore you have sent me those compilations,[2] and I have studied them, and have prayed God earnestly that the opinion about the truth, which has already made its home within me, may be still more confirmed, I will visit you soon, that with your assistance I may receive the pledge of faith in Christ. For I can no longer support the doctrine of my Fathers, shaken as it has been by your wisdom in so many proofs. Nor have I any more to say against the mystery of Christ, strengthened as it is by so much evidence.

I have indeed met many Christians ere this who tried to use our Jewish prophecies in order to pull down the opinion of the Jews, with regard to which prophecies Jews have contrived many answers (as I formerly[3] used to suppose), but, as I now see clearly from the nature of your enquiry, should rather be called excuses.

But the manner of your arguments is so concise and attractive, and leads so straight to the knowledge of the truth, as to persuade not Jews only, but every one who holds erroneous opinions, and not him only, but also to confirm one who is of the household of the faith, not about the difference between Jews and Christians alone, but in fact about all the wise and wholesome doctrine about God in all respects.

But I pray you to write down what has now been said—for you will be able to recall it to memory—and adding those other things,[4] to send them together, especially the portion about the only way to man's salvation. For in the former, I think, that, helped by the grace of Jesus, and having learned this way first from your wisdom, and then using your second compilation about the Gospel Law as a kind of stay or weapon, I shall not miss the end.

The Christian. I will do so. And may our Lord Jesus work with both of us, until I see you receive happily the pledge of faith in Him, and of access by Him unto our God and Father. So let us glorify the Divine grace. Farewell, my very thoughtful Friend.[5]

---

[1] See f. 150 v.
[2] *Supra*, p. 195 and *infra* and Appendix, p. 202.
[3] f. 174 v.
[4] The present Appendix.
[5] ἔρρωσο, φρονιμώτατε.

APPENDIX TO GENNADIUS' REFUTATION

A Selection of Prophecies about Christ[1]

The Greek inscription is, "The clearest prophecies about the Lord Jesus Christ are here set forth, there being very many in all the books of the Prophets."[2]

These few pages form the collection to which Gennadius refers two or three times in his *Refutation*,[3] and although it contains nothing that is new for our purpose it is worth noticing so far as to give an indication of its contents. It professedly does not attempt to give more than the more salient of the many prophecies about our Lord, and it will be sufficient to mention only some even of these. He gives[4] Gen. xlix. 10; then Micah v. 2 *sq.*, where he says that the phrase *whose goings forth are from the beginning of eternity* cannot refer to Zerubbabel (born in Babylon during the Exile), as the Jews affirm,[5] contrary to the belief of their forefathers, Matt. ii. 4–6.[6] Among other passages are Ps. cx. 3; Isa. liv. 1; ii. 1–4; vii. 13 *sq.*, which he examines at some length,[7] asking where was the sign to Ahaz if the mother was married, and the child was Hezekiah, and further, why should he be called Emmanuel? A Virgin could be called νεᾶνις, as Deut. xxii. 25 *sq.* shows (for Gennadius plainly knew no Hebrew), and also 1 Kings i. 3 *sq.* And who ever called Hezekiah Emmanuel? And could a mere man reject evil and choose the good before he even knew good and evil? But the King of Assyria[8] (i.e. the Devil) was taken as spoil by the Son of Mary. Isa. ix. 6 *sq.* is also discussed. For He is God who made the world, to whom was said Gen. i. 26; and of Him also *by the Word of the Lord were the heavens established*, as David said (Ps. xxxiii. 6); and as Adam was father of the present age, so shall He be of that which is to come, as the Apostle says: *If any man be in Christ he is a new creation, the old things passed away, behold, all things have become new.*[9]

And He is called *Prince of Peace*, and *Mighty God*, which in Jewish is Elgeb Môr (ἤλγεβ μῶρ, i.e. *él gibbór*), and He came and set up the throne and kingdom of David. But then they will not call Him Emmanuel, for they shall call Him Jesus, as it says *Thou shalt call*[10] both then and now, instead of *Call* (imperative).

---

[1] *Delectus Prophetiarum de Christo* (Jahn, pp. 56–68).

[2] Ἐκ τῶν περὶ τοῦ ἰησοῦ χριστοῦ προφητειῶν αἱ σαφέστεραι ἐνταῦθα ἐτέθησαν, πλείστων οὐσῶν ἐν πᾶσι τοῖς τῶν προφητῶν λόγοις.

[3] *Supra*, pp. 189, 195.   [4] f. 175 r.   [5] f. 175 v.

[6] The Talmudic Jews in general interpreted these verses in Micah as referring to the coming of Messiah. See Strack-Billerbeck, iv. 860. So also the Targum, Rashi, Aben Ezra, Kimchi. But Theodoret says that the Jews of his time referred Micah v. 2. to Zerubbabel, and Grotius maintained that this was the true meaning (*vide* Poole's *Synopsis* on Micah v. 2).   [7] f. 176 r.

[8] Isa. viii. 4. Cf. *Trypho*, lxxviii. 9 (*supra*, p. 41).

[9] 2 Cor v. 17.   [10] Isa. vii. 14; καλέσεις LXX.

Then Gennadius expounds Isa. lii. 6–10, 13–liv. 1 at some length;[1] and then Jer. xxxviii. 31–36, also rather fully; adding Isa. x. 22 (= Rom. ix. 27), on which he says that the Remnant is the Apostles with those Israelites who received the word through them, namely, the 3000 and the 5000 of Acts ii. 41; iv. 4. And the passage tells us that all shall know God, as He shines like the sun on all, moving towards Himself the hearts of all, wise and unlearned, private persons and rulers, slaves and free, small and great, by faith alone, and baptism the pledge of faith, and repentance for past sins, enlightened at once by the light of the knowledge of God—all this is clear in the utterance of the Prophet, and this prophecy is the clearest of all about the Law of the Gospel.

So also did Gabriel appear and say to Daniel ix. 23–25, 27.

With a discussion of the chronology indicated by this passage, including a reference to Philo[2] as confirming Gennadius' statements, the *Selection* comes to an end.[3]

[1] ff. 177 v–180 r.
[2] Cf. the *Refutation*, f. 145 v (*supra*, p. 193).
[3] ff. 181 v–182 v.

BOOK IV

SPANISH WRITERS

LITERATURE COVERING THE WHOLE PERIOD

1. JOSEPH JACOBS. *An Inquiry into the Sources of the History of the Jews in Spain.* 1894.
2. JOSEPH JACOBS. The article *Spain* in the *Jewish Encyclopedia*, 1905.
3. DON JOSE AMADOR DE LOS RIOS. *Historia social, politica y religiosa de los Judios de España y Portugal*, 1875.
4. H. GRAETZ. *Geschichte der Juden von den ältesten Zeiten bis auf die Gegenwart*, vols. IV–VIII, 2nd edition, 1871–1875.

CHAPTER XXI

EARLY SPAIN TO THE MOHAMMEDAN
CONQUEST

A.D. 711

The relativity of moral values is nowhere more evident than in the history of the Jews in Spain. That history is sad reading for the Christian, and inspiring for the Jew—if, at least, a martyr's death shames his murderers, and is the glory of his fellow-believers. For Spain stands out above all countries for the sufferings of Jews, inflicted, alas, by those who called themselves Christians, not all of whom were merely worldly or selfish. For in Spain the marriage of ignorance and piety has begotten a fanaticism eager-eyed for superstition and blind to God. Ethics have been of less importance than orthodoxy, and love a minor grace. Happy indeed is the Judaism which has produced so many staunch confessors; miserable the Christianity which has failed to spell out even the alphabet of the life and teaching of its Master.

When Jews first entered Spain is quite unknown. Legends tell us that Solomon's fleet carried some Jews thither, and that Nebuchadnezzar sent others. Besides, we are asked, is not "Toledo" only another form of the common Hebrew word for "generations", *Toledoth*? Of greater apparent evidential value is the word "Sepharad" in Obad. 20, with the common interpretation, due to Rabbinic exegesis, that it means "Spain". But the discovery at Sardis in 1916 of a bilingual inscription of "the tenth year of Artaxerxes" (either 455 or rather 394 or even 349 B.C.) in Aramaic and Lydian throws a different light on it, for in the Aramaic SPRD (also SPRB) refers almost certainly to the city where the inscription was found.[1] "Sepharad" in Obad. 20 is probably but another form of "Sardis".

Another allusion in the Old Testament is of a very different character, and perhaps convincing. For when Jonah takes his passage to "Tarshish" there is not a hint that the author of the book—whether he lived in the eighth or the fifth century B.C. is

[1] See especially the article by Dr S. A. Cook in the *Journal of Hellenic Studies*, 1917, xxxvii. 77–87, 219–231.

immaterial for our purpose—thought it in any way extraordinary that a Jew should go there. And the identification of Tarshish with Seville, naturally Seville in its oldest site, may be considered proved. The Book of Jonah suggests that there were at least some Jews in the south of Spain at the date when it was written. It is also unlikely that among the crews, or the prisoners, of those Phoenician ships which visited Spain in early days there were none of Jewish race, and that these never settled in the country. We can therefore hardly be wrong in believing that in the latter part of the days of the Roman Republic—before, that is to say, the commencement of the Christian era—many Jews lived in Spain.

There have however been times when this belief has been of value for propaganda purposes, and attempts have been made to prove it by direct evidence. A letter exists, and has found value in the eyes of certain historians, which purports to be signed by Jews of the synagogue of Toledo about A.D. 30 protesting to their brethren in Palestine against the crucifixion of Jesus of Nazareth. The document may be seen in full in the history of the Jews in Spain by Amador de Los Rios.[1]

But there is no reasonable doubt, both from its language and from its contents, that it was concocted by Spanish Jews of the fifteenth century. They hoped that by it they might convince their Christian persecutors of the falsity of the prevailing accusation that their ancestors had put Jesus to death. That is not true, they said—alas, that the reply was false!—we Jews of Spain at least had no share in that crime. Other Jews had, no doubt, others perhaps who lived away from Palestine, but not we. We did our best to save your Saviour when He was threatened, as this letter of our ancestors proves.

That witness to the existence of Jews in Spain may be dismissed. Who comes next? St Paul. For with his methods of evangelisation —going in every case to the Jew first—it is very improbable that he should have intended to visit Spain[2] if he had not expected to find there[3] not only Jewish inhabitants, scattered in different places, but even organised communities of Jews (with synagogues great or small, cf. Acts xiii. 5) whom he could use as the base of his missionary operations. Whether he actually did go to Spain or not is of no importance for our present purpose. He expected to find Jews there, Jews settled there, at the date when he wrote to the

---

[1] i. 504 *sq.*   [2] Rom. xv. 28.
[3] Even Graetz grants this, *Geschichte*, 1871, v. 396.

Christian community of Rome in the end of the sixth decade of the first century of our era.

Then the river of Lethe flows wide and deep for more than two hundred years, with but very few stepping-stones across it. There are one or two sepulchral monuments, and early Jewish writings containing some references to Spain and Spaniards which may belong to the second or third centuries. But that is all. Nothing of any importance is to hand until the Council of Illiberis (Elvira, a little north-west of the city of Granada), the date of which is now placed *c.* A.D. 300. Many Spanish bishops and clergy were present, and three of the canons passed at the Council show clearly that the Jews in Spain at that time were considered to be dangerous to the spiritual life of Christian people.

It seemed necessary to warn the faithful against inter-marriage with Jews as much as with heretics (Canon 16), and against making use of them to bless their fields (Canon 49), and even against partaking of meals with them (Canon 50).[1] Evidently the Christians were closely in touch with the Jews, and the Church rulers were afraid of Jewish influence on the weaker brethren.

The Council of Elvira was held in the very beginning of the fourth century, and we know nothing more about the Jews in Spain until its end, or perhaps the beginning of the fifth. For though the *Apotheosis* of Prudentius was written perhaps as early as 395 it was not published, as it seems, till A.D. 405.

Aurelius Prudentius Clemens[2] (to give the favourite Christian poet of the early Middle Ages his full name) was born probably at Saragossa, and in any case not very far from the Pyrenees, in A.D. 348. He was of a distinguished family, as his name implies, and his parents seem to have been Christians. He was well educated, especially in Latin literature, and possessed a little knowledge of Greek, but none of Hebrew. He became well known as an advocate, and was twice Governor of cities, and later was appointed by the Emperor Theodosius, himself a Spaniard, to a high office in his court. And then suddenly, about A.D. 395, when he was some forty-seven years of age, he gave up his appointment, with its prestige and its civil or military state, for the one object of consecrating his powers to God in strengthening the faith of his fellow-Christians, in combating error, and in singing of God and

---

[1] Mansi, *Concilia*, ii. 8, 14.
[2] See especially A. Brockhaus, *Prudentius in seiner Bedeutung für die Kirche seiner Zeit*, 1872.

the saints. It is probable that he joined some religious society. About A.D. 400 he went to Rome, where he published a collection of his works four or five years later, and from that time we know no more of him. He was of a lovable character, and unlike Tertullian, whose works he knew well, fond of art, and even ready to keep and admire statues, so long as there was no likelihood of worship being paid them.

His interest for us lies in his writings. They were all in verse, and some of his hymns are in every collection of sacred poetry, and are used to-day in our own Church. Four examples may be seen in *Hymns Ancient and Modern*.[1] He also wrote long didactic poems, and in one of these, the *Apotheosis*, perhaps the earliest of his works, he devotes 220 lines to the subject of the Jews. After combating the errors of the Patripassians and the Sabellians, he turns to the Jews, passing from them to the Ebionites, and, after a digression on the nature of the soul, finally to the Manichaeans. Perhaps the appearance of Sabellian Priscillianists in Spain at the end of the fourth century may have inspired him to this form of Christian endeavour.

What has he to say about the Jews, and how does he try to present Christ to them? The former question will be answered in due course; the latter briefly and at once. It is hard to distinguish exactly between writings designed primarily to win the Jews to Christ, and those which have for their principal object the desire to reassure believers that they are indeed the heirs of the Old Testament, while supplying them with arguments against Jewish attacks.

Prudentius' verses belong, no doubt, to the second category, but (perhaps for that very reason) throw much light on the manner in which Christians of the day regarded Jews, and were equipped for meeting their objections. A study of Prudentius' writings does not suggest that he knew much about either the Jews or the Judaism of his time. He is very different from Justin Martyr, for example, or the great controversialists of the thirteenth century. Still, we learn the theological attitude of the Christian layman towards them, and the arguments likely to be employed in controversy. The pity is that these show no sign of sympathy with Jewish difficulties.

In line 316 of the *Apotheosis*,[2] at the close of his arguments against

[1] 1909 edition.
[2] Taking J. Bergmann's edition (1926) as the standard.

the Sabellians, the poet had adduced the favourite text, "Then the LORD rained upon Sodom and upon Gomorrah brimstone and fire from the LORD out of heaven",[1] in proof of the twofold personality in the Godhead. He then turns directly to the Jews, and says that they ought to have understood the Gospel message, but were true children of their ancestors who had made the Golden Calf. They had not seen Christ proclaimed in the Law because they had covered their eyes with a veil lest they should behold His glory. They were like the olive tree whose branches had been broken off, that the wild olive slips should be grafted in. Yet the wild olive does not boast over them—would that this were true! —but only warns them not to remain bitter and contemptuous— "most ungrateful of all peoples, blaspheming Christ the Lord".[2]

You keep the Passover, you say! But how can you do so, when you are still in sin? Cannot you yet understand our Passover, with Christ's blood marking our forehead and so preserving us from the destroying angel? You are indeed unlike Abraham, who saw God and believed. No doubt you are his descendants after the flesh, as you boast of being, but it is only after the flesh; you see everything carnally.

Again, Christ has been proclaimed in all literature. Pilate's inscription in Hebrew, Greek, and Latin was a true symbol of the universal spread of the news of Christ. And then Prudentius gives us a really eloquent description of the sound of Christ throughout all nations, adding an address to Him from himself:

> Christ they publish, of Christ they sing,
> Voiceless, all utter "Christ",
> Living notes of the harp of God!
> O dearest of all Names,
> My Light, Renown, and Hope!
> My Guard, my Rest assured from toil,
> How sweet to taste, how fair to scent,
> My Spring of water sure!
> My spotless Love, my beauteous Form,
> My uttermost Desire![3]

Do Jews still refuse to hear? Then let them listen to the testi-

[1] Gen. xix. 24.
[2] "Blasphemas Dominum, gens ingratissima, Christum."
[3] "Christum concelebrat, Christum sonat, omnia Christum
muta etiam fidibus sanctis animata loquuntur.
o nomen praedulce, mihi lux et decus et spes,
praesidiumque meum, requies o certa laborum,
blandus in ore sapor, fragrans odor, inriguus fons,
castus amor, pulchra species, sincera uoluptas!" (ll. 391–396.)

mony of the demons, when Christ cast them out. For He is supreme over them: "Beaten! Be off! Thou windy vapour, Christ bids thee 'Go!'"[1]

They who entered the Gerasene swine confessed, "We know Thee who Thou art, Thou Son of God."

What a contrast you Jews are to the Gentiles! You have heard the Gospel, but it has not gone down into your hearts, for your minds are destitute of light. But in the West the inhabitants of Spain have listened to it, and those of the East, and Scythia and other countries in the North, and the Moors in the Atlas range. For these last have even given their long-haired kings to be ministers at Christ's altars.

Once more, consider the effect of Christ's coming upon the heathen religion. The Oracles have ceased since the Incarnation, and even in Rome the Emperors have become Christian. Do you retort, "Julian"? Alas, that most excellent of Emperors, in everything regarding the State, indeed broke his faith to God. But remember what happened. He renewed the heathen sacrifices, yet once when he was offering he found the omens failed him. Some Christian, he said, must be present. And then a young soldier with light brown hair—was he from the Danube or the Rhine?—came forward, flinging down his spear and confessing that the cross of Christ was on his brow. The Emperor is thrown into confusion and leaves the scene in haste, and all those present, regardless of their Emperor's orders, fall down and worship Jesus, Who has shown Himself supreme over the powers of evil.

Do you not repent even yet, O Jew? Christ broke the earthly sabbaths, but takes men to the heavenly! He now possesses the whole world!

Further, your temple is laid waste, and that rightly, for what begins has also an end. But our temple is the Body of Christ, and this you once attacked in vain, with stripes and cross and prison, for He rose again with it on the third day. He is our temple, and attended by angels He ascended to heaven, and the gates, as the Psalmist said, lifted up their heads to admit Him.

But your altars are in ruins, for Titus' and Pompey's soldiers have taught you what you deserve, and by them you have been dispersed throughout all lands, receiving the punishment due to you for your awful crime of putting Christ to death, with His blood scattered on you, as you invoked it.

[1] "Pulsus abi, uentose liquor, Christus iubet, exi." (l. 411.)

But we who once were heathen acknowledge the true Christ as King:

> Infidel once, believing now, she triumphs through the Christ!
> But she who then rejected Him, defeated prostrate lies
> Under the power, by heaven's decree, of those who trust in Him![1]

Prudentius then passes on to the subject of the Ebionites, beginning by saying they are the outcome of Jewish zeal, and are related half to Jews and half to Christians.

We may gather from this summary of Prudentius' arguments that while their foundation was the witness of the Scriptures both Old and New he yet used in practice the present position of the Jews, without city or temple or sacrifices, as evidence that God was no longer on their side. Christ, on the other hand, had shown His pre-eminence, not only by the direct witness of the spiritual world, but also in the failure of the heathen gods to maintain their power, and by winning the hearts of representatives of all nations, including the Emperors of Rome itself. If any of these opposed Him, His power was seen only the more plainly. Jews therefore ought to yield themselves to Him.

While however the *Apotheosis* is the only poem in which Prudentius deals directly with our subject, his other writings make so many allusions to the Old Testament (in order to prove the Divinity of our Lord) that he was evidently acquainted with the common Biblical arguments adduced in controversy with Jews. He appears to have had a thorough knowledge of Tertullian's *Adversus Judaeos*. Brockhaus[2] gives a list of such passages. Here it must suffice to notice his evidence that the Cross of Christ was prefigured in the Old Testament. Had not Abraham 318 servants (TIH in Greek), and is not the first letter of the number a cross?[3] Did not Moses heal the water at Marah by a tree?[4] Did not Joshua prevail against the Amalekites only so long as Moses held up his arms, thus making a cross?[5] But in fact the cross is as old as the world, to be seen in signs and letters, and is only brought into clearer light by the Old Testament.[6]

---

[1]   "Christum confessa triumphat
        gens infida prius; Christi sed victa negatrix
        subditur imperio dominos sortita fideles." (ll. 549–551.)

[2] *Op. cit.* p. 189 *sq.*

[3] *Psych. praef.* l. 57 *sq.* See *Barn.* ix. 7–9 (*supra*, p. 24).

[4] *Cath.* 5. 93 *sq.*

[5] *Cath.* 12. 170 *sqq.*; cf. Justin, *Dial. c. Tryph.* xc. 4 (*supra*, p. 40).

[6] *Perist.* 10. 621–635.

On the whole we may regard Prudentius as an interesting witness to the nature of the evidence for the truth of Christianity which the Church of his time desired to bring before the Jews. And there is no doubt that at least his writings served their purpose in strengthening the faith of those who were Christians already. This was why he chose verse rather than prose for his medium of self-expression. The schoolmaster was not then abroad among the rank and file of believers, but men and women hung on the lips of professional reciters, more so perhaps in Southern than in Northern lands. And as poetry is more easily remembered than prose, and has greater charm in itself, Prudentius cultivated his gift and put his arguments into verse. And more than this. Poetry lends itself to music, and as Bardesan of Edessa had promulgated his false doctrine largely by song as early as the beginning of the third century, and as Ephraim the Syrian, in the middle of the fourth century, had used the same means, sometimes employing the very tunes which Harmodius, Bardesan's son, had composed, that he might counteract his influence, so, we may suppose, Prudentius thought it well also to write in verse, supplying material for song, private and public. The result justified his hope. Not a little of Prudentius' work, like Ephraim's, was used in the worship of the Church.[1]

He appeals to us, however, much less than if he had reasoned out his thoughts in prose. For we are bored by versification when we wish to study theology. Yet Prudentius does occasionally rise to the level of poetry.

The hope of Prudentius that the power of Imperial Rome would continue to spread[2] was very soon to be belied. For on August 24, A.D. 410, only five years after the last we hear of him, the city was taken by Alaric the Goth, and Alaric's forces were but part of the great Gothic flood under which the civilisation of the Western Empire was gradually submerged.

The history of Spain during the whole of the fifth and the greater part of the sixth centuries is once again nearly blank, save that we get glimpses of the conquest of the peninsula by horde after horde of barbarians, beginning with the crossing of the Alani from Gaul in A.D. 409. The Visigothic conquerors were Arians who persecuted such Catholic Christians as remained, though they allowed Jews

---

[1] So the five books of Tertullian's *Treatise against Marcion* were put into hexameters for popular purposes. See Oehler, *Tertullian*, ii. 781–798.

[2] E.g. *Perist.* ii. 1–8.

to come to Spain more freely than ever. But near the end of the sixth century, in A.D. 587, Reccared the King of the Visigoths became an orthodox Catholic, and fresh materials for our study begin to be available. He put in force those Roman laws which were less favourable to Jews but had fallen into disuse. Hence the Third Council of Toledo (A.D. 589) in Canon 14 decrees that Jews were not to have Christian wives or concubines, that the children of such unions were to be baptised, that Jews could not hold any office which gave them power to punish Christians, and could not buy Christian slaves. Further, that if such slaves became Jews they were to be set free and to return to Christianity.[1]

The three names about which the rest of the history under the Visigoths revolves are Isidore of Seville, Hildefonsus of Toledo, and Julian of Toledo. The first is by far the most important.

In A.D. 612 Sisebut, who had recently succeeded to the throne of the Visigoths, strengthened the harsh laws of Reccared, and, further, ordered that all Jews were to be baptised under penalty of banishment, and of the confiscation of their goods. It has been said indeed[2] that this was one of the conditions of the peace made with him by Heraclius the Roman Emperor, but there is no sufficient evidence of this. Sisebut, in general a mild and intelligent man, seems to have been moved by his own mistaken piety, or by the more ignoble desire of personal gain.[3] In any case, he could not claim the highest ecclesiastical authority for his action, for Pope Gregory I had said in A.D. 591: "Conversions wrought by force are seldom sincere, and such as are thus converted seldom fail to return to their vomit when the force is removed."[4] So it is not surprising that Isidore wrote only five years after Sisebut's death (621) in his *History of the Gothic Kings*:[5] "Sisebut in the beginning of his reign urged the Jews to accept the Christian faith, for he had zeal, no doubt, but not knowledge. For he compelled by force those whom he ought to have incited by the arguments of the true faith."[6]

---

[1] Mansi, *Concilia*, ix. 996.

[2] See, for example, Lindo, *The History of the Jews of Spain and Portugal*, 1848, p. 12.

[3] See the *Cambridge Medieval History*, ii. 174.

[4] *Ep.* i. 34 *sq.*   [5] *Era* DCL. *ann.* 612.

[6] "Qui in initio regni *Iudaeos ad fidem Christianam permovens* aemulationem quidem habuit, sed non secundum scientiam: potestate enim conpulit, quos provocare fidei ratione oportuit" (see Mommsen's *Monumenta Germaniae Chronica Minora*, 1894, ii. 291, in the *Monumenta Germaniae Historica*).

Isidore was a remarkable man. He was born about A.D. 560, probably at Cartagena (where his father may have been prefect) shortly before his parents left for Seville. It is uncertain whether they were of Gothic or of Latin stock, though it has been asserted that the father was of the Visigothic royal family, and the mother a daughter of the Emperor Theodoric. His elder brother Leander was Archbishop of Seville *c.* 579–599, and his younger brother Fulgentius, Bishop of Astigi or Ecija in the province of Seville. The excellence of his early training, doubtless in a monastery, is shown by the brilliancy and width of his erudition in after life. He had indeed very little originality of thought, but he was unquestionably the most learned man of his day. His *Encyclopaedia*[1] was esteemed so highly that in the Middle Ages there was scarcely a library of a Chapter House or Monastery that had not a copy.[2] Mrs Humphry Ward says: "It is probably not possible to overrate the value and the usefulness of this treatise to the age in which he lived, and indeed for many ages it was the most available handbook to which the world had access."[3]

This gives greater weight to his work on behalf of the Jews. An extract from his *Origines* has already been given, but his interest in the Jews went far deeper than that. It is true that at the Fourth Council of Toledo, held under his presidency in A.D. 633, Canons were passed which were very strict indeed against anything like apostasy on the part of Jews who had already been baptised, and against Jews being allowed to have opportunities of influencing Christians unduly, but Canon 57 expressly forbids Jews to be brought to Christianity by force or by threat.[4]

He himself had taken what he believed to be the better way, the way which commends itself now to all right-thinking people, by endeavouring to convince the Jews by argument. When indeed he wrote his *Contra Judaeos*[5] is unknown, but the date is of little importance. His sister Florentina had asked him, as it seems, for

---

[1] *Origines sive Etymologiae*, written between 622 and 633.
[2] *Cambridge Medieval History*, ii. 192.
[3] *Dict. Chr. Biog.* iii. 308.
[4] "Non enim tales [Iudaei] inviti salvandi sunt, sed volentes, ut integra sit forma iustitiae: sicut enim homo proprii arbitrii voluntate serpenti obediens periit, sic vocante gratia Dei propriae mentis conversione homo quisque credendo salvatur. Ergo non vi, sed libera arbitrii facultate, ut convertantur suadendi sunt, non potius impellendi" (Mansi, *Concilia*, x. 633).
[5] *De Fide Catholica ex veteri et novo testamento contra Judaeos, Opera*, vol. vi, edition F. Arevalus, Rome, 1802; also in Migne, *P.L.* lxxxiii. 449–538.

arguments wherewith to meet Jewish objections to the faith, and he writes this treatise in two books, the first giving in great detail the history of Christ according to the Old Testament, and the second the prophecies in the Old Testament about the rejection of the Jews on the one hand, and the welfare of true believers under the new Covenant on the other. The Jews would believe in Christ at the end of the world.

It is perhaps the ablest and most logical of all the early attempts to present Christ to the Jews. These in general are of two kinds. There is the thoughtful but wordy *Dialogue with Trypho*, written by Justin Martyr, full of good matter, but ill arranged, (at least in its present form) and with many repetitions. There is also the collection of bare texts such as the *Testimonia* of Cyprian. Isidore takes the middle course. He adduces, it is true, innumerable proof-texts, leaving but few for others to glean after him, but he arranges them in an admirably clear order, and he also points out the bearing of each upon the point at issue. His weakness as compared with Justin is, alas, that he has no knowledge of traditional Judaism, and can hardly have come into close contact with Jews. It was not so with Justin, whose work shows on every page acquaintance with the mind and habits of the Jews of his day. Trypho may or may not have been a real person—though there is every probability that a discussion between Justin and some such Jew served as the basis of the book—but Justin must have had conversations with Jews again and again, to have learned so much about them as he continually shows. Isidore can have had no such experience. He was a monk, reserving his external activity to members of his own faith, shunning the difficult task of mixing with unbelievers. In spite therefore of his theological learning, and the use he had undoubtedly made of the works of his predecessors, he fails to perceive the nature of Jewish objections, and shows no sign of acquaintance with Jewish customs other than such as he could find in the Old Testament itself, or than such as were generally known to the Gentile world of the seventh century.

Still, he did his best, and the treatise is a storehouse from which, in all probability, many later tracts, perhaps even down to the nineteenth century, were ultimately drawn.[1]

The moderating force of Isidore's influence may be gauged by the change of policy made only two years after his death. For at the sixth Council of Toledo held in A.D. 638 under King Chintilla

[1] See Appendix, pp. 282–292.

it was ordered that no one should be allowed to stay in the land who was not a Catholic. But mercifully it is easier to pass bad laws than to carry them out, and in 672 the Jews were still there, and King Wamba had to pass a decree of banishment again.

Meantime a treatise had been written by Hildefonsus, Bishop of Toledo, A.D. 657–667. When still a boy he had run away from home to the monastery of Agali close to Toledo, eluding the search made for him there by his father, and, becoming a monk and eventually abbot, succeeded Eugenius II in the see of Toledo. His life, written more than a hundred years after his death, attributes to him so many miracles that he has become perhaps the most popular saint in Spain. For it is not learning but kindness of heart that makes for popularity. This is, in fact, the character that his book reveals to us. Its title is *Liber de Virginitate S. Mariae contra tres infideles*;[1] who are, in fact, Jovinian, who denied that the Blessed Virgin preserved her virginity in giving birth to our Lord; Helvidius, who believed that she had other children later, viz. our Lord's "Brethren"; and a Jew.

Hildefonsus dismisses the first two very briefly, and gives nearly all his space to the Jew. Mary, he says, was by nation Jewish, but Christian by her faith, honour, praise, and love. Prophecy joined her virginity to her motherhood, and she remained a virgin for ever. After adducing better-known texts he adds Ezek. xliv. 1, the gate which looketh towards the east remains always closed. Then, after speaking at some length about the *perfidia* of the Jews, and exhorting them earnestly to believe, though he adduces very little argument wherewith to convince them, he expounds the mystery of the Incarnation, quoting not only Ex. xxiii. 21, "My Name is in Him", but also Ecclus. xxiv. 3, "I came forth from the mouth of the Most High". He then shows that the Son of the Blessed Virgin is indeed God, as Baruch iii. 36 *sq.* implies: for "He hath found out all the way of prudence"...and as man "was conversant with men". Then he adduces many passages from the New Testament as well as the Old to prove his point, and passes on to narrate from both Testaments the whole life of Christ until the Holy Spirit was sent down upon the Apostles at Pentecost. Yet as Jer. v. 12 tells us, "They have denied Me, and said, It is not He". The Virgin's own words are quoted, as also Elizabeth's and others' about her, and the testimony of the angels. He closes with a fervid address to the

[1] Migne, *P.L.* xcvi. 51–110.

Blessed Mother and her glorious Son, and inveighs against "the impious profaners of her unsullied virginity".

Its spirit is earnest and not unkindly, in spite of its narrowness of outlook. But it shows no trace of personal acquaintance with Jews. In fact the impression which it gives is that it was not originally intended to be read, or even listened to, by Jews, but was a discourse addressed to a congregation of earnest Christians, already convinced of the truth on which Hildefonsus was insisting. He was plainly a good and devout man, but possessed neither originality of mind nor wide learning. It was doubtless only his name which secured immortality for the sermon.

The twelfth Council of Toledo was held in A.D. 681 under the presidency of King Erwig, who in flaming words appealed to the Bishops present to confirm the twenty-eight laws he had compiled, twenty-seven of which were against "the Jews". "So because the Lord charges us in the Gospel, saying, 'Verily I say unto you, If two of you shall agree on earth as touching anything whatever they shall ask, it shall be done for them of My Father who is in heaven', therefore do I address the venerable assembly of holy Fathers with tears streaming down my cheeks, that by your zealous rule the land may be purged from the pollution of vice. Arise! Arise! I beg you. Loose the knots of the guilty, correct the shameful habits of the wicked, apply the scourge of zeal against the disaffected, stamp out the backbiting of the proud, lighten the burdens of the oppressed, and, more than all else, pull up from the very roots that plague-spot which is ever bursting forth into new forms of virulence—the Jews. Examine therefore with the utmost thoroughness the laws which have been recently issued by Our Majesty against the treachery of certain Jews; make the purport of those laws inviolable; sum up the decrees concerning the outrageous actions of those treacherous persons, and issue them as one."[1]

The Bishop of Toledo at the time of this Council was the famous Julian, who therefore cannot be acquitted of responsibility for the heavy penalties laid down on Jews who refused to be baptised. It appears that there were then special reasons for fearing Jewish influence. The Jews were making much of certain books, which, it may be presumed, had reached them lately. For the eleventh Canon of the Council forbade their reading "those books which the Christian faith rejects". These may have been parts of the

---

[1] *Monumenta Germaniae Historica, Leges Visigothorum,* i. 475 *sq.*

Babylonian Talmud. It is at least noticeable in view of Julian's treatise that the treatise *Sanhedrin* contains a discussion on the signs of the coming of the true Messiah. According to one opinion the duration of the world is six thousand years, two thousand of chaos, two of Torah, and two of the days of Messiah. According to another, after 4291 years the wars of Gog and Magog will begin, and the rest of the six thousand years will be the days of Messiah. According to others, the world will be renewed after seven or five thousand years.[1] When therefore Julian desired to win the Jews to the true faith he chose the topical subject of the date when the Messiah was to come.

Julian himself is said to have been of Jewish extraction, the son, or descendant, of Jews who by force or free-will had been baptised, but he does not show any sign of great sympathy with them. He spent all his life in Toledo, and on the death of Hildefonsus was the most prominent Churchman in Spain. When Quiricus the Bishop of Toledo died in 680 "it could have astonished no one", writes Mrs Humphry Ward, "that Julian should succeed to the vacant see".[2]

His work was entitled "On the verification of the sixth Age"[3] and is dated the sixth year of King Erwig, i.e. A.D. 686, and Julian's dedication is: "To the renowned and glorious revered Lord King Erwig, Julian your humble servant."[4] He goes on to say that as skilful physicians cut away the putrefying parts of a wound before it can heal, so must it be with the language of the Jews, who say that Christ has not come because we are now in only the fifth age, and He is to come in the sixth. He then states his intentions. His First Book will show from the Old Testament that Christ must have come. Jews are injuring the faith of believers. We must therefore try to answer them, in the hope "that the rock of truth discharged from our mouth may break their teeth", and that "even if the Jew be not convicted at least the Christian may receive advantage". This, as has already been said, is a leading feature in most of the writings *contra Judaeos*. Julian, it should be noticed, does not accept the favourite interpretation of Ps. xc. 4, "a thousand years are as one day", implying that the six days of creation are the same as six thousand years. It is, he says, only a figurative expression,

[1] T.B. *Sanhedrin*, 97 a, b.
[2] *Dict. Chr. Biog.* iii. 477.   [3] *De comprobatione aetatis sextae.*
[4] "Inclyto et glorioso Reverendo Domino Eruigio Regi Iulianus servulus vester." The treatise is printed in Migne, *P.L.* xcvi. 537–586.

a thousand years being in God's eyes as nothing at all. Julian thus does not hold with that over-exactness in computation of times which has often taken a large place in the calculations of Jews and of Christians. Neither does he care to repeat—he may be thinking of Hildefonsus[1]—the evidence of the Old Testament to the details of Christ's life. But he does point out that Christ was to be called "peace", and His coming to be in a time of peace; that the Kings of Judah were to have failed, for "Herod, a foreigner, had succeeded". He also adduces (§ 11) a curious argument from Gen. xxxviii. 12, that whereas Judah there signifies Christ, his friend, *Iras ille Odollamitis*, represented John the Baptist. For Iras means "the sight of my Brother", and *Odollami* "testimony in water".[2] And John not only saluted Christ *ex utero*[3] but also, with the descent of the Dove, bore testimony to Him in the water.[4] Julian goes on to show that Christ was to come while the Temple was still standing, and that now the Jewish Kingdom, priesthood, and sacrifice have ceased[5]—in contrast to the Christian sacrifice which is spread everywhere—and he closes his First Book with a discussion of Dan. ix. 22–27. His Second Book deals exclusively with the evidence of the New Testament, claiming two miracles as of special importance, the Virgin Birth and Jesus' appearance to His disciples, "the doors being closed", after His Resurrection. The Third Book is devoted to a long technical discussion about the calculation of the ages, and the question why Christ ought to be born in the sixth age, as indeed He was. Julian's final words are, "Thou hast lost the Way, therefore follow the Way, that through the Way thou mayest come to salvation".

It should be noticed that Julian's learning appears throughout. He quotes again and again from Augustine's *De Civitate Dei*[6] and once at least from Tertullian,[7] Epiphanius[8] and Jerome.[9] But he also shows no sign of having come into direct contact with Jews, and thus of having learned the arguments likely to be adduced by them.

---

[1] *Supra*, p. 218.

[2] The English versions render correctly *Hirah the Adullamite*. Jerome says, "*Iras*, vidit fratrem meum, sive fratris mei visio" and "*Odollamites*, contestans aliquem, vel testimonium in aqua" (*De Nom. Hebr.*, Vallarsi, iii. 12 *sq.*). *Iras* seems to be derived from the Aramaic root *ḥur* "see" and Aram. or Heb. *'aḥ* "brother" (instead of *'aḥ*); *Adullamite* from the Hebrew *'dlmy* as "witness—to or of—who (someone) or water".

[3] Luke i. 41. [4] John i. 32 *sqq.* [5] Hos. iii. 4. [6] In iii. 18–24.

[7] In i. 26. [8] In iii. 17. [9] In iii. 25.

Julian died in A.D. 690, and although fresh laws were passed concerning the Jews, and especially baptised Jews, there is no later writer that concerns us now. For in A.D. 711 the Moors landed in the South, and Muza overthrew the Visigothic Empire by his success at Xeres.

The impression that one receives from a study of the attitude of the Church in Spain towards the Jews until the end of the Visigothic Kingdom is that it was not wholly unworthy of its Divine character. Politics and social intricacies played indeed their parts, and both ecclesiastics and Church laymen were often only too ready to apply the forces of the State. No doubt there were causes for opposition to the Jews. As a nation they take singularly little trouble to acquire, much less to retain, popularity. They believe themselves to be the cream of the whole earth, and hold it to be only proper that the cream should rise. They therefore readily become bumptious, and when they have power are but too often regardless of others. Add to this the facts of their innate ability in business and their solidarity as a people, and it is easy to understand that they are often disliked, and that this dislike shows itself in measures incompatible with true Christianity.

Yet, allowing for this feeling on the part of Churchmen, clergy and laity alike, there does seem to have been a sincere desire among the Spanish Christians of the seventh century not so much to get rid of the Jews as to win them to Christ. The better educated of the clergy were well aware that force alone was insufficient, and they endeavoured to obtain the heartfelt adherence of Jews to the dominant creed. It was no pretence that produced long treatises setting forth the claims of Christ upon the Jews. Christians could not understand how it was that they still opposed Him as in the days of His flesh, and they did their uttermost to present Him to them.

There were, however, two factors which ensured relative failure. The Christian apologists themselves did not understand the inner teaching either of Judaism or of Christ. They cannot be blamed severely for not understanding Judaism. Ecclesiastics and statesmen, even if the two are combined in the same person, do not as a rule come across learned Jews. Those Jews who are prominent in politics or social questions are seldom well acquainted with the doctrines of their own religion. They may not even be practising Jews, and if they are they may know little more than the way in which to observe certain forms. The thinkers in Judaism, as in most religions, are quiet folk, dwelling among their own people, and shrinking from intercourse with Christian students at least as much as these shrink from them.

The other fault is, in reality, more serious. Spanish Churchmen throughout this period failed in their endeavour to present Christ to the Jews because they did not understand what they had to present. Their subject is purely intellectual, and of the ethical character of Christ they have nothing to say. Christ is to them the fulfilment of the Old Testament, and the Son of God; but for all they tell us of Him, He might have had no heart overflowing with love, and might not even have been of spotless life. In other words, they do not present Christ at all. He Himself in His holiness and self-sacrifice is not shown. He is not so lifted up before the Jews as to attract them to Him.

Nor, finally, can another point be overlooked, not wholly unconnected with the last. They lay no stress, to put it mildly, on our own need of salvation and on Christ as our Saviour from sin. They are not ignorant of what He did for us, for occasionally they break out into personal thanksgiving to Him. But it is only personal, and does not enter into their argument. In fact, they neglect that weapon in the Gospel armoury which has proved to be the most effectual of all, and represents the innermost teaching of the Good News brought by Christ, however much misinterpreted to-day, that God in Christ purchased salvation for us by supreme self-sacrifice.

It is the lack of this truth that has weakened the presentation of Christ to the Jews, for it belongs to the very heart of the Gospel which Christians have to preach.

CHAPTER XXII

ALVARO AND BODO
Cent. IX

The Christian inhabitants of Western Europe were scandalised in the first half of the ninth century by the apostasy of a well-known Churchman to Judaism. Bodo,[1] the son of noble parents in France, and now the Deacon of the Palace of Louis the Good-natured (Le Débonnaire) (A.D. 814–840), desired in A.D. 838 to visit Rome, obtained permission from Louis, and was sent there (839) with valuable presents from the King and Queen. But soon after he arrived he was persuaded (by whose influence and by what means we are wholly ignorant) to become a Jew, and he "submitted to circumcision, and let his beard grow", changing his name Bodo for that of Eleazar, and wearing military dress. Apparently his morals had already been atrocious,[2] but he now married a Jewess, compelled his nephew to become a Jew, and went to Saragossa. From there he went in A.D. 840 to Cordova, the capital of the Moorish kingdom of Spain, and not only ingratiated himself with the King, but even urged him to compel all those of his subjects who were Christians to accept Islam or Judaism on pain of death. We cannot wonder that the Christians did their utmost to counter-act his influence.

His special interest for us is that a learned layman of Cordova, Paulo Alvaro *Cordobes*, who was himself of Jewish descent, wrote him four letters in the hope of convincing him of his error.[3] Eleazar also sent replies, but unfortunately the Christian copyists were so shocked at their contents that only small fragments of three of them have survived. Observe that there is no question here of the reason why Alvaro's letters were written. He was

[1] See H. Florez, *España Sagrada*, 1753, xi. pp. 20–23, and especially J. Aronius, *Regesten zur Geschichte der Juden im fränkischen und deutschen Reiche bis zum Jahre 1273*, 1902, § 103.

[2] See his own statement as quoted by Alvaro (*vide infra*), *Ep.* xvi. 2. See also the succinct statement of Amulo, *c. Judaeos*, xlii (*vide infra*, p. 363).

[3] They are printed in *España Sagrada* (*vide supra*), *Epp.* xiv, xvi, xviii, xix, together with the remnants of Eleazar's replies, *Epp.* xv, xvii, xx. Florez prefixes a full life of Paulo Alvaro on pp. 10–61. See also Migne, *P.L.* cxxi. 478–514.

composing no academic treatise, and had no idea of building up
Christians in the true faith. He was out for definitely missionary
work, winning a professing Jew to Christ.

Alvaro's first letter is quite a model of the spirit in which all
religious controversy ought to be conducted. "To my beloved
Eleazar....Besides, I ask you not to look down on this offering of
my love, by which I long to win you in the Lord."[1] But the kindly
feeling was hardly maintained, for Alvaro's last letter says: "Do
not call us mad dogs, but recognise yourself as a snarling fox."[2]

The first letter is chiefly concerned with showing that according
to the chronology, and various events foretold in the Old Testament, the true Messiah must have come about the time of our
Lord.[3] The chronology of the Septuagint no doubt differs from
that of the Hebrew text, but this is not of primary importance for
the argument. For Gen. xlix. 10 says that the kings of Judah's line
will have come to an end, and Hos. iii. 4 must be reckoned from
the time of Daniel, i.e. after, not before, the Captivity in Babylon.
Dan. ix. 22 says that after Christ has been killed the Jewish nation
is to be laid waste, and in the first year of Vespasian, the year of
your captivity, "the rest of the number of the weeks...was filled
up".

In his next letter (*Ep.* xvi) Alvaro blames Eleazar for thinking
that the seventy years were completed in the captivity in Babylon,
and chaffs him for pretending that he, a mere Gaul, knew more
Hebrew than the great scholars. The Latin then has discovered in
Hebrew literature what the Hebrew never knew![4] Eleazar should
study Jerome, whom however he has dared to attack bitterly, in
spite of his own immorality. Then follows a discussion of the
meaning of *'almah* in Isa. vii. 14, and it is pointed out that the
interpretation "virgin" is not only Jerome's, but also the Septuagint's. Besides, your people have mutilated the Canon, cutting
out the Wisdom of Solomon because of Wisd. ii. 12, 18–20, and
have falsified even the Hebrew text, adding in Deut. xxi. 23,

---

[1] "Dilecto mihi Eleazaro Alvarus....De cetero rogo ut non fastidium tibi
ingerat dilectionis nostrae oblatio, qua te lucrare (*sic*) in Domino cupio."

[2] "Vulpeum (*sic*) gannientem."

[3] In his third letter (*Ep.* xviii) he speaks of both Josephus and Philo as saying
that Herod the Great was a foreigner.

[4] Compare, on the other hand, Nachmanides' taunt at the disputation at
Barcelona 1263 and that Paulus Christiani understands the words of the
Talmudical writers better than they themselves (*Wikuach*, edition Stein-
schneider, p. 6).

"accursed *of God*". At the close of this letter he says: "You write at the end, 'Farewell, so hold your Jesus fast, here and for ever'. Hear then my short reply—'Amen, and again Amen, and a third time Amen. In heaven, Amen, and in the earth, Amen. And let not the Angels only, but all the people say, Even so, so be it.'"

Eleazar's second letter had plainly been abusive, for in Alvaro's third (*Ep.* xviii) there is a *tu quoque* for blasphemy. Gen. i. 26 is then discussed. Further, as the veil over the face of Moses signifies your blind intellect, so do you also put a silk veil over the Heptateuch.[1] Which then of us now has the greater claim to the name of Israelite? You, who turned from idolatry[2] to the worship of God, and are not a Jew by race but in faith only, or I, who am a Hebrew both in faith and in race? Observe that I do not call myself a Jew, because Isa. lxii. 2 promises, *Thou shalt be called by a new name.* You ask why we do not keep the ceremonies of the Law? Because Isa. xliii. 18 says, *Do not remember the former things.* The 20th verse adds, *The beasts of the field honour Me*, meaning by *beasts* the Gentiles. After dealing with Isa. lx. 2, Alvaro discusses the various Hebrew readings in Isa. xlix. 5, *not* or *to him.* He then argues for the doctrine of the Trinity, adducing among other texts Ps. xxxiii. 6, *By the Word of the LORD were the heavens made.* Eleazar had evidently uttered some coarse remarks about the birth of Christ, and Alvaro reminds him that, after all, our bodies were made by God. The very sufferings and death of Christ are trophies of glory.

An interesting piece of information about the religious liberality of Louis the Good-natured follows soon after, when Alvaro tells us that Eleazar said that he had seen in the palace fourteen men of different religions. Further, Alvaro adds, you say that the sayings of the Prophets compelled you to become a Jew. "Nay, it was women, who are very moths, corrupting soul and body."[3] After all, you had better have become a Mohammedan, for then you could have had several wives. Then Alvaro argues solemnly that the promise in 2 Sam. vii. 12 cannot have been fulfilled in Solomon, for it speaks of a ruler born after David's death, and Solomon was

[1] "Eptaticum." "Originally, a wrapping of fine silk was spread along the full length of the parchment, to protect the writing from dust and injury when the scroll was rolled up....The custom of completely covering the writing with silk, when the mantle is not in use, is still practised by the Sephardim in the Orient" (*Jew. Enc.* viii. 298).

[2] Presumably because Bodo's ancestors were heathen.

[3] "Femina, quae est animi et corporis tinea."

born before his death.[1] Then he adduces many texts to show that the Jewish nation is not acceptable to God (e.g. Mal. i. 10), and that this state of things will never cease, so that there is no use in praying that it may (Jer. vii. 16). To have Christ is the only way to peace.

The fourth letter of Alvaro to Eleazar is very short and contains nothing of interest.

Whether the letters produced any visible effect on Bodo-Eleazar we are not told; presumably they did not. The arguments used are not, alas, very convincing, and show little or no acquaintance with the intellectual difficulties in a Jew's acceptance of Christianity, especially in our own day. But the letters remain an interesting record of the zealous attempt of a godly and learned Spanish Christian layman in the ninth century to win back an erring brother to the faith.

[1] Cf. Peter Alphonsi, *Dialogue*, § viii (Migne, *P.L.* clvii. 622 D).

CHAPTER XXIII

"THE LETTER OF R. SAMUEL"

A.D. 1072 (?)

"The Golden Work of Rabbi Samuel the Jew, rebuking the error of the Jews, originally translated from Arabic into Latin, but now from Latin into the common tongue of the Greeks. Published at the expense of the most honourable and respected Master Nicholas Scurtes. In Leipzig of Saxony, at the printing press of Breitkopf, in the year 1769."[1]

"The blessed Jew of Morocco or a Blackmoor made white York 1649."[2]

The former is a translation of the title-page of a rare book; the latter a copy (presumably) of the title-page of another equally rare book;[3] both being editions of a work which is one of the most famous of all tracts written for the Jews, and also, as some think, one of the best known of mediaeval forgeries.

For it claims to be a Letter written in Arabic by R. Samuel of Fez about the year 1072[4] to R. Isaac, the Head Master of the Rabbinical School and the Jewish synagogue in Subjulmeta in Morocco, expressing at first his doubts about Judaism, and gradually his full acceptance of Christianity. Few scholars believe in its genuineness to-day, yet no one, on the other hand, is quite sure who the author really was. Steinschneider thinks that the name R. Samuel was taken from Sanuel ben Jehuda ibn Abbas, "the Moroccan and Spaniard" who in 1163 passed from Judaism to

[1] Πονημα χρυσουν Σαμουηλ Ραββι του Ιουδαιου, εξελεγχον την των Ιουδαιων πλανην. Πρωτον μεν ἐκ τῆς Αραβικης εις την Λατινιδα μεταφρασθεν· νυν δε εκ της Λατινιδος εἰς τὴν κοινὴν των Ελληνων διαλεκτον. Ἐκδοθὲν ἀναλώμασι τοῦ τιμιωτάτου, κα(ὶ) χρησιμωτάτου κυριου Νικολαου Σκουρτου. Εν Λειψίᾳ τῆς Σαξονίας Τυπογραφίᾳ τοῦ Βρεῖτκόπφ Ἔτει 1769. It gives the Latin and a translation into modern Greek in parallel columns. The translator into Greek appears to have been Nicephorus Theotokes, a somewhat voluminous writer of the period, who writes an interesting Introduction. The curious reader will find an account of him in Sathas, *Neohellenike Philologia*, 1868, pp. 583.

[2] See Steinschneider, *Bodleian Catalogue*, col. 2451.

[3] The first seems not to have been known to Steinschneider; the second was not in the Bodleian when he made his Catalogue.

[4] A thousand years and more after the destruction of Jerusalem by Titus, ch. 1.

Islam, and afterwards wrote against his former faith. The Latin version claims to have been made by Alphonsus Bonihominis 250 years after the (supposed) Arabic original, and Steinschneider suggests that this Alphonsus was no other than Abner of Burgos, who was afterwards Alphonsus of Valladolid.[1]

Little doubt, however, was expressed about the genuineness of R. Samuel's Letter until Steinschneider wrote his long article in the Bodleian Catalogue,[2] and, after all, that article is extraordinarily disappointing. It is learned to a degree, with minute enquiry into what is known of R. Samuel ibn Abbas,[3] but Steinschneider bases his argument of non-genuineness entirely on the three facts that both Samuels came from Fez, that both left Judaism, the one for Christianity in the eleventh century, the other for Islam in the twelfth ("A.D. 1163 Islamismum amplexus est prope Mosul"), and that both wrote against Judaism. Steinschneider therefore thinks that the forger of the Letter based it on the name and work of Samuel ibn Abbas. Yet he himself acknowledges that there is very little in common between the Letter and what we know of Samuel ibn Abbas' treatise against his former coreligionists.

No doubt the coincidence of name and place is rather remarkable, but there has always been a large Jewish quarter in Fez, and Samuel is a very common name among Jews. He does not suggest any reason why the R. Samuel of the Letter is put a hundred years earlier than Ibn Abbas. Nor does he ask why the forger (as he supposes the translator "Alfonsus Bonihominis" to have been) wrote the document first in Arabic (as is granted), and then put it into Latin. Nor, again, does he explain why he should have taken the trouble to render Bible texts into Arabic in such a way that these sometimes disagree with the Vulgate text of the fourteenth century.[4] Again, one would have supposed that the Christian theology of the fourteenth century would somehow have made itself felt, yet there seems to be nothing in the Letter which might not well have been written in the eleventh. I myself, therefore, cannot feel that the question is decided, in spite of the vast learning of Steinschneider, and his general fairness in judgment.

[1] *Vide infra*, pp. 259 *sq.* "Nisi plane fictus, forsan idem est ac Magister Alfonsus Vallisoletanus, inter Judaeos Medicus Abner de Burgos" (*Cat. Bodl.* col. 732; cf. his *Jewish Literature*, 1857, where he dates the tract A.D. 1339).

[2] Published 1852–1860, s.v. *Samuel Marokki*, coll. 2436–2451; cf. also col. 732.

[3] See further Steinschneider's much later work, *Die Arabische Literatur der Juden*, 1902, pp. 186–193.

[4] *Vide infra*, p. 230, note.

I know of no argument that tells with any decisive force against the original Letter having been written in Arabic about A.D. 1072, and translated into Latin in 1339.[1]

However this may be, the work is a clear and well-written tract of forty-three small octavo pages in English.[2] In chh. i–v the author discusses the reason why the present captivity of the Jews is longer than that in Babylon, and indeed worse, because no promise of release from it is to be found, and no sacrifices can be offered.[3] The real reason is shown in chh. vi–xiii, viz. the rejection of Christ. Amos hints at this, in selling the Just One for silver, and his words are "not to be understood as according to our teaching, which says that the righteous here is Joseph, the son of Jacob".[4] Nay, "I am afraid and fear, Sir, that Jesus, in whom the Christians believe, may be the Just One who was sold for silver...and I apprehend also that to him refers the testimony of the prophets".[5] The Messiah was to come the first time in humility, but the second time as Judge. For He was to ascend into heaven after He had trodden the wine press,[6] and "waged war with our fathers".[7] The

[1] I understand that my friend Mr Abinoam Yellin of Jerusalem is making an independent study of the question, based on a MS. of Samuel ibn Abbas now in Cairo. Steinschneider mentions several anti-Jewish works written in Arabic by Christians between the ninth and the thirteenth centuries, and still extant in MSS. (*Jewish Literature*, 1857, p. 125).

[2] The English edition (e.g. 1885), used by the Missionary Societies down to the end of the nineteenth century, has been somewhat bowdlerised, *bien entendu*, by omitting texts from the Apocrypha and phrases suspected of Roman Catholic teaching (*vide infra*, p. 231), but otherwise agrees essentially with the Latin. This was first printed at the end of the *Scrutinium* of Paul of Burgos (*vide infra*, p. 267). Migne reprints it, *P.L.* cxlix. 333–368.

[3] Each chapter generally ends with some such phrase as "Yet whatever may happen, we are all of God", in the Arabian manner.

[4] Amos ii. 6. Joseph's brethren sold him for twenty pieces, and each bought a pair of shoes with his two pieces (*Targ. Ps.-Jon.* Gen. xxxvii. 28; *Pirqe d'R. Eliezer*, § 38).

[5] E.g. Isa. xlix. 4; liii; Pss. ii. 2; xciv. 21; Jer. xxxi. 22; Zech. xii. 10; xiii. 6; Hab. iii. 13.

[6] Isa. lxiii. 3.

[7] "Quod gessit bellum cum patribus nostris sicut dicit David Psalmo 23, *v.* 8." The words do not occur in Scripture, but presumably are an expansion of *The LORD mighty in battle*, Ps. xxiv. 8. The Targum is, "Who is this glorious King? The LORD powerful and mighty; the LORD, lord of might and waging war". The addition, "cum patribus nostris", no doubt means that He fought on the side of our fathers. Cf. Aben Ezra, "and He fights on behalf of His saints." The Latin translator tells us in his preface that He purposely does not follow the Vulgate, but gives the exact translation of what he finds in the Arabic. I am told that Lagarde's Arabic Psalter refers to no such variant.

author quotes also "Aser the prophet", chapter iii, as saying, "I saw a man coming down out of the heart of the sea, and he came unto the heaven".[1]

In chh. xiv–xxvi the author deals with the subject of the rejection of the Jews, and the choice of the Christian Church in their stead, the usual texts being quoted. But concerning Christians he says:[2] "Now of these sons, who are the Apostles, Jesus the Wise, the Son of Sirach, says, Hear ye, my beloved sons, and work for your salvation. For God honours the father in the sons."[3] Further on, speaking of the bread and wine of Melchizedek, he says: "In which words the Lord showed clearly by the Prophet that the sacrifice of Aaron would come to an end when that sacrifice began for ever, and the Order of sacrificing; but this Aaron would come to an end when the sacrifice in bread and wine began, which was to last for ever."[4] In ch. xxiii is a description of the Church as the noble Hind of Prov. v. 19, with the application of the rest of the verse to the Sacraments.[5]

The last chapter (xxvii) is of a different kind, and the greater part may even have been taken from the writing of Samuel ibn Abbas (if any was), for it quotes several sayings from the Qoran about Jesus and the blessed Virgin Mary.

The modern English tract adds a note regretting that the author "unfortunately lived at the time of the Middle Ages, when the Christian Church was enveloped in darkness through manifold human traditions, and hence had not the advantage of that better and sounder teaching now happily adopted in most of the Protestant Churches, which allows to the predictions of the second coming of Christ, and the establishment of his kingdom of glory, as literal an interpretation as is done with regard to the predictions of his first coming in a state of humility". It naturally closes with the

---

[1] § 13. "Aser" must represent Ezra, for the reference is plainly to 4 (2) Esdras xiii. 3 in the Syriac, though omitted accidentally in the Latin. The Latin translator of R. Samuel's Letter adds, "because we have not this prophecy I have omitted many things that the author adduces on this point".

[2] Ch. xix.

[3] Ecclus. ii. 2 *sq.*: "Audite filii charissimi, et operamini in salutem; quia honorat Deus patrem in filiis." The modern English tract has mangled the quotation, no doubt for dogmatic reasons.

[4] Ch. xix. This also is mangled for the same reasons. But the Latin itself may be slightly corrupt. The edition of 1769 differs from that of 1591. See also Paul of Burgos' *Scrutinium*, p. 560 a.

[5] Most of this is omitted in the modern English tract.

desire that the example of R. Samuel's earnestness in studying God's word with sincerity may have many imitators.

We may well re-echo this wish, whether we regard R. Samuel as a real person, or as a lay-figure portrayed by a skilful artist, who was devoted to the cause of Christian propaganda among the Jews.

CHAPTER XXIV

PETER ALPHONSI AND HIS DIALOGUE

A.D. 1062–1110

The festival of St Peter and St Paul[1] in A.D. 1106 was a great day in the small but ancient town of Osca, or Huesca, in the north-east corner of Spain. Only ten years had passed since the Moors had been defeated at Alcoraz in 1096, and the town been claimed for his kingdom by Pedro I, King of Aragon (1094–1102). His brother and successor, Alphonso I of Aragon (1102–1134),[2] was present at this festival for a very different reason. His medical man, Moses, a Jew born in Huesca 1062, educated, and, as it seems, living there for most of his life, was being baptised at the hands of Stephen the Bishop, with the King as his godfather. In honour of the day the convert received the name of Peter, and in gratitude to the King surnamed himself Alphonsi.

He seems to have been a genial man, deeply read not only in Jewish but also in secular lore. For he composed a collection of moral tales, taken chiefly from Arabic and Jewish sources, which, under the title of *Disciplina Clericalis*, had a wide vogue in the mediaeval world.[3]

But it was only natural that he should also endeavour to win his former coreligionists to the true faith, by explaining to them the reasons for his own action. He therefore composed his *Dialogue*,[4] to show the untenableness of Gentile religions (particularly the Mohammedan in the midst of which he had lived for thirty-four

[1] June 29. But Peter Alphonsi's words are, "Mense *Julio*, die natalis apostolorum Petri et Pauli" (Preface to his *Dialogue*).

[2] I assume that as Huesca was in Aragon the Alphonso mentioned was the King of that country, who is sometimes called Alphonso VII of Castile, by virtue of his unhappy marriage to Urraca, who succeeded her father Alphonso VI of Castile in 1109. But it is possible that it was Alphonso VI of Castile, paying a visit to his namesake and future son-in-law.

[3] See the *Jew. Enc.* i. 377.

[4] "Dialogus Petri cognomento Alphonsi, ex Judaeo Christiani, et Moysi Judaei" (Migne, *P.L.* clvii. 535–672). In the library of Corpus Christi College, Cambridge, is a MS., "probably of cent. xiii early" (M. R. James' *Catalogue*, 309²), containing the whole *Dialogue*. The text (where I tested it) is identical with that in Migne.

years), and also to prove that the Christian law is superior to all others.[1] The Jewish disputant in the *Dialogue* is called Moses, after the author's name before his baptism, and the Christian Peter, from his baptismal name. The *Dialogue* is much too long to be summarised here at any length. But the headings of his divisions, which, as he tells us, he has made in order that his readers may find in it more quickly what they want, are as follows.[2]

I. This shows that the Jews understand the words of the Prophets in a carnal manner, and explain them falsely. II. This treats of recognising the cause of the present captivity of the Jews, and how long it must last. III. On confuting the foolish belief of the Jews concerning the resurrection of their dead, for they think that these will rise, and inhabit the Land (of Palestine) again. IV. To show that the Jews observe very little indeed of the whole Law of Moses, and that that little does not please God. V. Proving the fallacy of Mohammedanism, and confuting the folly of their opinions. VI. On the Trinity. VII. How the Virgin Mary conceived of the Holy Spirit, and bare a Son without human intercourse. VIII. How the Word of God became incarnate in the body of Christ, and Christ was man and also God. IX. That Christ came at the very time at which it had been foretold by the Prophets that He would come; and that all that they foretold of Him was to be seen in Him and His works. X. That it was of His own free will that Christ was crucified by the Jews and slain. XI. Of the Resurrection of Christ, and His Ascension into heaven. XII. That the Law of Christ is not contrary to the Law of Moses.

It will have been seen that these twelve chapters cover pretty well the whole ground of the subject, but, perhaps necessarily, they sometimes pass beyond the limits of controversy with the Jews as such. For Peter Alphonsi had unbelievers all round him, not Jews only and orthodox Mohammedans, but also philosophers, who, it may be suspected, sheltered themselves under the aegis of one or other of the three great creeds. He had therefore to bear all these classes in mind if he would make his treatise as widely useful as possible. The Jewish disputant, Moses, expresses his wonder that Peter had not become a Mohammedan, rather than a Christian, for he had always lived among the Mohammedans and had read

---

[1] Preface and chapter v.

[2] Observe that the disputants agree to stand by the Hebrew text, thus excluding the Septuagint and the Vulgate, which many less learned controversialists have not scrupled to employ.

their books. Peter therefore describes the Mohammedan religion, with its hope of a material paradise of sensual delights, and he asks if he can be expected to be attracted by that! He then states the salient points in the life of the false Prophet, and his connexion with heretical Jacobites[1] and two Jews, adding something about the Qoran, which was composed after Mohammed's death. He states also that according to Mohammed Christ was not killed, save in appearance.

But while this is almost all that he has to say about the Mohammedanism of the people, he has long essays on philosophical speculations (no doubt partly among Mohammedans of the learned sort), about, for example, the origin of the world, the nature of God, and His work in creation and in the government of the universe. These essays must have been intended for the perusal of the upper classes of all educated men of the period. Naturally they are out of date now, and it is not worth the trouble to any but a very few readers to try to understand the philosophy and the science of that time. But evidently Peter was fully abreast of the knowledge of his day, and did his best to use his knowledge for Christ.

To us it is easier to look at the scriptural arguments which he adduces in favour of Christianity as being consistent with the Old Testament, and fulfilling its prophecies. It is not necessary to attempt to repeat those of his texts which are found in almost all Christian polemical writings. But some are less common. For example, *Elohim* ("God") is the plural, he says, of *Eloha*, and implies a kind of plurality in the Godhead. Hence, if anyone wishes to say "my God" in Hebrew, the form is always *Elohay* (literally, "my Gods"), and no one addresses God in the Hebrew Scriptures as *Elohi*. If indeed Christ said *Elohi*[2] this was because He as the Second Person in the Trinity was addressing the First.

In connexion with his argument for the doctrine of the Trinity in Unity he gives a remarkable statement, and a diagram, derived, he tells us, from an explanation of the Sacred Name in the *Secret of Secrets*—presumably a Cabbalistic writing. The meaning may be seen from the diagram, three Names (JaH, Hu, Vah) making but one Name (JeHoVaH).[3]

[1] Col. 600 A: "Jacobitae autem sunt haeretici, a quodam Jacobo dicti, circumcisionem praedicantes", etc. (cf. *infra*, p. 236).

[2] Matt. xxvii. 46.

[3] Col. 611 A. Alphonsi seems to have used material afterwards incorporated in the Zohar (iii. 65 a and 162 a), translated in Ginsburg, *The Kabbala*, 1864, p. 238 (see *The Proceedings of the Literary and Philosophical Society of Liverpool* for

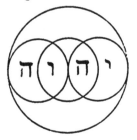

As to Ps. lxxii, the Jew grants that the reference is not to Solomon but to Christ, and says that "our doctors have taught this".[1] To the objection brought by the Jew that Isa. ii. 4 says that Christ will bring peace, and He has not done so, the Christian replies that the passage does not say the nations will actually make peace, but that this is what Christ bids them do.[2] Similarly, the lion and the lamb of Isa. xi. 6 and lxv. 25 cannot be taken literally; the terms really refer to men of different temperaments.[3] Chapter x is chiefly a long discussion on the nature of the devil, and on the question how it was that man fell under his power, and how God restored him. It was out of kindness that Christ did not avenge Himself on His murderers, but prayed for them, and one day, if God will, the children will confess the sin of their fathers.[4] One passage in chapter xii is curious, in saying that circumcision was forbidden lest it should be put on equal authority with baptism, adding that Nestorians and Jacobites assert that each is necessary to salvation.[5]

that year). See also Raymund Martini's *Pugio Fidei*, III. iv. 4, pp. 540–543, and Voisin's note, p. 707, which refers to Bechai on Num. vi. 24. The *Sepher Yetzirah*, i, gives many permutations of the Tetragrammaton. Cf. also Peter of Blois, v. 833 A (*infra*, p. 402).

[1] Col. 622 A. He is probably thinking of the Targum of Ps. lxxii. 1: "O God, give the rules of Thy judgment to King Messiah, and Thy righteousness to the Son of King David." But the application of Ps. lxxii. 8 to Messiah is given expressly in *Bemidbar R.* Par. xiii on Num. vii. 13.

[2] Col. 636 A.   [3] Col. 636 D.   [4] Col. 649 A.

[5] Col. 659 D: "Qui nullum hominem salvari posse putant, nisi per utrumque." This appears to be the doctrine of the Abyssinian Church to-day. For another reference to Jacobites *vide supra*, p. 235. I can find no support for the statement about the Nestorians and Jacobites. Probably our author was rather vague in his nomenclature, and confused them with the Copts (who at least generally practise circumcision to-day, Hastings, E.R.E. iv. 119) and the Abyssinians. The Nestorian "Amrus Matthaei filius", *c.* A.D. 1340, expressly says of his own religion "omissio circumcisionis, ejusque loco verae fidei subrogatio, sicut scriptura docet" according to Assemani's translation (*Bibliotheca Orientalis*, iii. 1728, p. 585).

By far the most noticeable trait, however, in the *Dialogue* is the
way in which the author attacks the Talmud. For this seems to be
the earliest example of what was afterwards so common, pillorying
the anthropological images of God, and the outrageous and para-
doxical tales, contained in the Talmuds and the Midrashim, as
though they were to be taken literally. It is true that they were
often taken literally by even the Jews of Peter Alphonsi's day, and
we cannot blame him for being no wiser than his contemporaries,
but it is impossible to believe that in their origin they were, for the
most part, other than pictures of great or trivial thoughts expressed
in the richness of oriental allegory. Christian readers of the
Apocalypse of St John ought to be the last to insist on the literalness
of Jewish Haggadoth.[1]

Among the many examples of errors of Jewish faith adduced by
Alphonsi the following may be mentioned.[2] A body is ascribed to
God.[3] He wears phylacteries.[4] He is only in the West.[5] He is
limited in space.[6] He is angry at the first hour of the day, though
no one has known the precise hour of his anger except Balaam.[7]
God weeps once every day, and His tears fall into the Great
Sea.[8] Because of His weeping He roars like a lion three times
a day, and beats the sky with His feet, and whispers like a
dove, grieving for His temple.[9] He prays every day that His pity
may surpass His anger.[10]

Tales of another sort which move Alphonsi to ridicule are these.

[1] This strange and unjust misapprehension of the facts has lasted to our own
time, not only among Anti-Semites, from whose ignorance nothing better could
be expected, but even among devout Christians who write tracts for Missions
to the Jews.

[2] Alphonsi seems never to give a literal translation, but only the general
sense of each passage. The references to the Talmud appear to be always to
the Babylonian form.

[3] Col. 541: "In prima parte vestrae doctrinae." *Berakoth*, 6 a. See further
Blau's article on *Shiur Komah* in *Jew. Enc.* xi. 298, and L. Ginzberg's brief
remarks in iii. 462. He speaks of it as "this vexatious piece of Jewish theosophy".

[4] Col. 541. *Ber.* 6 a, 7 a.

[5] Col. 545 D: "In doctrinarum libro." *Baba Bathra*, 25 a. The Shekinah was
in the West. This is discussed.

[6] Col. 549 A: "Vestri doctores in doctrinae libro tertio, Deum in loco esse
asserunt sex partibus terminato." I can find no direct reference for this.
Chagiga, 12 b, speaks indeed of God's dwelling and of the seven firmaments,
but this is not the same thing.

[7] Coll. 549 D, 550 A. *Ber.* 7 a.

[8] Col. 550 B. *Ber.* 59 a. Cf. Peter the Venerable, col. 622 A–B (*infra*, p. 390).

[9] Col. 550 D. Partly in *Ber.* 3 a, 6 b.　　　[10] Col. 551 A. *Ber.* 7 a.

The keys of the treasures were carried by the three hundred camels of Korah.[1] The son of Dan cut a big stone and threw it down on the hosts of Esau at his funeral, which was at the same time as Jacob's.[2] Og, King of Bashan, put a big mass on his head, wherewith to destroy Israel, but a hoopoe, "a very small bird", bored a hole in it, and brought the mass down on Og's shoulders, and his teeth stuck in it.[3]

Again, the angels objected to Moses receiving the Law.[4] Joshua ben Levi by a trick on the angel of death goes to Paradise without dying, and succeeds in not being forced out of it and lives (there) safe until now.[5] John ben Zakkai (*sic*) was so holy that birds which flew over his head when he was reading the Law were burned.[6] Hunni in a drought made a circle of stones, and said he would not step out from it until God sent rain.[7] The empty basket of Chanina ben Dosa was filled.[8] Nicodemus ben Gorion in a drought gets a cistern filled with water.[9] The holiness of Aqiba was foretold to Moses.[10]

Alphonsi also refers to the belief that Christ was a magician, and was born in incest, and led the whole people into error.[11] He mentions also, it may be added, the statement that forty years before the destruction of Jerusalem (i.e. about the time of the Crucifixion) strange portents took place, and that John ben Zakkai quoted Zech. xi. 1 as foretelling them.[12]

[1] Col. 564 c. *Pesachim*, 119 a (*vide infra*, p. 391).

[2] Col. 565 A. See also Peter the Venerable, *c. Jud. P.L.* clxxxix. 644 D. Alphonso de Spina (*infra*, p. 278). In *Sotah*, 13 a, Hushim the son of Dan throws a stone at Esau, who was hindering the burial of Jacob in Machpelah. See further *Jew. Enc.* vii. 24.

[3] Col. 565 c. Cf. *Ber.* 54 b, which says that the hole was bored by ants (*vide infra*, p. 390).

[4] Col. 566 B. *Sabb.* 88 b. Cf. *Jew. Enc.* ix. 50. See also Peter the Venerable, coll. 631 A–633 A (*vide infra*, p. 391).

[5] Col. 566 D. A little in *Derek Eretz Zuta*, i, end.

[6] Col. 569 A. Jonathan ben Uzziel is meant; see *Sukkah*, 28 a, where there is also a long account of Jochanan ben Zakkai.

[7] Col. 569 B. *Taanith*, 19 a. Honi (Onias) ha Meaggel lived in the first century B.C.

[8] Col. 569 B. *Taanith*, 25 a. Cf. Lull's *Blanquerna*, lxii (Peers' translation, 1926), where the Blessed Virgin repeatedly fills the granary of a godly farmer, who gives the corn away to the poor, during a famine.

[9] Col. 569 D. *Taanith*, 20 a.

[10] Col. 570 B. *Menacheth*, 29 b. Cf. *Jew. Enc.* i. 308; Strack and Billerbeck, ii. 344 *sq.*, 526.

[11] Col. 573 A. *Sabb.* 104 b; Mishna, *Yebamoth*, iv. 13 (49 a). Cf. Strack, *Jesus*, pp. 27* *sq.*   [12] Col. 573 c, D. *Yoma*, 39 b.

Again, Aqiba and others were put in prison because they had sold a Jew—who, the Rabbis say, was Joseph. In reality he was Jesus.[1] One of your doctors says that Messiah ben David will come to-day if you believe His words,[2] even as, says Alphonsi, the rejection of Him caused your captivity. Ezek. xxxvii. 1–12, says "Moses", refers to Ephraimites who had died in Philistia.[3] Those born after the Anointed has come will die at the end of His reign.[4] God is especially near us on the ten days from the Festival of the New Year—"so our doctors teach".[5] Passover is never to be observed on Monday, Wednesday, or Friday, because our doctors, and especially Gamaliel, so ordered it.[6]

There are many more references to Talmudic writings to be found in the *Dialogue*, but these will give some idea of the knowledge of Judaism which Alphonsi possessed, and of the method by which he endeavoured to convince his readers of the truth of Christianity. He, of course, like many Jews of mediaeval times, and like the Polish Jews of fifty years ago, had been brought up in the belief that the words of the Talmud were to be interpreted literally, and we cannot but admire the way in which he cut himself off from accepting them as true. But we wish that he had remembered that the Talmud is an Eastern book, compiled by people of vivid imagination for persons like themselves. Yet even if he had

[1] Coll. 575 D, 576 A. Alphonsi also says here that Aqiba and the others were killed in various ways, "quemadmodum mortes illas vestrae doctrinae liber exposuit". See *Berakoth*, 61 b; cf. *Jew. Enc.* viii. 355 *sq.*
[2] Col. 581 A, B: "Interrogatus enim quando filius David esset venturus, 'hodie,' ait, 'si verbis credideritis ejus'." Cf. *Sanh.* 98 a (end): "He said to Messiah, When wilt Thou come, my Lord? To-day.... But He has not come.... Nay, He said, To-day, if ye will hear His voice."
[3] Col. 583 D. See 1 Chr. vii. 20–22; *Sanh.* 92 b.
[4] Col. 592 D. In 2 Esdr. vii. 29 *sq.* Messiah and all human beings die after His reign of 400 years.
[5] Col. 629 D. Cf. *Rosh haShanah*, i. 2, and its Gemara 18 a.
[6] Col. 665 B. Peter explains that it was because Gamaliel knew that on Monday the Jews took counsel against Christ; on Wednesday the plan was made for His betrayal; on Friday was the crucifixion. The Feast of the New Moon may not be kept on a Sunday, a Wednesday, or a Friday (see Levy, *Neuh. u. Ch. Wörterbuch*, iii. 204), or the Passover on Monday, Wednesday or Friday, as Peter says. These prohibitions are secured by the very abstruse system of Intercalations in the Calendar. A still more important rule is that the Day of Atonement may not "fall upon either Friday or Sunday", for in either case the preparation for the Sabbath or for the fast would be put off two days (Joseph Jacob's "Explanation of the Jewish Calendar" in *The Jewish Year Book* for 1897, p. 17).

perceived the true meaning of these figures of speech it is possible that he would not have cared so to state it, for his readers would not have accepted his explanation. And since the question for him and them was really that of accepting such unphilosophical, and even irreligious, nonsense as the literal meaning often gives, or of rejecting it in favour of a religion, which, without danger of any misunderstanding, takes a high view of the holiness and transcendence of God, there can be no doubt that Alphonsi was right in ridiculing the Talmudic sayings. We must speak, and think, of God in terms that appeal to the best and highest that is in us, and in doing so we are led to that form of religion which presents God in His highest and best aspect. And for every Christian this means Christianity.

CHAPTER XXV

RAYMUND DE PEÑAFORTE, PAULUS CHRISTIANI AND RAYMUND MARTINI

Cent. XIII

Who can measure the dynamic of conversion? For spiritual life breaks out in energy for the Kingdom of God in all directions. One example of this is the missionary activity of the thirteenth century, which was the direct result of the dedication of themselves to God by the Italian St Francis of Assisi (about 1206), and St Dominic of Calaroga the Spaniard (about 1200). The spiritual level at which the former lived was, no doubt, higher than that of the latter, and St Francis has ever been the more attractive personality of the two. But he discouraged learning, while St Dominic enforced it.[1] And the Spaniard was right. For in Spain Jews and Mohammedans alike were among the chief thinkers of the day.

The thirteenth was a critical century for the Jews of Europe, but in Spain it produced the most learned of all literary efforts to win them for Christ. And this was not due to chance. It was the result of no little preparation more or less conscious.

The century did not begin well for the Jews. The decision of the Fourth Lateran Council of 1215, that all of them should wear a badge,[2] was a measurable stage in their social degradation in Spain as well as elsewhere. True that Pope Honorius III gave a dispensation in 1219, freeing the Jews of Castile from the obligation of wearing it, but James I of Aragon enforced it in 1228, and his action certainly represented the desire of the greater number of the less educated Christians of the Peninsula. For, in general, there was little love lost between Jew and Christian. Though the

---

[1] "Cum ab eo (Jordan, the second General of the Order) quidam quaereret, quam regulam haberet, respondit, 'Regulam fratrum praedicatorum. Et hec est eorum regula, honeste vivere, discere et docere'" (Reichert, *Vitae Fratrum Ordinis Praedicatorum*, 1896, p. 138). We can all sympathise with the complaint made in A.D. 1220: "Multi religiosi tanto zelo gubernant libros, ut non permittant, quod aliquis alius frater illos legere possit" (*Chronica Ordinis Praedicatorum*, 1897, § 37, p. 24).

[2] For pictures of Jews wearing it, in its various forms and colours, and for the facts connected with its imposition, see the *Jew. Enc.* s.v. *Badge*

Christian used the Jew, he despised and hated him, and more or less feared him.

A remarkable example of this hatred is seen in one of the earliest poems in the Spanish language, No. xviii of the *Milagros de Nuestra Señora*, by Gonzalo de Berceo, of about A.D. 1250.[1] It tells us that the Archbishop of Toledo was at the High Altar in his cathedral, with a large congregation, when suddenly a voice was heard complaining that the Jews were repeating their crucifixion of "my Son". All knew it was the voice of Mary. "The people stirred, with all the clergy, and rushed in haste to the Jewry, Jesus Christ and the Virgin Mary guiding them. Then was their sacrilege discovered! They found in a house of the Chief Rabbi a great figure of wax fashioned like a man—like the Lord Christ was it, set there crucified, fastened with great nails, with a great wound in its side."[2] The result may be imagined, and the poet gloats over the requital of imprisonment and death which was paid by the wretched Jews.[3]

But a better mind was abroad also. The leaders of the Christian Church began to see that mere violence and abuse were insufficient, and that means ought to be taken to ensure a real knowledge of Judaism if its adherents were to be won. The same Pope Gregory IX who in 1236 had protected the Jews of France from persecution by the Crusaders ordered in 1240 the princes of Spain to seize all the Jewish books, "on the first Sabbath next Lent", when the Jews were in synagogue, and to hand over the books so seized to the Dominicans and Franciscans for better security.[4]

The moving spirit, however, of Gregory IX in all that affected the Jews was, no doubt, the famous Raymund de Peñaforte.[5] This remarkable man, born in 1176 at the castle of Peñaforte near

---

[1] *Biblioteca Española*, lvii. 116. See also Lanchetas, *Gramatica y Vocabulario de las obras de Gonzalo de Berceo*, Madrid, 1900.

[2]   "Fallaron en una casa del rabi mas onrrado,
        Un grant cuerpo de çera commo omne formado,
        Commo don Xpo sovo, sedie cruçifigado,
        Con grandes clavos preso, grant plaga al costado." (Stanza 427.)

[3] Observe that this is not the same thing as the horrible Blood Accusation, i.e. the charge that the blood of a Christian child was necessary for the observance of the Passover, which seems to have been fabricated first in 1144. See A. Jessop and M. R. James, *Life of St William of Norwich*, by Thomas of Monmouth, 1896, Book i. v. The accusation is still very common in Europe.

[4] Amador de los Rios, i. 363.

[5] The materials for his life are collected in *Raymundiana* (*Monumenta Ordinis Fratrum Praedicatorum Historica*, vi, Rome, 1900).

Barcelona, and dying in Barcelona at ninety-nine years of age in 1275, had been professor of Canon Law at Bologna for several years, then been brought back to Spain by the Archbishop of Besançon, who had been sent by the Pope on a special mission to Spain, then had joined the Preaching Brothers, i.e. the Dominicans, in 1222, and afterwards been summoned to Rome as the Pope's Chaplain and Penitentiary. Here he collected and edited the Decretals, in a form which Gregory IX ordered the Universities to take as their standard, and he also wrote his *Summa* of Casuistry. He was elected Master General of the Order in 1238, but from bodily infirmity (as it appears) resigned his position in 1240, living the rest of his life in the convent of the Order at Barcelona, high in the King's counsels and universally respected for his piety and zeal.[1] For he was missionary-hearted, and was ready to use right methods in winning Mohammedans and Jews to the Faith. These, he writes, quoting Gregory I, "ought to be moved to adopt the Christian faith by authorities, reasons, and enticements, rather than by harsh dealing; and not to be brought by compulsion, for enforced services do not please God".[2] Even James the First of Aragon, the Conqueror, was himself anxious for the conversion of the Jews, but was opposed to the use of force, for this, he said, would be a sacrilege to the sacrament of baptism.[3] The King also forbade that converts should lose their property on their conversion.[4]

It is not surprising that before 1238[5] Raymund had, with the

---

[1] Bishop Grosseteste's appreciative letter to him in 1235 or 1236 can hardly be only formal.

[2] "Debent autem, sicut ait Gregorius, tam Iudaei quam Sarraceni auctoritatibus, rationibus et blandimentis potius quam asperitatibus ad fidem Christianam de novo suscipiendam provocari; non autem compelli, quia coacta servicia non placent Deo" (*Summa*, Lib. I. iv, *De Iudaeis et Sarracenis*, § 1, Verona edition, 1744). Gregory's words are: "Qui sincera intentione extraneos a Christiana religione ad fidem cupiunt rectam adducere (*Grat. dist.* 45, c. 3), blandimentis, non asperitatibus debent studere, etc." Also "Agendum ergo est ut, ratione potius et mansuetudine provocati, sequi nos velint, non fugere, ut eis ex eorum Codicibus ostendentes quae dicimus, ad sinum matris Ecclesiae Deo possimus adiuvante convertere." *Ep.* to Paschasius, Bishop of Naples, A.D. 591 (*Ep.* xiii. 12; Migne, *P.L.* lxxvii. 1267 *sq.*).

[3] Amador de los Rios, i. 413.

[4] This was the common custom in mediaeval times, strange though it appears to us. Don Jaimé followed the Canons of the Third Lateran Council (A.D. 1179). See Amador de los Rios, i. 412. Cf. L. I. Newman, *Jewish Influence on Christian Reform Movements*, 1925, p. 367.

[5] His action is mentioned before this date in a *Life* of Raymund de Peñaforte written before 1351; see *Raymundiana*, Fasc. i. p. 19.

permission of the Master of the Order and the help of the Kings of Castile and of Aragon, secured the study of Arabic by twenty or more members of the Order. The result was so successful that "more than ten thousand Saracens were converted by the Brothers preaching to them", including nearly all their teachers of Arabic. The document continues: "In Hebrew also by his advice and encouragement some Brothers were similarly instructed. Because they can refute the spite and errors of the Jews, who can no longer as aforetime presumptuously deny the true text, and the interpretations of their own scholars of the earlier days,[1] when these agree with our saints in such points as belong to the Catholic Faith."[2]

Among those Dominicans who received such instruction were, as it seems, both Paulus Christiani and Raymund Martini. The former of these claims our attention at once.

Nothing is known of the date of the birth of Paulus Christiani, and very little of his life,[3] but he was certainly a convert from Judaism, though his Jewish name has not come down to us. He was born probably at Montpellier in Languedoc,[4] and was trained by R. Eliezer of Tarascon. We are quite ignorant of the influence by which he was led to Christ. Possibly he joined the Dominicans in 1229 when Raymund de Peñaforte was sent by the Pope into Provence to preach on behalf of King James' expedition against the Moors of Majorca.

Be this as it may, Paulus became a typical follower of St Dominic, and, armed with royal authority, went throughout Provence,

[1] The meaning of this phrase becomes apparent in the Disputation at Barcelona and in the *Pugio Fidei* (*vide infra*, p. 248).

[2] "In lingua etiam hebraica cum ipsius consilio et favore, fratres aliqui taliter sunt instructi, quod possunt Iudeorum convincere malitias et errores, qui iam non possunt, sicut hactenus consueverant, audacter negare textum verum et glossas suorum sapientum antiquiorum cum sanctis nostris in hiis que ad fidem catholicam pertinent concordantes" (p. 32). Two colleges for the purpose were opened, one in Tunis, and another in Murcia (Strack in Hauck, *Realencyklopädie*, 1905, xvi. 413).

[3] The chief facts are given by Renan, *Les Rabbins Français*, 1877, p. 569. Paulus seems to have died at Taormina in Sicily about 1274.

[4] Montpellier was the birthplace of James I, 1208, the son of Pedro II of Aragon and Mary the Lady of Montpellier. He therefore succeeded to the Lordship of Montpellier, and visited it often during his long reign. It was a town of 10,000 houses in 1273, and was reckoned by James "one of the best in the world" (see Darwin Smith, *Life and Times of James the First, the Conqueror*, 1894, pp. 11, 232). A Jewish convert of Montpellier would therefore naturally have close connexion with Aragon.

about 1260 onwards, preaching to the Jews even in their own synagogues. So it was only natural that he came to be regarded by the Dominicans as their chief spokesman in arguing with the Jews, and was chosen to represent the Christian side at the famous Disputation at Barcelona in 1263, which King James attended with his nobility.

Unhappily for the reputation of Paulus Christiani, the protagonist put forward by the Jews was no other than R. Moses ben Nachman (Nachmanides),[1] one of the most famous of all mediaeval Jewish scholars and writers. Two accounts of the Disputation are extant, one in Latin, very brief, and signed by the King as correct, but doubtless drawn up by the Dominicans;[2] the other in Hebrew, much fuller, and written by Nachmanides himself.[3] They agree in substance, no doubt, but naturally the result as depicted in the Dominican version is that the Jew was defeated, while the Hebrew account is that he was overwhelmingly victorious. A dispassionate study of the two documents leaves little doubt that the latter is truer to the facts of the debate than the former. For, as Nachmanides says, though never speaking discourteously,[4] Paulus had no real knowledge of Jewish Law and Halakah, though he had had some practice in Haggadoth.[5]

[1] The name by which he was known among non-Jews was Bonastruc da Porta, and this has led to no little confusion, the two names being thought to indicate different persons. For a summary of his life and teaching see Broydé's article in the *Jew. Enc.* ix. 87–92.

[2] This and eleven other documents connected with the Disputation are given by O. P. Denifle in his "Quellen zur Disputation Pablos Christiani mit Mose Nachmani zu Barcelona 1263", printed in the *Historisches Jahrbuch im Auftrage der Görres-Gesellschaft*, 1887, pp. 225–244. Denifle, himself a Dominican, tries to show that the Disputation ended in Christiani's victory, but on quite insufficient grounds. The Disputation was spread over four days, not consecutive, but chosen, as it seems, to suit the King's convenience.

[3] Printed from a very imperfect manuscript, together with a Latin translation, by Wagenseil in his *Tela Ignea Satanae*, 1681. But the only trustworthy edition is by Steinschneider (Hebrew only), *Sepher Wikuach ha-Ramban b'inyan ha'emunah liphnê melek wsarim*, Berlin, 1860. The fullest account of the Disputation is by I. Loeb in the *Revue des Études Juives*, 1887, xv. 1–18. See also Schechter, *Studies in Judaism*, 1896, pp. 125–130; Hamburger, *Real-Encyclopädie des Judentums*, iii, Supplement v, 1900, pp. 53–56; Graetz, *Geschichte*, 1873, vii. 132–138 and 417–421.

[4] I.e. in Steinschneider's edition, for Wagenseil's MS. interpolates many abusive expressions.

[5] Steinschneider, p. 7; Wagenseil, p. 28. Similarly, Paulus cannot find a passage in Maimonides to which he himself refers, to the evident amusement of Nachmanides (Steinschneider, p. 17). Again, he is said quite to misunderstand the translation of a passage in a Midrash (*ibid.* p. 20).

The subjects agreed upon for debate were, Whether the Messiah has come; whether according to prophecy He was to be both God and man; whether He did in truth suffer and die for men's salvation; and whether the laws and ceremonies have ceased, and ought to have ceased, after the coming of the Christ. But, in fact, only the first two subjects were formally discussed, the third being touched upon only incidentally,[1] and the debate being broken off before reaching the fourth.

It is not possible to mention here, much less to discuss, most of the Biblical arguments adduced by Paulus, and Nachmanides' arguments against them;[2] but two new points were brought forward, one by Nachmanides, and the other by Paulus. The former is that Christians are mistaken in thinking that the doctrine of the Messiah is all-important in the eyes of Jews.[3] Nachmanides is right. The Messiah does not hold in Judaism at all the same place that He holds in Christianity. In fact, Judaism as a system of religion has very little use for Him. He is, no doubt, a Hope, a glorious Hope, the vividness of which depends on the expectation of the part He will take in bringing material and social, and even religious, welfare to the Jews, and, in measure, to the whole world through the Jews. But this is little more than a side issue. Judaism insists on God, His glory, His everlasting kindness, His uttermost claim on all we have and do and are.

With a Christian it is different. His sense of sin is far more developed than that of a Jew, and he realises his inability to do anything to deserve pardon, even with the help of God, and glories in the personal condescension of God in coming into the world as its Messiah. Christianity without God incarnate as Messiah is a contradiction in terms. Judaism as such does without Messiah, relegating Him to the future. Nachmanides was justified in calling attention to this. A Jew is not concerned much with finding out whether the Messiah has come or not.

The second point is an argument adduced by Paulus Christiani from the use of the Talmud. The Talmud, no doubt, had been

---

[1] See Steinschneider, pp. 11, 13 *sq.*; Wagenseil, p. 43.

[2] Nachmanides is ready enough to give detailed expositions of passages, but the King evidently became rather weary of the length of time he took up. With reference to Ps. cx. 1 he makes the interesting but very improbable suggestion that David *meant* "The LORD said *to me*", but as he could not sing it in the Temple himself he composed it in such a way that the Levites could sing it (Steinschneider, p. 18; Wagenseil, p. 53).

[3] Steinschneider, p. 12; Wagenseil, p. 39.

used by Peter Alphonsi in the twelfth century as a means of attack upon Judaism. He had taken its Haggadoth—a word which answers somewhat to our "illustrations"—in their literal sense, and had had no difficulty in showing their absurdity when so taken. Paulus' line is precisely the opposite. He takes the Haggadoth indeed quite as literally, and, we may be sure, sometimes employed them for the same purpose, and in the same way, as Alphonsi, but here he tries to show from them that their authors knew that the Messiah had already come, and corresponded in nature and activity with the account given in the New Testament. In other words, Paulus appeals from the Jews of his own day to the Jews of Talmudic times, and argues that these had accepted some of the great Christian facts, although they rejected their application.[1] We can sympathise with this view. There are certain statements in the Talmuds and Midrashim with reference to the Messiah which do require explanation, and it was well that the subject should be threshed out. Paulus attempted to do so, but had against him the massive knowledge and the controversial skill of Nachmanides, who says that had Paulus' argument been true the Talmudic doctors would have become Christians—"like Fray Paul, who understands their words better than they do themselves".[2] He adds also the important statement that the *Midrashim*, i.e. "*Sermones*", are not authoritative, even if they do represent the deliberate opinion of individual teachers.[3]

With the result of the Disputation we have nothing to do. According to Nachmanides' account—and we have no reason to doubt its accuracy—the King said he had never seen any one who was in the wrong argue as well as he had,[4] gave him money for his expenses, and sent him home to Gerona in peace.[5] But the influence of the Dominicans was too strong, and eventually he was exiled, and his pamphlet condemned to be burned.[6]

[1] Here we see the outcome of the teaching of Raymund de Peñaforte, *vide supra*, p. 244, note 2. Perhaps an adumbration of this may be seen in "Anastasius'" *Dissertation against the Jews* (of the eleventh century in its present form), in Migne, *P.G.* lxxxix. 1245 D (*supra*, p. 178).

[2] Steinschneider, p. 6.

[3] *Ibid.* p. 10. Nachmanides also includes such parts of the Talmud as are not directly explanations of the Law, i.e. such as belong to Haggada, not to Halaka.

[4] Steinschneider, p. 21; Wagenseil's text is corrupt.

[5] Steinschneider, p. 22; Wagenseil, p. 60.

[6] *Jew. Enc.* ix. 90.

We know little of Paulus Christiani, and we know but little more of his greater contemporary Raymund Martini. The latter was born at Subirato in Catalonia between A.D. 1225 and 1230,[1] of Gentile parents, as it appears. For early writers give no hint of anything else, and it is not until the fifteenth century that Peter Niger, a Dominican, says that Martini had been a Jew for forty years before his conversion, and part of the time a Rabbi.[2] He joined the Dominicans between, as it seems, 1243 and 1248, and he was one of the eight Dominicans chosen by Raymund de Peñaforte in 1250 to study Oriental languages in order to win Mohammedans and Jews to Christ.[3] He did not take any part in the Barcelona Dispute of 1263, but in 1264 he was one of the five Christian scholars appointed to erase blasphemies from the Talmud,[4] and he naturally had ready access to Jewish books, all of which the King had ordered to be confiscated to the Church.[5] Some Christians indeed might urge their destruction, but not he, for, as will be seen, the argument of his book requires their preservation. To him they are important witnesses to the truth of Christianity.[6]

He had already written smaller treatises, the *Capistrum Judaeorum*,[7] and something against the Mohammedans,[8] before he issued his great work, the *Pugio Fidei* ("The Dagger of the Faith"), in 1278. He lived until 1284 at least.[9]

The *Pugio Fidei* had a curious history. For it was plagiarised without acknowledgement by Geronimo de Santa Fé in his

[1] So it is generally said, but as he had worn "the habit of religion" for about fifty years (and he would hardly have taken it before the age of fifteen), and he died after 1 July 1284 (*vide infra*), his birth should be placed 1215–1220. See Carpzov's edition of the *Pugio Fidei*, 1687, Introduction, p. 106.

[2] Wolf, *Bibliotheca Hebraea*, 1727, iii. 900. So also Paul of Burgos, in A.D. 1432, speaks of "Raymundus, Rabbi tuus, in suo *Pugione*" (*Scrutinium*, i. 8, xv).

[3] Diago in Carpzov, *Introduction*, p. 105. Instead of "eight" the early *Life* of Raymund de Peñaforte says "twenty", *vide supra*, p. 244.

[4] Diago, *ibid*.   [5] *Vide supra*, p. 242.

[6] Perhaps it was this feeling that moved Alphonso X of Castile (A.D. 1252–1284) to desire translations to be made of the Talmud and the Qabbala (Amador de los Rios, i. 450).

[7] I.e. "A Muzzle for the Jews", against their errors. It is still only in manuscript. He went to Tunis in 1269, and stayed there for a short time, returning to Barcelona in September of the same year (Carpzov, *Introduction*, p. 105 *sq.*).

[8] *An Explanation of the Apostles' Creed* is also attributed to him in a marginal note in the MS.

[9] For he signed an Act in his convent in July 1284 (Diago, *Historia*, 1598, p. 136, followed by Carpzov, *Introduction*, p. 106).

Hebraeomastix,[1] and was used even more extensively, and with no more honesty, by Peter Galatin, another convert.[2] Victor Porchet de Salvaticis, indeed, who died, as is supposed, in 1315, had honourably acknowledged his source in his *Victoria adversus impios Ebreos*, published in 1520. His words are, Raymundus Martinus "…a quo sumpsi huius Libelli materiam in plerisque compilandi".[3] But even Scaliger in 1604 did not know who was the author of the quotations in Galatin, attributing them to one Raymund of Sebone (died 1432), who was neither a Dominican nor a Hebraist. Bosquet, writing to Voisin in 1651, says that he had, as a young man, read a manuscript of the *Pugio Fidei* at Toulouse, had identified Galatin's quotations as having been taken from it, and had, on careful inspection, seen in it the name of Raymund Martini. At last Voisin edited and published the *Pugio Fidei* in 1651, and finally Carpzov's edition appeared at Leipzig in 1687, embodying Voisin's invaluable notes and illustrations.[4]

Martini's Preface gives an admirable account of the aim and method of his work. St Paul, he says, urges in Tit. i. 9 the preacher

---

[1] *Vide infra*, p. 261 note.

[2] *De Arcanis Catholicae Veritatis contra Obstinatissimam Iudaeorum Nostrae Tempestatis Perfidiam*, 1518.

[3] Strack, *op. cit.* p. 414; Carpzov, *Introduction*, p. 104.

[4] Raymund Martini's own honesty has been impugned. For my dear and revered teacher, Dr Schiller-Szinessy, accused him in the Cambridge *Journal of Philology*, xvi. 130–152, of forging some of his alleged quotations in the interests of Christianity. They seemed to be too crudely Christian to have formed part of Jewish writings. It is sufficient to say here that some of the passages adduced as false have since been discovered, that it is doubtful whether any are too strongly Christian to have been included in some Qabbalistic writing, and that Dr Schiller-Szinessy's theory has not commended itself to scholars, Christian and Jewish alike. See Neubauer in the *Expositor*, 1888, pp. 101–105, 179–189; and also in his *Book of Tobit*, 1878, pp. xviii–xxiv; Abr. Epstein, *Bereshit Rabbati*, 1888. There is no real doubt that Martini copied all his Jewish quotations from Jewish books. The "R. Rachmon" whom he mentions is, no doubt, a mystery, for the name is quite unknown as that of a Rabbi. Dr Schiller-Szinessy suggested that it stood for Raymund himself, which is very improbable. May it be that the quotations attributed to "R. Rachmon" were ultimately taken from a Midrash in which the paragraphs were headed "*Bshem Rachman*", i.e. "In the Name of the Merciful One", as is the case with the Preface of the Yemenite *Midrash ha-Gadol* published by Schechter, 1902, p. xvii? It may be noted that in the *Pugio Fidei* the name of R. Rachmon seems to occur much more often in the Latin than in the Hebrew, which suggests that the mistake (if it be a mistake) was not originally made by Raymund Martini, but was copied by him from a source he used. Paul of Burgos A.D. 1432 refers to "Rabbi Rahamon", who writes on Gen. xv. 15 (*Scrutinium*, i. 6. iv); but he knew Martini's book (*vide supra*).

to exhort the faithful in sound doctrine, and to convince them that gainsay the truth. St Peter too (1 Pet. iii. 15) bids him be ready to give to every man who asks him a reason of the hope and faith which he believes and preaches. Now Seneca tells us that no plague can do more injury than an enemy in our own household, and no enemy of the Christian faith stands closer to us, and can less easily be avoided by us, than the Jew.[1] So, Martini continues, "I have been commissioned[2] to put together from those books of the Old Testament which the Jews receive,[3] and also from the Talmud and their own other writings acknowledged among them, such a work as may serve as a kind of *Dagger* (*Pugio*) which the preachers and adherents of Christianity can always have in readiness, either to divide the bread of the Divine word to Jews, or to slay their impious falsehoods, and put an end to their obstinacy towards Christ and their insensate shamelessness....So I will fashion this *Dagger*, not as I should have liked, but as well as I know how, chiefly against the Jews, but also against the Mohammedans, and certain other opponents of the true faith. Mistakes must be put down to my own ignorance, and may be freely corrected. The material for this *Dagger* is twofold: first and chiefly the Old Testament, secondly, "certain traditions which I have found in the Talmud, the Midrashim (i.e. the Glosses), and the Traditions of the ancient Jews, and have picked them out like pearls from a great dung-heap, to my no slight joy. But these with God's help will I translate into Latin, putting them into their proper places, as will seem best".

Now these traditions, which they call the Oral Law, were, they believe, given to Moses by God on Mount Sinai, and handed by him to Joshua, and so to his successors, until they were committed to writing by the ancient Rabbis. But it is folly to suppose that this is true of the whole Oral Law, because of its many absurdities. Yet of some such traditions we can believe it, for they agree with the teaching of the Prophets and the holy Fathers, and, as will be

---

[1] "Iuxta sententiam Senecae, *nulla pestis sit efficacior ad nocendum quam familiaris inimicus*: nullus autem inimicus Christianae fidei magis sit familiaris, magisque nobis inevitabilis, quam Iudaeus." It is really from Boethius, *De Consol. Philos.* Lib. III, prosa v. Boethius had just illustrated his statement by the "friendship" between Nero and Seneca. I owe this reference to Dr Jenkins.

[2] Presumably by the Head of his Order, or Raymund de Peñaforte, or possibly the King. The following paragraphs are a summary, not a verbal translation.

[3] I.e. exclusive of the Apocrypha. Ecclesiasticus and Wisdom are indeed referred to in Carpzov's Index, but not such a favourite passage as Baruch iii. 37.

seen in this Book, marvellously express the Christian faith, but utterly confound the treacherous opposition of the modern Jews. We must not reject good evidence from any source, and therefore we do not hesitate to wrest this weapon out of the hand of the Jews, and use it against them.

Following Jerome's example I shall use the Hebrew text, and not the Septuagint, or our Latin version, especially as it expresses the Christian truth more forcibly. St Paul himself used the Hebrew. I shall aim at brevity and yet clarity of expression, and the careful transliteration of Hebrew words.

"May the Son of God who moved me to begin, grant His poor servant the power to complete; that it may turn out to the glory and honour of God, the strengthening of believers and the defence of the Faith; and also to the true and profitable conversion of unbelievers; and to the eternal salvation of myself, the least of all in the Order of Preachers! May Jesus Christ grant it, who lives and reigns with the Father and the Holy Spirit, God for ever and ever. Amen."

The *Pugio Fidei* is long (more than 700 folio pages),[1] but so important that the attempt must be made to give our readers some account of it. A very brief summary of its contents in general must suffice.

It is divided into three Parts, of which the First is short (only sixty-six pages), and more or less introductory. It deals with those who err from the truth, and have only the natural, not the revealed, Law; viz. Epicureans, Men of Natural Science, and Philosophers. He shows these that God exists, that pleasure is not the chief good, that the rational soul is immortal, and that philosophers are to be blamed for putting philosophy before faith. They do, however, deserve praise for the way in which they have worked out certain sciences, e.g. Arithmetic, Geometry, Logic, and Astronomy, save that some concern themselves with Astrology. Finally, he considers in some detail their threefold error in saying that the world is eternal, that God is ignorant of details, and that the resurrection of the body is impossible. His arguments in this part are mainly philosophical, with copious quotations from Aristotle and Mohammedan writers.

Martini then turns to those who have the Law, and "because Jews arrogate to themselves the first place among such he attacks them first". He seems to intend to turn afterwards to the Moham-

---

[1] In addition to Voisin's notes at the end of several chapters.

medans, but does not do so. He limits himself to the Jews, save for occasional allusions.

In Part II (about 200 pages) he sets himself to prove that the Messiah has come. He begins by distinguishing the Jews from the Ten Tribes, who have been rejected for their sin in the Calves, and have become Gentiles. Similarly, the Jews proper have been rejected, one of their sins being their belief in two Messiahs, a sin comparable to that of the Calves. Martini then brings forward the usual texts from the Old Testament in favour of his thesis—considering each point at some length, and adducing such evidence from the Talmud and other Jewish writings as bears upon it. He brings forward the Seventy Weeks of Daniel, Gen. xlix. 10 (with much reference to Hillel, "Ben-Cosba", and R. Aqiba), the Image of Nebuchadnezzar, and the Stone throwing it down at one stroke. Further, he tells us that Gen. iv. 25, Jer. xxxi. 22, Ps. ii. 7 are all made to refer to the Messiah in the Great Midrash by Moses ha-Darshan.[1] Then come proofs from our Lord's miracles, which even the Jews acknowledge.

He then shows that Messiah was to come while the Second Temple was still standing, adducing Mal. iii. 1, 2, Ps. lxxxix. 36, Hagg. ii. 6–9 and other passages. He adds proofs from the Talmud that according to the computation of the duration of the world Messiah must have already come.[2]

Having thus completed his chief thesis he devotes the rest of this Second Part to a consideration of some of the objections brought forward by his opponents. The Jews say "Christ has not saved the Jews". He answers You mistake the meaning of salvation. This was to be spiritual, not carnal, and the promise is only to "one of a city and two of a family" (Jer. iii. 14), or even to "two out of six hundred thousand", as the Talmud says.[3]

---

[1] A French exegete living at Narbonne in the middle of cent. xi. His relation to the *Midrash ha-Gadol* is very uncertain. See the *Jew. Enc.* ix. 64.

[2] He here (II. x. 2) notes incidentally that he is writing in A.D. 1278, or 5038 from the Creation, according to the Jewish reckoning.

[3] T.B. *Sanh.* 111 a. There is a *Boraitha* (an unofficial Mishna); R. Simai said: "It is said, 'And I will take you to Me' (Ex. vi. 7 and Jer. iii. 14), and it is said, 'And I will bring you' (Ex. vi. 8 and Jer. iii. 14). He compares the going out from Egypt to the entering in to the Land. As the entering in to the Land was two out of six hundred thousand [only Caleb and Joshua, Rashi], so was it in the going out from Egypt [the rest died in the three days' darkness, Rashi]." Rabba said: "And so will it be in the days of Messiah, for it is said, 'And she shall respond there, as in the days of her youth, and as in the day when she came up from out of the land of Egypt'" (Hos. ii. 15 (17)).

Further, the Jews argue, "How could he who could not save himself, save others?" And how could Messiah be killed, or, as He feared death, be God? The answer to this difficulty involves the statement and discussion of the whole subject of a suffering Messiah, which Martini shows was taught both in the Old Testament and in the Talmudic literature. Again: "If Jesus was Messiah all peoples and nations ought to have accepted Him, and He have become their King and Ruler. But this is not the case." Martini investigates the passages alleged to prove this, and shows that the Jews interpret them much too carnally. Again: "There are to be no weapons of war in the days of Messiah." But the Talmud itself says that the days of Messiah are to be like our own. Again: "Christ did not come in the clouds of heaven, as was promised." There is a double Coming, says our author. Further, "The light of the sun and moon has not increased" (Isa. xxx. 26). But strange events did take place in the heavens at His death. "Wherefore," Martini adds, "let him who would defend the Faith, and attack the error of the Jews, pay watchful heed to whatever nonsense they allege against Jesus, from other places in Scripture in such manner as has already been stated, and carefully distinguish what suits the first, and what the second Coming of Christ, and in what way any prophecy belongs to His human nature, and any to His divine. Let him mark too what is said in Scripture about the good Israel and Jacob, and what about the bad. And so let him reply to each argument as is fitting and suitable in each case."[1]

The Jews argue also that "God promised that in the days of Messiah He would gather them from among the Gentiles, and He has not yet done so". Martini here falls in with the usual *praeiudicium* of his age, and repudiates altogether a restoration of the Jews in Christian times, though we in this twentieth century see it taking place before our eyes. He therefore says that all such promises were fulfilled by God in the time of Cyrus, and no further restoration is to be expected. He closes the Second Part of his book by reminding the Jews that all God's promises and threats are conditional, and that if they do not conform to the conditions they cannot expect to be blessed.

In the Third Part (about 450 pages) there are three Divisions, dealing respectively with the doctrine of the Trinity according to Holy Scripture and the Talmudic books; the Fall of man and the punishment of sin, showing also why men could not be freed from

[1] II. xiii. 8.

such punishment save by God incarnate; and the Restoration, Redemption, and Glorification of man.[1] This third Division of the Third Part contains not a little which has been considered before at greater length. Possibly parts of it were written first, but, in any case, their incorporation here makes for the completeness of the subject. God's Word, i.e. His Wisdom, i.e. His Son, was to be sent by Incarnation. The various names of Messiah in the Old Testament are collected, some of them directly implying His Divinity. Only because He is truly God and truly man can He suffice for men's salvation. Various objections to the doctrine of the Incarnation are stated and refuted. There follow considerations of our Lord's attitude to the Law, especially as regards Circumcision and the Sabbath. The Sacraments are then considered, Baptism, Penance (for there is to be *poenitentia* in the days of Messiah), and the Eucharist. After pointing out the necessity for the sufferings of the Messiah, the author discusses the Descent into Hades, where Christ redeemed the captives, His Resurrection, Ascension, and Session on the right hand of God. Messiah was also to give a New Law, and to send the Holy Spirit.

Martini closes this third Division of the Third Part, and so the whole Book, with again insisting that there can be no Restoration for the Jews, and that the Jews of his day were much worse than their forefathers, and had been smitten with judicial blindness to the Truth, and held grossly erroneous doctrines. The Jews will remain till the end of the world in ignorance of the true God, only a remnant of them being saved.

Would that Martini's chief argument were sounder! For, learned though he is, in the philosophy of his day and in Jewish literature—so far at least as regards its Haggadic portions, for he has given us little opportunity of knowing whether or not he was versed in the more fascinating, because more subtle, intricacies of Halaka, the substance of Talmudic Law properly so-called—he yet has followed, we believe, a will-o'-the-wisp in using the Talmud to prove the truth of Christian doctrine. He is, no doubt, quite within his rights in adducing its evidence to show the existence of Jesus and His disciples, and the truth of the statement that Jesus performed miracles, and even to show that the Messiah was expected to come about the time that our Lord did come. But that Talmudic Jews, apart from the possible influence of Christian thought upon individual Jewish teachers in Christian times, believed and taught

[1] "Humanae reparationis, redemptionis, et glorificationis."

such Christian doctrines as the Divinity and Incarnation of the Messiah, the Fall of man and the consequent sinfulness of the human race (in the Christian sense), or, again, the Passion and Death and even Resurrection and Ascension of the Messiah, is to misinterpret the meaning of the Talmud. Workers among the Jews of our own day dare not use arguments of this kind, for they are demonstrably false. Where Jewish writings do contain such evidence for Christian truths, they are not independent of Christian influence, and thus are worthless when adduced in support of the truth of Christian doctrine. There is no real opposition between the ancient Jews and those of Martini's day, or our own. Jews rejected the truth of old, as they reject it still, for reasons which go far deeper into the heart and conscience than the interpretation of texts.

Yet the *Pugio Fidei* is not only marked by wide learning and sound knowledge of Jews and Judaism, but is also so comprehensive as to leave hardly any part of the controversy between Jews and Christians untouched. No doubt it is limited in its outlook on many subjects by the faulty learning of its time. The thirteenth century was not the twentieth. But, when all is said and done, Martini's work remains well worthy of the careful study of those who desire to understand the differences between Jews and Christians, and to appreciate the reality of the efforts which Christian scholars have made from time to time to win the Jews to Christ.[1]

---

[1] It is much to be wished that an abbreviated edition of the *Pugio Fidei* were published, incorporating the Jewish quotations, with some of Voisin's notes, and adding notes and explanations more suitable to our own day. It would form a valuable introduction to the study of Jewish literature.

CHAPTER XXVI

RAYMUND LULL

A.D. 1266–1315

We see an afterglow of Raymund de Peñaforte's influence in Raymund Lull.[1] For though born of noble parentage at Palma in Majorca in 1236, and spiritually converted only in 1266, he yet came into close contact with the aged saint, and owed much to his advice. Few men have taken a wider range of subjects for their study than Lull, and few have written more about them all. But the charm of the *Doctor Illuminatus* lies not in his erudition or the clearness of his thought, but in the intensity of his love for Christ, as seen in both word and deed. This is not the place to speak of his missionary enterprise in general, or of the tragedy of his martyrdom by the Mohammadans at Bugia in North Africa (i.e. Bougie, a little east of Algiers) in 1315. He was as keen on winning Jews to the Saviour as on winning Mohammedans. But his methods differed from those of his contemporaries. It is indeed singularly unfortunate that of the three works referring to the Jews attributed to him, and perhaps surviving somewhere in manuscript—viz. *Against the Jews, On the Hebrew Reformation, On the Coming of Messiah*[2]—none seems to have been printed. For it is probable that they present to the Jews a picture of Christ and His teaching in a form infinitely more agreeable to that of the New Testament than is that of most controversialists. We are led to suppose this, not only from his works in general, but also from his treatise *On the Gentile and the Three Wise Men*,[3] the gist of which is as follows: Three men, a Jew, a Christian and a Mohammedan, meet and go into a forest to rest and meditate. They all come to a very fair meadow where is a

---

[1] I have retained the common English form of the name Raymund, derived from the Teutonic and Norman-French, which has been softened into Ramon in Catalan and Castilian. All earlier Lives are superseded by Prof. Peers' *Ramon Lull, a Biography*, 1929. It has a very full Bibliography. See also C. Ottaviano, "L'Ars Compendiosa de R. Lulle", in *Études de Philosophie Médiévale*, 1930, pp. 1–103. Lull's complete works are now being published for the first time in their original Catalan (1906–). The Latin translation was printed in 1721–1742 (8 vols. folio).

[2] *Liber contra Judaeos, Liber de Reformatione Hebraica, Liber de Adventu Messiae*, numbered 247, 248, 250 in the catalogue in the *Acta Sanctorum*, June, vol. v for the 30th day, p. 704. But in their case no notice is added to say whether they exist or not. Probably they do not.

[3] *De Gentili et Tribus Sapientibus* (*Opera*, 1722, ii. 1–94).

lovely spring (*fons valde decorus*) which waters five trees bearing fruit of various virtues and vices. By the spring is a lady called *Understanding*,[1] who speaks to them of the doctrine of God in general, and of the meaning of the trees and their fruit. Then a Gentile comes up, emaciated through his long wandering in the forest, with eyes bathed in tears, and sighing as he comes, who has to drink of the spring before he can even talk to the Sages. He then greets them, and they return his salutation, with their prayers that God as the Creator of all things, He who will also raise the good and the evil from the dead, will comfort him, and help him in his need. The Gentile marvels at their words, and at the trees with their fruits, and in reply to their questions says he has never heard of God or the Resurrection. They then give him instruction, beginning with a general statement referring to the Trees, and afterwards each from his own point of view. First, the Jew declares his faith in detail (the account seems to be admirably fair), then the Christian his faith, and last of all the Mohammedan, each adducing in his favour the fruit of the Trees. In the end the Gentile is convinced of the existence of the one true God, and offers to Him prayers of singular beauty. The other three part in a very friendly way, each expressing his hope that he has said nothing to grieve either of the others. They also arrange to discuss matters together often, "that they might be able to agree in one faith and law, and take their course through the world, giving praise and glory in the name of our God".[2]

Another extract from Lull's *Contemplation of God* indicates perhaps still better his attitude to all missionary enterprise, and its advice is as necessary to us to-day as ever it was. "I see many knights going to the Holy Land across the sea, and thinking to gain it by force of arms, but at last they all perish without attaining to their hope. Wherefore it seems to me that the gaining of that Holy Land may not be carried out save by that very same way in which Thou and Thy apostles gained it, namely, by love and prayers and pouring out of tears and blood."[3] He continues, "Since Thy holy

[1] "Intelligentia."

[2] "Ut in una fide et lege possent concordare, et percurrerent mundum, dando laudem et gloriam de nomine nostri Dei" (vol. ii, p. 94). There are many references to winning Jews to Christ by proper instruction and devotion in Lull's *Blanquerna*, e.g. xliv, lxxi, lxxx, lxxxiii *sq*.

[3] "*Gloriose Domine, pie, humilis, dulcis, simplex et suavis!* Multos equites video ire ad sanctam Terram ultramarinam, et putare ipsam acquirere per vim armorum, et in fine omnes consumuntur, quin veniant ad id, quod putant:

Sepulchre, O Lord, and the Holy Land across the sea must, as it seems, be gained rather by preaching than by force of arms—let all the holy knights of religion go forward, protecting themselves by the sign of the Cross, and filled with the grace of the Holy Spirit, and so go to preach to the Infidels the truth of Thy Passion, and for love of Thee pour out their very eyes in floods of tears, and all their body's blood, even as Thou didst for love of them."[1]

unde videtur mihi, quod acquisitio illius sanctae Terrae non debeat fieri, nisi eodem modo, quo Tu et tui Apostoli eam acquisistis, scilicet amore et orationibus et effusione lacrymarum et sanguinis" (cap. CXII. § 10, vol. ix, p. 250).

[1] "Cum sanctum Sepulchrum et sancta Terra ultramarina, *Domine*, videatur debere acquiri per praedicationem melius, quam per vim armorum, progrediantur sancti equites religiosi, et muniant se signo Crucis, et impleant se gratia sancti Spiritûs, et eant praedicare infidelibus veritatem tuae Passionis, et effundant pro tuo amore totam aquam suorum oculorum, et totum sanguinem sui corporis, sicut Tu fecisti pro amore ipsorum" (§ 11, vol. ix, p. 250). The date of the *Contemplation of God* does not seem to be known, but presumably it was much earlier than the strange *Liber de Fine* (A.D. 1305), in which Lull sets forth in detail a proposition for the conquest of the Holy Land by means of all the appliances and methods of the wars of his time. The natural doubt of the genuineness of this work is stifled by the fact that Lull appeared in person at the Council of Vienne (1311) to urge this his new plan. He seems to have thought in his old age that only after the Saracens were defeated would the Gospel be brought home to them with success. Yet he vindicated his earlier position by going soon after the Council of Vienne once more to Bugia, courting and receiving martyrdom for Christ. A. Gottron discusses the question fully, and gives extracts from the *De Fine*, in his *Ramon Lulls Kreuzzugsideen*, Berlin, 1912. It is observable that Gottron's summary of a small section in *De Fine*, "Against the Jews", is also marked by a harshness very unlike the spirit of Lull's writing quoted above. The change in Lull's opinions, if it really took place, may be compared with that of Augustine about the Donatists (see *Epp.* xxiii. 7 and xciii. 2 and 5), and with that of Luther, who desired in his treatise, *On the use of Christian Freedom*, 1524, to "bring a Jew in all kindness to believe in Christ", but in his later years advised the destruction of their synagogues. In *Blanquerna*, lxxxvii, § 4, Lull evidently favours the force of arms to compel unbelievers to allow the preaching of the Gospel in their land, but in § 5 he urges spiritual forces only.

CHAPTER XXVII

ABNER OF BURGOS
(ALPHONSO OF VALLADOLID)
c. A.D. 1270–1348

A brilliant young Jewish scholar, who also practised medicine, one Abner of Burgos, had a strange experience in A.D. 1295.[1] Two Rabbis of godly life appeared, one in Avila,[2] in the Province of Compostella where Abner himself was, and the other in Ayllon near Toledo, announcing that on the last day of the fourth month in that year the Lord would give a sign of His redemption of Israel. The Jews went in multitudes into their synagogues to pray, wearing their white robes—of linen or silk as the case might be—as on the Day of Atonement. But suddenly these were all marked with a cross, and not only those actually being worn, but those also which were still laid up in wardrobes. No wonder that the Jews were shocked, some consulting Abner about their own health, some asserting that it was the work of the devil by magic art, others hesitating to express any opinion (for they did not deny the fact), and a very few being led by it to consider the truth of Christianity more deeply, and even to be baptised.

Abner himself belonged to the last class, although it was very long afterwards that he was baptised, at sixty years of age (*c.* A.D. 1330), when he took the name of Alphonso, after the King, and then, because he was appointed Sacristan at Valladolid,

---

[1] He tells us of it himself in his *Wars of God*, ch. 27, a writing which has not been printed, though a MS. of the Spanish version is said by Rodriguez de Castro to be "en el monasterio de Religiosos Benitos de Valladolid" (*Biblioteca Española*, 1781, i. 195 *sq.*). Otherwise the work is known only by quotations. The incident here recorded is copied by Paul of Burgos in his *Scrutinium*, II. 6, x (*vide infra*, p. 275), who adds that though the miracle happened sixty years before his own birth, yet (speaking the truth before God) he well remembers the old people still talking about it. Some of the details given above are from the quotations in Alphonso de Spina's *Fortalitium Dei*, 1495, III. 10, x (*vide infra*, p. 279). De Spina appeals also to "Magister Johannes Conversus in libro suo *De Concordia legum*, IV. iv", who lived only forty years after the incident, as saying that the case was investigated by a papal nuncio, as well as by Paul of Burgos.

[2] See the *Jew. Enc.* i. 98, s.v. *Abraham of Avila*.

became known in Christian circles by the name of Alphonso of Valladolid.[1] He wrote much in Hebrew or in Spanish, for he knew no Latin, but all that concerns us is *The Wars of God* (partly an answer to Jacob ben Reuben's *Book of the Wars of the* LORD), *The Book of the Three Graces*, and *The Guide to Righteousness*. They are still unprinted. The aim of the last is chiefly "to convert the Jews by showing the truth of Christianity from the Talmud and the Midrashim without appealing to the Bible".[2] It is to be regretted that Abner-Alphonso allowed himself to accuse his former co-religionists of reciting in their synagogue services a prayer against the Christians,[3] and thus to lead the King of Castile (Alphonso VI) to publish an edict forbidding the Jews to use it. After the King's death the edict was ignored. Abner-Alphonso himself died about 1348.

[1] Much the fairest estimate of Abner-Alphonso is by Isidore Loeb (*Revue de l'histoire des Religions*, 1888, xviii. 141–144). He says: "Ses ouvrages firent sensation; ils sont considérés, par les juifs, comme le fondement de la nouvelle polémique chrétienne, et la plupart des controversistes juifs d'Espagne se croient obligés de les combattre." Graetz, as usually when he writes of "apostates", has not a good word to say of him (vii. 317–321, 485–489). Moses of Narbonne in his *Maamer ha Bechirah*, 1361 (see especially Munk, *Mélanges*, 1859, pp. 502–506), accuses him of becoming a Christian in order to satisfy his earthly ambition and desire for a living, and of defending his step by appealing to the compulsive influence of the stars. His books were much used by Servetus, see L. I. Newman, *Jewish Influence on Christian Reform Movements*, 1925, p. 191; cf. p. 550. Newman's study of the Jewish works that influenced Servetus (pp. 511–609) is of much interest.

[2] It would be interesting to see whether he used the arguments of Paulus Christiani and Raymund Martini (*vide supra*, pp. 247, 253 *sq.*). The special aim of *The Guide to Righteousness* seems to be the same as that of the first of the two treatises of Geronimo de Santa Fé (*vide infra*, p. 262). It may be guessed, not uncharitably, that the later writer used his predecessor freely.

[3] See Singer's *Authorised Daily Prayer Book*, p. 48, with Abrahams' note, and Justin, *Trypho*, xvi. 4 (*supra*, p. 34). The prayer was originally directed against Jewish-Christians only.

CHAPTER XXVIII
GERONIMO DE SANTA FE
FLOURISHED A.D. 1414

The work of the Dominican friar Vicente Ferrer does not come directly under our purview. Urged on by his friend Pedro de Luna, who had now become Benedict XIII, Pope at Avignon (1394–1424), he passed throughout Castile in 1411, "with a cross in one hand and the Torah in the other", preaching with a fiery zeal in the synagogues, to such effect that the number of converts was, according to one authority (Mariana), 35,000, according to another (Zacuto), more than 200,000![1] Probably even the lower number is exaggerated and in any case, one shudders to think of the severity of the persecution which gave rise to such mass movements. For our present purpose, however, the interest lies in the fact that he had among his most eager assistants one who in his Jewish days bore the name of Joshua Ibn Vives al-Lorqui (or Lorca, Lorka), and now the baptismal name of Geronimo de Santa Fé (Hieronymus de Sancta Fide).[2]

Beyond the fact that he was born at Lorqua in Murcia,[3] and was brought up as a Jew, and acquired at least some Jewish learning,[4] little is known of him until after his conversion.[5] He was afterwards

[1] Joseph Jacobs in the *Jew. Enc.* xi. 496 *sq.*

[2] Compilers of catalogues and dictionaries insert their notices of him under one or other of the many forms of his names, and seldom put cross-references!

[3] Or perhaps at Alcanes in Northern Spain, see Graetz, 1875, viii, Note before the Index.

[4] He can express himself well and clearly, and his quotations from Jewish literature seem to be generally trustworthy. But he is a tyro compared with Raymund Martini. It will be seen below that although Geronimo often used the *Pugio Fidei* he did not slavishly copy it, as did Galatinus later, who quotes whole passages from the *Pugio* without saying so (e.g. Galatinus, xi. 1). We cannot blame Geronimo much for not mentioning his indebtedness to Raymund Martini. Literary honour of that kind is modern, and Geronimo refers to hardly any recent writer. He does, indeed, in the end of ch. II, bid his reader turn to Nicholas de Lyra for further information on a certain point, but de Lyra's *Postilles* were very much shorter than the *Pugio Fidei*, and far more widely spread.

[5] It used to be supposed that he was the Lorqui who defended Judaism against Paul of Burgos (Steinschneider, *Jewish Lit.* 1857, p. 128), but the identification is now abandoned (Graetz, p. 402). See Kayserling's two articles on Ibn Vives al-Lorqui Joshua ben Joseph in *Jew. Enc.* vi. 551 *sq.*

the body physician of Benedict XIII, whom he induced to order a public Disputation at Tortosa between Jews and Christians. This began on Feb. 7, 1413, and lasted with many interruptions till Nov. 12, 1414.[1] But before the Disputation he wrote two treatises, probably by way of preparing both himself and the Pope with his adherents for the approaching discussion. They have come down to us under the titles of *To prove the perfidy of the Jews* and *Concerning Jewish errors drawn from the Talmud*,[2] the first quite courteously marshalling the evidence of the Talmudic writings to the truth of Christianity (for this, as we have seen already, was a common argument), and the second, alas, collecting together the worst parts of the same literature. The second need not detain us long, but the first deserves some consideration.

The aim of the treatise, *To prove the perfidy of the Jews*, is to prove the chief doctrines of Christianity from the words of the Prophets and the recognised authorities among the Jewish Doctors. Geronimo rightly begins by saying that in all discussions we must first of all see what principles are granted by both sides. For before physicians come to an agreement about their treatment they must agree first about the nature of the illness which is to be cured. There is much then in common between Jews and Christians. Both acknowledge the authority of the Prophets as well as of the Pentateuch;[3] both, that God was to send the Messiah; and both that He was to be of the seed of David. But there are also grave differences. A Jew observes the Mosaic Law literally,[4] and according to rules laid down in the Talmud; but the Christian not literally, for he interprets it according to the preaching of Jesus Christ. Again, the Jew affirms that the Messiah of the seed of David has not yet come, while the Christian is sure that He has. Yet, adds Geronimo, these two points of difference are really one, for the first depends on the second.

---

[1] See J. Jacobs, *Jew. Enc.* xi. 497. Geronimo was the leader on the Christian side. A short Hebrew account of the Disputation is given in Kobak's *Jeshurun*, vi. 45–55.

[2] *Ad convincendum perfidiam Judaeorum* and *De Judaicis erroribus ex Talmut*. The second was printed in 1552, and both together in 1602 under the common title of *Hebraeomastix* ("The Scourge of the Hebrews"). They may be found most conveniently in the *Bibliotheca Magna Veterum Patrum*, Lyons, 1677, xxvi. 528–554. Migne omits.

[3] This might have been qualified; for Jews set the authority of the Law far above that of the Prophets.

[4] P. 530 c: "Materialiter."

He is here careful to point out, and indeed it is an essential part of his argument, that while Jews generally insist on the literal words of Scripture they are also well acquainted with their more spiritual meaning, as is seen in their interpretations of "Sion", "Israel", "Jerusalem", etc.[1] He then says[2] in scholastic phraseology, that his major syllogism is that He in whom meet all the acts and conditions attributed to the Messiah by the Prophets is the true Messiah, and his minor, that because all these meet in Jesus, He, and no other, is the true Messiah. Geronimo then mentions twenty-four such acts and conditions, but as these are of the usual kind his list need not be repeated here.

In ch. ii Geronimo shows that the Messiah was to come shortly before the destruction of the Second Temple, and confirms his quotation of Mal. iii. 1 and Isa. lvi. 1 by an appeal to the *Breshith Rabba* of Moses ha Darshan.[3] At the end of the chapter he bids his reader refer to "Nicolas de Lyra and his gloss, where you will find it all stated plainly and sufficiently and in accordance with the true Faith".[4] In chh. iii, iv, v he shows that the Messiah was to be born at Bethlehem, of a Virgin, true God according to His Divinity and true Man according to His humanity. One of his quotations is from the Midrash *Tillim* on Ps. xxxvi. 10: "One lighted his lantern, and it went out; he lighted it again, and it went out; Then he said, How long shall I trouble with this lantern? I will wait for the light of heaven, and I shall walk in the light.... They were in bondage in Egypt and Moses arose; in Babylon and Daniel, etc.; in Elam and Mordecai, etc.; therefore said Israel.... No longer will we wait for redemption by flesh and blood, but for our Redeemer, the LORD of Hosts is His name, the Holy One of Israel; and we seek not henceforth for flesh and blood to give us light, but for the Holy One, blessed be He, to give us light, for it

[1] P. 531 B, C. He says that Rashi in a gloss on *Sanh.* § "All Israel" (i.e. *Perek* xi) says that Ezekiel in the end of his prophecy refers to the heavenly Jerusalem ("intelligitur de caelesti Jerusalem"). I cannot identify the passage, but perhaps the reference is to p. 100 a on Ezek. xlvii. 12.

[2] P. 531 E.

[3] P. 532 D: "In Bresit Rabi Moyse praedicatorio." Geronimo is very fond of this form of reference, but I do not know whether his use of it has ever been critically examined, to see whether he quotes Moses ha Darshan independently or not. I cannot find that this passage at least is taken from the *Pugio Fidei*. Abr. Epstein does not mention Geronimo in his stimulating *Bereschit Rabbati*, 1888, nor, as it seems, in his *Moses ha Darschan aus Narbonne*, 1891 (Hebrew).

[4] P. 534 G: "Require autem Nicolaum de Lyra et glossam ejus, ubi totum catholice ac realiter declaratum reperies et sufficienter."

is said, 'For with Thee is the fountain of life, and in Thy light shall we see light'."[1]

In ch. vi he argues that it was prophesied in the time of Abraham that the kings of the East should come before Messiah with incense, etc. In support of this he adduces a passage from Moses ha Darshan which is found in the *Pugio Fidei*, p. 603.[2] It is to the effect that *Saba* in Gen. xxv. 3 was among the children of Abraham, and that, when Solomon prospered, the men of Saba thought he might be Messiah, and therefore it was that the Queen of Sheba came. For she had prophets who prophesied to her "in the name of the LORD".[3]

A good deal of his ch. vii ("Before the coming of Messiah all souls were in hell, because of the first sin, but were rescued by Him") is also in the *Pugio Fidei*.[4] Among the passages adduced is one from *Chagigah*, showing that even the Wise go to Gehenna, but, like the salamander, are not injured by its fire, for they are already all on fire with the fire of God, as is said, "Are not My words as a fire?"[5]

Ch. viii deals with the resurrection of Messiah after three days and His ascension; ch. ix with the new teaching that He was to set forth.[6]

In ch. x he points out that even the Mohammedans believe much which is in the Law of Moses, thus fulfilling part of the prediction that the coming of the Messiah will bring the end of idolatry, and the recognition of God by all the Gentiles. For, as R. Chanina says in *Midrash Tillim* on Ps. xxi. 1, referring to Isa.

---

[1] P. 537 G, H. See *Midrash Tillim* on Ps. xxxvi. 10 (Buber, p. 125 b). Further, Geronimo uses the following illustration from the *Siphra* on Lev. xxvi. 12. It is like a king who went out to walk in his garden with his labourer, but the labourer hid himself. Says the king, Fear not, for I am like thee. So in the future will God walk in Paradise among the just, and when they are afraid He says to them, Behold, I am like you. Geronimo does not use here the phrase "in Paradise", but "Paradise" occurs in another quotation by him in the same context from T.B. *Taanith*, end.

[2] Yet it is not copied from the *Pugio Fidei*, if we may judge from the context in each.

[3] 1 Kings x. 1; p. 538 B.

[4] Pp. 538 E–539 F. Cf. *Pugio Fidei*, pp. 481, 483, 485. Yet here there is little verbal coincidence. Geronimo was no mere copyist.

[5] Jer. xxiii. 29. See *Chag.* 27 a; *Pugio Fidei*, p. 485.

[6] P. 540 D. Here again, a quotation from *Cant. R.* on Cant. i. 2 is to be found in *Pugio Fidei*, p. 689 *sq.*, but the context is different, again suggesting Geronimo's independence as a scholar.

xi. 10, "King Messiah comes only to give commands to the peoples".[1]

In ch. xi Geronimo speaks of the humility of the promised Messiah in riding on an ass; and in ch. xii he shows quite briefly that (a) the coming of Messiah was to be announced by a herald in the desert; (b) The Jews are in Captivity because of their ingratitude to Him; (c) God the Father having for that reason shut the doors of Heaven so that He should not listen to their prayers; (d) yet He always holds the door of conversion open for those who repent and desire to be baptised.[2]

The most original part, however, of Geronimo's first treatise is his *Anacephalosis*.[3] I have proved my case, he affirms. Yet some one will say, If the Talmud, etc. thus testify of Messiah, why do the Jewish scholars, "and in particular those who labour night and day in the study of this Talmud", refuse to listen to its teaching about Christ? There are two reasons. First, this doctrine about the Messiah is chiefly to be found in the part of the Talmud called *Haggadoth* ("narrationes") or *Midrassoth* ("sermocinationes"), which, however, are intermingled with the rest, and the Jews, in their study, do not pay much attention to *Haggadah*, "saying that it bears no fruit. For their aim is to read nothing but those material sayings which concern enquiries about food. For which reason the common and simple-minded populace give them honour". They therefore do not consider, and indeed are ignorant of, the authoritative passages I have quoted.

Secondly, perhaps on their reading they do note one or two, or even three, of these passages, and yet are not impressed. For they ought to consider many of these, and to compare them one with another. Besides, their studies being but worldly, they turn away from the truth. Yet some do consider, and do listen, and do yield to the message.

Geronimo is not very wide of the mark in the reasons that he here gives for their unbelief.

Geronimo's second treatise stands in sad contrast to his first, and might have been composed by an ignorant Anti-Semite of our own

[1] P. 542 B, C. "R. Chanina" in the ordinary text, but in Buber's "R. Tanchuma", and also expressly "six commandments". The *Pugio Fidei* (p. 516) adds "such as Tabernacles, the Lulab (the ceremonial palm branch used at the Feast of Tabernacles), and the Phylacteries, but Israel learns the Law from the Holy One, blessed be He". And so Buber's edition.
[2] Cf. de Spina, *infra*, p. 279.
[3] P. 544 C-G.

day. Its title, *On Jewish errors drawn from the Talmud*,[1] hardly expresses its real object, which is to show that in the Talmud are "lying, foul, foolish and abominable quibbles, contrary to the Law of God, to the Law of Nature, and to the Law as written".[2] Yet the Jews are governed by its precepts, which are not mentioned in the Law of Moses, and are held to be equal to those contained there. They who deny this do so on pain of death. But his holiness Pope Benedict XIII has bid me, his friend and physician, to look through the many volumes of the Talmud, ten times as large as our own Bible, and bring out to the world at least specimens of the abominations they contain.

Fortunately for our purpose it is not necessary to wade through the filth that Geronimo's second treatise contains.

Yet are his extracts trustworthy? Do the Talmud and the writings akin to it really contain these scurrilous sayings and tales? Yes, speaking generally, they do. But what of this? No doubt, if the Talmud is considered to be another Bible (as it has been considered at some periods and in some places), it may be necessary to show its unworthiness to hold such a position. But if it be judged fairly, as being in fact a collection of the sayings and opinions of all sorts of Jews, learned and unlearned, pious and ungodly, persecuted and blatantly dictatorial, it cannot fairly be blamed for containing some, or indeed many, things unseemly and even profane. No sensible or humble controversialist will try to make much of the moral failures of his opponent—much less do so in a flippant and boastful manner. For, alas, it must be confessed that writings like this second treatise have done, and are still doing, infinite harm to the cause of Christianity amongst the Jews. For they are engendered by moral ignorance, even though they be brought to the birth by pride of intellect.

A Note at the end of the treatise claims that it produced the conversion of five thousand Jews. It does not attempt to estimate the number of the persecutions of Jews caused by its effect on Gentile readers. One cannot but be sorry to have to say this, for Geronimo's first treatise was not unworthy of its aim, considering the date at which it was composed.

---

[1] "De Judaicis erroribus ex Talmut."

[2] P. 545 B: "In eo sunt intricabilia mendacia, turpia, fatua, abominabilia: contra legem Dei, contra legem naturae, contra legem scriptam." Cf. de Spina, *infra*, p. 279.

CHAPTER XXIX

PAUL OF BURGOS

SCRUTINIUM SCRIPTURARUM

A.D. 1350–1435

The *Scrutinium Scripturarum* by Paul of Burgos is of a calibre very different from that of the writings enumerated in the last chapter. It takes its place easily among the first three of Spanish treatises designed to attract the Jews to Christ, and, though it is the latest in point of time, has excellences of its own over the two earlier. For Isidore's *Contra Judaeos*,[1] comprehensive and well arranged though it is, shows little knowledge of Judaism, and Raymund Martini's learned *Pugio Fidei* is more of the nature of a thesaurus than a manual for enquirers or teachers. But the *Scrutinium* is comprehensive, learned, and so arranged that it can be read and remembered, and be suitable for ready reference. It is, in fact, precisely what we should expect from a man like Paul of Burgos, who was at once a learned Jewish Rabbi, and, as a Christian, a practical man of affairs. His book too contains comparatively little of the harshness which came out in his administration, and has made his name abhorrent to later Jewish writers.[2]

Solomon ha Levi,[3] for such was his name in Judaism, was born of rich Jewish parents of the tribe of Levi in the city of Burgos in

---

[1] *Vide supra*, p. 216.

[2] One never expects much fairness from Graetz when he writes of Jewish-Christians—"apostates", as he and others always call them—and unfortunately his opinions are generally accepted *en bloc*, without being tested. In the case of Paul of Burgos he is more prejudiced than usual, for he accepts at their face-value the bitter attacks on Paul made by his contemporaries. For some contemptuous remarks about the *Scrutinium* see his *Geschichte*, 1875, viii. 82, 148 (E.T. iv. 200, 252). The *Scrutinium* was much used by Servetus (L. I. Newman, *Jewish Influence, etc.* p. 550).

[3] Materials for his life are in Sanctotis' edition of the *Scrutinium* (1591), pp. 10–78 (*vide infra*); Steinschneider, *Bodl. Cat.* cc. 2087 *sq.*; Graetz, *Geschichte*, 1875, viii. 77–88, 148; Kayserling in the *Jew. Enc.* ix. 562 *sq.*; Amador de Los Rios, 1875, ii. 490 *sqq.* A. Fürst has an excellent account of him and his book in *Christen und Juden*, 1892, pp. 54–78; F. Heman, *Geschichte des jüdischen Volkes*, 1908, pp. 220–223, is also good. The *Scrutinium* is printed also in *Biblia Sacra*, Antwerp, 1634, vi. coll. 1793–2070.

A.D. 1350, and became known as a Jew deeply versed in all the traditional lore of his religion.[1] He says that he was led to Christianity through the study of St Paul's Epistles,[2] with the help of Aquinas' *De Legibus*.[3] He was baptised at Burgos on July 21, 1390 (or perhaps 1391), taking the name of Paulus de Santa Maria.[4] After studying theology for some years in Paris, where he took his Doctorate, he became Archdeacon of Trevino, Bishop of Cartagena in 1402, Keeper of the royal seal in 1406, and Archbishop of Burgos in 1415, holding office until 1435, when he was succeeded by his son Alphonso. He died on August 29 of the same year.[5]

He was very zealous for the conversion of his former coreligionists from the time of his baptism, corresponding with them on Christianity,[6] making Additions to the *Postilles* of Nicholas de Lyra on the Bible, which Paul finished in 1429, and taking, alas, a prominent part in the edict of January 2, 1412, "issued in the name of the child-king John II", which hindered Jewish commerce and compelled Jews to live in their ghettos.[7]

But our own interest in Paul of Burgos centres in his *Scrutinium Scripturarum*, evidently the outcome of thoughts and arguments spread over many years, but not written until 1433, three years before his death.[8] The title is based on John v. 39, "Search the Scriptures", "Scrutamini scripturas", etc.

[1] He visited London shortly before his conversion, writing a Hebrew letter thence at Purim, and possibly as a prisoner. See Isr. Abrahams, *Jew. Qu. Rev.* 1900, xii. 255–263.

[2] Sanctotis tells us (p. 12), on the testimony of many, that when Solomon ha Levi was asked at his baptism what new name he would have, he replied, "Paulus me ad fidem convertit, Pauli mihi indelebile nomen, una cum caractere assignari deposco". The extraordinarily interesting little autobiography in the Prologue to his Additions to Nicholas de Lyra's *Postilles* on the Bible, whilst attributing his conversion to the grace of God, makes no reference to the means used.

[3] Sanctotis, p. 21.

[4] Graetz insists that the baptism was in 1391, and the cause of it the severe persecution of the Jews in Castile and Aragon in that year (see Amador de Los Rios, ii. 349–396).

[5] Sanctotis, pp. 71, 76.

[6] See the note on Lorqua, *supra*, p. 261.

[7] *Jew. Enc.* s.v. *Spain*, xi. 496.

[8] "Quem composuit post Additiones per eum compositas ad Postillam Nicolai de Lira, Anno Dñi M.CCCC.XXXIIII. Anno vero aetatis suae LXXXIIII" (Sanctotis' edition, p. 101). In i. 3. iii (p. 145) and iv (p. 147) Paul says he is writing in 1432.

Now three things, he tells us, are required for the knowledge of Christ. (1) The mysteries of Him, which are handed down in Scripture, must be studied not perfunctorily but diligently; (2) and testimonies to Him must be gathered, not from the Scriptures of the sacred Canon only, but also "from other authoritative writings among the Hebrews...which are glosses or Talmudic authorities, and other writings authoritative among them".[1] These indeed have no authority in themselves, but from them can be taken powerful arguments against the Jews, who, like Caiaphas, sometimes uttered prophecies without intending to do so. It is true that the Talmud was written long after the time of Christ, but parts of it were in existence many years before it took its present form— just as Gratian compiled the Decretals and utterances of the saints, which, however, had been uttered long before. R. Moses (i.e. Maimonides) points this out in the Preface of his *Deuteronomos* (i.e. the *Yad ha Chazaqah*).[2] (3) We must study not the mystical but the literal meaning of Scripture, as Augustine points out when writing against the Donatists.[3] For it is quite a.mistake to suppose that this does not require strenuous "searching". It was because the Pharisees did not seek Christ with their heart that "they failed in diligently searching".[4]

The aim of Paul's treatise is, he tells us, twofold: I. To go through the principal errors of the Jews which hinder them from knowing the true Messiah, and thus to show that He is the very Christ. This part is in the form of a Dialogue between Saul the Jew and Paul the Catholic.[5] II. To enable true believers to understand the reasons for their faith. This follows the didactic method; the Disciple asks questions, and the Master answers them, "as being already trained in Catholic doctrine".[6] *Give me* (therefore) *understanding, and I shall keep Thy law; yea, I shall observe it with my whole heart.*[7]

[1] "Ab aliis scripturis apud ipsos Hebraeos autenticis....Quae quidem scripturae sunt glossae, seu autoritates Talmudicae, et alia scripta, apud ipsos autentica" (p. 101 *sq.*). Cf. the statements of Raymund de Peñaforte and Paulus Christiani, *supra*, p. 247.

[2] Maimonides begins by arguing that the traditional Law—the explanation of the written Law—was given to Moses, and taught by him orally to his successors, but was not written down till the time of R. Judah the Saint (*c.* A.D. 200).

[3] Apparently in the *De Unitate Ecclesiae*, § 9 (Migne, ix. 397).

[4] "Defecerunt scrutantes scrutinio" (Ps. lxiv. 6, Vulg. from the LXX).

[5] Cf. Acts ix. 1, 22.

[6] "A magistro jam in Catholica doctrina erudito."   [7] Ps. cxix. 34.

Part I has ten Divisions,[1] and discusses the following subjects. (1) Those who were to be saved, or redeemed, by Christ, who was promised in the Law. (2) The call of the Gentiles to the dignity enjoyed by Israel. (3) The Coming of Christ—is it past or yet in the future? (4) The Restoration of the Jews by Messiah—is it bodily, or, rather, spiritually? (5) The Redemption of Israel, and the manner of it. Redemption is both bodily and spiritual, but the latter is the more worthy and the more perfect. (6) The salvation wrought by Christ—was it only for His contemporaries and those of later times, or did it also extend back for the earlier saints? (7) Is the Kingdom of Christ that of which Daniel spoke? (8) Was a New Law to be given in the time of Messiah? (9) The Trinity. (10) The Divinity of Christ.

Part II has only six Divisions. (1) The Disciple states difficulties felt by him about the Divinity of Christ, and the Master resolves them. (2) Similarly with respect to the Blessed Virgin, especially why certain things are not told us about her in Scripture. (3) The Sacrament of the Altar. (4) The life of the Fathers before the coming of Christ and afterwards, especially as regards the "consilia evangelica" and monasticism. (5) The Book of Job. (6) The consequences to the Jews of their ruinous lack of faith.[2]

In view of the author's learning, it is worth while to give a brief summary of his arguments in one of the Divisions in each Part. The eighth Division in Part I is concerned with the giving of a new Law in the time of Messiah,[3] and has sixteen sections, filling forty-two pages. § i. Though man may not add to, or deduct from, the Law of Moses,[4] God can do so, and He may commission a Prophet to do so. § ii. God promised to give a new Law (for "covenant" does mean the Law),[5] as Jeremiah says,[6] the Talmudic doctors themselves agreeing that a more excellent Law was to be given by the Messiah than that given by Moses.[7] § iii. For the Law of Moses is vanity compared with that of the Messiah, as is said in *Eccles. R.* on Eccles. ii. 1, "The Law thou learnest in this world is vanity compared with the Law of the world to come."[8] § iv. God

---

[1] "Distinctiones."   [2] "Perniciosa perfidia."

[3] "Circa innovationem divinae legis tempore Messiae" (p. 242).

[4] Deut. iv. 2. See also § xii.   [5] Ex. xix. 4 *sq.*   [6] Jer. xxxi. 33.

[7] Paul gives no reference at this point, but see *Pesiqta d'Rab Kahana* (Buber, 1868, p. 79 a) about the abolition of some laws. Buber adds many references. Cf. *Lev. R.* § 9 on Lev. vii. 12; § 27 (end) on Lev. xxii. 29; *vide infra*, p. 272 note.

[8] Or, as Paul gives it, "Gloss. Omnis lex quam homo addiscit in hoc seculo *habet*, id est vanitas est, respectu legis Messiae" (p. 246).

was to raise up another Prophet as legislator. See Deut. xviii. 18, which is discussed at length. § v. The observance of the Law "for ever" means only so long as it lasts. § vi. And the giving of the new Law by Christ is the limit of the duration of the old, save in cases that belong to the Law of Nature. § vii. Yet everything in the Mosaic Law is still profitable for our learning; and, § viii, the whole Law hangs upon the two precepts of Love to God and Love to one's neighbour, as the Saviour said. § ix. The Talmudic Doctors say[1] that the 613 precepts of the Mosaic Law are really contained in a very few, and even in one, "the just shall live by his faith".[2] An objection indeed is raised that Habakkuk says "faith", and Jesus says "love". But Paul of Burgos replies that the faith mentioned by Habakkuk is really that faith which worketh by love.[3] § x. What then are the commandments of the Mosaic Law contained in Christ's command, "Keep the commandments"?[4] If those of real permanence are considered they are only the moral, viz. the Ten Commandments and such like. § xi. But which of these are in reality moral, and so are binding for ever in this life, and which are ceremonial and are terminated by the New Law? Saul, the Jewish interlocutor, urges that there is no such distinction in the Law of Moses; either all are binding and perpetual, or none. Not so, answers Paul, the Christian; for the Decalogue was given with special solemnity, and there are also many natural precepts, especially reverence for the aged. So Aristotle distinguished between those laws which are binding by law only, and those which are of force by Nature.[5]

§ xii. But some ceremonial and judicial ordinances are changeable, as the Talmudic doctors grant. By "ceremonial" laws we understand those which refer to duties towards God, such as orders about the sacrifices and the priests, and the "fringes", etc., connected with the cult. By "judicial", precepts referring to men, e.g. those in Ex. xxi, whose force depends solely on the fact that they were commanded. Consider in this connexion the arguments of Maimonides in Part iii of his *Moreh Nebochim*.[6] We may learn that while sacrificing to God belongs to the Law of Nature, the methods of sacrificing are merely ceremonial. Saul the Jew indeed argues that Maimonides elsewhere says[7] that the ceremonial and

---

[1] T. B. *Makkoth*, 24 a.   [2] Hab. ii. 4.
[3] Gal. v. 6.   [4] Matt. xix. 17.
[5] *Ethics*, I. 3.   [6] § 26.
[7] *Yad ha Chazaqah, Hilkoth Melakim*, § xi (1702 edition, iv. 306 b).

judicial parts of the Law are not to be changed. But Paul the Christian replies that God can change His own ordinances. For He once forbade the eating of flesh,[1] and afterwards allowed it,[2] and Jewish teachers far older than Maimonides say that some ceremonial laws do not last for ever.[3]

Our author then turns to a subject of greater interest to him than to those of us who are not mediaevalists in doctrine, and urges (§ xiii) that Christians are not to be accused by Jews of idolatry because they worship images. We put up images, he says, not for worship (strictly speaking) but for contemplation, as representing some specific truth. The Jew may argue, The commandment is clear, *Thou shalt not make unto thee a graven image*,[4] but the Christian reminds him of the carving of the Cherubim, and of the figure of a lion on the standard of Judah.[5] And, as the Philosopher (Aristotle) says, our minds are moved by what we see.[6] Besides, we give to images only such "worship" as we pay to men (*dulia*), not that which we offer to God alone (*latria*).

In § xiv Paul meets the difficulty of our observing Sunday and not the Sabbath. He points out that so far as the Sabbath is a moral command it is not tied to a particular day of the week. Maimonides himself permits one who is in the desert, and does not know which day is which, to work any six days and to rest on the seventh.[7] The foundation of the change from Sabbath to Sunday agrees with the fact that even the Sabbath was instituted to remind the Israelites not only of Creation but also of the redemption from Egypt. In the days of Messiah then we may well remember the greater redemption wrought for us.[8] § xv. Nor can the Christians be blamed for not practising circumcision. St Paul did not cir-

---

[1] Gen. i. 29. [2] Gen. ix. 3.

[3] "Breshith R. 41", referring to Ps. cxlvi. 7: "The Lord looseth the bound." The reference seems to be to the lost *Midrash ha Gadol* of R. Moses ha Darshan. See Buber's note on *Midrash Tillim*, Ps. cxlvi. 7, p. 535 *sq.* One explanation given there of the phrase in the psalm is that in the world to come God will remove all restrictions about unclean beasts. Cf. Justin's *Trypho*, § xx (*supra*, p. 41).

[4] "Non facies tibi sculptile."

[5] See Targum of Pseudo Jonathan on Num. ii. 3. The argument is common in the Eastern apologetic treatises, e.g. *Trophies* iii (*supra*, p. 163).

[6] "Ex visis enim secundum Philosophum movetur animus." See the beginning of the *Metaphysics*. Cf. Raymund Lull: "For as by seeing fair things [e.g. the cross and images] the soul is moved to love, even so by hearing pleasing words it is moved to desire" (*Blanquerna*, ch. xxv b, Peers translation).

[7] *De Sabb.* ii. 22. [8] Cf. Jer. xvi. 14 *sq.*

cumcise Titus, and, in any case, spiritual circumcision, that of the heart, is more important than physical.[1] Besides, circumcision as now performed in accordance with Pharisaic teaching is quite contrary to the meaning of the Old Testament, "as Raymund your own Rabbi declares at length in his *Pugio*".[2]

The last section (xvi) of this eighth Division is an explanation of Mal. iv. 4, *Remember ye the law of Moses*, in which Paul of Burgos reminds us that the prophet does not say "Keep", but *Remember*, hold in memory, so as to see the spiritual teaching of the Law. Nachmanides brings out the difference between "keeping" and "remembering" in his Exposition of Ex. xx. 8, comparing this verse with Deut. v. 12, and saying that the former passage means really "remember", and the latter is only a negative command to abstain from certain things on the Sabbath.[3] Besides, even if *remember* in Mal. iv. 4 did mean "keep" this would refer to observing the Law only while the Temple was standing, and until the Messiah came.

Another example of the style of argument employed by Paul of Burgos is to be seen in Part II, Division (6), the general subject of which is "The Consequences to the Jews of their ruinous lack of faith".[4] He first (§ i) shows that their punishment has been greater than that of Sodom, and that of Abiram, which were sudden and catastrophic, while theirs is long-lasting, and also proves to be advantageous to the Church. The Jews still applaud the attitude of their ancestors to Christ. See Maimonides.[5] In § ii Paul of Burgos adduces three particulars about their present Captivity: (*a*) it is both worse and longer than that of Babylon; (*b*) all Jews

---

[1] Deut. xxx. 6; Jer. ix. 26.

[2] "Prout Raymundus Rabbi tuus, in suo Pugione, large declarat." Observe that in 6. iv he refers also to "Rabbi Rahamon", whom Raymund quotes, *vide supra*, p. 249.

[3] Nachmanides urges that "remember" regards the Sabbath as a remembrance of God's work in creation, and refers to our observance of it in positive fashion, and that "keep" is connected in thought with "beware" (lit. "keep thyself"). A few lines further on he quotes an exposition that "remember" proceeds from God's quality of love, because it is a privilege to do God's will, and "keep" from God's quality of fear, because it suggests judgment, and he who refrains from doing wrong fears God. And as Love is greater than Fear, so is a positive command greater than a negative.

[4] "Sua perniciosa perfidia." Cf. *supra*, p. 270.

[5] *Hilkoth Melakim*, xi. 4 (1702, iv. 307).

share in it and in the sin that caused it; (c) they are ignorant of that sin.[1]

§§ iii–vi. The Jews are judicially blind, such blindness being a punishment for their Pharisaic hypocrisy. For in addition to Christ's words, Bede says, "Hypocrisy spreads like leaven",[2] and Theophilus, "Nothing so affects character as hypocrisy, namely, that of the Pharisees".[3] The marks of such Pharisaic hypocrisy are then enumerated. § vii. Because of their blindness they deny the Divine Providence, for God has brought good out of their darkness, the illumination of the Gentiles. §§ viii, ix. This blindness of theirs includes (a) ignorance of the time of Messiah's Coming, His Divinity, and the method by which He would redeem man; (b) the belief that the Law of Moses would last for ever, as regards its ceremonies. So the words of the Prophet are fulfilled, "Wisdom shall perish from the wise".[4] For this reason have they composed that Talmud of theirs, with its follies and absurdities. The *Disciple* indeed urges that these are to be understood metaphorically, but the *Teacher* denies this. Yet, adds the *Disciple*, Christ approved of what the Pharisees taught.[5] Nay, replies the *Teacher*, He was then speaking of the Law of Moses, not of the Talmudic Law, which they falsely claim to be a second Law given to Moses. § ix. They are indeed so blind as not to see the meaning of their own expressions.[6] For example, they say that the Patriarchs were not to enter Paradise till the son of Pharez (i.e. Messiah the son of David) should come, because of the sin of Adam,[7] and yet

[1] Paul here refers to the evidence of a Talmudic book called *Magnila* (*sic*, in both the text and the margin of the *Scrutinium*, p. 500, but I cannot identify it) that the present Captivity differs from that of Babylon in that the sin which caused the present one is not known, nor the limit of its duration.

[2] "Sicut modicum fermentum totam farinae massam corrumpit, sic simulatione animi tota virtutum sinceritas et veritas fraudabitur." I cannot find this.

[3] "Nihil sic alterat mores ut hypocrisis, scilicet Pharisaica." I cannot find this.

[4] Isa. xxix. 14.

[5] Matt. xxiii. 2 *sq.*

[6] He here refers to passages in the Talmud confirming the doctrines of Christianity, which he has already quoted in Part I. He compares the words of Caiaphas in the Preface (*Scrutinium*, p. 102), *vide supra*, p. 269.

[7] "Dicunt quod Patriarchae et omnes sancti ante adventum Messiae non intrabant paradisum, sed erant in ejus suburbio, donec veniret filius Phares id est Christus filius David, et hoc propter peccatum Adae." *Bereshith R.*, Par. 12 on Gen. ii. 4 (about the middle), speaks of the restoration of blessings lost by Adam, but says nothing precisely about him or the other Patriarchs entering Paradise. Perhaps however this is implied in *Shemoth R.*, Par. 30 (near the beginning) on

they deny original sin, and the need for it to be expiated by Christ!
Similarly, they do not follow out their own arguments with regard
to the date when Messiah must have come.

§ x. Yet we can often derive instruction from the opinions which
the Jews fail to understand, a method of learning from earlier but
mistaken writers which Aristotle praises.[1] Two limits of time for
Messiah's Coming may be found in the Rabbinic authors. First,
Maimonides says He will come at a date now 218 years ago.[2] And
indeed about that time SS. Francis and Dominic appeared, and
Scripture may well contain some reference to their appearance,
"for who can calculate how many souls have been redeemed by
the ministry of the preaching and teaching, in word and writing,
of the Preaching and the Minor Friars, from the captivity of the
devil, the grace of God working with them?" Secondly, Nachmanides[3] shows that Messiah is to come in A.D. 1358, and he is
followed exactly by R. Levi Begner,[4] who says that he has had a
Divine revelation on the subject. And indeed the Jews in Spain
were at that time held in great honour. At this point Paul of
Burgos quotes the incident in the life of Abner of Burgos (Alphonso
of Valladolid) which has been given above on p. 259. Thus all
these false computations of the date of Messiah's Coming have had
for their result the confirmation of the Catholic Faith.

§ xi shows that the Jews agree that Repentance is the most

Ex. xxi. 1, where we are told that Messiah will arise from Perez, and in His
days the Holy One, blessed be He, will swallow up death (Isa. xxv. 8). For
Perez see especially Schechter's *Midrash ha Gadol* on Gen. ii. 4. Burney, *The
Aramaic Origin of the Fourth Gospel*, 1922, has an interesting note (p. 46). Consult
also Prof. Burkitt in *J. Th. St.* April, 1929, xxx. 254.

[1] P. 521: "Secundum Philosophum in Metaphysica: veri Philosophi in
cognitione veritatis profecerunt, ex opinionibus antiquorum etiam a veritate
deviantium." This appears to be a deduction rather than an exact quotation.

[2] See Maimonides, *Iggereth Teman* (A.D. 1216), edition of 1859, p. 6 b, c.
Bacher defends the genuineness of the passage in the *Rev. d. Études Juives*,
xxxiv. 101–105.

[3] (A.D. 1194–1270), in his Preface to the Pentateuch, "in Expositione Penta-
theuci in parte prohemiali". So p. 522. I cannot find it, but it occurs in both
narratives of the Disputation with Paulus Christiani (Wagenseil, p. 47;
Steinschneider, p. 15; *vide supra*, p. 245).

[4] R. Levi ben Gershon (= Leon de Bagnols = Ralbag), in his commentary
on Daniel (xii. 4–13), finished as he tells us in A.D. 1338. He does not, however,
mention Nachmanides, and after saying that earlier calculators were in error
because they hoped the End would be near their own time, he himself places
it in A.D. 1403, i.e. 45 years later than the date computed by Nachmanides.
Paul of Burgos had already made the same statements about Nachmanides
and R. Levi (only there more expressly) in his *Scrutinium* on p. 149 (I. iii. 4).

important sign of the coming of the Messiah, but when He came they did not see their need of it. § xii. For the blindness foretold by Isaiah[1] is spoken of in the Gospel.[2] Yet (§ xiii) this does not prevent the conversion of the descendants of those early Pharisees. For in the times of the greatest strength of the Church, namely, at its beginning and its end, Jews were and will be converted in large numbers.[3]

§ xiv. Meantime, i.e. between the First and the Second Advents, how ought we Christians to feel? We cannot expect many Jews to be converted, but can expect that some will be—*as the shaking of an olive tree, two or three berries in the top of the uppermost bough.*[4] And, in fact, some Jews in leading positions have been thus converted, e.g. Evaristus, the seventh Bishop of Rome from St Peter,[5] Julian Pomerius, Archbishop of Toledo,[6] Peter Alphonsi,[7] Alphonso of Valladolid.[8] For Jeremiah's promise has been fulfilled, *I will take you one of a city, and two of a family, and I will bring you to Zion.*[9]

Finally the Disciple expresses his thanks for the instruction he has received. And so the whole *Scrutinium* comes to an end—not a perfect book, but marked throughout by the best learning of its day, and expressed (save for a few exceptions) in word and phrase not likely to give offence to those whom it was endeavouring to win.

---

[1] Isa. vi. 10.   [2] John ix. 39.

[3] Rom. xi. 26. See also Hos. iii. 4 *sq.*, with the Targum, "And they shall obey Messiah the Son of David, and shall fear before the LORD". "The Hebrew", Paul of Burgos adds, "has *And they shall flow* (fluent) *unto the Lord, and unto His goodness in the last days.*" Paul of Burgos explains the "goodness" as spiritual (p. 530 *sq.*). Paul's explanation of the Hebrew וּפָחֲד֖וּ is strange. The LXX has ἐκστήσονται, a corruption of which might give ἐκστάζονται, "are dripping", if the compound word existed.

[4] Isa. xvii. 6.

[5] See Eusebius, *Eccl. Hist.* iii. 34; iv. 1.

[6] Paul confuses Julian Pomerius (*c.* A.D. 500), an Abbot who lived at Arles, and, as it seems, an African Gentile by birth, with Julian, Archbishop of Toledo 680–690, who was of Jewish descent. For the latter *vide supra*, p. 220.

[7] *Vide supra*, p. 233.   [8] *Vide supra*, p. 259.

[9] Jer. iii. 14 (*Scrutinium*, p. 533).

CHAPTER XXX

ALPHONSO DE SPINA
"THE FORTRESS OF THE FAITH"
A.D. 1459

We now come to our last document, which need not detain us long. It is *The Fortress of the Faith, against all the enemies of the Christian religion, restraining the rage of Jews and Mohammedans*, etc., etc.,[1] written in A.D. 1459 by Alphonso de Spina, General of the Franciscans,[2] who is said to have originated the idea of the Inquisition in Spain. Its primary object was not to win the Jews to Christ—though it contains many arguments intended to do so—but to protect Christians from Judaism and all its abominations. For it is a venomous book, and, thank God, was not written by a Jewish convert,[3] but by as pure blooded a Gentile as could be found in Spain at that age. The writer shows indeed a certain amount of natural ability in searching out and marshalling his facts—though his facts are far from always being facts—but he is totally lacking in sympathy with his opponents.

After a comprehensive Table of Contents, and a short Preface beginning "A strong Tower from the face of the enemy",[4] and consisting of praise to God and the expression of the writer's intention in the form of a prayer, he divides his subject into five books. I. On the armour of all the faithful. II. On the war with heretics. III. On the war with Jews. IV. On the war with Mohammedans. V. On the war with demons. We are concerned with the third book only. This contains twelve chapters,[5] ch. 1 being on the blindness of the Jews, and considering how they can be led back to the light. Ch. 2 deals with "the parentage of

---

[1] "Fortalitium fidei in universos christiane religionis hostes Judaeorum et Saracenorum...rabiem cohibens", etc., etc., Lyons, 1525 (at the end of the book).

[2] Amador de Los Rios, iii. 136; Graetz, viii. 225 *sq.*; Kayserling in *Jew. Enc.* xi. 510.

[3] In spite of the assertions of Jost, *Gesch. des Judenthums und seiner Sekten*, 1859, iii. 96, and Amador de Los Rios, iii. 129, 136.

[4] Ps. lxi. 3.

[5] "Considerationes"; pp. cvi a–ccxxxix b in the edition of 1525.

the Jews according to the doctrine of the Talmud",[1] saying that this shows the Jews are children of demons. Ch. 3 insists on the great differences that may be seen in their faith and opinions, such as those of the Talmud and those of the Karaites, and of many others, the author here appealing to "Magister Alphonsus conversus",[2] in ch. xxxiii of his *Wars of God*. He then discusses at some length objections urged by the Jews against Christianity; in ch. 4 adducing thirty of their arguments taken from the Law of Moses, in ch. 5 twenty-four arguments from the Gospel, and in ch. 6 twenty-four things in Christianity deemed by Jews to be impossible —as, for example, that God should become incarnate and so be defiled.

Having dealt thus far with doctrines and abstract ideas de Spina turns to what he doubtless considered solid facts of more real importance. Ch. 7 states the cruelties committed by Jews[3] towards their Messiah, and thus towards themselves in their ensuing captivities and their eternal damnation, and, with full particulars, towards Christians; e.g. killing children, hanging up a Christian who had first been crowned with thorns and scourged through the city, poisoning the wells in Germany, and so on.[4] Ch. 8 deals with their nonsensical tales, "for the Holy Spirit suffers them not to lie except so patently that every one can see that what they say is false"[5] He refers in particular to the Haggadoth in the Talmud, and seems to have drawn upon Peter Alphonsi for his knowledge of them.[6] He arranges them under the headings of nonsensical tales against charity, against the Law of Nature, against the Divine perfection, and against the Law of Moses and the Prophets; also tales of events that were plainly impossible, or that referred to their foolish expectation of the coming of the Messiah; together with

---

[1] "De judaeorum parentela ex thalmud doctrina."

[2] Alphonso of Valladolid, *vide supra*, p. 259. He adds (p. cx a), "according to what R. Aben Ezra wrote in his commentary on the Law—secundum quod scripsit rabi abraham benesdra in libro suo quo legem glossavit". See Aben' Ezra's Introduction to the Pentateuch, with Bacher's remarks in his essay on this in the *Sitzungsberichte der philos-histor. Classe der k. Academie d. Wissensch.* 1875, lxxxi. 369, 398–414.

[3] "De crudelitatibus judeorum" (pp. clxxxiii b–cxcvi a).

[4] There does not seem to be any special reference to the use of Christian blood *at the Passover*.

[5] "Non enim permittit spiritus sanctus eos mentiri nisi ita clare quod ab omnibus cognoscatur esse falsum et mendacium" (p. cxcvi b, c).

[6] E.g. in the tale of the keys and the camels, and the big stone at Jacob's funeral, pp. ccv a–ccvi a (*vide supra*, p. 238).

various mistaken notions in the Talmud and various Rabbinic writers.[1]

In the 9th chapter our author dwells upon the expulsion of the Jews from various lands; first, the Holy Land, with the signs that preceded it and its terrible calamities; next, from France, then from England (with an account of the martyrdom of little Hugh of Lincoln),[2] and from Spain when Sisebut expelled them in the seventh century.[3] The 10th chapter relates miracles which have happened in connexion with Jews, and expresses the author's wonder at the obstinacy of the Jews in not being moved by them to turn to Christ. For did not the baptismal water disappear in the the time of Theodosius and Pope Innocent I (A.D. 401–417), when a Jew came for baptism hypocritically? Did not, more than once, an image of the Blessed Lord bleed when pierced by a Jew's weapon, or indeed was only struck by a Jew? And when a Jewish boy had received the blessed Bread in Church, and, for doing so, was thrown by his father into a furnace—did he not come out alive? Further, there was the incident of the crosses appearing on the clothes of the Jews, as Master Alphonso the convert tells us.[4] And indeed quite lately in A.D. 1455 a Jewish boy bought the most sacred Body of Christ from an avaricious sacristan at Segovia, and It wrought such miracles that It was afterwards restored to the Church.

Ch. 11 deals only with certain laws canonical and civil, and royal ordinances, regarding the Jews.

The last chapter (12) is longer and more interesting. For it grants that the conversion of the Jews is to take place in the end of the present age.[5] After discussing why the Jewish community is not converted to faith in Christ, the author asks whether they who wish to be converted are to be received. He answers, Yes, even though there be a danger of hypocrisy. In what manner then are they to be received? Only after eight months' catechumenate before baptism, unless indeed they be dangerously ill. He then discusses whether compulsion may be used. Duns Scotus (died 1308) says, Yes, in the case of children, even though their parents be unwilling—just as the King can take children from their parents

---

[1] E.g. Maimonides. For De Spina's abuse, cf. Geronimo de Santa Fé, *supra*, p. 266.

[2] P. ccxviii *sq.*   [3] *Vide supra*, p. 215.

[4] *Vide supra*, p. 259, with note.

[5] So also Isidore, *c. Judaeos*, II. v. See Appendix, *infra* p. 290.

to be trained for his purposes! But other Doctors forbid it. And with adults? Yes, says Duns Scotus again, "for it is better for them to be compelled to do good than to do ill with impunity as they do now"![1] One is sorry that a British scholar should have expressed such opinions! It is easy to guess the punishment adjudged to converted Jews "who return to their vomit of Judaism".

De Spina then tells us that the Jews will accept Antichrist, who is to be born in Babylon of the tribe of Dan[2] as the blessed Isidore[3] and Bede[4] inform us. But the Jews will afterwards recognise that they have been deceived by Antichrist, and be converted at last to the Catholic Faith. He then asks whether we can know with any accuracy the time of the coming of Antichrist and of the conversion of the Jews. His own answer is that it is presumptuous of us to try to find it out too particularly, as Augustine says.[5]

De Spina adds, however, that he has found in the Scriptures nine signs of the near coming of Antichrist, and, after mentioning them, bids the diligent reader consider whether he sees any such signs already injuring the world. And "let him resort earnestly to our strong Defender, Jesus Christ our Lord, who is a strong Tower from the face of the enemy. And may the Faith of us Christians remain by His special protection steadfast and untouched for ever and ever".

After all, even De Spina means well. He is, as has been said, often venomous, and he has little, if any, independent knowledge of Judaism. But he is of wider hope than many Christian writers in his expectation of the final conversion of the Jews, and according to his light—dim though it was—he had a sincere desire to win at least some of them to Christ in his own day.

CONCLUSION

One rises from this brief review of the literary efforts of the Spanish Christians to win the Jews to Christ with the feeling that those efforts have been underrated both by friends and foes alike. We

[1] P. ccxxxv a, b: "Quia melius est compelli ad bonum agendum quam male agere impune sicut ipsi agunt."

[2] P. ccxxxvi; Gen. xlix. 17. See Bousset, *Der Antichrist*, 1895, pp. 112, 115. The basis of the tradition is the connexion of the tribe with idolatry.

[3] On Gen. xlix. 17, "Alii dicunt Antichristum praedici per haec verba de ista tribu futurum" (Migne, *P.L.* lxxxiii. 282).

[4] *Explanatio Apocalypsis*, vii. 5; xvii. 12.

[5] *De Civitate Dei*, xviii. 52. He refers to Acts i. 6 *sq.* in the same section.

cannot indeed expect those who lived only in the first fifteen centuries of our era to attain to the standard of our own generation in Biblical scholarship or historical insight. But in most cases they knew their subject, and the arguments that Jews use against Christianity. For Jews were in such large numbers throughout the Peninsula that it was impossible for any Christians who desired to do so to fail to be acquainted with them and their doctrines. Hence we cannot wonder that some of the Christian Apologies with which we have been concerned attain a very high degree of intellectual success. The sincerity too of the writers is apparent. In fact we receive the impression in every case that they are doing their utmost to persuade the Jews that Jesus is the Christ.

But deeds speak louder than words. The action of the Church in Spain, the virulence of her persecution of the Jews, the horrors of the Inquisition (the first Auto-da-Fé was in 1481), the expulsion from Spain (March, 1492), from Navarre (August, 1492), and from Portugal (1496), burnt, like acid in an etcher's panel, always deeper and darker delineations of Jesus Christ as torturer and executioner; exhibiting Him as the very incarnation of a mediaeval Satan. We cannot wonder that those many Jews who in abject terror consented to be baptised still worshipped in secret their own God (and ours) whom they knew to be the God of holiness and pity. In our heart of hearts we cannot blame them.[1]

But when we Christians learn to present to them, in our actions as well as by our words, Jesus in His true character, as the full revelation of the one true God, then, but not before, they will accept Him. We cannot but honour the Jews for their faith in God despite all our ill-treatment of them. It is our part to show Him to them in Jesus of Nazareth, the Messiah, Very God of Very God, as Incarnate Love.

[1] Some Crypto-Jews or "Marranos" have survived in Portugal until the present year. See especially Mr Lucien Wolf's extraordinarily interesting *Report on the "Marranos" or Crypto-Jews of Portugal* (Anglo-Jewish Association, 1926). Mr Wolf points out that this survival was due to special circumstances, which did not exist in Spain. Hence in Spain "crypto-Judaism was in the course of years so ruthlessly tracked down that by 1560 it was almost completely extirpated, and when we read of Spanish Marranos at a later date we find, on closely examining the available Inquisition Processes, that they were, for the most part, Portuguese immigrants or their descendants" (p. 5). See now Cecil Roth, *A History of the Marranos*, 1932.

APPENDIX (see p. 217)

A SUMMARY OF ISIDORE'S *CONTRA JUDAEOS*

Isidore's treatise *Against the Jews* contains so many of the "proofs", good and bad, which are drawn directly from the Old Testament, and are sometimes used even down to our own day, that it seems worth while to transcribe the headings of all its chapters, adding the more important of the texts adduced, together with some of Isidore's comments.

FIRST BOOK

Isidore addresses his Preface to his sister Florentina, dedicating to her the work he had written at her request, "that the authority of the prophets may strengthen the grace of faith, and show the ignorance of the unbelieving Jews".

I. *Christ was begotten of God the Father.*

1. Though the Jews disbelieve the Prophets of the Old Testament and are deaf to those of the New Testament.

2. Ps. cx. 3, "from the womb, before the morning-star, did I beget Thee" (Vulg.).

3. As He Himself says, "My heart expressed the good Word" (Ps. xlv. 1 Vulg.), and "Thou art my Son, to-day have I begotten Thee" (Ps. ii. 7), which cannot refer to David because of the following promise, "Ask of me and I will give thee the nations", etc., etc. This must refer to Christ alone; see Ps. lxxii. 11, "All kings shall adore Him; all nations shall serve Him".

4. Prov. xxx. 4. Solomon hints at His name and the mystery of His birth.

5. Dan. iii. 25 says, "He is like the Son of God". If it be objected that in the Song of the Three Children (v. 26) the fourth person is called an angel ("But the angel of God went down with Azariah and his companions into the furnace"), this is only right, because Christ is called God's "angel" in Mal. iii. 1.

6. "Son of God" by origin, "angel" because sent. Cf. Ex. xxiii. 20 *sq.*, "I will send my angel before thee.... My name is in Him".

7. Who then is He to Whom God gave His power and His name? The Son of God; see Isa. lxvi. 9, "Shall I make others bring forth and I not bring forth, saith the Lord. And I who give precreation to others, shall I be barren, saith the Lord" (Vulg.). The unbeliever must choose whether he will believe that Christ is the Son of God, or deem the prophets liars.

II. *Christ was begotten of the Father before the ages* (ineffabiliter).

1. No need to ask *when* the Father begat Him: Mic. v. 2 and Ps. lxxii. 17 ("before the sun...before the moon").

2. Prov. viii. 24–30.

3. Or *how*, for it is beyond man's intelligence. Isa. liii. 8, "His generation, who shall declare?"

4. Job xxviii. 20 *sq.*, "Whence will you find (the) Wisdom (of God the Father)? For it is hid from the eyes of men, and kept close from the fowls of heaven", i.e. it is unknown to the very angels. Ecclus. i. 6, "To whom hath the root of wisdom been revealed?" i.e. the origin of the Son of God.

5. Christ shone forth from the Father, as brilliancy from light, a word from the mouth, wisdom from the heart.

III. *Christ is God and Lord.*

1 and 2. Ps. xlv. 6, "O God...God hath anointed thee", i.e. as "Christ". So He is called "Cyrus" (Isa. xlv. 1).

3. The King of the Persians, an impious idolater, cannot be called Christ, God, Lord. Therefore the LXX rightly has not "my Christ Cyrus", but "my Christ the Lord".[1]

4, 5. Gen. i. 26, in the image of angels! As though angels were equal to God! But of Him who has one "imago" with God and the one only name of divinity.

6. Gen. xix. 24, "The Lord rained...from the Lord".

7. Ps. cx. 1, "on My right hand"; 2 Sam. xxiii. 1 *sq.*

8, 9. Zech. ii. 8, the Lord of Hosts is sent from the Lord of Hosts "after the glory", i.e. after the glory which He had with the Father He was sent to the Gentiles; see *v.* 10 *sq.*

10. Job xxxiii. 4, 6, the Holy Spirit also is divine; "God made Me, as also Thee" (Vulg.).

IV. *On the meaning of the Trinity.*

1. Not contrary to Deut. vi. 4.

2–13. Many texts, e.g. Gen. i. 26; Isa. vi. 3. If the Jews object, "If the Father is God and the Son is God, then there are two Gods and not one", let them then hear Isaiah instead of me, when he says that each Person is the One God: "Thou art God, and in Thee is God." For when he says "Thou art God", he indicates the Father, but in adding "in thee is God" he manifests the Son.[2]

---

[1] But see Jerome *in loco* for the falsity of this reading.
[2] The reference apparently is to Isa. xlv. 14 *sq.*

V. *That the Son of God, though God, was made man.*

Isa. ix. 6; Ps. cx. 3; lxxxvii. 5; Dan. ix. 23 *sq.*, 26. He came because man sinned, and afterwards did not keep the Law of Moses. We shall now show that His name and all He did was foretold in Scripture.

VI. *His Name Jesus.*

1. That name *auses* (Oshea) was altered to *Jesus* (Joshua) by Moses, Num. xiii. 16. The name was altered because after the death of Moses (i.e. the Law) our Lord Jesus Christ would lead us through the flood of Jordan (i.e. by the grace of Baptism), and bring us to the Holy Land, the possession of eternal life, the sweetest thing there is.

2. Therefore Hab. iii. 18, "I will rejoice in the Lord, and exult in God my Jesus" (Vulg.).

VII. *Christ was of the seed of Abraham according to the flesh.*

Gen. xxii. 18.

VIII. *Christ sprang from the tribe of Judah.*

Gen. xlix. 10. The kingdom ceased with Herod the foreigner, but the Jews obstinately affirm that the time has not come yet, referring to some king or other of Jewish descent who rules in the extreme east. Their assertion is contrary to Hosea iii. 4.

IX. *Christ was born of the stem of David.*

2 Sam. vii. 12–16; Jer. xxiii. 5 *sq.*; Isa. xi. 10.
From Ruth of Moab, Isa. xv. 9 and xvi. 1, "a Lion from Moab... send out a Lamb, O Lord, to be the Ruler of the land from Petra of the desert to the mountain of the daughter of Sion". "For the spotless Lamb went forth from the race of Moab, Who takes away the sins of the world, and rules over the whole earth. Now Petra of the desert signifies Ruth, who was left bare by the death of her husband." The mountain is either Jerusalem or tropologically the Church, set on an eminence of virtues.

X. *Christ was born of a pure Virgin.*

Isa. vii. 14; xxviii. 16; Ezek. xliv. 1 *sq.*, which indicates the perpetual virginity of Mary.

XI. *Christ was born in Bethlehem.*

Micah v. 2; cf. Hab. iii. 3, "God shall come from the south", for Bethlehem is south of Jerusalem.

XII. *The birth of Christ is shown by a star.*

Num. xxiv. 17.

XIII. *The Magi offered gifts.*
Isa. xviii. 7; Ps. lxxii. 10.

XIV. *He was anointed by God the Father.*
Isa. lxi. 1; Ps. xlv. 7.

XV. *At His first advent He came as one poor and rejected.*
Zech. ix. 9; Isa. lii. 13–liii. 12; Jer. xiv. 7–9.

XVI. *He did signs and miracles.*
Isa. xxxv. 4 *sq.*; lxi. 1.

XVII. *(God) was to be visible in a human body.*
Isa. lii. 6; Ps. lxxxiv. 7, "The God of gods shall be seen in Sion" (Vulg.); Baruch iii. 35–37, "This is our God, and no other shall be accounted of by Him, who has found out all the way of prudence, and shown it to Jacob His servant, and to Israel His beloved. Afterwards did He appear in the earth, and had intercourse with men" ("in terris visus est, et cum hominibus conversatus est", Vulg.).

XVIII. *The Jews would not recognise Him.*
Jer. v. 11 *sq.*; Isa. liii. 2 *sq.*; and the Jews do not change, Jer. xiii. 23.

XIX. *As the Jews did not recognise Him they gathered together against Him.*
Ps. ii. 1 *sq.*; xxii. 16.

XX. *He was sold for money.*
Zech. xi. 12 *sq.* Judas hanged himself fulfilling "Isaiah's" words, "A false witness shall not be unpunished (Prov. xix. 5), because he sold the righteous for silver" (Amos ii. 6).[1]

XXI. *He was delivered up by His disciple.*
Ps. xli. 9; lv. 13, and his name Judas is suggested by Jer. xvii. 1.

XXII. *He was delivered up by Himself.*
Isa. liii. 7 ("He was offered up because He Himself wished it", Vulg.); Jer. xii. 7.

XXIII. *He was taken prisoner.*
Lam. iv. 20; Wisd. ii. 12, 13, 18–20.

XXIV. *He was judged.*
Ps. li. 4.

---

[1] So also in ch. xxvi, where too Mal. iii. 13 is attributed to Zechariah. Cf. ch. xxix, where Isa. l. 6 is attributed to Jeremiah. See also ch. xxxi; Book II, ch. xxii and ch. xxiv.

XXV. *He was deserted by the disciples at His Passion.*

Ps. lxxxviii. 8; Zech. xiii. 7.

XXVI. *He was accused by false witnesses.*

Hosea vii. 13; "Zechariah", really Mal. iii. 13; Ps. xxvii. 12; "And Isaiah says of Judas, a false witness shall not be unpunished (really Prov. xix. 5), because he sold the righteous for silver", Amos ii. 6. See ch. xx, note.

XXVII. *The Jews cried out that He should be crucified.*

Jer. xii. 8; Isa. v. 7.

XXVIII. *The Jews cursed their own posterity.*

Isa. xiv. 20 *sq.*, "Thou most evil seed! Prepare your children for slaughter for the iniquity of their fathers."[1]

XXIX. *He was scourged and smitten with the palms of men's hands.*

Job xvi. 10; Isa. l. 6; Lam. iii. 30[2].

XXX. *His head was struck with a reed.*

And He bore it patiently—Isa. xlii. 3.[3]

XXXI. *He was crowned with thorns.*

Cant. iii. 11. So also by Jeremiah does the Son say, "This people has surrounded Me with the thorns of their sins."[4]

XXXII. *He was clothed with a scarlet robe.*

Isa. lxiii. 1.

XXXIII. *He was silent while He suffered.*

Isa. liii. 7.

XXXIV. *He carried His cross.*

Isa. ix. 6; Gen. xxii. 6.

---

[1] Cf. the Septuagnit.

[2] Isidore also quotes another Latin version of part of Isa. l. 6, attributing it to Jeremiah. See ch. xx, note.

[3] Isidore's text of Isaiah here is very conflate.

[4] Doubtless an expansion of Jer. iv. 3; cf. Targum there. The *Dialogue of Silvester* has the same "quotation" from Jeremiah. See G. Cedrenus' transcript in Migne, *P.G.* cxxi. 525 B (*vide infra*, p. 342). Cf. ch. xx, note.

XXXV. *He was fastened to the cross.*

Jer. xi. 19;[1] Ps. xcvi. 10 ("The Lord reigned from the tree");[2] Hab. iii. 4 ("Horns were in His hand", Vulg.). "For what else does this mean than the trophy of the cross?"

XXXVI. *His hands and feet were fastened with nails.*

Ps. xxii. 16; cf. Cant. v. 5; Zech. xii. 10.

XXXVII. *He was crucified between two robbers.*

Isa. liii. 12; Hab. iii. 2 ("in the midst of two living creatures shalt Thou be known", LXX, not Vulg.).

XXXVIII. *His garments were divided.*

Ps. xxii. 18.

XXXIX. *He was given gall and vinegar to drink.*

Ps. lxix. 21; cf. Deut. xxxii. 32, 6.

XL. *They put a sponge full of vinegar round* (a stalk of) *hyssop.*

Ps. li. 7; Ex. xii. 22.

XLI. *The title on His cross was not spoiled.*

Ps. lvii Title, "Spoil not the inscription of the title."[3]

XLII. *When hanging on the cross He prayed for His enemies.*

Isa. liii. 12; Hab. iii. 2 (see ch. XXXVII, *supra*).

---

[1] Justin (*c. Trypho*, lxxii. 2, *supra*, p. 33) curiously includes this verse among the passages deleted by the Jews, though it is found in all the MSS. (as it seems) both Greek and Hebrew. It was perhaps in the *Books of Testimonies*, for it is often quoted (Lactantius, iv. 18; Cyprian, *Test.* ii. 20 and 15, Gregory of Nyssa, *Test. adv. Jud.* vi, our passage; Bar Salibi, *c. Jud.* iv. 19; vi. 8).

[2] Ps. xcvi. 10. The words "from the Tree" are quoted also in Justin Martyr, 1 *Apol.* xli. 4; *Trypho*, lxxiii. 1 (*supra*, p. 34); Tertullian, *c. Marc.* iii. 19; *adv. Jud.* 10 and 13; and in other Latin Fathers. The hymn *Vexilla Regis*, attributed to Fortunatus (died *c.* A.D. 600), has "Impleta sunt quae cecinit...Regnavit a ligno Deus." *Barn.* viii. 5 may allude to it (ἡ βασιλεία Ἰησοῦ ἐπὶ ξύλῳ). The words are not in the LXX, save in one Greek MS. (156, an uncial), which reads ἀπὸ τῷ ξύλῳ (*sic*), and in the Sahidic version, and in the Latin (only) of the bilingual MS. *Veronensis* (R), and some other old Latin texts (see Swete, *Introd. to LXX*, 1900 and 1914, p. 424). There is nothing equivalent in the Hebrew. The phrase is doubtless a Christian interpolation.

[3] Heb. is "Altascheth (A Psalm) of David: Michtam". Cod. Amiatinus of the Vulg. has the title: "In finem, Ne disperdas, David in tituli inscriptione. Propheta de senioribus Judeorum dicit." The writer of Amiatinus evidently knew the interpretation recorded by Isidore. Augustine adopts it, and also, apparently, the *Breviarium in Psalterium*, wrongly attributed to Jerome.

XLIII. *He was crucified for our sins.*
Isa. liii. 5 *sq.*

XLIV. *He died.*
Isa. liii. 8; Jer. xxxi. 26;[1] Dan. ix. 26; Wisd. ii. 19 *sq.*

XLV. *There was darkness at His passion.*
Amos viii. 9; Jer. xv. 9.

XLVI. *They did not break His legs.*
Ex. xii. 46.

XLVII. *He was pierced with a lance.*
Job xvi. 14 ("breach upon breach", in addition to the nails); Zech. xii. 10.

XLVIII. *Out of His side flowed blood and water.*
Zech. ix. 11; Ezek. xlvii. 2 ("Waters pouring out on the right side", i.e. of Christ).

XLIX. *He was buried.*
Ps. cxliii. 3; Isa. xi. 10 ("and His tomb shall be glorious", Vulg.).

L. *A stone was set at the entrance of His sepulchre.*
Lam. iii. 53; *vv.* 9, 7 ("He hath fenced up my ways with hewn stone, he hath fenced me about, that I should not go forth").

LI. *He descended into hell.*
Ecclus. xxiv. 32 (45) ("I will penetrate all the lower parts of the earth, and consider all that sleep, and enlighten them that hope in God", Vulg.); Ps. lxxxviii. 3 *sq.*

LII. *On going down He set those, whom He would, free from death.*
Hosea v. 14 *sq.*; xiii. 14.

LIII. *The body of Christ in the tomb did not see corruption.*
Ps. xvi. 9 *sq.*

LIV. *He rose from the dead.*
Hosea vi. 1–3.

LV. *The Apostles were sent to preach.*
Jer. xvi. 16; Isa. lxvi. 18 *sq.*; Ps. xix. 4.

LVI. *He ascended into heaven.*
Dan. vii. 13 *sq.*; Ps. lxviii. 18; Cant. ii. 8.

[1] I.e. I awaked from the sleep of death.

LVII. *He sits on the right hand of the Father.*
Ps. cx. 1; ciii. 19.

LVIII. *Christ's kingdom will be for ever.*
Dan. vii. 13 *sq.*; ii. 44; Isa. ix. 7; Ps. lxxii. 7.

LIX. *Christ after His ascension sent the Holy Spirit on the Apostles.*
Ps. lxviii. 18; Joel ii. 28.

LX. *The Apostles spoke in different languages.*
Ps. xix. 3 *sq.*

LXI. *He will come to judge.*
Ezek. xxi. 26 *sq.*; Isa. xxx. 30 ("The Lord...shall show the terror of His arm", for, adds Isidore, the arm of God is Christ); Job xix. 25 *sq.*

LXII. *The Epilogue of the work*, i.e. of Book I.
"We have shown from the Prophets that Christ is the Judge and King of the New Covenant, and that He is Lord of all in accordance with the Law." The books of the Hebrews contain all the details, and the Jews read all these, but do not understand. For to them they are sealed, as Isaiah says (xxix. 11). These are the seals of the Old Testament, which the Son and Heir unsealed, enlightening the eyes of our heart, as it is written, "Bind thou up the testimony, seal the law among My disciples" (Isa. viii. 16).

SECOND BOOK

Preface. As Book I gave a summary of Christ's history in the Old Testament, so Book II will give the prophecy about each people, viz. the rejection of the Jews and their ceremonies (chh. i–xiii), and the praise of the people of the New Testament (chh. xiv–xxvii). Many texts under each heading.

I. *Concerning the call of the Gentiles.*
E.g. Ps. xxii. 27; xcviii. 1 *sq.*; Isa. xlv. 20; lxvi. 18.

II. *All nations were bid believe on Christ.*
E.g. Gen. xlix. 10; Isa. xi. 10; Hagg. ii. 7 ("I will move all nations, and the Desired of all nations shall come", Vulg.). If an unbeliever understands this prophecy of Antichrist, he is plainly wrong. For the Gentiles do not desire Antichrist, but the Jews alone expect him.

III. *Both Jews and Gentiles are bid come to Christ.*
E.g. Isa. vii. 21, "A man shall nourish a cow of the herd and two sheep." The cow is the Jewish people of the seed of the patriarchs; the two sheep are the Church from the Gentiles, which is more in number than that from the Jews.

IV. *Concerning the call of the Gentiles to the faith before the Jews.*

Ps. lxviii. 31, "Ethiopia shall haste to stretch out her hands unto God."[1]

V. *The Jews will believe on Christ in the end of the world.*

God calls the Jewish people "halting" (see Ps. xviii. 45 Vulg.) but He promises to save them in the last days, "I will save her that halteth" (Zeph. iii. 19). See also Mal. iv. 5 *sq.*

VI. *Very many of the people of the Jews would not believe.*

E.g. Deut. xxviii. 66, "Thy Life shall be hanging before Thine eyes... and thou shalt not believe thy life" (Vulg.).[2] Cf. Isa. liii. 1; lxv. 1 *sq.*

VII. *Because of the unbelief of the Jews, Christ would pass to the Gentiles.*

Jer. xiv. 8 *sq.*; Mal. i. 10 *sq.*

VIII. *The Jews were cast forth and the Gentiles came in.*

Isa. xliii. 8 *sq.*, "Lead out the people....Let all the nations be gathered together"; xxvi. 1–6; lxv. 15 *sq.*

IX. *The Jews were vanquished because of their sin against Christ, and were scattered.*

Jer. xii. 8–11, "She hath uttered her voice against Me....Has My inheritance become a speckled bird?...because of Me (*sic*) the whole land is made desolate."[3] For this sin has been unlike other sins, involving a far longer captivity.

X. *Concerning the desolation of Jerusalem.*

Jer. v. 10–12; Dan. ix. 26, "Both the state and the sanctuary shall a people destroy, (acting) with a leader who is to come" (Vulg.), i.e. the Roman army with Vespasian.

XI. *On the Jews being spurned, and the Synagogue rejected.*

Isa. i. 7.

XII. *On the perpetual desolation of Jerusalem.*

Isa. xxv. 1–6; Jer. xix. 10 *sq.*

XIII. *On the irreparable abandonment of the Jews.*

Jer. xiii. 19; xviii. 15–17; xxiii. 39 *sq.* Such texts refer, however, to the carnal Kingdom; there are promises for Jews who believe on God.

XIV. *When the old covenant was cancelled, there was to be a new one.*

Isa. xliii. 18 *sq.*; Jer. xxxi. 33.

---

[1] Cf. Aprahat, xvi. 1 (*supra*, p. 98).

[2] See the *Altercatio Simonis Judaei et Theophili Christiani*, vi. 22 (Harnack, 1883, p. 30); *Sargis d'Aberga* (the Ethiopic form of *The Teaching of Jacob*), i. 42.

[3] Aphrahat, xii. 4, gives a different turn to *v*. 9 (*supra*, p. 97).

XV. *On the cessation of the Sabbath.*

Jews suppose the Sabbath should be observed literally ("carnaliter"). They are wrong, for the Lord says through the prophet, Ps. lxxviii. 2, "I will open My mouth in *parables*, I will utter *dark sayings* from the beginning of the world." Its observance therefore was intended to be spiritual. If it is a crime not to observe literal rest on the sabbath why does God work on it? Gen. ii. 2, "God completed His work on the seventh day." Cf. Josh. vi. 15, of Joshua and his army; and 1 Macc. ii. 41. See Isa. i. 13, "New moons and your sabbaths (*sic*) My soul hateth." Why then did God order Ex. xx. 8–10? To remind the people of the 6000 years of work, ending with the seventh thousand of "sabbath", the end of the age and the Rest of the saints. Jer. xvii. 21, "Bear no burden on the sabbath day." Hear the mystery of prophecy. He bears burdens on the Sabbath, whom the day of Judgment shall find with his transgression; he bears burdens on the Sabbath, who, though he believes in Christ, does not cease from sin. Similarly, the man who was gathering sticks on the Sabbath was slain at God's command (Num. xv. 32–36), for he was a type of him who gathers "wood, hay, stubble" (1 Cor. iii. 12) against the day of Judgment.

XVI. *Concerning the closure* (consummatio) *of circumcision.*

Circumcision was instituted as a sign of nationality, but in the latter days there was to be only circumcision of the heart, Deut. xxx. 6; Jer. iv. 3 *sq.* Baptism takes its place, Isa. xliii. 18–21. Cf. Jer. ix. 26, "All nations are uncircumcised, but all the house of Israel is circumcised (*sic*) in heart." Also Joshua, the second leader, circumcised with knives of stone (Josh. v. 2), because the Stone means Christ, by whom believers are cleansed from all lusts by spiritual circumcision.[1]

XVII. *Concerning the sacrifices.*

These also were rejected, Isa. i. 11; Mal. i. 10 *sq.*

XVIII. *Concerning foods.*

Elijah lived on Gentile foods (1 Kings xvii. 15). All things were pronounced "very good" by God; therefore the real reference of "unclean" foods is to character.

XIX. *Concerning the sacraments of the Christian faith.*

We now turn to show that the Covenant was given not for the Jews only but also for all nations. Ps. xxii. 31; cxxvi. 2.

XX. *Scripture must be understood not historically only, but also mystically.*

Ps. lxxviii. 1; Prov. xxii. 20 ("Write the law doubly, yea, trebly in thy heart", *sic*),[2] i.e. historically, sacramentally or mystically, and

---

[1] Cf. *Trypho*, xxiv. 2 (*supra*, p. 38). See also Aphrahat, xi. 12.

[2] Isidore's version is connected with the LXX, "And do thou record them for thyself trebly." The Vulg. has, "Lo I have described it for thee trebly."

morally. Thus Noah's ark was built of two chambers, or rather of three, for within the Church *History* and material for law should find a place, and receive a *mystical* meaning, and give guidance for *morals*. The Jews, who believe not, cannot understand this.

XXI. *The Jews do not understand the covenant of the Law.*

Isa. xxix. 11. The veil is on their hearts (2 Cor. iii. 15).

XXII. *The Jews do not understand the Scriptures unless they believe in Christ.*

"If ye do not believe ye will not understand, for the just shall live from faith in Me."[1] Righteousness without faith on Christ is useless, as the Lord testifies through Jeremiah (really Isa. lvii. 11 *sq.*).[2]

XXIII. *Two covenants were given by God.*

Cant. vii. 13; Deut. xi. 14 ("the former and the latter rain").

XXIV. *The remission of sins was to take place through baptism.*

Isa. xii. 3; Zech. xiii. 1; xiv. 8–10; Ezek. xlvii. 1–12 (which is also attributed to Zechariah);[3] xxxvi. 24–27.

XXV. *That the Gentiles must be sanctified by anointing.*

Ex. xxx. 23–31. The first tabernacle with its various vessels was a figure of the Church with its different peoples.

XXVI. *That believers should be saved by the sign of the cross.*

Ezek. ix. 3–6. Cf. the blood sprinkled on the door posts in Egypt, and Ps. iv. 7 ("The light of Thy countenance has been signed over us", from the LXX). Ezek. xxi. 10 *sq.*, "Thou (sword) art sharpened, which movest the sceptre of My Son; thou hast cut down wood, and I have given it (the sword) to be polished that it may be held in the hand" (nearly = Vulg.). Here we have the crucifixion of the Son of God, and the sign of His cross which is to be accepted by all. For the fact that the cross also was to be of two parts see Ezek. xxxvii. 16 (the two sticks), and 1 Kings xvii. 12 (the two sticks which the widow who fed Elijah was gathering).

XXVII. *How the sacrament of the Eucharist was prefigured.*

Melchizedek's bread and wine. Areval (the editor of the edition of Isidore's works, 1802) compares with Isidore's language here "the Isidorian or Mozarabic Breviary" on SS. Simon and Jude's Day. Ps. cx. 4; Prov. ix. 1–6; Isa. lxv. 13–16, which also shows that God's servants are to be called by a new name, viz. that of "Christians".

XXVIII. *A Recapitulation of the Work.*

A very short summary. Christ has fulfilled all the types; when truth arrives the shadow ceases. We keep the realities prefigured of old. The last example given is, "We do not observe the Feast of Tabernacles, because the tabernacle of God is His saints, in whom He dwells for ever."

[1] "Si non credideritis, non intelligetis, justus enim ex fide mea vivet", Isa. vii. 9 (from LXX) with Hab. ii. 4 (from LXX).

[2] See Book I, ch. xx, note.   [3] *Ibid.*

BOOK V

LATIN WRITERS

c. A.D. 384–1349

CHAPTER XXXI

THE DISCUSSIONS OF
ZACCHAEUS THE CHRISTIAN AND
APOLLONIUS THE PHILOSOPHER

c. A.D. 384

There is not much to be said about the *Three Books of the Discussions of Zacchaeus the Christian and Apollonius the Philosopher*,[1] for they are not concerned directly with the Jews. But although they are addressed to Gentile readers they so far fall under our purview that the author has often in his mind objections brought forward by Jews, and even deals with them expressly in Book II. iv *sq.* Further, in two or three particulars his matter is of special interest. The three books represent the discussions of three days. "The first book replies to the Pagan objections of Apollonius, the second expounds the doctrines, and the third the practice of the Christian religion."[2]

The author presents us with two strange quotations from the Old Testament. The first is in a chapter entitled "Against the Patripassians, who think the Father suffered"; "David itaque sub verbis Domini ipsius dicit: *Obediens factus sum usque ad mortem*",[3] which seems to be an adaptation of Phil. ii. 8 foisted into the writer's copy of the Psalter, perhaps at Ps. xxii. 15.

The other is in a passage where the author is insisting on the

---

[1] *Consultationum Zacchaei Christiani et Apollonii Philosophi Libri Tres*, first published by Dom d'Achery (Acherius) in his *Spicilegium*, vol. x, 1671; also in Migne, *P.L.* xx, 1071–1166. Its date is placed by Batiffol as, probably, A.D. 384 (*Revue des Sciences Religieuses*, 1922, ii. 114–120), and it is therefore rather later than the *De Errore* of Firmicus (*c.* 350), whom Dom Morin suggested as its author, chiefly on the ground of verbal similarities (*Hist. Jahrbuch*, 1916, pp. 229–266). Batiffol thinks the writer was not a professional theologian, but a literary man, who failed to see the theological implications of some of his statements. Nothing is known either of Zacchaeus or of Apollonius, and probably both are symbols, the former as a favourite name of a Christian, the latter as perhaps alluding to the cultured philosopher at Rome who was martyred in the time of Commodus (A.D. 180–192). See Eusebius, *Ch. Hist.* v. 21. In our treatise also he becomes a Christian, but his Confession (I. xxxvii [xxxviii]) has nothing in common with the short account in Eusebius, or his Apology in the Armenian narrative (F. C. Conybeare, *Monuments of Early Christianity*, 1896, pp. 35–48).

[2] Dr Salmon, *Dict. Chr. Biogr.* 1887, iv. 1207. Morin has a very full account of the contents. [3] II. xv.

need for perseverance, for unless the combat is finished the palm of victory is not awarded: "unde in Salomone: *Laus in exitu canitur*". This "mumpsimus" indeed is almost better than the original "sumpsimus". For Prov. i. 20 is, according to the Hebrew, *Wisdom crieth aloud without*, which the Septuagint renders, *Wisdom is sung in the ways outside* (σοφία ἐν ἐξόδοις ὑμνεῖται). The Latin of Irenaeus (*Adv. Haer.* v. xx. 1) has *Sapientia in exitu canitur*.[1] Then *Sapientia* became popularised into *laus* because of *canitur*, and a new meaning was given to the whole phrase.[2]

In I. iv Zacchaeus tells Apollonius that he ought to remember that even heathen authors bear witness to the Divinity of Christ, and to His Cross which Apollonius derides. And he quotes two examples, Plato and the Sibyl. "For when Plato, whom you call most learned and most wise, was speaking about the revelation of the majesty of Christ, with these words he was also constructing, as a sign of Him, a future God to come into being, whose sign is rounded in a circle and divided crosswise."

The reference is doubtless to the *Timaeus*, 35 A, 36 B, and it is probable that our author "is thinking of this globular divine universe, the first begotten of the divine δημιουργός, the Creator. It has two circular motions, one on an axis running through the North and South poles, and the other in a plane inclined to the equator. The first circle generates the sphere of the universe, and Plato thinks of the two circles as arising from two straight strips, placed cross-wise at an acute angle (to get the inclined path of the sun through the heavens), and then, while fastened together at their central points, having their ends bent round to form two circles."[3]

The second quotation is from the Sibyl:

Felix ille Deus, ligno qui pendet ab alto,[4]

[1] So also Hilary on Ps. cxix. 32 (Migne, *P.L.* ix. 532), and Vigilius Tapsensis (*c.* A.D. 508) in his *De Trin.* xii (Migne, *P.L.* lxii. 327).

[2] III. ix. I owe the explanation to Prof. F. C. Burkitt. Our form of the quotation, however, does not occur anywhere else, as it seems.

[3] "Plato enim, quem doctissimum ac sapientissimum perhibetis, cum de revelanda Christi majestate loqueretur, his verbis etiam signum illius intimavit, futurum adstruens Deum, cujus signum circumrotundatum et decussatum est." I owe the reference, translation, and explanation to the kindness of the well-known Platonist, Mrs A. M. Adam. See also Justin, 1 *Apol.* lx, who quotes Plato as saying in the *Timaeus*: "He placed Him in the universe after the manner of the letter χ" (ἐχίασεν αὐτὸν ἐν τῷ παντί). Cf., further, C. H. Sharpe in *The Times* of April 2, 1931.

[4] This fragment from one of the many forms of the Sibylline Oracles seems to be found here only.

which is evidently based on the well-known addition to Ps. xcvi. 10.[1]

In ii. iii, *In the Beginning* (Gen. i. 1) is once more interpreted of Christ;[2] and in viii, the stone knives of Josh. v. 2 are made to refer to the disciplinary commands of the Gospel.[3] In vi our author follows Cyprian (*Test.* ii. 20) closely in his Old Testament evidence for the Crucifixion, when he quotes Deut. xxviii. 66, *Erit pendens vita tua ante oculos tuos*; and, even more strangely, Num. xxiii. 19, *Non quasi homo Deus suspenditur, nec quasi filius hominis minas patitur.*[4] In ix the Blessed Virgin is the *Shoot*, and Christ the *Flower* of Isa. xi. 1.[5] In x, *Homo Juda* (Isa. v. 3), the too literal translation of the Hebrew (Vulg. *viri Juda*), is made to refer to Christ: "Homo Juda Salvator"; and the "people of Jerusalem", to those whose hope is in the faith of the Church.

Another passage is interesting for a different reason. In ii. xix Zacchaeus is warning Christians against enquiring too closely into things unrevealed, whether in heaven or in hell. For those whom the devil cannot deceive by sins of the flesh he trips up by that kind of empty learning, "and appointing diviners of this hidden knowledge he bids them make enquiries of a stone set under a stone, that they may find—a serpent".[6] Is it possible that this curious magical ceremony has any connexion, either by origin or by way of heathen protest, with the famous Saying of our Lord discovered in 1897: "Raise the stone, and there thou shalt find Me"?[7]

[1] Which is quoted in ii. vi. See further the notes in my edition of the *Dialogue with Trypho*, 1930, lxxiii. 1 (*supra*, p. 34). Cf. note on Isidore, *c. Judaeos*, 1. xxxv (*vide supra*, Appendix, p. 287).

[2] See *Jason and Papiscus*, *supra*, p. 29.

[3] "In abscisionibus petrinis evangelicae conveniunt disciplinae." Justin understands them in nearly the same way, as Christ's words by which hearts are circumcised (*Dialogue with Trypho*, cxiii. 6; cf. xxiv. 2, *supra*, p. 38), but he tends to connect "stone" with Christ Himself.   [4] *Vide supra*, p. 63.

[5] "In *virga* Mariae venerabilis monstratur integritas; in odore *floris* et gratia signatus est Christus." For the *Flower* see the *Dialogue with Trypho*, cxxvi. 1 (*supra*, p. 40).

[6] "Occultaeque scientiae arbitros statuens, lapidem sub lapide cogit inquirere, ut inveniant serpentem."

[7] ἔγειρον τὸν λίθον κἀκεῖ εὑρήσεις με (Grenfell and Hunt, 1897, p. 9). For the phrase, though not for the thought, compare, "Underneath most of the cloths or mats covering the graves (of some five hundred and fifty Amoraim near the grave of the Prophet Ezekiel by the Euphrates) a serpent is coiled, which guards the grave. Therefore they say to every one, 'When thou raisest the mat, beware of the serpent'" (*The Travels of R. Petachiah of Ratisbon*, in the twelfth century, ed. Benisch, 1861, p. 37).

CHAPTER XXXII

EVAGRIUS

THE DISCUSSION CONCERNING THE LAW BETWEEN SIMON A JEW AND THEOPHILUS A CHRISTIAN[1]

? c. A.D. 400

There are few writings connected with our subject to which so much attention has been paid as to this. For it has had the honour of being critically edited and examined by Harnack.[2] Unfortunately he possessed only the bare beginning and the closing words of a MS. at Monte Cassino,[3] and also knew nothing of another MS. at Reichenau, which, however, is not very good.[4] He tried to show that the Dialogue was based upon the lost *Discussion of Jason and Papiscus*,[5] which it incorporated to a great extent. But his evidence is lamentably weak, and his theory is vitiated by his failure to perceive that similarities in the strange use of Old Testament passages do not point to the literary employment of one writer by another so much as to the existence of a common method of interpretation. On the other hand his edition contains an invaluable investigation of the facts of such similarities between Evagrius and other writers, which Bratke indeed tabulates (with many additions) but does not study. A cursory examination of Bratke's references to the Latin translation of twenty Homilies by Origen[6] shows that these addresses were well known to our author. Yet Evagrius does not quote directly from them (much less mentions them by name), but incorporates ideas and phrases that are found there. This illustrates exactly what has been said, that

---

[1] *Altercatio Legis inter Simonem Judaeum et Theophilum Christianum.* E. Bratke in *Corp. Scriptorum Eccl. Lat.* vol. xxxv, Vienna, 1904. See also Migne, *P.L.* xx. 1165–1182. Juster, *op. cit.* i. 64, has many references to studies of this document. For a discussion of some details, especially in its Latinity, see Th. Stangl in *Berliner Philologische Wochenschrift*, 1915, coll. 733–736; 829–832.

[2] *Texte u. Untersuch.* i. 3 (1883).

[3] No. 247 (cent. xi–xii). Published in full in *Bibliotheca Cassinensis*, 1894, v. i. 21–33.

[4] Bratke, p. vi.   [5] *Vide supra*, pp. 28 sq.

[6] *Tractatus Origenis*, ed. Batiffol, 1900, who shows that it may well be attributed to Origen.

Evagrius followed the current usage of the Church in his interpretation of Scriptural passages, not that he made direct use of his
predecessor as a "source".

Who Evagrius was, no one knows. Gennadius of Marseilles,
when making (about A.D. 480) some additions to Jerome's *De Viris
Illustribus* (§ 51), tells us that "another Evagrius wrote the Discussion of Simon a Jew and Theophilus a Christian, which is
known to almost everybody". The word "another" is inserted to
distinguish him from a monk of that name whom Gennadius had
mentioned in § 11, and from the Evagrius who was Bishop of
Antioch and a friend of Jerome.[1] Our author doubtless lived in
the West, and it has been suggested that he lived in Spain, and
even that he is to be identified with Gregory Baeticus, Bishop of
Elvira (Illiberis), *c.* A.D. 357–384.[2]

In giving a brief summary of the tract it will be convenient to
refer to it by Harnack's thirty sections, even though these are
neglected by Bratke. After Evagrius has saluted his brother
Valerius he says that he is sending him an account of an interesting
discussion that took place before his very eyes,[3] between one Simon
a Jew and Theophilus a Christian. The Jew begins by saying,
"Thou worshipper of the cross, who bearest the cross on thy forehead,[4] and professest to be a teacher of the Law", convince me
of the truth (for I will listen patiently) out of the Law. If you
overcome me, make me a Christian, but if I you I will make a
Nazarene become a Jew (§ 1). On Theophilus undertaking to
prove that the crucified Christ is God (§§ 2, 3), Simon adduces the
passage, *There is no other God beside Me* (Deut. xxxii. 39), and, *I am
the first and I the last, and beside Me there is no God* (Isa. xliv. 6) (§ 4).
Theophilus replies that *first* and *last* refer to Christ's two advents,
and that the words *beside Me*, etc. were really said by Christ Himself,
but directed against the false claim of Antichrist, to whom Zech.
xi. 16 *sq.* refers (§ 5).

So, says Simon, there are two Gods! No, replies Theophilus,
"There is one God, of whom is Christ and in whom is God",[5] just
as Three appeared to Abraham in Mamre, where the tree prefigured the tree of the cross. Besides, Ps. lxxxi. 1 says, *God stood*

---

[1] Harnack, *op. cit.* pp. 1–3.
[2] G. Morin, *Rev. d'Hist. Ecclés.* 1900, pp. 266 *sqq.*
[3] Yet there is no sign of an eyewitness throughout the Discussion.
[4] Cf. *infra*, § 24, p. 303.
[5] "Deus unus est, ex quo Christus et in quo deus."

in the synagogue of the gods, and was judging gods in the midst, a plain reference to Christ, who taught in your synagogues, and performed great miracles. See also Ps. xlv. 6 *sq.,* and Jer. (Baruch) iii. 35–37 (§ 6).

But where does God definitely appoint Christ to be God?

Theophilus answers that as God appointed Moses to be God to Pharaoh, an unbelieving heathen (and Moses was a type of Christ), how much more is Christ the God of believers (§ 7).

Then comes the interesting passage, recalling the *Dialogue of Jason and Papiscus,* in which Gen. i. 1 (*in principio*) is identified with Christ.[1] For God made heaven and earth in Christ's decision and at His will, in Whose image and likeness God deemed it well to make man. For He says Gen. i. 26 *sq.* (§ 8). But, urges Simon, this could have been addressed to the angels! You are wrong, is the reply, "for to which of the angels did God say, *Thou art My Son,* etc. (Ps. ii. 7)? And again, *I will make Him My Princeps*" (Ps. lxxxix. 27) (§ 9). See also Josh. v. 13 *sq.* (§ 10).

Yet, says Simon, In what sense is Christ the Son of God, for all the saints are called so? You surely cannot mean that He is Son by natural generation.

No indeed, is the reply, but by a generation far more perfect, from the womb of His very heart. So God promised to be Father to David's seed (2 Sam. vii. 14; cf. Ps. ii. 7). See also Ps. xlv. 1, *My heart poureth forth a goodly Word,* and Ps. cvii. 20, *He sent His Word and healed them.* And Ecclus. xxiv. 5 (Vulg.), *I came forth from the mouth of the Most High, the First-Born before every creature,* and Prov. viii. 22, *The Lord formed Me at the commencement of His ways, in the Beginning*[2] (§ 11).

Simon. This may refer to Wisdom.

Theophilus. Nay, for Christ Himself is the Power of God and the Wisdom of God. Even your kings required the use of the word Christ ("anointing"), and Dan. ix. 24 *sq.* says of Him, *The Holy One of* (all) *the Holy Ones shall be anointed...and thou shalt understand ...in building Jerusalem until Christ is reigning.* "But when the Christ of (all) the Christs (i.e. anointed ones), and the Lord of lords, and the King of your kings, came from God, the anointing oil of

---

[1] *Vide supra,* p. 298.

[2] *In principio.* The Vulg. has *in initio,* but the MS. Amiatinus reads *initium* only, and this, as the literal translation of the Hebrew, probably represented the old Church exposition that *Beginning* was one name of Christ. Cf. the Haggadic explanations in Rashi on Gen. i. 1.

Samaria failed,[1] together with the horn containing it from which your kings were anointed; and all the prophets were silent, for He came of Whom they used to speak."[2] For Isaiah says (xlv. 1), *The Lord says to Christ my Lord, whose right hand I have holden*, etc.[3] And He gives the sign to Ahaz (§ 12).

The Jew argues that this referred to the virgin daughter of Sion (Isa. xxxvii. 22). To this the Christian replies, But what then of the Child? Who was it that ate the *butter* and *honey*, and took *the wealth of Damascus and the spoils of Samaria against the king of Assyria* (Isa. viii. 4) (§ 13)? *Butter* and *honey* are to be understood literally, for Christ was like other babes, and also *butter* means the anointing of the Spirit, and *honey* the sweetness of His teaching. And taking *the spoils of Samaria* refers to the gifts of the Magi, and also to the fact that both *Samaria* and *Damascus* left their idols and became good believers, forsaking the Assyrian, i.e. the devil (§ 14).[4]

Simon. You have proved to me that the Son of God was born of a virgin, yet, How do you assert that He was born of David's seed in Bethlehem?

Theophilus. Isaiah (xi. 1) says, *A Shoot (virga) from the stock of Jesse.* For the *virga* is the Virgin *(virgo)* Mary, who was of the seed of David, from which Virgin is born Christ, the Flower of the patriarchs according to the flesh.[5] God who made an ass speak (Num. xxii. 28) made a much greater sign that Christ should be born of a virgin. For what sign was it except that she who bare was a virgin (§ 15)?

Simon. If indeed a virgin can bear!

Theophilus. God could break the rock and bring out water in plenty! But will you believe Baruch (§ 16)?

Simon. Do you take me for an unbeliever?

Theophilus. He prophesies near the end of his book, *This Mv Anointed, My Elect, is said to be the offspring of an unsullied womb, to have been born, and to have suffered.* For His *robe* also was *woven from the top throughout.*[6] As to His birth at Bethlehem, see Micah v. 2 (§ 17).

---

[1] "Unctio Samariae defecit." A curious phrase, suggesting (it seems) that the anointing of all the kings of Israel and Judah was alike imperfect, and suitable only to imperfect notions of God. Is the phrase unique?

[2] *Trypho*, lii. 4 *et al.* (*vide supra*, p. 36).

[3] See *Barn.* xii. 11 (p. 26); Tert. *c. Jud.* vii (p. 47).

[4] See *Trypho*, lxxviii. 9 *sq.* (*supra*, p. 41).

[5] *Trypho*, cxxvi. 1 (*supra*, p. 41).

[6] From some unknown Book of Baruch. Dr M. R. James notices our quotation in his *Lost Apocrypha of the O.T.* 1920, p. 78.

Simon. Yet how can you expect to persuade me when you forbid Circumcision in spite of God's charge to Abraham?

Theophilus. That was given to Abraham after he had believed, not before. Circumcision therefore is only a sign of race, not of salvation (§ 18).

Simon. Yet the angel had choked Moses' uncircumcised child unless Zipporah had circumcised the boy with a stone, and prayed, *Let the blood of the boy's circumcision stay.*[1]

Theophilus. Yes, and it has stopped altogether since Christ came (§ 19)! For the circumcision God desires is that of the heart (Jer. iv. 3 *sq.*), and the stone knives of Joshua (Josh. v. 2) point to Christ circumcising the hearts.[2] Now that is the circumcision which Enoch, Noah, Job and Melchizedek had (§§ 20, 21).

Simon. Can the Christ possibly have suffered such a shameful death—if at least what you say is true, that He was fastened to the gibbet of a cross at the hands of our fathers? Haman and Absalom, yes; but Christ! We never learned that, nor can we find it in our Scriptures. Deut. xxi. 23 says, *Cursed is every one who hangeth on a tree.*

Theophilus. That refers to a criminal, which Christ was not. *He did no sin,* says Isa. liii. 9. But for His crucifixion see Ps. xxii. 16–21, and other passages, e.g. Deut. xxviii. 66; Num. xxiii. 19.[3] So also the Bunch of Grapes brought back by the two spies prefigured Christ hanging on the tree, with you turning your back on Him, and us looking towards Him (§ 22).[4] The Pomegranate also, which was brought at the same time, is a figure of the Church, with its people marked out by the Red of the blood of Christ (§ 23).[5]

Simon. Figs were brought also, and they represent sin! For when Adam fell he covered himself with fig-leaves.

Theophilus. You judge by the outside. For the fig-tree and the covering by its leaves represent the old man. But if you think of the inner man you will find that the fig-fruit itself means spiritual life. For so the plaster of figs brought life to Hezekiah (Isa. xxxviii. 21).

But let me resume the subject of the Humility of Christ's first Advent. Consider Isa. liii. 1–12. So in Egypt a lamb had to be

---

[1] Ex. iv. 24–26: "Stet sanguis circumcisionis pueri." Cf. LXX, ἔστη τὸ αἷμα τῆς περιτομῆς τοῦ παιδίου μου. The Vulgate follows the Hebrew.

[2] See *Trypho,* xxiv. 2; cxiii. 6, where see my note (*supra*, p. 38).

[3] For these passages see Index.   [4] Num. xiii. 23.

[5] *Tract. Orig.* xi. 121–126 works this out at a greater length.

slain, and its blood marked on the threshold for the household to be saved. And a lamb of one year old is mentioned, for from Christ's baptism to His passion was one year (only).[1] And the mark of the Cross on our foreheads is mentioned in Ezek. ix. 4.[2] So also Hosea (Hos. i. 2) is bid take a wife of fornication, i.e. the Church, which turned from the fornication of idolatry to Christ (§ 24).

Simon. So the Church is a harlot!

Theophilus. Only in refusing none who comes to her. Christ rejected the Synagogue, and took to Himself the Church. The Jews had deserved this rejection, for, as Solomon said in Wisd. ii. 12–22, *Let us lie in wait for the Righteous One*, etc.

That He rose from the dead is taught in Ps. xvi. 10 *sq.*, and elsewhere. His Ascension also is often foretold, e.g. Ps. xxiv. 7–10; cx. 1; and also Ps. lxxii, for this cannot refer to Solomon (§§ 25, 26).

The Jew confesses that his blindness is departing, and the Christian assures him that so he will be loosed from his chains (Isa. lxi. 1), and that when Christ, who is the Light, comes to him the darkness of his ignorance will remove, Gen. i. 2 *sq.* (§ 27).

Simon. I still have a difficulty, that you neglect the Sabbath, and also take food and wine[3] as do the heathen, without regard to God's specific directions.

Theophilus. You are a true son of your fathers, who, after their deliverance from Egypt, etc., dared to demand strange gods.

As for the Sabbath, its rest was only figurative.[4] For Joshua went round Jericho seven days, and seven times on the seventh day, and the Maccabees fought on it. Consider also Isa. i. 13 *sq.*; lviii. 13, where God desires rest from evil works, as in the seventh millennium, the Sabbath of sabbaths.[5]

As for Foods, it is not a question of eating pork, but of refraining from pig-like actions, such as incest, robbery, proclaiming your festivals openly, praying in the streets.[6] And Ps. xvii. 14 says,

---

[1] Eusebius, *Ch. Hist.* iii. 24.

[2] Ps.-Aug. *De Altercat.* col. 1134 (*infra*, p. 330).

[3] The Mosaic Law says nothing about drinks. Evagrius may be speaking vaguely, or may have thought that Judaism taught asceticism. See the next page.

[4] "Sabbata scilicet imaginaria septimi diei tradita fuit." Cf. *lex imaginaria, Tract. Orig.* x. 109, 114.

[5] See *Barn.* xv; and the beautiful sermon, *Tract. Orig.* viii. 86–95, where the rare phrase *sabbatum sabbatorum* recurs, pp. 94 *sq.*

[6] Cf. Matt. vi. 5. Cf. Novatian, *De Cibis Judaicis*, § v: "Deus ventre non colitur, nec cibis" (Migne, *P.L.* iii. 960).

They are satiated with pork, and have left the rest to their little ones.[1] But show me where in your Scriptures Christian wine is forbidden, and I will show you where Jewish wine is forbidden, and we are charged not to eat your food. *The wine of Sodom is their wine,* etc. (Deut. xxxii. 32–34).

If you do not believe, you contradict your own salvation. Recognise the Son of God, as did Nebuchadnezzar who was a heathen. Take heed lest the warning of Hab. i. 4 *sq.* be fulfilled in you (§ 28).

Simon then yields fully, asking to be examined,[2] and consecrated with the sign of faith in Jesus Christ, "for I think I shall receive the washing away of my sins by the laying on of hands".

Theophilus. Yea, and blessing also! As with Ephraim and Manasseh (Gen. xlviii. 13–20) (§ 29).

Then Theophilus anointed[3] Simon, who rendered thanks to Jesus. "Jesus, whom I have never seen face to face, but now I believe in Thee; I give thanks to Thee, O Jesus, whom I have never heard, but now hear. I call upon Thee, O Jesus, for Whom I had no feeling heretofore, but now long for that feeling of mine to be for Thee, by Whom it recognised Theophilus as Thy servant. O Lord Jesus, if I am worthy to have faith, strengthen me also for the full knowledge of Thyself. For Thou showest the way to them that wander, and callest home the lost, and raisest the dead, and strengthenest the faithless in Thy faith, and to the blind Thou givest light in the eyes of their heart. Thou Thyself art the holy Tabernacle who wast with our Fathers in the desert.[4] Thou art the Candlestick, Thou the Golden Altar and the Shewbread, Thou the Altar and the willing Victim. Thou too, O Lord, art Life and Pearl,[5] Crystal, Yoke and Plough.[6] I pray Thee, O Lord, remember not my ignorance and unbelief. For Thou art ever giving the hidden treasures of Thy kindness, Who hast deemed it well to

---

[1] "Saturati sunt porcina." The Latin version used by Evagrius was evidently made from a LXX MS. which read υἱῶν instead of υἱῶν (υἱέων).

[2] "Catecizari."　　　　　　　　　　　　　[3] "Unxit."

[4] So also it was Christ who went with Simon's fathers in the column of the cloud (§ 11).

[5] See M. A. Canney, "The Life-giving Pearl", in the *Journal of the Manchester Egyptian and Oriental Society*, 1930, xv. 43–62. "Margarita appellatur, ut nihil illa pretiosius habeatur", Phoebadius, *De Filii Divinitate*, vi (Migne, *P.L.* xx. 42 D).

[6] Cf. a Poem attributed to Orientius (cent. iv), ed. Ellis, *Poetae Christiani Minores*, 1888, p. 243.

bestow everything upon me. To Thee be honour, power, praise and glory, both here and unto all the ceaseless ages of eternity. Amen" (§ 30).

The impression that the treatise makes is that it was more than a merely academic essay. The author appears to know something about Jewish practices. Yet he has no intimate knowledge of Jewish learning, and his Jew knows no more than his Christian. It is well-meaning, and not unkindly, if the vituperation common to the age be excluded. He appears to have had earlier writers in front of him (though not exclusively writings against the Jews), especially Tertullian and Cyprian, and the Homilies called *Tractatus Origenis*. But there is no reason to suppose that he took any one treatise, e.g. the *Dialogue of Jason and Papiscus*, as the basis of his work, or indeed that he used that particular Dialogue at all.

CHAPTER XXXIII

AN ARIAN TREATISE AGAINST THE JEWS

BY MAXIMINUS THE ARIAN BISHOP OF HIPPO
(flor. A.D. 427)

(Commonly attributed to St *Maximus of Turin*[1]
flor. A.D. 451)

Although difficulties about the complete orthodoxy of this treatise
have been raised these many years,[2] it is only since 1922 that its
Arian authorship has been demonstrated. Hitherto it has always
been credited to St Maximus,[3] the orthodox Bishop of Turin who
was present at the council held there in 451 and signed the letter
to Pope Leo I. But a comparison of its language, style, and even
doctrine, shows that it is by the same author as that of the tractate
entitled *Against the Heathen* (*c. Paganos*) and certain sermons and a
fragment of a definitely Arian sermon. And, further, there are
found to be "astonishingly close and complete" parallelisms in
this group with the arguments employed by Maximinus, the Arian
Bishop of Hippo, in his discussion with Augustine in that city in
the year 427 or 428.[4] Other writings in the group, though not,
it would seem, the one in which we are especially interested,
suffered mutilation for their unorthodox terms, thus preparing the
way for the identification of their author with "one of the two most
celebrated preachers of the North Italian Church".

The interesting points about this Arian endeavour to win the
Jews to Christ are, first, that it proceeds along the old and orthodox

[1] *Contra Judaeos.* Dr C. H. Turner has published a critical text in *J. Th. St.*
1919, xx. 289–310; and a consideration of the authorship in *ibid.* 1922, xxiv.
76–79, accepting the arguments and conclusions of D. B. Capelle in the *Revue
Bénédictine*, April, 1922, xxxiv. 81–108. The common text is in Migne, *P.L.* lvii.
793–806.

[2] See the explanatory note in Migne at the end of ch. x (col. 805).

[3] "S. Maxime eût frémi à la pensée qu'on pût jamais le [l'auteur] confondre
avec lui" (Capelle, p. 90).

[4] Migne, *P.L.* [Aug. viii], 708–742, and Augustine's further reply to his
adversary's arguments in his two books against Maximus, 743–814. The discussion was recorded by official notaries, to whose records appeals were made
during it.

lines of verbal proofs from the Old Testament; secondly, that it includes appeals to supposed facts in nature (ch. iii); and, thirdly, that it is marked to an astonishing degree by warnings against the employment of physical force to win the Jews, and by insistence on our warfare being only spiritual (ch. viii). The author might, in fact, have taken lessons from Raymund Lull himself (in his better mood), who lived eight hundred years later.

The author is determined to show that the Old Testament, if it be understood aright, supports the claims of Christianity even from its earliest pages. For if we begin with Adam we find that Cain, the elder brother representing the Jews, was rejected of God, who accepted the sacrifice of Abel, the younger brother who stands for Christians. And when Abel was slain (for his name means "sorrow", *luctus*) Seth was born in his stead, and Seth means "resurrection". So here in those two younger brethren there was indicated Christ's Passion (i.e. death) and Resurrection, in which the Christian people has its being ("in qua consistit populus Christianus").

The histories too of Ishmael and Isaac, of Esau and Jacob, of Jacob's elder sons and Joseph, of Manasseh and Ephraim, all tell the same tale—as does also the fact that of the two sets of tablets given to Moses, the first was broken, and the second kept, "whence", Maximinus adds quaintly, "it is called Deuteronomy, i.e. the second Law" (ch. i).[1]

He then recites the teaching of Moses himself about the Christ. For Moses said that God would raise up a Prophet like himself. Not only that, but in the opening words of Genesis Moses writes: "*In the Beginning God made the heaven and the earth*, by the word *Beginning* dealing with ('taxans') the Son, in Whom God the Father made the heaven and the earth."[2] So also says "our Apostle Paul" (Col. i. 16), and Solomon in Prov. viii. 22 *sq*. To the Son again God said, *Let us make man* (Gen. i. 26 *sq*.), not to the

---

[1] This may be taken from some Midrash on Ex. xxxiv. 1–27, *And I will write on the tables the words*, etc. The Hebrew title for Deuteronomy is *These are the words* (דְּבָרִים). R. Acha (*c*. A.D. 350) distinguished between the contents of the first and the second sets of Tables, the first containing the Ten Commandments only, the second including Halakoth, Midrashim and Haggadoth, illustrating this by Job xi. 6 (*Ex. R.* Par. 46 on Ex. xxxiv. 1). For a further explanation of "Deuteronomy" see *Timothy and Aquila*, fol. 77 r⁰ (*supra*, p. 72).

[2] So the *Dialogue of Jason and Papiscus*. See my note there, p. 29. Maximinus appears to have had this interpretation in mind when he insists in the *Discussion with Augustine* that it was the Son, not the Father, who "made man" (Migne, 734); but if so Augustine had never heard of it, for he asks how Maximinus knew that it was the Son who made man (Migne, 804 *sq*.).

angels, as a Jew perhaps asserts. For "God spake" and "God made", i.e. the Father commanded, and the Son accomplished. So again at the destruction of Sodom, *The Lord rained from the Lord*, i.e. at the Father's command, the Son rained down fire (Gen. xix. 24). Other Old Testament passages are adduced, especially Ps. ii. 7, for though the Jew cries, "Has God then a son?" the answer is, "Certainly He had a Son, whom He begat not after the manner of men, but as it became God to beget, without passion, without corruption, in the manner of God ('inpassibiliter, incorruptibiliter deifice')." See also Ps. cx. 1. And in Ps. cxxxii. 17 *sq.* the Father says, *I have prepared a lantern for my Christ*, i.e. I have prepared the Church, which shines and glows by His light, for it is the number of the faithful who have received in their heart the light of truth and belief, and have left the darkness of unbelief and ignorance. Such also was John the Baptist, a lamp illuminating the people (John v. 35) (ch. ii).

The writer then turns to the Incarnation. He quotes Isa. xxxv. 3–5; Baruch (as "Jeremiah") iii. 35–37;[1] Isa. lii. 10; with vii. 14 (all these being in Cyprian's *Testimonia*), and also Ps. lxxii. 6 of the silence of His coming, though, as he says, neither Jew nor Heathen believes in this Virgin birth. Yet if the angels, and some birds, and other creatures, are born in like fashion,[2] why should not God make the temple of His body in such strange manner? But in flesh He died and rose again, that we too should have hope of a future resurrection. For there is no pollution (as the old Jewish objection says) in God being born of a woman. The sun's brilliancy is not defiled whatever it may touch (ch. iii).

For the Jews have always been stiff-necked and uncircumcised of heart, as Scripture says, in spite of their claim to be circumcised. But we tell them, Would that you were circumcised indeed, and had the fragrance of Abraham and not the stink of your faithlessness.[3] Abraham was not justified by circumcision, but by faith, and the saints before him were never circumcised. For true circumcision is of the heart. For you should notice that Joshua was bid make knives of flint, and circumcise the children of Israel

[1] See Cyprian, *Test.* ii. 6 (*supra*, p. 61). The original reference was to the Law (cf. Whitehouse in Charles, ii. 591).

[2] Mr T. H. Baxter illustrates this point from earlier writers in *J. Th. St.* 1920, xxi. 175–177.

[3] "Utinam haberetis odorem fidei Abrahae et non bromositatem perfidiae vestrae." The allusion seems to be to the scents always characterising feasts, and therefore used at the feast after a circumcision.

"a second time". Understanding this spiritually it means that by the Law they had been circumcised from idolatry, but still need to be circumcised a second time by the Gospel[1] (ch. iv).

You may indeed say you are children of Abraham. Yes, but your mother is Hagar, and the blessing is in Isaac. The author alludes again (cf. ch. i) to the rejection of the elder sons, and also to the breaking of the first tables of the Law, this time to show that the Jewish heart is broken and rejected, but the Christian is fit for the divine laws and is to be preserved. St Paul therefore committed himself to Christ that he should no longer live under Caesar but under Christ as his King (ch. v).

Our sign of salvation, unlike yours, is for both men and women; the cross is on the two posts marked by the blood of the Lamb. His blood is, as you cried, on you and your children, but for condemnation. You chose a robber, for *every living creature loveth his like* (Ecclus. xiii. 15); we chose the Lord. You thought you slew the Lord, but He was not to be held in a narrow rock, no, not even His soul, much less His divinity. For Christ lives and reigns for ever, as Gabriel told Mary (ch. vi).

He has come to give abundance of peace (Ps. lxxii. 7), for He is the very fount of peace, in Whom are no storms of quarrel nor bitter spite, but only sweet and restful goodness. For there is *abundance of peace as long as the moon is exalted*—and by moon is meant the Church, which waxes in time of peace and wanes in persecution. So will He *reign from sea to sea*, and at His presence shall the Morians fall down, *and His enemies shall lick the dust* (Ps. lxxii. 9)—for the Morians are the spirits of darkness, who are troubled at His presence. But that Psalm is fulfilled in many details. For *the whole earth shall be filled with His glory* (Ps. lxxii. 19). The Jews then are plainly convicted (ch. vii).

By God's help, then, we say this, not to injure and destroy them. God forbid! It is a spiritual warfare that we wage, not carnal. So we seek to bring them back and save them, bring them under the dominion of Christ our King. For we fight under a peaceful King, and follow the camp of peace.

But the Jews would rather die than be convinced, saying that they worship one God, and they cry that this command, *Hear O Israel*, etc., was given to their fathers, and that they must keep it. We ask them then, Why did your fathers leave that one God of yours and turn to idols? (Ps. cvi. 19 *sq.*). They say: "Let them see

---

[1] This is suggested in Cyprian, *Test.* i. 8.

to that; we know nothing of it." The command was really given to keep the Jews from the worship of heathen gods and immoral practices. But we worship the one God of you Jews, invisible, incorporeal, immortal, without beginning or end (ch. viii).

Then follow many proofs from the Old Testament that Christ is both God and the Son of God, amongst them Gen. i. 1, again, for we repeat these texts lest you forget (ch. ix).

"But", cries the Jew, "how can you Christians say that God has a Son? Did the invisible and incorruptible God beget a Son?" Yet David said, speaking doubtless in the person of Christ, *The Lord said unto me, Thou art My Son, to-day have I begotten thee* (Ps. ii. 7). And again David speaking as a prophet in the person of the Father to the Son said, *With Thee, the Beginning, in the day of Thy power in the splendours of the Saints, from the womb before the morning star did I beget thee.*[1] Of course we do not mean that God begat in carnal fashion. But observe that when the Father says "thee" it shows that it is Another than Himself whom He is addressing. Also that "womb" suggests the ineffable fulness and the deep mystery of God, His incomprehensible wisdom. And *before the morning star did I beget thee* means either before the decorations of the heavens, or "before the beginning of the Holy Spirit,"[2] because the Holy Spirit Himself is called 'the morning-star', for He pours into men's minds the light of truth and sound faith, and has announced by the prophets again and again, like the morning-star, the coming of Christ the everlasting sun" (ch. x).

It was no strange thing that Christ should appear, for He had appeared before—to the children of Israel in a pillar of fire and smoke, as God the Father said: "Behold I send My Angel", etc. (Ex. xiii. 21; xxiii. 20). So also He appeared to Joshua (Josh. v. 14), and to Abraham; see especially the phrase, *The Lord rained fire and brimstone from the Lord*, i.e. the Son rained it from the Father (Gen. xix. 24, see also above, ch. ii). Jacob also saw God face to face, seeing Christ in that form of body which He was afterwards to assume, and wrestling with Him (Gen. xxxii. 24, 30). Moses also saw Him in the bush, and (once more) Joshua saw Him as Prince,

[1] "Tecum principio in die virtutis tuae in splendoribus sanctorum, ex utero ante luciferum genui te" (Ps. cx. 3).

[2] "Ante Spiritus sancti initium." This may be purely Arian, the idea being that the origin of the Holy Spirit was later than that of the Father and the Son. But possibly the writer refers to Gen. i. 2, the initial action of the Holy Spirit, which was later than the work of the Son, the *Principium*; see the preceding note and *supra*, p. 307. In this case, cf. John vii. 39, οὔπω γὰρ ἦν πνεῦμα.

who was appointed King, as He Himself says in the second Psalm. Notice also how David speaking in the person of Christ says, *Offer to God sacrifice...and call upon Me* (Ps. l. 14 *sq.*).

We Christians therefore believe that there is one God the Father, and one Lord Jesus Christ His Son, of whom both Law and Prophets spake, and through Him we pray to God the Father, and to Him we give thanks, as He Himself enjoined (John xvii. 3). Knowing therefore the commands of our Saviour Christ let us ever praise the One God the Father through Him, to whom is glory for ever. Amen (ch. xi).

The ending is characteristically Arian, without any reference to God the Holy Spirit. Yet the general effect of the tract is pleasing. It is written with so mild an Arianism that it suggests rather Pre- than Anti-Nicene thought. The author shows sincere faith in Christ, and longs to win Jews to Him by means that are never incompatible with His teaching, but appeal to Scripture only. Happy had it been for the Church if it had always followed the methods of Augustine's controversialist Bishop at Hippo.[1]

---

[1] It is generally assumed that Maximin used the *Testimonia* of Cyprian as one of the chief sources of his argument against the Jews. It may be so, but the fact of there being many quotations from the Old Testament common to both writings is too slight evidence. For both Maximin and Cyprian use the method of exposition and of controversy that was common to the early Church (*vide supra*, p. 11). The order of subjects and the order of texts under those subjects differ as widely as possible. Also, identity of words and of style in the quotations may be due to a common version current in North Africa. But Dr C. H. Turner brings evidence for the other writings of the same author (*vide supra*, p. 306) that he used Cyprian (*J. Th. St.* 1916, xvii. 232–235).

CHAPTER XXXIV

AUGUSTINE

A DISCOURSE IN ANSWER TO THE JEWS[1]

A.D. 354–430

What a wonderful person St Augustine is! It is almost impossible to turn to him without finding something of profit, and spiritual profit at that. Here he is preaching a sermon to a Christian congregation (§ 15)—where and when is quite unknown—about the duty of Christians towards Jews. He is, therefore, properly speaking, not attempting to win Jews directly to Christ, although his arguments why they should believe on Him are such as Augustine himself would use, and would wish his congregation to use. For Christian people have duties towards Jews, and must do their best to lead them to Christ.

It is a delightful little sermon, strange and out of date though its arguments may be. For, unlike the Homilies of Chrysostom, his rather older contemporary, Augustine breathes love and not severity. Perhaps he had not the same reason to complain of his people that Chrysostom had; he at least says nothing of Christians visiting Jewish synagogues from superstitious motives.[2] But that is hardly sufficient to account for the difference between the two writers. Chrysostom, with all his charm of unmatched eloquence, and his employment of a language capable of expressing finer shades of thought than were possible in Latin, was, when all is said and done, a monk, unversed in human affairs, and unmoved in the depths of his spiritual life. St Augustine had passed through bitter stages of sin and conversion, and his heart was very tender towards those who were still in ignorance. Jews were in ignorance —of that, at least, he was quite sure—but he dealt with them in a spirit of Christ-like love. Chrysostom, when he thought of the Jews, was the ecclesiastic; Augustine was the Christian.

He begins by referring to Rom. xi. 18–23, which may well have been the text of his sermon, though it is not printed as such, and

---

[1] *Tractatus adversus Judaeos*, Migne, *P.L.* [Aug. viii], 51–64.

[2] Cf. the chapter on Chrysostom, p. 132. See, however, Augustine's *Letter to Asellinus*, *infra*, p. 318.

he says that the passage tells us that because of unbelief the Jews are now cut off from the root to which the Patriarchs belong, and that Gentiles have been grafted in by humble faith instead, and now partake of the richness of that olive-tree (I. 1).

Yet Jews reject this statement! For they do not understand the meaning of Isa. xlix. 6, *I have given Thee for a light of the Gentiles, that Thou mayest be My salvation as far as the ends of the earth*, or they would recognise Christ as that light. Nor, when they sing, *Their sound is gone out into all the earth, and their words to the end of the world* (Ps. xix. 4), do they wake up at the *sound* of the Apostles, or feel their *words* to be Divine! We must therefore bring testimonies[1] from Scripture (I. 2).

Yet Jews ask, What have we Christians to do with the Old Testament, now that we have discarded its sacraments and keep new ones; when we Christians do not practise circumcision of the flesh, and we eat food forbidden by the Law, neglect Sabbaths, New Moons, and Feasts, and do not sacrifice or observe Passover with lamb and unleavened bread? The answer is that we do keep and observe all these things in a way that goes deeper than carnal observance. For we keep them all in their spiritual significance. Thus the Old Testament belongs in truth more to us Christians than to Jews.[2] For, again, we find all these sacrifices, etc., fulfilled in Christ, the Bull whose horns form the Cross;[3] the true Paschal Lamb, with the unleavened bread of sincerity of truth (II. 3).

The important thing to bear in mind is that Christ did not deprive those former symbols of spiritual things of their authority only by arguing against them; He changed them by fulfilling them. And this change was foretold in the Psalms. See, for example, the title of Ps. xlv: *For those things which shall be changed*[4] (III. 4. 4).

[1] Notice this common use of the word "testimonies" (*testimonia*). There is plainly no reference here to a book so called.

[2] Cf. Augustine, *Enarratio in Ps.* xl, § 14. "The Jews are our attendant slaves, who carry, as it were, our satchels, and bear the manuscripts while we study them.... When we argue with the heathen we adduce the predictions found in manuscripts written by Jews." Cf. pp. 327, 401 and Chrysostom, *Demonstratio*, ii (*supra*, p. 136).

[3] Cf. Tertullian, *Adv. Judaeos*, x (*supra*, p. 49).

[4] "Pro iis quae immutabuntur." Heb. *al shoshannim*, lit. *upon lilies*, the name either of instruments so shaped, or, possibly, a tune. The Septuagint refers the word to the root Sh N H, which may mean *change*, and translates ὑπὲρ τῶν ἀλλοιωθησομένων, which Augustine follows. The ordinary Vulgate text is similar, but reads *on behalf of those* (persons) *who*, etc. Almost the same phrase recurs in the titles of Ps. lx, lxix, lxxx, in Hebrew, Septuagint and Vulgate.

Further, the whole of that forty-fifth psalm refers to Christ, as a brief exposition of it shows us. Even the very word for *anointing* (*v.* 7) is *Chrisma* in Greek, which gave Christ His name. And *v.* 11, for fear lest you should think you must put your trust on a mere man, expressly says: *For He is the Lord, thy God*[1] (IV. 5).

Augustine then quotes the similar title of Ps. lxix, and expounds the whole psalm of Christ. *The cities of Judah* (*v.* 35) are *the churches of Judaea which are in Christ* (Gal. i. 22). But the Jews interpret the passage of the earthly Jerusalem, not of *our Mother*, eternal in the heavens, Gal. iv. 26; 2 Cor. v. 1 (*v.* 6).

The eightieth psalm, again, has the same title, and Augustine expounds much of it of Christ and His work. *Look down from heaven and visit this vine* (*v.* 14) which He had brought out of Egypt (*v.* 8). For Christ did not root up that vine and plant another vineyard. But He did assign it to other husbandmen (Matt. xxi. 41). So, again, the saints of the Old Testament and those of the New form one sacred Vine, the Church. And again in *v.* 17 of this psalm we read, *Let Thy hand be upon the Man of Thy right hand, and upon the Son of man Whom Thou madest strong for Thyself.* This means the coming of the Gentiles to Christ the true Vine. For "through this Son of man, i.e. Christ Jesus, and from the others who belonged to Him,[2] i.e. the Apostles and many others who believed on Christ as God from among Israelites, when the *fulness of the Gentiles* (Rom. xi. 25) comes in, then the Holy Vine is perfected. Thus in the removal of the old sacraments and the institution of the new, the title of this psalm is fulfilled—*for those things which shall be changed*" (VI. 7).

There are, however, even clearer testimonies than these. In particular, Jer. xxxi. 31 *sq.* says that the Lord will give a new Covenant (*testamentum*), not like that which He had given of old. Even so, urge the Jews, why should not Jews observe the old precepts even though Christians observe the new? But, as the Song of Solomon says (ii. 17): *The breath of day has come, let the shadows be removed.*[3] "Let the spiritual meaning grow brighter and brighter, and the carnal observance cease."[4] Again, Ps. l. 1 says that God called the earth from east to west—the New Covenant was for all. And the same psalm clearly foretells the change of the old sacrifices, and the showing forth of the Salvation of God. "And

---

[1] "Quoniam ipse est Dominus Deus tuus." So the ordinary Vulgate text, but both Hebrew and Greek (B) omit *God*.

[2] "De suis reliquis."   [3] "Aspiravit dies, removeantur umbrae."

[4] "Spiritualis significatio jam lucescat, carnalis celebratio jam quiescat."

what else is the Salvation of God save the Son of God, the Saviour of the world; the Son who is Day from the Father Who is Day; namely Light of Light, whose coming has shown to the world the New Covenant? *Sing to the Lord a new song....Bring the good news of His salvation to day after day*"[1] (vi. 8).

Yet the Jews affirm that these blessings refer to them, and that they are the people of God. What? Do you Jews belong to the people whom *the Lord has called from the rising of the sun to its setting* (cf. Ps. l. 1; cvii. 3)? You were brought out of Egypt only, and have been not *called from*, but scattered *unto the rising of the sun and to its setting*. We do not deny that Jesus and His Apostles were of Jewish descent and we might claim the passage in this way, but the prophecy plainly refers to us Christians, who fulfil Isa. ii. 2, 3, *Come ye and let us go up*, etc.[2] "For indeed as that Law which came forth from Mt Sinai was written by the finger of God, i.e. the Holy Spirit, on the fiftieth day after Passover, so that Law which came forth from Sion and Jerusalem was written not on tablets of stone but on tablets of the heart of the holy Evangelists by the Holy Spirit, on the fiftieth day after the true Passover of the Passion and Resurrection of our Lord Christ; on which day the Holy Ghost was sent, who had been promised before" (vii. 9).

If indeed you do claim to be the people, then acknowledge that it was by your iniquities that He was led to death (Isa. liii. 8); that you in the persons of your ancestors led Christ to death. If you still make the claim, then acknowledge that you are the people whose *heart is fat*, etc. (Isa. vi. 10), the *unbelieving people* to whom God says, *All the day have I stretched out My hands* (Isa. lxv. 2). But you are so blind that you claim to be (spoken of) where you are not, and do not recognise yourselves where you are (vii. 10).

When you read in Isa. ii. 5, *And now as for thee, O House of Jacob, come ye, let us walk in the light*[3] *of the Lord*, you say it refers to your-selves, but when the Prophet adds, *For He forsook His people, the House of Israel* (*ibid. v.* 6), you refuse to acknowledge it. Yet He still invites you: *O House of Jacob, come ye!* You still have time to repent, for you are still in the body; therefore come now. Reject not the Corner Stone, but cleave to It (Isa. xxviii. 16; Ps. cxviii. 22). For circumcised and uncircumcised peoples are like two walls coming

---

[1] "Bene nuntiate diem ex die salutare ejus" (Ps. xcvi. 2).
[2] Cf. *Dial. of Athanasius and Zacchaeus*, § 65 *sq.* (*supra*, p. 122).
[3] A variant reading is *to the Light* ("in lucem"), thus identifying the Light with Christ.

from different directions, which meet at the one corner—as with the kiss of peace. Hence the Apostle says: *For He is our peace, who made both one,* Eph. ii. 14 (VIII. 11).

The fact of your rejection is stated even more plainly in Mal. i. 10 *sq.*, which marks distinctly the repudiation of your sacraments and the acceptance of ours. For indeed yours were to be accepted in Jerusalem only, but ours everywhere. And it will not do for you to say that though you cannot now offer sacrifices with your hands you can and do offer them with your hearts, as it says in Ps. iv. 5, *Offer unto God the sacrifices of praise.*[1] For it says there: *I have no pleasure in you, saith the Lord of Hosts, neither will I accept an offering at your hand. For from the rising of the sun even unto the going down of the same My name is great among the Gentiles; and in every place incense is offered unto My name, and a pure offering: for My name is great among the Gentiles, saith the Lord of Hosts,* Mal. i. 10 *sq.* (IX. 12).

Do not, however, think that sacrifice cannot be offered now. *Search the Scriptures,* as Christ said (John v. 39). Yes, search them through and through. For they bear testimony to the clean sacrifice which is now offered to God in every place, including even Jerusalem—not after Aaron's priesthood which no more exists, but after Melchizedek's, for Christ's priesthood continues for ever in heaven (IX. 13).

Come, therefore, *O House of Jacob, and let us walk in the light of the Lord* (Isa. ii. 5). For that Light is not in you Jews, but in Christ; *I have given Thee for a light of the Gentiles* (Isa. xlix. 6). *Come ye unto Him and be lightened* (Ps. xxxiv. 5). For He is the Stone of Daniel (ii. 35), which becomes *a great mountain, filling the whole earth, every person worshipping Him from his own place* (Zech. iv. 7; Zeph. ii. 11). "It does not say, Prepare ye ships or beasts of burden, and load them with the victims for your sacrifices, and make ye your pilgrimages from afar to the place where God can receive the offerings of your worship. But, *Come ye unto Him* who is preached in your very ears; *come ye unto Him* who is glorified before your very eyes. You are not to toil by walking far. In the place where you believe on Him, there you come to Him"[2] (IX. 15).

---

[1] For the Jewish belief in the "meritorious" value of Prayer, Fasting, etc. see my essay on "Atonement in Jewish Literature from *c.* 400 B.C. to *c.* A.D. 200" in *The Atonement in History and in Life,* S.P.C.K. 1929, pp. 105–113.

[2] Cf. St Paul's argument with his quotation from Deut. xxx. 11–14 in Rom. x. 6–8, where Strack and Billerbeck give many illustrations from the Talmudic literature.

"This, my dear Friends,[1] let us preach to the Jews, wherever we can, in a spirit of love, whether they welcome our words or spurn them. It is not for us to boast over them as *branches broken off* (Rom. xi. 17 *sq.*). Rather let us consider by Whose grace, and with what loving-kindness, and into what kind of Root it was that we were grafted. For then, *as not minding high things, but agreeing with the humble* (Rom. xii. 16), we shall be able to say to them without exulting over them,—though we exult in God—*Come, let us walk in the light of the Lord.*" They may indeed refuse, "*but as for me, says the Church to Christ, I am like a fruitful olive-tree in the house of the Lord; I have placed my hope in the mercy of God for ever, even for ever and ever*", Ps. lii. 8 (x. 15).

[1] *Vide supra*, p. 312.

NOTE

One other genuine writing by Augustine having some reference to
Jewish matters may be mentioned, his *Letter to Bishop Asellinus*.[1] It
hardly concerns us, however, for it is not addressed to Jews, even indirectly, nor does it contain arguments for winning Jews. It is a letter
written to prevent Christians judaising in practice, as one Aptus had
done (§ 16), or in using the name Jews or Israelites without understanding their spiritual application to Christians (§§ 9 *sq.*), or in accepting
the teaching of Pelagius, which was, in fact, Jewish (§ 7).

"AMBROSIASTER"

One would have liked to have included the name of "Ambrosiaster"
among the authors of treatises against the Jews, direct or indirect, but
there is not sufficient to warrant this being done. The short papers on
various theological subjects known as Augustine's *Quaestiones Veteris et
Novi Testamenti* (Migne, *P.L.* xxxv [Aug. iii, Appendix], 2213–2386,
2386–2416, and especially Souter's Text and Introduction in the *Corpus
Scr. Eccles. Lat.* vol. L, 1908) are now generally attributed to "Ambrosiaster", but only § xliv *sq.* in the Old Testament part and § lxi in
the New deal with our subject.

---

[1] *Ep.* cxcvi; Migne, *P.L.* xxxiii [Aug. ii], 891–899. The Benedictine editors
say it was written in the end of A.D. 418 (col. 43). Pelagius and Caelestine had
just been excommunicated (§ 7) "by God's faithful servants", presumably at
the Council of Carthage A.D. 418 (Mirbt, *Quellen*, 1924, § 152). Augustine's
arguments (*Ep.* lxxxii) against Jerome's opinion that the incident at Antioch
(Gal. ii. 11–14) was a pre-arranged scene, suggest that Augustine had in mind
the danger of retaining Jewish customs in his own time. A convenient summary
of Augustine's views may be found in W. Montgomery, *St Augustine, Aspects of
his Life and Thought*, 1914, pp. 84–87.

CHAPTER XXXV

PSEUDO-AUGUSTINE
Cent. v

In the same volume (viii) of Migne's edition of St Augustine's works (*P.L.* xlii) is an Appendix containing several sermons and treatises which were long supposed to have been written by Augustine; and though this undoubtedly was not the case, they probably owe their survival to that pious belief. Among these are three which are of interest to us: (1) *A Treatise in answer to Five Heresies*, (2) *Against the Jews, Heathen, and Arians, a Sermon on the Creed*, and (3) *Concerning the Dispute between the Church and the Synagogue, a Dialogue*. It will be convenient to examine these in the order in which Migne presents them, without referring, for the moment, to the dates of their composition.

A TREATISE IN ANSWER TO FIVE HERESIES[1]

At a time when the Arians were supreme in North Africa (i.e. after A.D. 429), and faithful ministers had been driven out (ch. vi), this treatise was composed in fulfilment of a promise made some little time earlier in answer to a request that the author[2] should give his audience guidance as to how to meet the attacks of enemies of the Christian faith. They are powerful, but the Christian need not be afraid. They that are with us are more than they that are with them.[3] The Heresies are of five kinds, which the author considers in the following order: Heathen (ch. iii), Jewish (ch. iv), Manichaean (ch. v), Arian (ch. vi), and Sabellian (ch. vii), with a Conclusion (ch. viii).

We, therefore, are concerned only with the fourth chapter.

A Jew says, We have one God, and we know no other beside Him. But him whom you Christians affirm to be God our fathers slew, not as God but as man. Yes, precisely so, replies our author, would that as the demons recognised Him as their Judge, so men

---

[1] *Adversus Quinque Haereses, seu contra quinque hostium genera, Tractatus* (coll. 1099–1116).
[2] Bardenhewer (iv. 522) thinks that he was Quidvultdeus of Carthage, Augustine's friend (*Epp.* 221 and 223), who died in A.D. 453.
[3] 2 Kings vi. 16.

would recognise Him as their Saviour! Lo, the demons saw, and trembled; men saw, and slew Him. Yet men are saved, and demons punished! This *exchange* is due to *the grace of the right hand of the Most High.*[1] It is not due to a man presuming on his own strength.

Yet it is not I that strive with the Jew. It is his own books, the Law and the Prophets, and he will either be saved by being overcome and brought low, or will be punished if he continue proud and obstinate. The Lord said to Moses, *I will send My Angel.*[2] Hear Him, recognise Him as the Lord. For Gen. xix shows that the Angel was God. Observe that Lot addresses the *two* Angels as God.[3] Lot could see; he was not blind like the Jews and the Sabellians, nor blear-eyed like the Arians; but he had sound eyes like catholic Christians. "I see (says holy Lot) two, and them as equal; I address One and insult neither; because I divide not the Father from the Son." And how many reply to him? The words of the Book are, *And He said to him,* in the singular number. Yet there are two. *The Lord rained...from the Lord out of heaven,*[4] i.e. the Son from the Father. Imitate Joshua who fell on his face before the Captain who appeared to him.[5] At the end of the section our author quotes Isa. xlv. 24, *To Him shall men come, and all who oppose Him shall be confounded.* Go to now, all of you, Heathen, Heretics, Jews! Ye withstand, and oppose the Son of God. Unto Him shall ye come, and all ye who oppose Him shall be confounded.

[1] Cf. "Haec mutatio dexterae Excelsi" (Ps. lxxvii. 10).
[2] Ex. xxiii. 20 *sq.*
[3] "Dixit Loth ad eos, Domine mi" (Gen. xix. 18).
[4] Gen. xix. 24.   [5] Josh. v. 13 *sq.*

CHAPTER XXXVI

PSEUDO-AUGUSTINE *(cont.)*

CENT VI

AGAINST THE JEWS, THE HEATHEN, AND THE ARIANS: A DISCOURSE ON THE CREED[1]

It would hardly have been supposed that knowledge of the early history of the Drama on the Western Stage would be of any assistance to a writer upon *Anti-judaica*! Yet such is the case. For the treatise before us was used as the basis of a religious play at least as early as the eleventh century. Nor is this the most famous example, for the subject of the next chapter, the *De Altercatione Ecclesiae et Synagogae Dialogus*, is much better known than that of this.

Our treatise, i.e. the greater part (chh. xi–xvi) of the portion of it (chh. xi–xviii) which affects us, was followed very closely in a MS. of the eleventh century at the Abbey of St Martial of Limoges in a play *Ordo Prophetarum*, which E. N. Stone reproduces in full with an English translation.[2] It is very short, and as a play can hardly have taken more than half an hour to act, but is quite interesting. The dramatist takes the same prophets as our treatise mentions, and summons them forth on the stage, each to give his testimony. The only addition in the play which is not in the treatise is Israel's (i.e. Jacob's) testimony in Gen. xlix. 10, and the one omission is that of Zechariah before that of Elizabeth, but the quotations are shortened. In only one case is there a different quotation, where an earlier verse of the same context in "Jeremiah" is adduced in the play (Baruch iii. 35 instead of 37). Simeon and Elizabeth, John the Baptist, Vergil and the Sibyls all appear.[3]

[1] *Contra Judaeos, Paganos, et Arianos: Sermo de Symbolo* (Migne, *P.L.* xlii [Aug. viii], 1115–1130).

[2] *University of Washington Publications in Language and Literature*, Seattle, 1928, pp. 195–213. See also Karl Young, *The Drama of the Medieval Church*, 1933, ii. 125–171.

[3] The third part of *The Mystery of Adam* contains an Anglo-Norman play of about the middle of the twelfth century, written in Norman-French. It also consists of the testimony of various witnesses from the Old Testament, but they are not the same as in our Tract. The original may be studied in P. Stuber, *Le Mystère d'Adam*, Manchester, 1918, and in an English translation by E. N. Stone, *Adam*, University of Washington Press, Seattle, 1926, pp. 155–193.

A portion of our tract was used in many Churches as a Lesson for some part or other of Divine Service.[1]

What then is this little tract which lends itself so easily to the simple representation of a religious "pageant"?[2] It is part of a sermon delivered on the day following a special all-night service, in preparation, it would seem, for Baptism.[3] For we spent not last night, the preacher says, in sleep or dreams or warm rest upon our beds, but in watching, praying, singing psalms, in fighting against the devil, and receiving light in our very hearts, carrying out in the night the works of the day (cf. 1 Thess. v. 7 *sq.*). *Laying aside therefore the works of darkness, put ye on the armour of light* (Rom. xiii. 12), i.e. Renounce the devil and his angels, and Believe on God the Father, Almighty.[4]

The author then describes what is meant by the devil (ch. ii) and by renouncing him (ch. iii), and warns his listeners against the danger and awfulness of falling away after Baptism (ch. iv). In the next five chapters (v–ix) he treats of the doctrine of the Trinity, chiefly with reference to the Arians. In the course of his discussion (ch. vi) he illustrates the fact that "the Son was born from the Father without a mother" from Isa. liii. 8 ("nativitatem ejus quis enarrabit"). He draws also (ch. vii) a curious deduction from Ecclus. xxx. 5, 4 (*sic*): *The father rejoices in a wise son; he saw him in his life, and in his death he sorrowed not. For the father died, and is as though he had not died; for he left one behind him like himself.* "Behold," says our author, "the Prophet says that a man's wise son is like his father—and dost thou, O Heretic, dare to say that

---

[1] See E. K. Chambers (*vide infra*), ii. p. 52 *sq.*, who says it was so used at Arles on Christmas Day, Rome Christmas Eve, Rouen just before Christmas, and in the Sarum Breviary on the fourth Sunday in Advent. For the interesting *La Infancia de Jesu-Christo* see *Beiheft zur Zeitschrift für Romanischer Philologie,* No. 72, 1922.

[2] Its importance for the history of the development of the Drama is emphasised by E. K. Chambers, *The Mediaeval Stage,* 1903, ii. p. 52 *sq.* On the subject generally see especially Karl Pearson's essay on "The German Passion-play: a study in the evolution of Western Christianity", in his *The Chances of Death and other Studies in evolution,* 1897, ii. pp. 246–406. For much detail see Karl Young (*supra*).

[3] Both the date and the locality of its composition are quite uncertain. Juster (*Les Juifs dans l'Empire romain,* 1914, i. 74 *sq.*) places it later than the *De Altercatione* (to be mentioned next), but before A.D. 600 when Arianism disappeared from Gaul and Africa. The treatise is very full of many curious quotations from Scripture, which do not agree with the ordinary text.

[4] Ch. i, an adaptation of the first words of the Apostles' Creed.

Wisdom itself, i.e. the Son of God, is unlike the Father? The Prophet says that a dead human father, because he left a son like himself, lives in his son—and dost thou dare to separate that Eternal Life itself, which is the Son of God, from that Father who never dies?" The tenth chapter speaks of the joy in heaven at the birth of Christ, of the coming of the Magi, and Herod's massacre of the Infants—to whom Christ has given eternal life.

Then (chh. xi–xvi) our author challenges the Jews, who still deny the Son of God. Christ Himself bade them attend not to His words but His works (John x. 24 *sq.*), and in particular to their own Law, from which come not two but many witnesses. "Give, O Isaiah, thy testimony to Christ!" He utters Isa. vii. 14.[1] Let another witness come forward! And Jeremiah gives Baruch iii. 35–37 (ch. xi). Let that holy Daniel come forward! He says, *The anointing shall cease* (Dan. ix. 24), and *the great mountain* (Dan. ii. 34 *sq.*). This is *the mountain of the Lord* (Isa. ii. 3), which Peter recognised in Christ. "He recognised the mountain, and *went up into the mountain*; he gave testimony to the Truth, and was beloved by the Truth. Upon the Rock was Peter founded, that he might accept death in his love for Him whom in his fear he had denied thrice" (ch. xii).

Other witnesses are summoned. Do thou, O Moses the Lawgiver, the Leader of the people of Israel, give thy testimony to Christ! He says Deut. xviii. 15, 19. Let David come forth! He utters Ps. lxxii. 11; cx. 1; ii. 1. Do thou also, O Habakkuk the Prophet, give thy testimony to Christ! He says Hab. iii. 2: *O Lord, I heard the report of Thee, and feared; I considered Thy works, O God, and was afraid.* Why? Because *in the midst of two animals Thou wilt be recognised.* "Because Thou, the Word through whom all things were made, hast lien in a manger." *In the midst of two animals Thou wilt be recognised.* What (again) does this mean save that He will be recognised either in the midst of the two Testaments, or of the two Thieves, or of Moses and Elias when they descended with Him on the Mount?[2] Further in Hab. iii. 5 we have *The Word walked*

---

[1] This and the following verses have been quoted and discussed so often that it does not seem necessary to do more here than refer to Tertullian, *Adv. Jud.* ix (*supra*, p. 48).

[2] Cf. *De Civit. Dei*, xviii. 32 (Migne, *P.L.* xli [Aug. vii], 588). It seems that the Nativity begins to appear as a subject of Christian art in the fourth century, and from the first the ox and the ass are present, perhaps as emblems of the Jewish and Gentile world. Woodcuts will be found in *Dict. Chr. Antt.* 1880, ii. 1380 *sq.*

and went out into the fields.[1] Our author then returns to his Baruch iii. 37 (ch. xiii).

Holy Simeon is then brought forward, who, though very old, was kept back in the light of earth until he should see the true Light. Then come the parents of John the Baptist, Zechariah and Elizabeth (ch. xiv).

The last two chapters that deal with the Jews contain the evidence of non-Biblical and indeed Gentile witnesses. Did not that most eloquent of all poets say: "Now from the heaven on high is a new race sent down", referring to Christ?[2] Tell us too, O Nebuchadnezzar, what it was thou sawest in the furnace. Who told thee that it was the Son of God[3] (ch. xv)?

Two quotations from the Sibylline Books close the series, both taken, no doubt, from Augustine's *De Civitate Dei*, xviii. 23,[4] both being certainly Christian interpolations in the older heathen source. The first is remarkable because it forms an acrostic of the first letter of each line, making up (in Greek) the words "Jesus Christ, God's Son, Saviour".[5] It describes the terrors of the Day of Judgment.

The second portrays the details of our Lord's Passion, ending with the mention of the Resurrection.[6]

In ch. xvii our author tells the Jews that he thinks they must be so utterly confuted by the evidence he has adduced that they can ask for nothing more—although they did say to the Truth Himself, *Thou bearest witness of Thyself, Thy witness is not true* (John viii. 13).

---

[1] The Hebrew is rendered rightly in the R.V., *Before Him went the pestilence, and fiery bolts went forth at His feet,* but the LXX reads, "Before His face a word shall go forth, and shall go out into the plains" (πρὸ προσώπου αὐτοῦ πορεύσεται λόγος καὶ ἐξελεύσεται εἰς πεδία), misunderstanding DeBeR ("pestilence") as DaBaR ("Word"). The Vulgate has (very curiously in our connexion) "ante faciem ejus ibit mors, et egredietur diabolus ante pedes ejus". For a possible explanation of the Septuagint and the Vulgate renderings see an article by Mr G. Bousfield in *J. Th. St.* 1930, xxxi. 397.

[2] "Jam nova progenies caelo demittitur alto", Verg. *Eclog.* iv. 7.

[3] Dan. iii. 25.

[4] There are some unimportant variants in the second quotation.

[5] Marcus Dods gives a metrical version in his translation of the *De Civitate.* Eusebius presents the same passage of the Sibyl in a shorter acrostic (*Const. Magn. Orat. ad Sanct. coetum,* xviii, Heinichen, ii. 225 *sq.*). See also S. Terry, *The Sibylline Or.* 1899, pp. 171, 274. The acrostic was written in the time of Hadrian (Heinichen, *Notes,* iii. 580). For Peter of Blois' quotation from this *Sermon* see below, p. 406.

[6] Augustine says he has taken this from Lactantius (*Inst.* iv. 18 *sq.*). The *Ordo Proph.* of the Limoges MS. ends here.

But the author adds witness from the heavens, the sea, the earth, and the shades below (Matt. xxvii. 45, 51 *sq.*).[1]

Lastly (ch. xviii), he says, Your own actions brought about Christ's life-giving death, and fulfilled the prophecies about Him. In your Dispersion you unwittingly bore the lamps of the light, and the Dispersion itself fulfilled the Psalmist's words: *Slay them not, lest they forget Thy law, but scatter them in Thy power* (lix. 11). You hope for One to come! He will come, but not as you desire. What will be the answer of your heart, when He will show you no more longsuffering, because He Who will come to judge the living and the dead will find you dead in soul?

The rest of the Discourse (chh. xix–xxii) is concerned with the Arians only.[2]

[1] Curiously, the earth bore witness when the Lord's spittle was sprinkled on it, and thus the earth restored the blind man's sight (John ix. 6 *sq.*).

[2] Ch. xxii is especially interesting.

CHAPTER XXXVII

PSEUDO-AUGUSTINE (*cont.*)

CENT. V

CONCERNING THE DISPUTE BETWEEN THE CHURCH AND THE SYNAGOGUE—A DIALOGUE[1]

"I am in the position of one who has undertaken to bring the case of two ladies before you as the Censors,[2] and I propose laying open the claims of each in their wide relationships, in order that, by my doing so, whatever the truth, after full examination, shall in your judgment have determined, one of the two ladies shall be found to correspond to it. For this reason I recite in this your conclave the Law, and produce the documents. Let it be treated as a matter of Law, for the dispute concerns property. I shall at once unroll the decisions made by Imperial decree, in order that whatever the course of truth shall have ascertained may be published by the verdict of your assembly, in accordance with the Law of God.

"One of the two ladies was caught out in adultery more than once[3] and had violated by premature usurpation the legal rights of the possession that we claim as ours. The other,[4] in reward for her chastity in accordance with the verdict of Him who gave it, had deprived that possessor (who appears, as you listen to the evidence, to have been driven out) of some things in the world which she had gained by an earlier and secret deception. But by the law of restitution she is compelled to give it back every day,

---

[1] *De Altercatione Ecclesiae et Synagogae Dialogus* (Migne, *P.L.* xlii [Aug. viii], 1131–1140). In this chapter I owe much to Dr E. J. Thomas, of the Cambridge University Library, in response to many enquiries I made of him.

[2] The term "Censors" is part of the imagery. For although Gibbon writes "Every act of a citizen was subject to the judgment of the censors" (*Rom. Emp.* xliv, Bohn's edition, v. 56) the Censorship had long since been abolished, and although its revival was proposed towards the end of the fourth century this was never carried into effect. Further, "Women, as not included among the *tribules*, did not come at all under the control of the censors" (Smith's *Dict. Class. Antt.* 1890, i. 399 a, 402 a).

[3] I.e. the Synagogue; cf. Hos. ii. 2; *al.*

[4] The Church.

and she still owes as much as she has restored.[1] For we utterly deny the whole of her claim to possession.

"If therefore you wish to learn the outline of the case, the visage of the allegory—it is this.

"The Lady who is the Synagogue, once powerful and wealthy, usurped by her gold the Gentile nations, who are our inheritance, our property, granted to us—even to the very ends of the earth— by the law of the Supreme Emperor.

"We have laid our supplication before you; our prayers are written out; a pleader has been straightway brought forward; the fact that we hold the property takes its place in our legal right. Yet we desire[2] that whatever ornaments that restless woman[3] has usurped be given back to us. But though requisition has been made of her, she has returned them more slowly than she ought.[4]

"Now therefore to this Mother and Widow, namely the Synagogue, our Mother, the Church said: State your rights, and I will state mine."

The Synagogue begins by claiming that undeniably the Prophets came to her. Yes, indeed, replies *the Church*, but only as to a landlady. For they were the forerunners to arrange the dwelling for my Bridegroom, and, again, they were the servants who carried the children's books,[5] and were slain by you out of envy. Yet they did come to me, and I received them.

Anyhow, says *the Synagogue*, I acted honestly. I knew the King when you were but barbarians; I ruled great nations when you were mere herdsmen; I slew Pharaoh in his chariots; I slew Egyptian, Canaanite, Jebusite, Hittite and Perizzite kings.

Yes, is *the answer*. For you were warlike and cruel, and slew innocent men.[6]

But, argues *the Synagogue*, had I not the right to do what I would with my own kingdom?

The Church. Yes, you were mistress in the world, but now are only maid.

---

[1] A difficult phrase. It seems to mean that the Jews had not given up their claim to such Gentiles as they had won to God before the time of Christianity. It may also include a reference to certain "Jewish" tendencies among the unorthodox. Cf. *supra*, p. 318, of the Pelagians.

[2] "Volumus." So Monte Cassino MS. (*vide infra*, p. 336). Migne has "nolumus".

[3] The Synagogue.

[4] So the Monte Cassino MS.

[5] Cf. p. 401, *infra*.

[6] Coll. 1132; Gen. xxxiv. 26.

The Synagogue. You boast aloud, but prove that I am maid, and I will acknowledge you as mistress.

The Church. I have the documents, I read the grant[1] which Moses, your great Scribe and true Prophet, writes,[2] and Aaron signed in the presence of the Judge.

The Synagogue. Yet where did the Author of the Roll[3] bid me serve?

The Church. Read what was said to Rebecca, *The elder shall serve the younger.*[4] And when you ask how you serve,[5] look at the legions' standards, mark too the name of the Saviour,[6] bear in mind that the Emperors are worshippers of Christ,[7] and that you are cast out from your kingdom. You pay tribute to me. No Jew may be Emperor, Prefect, Comes, may enter the Senate, be admitted to military service, or to the tables of the wealthy. You have lost the rank of the membership of the higher nobility.[8]

The Synagogue. But what had I done to be deprived by God of my superiority?

The Church. When Moses received the Tables,[9] you demanded idols![10]

The Synagogue. I acknowledge my grievous sin, but they who committed it were punished by death. What have their descendants done?

The Church. You forget your own Scriptures, which say: *And let the sons announce to their sons that the sins of their parents have increased in the sons, and I will now not ease them for them, saith the Lord.*[11] And elsewhere He says, *The fathers have eaten sour grapes, and the children's teeth are set on edge.*[12]

The Synagogue. Any how, Christ came to me first!

The Church. Yes, and rightly. For if He had come first to me, you would certainly have rejected Him. You would say, If He had

[1] "Testamentum."
[2] So the Monte Cassino MS.   [3] "Dictator voluminis."
[4] Gen. xxv. 23.   [5] Col. 1133.
[6] "Sotēr" was a common title of the Emperors.
[7] "Christicolas" (*vide infra*, p. 337). Cf. "Et pia Christicoli semina fervet agri", Venantius Fortunatus, *Misc.* II. xii. 12 (Migne, *P.L.* lxxxviii. 101).
[8] For "charismatis" (Migne) read with the Monte Cassino MS. "clarissimatus".
[9] "Charaxatas", i.e. graven (Gk. *charasso*) (*vide infra*, p. 337).
[10] Ex. xxxii. 1.
[11] For the reading see Monte Cassino MS. The quotation is apparently a form of Jer. xxv. 29 (xxxii. 15).
[12] Ezek. xviii. 2.

only appeared first among my people, I would confess Him to be Him Whom the Prophets called God. Yet when He came to you, raised your dead, etc., etc., you rejected Him! Read what Esdras said, speaking in the person of the Saviour: *I came unto Mine own, and Mine own knew Me not. What shall I do to thee, O Judah? Judah refused to hear Me; I will remove Myself to another nation.*[1] If you would defend yourself by saying, I did not see the Lord;[2] I knew not what to do; I supposed the Prophets were liars[3]—all this is no excuse for your behaviour.

The Synagogue. The Prophets indeed said He would come, but as the Anointed of God, and the holy son of a virgin; but I was completely ignorant whether the Lord Himself chose to come.

The Church. Rightly does Isaiah[4] blame your obstinacy and ignorance.[5] If you read Isaiah and the Prophets you often hear Christ spoken of as God.[6]

The Synagogue. I do not grant that the passages bear you out. But turn to what, I think, will help my case. I, not you, received the Law; I, not you, had the advantage of circumcision, the sign by which Gentiles are separated from us. Therefore it is that I both keep my own sign and also do not part with the Law which Moses promulgated.

The Church. Yes, you have the Law of the Old Testament, but I the new Law of the Gospels. The old is squeezed out by the new, as Isaiah says.[7] And as for circumcision being for salvation you are mistaken. If it had been, what of your women? They then cannot be saved! So they are neither Jews nor Christians, but pagans! True circumcision is of the heart;[8] that you should not be immoral.[9] "For do you think that to be a sign which is covered with clothes out of modesty, and is recognised as being only for sexual purposes? For I have often seen even your women condemned for their crimes riding on asses with their hair plucked out and their heads bald.[10] Certainly, if that is a sign of salvation which commits adultery and rape, a woman who plays a disgraceful part

---

[1] 2 (4) Esdras i. 24. The first sentence is not in the text of 2 (4) Esdras, and is evidently an adaptation of John i. 11.

[2] I.e. Christ.   [3] So Monte Cassino MS.   [4] Col. 1134.

[5] Isa. vi. 9 *sq.*; see also Jer. ii. 13; viii. 7; Prov. i. 28 *sq.*

[6] Isa. vii. 14; Ps. xlv. 7; Gen. i. 27 (*God made man in His image*).

[7] Isa. xliii. 18.   [8] Jer. iv. 3 *sq.*; Deut. xxx. 6; Col. ii. 11.   [9] Jer. iii. 9.

[10] I have accepted Dr B. F. C. Atkinson's emendation of *officina* to *ob facina* (i.e. *facinora*). The printed text is "quia officina et mulieres tuas depilato capite ac decalvato in asinis saepe vidi damnatas". There seems to be no variant reading.

with this means of salvation, i.e. circumcision, ought not to be condemned, nor[1] ought he to be punished who casts off even to her death his adulterous wife violated by this salvation-bearing sign of circumcision. I know not how in such a case that could have been a sign of salvation for which admitted criminals are punished. But my people, by bearing the sign of salvation on their foreheads,[2] protect the whole man—both men and women— through the heavenly origin of the symbol, with a freedom recognised by all and kept inviolate through its source above."[3]

The Synagogue. How did you get your sign on the forehead?

The Church. Ezekiel cries, speaking in the very presence of the Supreme Royalty: *Go and slay...but do not touch any one on whose forehead you shall find the sign written.*[4] This was the sign of the Cross, which the Saviour's Passion adorned.[5]

The Synagogue. You imply that the ancient Prophets foretold the Cross. Do you read that Christ was to suffer and hang on a cross?

The Church. Attend, not indeed that you may be taught, but that you may be punished, and you will find where the Saviour foretold the Cross in the figurative action of His hands stretched forth. So Isa. lxv. 2. See also Jer. xi. 19: *Come, let us put wood into his food.* And in Deut. xxviii. 66: "because you were using the Pentateuch",[6] *And thy Life shall be hanging before thine eyes by day and night.* So also the Psalmist:[7] *A whole day have I stretched forth My hands unto Thee* (Ps. lxxxviii. 9). And Num. xxiii. 19: *God is not hung up like a man, nor suffers threats like the Son of man.* And the Prophet says elsewhere: *The Lord reigned from the Tree* (Ps. xcvi. 10).[8]

---

[1] Col. 1135.

[2] I.e. the sign of the Cross applied in Baptism. The sense is clear, but the author appears to have forgotten the construction of the sentence.

[3] "Populus autem meus signum salutis in fronte gestando, totum hominem, viros ac mulieres, de alto signaculi, casta de sublimibus et publica libertate defendit." Cf. Hooker, *Eccles. Pol.* v. lxv. 7. "In the forehead nothing more plain to be seen than the fear of contumely and disgrace. For which cause the Scripture (as with great probability it may be thought) describeth (Ezek. ix. 4; Apoc. vii. 3; ix. 4) marked of God in the forehead, whom His mercy hath undertaken to keep from final confusion and shame." Hooker adds references to Tertullian (*de Resurr. Carn.* viii). See also Tertullian, *De Corona*, iv and Cyprian (*Ep.* lviii. 9, Hartel, p. 664). 　　　[4] For the reading see Monte Cassino MS.

[5] The mark of Ezekiel was the same as the last letter of the Hebrew alphabet (*Taw*), at that time (X). Hence St Francis of Assisi's love for *Taw* (Thomas of Celano, *Legenda secunda*, § lxxii (106); *Tract. de Miraculis*, ii. 3, edit. 1906, pp. 250, 343). 　　　[6] "Quia Pentateucho utebaris"; *vide infra*, p. 331.

[7] "Psalmidicus." Cf. p. 337, *infra*.

[8] See Justin Martyr, *Trypho*, § lxxiii. 1 and my note there.

The Synagogue. I grant the facts and recognise the sayings, but who are you to find fault with me? You were ignorant, and living as heathen; I was trained in the Law, and the Prophets came to me with their commands and orders.

The Church. Listen, thou widowed and forsaken Woman! I am what you have not been able to be. I am the Queen who have removed thee from thy throne, the Bride who, leaving idols behind, have come down from the forest and the mountain. My Bridegroom is fair beyond the sons of men, the King of kings, who has set the marriage crown[1] on my head, and has clothed me with purple, and has welcomed me when I came to Him.

The Synagogue. What kind of evidence can you bring to prove that you are the Bride, and that Christ is seen in the Law to be your Bridegroom?

The Church. If the Prophets had come to me first, you would say to-day that you were ignorant of the Law, that you had not had the Prophets, that you did not know what was written.[2] Learn therefore your defeat from the lips of your own Prophets. Hear the charge the Prophets gave concerning the Bride and the Bridegroom: *Blow ye the trumpet in Zion, sanctify a fast... let the Bridegroom go forth from His chamber, and the Bride from her closet.*[3] For I am sure that you are that Jerusalem from which the Bridegroom and the Bride came forth,[4] as David says: *And He is as a bridegroom going forth from his chamber*, etc.[5] And John says in the Apocalypse: *Come, I will show thee the newly married, the Bride of the Lamb*, etc.[6] And: *The Marriage of the Lamb has come, and His wife hath made herself ready.*[7] You see then that the Law speaks of a *Bride* and *Wife*;[8] *Bride*, because I pledge myself to place my faith in the Lord my Saviour; *Wife*, because of my children at Baptism.

The Synagogue. Please explain your quotation from Deut. xxviii. 66.[9]

The Church. It means, The Saviour hung on the cross by day and by night, i.e. on the sixth day of the week and throughout the night of this day until[10] the sabbath, on which you say that according

---

[1] "Mitra." In both the Greek and the Latin Church it was usual to place a crown on the head of both Bridegroom and Bride (Smith and Cheetham, *Dict. Chr. Antt.* ii. 1110), and similarly in the Synagogue (*Jew. Enc.* iv. 372).

[2] Col. 1136.   [3] Joel ii. 15 *sq.*   [4] So Monte Cassino MS.
[5] Ps. xix. 5 *sq.*   [6] Rev. xxi. 9–11.   [7] *Ibid.* xix. 7.
[8] "Sponsam quod spondeo."   [9] *Vide supra*, p. 330.
[10] Our author seems to have lived far from a Jewish population, and to have thought that for the Jews, as for himself, the Sabbath began in the morning.

to the Law a man may not hang on a tree. And, further, the words may strictly mean "on a day and night". For there was day and night on one day. The darkness of night suddenly divided the light of day with the horror of darkness.

The Synagogue. If He was killed, how did He rise? How can you say He lives, rose, and sits on the right hand of the Father? Tell me in such a way that you can seal your evidence from the Prophets.

The Church. Listen, poor and unhappy Lady! Thou woman murderer,[1] who still hast doubts about Christ's death and resurrection! Read what David says in the person of the Saviour: *Thou wilt not leave My soul in hell, nor give Thy Holy One to see corruption.*[2] And: *Lord, Thou hast brought back My soul from Hades.*[3] And: *I slept, and took sleep; and I arose, for the Lord helped Me.*[4] And David says again, speaking in the person of the Father to the Son: *Awake, My Glory, awake! I will awake with the dawn,*[5] i.e. after the third day He restores men alive from the dead,[6] as the Prophet says: *Weeping shall endure till the evening, and at morning there is joy.*[7]

The Synagogue. Why "the third day"?

The Church. You really remember, but will not say so. Read Hosea, *He gave us life on the third day.*[8] So in Deuteronomy:[9] *The Lord said to Moses...and let them be ready against the day after to-morrow,*[10] *for the third day the Lord will come down in Mount Sinai.* See also Matt. xii. 39 *sq.*

The Synagogue. I acknowledge the truth of all this, but I would know now where Christ is, where hidden. For I wish to see whether He has, according to the Prophets, any power afterwards, i.e. after His passion or even after His resurrection. For I have read that Elijah,[11] the anointed of God, would come to save the People.

The Church. Confess then, O unhappy Woman, what you cannot deny. His authority reaches to the very heavens of glory.[12] Daniel

---

[1] *Vide infra,* p. 337.   [2] Ps. xvi. 10.   [3] Ps. xxx. 3.

[4] Ps. iii. 5: "et resurrexi, quoniam Dominus auxiliatus est michi" (Monte Cassino MS.).   [5] Ps. lvii. 8.

[6] "Reciduat vivus (= vivos) ex mortuis venturus (= venturos)." Cf. "Quantus filius habuit exceptis Kam (*sic*) et Habel" ("How many sons had [Adam] besides Cain and Abel"), P. Meyer, *Basdatin,* 1877, p. 16. See further C. H. Grandgent, *An Introduction to Vulgar Latin,* 1908, § 244. He says "*os* and *us* were interchanged from the third century on". "The accusative plural in *us* was particularly common in Gaul."

[7] Col. 1137; Ps. xxx. 5.   [8] Hos. vi. 2.

[9] A mistake for Ex. xix. 10 *sq.*   [10] "In perendinum diem."

[11] Elijah. Cf. Justin, *Trypho,* viii. 4 (*supra,* p. 32).

[12] "Tota se usque ad caelos claritatis libertas extendit."

says "I saw in a vision by night, and behold[1] *One like the Son of man
...and royal power was given to Him, and all the kings of the earth in each
race of men, and all glory was obedient to Him* ".[2]

The Synagogue. I cannot deny that the Anointed of God, i.e.
Christ, has glory, but can He acquire it and hold it after His
Passion and Resurrection?

The Church. See Isa. xxxiii. 10: *I will arise*, etc., and Ps. cx. 1 *sq.*:
Sit Thou, etc.

The Synagogue. So He is both God and the Son of God!

The Church. Of course, thou foolish Woman! He who is born
of man is man; so He also who springs from God is assuredly
marked out as God.

The Synagogue. I don't believe assertions, but I wish to be convinced by the Law. It is not you but the Prophets whom I long
to hear.

The Church. Recall what the Psalmist[3] says, and you will know
that the Saviour is the Lord God: *Let God arise....Sing ye to God,
sing praises to His Name; make a way for Him who ascends above the west,
the Lord is His name.*[4] And again, *Arise, Lord, and judge the earth.*[5]
And, *The God of gods, the Lord, hath spoken.*[6] And, *A virgin shall bear
a Son, and His name shall be called Emmanuel, which is interpreted, God
with us.*[7] And, *Therefore God, Thy God, anointed Thee.*[8] So you have
Him both *God*, and *Lord* and *King*.

The Synagogue. How is He King?

The Church. If He is God, surely He must be King?

The Synagogue. Yes, but for myself I wish (His Kingship) to be
marked clearly by the truth given to Israel.[9]

The Church. See Ps. lxxii. 1; lxxiv. 12; ii. 6 *sq.*; Mal. i. 14;
Ps. xcvii. 1; xlv. 1.

On the *Synagogue* confessing that she is convinced, the *Church*
offers to answer any further question. Whereupon the *Synagogue*
asks, If Christ is the God of Abraham, and Abraham was a Jew,
how can you say I must be condemned?

---

[1] The Monte Cassino MS. 247 ends with these words.
[2] "Et omnis claritas serviens ei" (Dan. vii. 13 *sq.*). The passage resembles
the Septuagint proper, rather than the common Theodotion text, which the
Vulgate follows. But, as Dr Burkitt pointed out to me, it is the text followed
by Cyprian, *Test.* ii. 26.
[3] "Psalmidicus." *Vide infra*, p. 337.
[4] Ps. lxviii. 1–6.   [5] Ps. lxxxii. 8.   [6] Ps. l. 1.
[7] Isa. vii. 14 (Matt. i. 23).   [8] Col. 1138; Ps. xlv. 7.
[9] "Sed volo mihi Israel veritate signari."

The Church. My Peter and Paul were Jews, but, leaving you, came to the Spring of Life. For Abraham, who broke his idols[1] and fled to friendship with God, came to you, but was afterwards bidden return to the Gentiles, i.e. to us. For God says: *Go out from thy land...and I will make thee a great nation.*[2] And, moreover, Isaac blessed Jacob in the person of the Saviour: *The Gentiles shall serve thee,* etc.[3]

The Synagogue. So all have come to thee! And I, who had so many children, and such great ones, and boasted of their number, am looked down upon as forsaken, who was a mother to the peoples! Yet prove from the Law that you were to have more children than I.

The Church. Now you are trying to get out of it, and the old stiffness of your neck is beginning to lift you up; you will soon be even twisted back to your former roguery. For the Lord says: *Enlarge the place...and thy seed shall possess the Gentiles,* etc.[4] I was indeed accursed when I followed idols; now I am raised up to have children, as it says: *The barren hath borne seven.*[5] And the Apostle sends letters to seven Churches.[6] So Rachel, younger but fairer than Leah, was at first barren, but after bare children and received a blessing, as in Gen. xxv. 23: *The elder shall serve the younger.*[7] Compare Hos. ii. 23: *I will call* (them who are) *not My people, My people; and her who is not beloved, beloved.*

Certain MSS. add here:[8]

You read in Isa. i. 7: *Your country is desolate...as a besieged city.* If then you are left desolate in accordance with the Law, why blame me for believing the records of my dowry, and receiving a great kingdom, which you could have had without any doubt, if you had not already condemned yourself by your violent crime and godless murder.[9]

For you remember what your own Prophet Ezra cries out respecting you, where you foretold to your children wretchedness and slavery: *Go your way, O my children; for I am a widow and forsaken.*

---

[1] *Gen. R.* § 38, on Gen. xi. 28.
[2] Gen. xii. 1 *sq.*   [3] Gen. xxvii. 29.
[4] Isa. liv. 2–4.   [5] Col. 1139; 1 Sam. ii. 5.
[6] On the importance of "seven" see Cyprian, *Ad Om.* i. 20.
[7] Said to Rebecca.
[8] The large print in Migne therefore also ends here. Small print follows from here to the end.
[9] "Profano parricidio." *Vide infra,* p. 337.

I brought you up with gladness, and with grief and sorrow have I lost you.[1]

The Synagogue. Did I ever slay anyone!

The Church. I see that, if on your own evidence you have persecuted men to their death, you have admitted the charge of murder. For you cannot deny that you have killed the righteous Prophets of God.

The Synagogue. Who can prove that I have stained my hands by doing this?

The Church.[2] Your sword is still dripping to its very point with wet gore, and does it long to be repressed? Listen then to Elijah: *I have been very jealous for my Lord Almighty, for . . . they have slain Thy Prophets with the sword,* etc.[3] See too what Ezra has foretold: *They departed from Thee, and went off behind Thy Law, and slew Thy Prophets who testified against them to turn them unto Thee.*[4] So also Jeremiah wrote: *I sent unto you My servants the Prophets; before the Dawn did I send them; and ye did not hear, nor incline with your ears, that ye should not walk after strange gods, to serve them, and ye would not hear My precepts.*[5]

The Synagogue. I grant this now. But I do not know the context just preceding, for I have listened but carelessly to those Prophets you quote.

The Church. The fact is that it is not what you say, but what you understand to be the Law, is itself evidence, as Isaiah says: *All these words will be as the words of a book which is sealed. And if you give it to be read by a man who cannot read, he will say I cannot read it for it is sealed.*[6] *But in that day the deaf shall hear the word* (sic) *of the book, and they who are in darkness, and they who are in a cloud, even the eyes of the blind shall see.*[7] And as Jeremiah says: *In the last day ye shall know Him.*[8] So also Daniel wrote: *Shut up the words, seal the book, even to the time of the end, that many may be brought forward, and knowledge may be fulfilled, for when the Dispersion takes place, they shall know all things.*[9]

All these things are known, and all things have taken their course happily, in their own order. And so know thou that thou art

[1] 2 Esdras ii. 2 *sq.*   [2] Col. 1140.
[3] 1 Kings xix. 10.   [4] Neh. ix. 26.
[5] The quotation seems to be conflate, resembling Jer. xxxv. 14 *sq.* most.
[6] Isa. xxix. 11 *sq.* But the text is curiously muddled.
[7] *Ibid. v.* 18.   [8] Cf. Jer. xxiii. 20.
[9] Dan. xii. 4, 7. Here again the last words agree with the LXX (Theodotion) rather than with the Vulgate. But, again, they are in Cyprian, *Test.* i. 4.

condemned by thy sword, stricken by thy Testament, by the utterances of thy Prophets, all of whom were Jews.

For it is with this object that I have brought forward my proofs, while keeping back the Gospels and the Apostles for myself and my own people. For if you had read these you would have bellowed at it[1] the more. Rejoice, O ye Peoples: rejoice, ye Worshippers of Christ; the barren has borne, and she who had children has failed with her children of old.[2]

It will have been noted that here the Summary of the treatise has preceded any remarks upon it. The reason is that its opening paragraph is in itself so interesting that it can hardly fail to secure the attention of the reader, and entice him to further study of the argument. For this is one of the abler Tracts, not indeed for its knowledge of Judaism, of which the author is as ignorant as Augustine himself, but for its crisp and clear-cut method in the presentment of the case, so far as its author understands what that case really is.

Yet a few questions must be asked, even though the answers will be incomplete.

1. What are the materials for the Text, and how far are they trustworthy?

2. What are the Date and the Place of Origin?

3. Lastly, what is the relation of the Tract to early Mediaeval Drama?

1. The Text.

The Benedictine editors, followed by Migne, do not appear to state expressly the sources of their text, but presumably these are the same as those of the first of these three Pseudo-Augustiniana, viz. ten MSS. at the Vatican, and eleven others in the south of Europe. Besides this Benedictine text F. Cumont collated MS. No. 247 at Monte Cassino[3] and the variations have been reproduced by G. Morin.[4]

---

[1] "Immugisses."　　　　　　　　　[2] "Cum filiis suis ante defecit."

[3] Juster (*Les Juifs dans l'Empire Romain*, 1914, i. 73) gives the reference as *Reliquiae Taurinenses: Un dialogue judéo-chrétien du temps de Justinien*, dans *Bulletin de la Classe des Lettres et des Sciences morales et politiques de l'Académie royale de Belgique*, 1904, pp. 81–96. The MS. is of cent. xi or xii, and ends with the words "videbam in visu nocte et ecce" (*supra*, p. 333) and is described briefly in *Bibliotheca Casinensis*, 1894, v. 3, and in the *Catalogus MSS. Casin.* II. i, 1928, No. 247.

[4] In *Revue d'histoire Ecclésiastique*, 1900, pp. 270–273.

So far as can be judged from the examples given, this MS. presents a better text than that of the Benedictine, but it is much to be desired that a competent scholar should publish a critical edition of the tract, paying attention not only to the text, but also to the many questions which the tract raises. The Monte Cassino MS., it may be observed, seems to throw little light upon the curious form of several Biblical quotations, save that (as is to be expected if the text be more original) it is on the whole further from the printed Vulgate than is the Benedictine text.

2. The Place of Origin and the Date.

The solution of the problem of the place depends largely, I should suppose, on the nature of the Latin, on which I am not competent to form an opinion. It is certainly legal (unless it is only pseudo-legal), and apparently strongly provincial.[1]

The date is slightly more certain. For the statement (col. 1133, top, cf. *supra*, p. 328) that no Jew can be a Comes, a member of the Senate, hold a Prefectship, enter the army, be reckoned a noble, suggests (though it hardly proves, in our ignorance of what the law was in earlier years) that the tract was written after the Code of Theodosius II was published in A.D. 418 (XVI. viii. 24; see also III. i. 4).

The later limit of date may legitimately be found in the frequent references to the Emperors, pointing to the existence of the Empire of the West. But this was abolished by the conquest of Odoacer in A.D. 476. It has been said also that the term *Christicolas* applied to them indicates Orthodoxy.[2] But presumably it could be used of Arians, such as Odoacer was.

It is then fairly safe to date the tract between the years 437 and 476, but more cannot be said. In any case the verdict of the Benedictine editors holds good, that the tract has nothing of Augustine's diction, and that its author was probably a courtier or a lawgiver of some kind.[3]

[1] Among unusual words may be mentioned *charaxatas* ("inscribed", see p. 328) from the Greek *charasso*; *Psalmidicus* ("Psalmist", see pp. 330, 333); *mitra* (an effeminate head-dress, see p. 331); *parricida* ("murderer", see p. 334); *reciduat* ("restore") and perhaps the accusative plural *-us* for *-os* (see p. 332). For *officina* see p. 329. For *Christicola* see p. 328.
[2] Cf. Juster, *op. cit.* i. 74, N. 1.
[3] "Nihil habet phraseos Augustinianae. Auctor videtur aulicus aut jurisconsultus quispiam fuisse" (Migne, col. 1131).

3. Lastly, what is the relation of this Tract to the early history of the Mediaeval Drama?

Its form so easily lends itself to dramatic representation that it would almost seem to have been composed with this object. But there is no evidence that the Church used Drama as early as the fifth century.[1] Yet, as the power of the Christian authorities increased, and the spiritual fervour of the majority of Christians diminished, attempts would be made to turn the gaiety of the old heathen festivals (e.g. the Saturnalia in December at Rome, and the Yule Feast[2] originally held in February among the German races) into something more seemly for Christian people. While, however, it is possible that such religious plays began as early as the fifth century, there seems to be no direct evidence for them at all until many centuries later, hardly, in fact, before the eleventh century. P. Weber shows that there was a close relationship between their development after the first Crusade (A.D. 1095) and the representations in Art. For these depict both the witness of the Prophets,[3] and the contrasted figures of the Church and Synagogue.[4]

NOTE

The multiplication in all parts of Western Europe of popular dramas depicting the triumph of the Church over the Synagogue, from the eleventh century till the Reformation, shows that the people still took some interest in the Jews. But, alas, we cannot assume that this was often an interest founded on right motives, or on spiritual desires for their conversion. The plays gradually became only verbal relics of past controversies. They testify, however, to a time, presumably past, when Christians were in danger of being led away by Jewish arguments. The people could not read, and the plays and the sculptures took the place of literature.

[1] The chief book on the subject is Paul Weber's small but very attractive *Geistliches Schauspiel und kirchliche Kunst in ihrem Verhältnis erläutert an einer Ikonographie der Kirche und Synagoge*, Stuttgart, 1894. Juster (i. 73, N. 3) refers to other works bearing on the subject. Weber connects both the Drama and the Art chiefly with the district bounded by the Maas, the Moselle and the Scheldt, say from Coblenz to Antwerp.

[2] Juster, i. 75, N. 1; P. Weber, p. 61.

[3] Cf. *supra*, pp. 320 *sqq.*

[4] P. Weber gives pictures of many, of which the most beautiful are at Strassburg (thirteenth century). See also the frontispiece to this book. Since this was in print H. Pflaum has published *Die Religiöse Disputation in der Europäischen Dichtung des Mittelalters*, which, as it seems, deals especially with the *De Altercatione* (Olschki, Florence, 1935).

CHAPTER XXXVIII

THE DISCUSSION OF ST SILVESTER

WITH THE JEWS AT ROME, IN THE PRESENCE OF
CONSTANTINE AND THE EMPRESS HELENA

c. Cent. v

"Now in the fourth year of the most pious Constantine the Great there was a *Discussion* in Rome between Christians and Jews. Of the Christians my Lord Silvester was the leader, being Pope of Rome, and of the Jews, along with many others learned in their Law, was chiefly Zambri the magician, of Hebrew race and a sorcerer, in whom the Jews had the greatest confidence."

Such is the beginning of the account of the *Discussion* incorporated by George Cedrenus in his *Compendium of History*. Not much is known of Cedrenus, but, as his book narrates events as late as A.D. 1067, his death may be placed slightly before 1100. He wrote in Greek, and lived under the Byzantine Empire.[1]

Cedrenus is convenient to consult, for Migne's *Patrologia Graeca* is accessible to the student in all large towns. But in this case he is far from satisfactory, for he omits large portions of the *Discussion*. And, besides, the *Discussion* itself is only a part of the *Acts of Silvester*, though the only important part for our purpose. No critical edition of them, or even of the *Discussion*, seems to exist. But they were printed, in full, as it seems, and in their Latin form, by Mombritius in his *Sanctuarium seu Vitae Sanctorum*, *c.* 1490. This book, however, is so very rare that a new edition was published in Paris in 1910, the *Discussion* being in vol. ii, pp. 508–529, with a few variant readings of some importance on p. 736 *sq.*

The Latin was also published by Wicelius at Mainz in 1544 containing nearly the same text as Mombritius. Francis Combefis published the Greek and Latin in his *Illustrium Christi Martyrum lecti Triumphi*, etc., 1659 (pp. 290–336).[2] It is found also in Syriac,

---

[1] George Cedrenus, Σύνοψις Ἱστορίων (*Historiarum Compendium*). The Διάλεξις τοῦ ἁγίου Σιλβέστρου is in Migne, *P.G.* cxxi. 521–540. *Disputatio Christiani et Judaei, super Evangelica religione* (Wicelius, *vide infra*).

[2] Georgius Monachus (Syncellus, cent. viii) has a very short summary. See Migne, *P.G.* cx. 596–604. For a brief account of him see *Dict. Chr. Biogr.* ii. 650.

and was published by E. W. Brooks in the *Historia Ecclesiastica Zachariae Rhetori vulgo ascripta*, 1919, with a Latin version 1924.[1]

Juster, who is always informing, is of opinion that the *Discussion* had its origin in the East, and was brought to the West in the end of the fifth century.[2] If so, its original language was presumably Greek. But though the Greek had many latish technical theological terms the Latin form is fuller, and will be followed in this chapter with the pagination of Mombritius (1910).

We learn that Helena, the wife of Constantine, was surrounded by Jews, and was in great danger of being converted by them from heathenism to Judaism.[3]

The *Discussion* was held in Rome, and attended by seventy-five Bishops and a hundred and twenty Jews, of whom twelve were the leaders: viz. Abiathar and Jonas (Rabbis), Godaliah and Aunan (Scribes), Doeg and Chusi (Teachers of the Synagogue), Benjamin and Aroel (Interpreters), Jubal and Thara (Doctors of the Law), Sileon and Zambri (Elders). The Jews chose two Judges who were neither Christians nor Jews, and thus were unprejudiced; one, Crato the philosopher, learned in Greek and Latin law and scrupulously just; the other, Zenophilus, a man of Prefect rank. Their joint opinion formed a legal decision.

Constantine speaks, and Crato, and then Zenophilus, each making his own position clear, and insisting on his own impartiality in decision. The names of the disputants are read out, including those of the twelve whom Issachar the High Priest of the Jews (unable to come himself) had sent, their leader being Zambri, a very clever magician.[4]

The treatise goes on to say that though the Jews urged Silvester to choose twelve Christians to argue the case, he refused, for he relied upon the help of God, and appealed to Ps. lxxiv. 22, *Arise, O God, plead Thine own cause.* To this Abiathar objects, claiming that the words were spoken by "our" prophet. Yes, answers Silvester, for we will prove everything from your own books, and so our victory be evident. Zenophilus and the King intervene, affirming that the judgment will be just if a man is defeated by the authority of the very religion he professes.[5]

---

[1] In the *Corpus Scriptorum Christianorum Orientalium (Scriptores Syri*, III. v. 56–93).
[2] *Les Juifs dans l'Empire Romain*, 1914, i. 66 *sq.*
[3] Mombritius, p. 515, ll. 1–21. Wicelius begins after this point, but the end of his *Discussion* tells us of Helena's repentance and conversion.
[4] P. 515, l. 46–p. 517, l. 19 (? = "Jambres").   [5] P. 517, ll. 21–34.

Then follows a discussion on the Trinity, Abiathar adducing Isa. xli. 21: *Behold, behold, I am God and there is no other God beside Me.* Silvester replies: We say that His Deity does not exist in such a desert as not to have the joy of a Son. And, referring to Ps. ii. 7, he argues: God is yesterday and to-day and has no end. Gen. i. 26 is also quoted.[1]

To Silvester's contention that Christ claimed to be God in raising the dead (in accordance with the words of the Prophets: *This is our God who raises the dead*,[2] and, *I will kill and I will make alive*)[3] Abiathar objects that Christ never slew any one and restored him to life! Crato, however, decides that it was sufficient for Silvester to have shown that Christ restored the dead. Abiathar further argues that none of the Prophets, who performed more wonderful miracles than Christ, ever claimed to be divine. Silvester replies that it cannot be denied that Christ raised the daughter of the ruler of the synagogue, and the widow's son, and Lazarus. "And, if I mistake not, your own historian Josephus relates all this of Him."[4] Caiaphas too blazed out in jealousy, and Pilate confirms it all in his report.[5] Silvester shows that those who opposed Moses were punished. Christ's claims were confirmed by His miracles. Zenophilus and Crato decide in Silvester's favour, for if Christ was speaking contrary to God He could not have raised the dead.[6]

Then comes Jonas, who says: Human reason cannot accept a faith which would persuade us that this man is God. For in what kind of God does Silvester bid us believe, who, he confesses, is Father, Son, and Holy Ghost? Read Ps. ii. 7, Silvester replies, and Ps. lxxxix. 26, and, for the Holy Ghost, Ps. li. 11; xxxiii. 6. Then Circumcision is discussed, and the means of Justification. Constantine expresses his surprise at the shamelessness of the Jews in not accepting the evidence of their own Scriptures about the Trinity. Let them bring forward any other objection![7]

Godaliah the third Jew asks for proof about the whole life of Jesus from His birth to His burial. Silvester says that he will show that all was proclaimed beforehand at the hands of the Prophets. He quotes Isa. vii. 14 and Baruch iii. 35–37.[8]

He then goes into details. The Temptation was foretold in Zech.

[1] P. 517, l. 40–p. 518, l. 4.
[2] Cf. 1 Sam. ii. 6; 2 Kings v. 7.   [3] Deut. xxxii. 39.
[4] "Mentior, si historiographus vester Josephus non de illo ista facta retulerit."
[5] "Sua relatione significaverit."   [6] P. 518, ll. 4–49.
[7] P. 518, l. 49–p. 519, l. 50.   [8] P. 519, l. 50–p. 520, l. 5.

iii. 1, 2 (Joshua the High-Priest and Satan). As for His being taken prisoner, this was foretold by Solomon. For we read, *Let us bind the Just One, for He is burdensome to us.*[1]

Other texts having been quoted as referring to the Passion, Silvester continues: But that He was also to be crowned with thorns Jeremiah has foretold, saying, *With the thorns of their faults this people enclosed Me.*[2]

His quotation of Jeremiah, *I was made a laughing-stock to this people,*[3] is doubtless taken from Lam. iii. 14. But his next quotation from Esdras, *You bound Me not as the Father, who set us free from the land of Egypt, when we were crying before the seat of the Judge; you humbled Me when I was hung on the tree; you delivered Me up,* cannot be traced.[4] The proof for the Burial taken from "Jeremiah", *For in (His) burial the dead come to life again,*[5] also cannot be traced, though it may be illustrated from Justin's *Trypho,* lxxii. 4, where see my note.

Godaliah falls back on his astonishment at the impudence of a Gentile presuming to claim knowledge of the Jewish Law. But Silvester appeals to the two assessors, who decide that not God but Godaliah said what was false, and Constantine agrees with them.

Then Aunan ("Ananias", Wicelius) comes forward. He wants proof of the details of Christ's life, but says also that Christians apply to Jesus words that in reality referred to others. To this Silvester replies fairly enough by saying, Show me any one else who answers to them!

The fifth Jew is Doeg, who urges that as Christ was God there was no need for Him to be baptised. To this Silvester replies that

[1] Wisd. ii. 12. See also Isa. iii. 10 in the Septuagint. The Hebrew of the last passage is *Say ye of the righteous,* the Greek translators reading *'imru* as *'iṣru.*

[2] "Spinis peccatorum suorum circumdedit me populus hic." No doubt this is an expansion of Jer. iv. 3, where for *And sow not among thorns* the Targum paraphrases: "And ask not redemption in sins" (*bḥobin*). The same quotation is given by Isidore of Seville (*c.* A.D. 600), *Against the Jews,* I. xxxi (*vide supra,* p. 286). It occurs also in a Syriac MS. in the British Museum Add. MS. 17199, "the Letter of the Blessed Sergius".

[3] "Illusioni factus sum populo huic."

[4] "Vinxistis me non sicut patrem: qui liberavit nos de terra aegipti clamantes ante tribunal judicis: humiliastis me suspensum in ligno: tradidistis me" (p. 520, ll. 21–23).

[5] "In sepultura enim reviviscunt mortui" (l. 24). Cf. also James, *The Fourth Book of Esdras* (*Text and Studies,* 1895, p. xli). Silvester does not directly include the Descent into Hades and the "Harrowing of Hell", as does Justin.

as Circumcision had its fulfilment in the circumcision of Christ, so Baptism had its beginning in His baptism.[1]

Chusi, the sixth Jew, asks why Christ was born of a virgin, whereon Silvester argues ingeniously that as the first man was of the earth before it had received any corruption, either by the curse of thorns and briars or by a human body being buried in it, so was it needful that the new Adam should be born of an uncorrupted Virgin.[2]

The seventh Jew is Benjamin, who says that it is too soon for all present to applaud Silvester, yet, if he replies to all the objections, then he will himself yield. Silvester expounds the doctrines of the Incarnation and the Temptation.[3]

The eighth is Aroel: What need had God to be born in Christ? Silvester's reply begins with stating that it was the Son of God who made the world, thus suggesting (as it seems) that the Incarnation was not the first time that He had to do with us. For *by the Word of God the Lord were the heavens made* (Ps. xxxiii. 6), and He is identified as the Son of God in Ps. cx. 3. Further, God was always Father. Consider Ps. xlv. 1: *My heart emitted the good Word*, and Wisdom says of herself: *I came forth from the mouth of the Most High* (Ecclus. xxiv. 3).[4]

The ninth was Jubal the Pharisee, who asks whether God has spoken ill of marriage, for, if not, why do Christians say that Christ was not born by marriage? When Silvester says that this doctrine has no intention of condemning marriage, Jubal asks: Why then do you praise virginity so much? He then passes on to attack the supposition that the Son of God should suffer, etc., and a discussion of the hypostatic union follows. Silvester adds an illustration. In the Emperor's robe are both the common wool and the purple dye; it was the former that suffered being twisted, etc., not the latter, which, however, gives the dignity.[5]

The tenth Jew, Thara the Pharisee, objects to this similitude, so Silvester gives another. Can a tree, he says, in which is sunshine, be cut into? Certainly, says Thara. Do you not see then, answers Silvester, that the sunshine receives the blow of the axe before this reaches the wood? Yet it can neither be cut into nor divided from the wood. Likewise the Deity can neither be separated nor cut into.[6]

---

[1] P. 521, ll. 1–10.

[2] P. 521, ll. 13 *sqq.* See also Bunyan's *Pilgrim's Progress*, II (Prudence and Matthew). The comparison of the womb to the earth is as old as Ps. cxxxix. 15.

[3] P. 521, l. 39–p. 523, l. 9.   [4] P. 523, ll. 9–45.

[5] P. 523, l. 45–p. 524, l. 29.   [6] P. 524, ll. 29–40.

Sileon, the eleventh Jew, desires to know the reason why Christ should have suffered, and in answer Silvester desires to expound the whole matter at length. After the misery caused by Adam's Fall, Abraham alone was found faithful, and to him therefore the promise was given that in his seed all nations should be blessed. For thus is it said in the Heptateuch:[1] *He set the bounds of the Gentiles according to the number of His angels, and the Lord's portion became Jacob, and Israel the line of His inheritance.* Later He gave to Israel through Moses the Law of Sacrifices. But the devil turned all these to his own idols. For this reason was He born of a Virgin—Silvester means apparently, that there should be a new start—that we should be re-born of the womb of the Virgin-Church. Then Silvester mentions all the details of Christ's life, death, resurrection, and ascension, showing the connexion of each with our salvation. At the end Sileon himself acknowledges he is satisfied.[2]

Up jumps Zambri, the twelfth and last Jew, crying out in indignation, Not words, but deeds! "Let the Emperor bid a bull exceeding fierce be brought us, that I may show before him the power of Almighty God." Silvester joins in the request. While the bull is being brought, Zambri says that no living thing can hear the Name of God and live; and that no material can receive it in writing without being destroyed. How then do you know it? asks Silvester. Zambri replies: I fasted seven days, and then spring-water was poured into a new silver dish. It was blessed, and letters were formed in the water by a Finger, to teach the Name of the Lord to the soul in silence. I wrote it again and again in the water until the evening, and could scarce grasp and withhold it in my heart.[3] What need then for these long discussions?

Then was an exceeding fierce bull brought forward by many soldiers, fast bound with cords. Now, boasted Zambri over the blessed Silvester, your arguments will come to an end! Either say the Name of your God in the bull's ear, and you will be proved to be a worshipper of the Almighty, or I will say it, that all may

---

[1] "In Eptatico" (Deut. xxxii. 8 *sq.*). The quotation is nearer the Septuagint than to the ordinary text of the Vulgate.

[2] P. 524, l. 40–p. 525, l. 47.

[3] "In aqua ipsa digito fiunt litterae: quae nomen domini erudiant tacentis animum. Tunc ab hora prima diei usque ad vesperum scripsisse in aqua recolo: et vix illud potui elimare (MS. R.) in secreto pectoris mei retinere", (p. 526, ll. 20–23). The text is "climate", which gives no good sense. Perhaps "elimate" ("elaborately" = "perfectly") should be read, but the precise form does not seem to occur.

agree to the truth of our religion! Then were all the followers of our faith much troubled. But Silvester stood up boldly, and said with glad heart, The greater efforts of demons are overcome by the greater help of God.

Then Zambri whispers the Name in the bull's ear, and at once the poor thing bellowed, and, throwing his eyes round wildly, gave up the ghost. The Jews are triumphant, and noisy altercation lasts about two hours, but Silvester was seeking help from the Lord Jesus Christ in earnest prayer. Then he says, Listen, ye Princes, that all the People of Rome may learn it well! The Lord Jesus Christ again and again gave health and restoration and life. But that name which slew the bull is the name of the devil, not of God, if it cannot restore the dead to life!

Then Zambri rent his garments, and said, O Lord Augustus, No one can overcome Silvester in words, but I have overcome him by action. Bid him say no more. His talk is a burden to your whole Empire!

After some verbal fencing Zambri says: Then let Silvester raise the bull to life by calling on the name of that Galilean, Jesus of Nazareth, that we may be able to accept the claim to his Divinity! "But", he says to Silvester, "you won't do it, even if you fly." Zambri solemnly professes that if Silvester does it he and all the Jews will abandon Judaism and yield to Christianity. And each of the eleven other Jewish protagonists makes personally the same affirmation.

Silvester bids the Christians separate themselves from the unbelievers, and in one group kneel and pray to the Lord together, "that He may assent to our prayers, and show that our Lord Jesus Christ is indeed His Son". But the Jews only laugh and ridicule. Then Bishop Silvester lifted up his hands to the Lord, and prayed at some length. Then he turned to that ear of the bull in which Zambri had said some name or other, saying, O thou name of cursing and of death, as thou didst enter into the ear of this bull, so come out at the command of our Lord Jesus Christ of Nazareth, in whose Name is now said to thee, "O Bull, arise!" And at once the bull received its breath once more, and arose gentle and quiet. And St Silvester loosed its bonds, saying, Go in all gentleness to thy herd; and thus it went away.

At once all the Jews fell down at the feet of Silvester, confessing they believed in Christ, and besought him to pray for them that no evil might befall them. And on that day more than three thousand Jews were converted to faith in Christ. So also was the Empress Helena, and her sons and daughters, with the chamberlains, and Zenophilus and Crato, the two assessors. On the holy day of the Passover they were born again in holy Baptism.[1]

Our subject ends here, and is followed by a wonderful story of Silvester delivering the people of Rome from a dragon.

This *Discussion*, as the reader will have seen, is more interesting than many. No doubt the final duel between Zambri and Silvester is a bit of folk-lore, but, as often, it hides truth under a fictitious tale. For the Name always stands for the completeness of that which it describes. Hence, as the vision of God in His perfection is more than the eye can bear (Ex. xxxiii. 20), so is the audition of Him too much for the ear. Neither beast nor man can hear it and live. The bull therefore must die when he hears it. And no material could have borne the inscription of it that Zambri might read it. But, by an ingenious subterfuge, the Name is written by a Finger in holy water, and only the thought of its sound therefore is conveyed. Again, that Name had to be whispered. But the Name of Jesus—with all It stands for—may be proclaimed aloud; and this Name does not kill, but gives life to what is already dead. The allegory of the tale has its charm; mere magic is of the devil, the Gospel message is of God.

In this connexion it may be noticed that the *Discussion* never mentions the Eucharist, though the writer must have lived at a time when phrases suggesting a miraculous change in the elements were freely used, and were easily so interpreted. A few centuries later the treatise would almost certainly have contained a further development, some example of the miracle-working power of the consecrated bread and wine.

What again of the arguments in the *Discussion*? Most of them, no doubt, only repeat the old method of proving the truth of Christianity from passages in the Old Testament, which are quoted without any regard to their context, and applied without a qualm to any Christian doctrine which they verbally fit.

But occasionally a reason is demanded. Why was it, after all, that the Incarnation was necessary? And, in particular, Why was it that Christ should suffer? Silvester tackles the problem bravely, and at some length, and not without success. For he tries to show that the suffering was by no accident, but was part of the necessary state of things. There was one awful fact with which the Saviour

[1] P. 525, l. 47–p. 529, l. 5.

had to deal, the fact of sin. This was so great that ages elapsed from the Fall before Abraham showed himself almost perfect. Him and his descendants therefore God could use. Then at last One of these, i.e. One of Abraham's line, though the very Son of God, was born of a Virgin, who was herself therefore as incorrupt as the virgin earth from which the First Adam was formed (*infra*, p. 378). He came and passed through the vicissitudes of human existence. "He received on Himself our curse, that He might pour out His own blessing upon us and take away our curse from us. He took our mortality on Himself, and restored to us His own life together with eternity. He was buried that He might bless the burials[1] of the saints. He rose that He might give life to the dead. He ascended into heaven that He might not only give back to man that paradise which he had lost, but even also open the door of heaven. He sits now at the right hand of the Father, that He may grant the prayers of believers."[2]

The argument underlying the rhetoric is sound: viz. that "it behoved the Christ to suffer these things, and to enter into His glory" (Luke xxiv. 26).

[1] "Sepulturas." Perhaps, the tombs.
[2] P. 525, ll. 24–30.

CHAPTER XXXIX

AGOBARD:[1] LETTERS

Between A.D. 824 and 828

The early part of the ninth century was a remarkable period in the history of France, for thoughts came to the surface then, and ideals were seen, which afterwards were long lost sight of, not to say buried, and were revived and put into practice only after nearly a thousand years had passed away. It was wrong, said Agobard, to settle disputes by duels,[2] or to determine innocence or guilt by ordeal.[3] And it was wrong, wrote Smaragdus to Charlemagne (c. A.D. 742–814) or his successor Louis le Débonnaire (814–840), to hold slaves at all, for all men have equal rights.[4] The claim, says Jonas Bishop of Orleans (ob. 843), to superior intellect, or to greater wealth, does not do away with the natural rights of every man. There is no justification for mastership on the one side and servitude on the other.[5]

These doctrines, which must then have seemed strange to many, were the outcome of Charlemagne's reign. With all his strength and success in warfare, spreading as he did his dominions south-ward over the Lombards, north-west over the Saxons, and eastwards as far as Bohemia and Pannonia,[6] he had time (like Napoleon, but with less self-seeking) to attend to the details of his subjects' comforts, and their advancement in education and religion. For he seems to have been a really religious man. He may also have been

---

[1] Graetz, *Gesch. d. Juden*, 1871, v. 226. Agobard was Archbishop of Lyons, c. A.D. 823–840. His works were edited by Baluze, 1666, and are in Migne, *P.L.* civ. 9–352. See also *Agobard von Lyon und die Judenfrage, in Festschrift...dem Prinzen Luitpold*, by Friedrich Wiegand, Erlangen, 1901, i. 221–250.

[2] *Adv. legem Gunobardi*, Migne, coll. 113–126.

[3] *De Divinis sententiis*, Migne, coll. 249–268.

[4] "Prohibe ergo, clementissime rex, ne in regno tuo captivitas fiat.... Conditione enim aequabiliter creati sumus, sed aliis alii culpa subacti" (*De via regia*, xxx, Migne, *P.L.* coll. 967 b, 968 b).

[5] *De institutione laicali*, ii, 22 (Migne, *P.L.* cvi. 213–215). See further P. Allard, *Origines du servage en France*, 1913, pp. 315 *sq.*, 322–324.

[6] See Gibbon, ch. xliv (Bohn's ed. v. 410), and in more detail, W. T. Waugh, *Germany*, 1916, p. 32.

moved by the missionary influences of the eighth century, in which our own English Church took so leading a part.

For England had been comparatively free from wars, and education had not suffered as much there as on the Continent. So Charlemagne brought Alcuin of York to his court, and listened to his advice. Perhaps it was due to Alcuin, perhaps to the Emperor himself, that the serfs of all degrees (and there appear to have been many degrees of serfdom then) were so cared for as to have churches provided for them and opportunities of worship. Their lords' powers were also limited.[1]

We must distinguish carefully between serfs (villeins) and slaves. The former, though bound to the soil and subject to the control of their lords in most departments of their lives, were free against all other persons, serfs or others. But slaves as such were mere chattels, and could be sold from master to master, or even sent abroad. What the proportion of the two classes was in the Frankish Empire at the beginning of the ninth century is not easy to determine. The Church, with its monasteries and Church lands, had no slaves, though many serfs. Alcuin himself, when twitted with holding so many of the latter, for he was now a wealthy man with many monasteries under him, replied that he had never purchased a single slave for his own personal use. Slaves in the proper sense of the word seem to have been comparatively few.

Who and what then were the slaves? A hundred years later, the wholesale importation of Slavs as captives in war, numbering (it is said) eighty thousand, gave the familiar name. But at the beginning of the ninth century slaves appear to have been seen in any quantity only in the hands of slave-dealers, partly Venetians but chiefly Jews, who bought and sold them like any other beasts. In the great majority of cases they must have been heathen, for according to the laws no Christian might be a slave to a Jew.[2] They were only heathen chattels, and might be sold at the ports of the Mediterranean into slavery among Turks and North African

[1] See P. Allard, *op. cit.* pp. 157 *sqq.* Yet Dr G. G. Coulton gives a terrible picture of the power of the lord over his serfs (*The Medieval Village*, 1925).

[2] Agobard, alas, had to remind Christians not to sell Christians to Jews (Migne, col. 72). The Council of Châlons (743) seems even to prohibit the sale of any one (heathen as well as Christian) to a Jew (*Dict. Chr. Ant.* ii. 1909 a). On Gregory the Great's horror of the Jewish slave-trade *vide* Sol. Katz, "Pope Gregory the Great and the Jews" in *J.Q.R.* Oct. 1933, pp. 128 *sqq.* Parkes gives much information. See in particular his Appendix I, ii. 391.

potentates.[1] Or a Jew might retain these poor heathen as his own personal slaves, with the intention of making them become Jews.[2]

This it was[3] that led to Agobard's famous letters and diatribes.[4] In the first (A) he asks advice on the subject generally. In the second (B) a concrete case had arisen. A heathen girl, a slave in a Jewish household,[5] had been won to Christianity and been baptised, and had, in consequence, been persecuted. As a Christian she could no longer be in slavery to a Jew, so she must be released. There was, however, no question of this being done without payment. Agobard makes it clear that in such cases the Church was ready to recoup the owner with the price he had paid for the slave, perhaps some twenty or thirty *solidi*.[6] The Church could not well

[1] Cf. Migne, col. 76.

[2] Bass Mullinger in *Dict. Chr. Ant.* ii. 1902–1910 (s.v. *Slavery*) is excellent, but barely reaches our period.

[3] For, as Wiegand says (p. 239), a Church (*Geistlichkeit*) which was at that time doing missionary work among Saxons and Danes, Slavs and Avars, would naturally direct its attention to the members of the heathen diaspora within the Empire.

[4] The standard investigation of their relative chronology is by B. Simson in *Jahrbücher des fränkischen Reichs*, 1874, i. 393–396. He bases his conclusions on the dates of the deaths of some of the persons mentioned, and on the statements about the Commissioners (*Missi*) of the Emperor. All five documents fall within the years 824 and 828 (Wiegand, p. 244).

A. *Consultatio et Supplicatio...ad Proceres Palatii de baptismo Judaicorum mancipiorum. Reverendissimis...Adalardo, Walae, et Helisarcho* (before 826, when Adalard died, *Missi* are not mentioned). Baluze, i. 98–102; Migne, *P.L.* civ. 99–106.

B. *Epistola ad Proceres Palatii contra Praeceptum impium de baptismo Judaicorum mancipiorum* (826, a threat of *Missi* being sent). Baluze, i. 192–197; Migne, coll. 173–178.

C. *De Insolentia Judaeorum* (826–827, *Missi* have been sent). Baluze, i. 59–66; Migne, coll. 69–76.

D. *Epistola Agobardi, Bernardi, et Eaof* (or *Eaor*) *de Judaicis superstitionibus* (same date). Baluze, i. 66–98; Migne, coll. 77–100.

E. *Epistola...ad Nibridium Episcopum Narbonensem de cavendo convictu et societate Judaica* (828, the year Nibridius died). Baluze, i. 102–107; Migne, coll. 107–114.

[5] The phrase implies that she was not a Jewess by birth and upbringing, though completely in Jewish surroundings. "Quandam feminam ex Iudaismo ad Christianismum gratia Christi translatam, graves persecutiones sustinere propter fidem quam suscepit Christi, quas per ipsius feminae breviculum potestis cognoscere" (Ep. B, Migne, col. 175).

[6] Ep. A, Migne, col. 103. The Council of Mâcon (581) "directs that Jewish or pagan proprietors shall be bound to surrender Christian slaves for a ransom of 12 *solidi*" (Bass Mullinger, *Dict. Chr. Ant.* ii. 1907 b). It may be noted here that Agobard expressly states that neither the children nor the slaves of Jews ought to be taken by force (Ep. B, Migne, col. 178).

do more. To have paid what the Jew hoped to receive by a future sale, or what he estimated the slave's value for work in the household, was not practical. It was only possible to see that the owner suffered no direct pecuniary loss. This much the Church would do, and there is no evidence that the number of such cases was as yet too great for the Church to meet.

But the Jews of Lyons were in an uproar at once. Had they not managed to secure a law from Louis le Débonnaire[1]—at least they said so, and probably with truth, though Agobard affects to doubt it—that no slaves should be baptised unless the owner had given his consent? What! cries Agobard, Had the Christians of Caesar's household (Phil. iv. 22) asked Nero's leave before being baptised? The requirement is unreasonable, and contrary to history.

The Jews, headed by Everard their "Magister", doubtless a Gentile Christian official appointed over them by the Emperor, threatened to get Commissioners sent from the Court, who would speedily bring Agobard to a better mind.[2] They came, and bullied the Christians and Christian priests in Lyons, but Agobard himself happened to be away. He writes another letter (C) to the Emperor in consequence, complaining of the "insolentia" of the Jews, sending at the same time a joint letter composed by himself and other Bishops (D), recapitulating the Canons of Councils and the decrees of Kings, and enumerating at some length the grievous superstitions of Jews in general. Lastly, there is a short letter to Nibridius the Bishop of Narbonne on the same subject, bidding him warn his people against all social intercourse with Jews (E).

We may now turn to some of the chief points in Agobard's criticism of the Judaism and Jews of his day.

1. He says that they hold that the Letters of the Alphabet are eternal, existing before the beginning of the world,[3] and that the

[1] The Germans call him Louis the Pious, presumably because he ended his days in a monastery, but it is more in accordance with his actions to call him Louis the Good-natured. He seems in fact to have been very squeezable.

[2] Charlemagne had "established as a regular part of the state machinery an institution which his forebears had used only occasionally. From the ranks of his nobles, counsellors, and clergy, he annually chose a number of trustworthy and experienced men whom he sent, by twos or threes, on tours of inspection through the realm. These *missi*, as they were called, held very wide powers. It was their duty to promulgate new laws, to communicate royal instructions to the counts, to hear and investigate all complaints, to enquire carefully into the conduct of the count and his subordinates, to collect information as to the state of the Church, and even to report on the morals of the people in general" (Waugh, *op. cit.* p. 33). [3] Ep. D, Migne, col. 87.

Law of Moses was many cycles of years earlier than the world.[1] Further, there is not a page or a sentence in the Old Testament on which the Jews do not make up lies and superstitions.[2] He also quotes Jerome's allusion to the great "number of traditions of the Pharisees which they to-day call Deuterosis".[3]

2. Their opinions about God are unworthy. He has a body.[4] He sits on a throne like an earthly king, "and is within, as it were, a great palace".[5] One of his seven trumpets is a thousand cubits long.[6] Observe that we can hardly blame Agobard for taking these and other Homiletic and semi-playful illustrations (*Haggadoth*) literally, for many Polish Jews of the first half of the nineteenth century were equally mistaken, and several learned Christian writers of the same period agreed with them.

3. Of special interest are Agobard's own statements of the opinions of the Jews about our Lord. For they form the earliest existing evidence of the Jewish life of him which is known as the *Toledoth Jeshu*.[7] He was, it says, a worthy man and a pupil of John the Baptist, and had Disciples, among whom was one named Kephas, i.e. Peter, so called because of the hardness and dullness of his intelligence.[8] When Jesus was expected by the people on a feast-day certain boys of his school met him, singing out of respect for their master, "Osanna to the Son of David". But at last he was accused of speaking many lies, and was condemned by Tiberius (*sic*) to be thrust into prison. For though he (Jesus) had promised his daughter that she should bear, though still remaining a virgin, she had only brought forth a stone.[9] For this reason as a detestable magician was he hung on a pole, where too he was struck on the

[1] Ep. D, Migne, col. 87, " multis annorum curriculis ante mundum".

[2] *Ibid.*

[3] Ep. D, Migne, col. 88: "Quantae traditiones Pharisaeorum, quas hodie Deuterosis vocant." See Jerome, *Ep.* cxxi. 10 (Vallarsi, i. 883 *sq.*). Δευτερώσεις (Jerome) represents *Mishnaioth*. Jerome in this passage has much to say about the traditions of the Jews.

[4] *Ibid.* "corporeum", quoting Jerome, "in quodam loco". I have not been able to trace this reference.

[5] Ep. D, Migne, col. 87: "et magno quamvis palatio continetur".

[6] *Ibid.*

[7] This part (Ep. D, Migne, col. 87 *sq.*) is quoted in Strack, *Jesus, die Häretiker und die Christen*, 1910, p. 14* *sq.* See also S. Krauss, *Das Leben Jesu nach jüdischen Quellen*, 1902, pp. 5–7.

[8] "Propter duritiam et hebitudinem sensus."

[9] This is evidently a Jewish perversion of the Christian insistence on the Virgin Birth, and on the Stone (i.e. Christ); cf. Justin's *Dialogue with Trypho*, lxxvi and elsewhere (*vide supra*, p. 38).

head by a stone, and so was killed.[1] Then he was buried near a certain conduit (*aquaeductus*), and entrusted to the charge of a certain Jew, but he was carried away at night by a sudden flood of the conduits. Although search was made for him at Pilate's command for twelve months, he was not found even then. So Pilate put them forth a law to this effect: "It is clear", he said, "that he who was put to death by you through envy, and has not been found either in the tomb or in any other place, has risen as he promised. Therefore I order you to worship him. And he who refuses to do so must know that his future shall be in hell."

All this, adds Agobard, have the elders of the Jews made up, and the Jews still read in their stubborn folly, in order that by such interpretations all the truth of the power and suffering of Christ may be made void, and worship may not be rightly addressed to him as God, but be ascribed to him by Pilate's law alone.

It is also said that Peter was in no wise led forth from prison by an angel, as we believe, but was released by the compassion of Herod, by whom Peter's wisdom was greatly praised.[2]

4. The attitude of Jews towards Jesus and Christians in general. They curse him and Christians by name in all their prayers daily, as Jerome says and many Jews confirm.[3] Elsewhere Agobard says only that they persecute him "in the synagogues of Satan" (Rev. ii. 9; iii. 9), quoting Jerome also for this.[4] They even assert that Christians worship idols,[5] and that miracles obtained by the intercessions of the saints were in reality wrought by the devil.[6]

5. Lastly, we must notice what Agobard tells us of the behaviour of the Jews in his time. He says that they "began to be carried away with detestable insolence, threatening us with all kinds of

---

[1] Cf. S. Krauss, *op. cit.* p. 164. Not "crucified". Agobard has already quoted the Jews as saying that Jesus died by compulsion, and not of His own free will prompted by pity ("ex necessitate naturae, non ex voluntate misericordiae", IX, Migne, col. 86).

[2] Is there here confusion with Herod's admiration for John the Baptist?

[3] Ep. C, IV, Migne, col. 73. Cf. "They curse the Lord and his body in all their prayers...as had been prophesied 'by the voice of the Lord speaking to the Father. They will curse, but thou wilt bless'" (Ps. cix. 28). Ep. D, IX, Migne, col. 86. See Jerome on Isa. lii. 4. See Justin's *Dialogue with Trypho*, xvi. 4, with my note, *supra*, p. 34.

[4] Ep. D, Migne, col. 88. I cannot find a definite reference in Jerome.

[5] Ep. D, Migne, col. 88.   [6] *Ibid.*

harm through the Commissioners they had obtained to pay off their revenge on the Christians".[1]

Further, "We suffered at the hands of the partisans of the Jews, for no other reason than that we preached to Christians that they should not sell to Jews Christian slaves, and not permit the Jews themselves to sell Christians into Spain, nor to have hired servants (evidently Christians), for fear that Christian women should observe the Sabbath with them, or should work on the Lord's Day, or have meals with them in Lent, and hired servants eat their meat in the same period, and that no Christian whatever should buy meat slain and porged by Jews and sell it to others, nor drink their wine, and such like."[2]

For if their animals are not slain in strict Jewish fashion or prove to be unfit for Jews, they sell the meat to Christians, and the wine which they have mopped up from the floor.[3] Further, they claim that after examining the Canons they do not see why Christians ought to abstain from Jewish foods and drinks.[4] Again, "the Commissioners aforesaid (plainly at the instigation of the Jews), lest they (the Jews) should be hindered in their observation of the Sabbath, ordered the usual Saturday markets to be changed, and fixed them for such days as the Jews chose. They say that this change suits the convenience of Christians because of their leisure upon the Lord's day (i.e. they have time for marketing). Whereas (on the contrary, this suggested change) is shown to be [to the profit] rather of the Jews and unprofitable [to the Christians]; for (as things are at present) those who live near (the town) buy what food they need on Saturday, and are the more free to attend the masses and preachings on Sunday; and if any come from far, by reason of the market, they attend both vespers (on Saturday) and

[1] "Coeperunt autem efferri quadam odibili insolentia Judaei, comminantes omnibus injuriis nos afficiendos per Missos quos adepti fuerant ad exsolvendam vindictam de Christianis" (Ep. C, Migne, col. 71).

[2] "Haec passi sumus a fautoribus Judaeorum, non ob aliud nisi quia praedicaverimus Christianis, ut mancipia eis Christiana non venderent, ut ipsos Judaeos Christianos vendere ad Hispanias non permitterent, nec mercenarios domesticos habere, ne feminae Christianae cum eis sabbatizarent, et ne diebus Dominicis operarentur, ne diebus Quadragesimae cum eis pranderent, et mercenarii eorum iisdem diebus carnes manducarent, ne quilibet Christianus carnes a Judaeis immolatas et deglubatas emeret, et aliis Christianis venderet, ne vinum illorum biberent, et alia hujusmodi" (Ep. C, Migne, col. 72 *sq.*).

[3] Ep. C, Migne, col. 73.

[4] "Et recursis canonibus non inveniri quare Christiani debeant abstinere a cibis eorum et potibus" (Ep. C, Migne, col. 74).

matins (probably on Sunday, but possibly on Monday), and then after mass has been solemnised they return home edified."[1]

Further, "they irreverently dare to preach to Christians what they ought to believe and hold, blaspheming in their presence our Lord God and Saviour, Jesus Christ".[2] They boast of their ancestry,[3] and (against the law) are allowed to build even new synagogues, and—especially galling to human nature—"it comes to such a pass that uneducated Christians say that Jews preach better to them than our priests".[4]

Agobard also quotes an edict of Childebert which implies that at Easter Jews were wont to march about the streets.[5] But he does not seem to say that this took place at Lyons or in his own day.

No doubt most of Agobard's charges against the theological opinions of the Jews are erroneous, and are due to his ignorance of Judaism from within.[6] Yet he cannot be altogether blamed. It was not an age of mealy-mouthed civilities. Jews themselves have never encouraged dissimulation in attack on either side, and everyone is liable to make exaggerated statements and unintentional mistakes.

[1] "Et supradicti Missi, ne sabbatismus eorum impediretur, mercata, quae in sabbatis solebant fieri, transmutari praeceperint, et quibus diebus deinceps frequentari debeant in illorum opinione ('optione', Baluze) posuerint, dicentes hoc Christianorum utilitati propter diei Dominici vacationem congruere; cum Judaeis magis probetur [utile et Christianis] inutile: quia et hi qui prope sunt, sabbato ementes victus necessaria, liberius die Dominico missarum solemnitatibus et praedicationibus vacant; et si qui de longe veniunt, ex occasione mercati, tam vespertinis quam matutinis occurrentes officiis, missarum solemnitate peracta, cum aedificatione revertuntur ad propria" (Ep. C, Migne, col. 75). The three Latin words in [ ] were suggested to me by Dr G. G. Coulton, who also inserts a comma after *mercati*. All earlier writers on Agobard appear carefully to have avoided translating this obscure passage.
[2] "Ut auderent irreverenter praedicare Christianis quid potius credendum esset ac tenendum, blasphementes coram eis Dominum Deum ac Salvatorem nostrum Jesum Christum" (Ep. C, Migne, col. 71).
[3] "Exponunt gloriam parentum suorum" (Ep. C, Migne, col. 74); cf. "Dum se patriarcharum progeniem, justorum genus, prophetarum sobolem, superbo ore proloquuntur" (Ep. E, Migne, col. 111).
[4] "Ad hoc pervenitur, ut dicant imperiti Christiani, melius eis praedicare Judaeos quam Presbyteros nostros" (Ep. C, Migne, col. 74 *sq.*).
[5] Was this really due to the Jewish Passover holidays sometimes coinciding with the Christian? Childebert I, son of Clovis, reigned from 511 to 558 (Ep. D, VI, Migne, col. 84; cf. VII, Migne, col. 85).
[6] In spite of his claim to have talked with Jews almost every day and to have listened to the mysteries of their erroneous belief. "Nobis...qui quotidie pene cum eis loquentes mysteria erroris ipsorum audimus" (*De Jud. Superstit.* ix, end).

We are now in a better position to estimate the character of Agobard in his general attitude towards the Jews. An unprejudiced mind will surely grant that he could hardly have refrained from acting as he did in those times and circumstances. He, as Arch-bishop, was the guardian of the Church's interests in Lyons, and was responsible for the spread of Christianity in at least his own Arch-diocese. Was he then to be slack in endeavouring to win heathens to the Saviour even though they did happen to be slaves in a Jewish household? He was ready, it must be remembered, to pay the legal price for their redemption.

That was the immediate occasion of the chief part of the dispute, and for Agobard's direct action in this few modern Jews would be inclined to condemn him. The question, however, does not stop there. Agobard was also the principal producer of the joint letter (and the sole writer of the letter enclosing it) in which are collected decrees of kings and Canons of Councils enumerating Jewish errors, and warning Christians against being led away by them.

But the real reason for the Jewish dislike of Agobard lies deeper than even this. Charlemagne had encouraged Jewish settlers in his dominions for economic reasons. While the upper classes of Christians thought only of war, the farmers of corn and wine, and the poor of their daily work and ability to live at all, the Jews were keen on trade, and by their interdependence were able to succeed in it. Besides, some scholars think that Charlemagne had per-suaded at least one family of Jewish scholars (Kalonymus) to come to Mainz, in the hope that they would improve the intellectual standard of their coreligionists. Again, the third member of Charlemagne's embassy to Haroun al Rashid (797) was a Jew named Isaac, who survived his two chiefs, and returned to Charle-magne in honour. The same policy of encouraging the Jews was followed by Louis le Débonnaire and Judith his second wife. She, a very able woman, was doing her best to secure the succession to her own son, a desire which the three elder sons of Louis by the first wife naturally resented. The Jews sided with Louis and Judith, while presumably the Church in general, and certainly Agobard in particular, supported the three half-brothers.

Thus before his activity, and the influence that he brought to bear on Court and Church, the Jews were acquiring a high and important position in the State, and his work and writings did tend to prevent their prestige growing, and even to make their condition a good deal worse than it had been before. Yet no one

in those days had any idea of toleration in the modern acceptance
of the word. Jews had no more notion of it than Christians.
Mohammedans were better, at least as regards their Jewish subjects. Agobard was in this respect no further advanced than other
Jews and Christians of his day, although he had gone far ahead
of them, as we have seen, in certain non-Jewish directions. He was
a keen and able ecclesiastic, doing his best to spread the Gospel,
and to make Christians become more worthy of their name. He
found his efforts for the Truth, and even for the diminution of
slavery, hindered by Jews, and he resisted their manœuvres in
what was perhaps the only way available to a man of his time. It
is not our way, let us hope. Nor is it the highest way. But we can
hardly blame a man of Agobard's antecedents—he had come from
Spain—when he saw himself and his cause opposed by prosperous
Jews who were not merely in will but also in fact influencing
Christians against Christianity. He struck hard and almost too
efficiently,[1] but he was a godly and an earnest man, living and
working up to the measure of his enlightenment. He was not a
Haman; he was, as his times went, a Saint.

[1] Even so it must be remembered that his diatribes contain none of the
venom which disgraces the later Spanish writers, e.g. de Spina in his *Fortress
of the Faith* (A.D. 1459).

CHAPTER XL

AMULO, ARCHBISHOP OF LYONS
A.D. 841–852

THE LETTER OF AMULO, OR A TREATISE AGAINST THE JEWS, ADDRESSED TO KING CHARLES[1]

If there was some doubt whether Agobard's fulminations might fairly be discussed in these articles, there is none about the inclusion of Amulo's treatise. Not, however, that it was written with the direct object of winning Jews to Christ, but he did compose it with the object of providing Christians with arguments against Jewish opponents, and so indirectly serve the cause of Christ against Jews. For if Agobard felt the danger of Jewish influence negatively, in that Jews were hindering the conversion of the heathen, Amulo had before him a concrete example of their success in winning an eminent Christian over to Judaism. The Apostasy of Bodo (838), deacon at the court of the Emperor Louis le Débonnaire, had shocked the Christian world,[2] and we cannot be surprised that learned Christian men did their best to counter its effect.

"Detestanda Judaeorum perfidia", which may be rendered colloquially, "How abominably crafty these Jews are!"[3] So

---

[1] *Amulonis Epistola, seu Liber contra Judaeos, ad Carolum Regem* (i.e. Charles the Bald, king of the Frankish kingdom A.D. 843–877), Migne, *P.L.* cxvi. 141–184. It had been published by P. F. Chifflet (1656), who attributed it to Rabanus Maurus (*vide infra*, p. 365). See Strack, *Jesus, die Häretiker, u.s.w.* 1910, p. 15*. Graetz gives some account of Amulo (Amolo) in his *Gesch.* 1871, v. 237–242. He thinks him nearly as bad as Agobard. Other forms of the name are Hamulus, Hamularius. He was a Gaul. The treatise was written in 846 (*Amulonis Ep.* ch. xix).

[2] See the chapter on *Alvaro and Bodo*, pp. 224–227. Also *infra*, p. 363.

[3] The passage is worth quoting in full: "Detestanda Judaeorum perfidia, et eorum inter Christianos conversatio quantum sit noxia fidelibus, et ecclesiarum doctoribus periculosa, apud multos incognitum est, non solum vulgares et plebeios, sed etiam nobiles et honoratos, doctos pariter vel indoctos: et apud eos maxime, inter quos nulla praefatorum infidelium habitatio aut frequentatio est." It is, perhaps, impossible to translate *perfidia* satisfactorily. It includes the untrustworthiness of the Jews towards God as seen in the Old Testament, and especially in their rejection of His Christ, and their pretence of conversion, and perhaps even their craft towards men in their devices to lead Christians into Judaism. The word is discussed by F. Vernet in the *Dict. Apologétique de la Foi Catholique*, 1924, ii. col. 1733.

Amulo begins his treatise, and he goes on to say that few people, poor or rich, learned or unlearned, know how hurtful to believers and dangerous to teachers is intercourse with Jews. Much later (ch. xliii) he says expressly that he is following in the steps of his saintly predecessor Agobard. But Amulo's treatise is not only much fuller in quotations of Canons and Royal decrees, but also gives long quotations from the Fathers, and, further, adduces many quotations from the Old Testament. Besides, Agobard's letters are little more than short appeals based on immediate needs. Amulo combines all his arguments into one formal document.

To whom it was actually sent is not quite clear. The title, no doubt, is simply *ad Carolum regem*, "to King Charles". But once the reader is addressed as "religiosa sanctitas vestra" (ch. x), and a second time we find "vestrae sanctitatis unanimitas" (ch. xliii); and these phrases suggest that the treatise was sent primarily to high ecclesiastics at Charles' court, as in the case of Agobard's Letters.

Chapters ii–ix of the work are concerned with evidence of the evil-doing of the Jews in general, use being made of Augustine, the attitude of Polycarp towards Cerinthus (all heretics at that time being Jewish), Jerome,[1] and of our Lord's own words.

Amulo then states some of the blasphemies that Jews utter (chh. x–xiii). They speak of the Apostles as "Apostates"; of the Gospel (*evangelium*) as "the revelation of iniquity" (*havongalion*), by which the world was sent into error.[2] But they forget that even this would be testimony against them, for in Job xx. 27 it is said that *the heavens shall reveal his iniquity*. They forbid also the recitation of the twentieth psalm (*the Lord answer thee*) in their synagogues in all parts of the world, lest they should seem to bless Christ as now present.

Further, they have been so blinded as to imagine two Messiahs. One of these, they say, was born in Judaea of David's line on the night of the destruction of the Temple under Vespasian and Titus, but, somehow or other, was carried off to Rome. He is there still, but hidden away in caves, and "in such a slave-house He remains,

---

[1] On Matt. xii. 43 (Vallarsi, vii. 84 *sq.*); Amos i. 11 (vi. 235); Amos v. 23 (vi. 304); *Ep.* cxxi, Quaest. 10 (i. 883 *sq.*) (for this last reference see also Agobard, *supra*, p. 352); Isa. viii. 14 (iv. 122 *sq.*).

[2] T.B. *Sabb.* 116 a. "R. Meir called it *'āven-gillajôn* (Roll of Emptiness); Jochanan called it *'avôn gillajôn* (Roll of Sin)." See further Strack, *Jesus, die Häretiker und die Christen*, 1910, pp. 2, 19*. Strack also quotes much of Amolo (pp. 15*–17*).

bound with iron, burdened with chains, and wounded in His whole body". And they are confident that through these wounds they themselves have pardon for their sins, in accordance with the promise of Isa. liii. 5: *And in His wound shall be our medicine.*[1]

It is also written in their traditions that this Messiah appeared of old to a great doctor of theirs, Joshua ben Levi, and in filthy raiment. But when Joshua, not knowing who He was, asked Him why He went along so unwashed and unkempt, He suddenly changed His form, and appeared like an old man of handsome countenance, with a sapphire jewel in His hand. On being questioned He replied, "I am Messiah, who bear many punishments for you, and I shall redeem you from captivity; and you shall all receive a sapphire stone such as you see I hold. And then shall there be fulfilled in you what is written in Isa. liv. 11 *sq.*: *O thou afflicted*, etc."[2] This Messiah they hope will come hereafter in the clouds of heaven (Dan. vii. 13).

The second Messiah is Ben Ephraim, the Son of Ephraim (Jer. xxxi. 9), who will come when Israel has been restored to Palestine, will fight against Gog and Magog, be slain, and be lamented by all Jewry with great lamentation (Zech. xii. 10). But here the Jews have even altered the wording of the prophecy, for instead of reading (as we Christians do) *Me whom they have pierced* they read *Him*, etc.[3]

With ch. xiv Amulo begins an elaborate argument against this belief in two Messiahs (chh. xiv–xviii). He first enlarges his criticism of Zech. xii. 10, pointing out that it is on Jews themselves that the Spirit of grace and prayers is to be poured out, and that it is they who will look at *Me whom they have pierced*, this being the only Begotten of God the Father, the First-born who will be set above the kings of the earth (Ps. lxxxix. 27). Amulo adds the interesting remark, which shows that he either could read Hebrew himself or obtained his information from some one who could, that though the Jews did not dare to alter the *Me* of the text itself, they place *Him* in the margin, and read the passage aloud accordingly; telling

---

[1] "Et in vulnere ejus medicina erit nobis." The ordinary text of the Vulgate is: "Et livore ejus sanati sumus."

[2] This story may perhaps be based upon Joshua ben Levi's interview with Messiah, who was sitting among the poor and sick at the gates of Rome, narrated in T.B. *Sanhedrin*, 98 a, but it differs in important details. Cf. Peter the Venerable of Cluny, *c. Jud.*, Migne, *P.L.* 549 D (*vide infra*, p. 386).

[3] *Vide infra.* Cf. Justin's *Trypho*, xiv. 8; lxiv. 7; lxxi. 2.

also their disciples to treat the writing and the reading thus.[1] It is an early example among Gentile writers of the traditional *Cthib* ("written") and "*Qri*" ("read") of our Hebrew Bibles.

Again, Amulo says, Where is it stated in Scripture that Messiah was to be born in the night that the Temple was destroyed? On the contrary, He was to come to it while it was still standing (Mal. iii. 1). It was His rejection that was the cause of the destruction of the Temple (ch. xv). For it was prophesied that Israel would be destroyed, e.g. Jer. xix. 11 (ch. xvi). Why then say such tales about Christ being ill-treated at Rome? It was not by the Romans but by the Jews that He was to suffer. See Mal. iii. 8: *If a man pierces God, because ye pierce Me, and ye—the whole nation—pierce Me.*[2] Again, has Christ been hidden for almost a thousand years (ch. xvii)!

As for the appearance to Joshua ben Levi, it was either wholly imaginary, or Satan himself appeared as an angel of light (ch. xviii). For Rufinus mentions other such appearances of Satan. Remember also Julian's attempt to rebuild the Temple,[3] and what took place —how some were terrified, and had to confess Christ against their will. And, lest they should think it happened by chance, there appeared next night the sign of the cross on their clothing.[4]

Further, calculations from Ezekiel (see Jerome on Ezek. iv. 4–6) show that the Captivity from A.D. 70 was to last only 430 years. Yet this period has been nearly doubled. "For from the coming of the Lord our Saviour we reckon 846 years to the present time" (ch. xix).[5]

The next subject of interest in Amulo's argument is that he acknowledges the learning of Josephus and Philo, yet points out that in spite of this they were but unbelieving Jews, although some Christians admire them more than the Bible. He here refers to Augustine who mentions Philo in *c. Faustum*, xii. 39 (Migne, *P.L.* xlii [Aug. viii], 274) (ch. xxiv).

---

[1] For a discussion of Zech. xii. 10 see my *Christian Evidences*, 1911, §§ 259–262.

[2] "Si configit homo Deum, quia vos configitis me, et me vos configitis gens tota." The Vulgate is: "Si affliget (var. lect. affiget) homo Deum, quia vos configitis me?...et me vos configitis gens tota." The Hebrew verb (*qāba'*) occurs only here and in Prov. xxii. 23, and is usually translated *rob*.

[3] Cf. Chrysostom, *Hom.* v. 11 (*supra*, p. 134); *Demonstr.* xvi (*supra*, p. 139).

[4] Cf. the appearance of crosses on the robes of Jews who were expecting some sign of redemption in 1295, as narrated by Abner of Burgos, *Wars of God*, c. 27, copied by Paul of Burgos in his *Scrutinium*, II. 6. x (*vide supra*, p. 259).

[5] "Nam ab adventu Domini Salvatoris octingenti et quadraginta sex impraesentiarum computantur anni."

Amulo then refutes at some length the Jewish objection, based on Deut. xxi. 22 *sq.*, that Christians believe on one who was accursed of God. Jews say that "at the loud command of their master Joshua Jesus was taken down quickly from the tree, and thrown into a tomb in a certain garden full of vegetables, for fear lest their land should be polluted" (ch. xxv).[1] Here too Amulo makes use of Jerome on Gal. iii. 13 *sq.*, and returns to the subject later on in chh. xxxvi to xxxviii. In ch. xxxvii he again refers to Augustine, *c. Faustum*, xiv. 6.

By rather a pretty use of allegory he says that "the Hind of the morning" (Ps. xxii, title) means, first, that the Body was not to remain on the cross at night, and, secondly, that Christ's crucifixion must be appropriated while it is still day, and not when the night comes for judgment (ch. xxxi).

Christ took our curse upon Himself, God having foretold this long ago by the Prophets. And it was not Christ's death, but the Jews themselves, who polluted their land, when they shouted: *His blood be upon us and on our children* (ch. xxxiv). Further, if they think they so scrupulously prevented their land from being polluted, why is it that it has through so many centuries vomited them forth as if they were unclean (ch. xxxv)?

In chh. xxxix and xl Amulo deals with other blasphemies of the Jews. "They call Him in their tongue *Ussum Hamizri*, which means in Latin, *The Egyptian Disperser*...affirming that He is the Egyptian Disperser of His people" (ch. xxxix).[2]

And, Amulo continues, they term our worship "the worship of Baal, and the religion of a strange God". And they say that the awful stink which rises on summer mornings is due to the torments which He is enduring in hell. In fact, they speak of Christ as Lucifer (Isa. xiv. 12–20). Jesus' body, they allege, was taken out from his tomb and dragged through the whole city, that all men might know that He was dead; and the tomb itself remains empty

---

[1] "Et conclamante, ac jubente magistro eorum Josue, celeriter de ligno depositum; et in quodam horto caulibus pleno, in sepulchro projectum, ne terra eorum contaminaretur."

[2] "Nuncupant eum sua lingua Ussum Hamizri. Quod dicitur Latine, Dissipator Aegyptius...affirmantes eum gentis suae Dissipatorem Aegyptiacum." Cf. Jerome on Isa. viii. 11 (Vallarsi, iv. 123): "Sammai et Hellel (Shammai and Hillel)...quorum prior dissipat interpretatur sequens profanus"—as though from the roots *Shāmēm* and *Chillēl*. Maimonides says that Jesus *dispersed* Israel, but uses a different Hebrew verb, i.e. PZR (*Yad hachazakah, Hilkoth Melakim*, Amsterdam, 1702, iv. 307 a).

and unsightly unto this day, with the stones and the filth that they ever throw upon it. And they even say that He is the adulterous issue of His Mother and a Gentile named Pandera.[1]

Amulo then turns to speak of the ill behaviour of the Jews at the present time (chh. xli, xlii), making the same statements as Agobard, whose Letters he was doubtless copying. In fact there is so little new matter here that it is sufficient to refer the reader to pp. 353 *sq.* above.

But at the end of ch. xlii he tells us of the terrible example of Jewish influence that had happened eight years before he wrote, viz. in A.D. 838, and thus some ten or twelve years after Agobard had sent his Letters. It was the well-known case of Bodo, and although he and the correspondence to which his apostasy led have been dealt with in the Spanish section of this book,[2] Amulo's statement is so concise that it is worth giving in full.[3]

The last section of the treatise need not detain us long, in spite of its containing eighteen chapters (xliii–lx). It begins with a strong expression of Amulo's desire to protect his people from Jewish impiety. He has already, this very year, bidden them again and again to separate themselves from Jews. And he here definitely takes Agobard as his model, and desires to complete his work both in word and in writing.[4]

[1] See Origen, *c. Celsum*, i. 28 and 32 (*vide supra*, p. 82).

[2] *Supra*, p. 224.

[3] "Quantum autem eorum nefanda societas, et venenatum colloquium proficiat ad impietatem, dum 'sermo eorum', dicit Apostolus, 'sicut cancer serpit' (2 Tim. ii. 17), in uno ab eis miserabiliter et horribiliter decepto omnibus considerare licet. Quod enim nunquam antea gestum meminimus, seductus est ab eis diaconus palatinus, nobiliter natus, nobiliter nutritus et in Ecclesiae officiis exercitatus, et apud principem bene habitus, ita ut eorum diabolicis persuasionibus abstractus et illectus, desereret palatium, desereret patriam et parentes, desereret penitus Christianorum regnum: et nunc apud Hispaniam inter Saracenos Judaeis sociatus, persuasus sit ab impiis Christum Dei Filium negare, baptismi gratiam profanare, circumcisionem carnalem accipere, nomen sibi mutare, ut qui antea Bodo, nunc Eliezer (*sic*) appelletur. Ita ut et superstitione et habitu totus Judaeus effectus, quotidie in synagogis Satanae barbatus et conjugatus, cum caeteris blasphemet Christum et Ecclesiam ejus." Amulo, *c. Judaeos*, xlii (Migne, *P.L.* cxvi. 171). Compare the case of a Dominican Deacon who apostatised to Judaism, and was called Haggai. He was burnt (by Fawkes of Bréanté) on Sunday, April 17, A.D. 1222. A tablet to him was set up by the Jews in the ruins of Osney Abbey, Oxford, in 1931.

[4] "Et aliqua austerius jussi, ut inveteratum malum funditus eradicarem, cupiens, Domino adjuvante, pii pastoris, et institutoris ac decessoris nostri, viri probati et orthodoxi, bonum imitari exemplum: qui pro hujus mali emendatione, dum adhuc regni hujus aliquantula esset tranquillitas, plurimum laboravit,

So he appeals to the high ecclesiastic through whom he is addressing the king, that he and others with him should do their utmost to win their pious rulers, and so secure in their dominion the observance of the sacred canons and the ancient laws in this matter of the Jews. For lay and sacred rulers alike must give account to the King of kings.

It is all very well, as Augustine says (in *Joann.* xi), for Jews to complain of being persecuted! But persecution by Jews is worse, for such persecution as they receive is only on the body, theirs of us is on the spirit. St Paul does not call Sara's actions towards Hagar persecution, but he does so call Ishmael's towards Isaac. Jews kill souls, but are ill-treated only in body.[1] And Augustine urges the words of our Lord in the parable (Luke xiv. 23), *Compel them to come in* (ch. xlvi).

Amulo then quotes certain harsh laws of Theodosius and Valentinian, being careful to add "we do not recall these because we desire (God forbid!) that any man's blood should be shed".[2] Constantine, Childebert, Reccared, Sisebut, Pope Gregory, and others are quoted. Hilary would not even return a Jew's greeting. Ambrose, Viventiolus (Bishop of Lyons, 516), Caesarius, Bishop of Arles (*c.* 469–542), and many others are added. What else, says Amulo, could I do (ch. lix) but try to imitate them, and thus preserve the people committed to my charge from being mixed up with the infection and sacrilege of Jews?

For (ch. lx) we must not either flatter men who are now lost, and are ignorant of their state—I mean the Jews—or (which God forbid) leave them wrongly confident in their own arguments. But let us try to follow St Paul, who says: *I have great sorrow and unceasing pain in my heart for my brethren who are my kinsmen according to the flesh, who are Israelites* (Rom. ix. 2 *sq.*). And again: *Brethren, my heart's desire and my supplication to God is for them, that they may be saved* (*ibid.* x. 1). And elsewhere: *Inasmuch then as I am an apostle of Gentiles, I glorify my ministry: if by any means I may provoke to jealousy them that are my flesh, and may save some of them. For if the casting away*

non solum verbis, sed etiam scriptis. Sed quia opus ab eo coeptum, perturbatione temporum est impeditum; nunc in quantum Deus facultatem tribuit, si hoc negligenter omitto, timeo divinum judicium, ne illi qui ex hac occasione contaminantur, et deprivantur, vel etiam pereunt, meae incuriae et reatui ascribantur." Amulo, *c. Judaeos*, xliii (Migne, *P.L.* cxvi. 171 *sq.*).

[1] "Nam occidunt animas, affliguntur in corpore."

[2] "Haec non ideo ad memoriam reducimus, quasi alicujus hominis sanguinem (quod absit) fundi optemus" (ch. xlviii).

of them is the reconciling of the world, what shall the receiving of them be, but life from the dead (ibid. xi. 13–15)?

Lastly, we must take our utmost heed lest as Christ was at His Passion "sold by a false disciple and carried off by false persecutors to be mocked and crucified, so He be now carried off by impious Jews to be in a kind of way reviled and blasphemed still more freely".

So the treatise ends. But it is to be regretted that Amulo added the last paragraph, for it leaves a nasty taste in one's mouth after the noble utterances of St Paul.

RABANUS MAURUS, ARCHBISHOP OF MAINZ
A.D. 847–856

A treatise against the Jews by Alcuin's distinguished pupil Rabanus Maurus, born in Mainz about A.D. 776, would certainly have been interesting, especially as he received the help of Jews in writing some of his commentaries, even though (judging from his writings in general) it would not have shown much originality of thought. But of the two treatises on the subject which have been attributed to him, one really is that of Amulo (*vide supra*, p. 358), and the other is worthless and cannot well be his. It may be found in Edmond Martène's *Thesaurus Novus Anecdotorum*, 1717, v. 401–594, printed from a manuscript (? cent. x) in the monastery of St Sergius at Angers. His name is on the MS. but the beginning of the preface is lost. It is little more than a long catena of passages from the Old and New Testaments, with an occasional patristic quotation, and shows no knowledge of Judaism or of the condition and influence of the Jews in the writer's time.

CHAPTER XLI

PETER DAMIANI[1]

A.D. 1007–1072

"Beloved Brother Honestus",[2] a busy layman of no great intellectual power, and probably quite unversed in theological training, had been often beset by Jews, whom perhaps he met in the way of business, demanding from him answers to their objections to the Faith. Presumably he did his best to answer them, but he thought it well to obtain from some one more skilful than himself advice as to his procedure. So he asked his friend Peter Damiani, who was already an ecclesiastic of some position, what reply he should make when he was questioned. For Honestus desired proper reasons, and plain passages from Scripture.[3]

Peter was not very keen on answering him at all, and would much have preferred a request for assistance in overcoming the vices of the age—"for these enemies are always with us, while Jews have now almost ceased to exist".[4] However, it seemed unworthy for an ecclesiastic to be asked to help, and to refuse to do so. So he writes these two treatises, very conscious of his superiority to Honestus in mental and literary equipment, but sadly unconscious of his own limitations. For he certainly knew nothing of Judaism, nor of Jewish methods of argument, and even (so far as may be gathered from these two treatises) of Hebrew itself.[5]

Yet Damiani was a learned man, highly thought of in the Papal Court, and indeed has been described as "the most important and

---

[1] A. *Antilogus contra Judaeos.* B. *Dialogus inter Judaeum requirentem, et Christianum e contrario respondentem.* The first complete edition of the works of Peter Damiani was drawn up by Constantine Caietan and published at Bassani, 1783. The two little treatises may be found in vol. iii. coll. 23–40 and 41–50. They were copied (very inaccurately) by Migne, *P.L.* cxlv. coll. 41–58 and 57–68. As Caietan's columns are the shorter and are enumerated also by Migne it has seemed well to refer to them only.

[2] "Charissime frater Honeste" (col. 50).

[3] "Rationalibus argumentis...evidentissimis sacrae Scripturae testimoniis."

[4] "Jam de terra pene deleti sunt" (col. 23).

[5] Jos. Kleinerman indeed thinks he knew Hebrew, and gives three or four references, but none to our treatises (*Dam. Petrus, Leben und Wirkung,* 1882, p. 206).

persistent champion of the Church in the eleventh century".[1] He had been born in Ravenna 1007, was Cardinal-Bishop of Ostia 1058–1062, and was to die at Fuenza in 1072, on a mission to his native city. Now, when he wrote these two treatises—or rather these two Parts of his one Answer—he was, presumably, in the prime of life, though the only indication of the date of writing seems to be his assertion that more than a thousand years had elapsed since the Jews had had a king, i.e. since the death of Herod (col. 28).

I. A REPLY TO THE JEWS

After saying that faith is the basis of all virtues, and also that controversy with Jews must not be undertaken out of vainglory or the love of strife, but only in the hope that the opponent may receive the spiritual benefit of conversion, Damiani reminds Honestus of St Paul's words. For in 2 Tim. ii. 24–26 the Apostle urges the Lord's servant to be *apt to teach*. He continues: Now almost all the books of the Old Testament bear witness to Christ, and without wasting words we will give some of the *testimonia*. But as an arrow flies straighter to its mark if this be set up first, we introduce a Jewish objector (col. 24).

The subjects of the First Treatise are the Trinity and the Incarnation. To prove the former (this is still part of his Introduction) he quotes the ordinary texts, and says nothing new about them. With chapter 1 he turns definitely to the Incarnation ("Concerning Christ, who is the Son of God"). Here again the usual texts appear. But there are others of more interest. Isa. lv. 11: *Mv Word shall not return unto Me void*. For, says Damiani, God would not say this of a temporary word. He was speaking of the Word by Whom earth and sky and sea were made.

Again, Damiani is like Pseudo-Augustine[2] in quoting Hab. iii. 5: *Before His face shall the Word go, and shall go out in the fields.* And, again, Hab. iii. 18: *But I...will rejoice in God, my Jesus.*[3] After

---

[1] "Der bedeutendste und ausdauerndste Streiter der Kirche im elften Jahrhundert" (*R.G.G.* 1909, i. 1956). His spiritual earnestness and his high significance in the Church life of his time may be seen best in Dr J. P. Whitney's study of "Peter Damiani and Humbert" (*Hildebrandine Essays*, 1932, pp. 95–142).

[2] See *de Symbolo*, xiii, with my note there (*vide supra*, p. 324).

[3] The Hebrew is *in the God of my salvation* (*b'elohe yish'i*). But the LXX reads *in God my Saviour* (ἐν θεῷ τῷ σωτῆρί μου), which by an easy transition became in the Vulg. *in Deo Jesu meo.*

quoting Baruch iii. 35–37 as usual,[1] Damiani says triumphantly: "If, as you assert, Christ is not God, show me from your books when God appeared on earth after the Law was given to Jacob (*v.* 36), and was conversant with men (*v.* 37). But if you cannot find this, you must confess that you are wrong in everything."

To show that Christ must have come before now, he quotes Daniel: *When the Holy of holies shall have come, anointing will cease.* "You will say, 'The Holy of holies has not yet come, (therefore) Messiah has not yet come. But He will come.' If so, show me the anointing (that you still have). But if, as is the fact, your anointing has ceased (for you no longer have temple or king or priest), you must acknowledge that the *Holy of holies* has come."[2] Then, after adducing Isa. xlvi. 11–13, he claims the testimony of Jacob in Gen. xlix. 10 (col. 28). When too did you see *your life hanging in front of you* (Deut. xxviii. 66),[3] save when, as you wagged your head in front of the cross, you said: *He saved others, himself he cannot save,* etc. (Mark xv. 29–32). On Ps. xxii. 16 Damiani writes: "if thou knowest not, O Jew (who is meant), He is thy bullock which was then being sacrificed in thy presence on the altar of the Cross. But, although thy deserts required this, He is not yet being eaten by thee. As in fact Moses says against thee in Deut. xxviii. 31: *Let thine ox be sacrificed in thy presence, and thou not eat thereof.* He, again, was thine ass, of whom Moses says, *Let thine ass be carried off in thy sight and not be restored to thee.* For our Redeemer is rightly in figure called an ass, who, as it were, put His back to bear the load of our iniquity, as the Prophet says (Isa. liii. 4): *He Himself bare our sins.* And there too is fitly added: *Let thy sheep be given to thine enemies, and there be none to help thee* (Deut. xxviii. 31). By these *sheep* the Apostles are meant, for their innocency, and because although they were Israelites, they were handed over to another people; as is said in Acts xiii. 46: *Lo, we are turned to the Gentiles*" (col. 29).

Further, in Isa. xlv. 13–15 the Lord of Hosts is speaking and says, *Thou art God.* Thus it is plain that the Person of the Father is speaking to the Son. And when He also says *God is in Thee,* and *Thou art a God that hidest Thyself,* He is plainly pointing out the human nature of our Redeemer. For in Christ Jesus, as our Apostle says, *dwelleth all the fulness of the Godhead bodily* (Col. ii. 9).

[1] See Index.

[2] The passage quoted from "Daniel" seems to be a vague reminiscence of Dan. ix. 24–26, but evidently it already existed in some book before Damiani quoted it.   [3] See Cyprian, *Testimonia,* ii. 20 (*supra,* p. 62).

So all nations are to be converted to faith in Christ; see Isa. xlv. 22 *sq.*, and other passages.

Now that the human nature and the Divine were to be present in one Mediator is clear. See Jer. xxiii. 5 *sq.*: *And this is the Name which they shall call Him, the Lord our Righteous One.* See also Isa. xlv. 8 and elsewhere (col. 30). Obadiah 18 is quoted, and explained as meaning, The House of Jacob and of Joseph (i.e. the Church) is inflamed by the fire of the Holy Spirit, and then burns up the house of Esau like chaff, purging it from the concupiscence of this present age to long for its Creator. *I have come to send fire on the earth, and what would I, save that it blazes* (Luke xii. 49) (col. 31).

The second chapter is devoted to the subject of Christ being the Stone—about which the present writer's note in his Justin Martyr's *Dialogue with Trypho*, lxxvi. 1, may be consulted. Here Damiani explains *cut out without hands* as meaning that He was born of an undefiled Virgin[1] (col. 31). He points out further that David died long before Isaiah prophesied that he was to be given as *witness of the people*,[2] etc. (lv. 3 *sq.*), so that the words cannot refer to him personally but to Messiah. Similarly Mal. i. 1 and Ps. lxxii. 1, 5 refer to the call of the Gentiles, and not to Solomon but to Christ (col. 32).

In the third chapter "the errors of the Jews are refuted", but only those that refer to the Incarnation, the others being reserved for the Second Treatise. Zech. vi. 12, *Behold, the man whose Name is the Dawn* (Oriens), is interpreted of Christ; as also in iii. 8, *And the seven eyes on the one Stone* (iii. 9), of the gifts of the Holy Spirit (col. 34). On Ps. lxxxvii. 5: *Mother Zion shall say, A man, and a man was made in her, and the Most High Himself founded her*, Damiani asks, Who is this *Most High* who is called both *man* and *Most High*? Turn over all the pages of Scripture, if you will, and weigh the fact that the term is used everywhere of God, and nowhere of a mere man. Hence it refers here to Him who is both God and man. He must have founded the city before the man was born in it. But who else could found it, and then Himself be born there, save our Redeemer? A curious and very far-fetched example of Damiani's use of mystical interpretation!

---

[1] "Sine opere complectentium, de incorrupta Virgine procreatus."

[2] "Testem populi." Is this a copyist's mistake for *populis* (Vulg. LXX), or another reading based on the Hebrew, where "peoples" is the second substantive answering to our genitive?

The fourth chapter continues the proof of Christ being the Son of God, beginning with an appeal which in its form[1] recalls that of the early Plays: "Wilt thou, Jesus, son of Sirach, be silent?" Four or five verses of Ecclesiasticus are quoted. After xxiv. 23 b–27 he says: "Ah, that is one testimony about Christ, good Jesus (son of Sirach); give us another of the same sort."[2] Then follow xliii. 23, 26, 28: *In His Word the wind was hushed; by His Thought He stilled the deep; and the Lord Jesus planted it....Because of Him the end of the journey was completed, and in His Word all things were summed up.*[3] Damiani naturally makes much of these verses (col. 35). So also he quotes xlvii. 11: "Christus (Vulg. Dominus) purgavit" (col. 36).

On Isa. xvi. 1, *Send the Lamb, O Lord*, Damiani points out that the Immaculate Lamb came from Ruth, who was of Moab.[4] And of course he quotes Dan. iii. 25: *And the form of the fourth is like the Son of God*—"See, O Jew, you have *the Son of God*. Why do you strive any longer to deny the Son of God? Speak! Reply! What can be said more clearly, more plainly about the Son of God, than to say *the Son of God*? But if you have now no objection to make against this, and can find no escape, yield up! Hand yourself over to the Conqueror right humbly, and acknowledge that you are overcome and utterly vanquished."

Similarly with Dan. ix. 25, 26 a: *After sixty weeks Christ shall be slain.* "What can be said more openly, or in clearer language, about the death of Christ, than that *Christ shall be slain*? This is no hidden and mystical figure of speech, no dark saying, but certainly open; history is now being told, though its facts be still in the future" (col. 37). He goes on to say that *vv.* 23 b, 24 foretell the exact time, as Tertullian shows.[5] He then quotes Isa. liii (col. 37).

After quoting Wisd. ii. 12–22, and Lam. iv. 20 (*The breath of our nostrils, Christ the Lord, was taken in our sins*), he cites Job xvi. 9–12, 14, adding: "Now evidently all this was outside the direct experience

---

[1] *Vide supra*, p. 323. on Pseudo-Augustine, *c. Judaeos*, etc. c. xiii.

[2] "Ecce, bone Jesu, unum de Christo testimonium, da consequenter et aliud."

[3] *Jesus planted it* (see R.V. marg.). In the LXX it was doubtless originally ἐφύτευσεν ἐν αὐτῇ νήσους, and so the Hebrew. But ℵ A B C have ἐφύτευσεν αὐτὴν Ἰησοῦς.

[4] Cf. Peter of Blois, x (*infra*, p. 403).

[5] "Lege Tertullianum." See his *Adv. Jud.* viii (*vide supra*, p. 47). Cf. Peter of Cluny, *Adv. Jud.*, *P.L.* clxxxix. 565 *sq.* (*infra*, p. 387).

of blessed Job, but is found, more clearly than the light itself, to have been fulfilled in Christ." Then, "I marvel, O Jew, that although you see so many rays of heavenly constellations shining before you, such dense darkness of utter blindness cannot find any place even in your eyeless sockets." You should at least follow blind Balaam (Num. xxiv. 15), who falling down has his eyes open, and says that the *Star shall arise out of Jacob*, etc. (Num. xxiv. 17). So ends the first treatise.

II. A DIALOGUE BETWEEN AN ENQUIRING JEW AND A CHRISTIAN ANSWERING HIS QUESTIONS[1]

This part of Damiani's reply to Honestus consists of Ten Questions and Answers, with a long Epilogue. It is a conscientious, and sometimes even thoughtful, attempt to solve the difficulty: Why, if Christ came not to annul the Law but to fulfil it, are the ceremonies of the Law neglected by Christians?

The First Question, naturally enough, refers to Circumcision. The Answer is twofold: Christ fulfilled by His resurrection its figurative meaning of stripping off the carnal life; and again Baptism in a sense corresponds to it, for by baptism we profess expectation of what will happen in our own resurrection. Thus its spiritual meaning is still observed.

Question Two is about the Sabbath. We keep the true Sabbath of that spiritual rest which Christ offered us in Matt. xi. 28 *sq.* (col. 41).

The Third Question deals with the Dietary Laws. Here also what they represented was fulfilled by Christ. All uncleanness in human ethics must be put aside, and all unclean persons avoided.

The Fourth Question refers to Animal Sacrifices. The Answer is: Whatever they meant typically was completely fulfilled in the offering of the Lamb. Besides, everyone knows that the sacrifices were only appointed for a disobedient people, to keep them from worshipping idols[2] (col. 42).

Question Five. Why does not a Christian man observe Unleavened Bread? Because the leaven of the old life is purged away, and the meaning of the new dough (*conspersio*) is being fulfilled.

---

[1] *Opusc.* iii. coll. 41–50.
[2] See *The Trophies of Damascus*, i. iii. 2 (*supra*, p. 164).

Question Six. If Christ came to fulfil the Law why does not the Christian celebrate the Passover with the blood of the Paschal lamb? Because the true Lamb has come, and we mark His blood, not on the lintels of our houses, but on the bowels of the inner man.

The Seventh Question is: Why do you not keep the New Moon? The Answer is, Because Christ fulfilled the whole object of its appointment. It represents the new creation in a man, of which the Apostle says 2 Cor. v. 17.

The Eighth Question is: Why does not a Christian observe the ceremonial Washings which the Law enjoins? Because he possesses the reality of which they were but the shadow (Rom. vi. 4).

Question Nine. Why do not Christians keep the holy Feast of Tabernacles? The Answer is: "The Tabernacle of God is the Society of Christian people, and since the Tabernacle of which you speak prefigured Holy Church, the mere sign is no longer of any account."

The Tenth Question. If Christ did not wish to annul the Law but to fulfil it, why does not a Christian observe the seventh year of Release?[1] Answer: The Truth and very Wisdom of God, who teaches the Angels in heaven, and yet came to teach men on earth, bade His disciples to understand spiritually what had formerly been ordered to be observed carnally, by way of figure. And so with the seventh day, the seventh year, the year of Jubilee—all indicate spiritual rest (col. 43). And again, when the true year of Jubilee comes, the Trumpet will sound (1 Thess. iv. 16), and we shall all return to our own possessions, i.e. we shall receive our bodies again.

After all, Scripture itself teaches you that the things ordered in the Law were only shadows, not the things themselves. See Ex. xxvii. 8: "What Moses then saw in the Mount is Holy Church, the very truth of reality itself." Damiani works this thought out in details (col. 44).

The last six columns (45–50) form a long "Epilogue", in which the author proposes to set forth summarily the testimonies of the Prophets.[2] In fact he quotes many of the well-known passages at their face value as verbal predictions of details of our Lord's life, from His Birth to His Ascension, and of the outpouring of the gifts of the Holy Spirit, and of the future Judgment. For as Ps. xcvi. 10

[1] The text seems to be faulty here, but the general sense is plain.
[2] "Prophetica testimonia."

says: *The Lord reigned from the Tree,*[1] so the end of the same psalm says of Him: *He shall judge the whole world in equity, and the peoples in His truth* (col. 48).

So then, O Jew, you plainly ought to believe. What is the great sin that has brought on you punishment for so long a time and on so many persons? Read Josephus, for there you will find that in that revenge for the death of Christ, which Titus and Vespasian took, a million Jews were slain, and eleven hundred thousand were taken captive[2] (col. 49). What was the cause of such awful punishment? Nought else save the death of Christ, and your continued unwillingness after committing this crime to return to the fountain of life.

The book closes with a solemn exhortation. Hear my counsel; leave your error; turn to faith in Christ and be baptised. "Yet since perhaps I can avail more with you by invoking God than by preaching—May the God of thy fathers throw off from thy heart the old veil of ignorance, drive away the darkness of errors, and bathe thee in the new light of the knowledge of Himself, for He promises by His prophet: *If the number of the children of Israel be as the sand of the sea, the remnant of Israel shall be saved* (Isa. x. 22)."

In a few closing words to Honestus Damiani says that he has purposely avoided flowers of speech and dialectic subtleties, in fact all ornaments of secular wisdom, out of respect for Honestus being engaged in so much secular business. He prays Almighty God to keep him, his greatly beloved brother, from the snares of all unseen foes, and to bring him safe out of all this present contest into the realms above (col. 50).

Of what value then to us is Damiani's whole Treatise? To speak quite frankly its value is very slight if it be regarded as a storehouse from which arguments may be drawn for controversy with Jews of to-day. The texts of Scripture are of force only for Christians, and even to them only so far as they recognise in them a secondary and "mystical" meaning. Like the Haggadoth of the Midrash they are often interesting, and one cannot say dogmatically that in inspiring the language of the Bible the Holy Spirit never intended to suggest more than what the plain, grammatical and strictly exegetical exposition can convey. He to whom past, present and future are all equally known may have seen fit to indicate distant

[1] See Justin Martyr's *Dialogue with Trypho*, lxxiii. 1 (*supra*, p. 34). Cf. the note on Isidore, *c. Judaeos*, I. xxxv (*vide supra*, Appendix, p. 287).
[2] Cf. Josephus, *War*, VI. ix. 3 (§ 420), where the numbers differ slightly.

truths concealed under present information. They are certainly often visible to a studious eye. But one cannot say more. On the other hand, when Damiani points out that the written Law and its various parts were fulfilled in Christ, and are now represented in deepest and truest meaning by Christian life and Christian Sacraments, his arguments are not out of date. In any case we can agree with his closing words, that more potent than any argument with other men is earnest prayer for them.

CHAPTER XLII

GILBERT CRISPIN, ABBOT OF WESTMINSTER

A DISCUSSION OF A JEW WITH A CHRISTIAN CONCERNING THE CHRISTIAN FAITH[1]

PROBABLY BEFORE A.D. 1098

The Disputation "is not cast in the form of a conversational dialogue, but consists of seven set speeches on either side; those of the Jew, who raises the objections, being much shorter than those of the Christian, who has to make somewhat elaborate replies, and also to carry on a counter-attack. The whole treatment is eminently fair: the difficulties propounded by the Jew are genuine difficulties, and to some of them a fully satisfactory reply cannot easily be given. There is no loss of temper on either side, and at the end there is no token of surrender and no note of triumph."[2]

So writes the late Dean of Wells, and one is glad to have the unbiassed opinion of so first-rate a scholar. Would that the latter part of his remarks were true of all the documents which we are examining!

Prefixed to the treatise is a short letter to Archbishop Anselm, hoping for his approval of it. Gilbert says that it contains a statement of what a certain Jew when discussing the subject with him brought against our faith out of his Law, and the replies that he made. "I know not where he was born, but he had been trained at Mainz, and had a good knowledge both of the Law and even of our own writings, and possessed both practice and skill in the Scriptures and in arguments against us." He often came to see me on business, and we often talked on religion, and one day, when we had more leisure than usual, some who were present asked me

---

[1] *Disputatio Judaei cum Christiano de Fide Christiana* (Migne, *P.L.* coll. 1005–1036). See also J. Armitage Robinson, *Gilbert Crispin, Abbot of Westminster—a study of the Abbey under Norman Rule*, 1911, especially pp. 52–54, 62–67. Gilbert was of a good Norman family called Crispinus because of its "hair which stood on end, bristling up like pine branches". He had been trained at Bec, was with Archbishop Lanfranc at Canterbury from 1079, and was appointed Abbot of Westminster in 1085. For the date of our treatise (before A.D. 1098) see coll. 1023 (*infra*, p. 378) and J. A. R. p. 64. He died Dec. 6, 1117.

[2] J. A. R. *op. cit.* p. 62.

to write down the discussion. I have done so, purposely mentioning neither my name nor his. I will make such corrections as
you suggest. "Still, a certain Jew, who was then in London,[1]
turned by the aid of the mercy of God to the Christian faith at
Westminster, professed faith in Christ in the presence of all, and
asked for and received baptism. And when he was baptised he
then and there consecrated himself to the service of God, and
became a monk and remained on with us."[2]

Thus then did the Jew challenge me.

The Jew. I would that you would confer with me patiently, and
tell me by what arguments of reason, and by what authority of
Holy Scripture, you blame us Jews because we observe the Law
which was given us by God, and follow implicitly Moses our Lawgiver. For if the Law is good, and was given by God, it should be
kept. Why then do you drive us out, who observe it, with cudgels
as though we were dogs, and chase us everywhere? But if the Law
is not to be observed, then blame Moses, and tell us how we are
to escape the curse of Deut. xxvii. 26. You Christians choose this
and that part of the Law of your own sweet will.[3]

The Christian. Right! So also do I ask for patience on your part.
But be willing to yield to the testimony of Scripture. Then I am
ready to argue with you, but more for the sake of truth and love of
yourself than from any love of argument.[4]

First, we Christians grant that the Law is good, and was given
by God, and is to be observed in its own time, but not necessarily
in its letter, because this is often self-contradictory. For example,
God made everything good (Gen. i. 31), yet afterwards some
animals are said to be unclean! And among these are some which
are not harmful as food. There is therefore some hidden meaning
(*sacramentum*).[5] Sometimes too the Law tells us of things that were
to take place in the future. See Gen. xlix. 10. "At length therefore
in times preordained by God, the Mediator of God and men came,
the Man Jesus Christ, opening our intelligence that we might
understand the Scriptures, and solving the deep mysteries which
had been spoken concerning Him in the Law and the Prophets.
And on Him you ought to believe."[6]

---

[1] Not therefore a Londoner bred and born. It is not likely that he was in
reality the Jew from Mainz.

[2] Gilbert's addition of this example is curious. Did he wish the Archbishop
to know that whatever criticisms he might have to make, Gilbert's arguments
had been effectual in one case at least?　　　　　　　　　[3] Col. 1007 A, B.

[4] Col. 1008 A.　　　　　　[5] Col. 1008 B.　　　　　　[6] Col. 1010 C.

The Jew. If things ordered in the Law are, as you say, for different times, how shall Ps. lxii. 11 stand: *God spake once?* What does it matter *why* God says this animal is clean and that unclean? He commands, and we must obey.[1] "Let us keep the letter, let us keep also what the letter signifies", e.g. abstain from pork, and also from what (if anything) is signified by pork, viz. sin.[2]

But you say that Christ is the author of a new religion, and a new Law. "I believe that Christ was a prophet at least of surpassing prestige in every virtue, and I will believe Christ's words. But believe in him I neither do nor will, because I believe in none save God, and in God as One (cf. Deut. vi. 4). God is One, not three-fold (*triplex*) as you Christians say while you deny it, and deny it while you say it;...'Not three Gods but One God'."[3]

Again, Isa. ii. 2, 3 speaks of going up to the *Mount of the Lord, to the House of the God of Jacob* But some of you say: "Let us go to the house of Peter, or of Martin." Also Isa. ii. 4 speaks of war ceasing, and it has not![4]

The Christian. Yes! What *God spake once* holds good, for Christ came not to abolish the Law but to fulfil it. *Not one jot or tittle,* etc., Matt. v. 18. "The Law forbids murder; Christ, even anger and hatred." One may abstain from pork if one likes, and indeed many of us abstain from all flesh. But what is really meant by pork is uncleanness.[5]

Every one knows that "the house of Peter" does not mean that it is consecrated to Peter. It is consecrated to God.[6] Again, it is easier to beat a sword into a ploughshare than to curb one's temper. Yet one does see many proud people of high position leave everything and serve God.[7] Again, that peace of which you speak existed in the primitive Church, and endured for a long time and over a wide extent, but we were told that fierce tribulation would arise, and this has already begun.[8]

Further, while I grant that we may not believe otherwise than in God and one God only, yet you ought to believe in Christ, for we do not call a man God; because "it is certain that Christ is God and man" Gilbert then expounds the doctrine of the Incarnation. By the by, he says, we do not speak of God as threefold (*triplicitatem*) but as a Trinity (*trinitatem*)[9]

---

[1] So *Yoma* 67 b of certain commands (*chuqqôth*); see Rashi there.
[2] Col. 1011 A. The Jew's standpoint here is that of Philo.   [3] Col. 1011 B.
[4] Col. 1012 A, B.   [5] Col. 1013 A.   [6] Col. 1014 B.   [7] Col. 1015 B.
[8] Col. 1016 D.   [9] Coll. 1017 A–1018 A. Cf. col. 1026 A.

The Jew appeals to James i. 17, and asks how there could be such a change (*alteratio*) as that God could become a man, the Creator a creature. And be born! For God forbid that you should say there was anything of mere appearance in connexion with God.[1] He then turns to Isa. vii. 14 and to the perpetual virginity of the Blessed Virgin.[2]

The Christian quotes "Jeremiah" (Baruch iii. 35–37), and Ezek. xliv. 2 of the Perpetual Virginity (*porta clausa*), and other passages.[3] With reference to the Fall he says that by it the Enemy (the Devil) acquired juridical rights over sinful men, but that God by the Incarnation satisfied those rights, thus making Atonement. In His death the entrance to Paradise was unlocked; the flaming sword that turned every way was removed.[4]

The Jew. "You do violence to Scripture, and wrest it to maintain your faith." Ezekiel refers to a gate, not a woman! You say Christ was of Abraham's seed, and yet not of human generation!

The Christian. Ezek. xliv. 2 cannot be understood literally. How can God go through a gate? The verse must refer to the Incarnation, and the Perpetual Virginity. For otherwise Christ would not be free from original sin. And the words are: *The gate shall be shut, because it will be shut to a man, and no man shall pass through it.*[5] Similarly Isaiah says: *The earth* (viz. the Virgin's womb)[6] *was opened, and brought forth the Saviour.* As for the Holy Ghost, Ps. xxxiii. 6 says: *By the Word of the Lord were the heavens made, and all the host of them by the Spirit of His mouth.*[7]

[1] Col. 1018 D: "Absit enim ut circa Deum aliquid phantasticum fuisse dixeris." The Jew means that Docetism is very unworthy of God. It would be a pretence and a sham.

[2] Col. 1019 B.   [3] Coll. 1019 C–1021 A.

[4] Coll. 1021 B–1024 A. This seems to be Gilbert's meaning, and, if it be, he could hardly have written this treatise if he had seen Anselm's *Cur Deus Homo* published in 1098, for that insists that the Devil had no rights over fallen man. Yet it may be argued that he would have stated the Devil's "feudal" claims more strongly if he had not been in close touch with Anselm. The strongest sentence perhaps is: "Jure amisit eam jurisdictionem, quam peccato primi hominis in hominem primum ejusque posteritatem obtinuerat" (col. 1023 B).

[5] "Porta clausa erit, quia viro clausa erit, nec vir transibit per eam." Cf. Pseudo-Gregory of Nyssa, iii (*supra*, p. 127). Perhaps the most beautiful use of this text is in Cynewulf's *Elene* (? *c.* A.D. 800) in C. W. Kennedy's translation (1910), p. 162. Although Cynewulf has embodied the chief Old Testament passages used against the Jews his poems have not Jews so definitely in mind as to require examination for our purpose.

[6] Probably a Midrashic explanation of Isa. xlv. 8.

[7] Col. 1025 D.

The Jew retorts politely but severely: "If it is right for Christians to read the Scriptures in this fashion, and interpret them of Christ, you will find many more passages which you can somehow or other interpret in this way. We do not know your sacred books, and perchance you say that you have many passages which we do not believe are contained in our scriptures." You quote from Jeremiah (Baruch iii. 37). But Jeremiah neither said it nor wrote it. Similarly Isaiah did not say *Virgin*, but *one hidden* (*abscondita*), and anyhow neither he nor any other prophet spoke of her perpetual virginity.[1]

The Christian. We do not need any false arguments. Our Scriptures came from you, by means of the Seventy Elders. And as for Jeremiah, Baruch *wrote from his mouth* (Jer. xxxvi. 4).[2]

The Jew. We know only of the Seventy Elders in Moses' time, and only the Hebrew books. As for other things, you have not got them from us.

The Christian. The Seventy we mean are those sent by the Jews to Ptolemy, King of Egypt, to translate the Hebrew Scriptures into Greek, and you must grant that their work was acknowledged by you Jews, and we only received it from you.[3] As to Isa. vii. 14, where was the marvel and sign if the word translated *Virgin* means only *hidden*, i.e. a girl of suitable age? And what is the literal meaning of a boy eating bread and butter and honey?[4]

Gilbert then expounds Isa. liii. 1–10, and quotes other well-known passages.[5] He then quotes Ps. xcvii. 7: *Ashamed be all who adore graven images.*

The Jew. You are condemned out of your own mouth! For Christians *adore graven images.* And he goes on to describe pictures of a cross with quaint mediaeval symbols, and of God as seated on a throne with outstretched hand, and figures of an eagle, a man, a calf, and a lion.[6]

The Christian. If the Law forbade all images, then Moses sinned. See Ex. xxv. 19 and elsewhere, and for the four animals see Ezek. i. 10. Besides, although we make pictures and sculptures we do not worship them with such worship as we pay to God. We use the words "worship", "adore" in various meanings, as when Bathsheba "adoravit regem" (1 Kings i. 16). When then a Christian "adores" the Cross, "he with the Divine worship of true religion adores in the Cross the Passion of Christ".[7]

---

[1] Col. 1027 A.   [2] Col. 1027 D.   [3] Col. 1028 A, B.
[4] Coll. 1029 C–1030 A.   [5] Coll. 1031 A–1033 D.
[6] Col. 1034 B.   [7] Col. 1036 A.

So Gilbert comes to his concluding words: Read the Scriptures again and again, and you will see that what I have said is true. Look especially at the signs by which we are to recognise the true Christ when He comes. "For He of whom it was promised that He should be sent, has come, having been sent, as the signs by which He was foretold prove—Jesus Christ, the expectation of the Gentiles, to whom be honour and dominion throughout the ages of eternity. Amen."[1]

What can one say of Gilbert's production? He has given us a nice little tract, free from all bitterness, and he has done his best to be fair to his opponent. Yet, save for his inclusion of the Jew's confession of the high personal ethics of Jesus (col. 1011 B), he has not gone outside the common rut of evidence supposed in his day to be likely to win Jews to our Faith. He is still in the mechanical stage of proving by reason that the Old Testament foretold Jesus and no other. And, further, with the above exception, he says nothing of what appeals so much to us now, the character of our Lord, and the power which they receive who enlist in His service. In other words, Gilbert belonged to his own time, not to ours. But this suggests also that he was not a man of any great spiritual power, or one who, like many mystics, had become inebriated in fellowship with Christ. Otherwise he could hardly have failed to write more impressively.

[1] Col. 1036 B.

CHAPTER XLIII

PSEUDO-GILBERT CRISPIN

A DISCUSSION BETWEEN THE CHURCH AND THE SYNAGOGUE[1]

c. A.D. 1150?

Another little tract has for some unknown reason been attributed to Gilbert Crispin. It has nothing in common with the genuine *Disputatio*, save that it is, comparatively speaking, of a kindly tone, though here both disputants express themselves very strongly! It contains nothing to mark the date of its composition, except that it evidently knows the Athanasian Creed, which is not surprising. The fact that it is attributed to Crispin suggests that it was written not very long after his death. We may therefore place it about A.D. 1150.

"From the time that the fig-tree flourished under which Nathanael stayed hidden, began the misery of the Synagogue." She stood deriding God on the Cross, while the Church waited with Him, shared His Passion and Death and Resurrection, clothed with the marriage garment, and affianced with the ring of faith.[2] "For", says the Church, "me anulo isto sibi desponsavit virginem"—"with that ring He betrothed me as a virgin to Himself"

The Church and the Synagogue argue, the Church affirming that the Law condemns the Jews for not keeping the Law. But the Synagogue urges that if Christ were God He would not act contrary to the Law. Then the Synagogue bewails the errors of her daughter, the Church, which has been deceived by magic arts. She, however, bids the Synagogue remember how the God whom she betrayed by Judas blessed and enriched her in the person of Jacob. The Synagogue cries: That God whom the Nazarenes worship never enriched me! Yes, answers the Church, it was indeed none other but He. Where, then, did you learn this? asks the Synagogue.

---

[1] *Disputatio Ecclesiae et Synagogae* in Martène and Durand, *Thesaurus Anecdotum*, 1717. Vol. v. coll. 1497–1506. It has not been reprinted by Migne.
[2] "Et anulo subarrata fidei."

The Church. You have the Law, I the Gospel; repent, while you have the time.

The Synagogue. Nay, do thou return! It is fitting that a daughter ever obeys her Mother.

The Church. I cannot obey thee, for thou hast bid me drink the cup of death.

The Synagogue. Will you teach me! You are drunk with the wine of the marriage in Galilee.

The Church. Satan has made you drunk, with the false libations of the Baalim. And so you suffered under Titus (col. 1503 c).

Then comes the serious Jewish objection against Christianity, that, for all its claims to produce holiness, its rulers and clergy do not show this in their lives. The Church, alas, can only reply with a *Tu quoque*: "There is no counting thy avarice! There is no limit to thy roguery!"[1] This tract, it will be noticed, makes very little use of the Old Testament.

The Synagogue then asks, What is it that God is? The Church replies: He is only spiritual, the very Light on which the angels desire to gaze. Look at the Sun, and learn that the substance of fire represents God the Father; the Splendour, the Son; the Heat, the Holy Spirit—"Lo! poor blind Mother, you here have what God is!"[2]

At once the harsh tone of the Synagogue towards her daughter is changed into tender love, and she confesses: "I was ignorant, for I understood not that God was this. I pray thee for full enlightenment."[3]

Yet "show me how the Son of God became incarnate". After a very brief exposition of what the Incarnation really means the Synagogue asks: "Since the Father is God, the Son is God, the Holy Ghost is God, it seems to me that there are Three incarnate, and Three have taken flesh." The Church shows the falsity of this argument, and the Synagogue accepts the Truth.[4]

That is all the tract—brevity itself. Neither is it powerful, but only pleasing, which, confessedly, is much in its favour. Was it ever intended, one wonders, to be complete? Or was it a

---

[1] "Non est numerus tuae avaritiae, nec finis tuae malitiae."

[2] Col. 1505 A: "Ecce habes mater caeca et misera, quid sit Deus."

[3] "Nescivi nec intellexi sic esse Deum. Peto a te illuminari" (col. 1505 B).

[4] Col. 1506 D.

Prologue to some longer work? May it have been the case that as a minor poet to-day will write a masque for a Commemoration at a seminary for young ladies, so this graceful little tract was originally but the Introduction to a Drama, perhaps a Passion Play, or, more probably, a Miracle Play in which the Nativity was all-important?

CHAPTER XLIV

PETER THE VENERABLE, NINTH ABBOT OF CLUNY[1]

A TREATISE AGAINST THE CHRONIC OBSTINACY OF THE JEWS[2]

BEFORE A.D. 1143

"You are the only man in our time who has slain the three chief enemies of our holy Faith, I mean the Jews, the heretics, and the Mohammedans, with the sword of the word of God."[3]

So wrote Peter of Poitiers about A.D. 1143 to his superior, Peter, Abbot of Cluny, afterwards designated the Venerable.[4] For, as Peter of Cluny himself says, even if his opponents should not themselves be converted, yet at least a Doctor of the Church ought to think of the needs of the weaker brethren, and do his best to protect them. In this desire, as he tells us, he was but following Augustine, who wrote against Julian the heretic, Faustus the heathen Manichaean, and also against the Jews.[5] And so, in fact, did Peter of Cluny. For, though he was ignorant of Arabic, he went to Spain in 1141, and got the Qoran translated for him into Latin, and then composed a treatise showing up its faults.

Only two books out of the four have come down to us, and probably experts would tell us that these are quite valueless for controversy with Islam to-day. But the good man did his best.[6] As to the Heretics he wrote a longish treatise against the followers

---

[1] Born 1092 or 1094; died A.D. 1156.

[2] *Tractatus adversus Judaeorum inveteratam duritiem*, Migne, *P.L.* clxxxix. 507–650. It was written before A.D. 1143.

[3] "Solus enim vos estis nostris temporibus, qui tres maximos sanctae Christianitatis hostes, Judaeos dico et haereticos et Saracenos, divini verbi gladio trucidastis" (col. 661 c).

[4] The title "Venerable" when formally granted is the first stage in Beatification (Hastings, *E.R.E.* ii. 443 b; iii. 210 a), but Frederick Barbarossa (*ob.* 1190) was the first to call him the Venerable (Hauck, *Realencyclopädie*, 1904, xv. 226)

[5] Col. 651 A.

[6] It is interesting to note that he already knows that Mohammed derived his doctrines partly from Judaism. For one of the *capitula* (col. 661) says that Book iv, ch. 5 used heresies "praecipue Thalmuth exsecrandi libri Judaeorum".

of Peter de Bruis,[1] a priest who had been burnt by the populace at St Gilles in A.D. 1132.[2] We ourselves can hardly call them heretics. For they seem to have been quite orthodox about Christian theology proper, and to have denied only such matters as the rightfulness of Infant Baptism, the need of special Buildings for Worship, the Adoration of Crosses, the Sacrifice of the Mass,[3] and especially Prayers for the Dead. They were, in other words, much like many of our English Nonconformists. But all these things seemed to the mediaeval Church to be shockingly Antichristian in both practice and theory.

However, our business is only with Peter the Venerable's work against the Jews.

"You, you Jews, I say, do I address; you who till this very day deny the Son of God—how long, poor wretches, will ye not believe the truth? How long will ye fight against God? How long before your hearts of iron are softened?"[4] It is not a very tactful opening for a treatise designed to win Jews over to the Faith! But it is only rarely that Christian writers have regarded Jews otherwise than from a level presupposed to be immeasurably higher than the Jewish, and have been able to keep out of sight their conviction that the unbelief of Jews was due to sheer obstinacy! Christian writers often lacked the knowledge, and too often even the love, which would have made their zeal effective.

Peter then says that he will refer the Jews to their own people, and to the Scriptures they had received from God, and will bring testimonies from them to which they must yield. To this plan he adheres fairly closely in his first four chapters, though with a good deal of verbiage. But the fifth he devotes to "the ridiculous and utterly foolish fables" which the Jews believe.

The first three chapters will not detain us long. For, with few exceptions, the passages that he adduces have often been before us. But occasionally he contributes new examples of exegetic ingenuity.

---

[1] *Tractatus contra Petrobrusianos*, coll. 719–850.

[2] Col. 725 A. See Neander, *Ch. Hist.* (Bohn), viii. 338–341; Hardwick, *Ch. Hist.* (*Middle Age*), 1874, p. 290.

[3] "Negat corpus Christi et sanguinem divini Verbi virtute vel sacerdotum ministerio confici; totumque inane ac supervacuum esse quidquid in altaris sacramento altaris ministri agere videntur, affirmat" (col. 987 c).

[4] "Vos ego, vos, inquam, ego convenio, O Judaei, qui usque in hodiernum diem negatis Filium Dei. Quousque, miseri, veritati non creditis? Quousque Deo repugnatis? Quousque corda ferrea non emollitis?" (col. 507 c).

Chapter I proves "That Christ is the Son of God". Among the passages is Isa. lxvi. 9: *Shall I who make others bear, Myself not bear? saith the Lord. Shall I who cause others to bring forth, Myself be barren? saith the Lord.*[1] Peter improves the occasion by adding: "For if God begat, then with reference to Him whom He begat He is necessarily Father; and the Son of God, with reference to Him who begat, is necessarily Son." It is fairly clear that Peter knew no Hebrew, or, if he did possess some smattering of it, had not the scholarly feeling to test the Vulgate by it.

Chapter II proves "That Christ is God in the proper sense of the word".[2] "Come forward, then, Holy Moses, come forward, I say, thou special friend of God." And Gen. xix. 24 is once more adduced. Finally, after quoting the predictions of Jewish writers, Peter bids his readers hear the testimony of the Sibyl prophesying from among the Gentiles, "that even by the mouth of a Gentile woman the Spirit of God may crush the foes of God".[3]

Chapter III proves "That Christ is not a temporal king, as the Jews suppose, but an everlasting and heavenly king".[4] "You dream that He will sit on David's earthly throne."[5] But "How long, ye Jews, shall this mental pig-headedness stay with you?"[6] What a contrast Zech. ix. 9 is to your expectations! Will you think of Herod! Will you accept the King of Morocco, a member of the Mohammedan sect![7]

After a long exposition of Isa. liii[8] Peter tells us of the Jewish legend that their Christ once appeared to one of their great teachers as a beggar, and then had His rags changed into splendid robes, with a sapphire and a diamond in His hands.[9] Amulo had much the same tale, but the difference in details prevents any positive assertion that Peter got his information directly from Amulo's treatise.[10]

I suppose I must continue my argument, adds Peter, though

---

[1] Col. 510 A. So, practically, the Vulgate, but not the LXX. Cf. Peter of Blois, *infra*, p. 402.

[2] Coll. 519–538 D: "Quod Christus specialiter Deus est."

[3] The whole passage seems to be based on *Sib.* viii. 256–320 (J. Geffcken, 1902, pp. 158–162).

[4] Coll. 538 D–558 C.   [5] Col. 538 D.

[6] "Quamdiu, O Judaei, hic bovinis intellectus cordibus vestris insederit?" (col. 539 D).

[7] Col. 540 D.   [8] Coll. 544 A–549 D.

[9] Coll. 549 D–550 A.

[10] Amulo, *c. Jud.* xii (*vide supra*, p. 360, with note).

really I doubt whether a Jew can be human, for he will neither yield to human reasoning, nor find satisfaction in authoritative utterances, alike Divine and Jewish. Can he be human from whose flesh the heart of stone has not yet been taken; who has not received the heart of flesh; within whom that Spirit of God has not yet been placed, for apart from that Spirit no Jew can ever be converted to Christ?[1]

It is worthy of notice that Peter has some idea of the development of revelation. For, speaking of Eternity, he says that it was not possible to bring everything at once before persons lately born into a new world, and wholly ignorant of Divine things; and he continues: "Seldom is this Eternity mentioned in the Pentateuch or Heptateuch (*Heptatico*); it is often brought before us by the Prophets; very often indeed, and very earnestly, is it proclaimed by the Gospel of Christ."[2]

"To bring this chapter to a close: either deny the temporal kingdom of Christ and reject the Scriptures, or if you dare not do that, take upon you the everlasting kingdom of the Christ we ourselves accept."

With chapter IV we come to more interesting matter. Its title is: "That Christ is not, as Jews fondly think, still to come, but has come already, at the sure and long since ordered time, for the world's salvation."[3] "Listen, I say, listen, not to any chance prophet, but to the great father of the prophets himself, the great prophet, I mean Jacob, the great patriarch";[4] and there follows a long exposition of Gen. xlix. 10.[5]

The subject involves chronology, and much therefore is made of Dan. ix. 25 *sq.*,[6] in the exposition of which Tertullian, *c. Jud.* 8, is quoted at length.[7]

The Jews urge that the term "for ever" implies the perpetuity of the Law.[8] To this Peter replies that this depends really upon the nature of the thing ordered. Moral commandments endure by their very nature; not so with others. Palestine was promised *as long as the heaven is above the earth*,[9] yet it has long since been taken away from the Jews. Again, you refer to the curse on *him who does*

---

[1] Coll. 550 D, 551 A.
[2] Col. 555 D.
[3] Coll. 558 C–602 A.
[4] Col. 558 D.
[5] Coll. 559 A–563 C.
[6] Coll. 563 C–568.
[7] Cf. Peter Damiani, *Dial.* i. 32 (*vide supra*, p. 370).
[8] Col. 574 D.
[9] Col. 581 D: "Quamdiu caelum imminet terrae"; Deut. xi. 21.

not abide in the words of this law nor performs them.[1] But there this passage refers only to you Jews, and the ceremonies were the only way by which you could be tamed to God's service.

He then says that, at any rate, the Miracles wrought by Christians ought to convince the Jews, and he mentions in particular the annual miracle of the Fire at the Holy Sepulchre. "Christ visits His sepulchre by a light sent down from heaven every year, and not on any day, but on that very day in which He lay in the tomb, He lights it up by a flash from on high."[2]

Chapter v is concerned with "The absurd and utterly foolish fables of the Jews".[3] *Man,* says the Psalmist (xlix. 20), *that is in honour, and understandeth not, is compared unto senseless beasts, and has been made like them.* This was said generally, but specially of thee, O Jew, yea of thee in particular. Take an ox or an ass, the stupidest animal there is. What difference is there from thee? An ass will hear but not understand; and so also is it with a Jew. I have already shown this in the first four chapters, but now in the fifth it will be clear, not to Christians only but to the whole wide world, that you are indeed such an animal,[4] and that I do not exceed the truth when I say so. "I lead out then a monstrous animal from its den, and show it as a laughing-stock in the amphitheatre of the whole world, in the sight of all peoples. I bring forward, thou Jew, thou brute beast, in the sight of all men, thy book, yea, I say, that book of thine, that Thalmuth of thine, that thy precious collection of doctrine, which, forsooth, is to be preferred to the books of the Prophets and all Divinely approved opinions. But do you wonder, since I am not a Jew, from what source the name of it became known to me, whence it was that it sounded on my ears? Who betrayed to me the mysteries of the Jews? Who laid bare before me your most secret and hidden doctrines? None other, I say, none other, but that very Christ whom you deny. The Truth itself laid bare your falsehoods, uncovered your disgrace, in saying: *There is nothing covered that is not to be revealed; and hidden that is not to be known* (Matt. x. 26)."[5]

Listen to your mad blasphemy! God, you say, does nought else in heaven but read the Talmud, and discuss it with the Jewish

---

[1] Col. 582 c; Deut. xxvii. 26.

[2] Col. 601 A. Our earliest authority for the Fire appears to be the monk Bernard the Wise c. A.D. 865 (Migne, *P.L.* cxxi. 572 B).

[3] Coll. 602 A–650 B: "De ridiculis atque stultissimis fabulis Judaeorum."

[4] "Te vere jumentum esse."   [5] Col. 602 A–D.

Scholars who composed it! But why should He? To become more learned? To remind Him of what He has forgotten?[1] And, pray, what kind of book is it? Of skins, or papyrus, or rags?[2]

Then follows a long quotation from the Talmud,[3] giving a detailed account of God's discussion with the Scholars about leprosy, for He said that fox-mange was leprosy, and they said it was not. After a long and heated argument they could come to no decision, but agreed to accept the opinion of R. Nehemiah. An angel was sent down and found him reading the Talmud, "which the Jews think so holy that so long as a man is reading it he cannot die". The angel of death bids him come, and he refuses, in spite of the assurance that it would be better for him in heaven. But in vain. The angel returned to heaven alone, and God bade him go again, raising a storm as of hail and stones about R. Nehemiah's head, so that the Rabbi should look away for one moment from his book. So he was caught up to heaven, and there he finds the discussion still going on. Then he shouted out, "It is clean; it is clean", meaning by this, Thou, O God, art beaten by the Jews in this discussion, because fox-mange is not leprosy, as thou didst say, but a "clean" kind of illness. So God blushed somewhat, but not daring to contradict the testimony of so great a man, playfully answered the Jews who were disputing with Him, *Naza huni benai*, i.e. My sons have defeated Me.[4]

Peter then proves at some length from Scripture the absurdity of the tale.[5] But it never occurs to him that there is any truth underlying it. For, after all, is the statement that God studies the Law quite meaningless? Must not He who gave it take a deep interest in its application to fresh needs? Is He not present in the discussions that His servants hold? May it not sometimes be the fact that old orthodoxy—the mind of God for the elders—is shown to be untrue in some particular? And may not such changes in the doctrine and practices of godly people be quite fairly

---

[1] Coll. 603 B–606 B. For various anthropomorphic representations of God's actions see the *Jew. Enc.* vi. 6 b.

[2] Col. 606 B.   [3] "Inquit Talmuth."

[4] Coll. 607 B–608 A. Cf. R. Joshua ben Levi's refusal to die, coll. 631 A–633 A (*infra*, p. 391). The inability of the Angel of Death to touch certain saints is a very common theme. Cf. *The Testament of Abraham*, Long Recension xv. Peter's story may be based on *The Letter of R. Joshua b. Levi to Rabban Gamaliel and the elders of Israel*, to be found conveniently in Eisenstein, *Ozar Midrashim*, 1915, p. 212. The Hebrew words at the end are in T.B. *Baba Mezia*, 59 b (*Ntzachuni bānay*)   [5] Coll. 608 A–617 B.

described under figurative forms? May it not be the case, in other words, that Peter the Venerable represents the crasser Western mind, which does not possess the wit or the imagination of the Oriental? Jewish "fables" are often not so inane as the first impression of them suggests.

Again, you say in your heavenly Talmud that God weeps every day, and two tears fall from His eyes into the Great Sea, and these tears are the evening lightning. He weeps for the Captivity of the Jews, and roars like a lion, beating the heaven with His feet like men treading a winepress. And He sighs like a dove as He utters His grief. And you say too that some of your doctors have heard His voice in some ruin-covered spot, as He prays daily that His pity may prevail over His anger, and that He may deal with His people in pity.[1]

But God forbid that I should answer these shameless and indecent tales, worthy of dogs and swine—as our Lord calls such people (Matt. vii. 6).

Again, do you think that story which your Talmud relates of Og the King of Bashan is really true? Yes, I know you do, and believe it is even more true than the words of the Law or the Prophets! Let it come forward then! And he repeats the story of Og and the Hoopoe, almost word for word as it is found in Peter Alphonsi.[2]

The next excerpt from the Talmud resembles the one already quoted in col. 607 B (*vide supra*, p. 389), in that R. Joshua ben Levi refuses to obey the summons of the Angel of Death, for he was studying the Talmud. God bids the Angel return and tell the Rabbi to come up and feast with Him, but he still refuses to go unless God covenants with him to grant him his desire. God unwillingly agrees, and R. Joshua ben Levi says he wishes to see the gates of Hell and of Paradise, while he is still alive. Yet he will not go unless the Angel gives him his sword, for fear that he should be slain on the way. On receiving it he accompanies the Angel, and sees in Hell the Christians and all the Canaanites, etc., Jabin, Sisera, Eglon, Nebuchadnezzar and Holophernes. But why are the Christians there? he asks. "Because they believe on the Son of

---

[1] Col. 622 A–G. This Haggada may be found in T.B. *Berakoth*, 59 a. Cf. my *Talmudic Judaism and Christianity*, 1933, p. 27 *sq.* Cf. also Peter Alphonsi, col. 550 B (*supra*, p. 237).

[2] Coll. 625 D–626 A, but the consideration of it lasts till col. 631 A. Cf. Peter Alphonsi, *Dial.*, Migne, *P.L.* clvii. 565 D–566 A (*vide supra*, p. 238).

Mary, and do not keep the Law, and especially because they do not believe the Talmud." The story is continued for some time, giving the vision of Paradise and consequent discussions with the Angel. Eventually R. Joshua ben Levi remains in Paradise (after the record of his life has been examined), having restored the sword to the Angel of Death, on condition that he does not use it to slay men in the way that he had done before.[1]

The next tale is of Eliezer and Rebecca, but is quite unprintable in English.[2] Then there follows the well-known Haggada on Ps. lxviii. 18 to the effect that when Moses went up to heaven the angels wished to kill him out of jealousy at the Law being given to him rather than to them.[3]

Two other stories follow. Three hundred camels bore the huge weight of the keys of Korah, with which he could open his treasures that were hid in different caves—yet the keys themselves were not of iron or wood, but of the dry hides of calves.[4] And again, at the burial of Jacob the sons of Esau were also burying their father, and on them and their attendants, who formed a great host, Dan threw down a stone, which slew them all. He afterwards threw it into the sea, and submerged the cities of Phitom and Ramesses, which Pharaoh rebuilt after forty years by the toil of the Israelites.[5]

Peter quotes one more out of "the huge mass of similar tales"[6] about the daughter of Jeremiah (of whom, as Peter points out, there is no mention in Scripture) and her marvellous son. But this again is too coarse to be printable.[7] Even Peter felt some qualms about repeating it. He adds a final tale to confirm it—though he confesses that this is not taken from the Talmud itself, but "from a book of no less authority"[8] It is to the effect that Nebuchad-

---

[1] Coll. 631 A–633 A. Peter's criticism of the tale (often quite interesting) lasts till col. 643 A. Peter Alphonsi omits the beginning of the story. See his *Dial.* I, Migne, *P.L.* clvii. 566 D–567 B. See also T.B. *Sabb.* 88 b; *vide supra,* p. 238.

[2] Col. 643 A–D.

[3] Coll. 643 D–644 C. Peter Alphonsi's account is much shorter (col. 566 B–D), but in it God explains to the angels that the Law was to teach the government of bodies which they did not possess. Cf. *Jew. Enc.* ix. 50.

[4] Col. 644 C, D. Peter Alphonsi quotes this legend also, but much more fully (Migne, *P.L.* clvii. 564 C–565 A), *supra,* p. 238. Cf. *Jew. Enc.* vii. 556.

[5] Col. 644 D. This story is almost word for word in Peter Alphonsi, col. 565 A, B (*vide supra,* p. 238, with my note).

[6] "Immensa congerie similium fabularum" (col. 645 B).

[7] This tale is in the *Second Alphabet of Ben Sira* (Eisenstein, *Ozar Midrashim,* 1915, p. 43).   [8] Col. 648 B.

nezzar sent a thousand armed men, "each of whom carried down one soldier on his finger nail",[1] and, wishing to know whether what he heard of the son was true, ordered him to come to him. The son refused, but sent him a hare on the forehead of which he had written all the questions which Nebuchadnezzar was intending to ask him. When the King saw this he acknowledged that he was wiser than all men.

Peter then adds a few closing remarks jeering at the supposed mysteries, secrets, and wisdom which the Jews claim to be superior even to Divine wisdom. In reality the prediction of Isa. lix. 5 is fulfilled. For you hatch basilisks' eggs, which infect you with the mortal poison of ungodliness. "And at length (as will happen near the end of the present age) they will be so evilly hatched by you as at last to produce Antichrist, the king of all the ungodly, the chief ruler, as it were, of all poisonous creatures."[2]

He ends the treatise complacently: "I think that you have now been so overwhelmed by both witnesses and reasonings of such great value, and have been so completely refuted by the Truth itself, that you are bound to make no further objection, and ask no further question."[3]

What contribution then does Peter the Venerable make towards the subject of controversy with the Jews? The answer must be, Very little, if anything at all. He adds nothing to our understanding of the Scriptures, for, it would seem, he knew no Hebrew, and possessed, with all his evident desire to help others, no

---

[1] "Quorum unusquisque militem unum deferebat super unguem digiti sui." This story seems to be taken from the legend of Barcochba, who tested the worth of his soldiers by ordering each to cut off a finger, and also every horseman to tear up a cedar when riding at full speed (T. J. *Taanith*, iv. 5 (6), 68 d). Another form of it is related in the *Second Alphabet of Ben Sira* (Eisenstein, *ibid.* p. 45 b). It speaks of the thousand horsemen having a finger mutilated and as uprooters of trees (אילנות) where the *Pesikta Rabbathi*, § 31 (Friedmann, 1880, p. 144 a), has אליוני ידיהם, "thumbs". "Militem...digiti" is presumably a copyist's error for "mutilum digito", and the rest of the Latin clause may be due to belief in onychomancy, the white marks sometimes found on finger-nails (the so-called "gifts" of English *Folk-Rhymes* (G. F. Northall, 1892, p. 171)), which are regarded as auguries of the future. See also the *Zohar*, ii. 76 a. Dr E. J. Thomas tells me that the Council of Treves (1238) formally condemned such onychomancy.

[2] "Et tandem, quod juxta saeculi finem futurum est, omnium impiorum regem Antichristum, velut omnium venenatorum animantium principem regulum, diu a vobis male fota producant" (col. 648 c).

[3] "Credo enim jam vos tantis testibus, tantis rationibus ita obrutos confutatosque esse ipsa veritate, ut nihil ultra repugnare, nihil quaerere debeatis."

originality of mind or special insight into Holy Writ or Christian truth. But his quotations from the Talmud, and a book akin to it, are of some interest, if only that they serve to explain the hatred of Christians for Jewish non-Biblical writings, and the terrible destruction of these in the next hundred years after Peter wrote.

Yet, if Peter the Venerable knew no Hebrew, how was he able to quote from these Jewish books? They had not even been translated as books into any language, so far as we know Whence then did he get his knowledge of them? It will have been seen from the notes given above that some of his quotations are found also in the *Dialogue* of Peter Alphonsi, a learned physician and scholar before his conversion from Judaism, who was an older contemporary of our Peter.[1] We know also that Peter the Venerable went to Spain in 1141,[2] and it is possible that his treatise was composed soon after he had been there. Even if he wrote it earlier he had probably been in touch with Spanish ecclesiastics, and may very well have received a copy of Peter Alphonsi's work. Yet the quotations from the Talmud are not sufficiently identical to warrant the conclusion that Peter the Venerable made direct use of Peter Alphonsi, or at least of him alone. We must suppose the existence of one or more other books of extracts written in Latin, which have not survived, or perhaps of some extracts procured from a Jewish convert. In any case Peter the Venerable himself had no personal knowledge of Jewish literature. He may therefore be the more readily pardoned for misunderstanding it.

Lastly, one wonders what effect this treatise had upon the Jews. None whatever, so far as we know. At all events, at a later time, probably in 1146, Peter is so far from hinting at any good done by it that he writes a furious letter to his king, Louis the Seventh.[3] He begins by saying that although he cannot accompany the Second Crusade (1147–1149) he will follow it in prayer. For who is not moved at the astounding movement of the army of the Lord of Sabaoth? As Moses slew the Amorites, and Joshua the Canaanites, giving their land to the people of God, so shall this great army overthrow the Saracens.[4] Yet what advantage will it be to vanquish these enemies of our Christian Hope who live in distant countries, if blasphemers who are far worse than the

---

[1] Peter Alphonsi was born in 1062 and died in A.D. 1110.
[2] *Vide supra*, p. 384.
[3] Migne, *P.L.* clxxxix. 566–568.
[4] It was, in fact, a disastrous failure.

Saracens, viz. the Jews—living not far off but in our very midst—
so freely and boldly, and without any fear of punishment, blaspheme, abuse, and even defile Christ and all our Christian
mysteries? I do not say this to sharpen the royal or the Christian
sword to slay them. God does not wish this, but rather that they
should be preserved like Cain, in a life that is worse than death.
God's punishment has ever answered to their crime, and so will it
be to the end of the world. And so let it be now. We all know the
facts! It is not from their work on the land, nor from service in
the camp, nor from any honourable and useful position, that they
fill their barns with produce, their bins with wine, their purses
with money, their chests with gold and silver, so much as from
those things which they treacherously filch from the worshippers
of Christ, and the things that they secretly buy from thieves, pro-
curing most precious articles for a mere song. If a thief breaks into
a church by night, and dares commit sacrilege and carry off
candlesticks, vessels, thuribles, and even the holy crosses or the
chalices, he escapes to the Jews, and sells to the synagogues of
Satan what he has stolen from God's house. And Jews will use,
as I have heard from trustworthy persons, the sacred vessels for
the vilest purposes.

And there is no redress! A law already antiquated but truly
diabolic, though issued by Christian princes, forbids Jews to be
compelled to restore any Christian vessel found among their
belongings, even though it was stolen—or even to produce the
thief. In fact, Jewish criminals are treated much more leniently
than Christian. But, on the contrary, let the Jews pay for the army
that is going against the Saracens! "Let their life be spared them,
but their money taken away, in order that, by Christian hands
helped by the money of blaspheming Jews, the boldness of unbelieving Saracens may be vanquished!"

"All this, most gracious King, have I written to thee from love
to Christ, and to thee, and thy Christian army, since it were foolish
and displeasing, I believe, to God, if so holy an expedition, on
which the property of Christians is to be spent as each can afford,
were not assisted much more copiously by the wealth of the
ungodly."

Poor Peter the Venerable! It is seldom that a man writes so
scathing an exposure of his own ignorance of Christian truth and
Christian ethics as he does in this Letter to King Louis.

CHAPTER XLV

AN ANONYMOUS TREATISE AGAINST THE JEWS[1]

A.D. 1166

The unknown author of this tract disarms all criticism by his humble opinion of his own learning. I write, he says, not for the learned, "but for those for whom, as for me, faith alone suffices and godly sincerity".[2] Yet he stands above many of our writers both in learning and in Christian character. He has some knowledge of Hebrew (§§ 12, 19, 31, 77); he knows how to give a philosophical turn to some of his arguments; he is not grossly unfair or abusive; he has had a good deal of intercourse with Jews;[3] and he can set forth his subject in a plain and straightforward way Altogether he is a person of whom we would gladly know more.

His method is to use only the Old Testament, and to base his answers to Jewish objections on passages taken from it, and not to refer to verses in the New Testament. And as a rule he follows the order of the Old Testament books, though in the latter part of his treatise he is not so particular. It should be noticed that his treatise is evidently unfinished, either because death, or some other external cause, prevented his completing it, or because the end of the manuscript perished.[4]

The text appears to rest on one old manuscript, preserved, when Martene wrote, in the Benedictine monastery founded in A.D. 1035 at Conches-en-Ouche, in the diocese of Evreux (Eure).[5]

He begins[6] with the first words of Genesis: *In the Beginning God created the heaven and the earth; the Beginning* in which He created being none other than Himself. And that was Wisdom (Ps. civ. 24).

---

[1] *Tractatus contra Judaeos*, in Martène and Durand, *Thesaurus Anecdotum*, 1717, vol. v, coll. 1507–1568. It is dated A.D. 1166, see § 34. Migne has not reprinted it.

[2] "Sed illis quibus mecum sola sufficit fides et sancta simplicitas."

[3] § 10. Cf. § 70, although there it is not said directly that the Jewish arguments were spoken in personal intercourse.

[4] He had written an earlier tract (§ 12).

[5] "Quem ex veteri codice monasterii S. Petri Conchensis in dioecesi Ebroicensi annorum circiter 500 descripsimus."

[6] § 2.

"But whatsoever is in God is God; therefore the very *Beginning* in which He created all things is God." So there is God in God. "Two Gods!" you cry? Yes, as Light and its effulgence ("Lux et lumen ejus") are one substance.

It is interesting to see how this late writer returns to the old vision of Christ seen in Gen. i. 1 by the author of *Jason and Papiscus*.[1] Further, in well-phrased argument, he sees the Third Person of the Blessed Trinity in the Spirit of God moving upon the face of the waters (Gen. i. 2).

Again, he shows[2] that the thought of Personality is inherent in the expression *the image* of God (Gen. i. 26), comparing Prov. viii. 27 and Ecclus. xxiv. 4, all the other terms used of Him being summed up "in the name you hate, that of Son" (Ps. ii. 7).

In § 10 our author turns to speak of the Sabbath, and points out that Scripture says that God Himself broke it. For he finished His work on the Sabbath day. Of course our Anonymous writer was not the first to discover this difficulty. At least it is found in Rashi (A.D. 1040–1105), the Jewish commentator slightly earlier than himself. He goes on to say that when someone once told him that God ceased work at midnight, he could not but smile, and reply: "Had the Lord no time then to finish His work by day? Such arguments are frivolous and mere child's play."

Then in § 11 he observes that the Jews break the Sabbath law in its strict meaning. For it[3] permits only "sitting" in the house, "but you say that Barachibas (R. Aqiba) and Symeon (? Shammai) and Helles (Hillel), our Masters, handed down to us the rule that we might walk 2000 steps on the Sabbath". And you prefer their definition to the Law of the Commandments of God. He adds jokingly, Suppose you go 2000 steps, and back again? That would make 4000 steps. Will Barachibas, Symeon, and Helles take you (like Habakkuk) by the hair of your head and carry you home? But even flying on Sabbath is nowhere permitted in the Law!

In § 12 he points out that the Hebrew of Gen. iii. 15 should be rendered *ipse conteret*, not *ipsa* as the ordinary text of the Latin Version runs. And he explains in § 14 that it was a spiritual serpent that seduced Eve, and that no mere man could crush him.

In §§ 16–19 he passes on to various verses in the Psalms, dwelling

---

[1] *Vide supra*, p. 29, where see the note.   [2] § 4.
[3] Ex. xvi. 29. The Hebrew word (*Shbu*) means "dwell", "abide", "sit" Here the LXX reads καθήσεσθε which our author follows, though the Vulgate has only *maneat*.

particularly on Ps. lxxxiv. 7: *The Lawgiver shall give a blessing; they shall go from strength to strength; the God of gods shall be seen in Sion.*[1] Now, how can God be seen save in human flesh? And he quotes Virgil's "Jam nova progenies", etc. (*Eclog.* iv. 7), and the Sibyl's

> E caelo rex adveniet per saecla futurus,
> Scilicet in carne praesens ut judicet orbem.[2]

Jer. xxxi. 22 (§ 20) can refer only to the Virgin birth, for otherwise it means nothing strange or new.

§§ 24, 25. Examine Amos iv. 12: *Prepare to meet thy God*, etc., in detail. Our author then quotes the inevitable Baruch iii. 37 once more.

In § 31 he quotes Hab. iii. 3, as showing that Christ comes in the temporal sense *from the South* ("ab austro", Vulg.), for Bethlehem is south of Jerusalem; and in the eternal sense *from Mount Paran*, for this word means from the "mouth"[3] of the Father.

Again, in § 33, Hab. iii. 4 speaks of *horns in his hands*, signifying that "His hands were fastened with nails on each horn of the cross".

Observe also, he says in § 34, the Prophet tells us that Christ will come *in the midst of the years* (Hab. iii. 5), not at the end of the Age, as you Jews falsely say. It is already A.D. 1166.

Who then is He, our author asks in § 36, *Whose strength is like that of the unicorn* (Num. xxiii. 22)? "For a unicorn cannot be taken by any hunter. Yet if a maid opens her bosom towards it as it comes up, it at once rushes towards her, moved more by love than by violence." So the Lord inclined His head "in the midst of the bosom of the daughter of Jerusalem, viz. the Church. And she has received in her bosom Him whom the Synagogue could not capture (when hunting) in the field."[4]

In § 37 the writer makes much of the false translation *the Desire of all nations* (Hagg. ii. 7), and, again, of the curious misinterpretation, *Send forth the Lamb, O Lord* (Isa. xvi. 1).[5]

You Jews expect (§ 39) a King to reign in glory in Jerusalem for

---

[1] "Benedictionem dabit legislator, ibunt de virtute in virtutem, videbitur Deus deorum in Sion." So the Clementine Vulgate, following the LXX.

[2] Cf. Peter of Blois, *infra*, p. 406, and especially Augustine, *De Civitate Dei*, xviii. 23. Cf. also Pseudo-Augustine, *Against the Jews, the Heathen*, etc. (*supra*, p. 324).   [3] "Mouth" is *Peh* in Hebrew.

[4] See more fully Hugo of St Victor (*c*. A.D. 1100–1141), *De Bestiis*, ii. 6 (Migne, *P.L.* clxxvii. 59); *Dict. d'Archéologie Chrétienne*, 1930, s.v. *licorne*. See also the ancient window in the War Memorial Chapel in King's College Chapel, Cambridge.

[5] Cf. Peter of Blois, vii (*infra*, p. 403).

a thousand years! But really His poverty, when He came, was the royal standard of His heavenly power, for by the King's poverty Justice and Salvation were to come to the human race.

In §§ 41–43 the author discusses Mal. iii. 1 and iv. 5. The Jews say that the Messenger is Elijah, who will prepare the way before "Haymenon", i.e. their Christ, who will come immediately after Elijah. Who then is this Haymenon of yours? Is He God? But the Prophet does not say that the Messenger will come before Haymenon's face, but before My face, i.e. God's. Do you make Haymenon a second God?[1] And can you really expect Elijah to come now, when the Temple has been destroyed? Yet it is true that he will come before the Day of Judgment (Mal. iv. 5) to convert the Jews to Christ.

In §§ 44–50 he discusses at some length the Seventy Weeks of Daniel, showing that Christ came at the proper time, concluding his argument by saying: If you reject all this, "Phyllida solus habeto"—"You have your charmer to yourself."[2]

The Jews, however, raise a further objection (§ 51), that if Jesus is everlasting righteousness, then sin and transgression ought to have been brought to an end. To this our author's reply is well-intentioned, and indeed indirectly goes to the root of the matter. For he says that "all sin and transgression are indeed brought to an end in those to whom Christ has become everlasting righteousness, for they are all one (*unum*) in Him". Cf. Rom. viii. 1. This is true, but as, after all, it asserts only the potential destruction of sin in the individual during this life, it hardly meets the Jewish objection.

§§ 52 to 77 are occupied with passages in Isaiah, but do not contribute much of special interest. On Isa. iv. 2 (§ 63) he says that Christ is rightly called the *Germen Domini*, because He is the perfection (*virtus*) and the image of the Father.

Before discussing Isa. vi he asks the Jew in § 64 what the form was in which the Prophets or the Patriarchs saw the Lord? Then he urges that "if He was seen of them in the figure of a man the Jew should let us say that in these latter days God appeared to us through a man"

---

[1] There does not seem to be any evidence that Haymenon was ever a name given by the Jews to their true Messiah. Mr H. Loewe suggests that it may be connected with *Ra'ya Mehemna*, "the Faithful Shepherd", the title of a Cabbalistic treatise incorporated in the editions of the Zohar, e.g. ii. 157 b.

[2] Virgil, *Eclog.* iii. 107.

In § 69 to § 77 he considers Isa. vii, arguing, quite rightly, that Hezekiah could not have been the Child, for he was too old; nor Isaiah's own son. And, further, he affirms, again quite correctly, that the *'almah* of vii. 14 cannot mean any girl, much less a married woman (for the word is never used of such), but can be only a young girl still carefully guarded by her parents, and never exposed to the gaze of men.

"Let it suffice to have made these short statements against the Jews concerning this chapter under discussion."

And so the manuscript ends! No doubt the author intended to continue his work. But whether, as has been said, he did so and the rest has perished, or he was prevented from doing so by circumstances or death we cannot tell. But we are glad to have met with so much sound learning (sound, that is to say, after the standard of his day), expressed in a sympathetic manner.

CHAPTER XLVI

PETER OF BLOIS[1]

AGAINST THE UNBELIEF OF THE JEWS[2]

c. A.D. 1200

Poor Peter of Blois! He had, we are told on good authority, such an excellent opinion of himself and his literary powers, and was for ever grumbling that he had not been properly rewarded;[3] for he was never more than an Archdeacon, first of Bath and afterwards of London. Nor, alas, does this treatise of his against the Jews support his claims. For beyond testifying to his study of earlier writers, particularly Jerome, and to his ability to arrange his arguments clearly, it gives no hint of independent study of Judaism, of spiritual sympathy with Jews, or of insight into the meaning of either the Old Testament or the New.

The reason why Peter composed this defence against Jewish lack of faith—only *perfidia* includes more active unbelief than this —is stated plainly in the opening words of the treatise, addressed to a correspondent whose name is unknown to us. "You have framed", he writes, "a long and troubled complaint that you are surrounded by Jews and heretics, and are continually being attacked by them, and yet have no authoritative statements of Holy Writ ready to hand, wherewith you can rebut their false accusations, and answer their crafty subtleties." He goes on to say that the Apostle tells us there must be heresies and schisms, and

---

[1] Born at Blois, *c.* 1135; studied at Bologna, 1160; Cancellarius to the Archbishop of Canterbury, *c.* 1173; Archdeacon of Bath, *c.* 1175; Archdeacon of London, *c.* 1192 (*Nat. Dict. Biog.* vol. xlv).

[2] *Contra perfidiam Judaeorum*, Migne, *P.L.* ccvii. 825–870; J. A. Giles, *Peter Blesensis...opera omnia*, Oxford, 1846, 8vo, iii. 62–129.

[3] "Peter's letters reveal him as a man full of literary vanity, ambitious for worldly advancement, and discontented with his preferments, which he thought unequal to his merits." He had, however, one experience like St Paul's (2 Cor. xi. 31), for he was "ill-treated by followers of the anti-pope Victor IV, but escaped by being let down the wall in a basket" (*Nat. Dict. Biogr.*). "It is pointed out by the Rev. Michael Adler (in his excellent account of the *Jews in Canterbury*) that Peter of Blois had been involved in financial transactions with those whom he attacks" (H. P. Stokes, *A Short History of the Jews in England*, 1921, p. 36)

he uses the interesting figure of the Jews, found as far back as Augustine,[1] saying, "even to Jews life is granted by God's kindness to-day, because they are our satchel-bearers (*capsarii*), carrying round the Prophets and the Law of Moses to prove the truth of our Faith. And", he adds, "we read the Passion of Christ, not only in their books, but also in their very faces."[2] Yet he wishes that no one who is not sufficiently trained would dispute with a Jew or a heretic. For logical victory does not include heart-conversion. It is better to leave Jews alone, for they are "people of hard neck and truly animal obstinacy". Yet, he says, I will do what you wish, for St Peter writes that every one ought to give a reason for the faith and hope that is in him.[3] So he will set forth the various heads of the Faith briefly, that his correspondent may be able to confirm argument from Scripture.

The treatise is divided into thirty-eight chapters, consisting almost entirely of passages from the Bible (chiefly the Old Testament), and dealing with the following subjects: II–VI, The Trinity. VII–XIV, The Incarnation. XV–XXIV, The life of Christ from His Birth to His Ascension, and the coming of the Holy Ghost, including some non-Biblical evidence, especially for His Resurrection. XXV–XXVII, The New Law and the Sacraments. XXVIII–XXXI, The Call of the Gentiles and the future salvation of the Remnant of the Jews, with the glory of the Church. XXXII, Scripture is not to be understood literally. XXXIII–XXXVII, Antichrist, the Second Coming of Christ, and the Final Judgment. XXXVIII, The testimony of Virgil and the Sibyl to the Coming of Christ and the future Judgment.

It will be seen at once that our author is quite comprehensive in his subjects, but writes entirely on old lines, without, it is to be feared, one single new suggestion, or any thought beyond that of proving, in a merely formal and external manner, that the Gospel was foretold in the Old Testament, and indeed even by a heathen poet and a heathen prophetess, and also that two or three contemporary non-Christian writers bear witness to its chief facts. He says nothing that appeals to the heart, and makes very little use of reason, save in well-worn illustrations of the doctrine of the

---

[1] On Psalm xli. 12: "Nobis serviunt Judaei, tanquam capsarii nostri sunt, studentibus nobis codices portant" (cf. *supra*, pp. 313, 327).

[2] Col. 825 c.

[3] Cf. the beginning of the anonymous *Treatise Against the Jews* in Martene (*vide supra*, p. 395).

Trinity. On the other hand he is no mere redactor of recent treatises, for he has studied his Jerome, and reproduces some of his more interesting remarks.[1]

There is not much to interest us in chh. II–VI. Peter, however, makes the same curious use of Isa. lxvi. 9 that we saw in Peter the Venerable.[2] He knows also that in Hebrew both *El* and *Adon* mean God and Lord, and he tells us that in the singular each points to the Unity, whereas the plural forms *Eloi* and *Adonai* indicate a plurality of Persons.[3] He has also an interesting explanation of the Tetragrammaton, "which, though of four letters, has only three elements, *Io, He, Vaf, He,* for the *He* comes twice. If then you look at this Name carefully, it is in Hebrew both threefold and one (*trinum et unum*). For if you join only the first and the second letters (namely *Io* and *He*) one name of God is the result. But if you put the second and the third together (i.e. *He* and *Vaf*) you have another name of God. But if you write the third letter and the fourth (i.e. *Vaf* and *He*) you have a third. Again, if you join all together in due order, you will find one Name. He who ordained that three names should be one name, Himself wished you to understand the Unity of the same Substance in Three Persons."[4]

Peter adds an illustration from the Blessing by the Priests in Num. vi. 23–27. The raising of the thumb, index, and middle fingers signify the excellence of the Trinity, and with Christians the sign of the Cross is always given at the same time. With these three fingers the dust of the earth[5] was taken, and Pharaoh's magicians acknowledged the Finger of God, i.e. the Holy Spirit, which the Jews so obstinately deny.[6]

He also[7] brings forward the old charge that the Jews altered the Scriptures to suit their purposes, referring to Jerome's remarks on

[1] We should have expected Peter at least to have made use of the charming *Dialogue* of Gilbert Crispin, Abbot of Westminster, about a hundred years earlier (*vide supra*, p. 375), or of the pretty little Play-Prologue (?) falsely attributed also to Gilbert (*vide supra*, p. 381).

[2] Ch. III, col. 829 A (*vide supra*, p. 386).

[3] Ch. V, col. 832 B.

[4] Ch. V, col. 833 A. Cf. Peter Alphonsi, *Dial.* col. 611 A (*supra*, pp. 235 *sq.*)

[5] "Moles terrae." The Vulgate has "pulverem terrae" in Ex. viii. 16 (Heb. 12), but translates the same Hebrew expression in Isa. xl. 12 by "moles terrae". The Septuagint has το χῶμα τῆς γῆς in Exodus.

[6] Col. 833 C.

[7] Ch. V, col. 833 D. Cf. Justin's *Dialogue with Trypho*, lxxi–lxxiii, with my notes (*vide supra*, p. 33).

the Jewish translation, called the Septuagint, in his Prologue to Genesis.[1]

Lastly, a quaint illustration of the Trinity may be mentioned A certain hermit, the Archdeacon tells us, when asked about that doctrine, made folds in his cloak and said: "This fold is cloth, and this, and also this—none of those folds is another of them, so those three folds are three cloths. But for all that there is one cloth."[2]

Chh. VII–XIV: The Incarnation. The usual passages are quoted to show that Christ's descent was from David. Also that by the fact of Ruth the Moabitess being His ancestress the prophecy of His Gentile origin in Isa. xvi. 1 was fulfilled: *Send, O Lord, the Lamb, the Ruler of the earth, from the rock of the desert to the mountain of the daughter of Sion.*[3] For the conversion of heathen kings he refers to Jerome on Isa. lii. 13, and says that "*Kings and the wise of this world shall shut their mouth,* i.e. they shall not abuse Him, but they shall agree to the Law of Christ, who will sprinkle the Gentiles with His own blood and baptism".[4]

In ch. XIII our author states the evidence for the place and the time of Christ's birth, and, after quoting several of the usual texts, he refers to Bede's explanation of the Seventy Weeks as meaning 490 years.[5] He says also that Jerome on Hosea[6] says he can find no other reason for the length of the present Captivity than the crucifixion of Christ. "Josephus, however, wrote in the eighteenth Book of the *Antiquities* that Jerusalem was destroyed because of the murder of James, yet all redounds to the glory of the Saviour."[7] In ch. XIV Peter gives us the gist of Jerome's strange exposition of Isa. lxiv. 1: *Oh, that Thou wouldest rend the heavens, that Thou wouldest come down, that the mountains might flow down at Thy presence,* viz. "*Come down,* because the Word was made flesh...*flow down,* i.e. the unbelieving and the proud."[8]

[1] See his Preface to the Pentateuch addressed to Desiderius, generally prefixed to editions of the Vulgate.
[2] "Haec plica est pannus, et haec, et tertia. Nulla istarum plicarum est altera, ergo istae tres plicae sunt tres panni. Immo unus pannus" (ch. VI, col. 834 D).
[3] Ch. x, col. 837 B: "Emitte agnum, Domine, dominatorem terrae de petra deserti ad montem filiae Sion." Cf. Peter Damiani, § 37 (*supra*, p. 370).
[4] Cf. Vallarsi, iv. 613.
[5] Col. 843 A. Where does Bede say this?
[6] Col. 843 C: "super Hosee" I cannot discover this reference.
[7] Our learned Peter is really quoting from Jerome's *De Viris Illustribus*, xiii (Vallarsi, ii. 851). Josephus refers to the death of James in *Antt.* xx. ix. 1 (§ 200), and to our Lord in XVIII. iii. 3 (§§ 63 *sq.*)   [8] Vallarsi, iv. 759.

Chh. xv–xxiv: The life of Christ from His Birth to the Ascension, with the Coming of the Holy Ghost, including some non-Biblical evidence, especially for our Lord's Resurrection. Most of this is quite ordinary, and calls for no special remark. In ch. xvii Peter speaks of the rejection of the legal Sacrifices. In ch. xix he quotes Isa. xi. 10, *The Root of Jesse, which standeth for a sign of the peoples*, and says, This is the sign of the Cross; and Peter goes on to speak of its present glory in much the same way as Chrysostom.[1] "This sign has been removed from the mortal punishment of robbers to the brows of Emperors and Princes, to the brows and heads of the Highest Pontiffs. Without this sign nothing is secure, nothing is inviolable."[2]

In ch. xx, Cant. v. 10: *My cousin* (patruelis) *is white and ruddy*, is explained as "*ruddy* in His Passion, *white* in His Resurrection".[3] On Isa. lxiii. 2 Jerome is once more used. In ch. xxi, Hos. v. 14: *I will take...and raise up*, means "from hell and earth into heaven".[4] That the Holy Ghost is given in Baptism and Confirmation is shown in ch. xxii by the Psalmist in Ps. civ. 30: *Send forth Thy Spirit*, etc.[5]

Ch. xxiii is interesting for its long quotation of the Letter of Pilate[6] to the Emperor Tiberius about our Lord and His miracles, His crucifixion by the Jews, and the Resurrection, with the evidence of Pilate's soldiers to it. This Letter may be seen most conveniently in M. R. James' *Apocryphal New Testament*, 1924, p. 146. Peter of Blois also quotes Tertullian's *Apology*, v, as to which Dr James writes: "Tertullian states it as a fact that Pilate reported all the events of the Passion to Tiberius, and the Emperor tried, without success, to induce the Senate to declare Jesus a God. What the source of this story was is unknown, but it is a very obvious one to invent."[7]

In ch. xxiv our author quotes the testimony of Josephus (*Ant.* xviii. iii. 3) to our Lord and to John the Baptist from Jerome's *De Vir. Illustr.*[8] He also quotes Philo[9] and Josephus as recording the miseries that came on both Pilate and the Jews. Like Eusebius

---

[1] Cf. Chrysostom, *Demonst.* viii (*supra*, p. 137).
[2] Col. 847 B.   [3] Col. 848 B.
[4] Col. 849 A.   [5] Col. 849 D.
[6] Col. 850.   [7] *Op. cit.* p. 153.
[8] § xiii (Vallarsi, ii. 851–853). Peter's quotation is not quite exact verbally; presumably his MSS. were different.
[9] *De Virtutibus et Legat. ad Caium*, ii. 38; Mangey, ii. 590.

(*Ch. Hist.* ii. 6) he sees in these the punishment for the rejection of Christ.[1] Our writer now turns to deal with the New Law and the Sacraments (chh. xxv–xxvii). Naturally he quotes Jer. xxxi. 31 *sq.*, and also discusses the Dietary Laws, and jeers at the deep and necessary teaching how to avoid eating crocodiles, bats, and moles.[2] But Ezekiel saw a wheel in the midst of a wheel,[3] meaning that the New Testament lies hid in the Old. So Pope Leo in his *Moral Precepts* tells us that no decrees of the former Testament are rejected, but have been augmented for the better by the method of the Gospel.[4] In reality, Peter adds, the spiritual meaning is far better than the literal, and is often insisted upon in the Old Testament itself.[5]

As to Baptism (ch. xxvi) Peter says: "The Jews even believed, and still believe, that they get their sins forgiven by the use of cold water. For this reason they themselves are wont to practise many baptisms."[6]

In chh. xxviii to xxxi Peter considers the Call of the Gentiles and the future salvation of the Remnant of the Jews, and the glory of the Church. *Lebanon*, says Isa. xxix. 17, *shall be turned into Mount Carmel.* How can that be? asks Jerome, and answers his question by saying that "Lebanon, which means whiteness, indicates the people of the Gentiles, which, when washed in Baptism, is made white in Christ".[7] Among the greater curiosities of mediaeval exegesis may be mentioned Peter's explanation of Ps. lix. 6: "For the Jews, when converted *at the evening* of the world, and hungering for the word of God, will *bark* against unbelievers, *and go round about the city*, i.e. the Church, to protect and defend it."[8]

But of greater interest is Peter's language in ch. xxxi about Isa. lx. 10: *And the sons of strangers shall build thy walls*, etc. "This cannot refer, O Jew, to thy Temple and thy State, but to-day we

---

[1] Coll. 851 c–852 b.　　　　　　　　　　[2] Col. 855 c.

[3] Ezek. x. 10.

[4] Col. 855 d: "Nulla Testamenti prioris decreta reprobata sunt, sed evangelico magisterio in melius sunt adaucta. Perfectiora enim sunt dantia salutem, quam promittentia Salvatorem." Cf. Gregory the Great, *Hom. in Ezek.* 1346 (Migne, *P.L.* lxxvii. 978).

[5] E.g. Jer. vi. 10; ix. 26. Peter quotes Origen on the former of these two passages to illustrate his point, but Origen deals with the subject at iv. 4 (Migne, *P.G.* xiii. 316–320).

[6] Col. 859 a.

[7] Col. 861 d. See Vallarsi, iv. 397 a.　　　　[8] Col. 864 c.

see the Kings of the earth and the Caesars themselves yielding their necks to the yoke of Christ, building churches with public funds, and issuing laws against heretics and those who persecute the Church."[1] Peter says further that to the words in Isa. xlix. 16: *Behold, I have graven thee upon the palms of My hands; thy walls are continually before Me,* the LXX has added another clause: *Thou shalt be built quickly by those by whom thou wast destroyed.*[2]

In ch. xxxii Peter insists more at length on the impossibility of interpreting Scripture literally. Would you, he asks, understand the Song of Songs so? St Paul in 1 Cor. x. 6 warned us against such an error: for "all things", he says, "happened to them *in a figure*".[3] So Esdras the Prophet added by the revelation of the Holy Spirit Titles to Psalms, in order that although sometimes history is touched upon in a Title, not the history as such, but the spiritual meaning of the history, might be considered.[4]

Chh. xxxiii to xxxvii: Antichrist, the Second Coming and the Final Judgment. Peter's doctrine of the resurrection of the body is very precise: "Suppose a man's limbs torn, scattered, burnt to ashes, and given to the winds—cannot He who could create all things out of nothing, remake that body out of even that slight and meagre stuff?"[5]

The last chapter (xxxviii) is chiefly concerned with the witness of Vergil, in his well-known Fourth Eclogue,[6] and of the Cumaean Sibyl.[7] This Peter quotes from (Pseudo-) Augustine,[8] but as it has already been discussed[9] it is not necessary to say anything here.

Peter concludes his treatise thus: "Here you have weapons sent you to defend the Faith; use them with care. For a Jew is always capricious and changeable. Now he affirms, now he denies; now

---

[1] Col. 865.

[2] This sentence in *v.* 17 is not an addition to the Hebrew but a translation due to a different pronunciation. The ordinary Massoretic text is *banayik,* "*thy children* make haste", but the St Petersburg cod. of A.D. 916 reads *bonayik,* and this reading was accepted by the LXX. Observe that the *Epistle of Barnabas* (xvi. 3, 4), written in the end of the first century, has, almost certainly, the same interpretation as Peter's. See the chapter on *The Epistle of Barnabas (supra,* p. 17).

[3] Col. 866 c.   [4] Col. 866 D.

[5] Ch. xxxiv, col. 868 A.

[6] Col. 869 B.   [7] Col. 869 D–870 c.

[8] "In sermone illo, qui sic incipit: Vos convenio, O Judaei." This is the beginning of § xi of the *Sermo c. Judaeos, Paganos et Arianos,* the quotation occurring in § xvi.

[9] *Vide supra,* p. 324.

he pretends to defend the letter, now he refers the whole subject to the times of his own Messiah, i.e. Antichrist; and, like his father the Devil, again and again fashions himself into unnatural forms. If therefore you would fully detect and destroy his tricks, get the Library of the Spirit set between you, so that he may neither take his refuge in it, nor turn his back upon it, but, like Goliath, be slain by his own sword."

CHAPTER XLVII

NICOLAS DE LYRA

TWO TREATISES

1270–1349

The relevant facts about Nicolas de Lyra[1] are few, and the dates not absolutely certain. He was born in A.D. 1270 at Lyra near Evreux in Normandy, presumably of Gentile parents. For the legend that he was of Jewish stock has no early evidence, and is due to the supposition that no one who possessed so much knowledge of Hebrew could have himself been other than a Jew. He became a Franciscan (probably in 1301), was a teacher in the Sorbonne, and died "certainly not before 1349". In his *Postillae*, or running commentary on the whole Bible, he insists primarily on the literal meaning of each passage. He made much use of Rashi, and also was well acquainted with the *Pugio Fidei* of Raymund Martini (written A.D. 1278)

In the Library of the London Society for Promoting Christianity amongst the Jews (now called "Church Missions to Jews") there were formerly two small quarto volumes bound in vellum, with inscriptions stating that they were given to the Society by Charles Farish, B.D., Fellow of Queens' College, Cambridge, in the year 1813. They both contained "Nicholas de Lyra's Method with his countrymen the Jews to Convert them to Christianity". The first volume was a manuscript copy by Mr Farish of the original Latin of the First (only) of our two treatises (from the Basle edition), with additions from another copy of the tract affixed to the *Hebraeomastix* of Hieronymus de Sancta Fide (1412), printed 1602.

---

[1] See especially F. Vernet as cited on *infra* p. 412, n. 2. Consult also Neubauer, *Expositor*, III. vii. 190 (1888). Chajim b. Musa wrote in A.D. 1456 a refutation of Nicolas de Lyra's work, which, however, is still unprinted. See Graetz, *Geschichte*, vii (1873), 490; viii (1875), 152 *sq.*, 407–410. Chajim b. Musa strongly advised Jewish disputants (1) to insist on the literal meaning of Bible passages; (2) not to recognise the inspiration of the Targumim; (3) not to admit proofs from the Haggada or Josephus; (4) to reject the Septuagint or the Vulgate when they differ from the Hebrew; (5) not to discuss Bible passages of doubtful meaning; (6) to reject all proofs from the New Testament; (7) not to admit philosophical discussions in Scripture exposition.

The second volume contained Mr Farish's translation. Both volumes had some notes by Mr Farish, but those in the first were more copious as well as more valuable.[1]

I. AGAINST THE JEWS

A PROOF OF THE TIME OF THE INCARNATION OF CHRIST; OR, PERHAPS, AN ENQUIRY INTO THE DIVINITY OF CHRIST[2]

In the first and better known treatise Lyra begins by saying that the first question is whether it can be effectively proved from the Scriptures accepted by the Jews that our Saviour was both God and Man. He also points out that this includes two enquiries, whether Christ is God and Man, and also whether the time of His appearance on earth corresponds with the time announced. He further mentions that in addition to the Hebrew Scriptures evidence can be obtained from the Targums, the Septuagint, Josephus, and the Talmud.

Among the usual proof-texts for the Incarnation[3] may be quoted Zech. ix. 9, with Lyra's exposition. For this will serve as an illustration of his method generally in the other examples or "proofs", which it is impossible to quote at length.

"The Divinity of Christ," he says (I use Mr Farish's translation), "and His humanity, is proved by the authority in Zech. ix: *Rejoice greatly, O daughter of Zion; shout, O daughter of Jerusalem; behold thy King cometh to thee, just, and a Saviour, poor, and riding upon an ass.* According to the doctors of the Hebrews, that authority cannot be expounded literally but of the Messiah.

"By that which is said here, *Poor, and riding upon an ass*, is shown His humanity, in which, as a lowly man, He conversed with men. But by that which is said, *A just King, and a Saviour*, is shown a nature more excellent in Him, by which He can save and reign, because a poor man, inasmuch as he is so, is impotent for such things; and therefore He was at once both rich and poor—rich in the Divine nature, and poor in the human nature.

"And that this authority of Zechariah should be so understood appears by the gloss of the Hebrews authentic among them upon

---

[1] Both volumes, together with many other more important books, were, alas, sold by an unhappy blunder in 1914. The information given above is taken from a short article by myself in *Jews and Christians*, Nisbet, 1894, p. 77. I do not know where the two volumes are to be found to-day.

[2] For the edition used see p. 412 note 2.   [3] Pp. 276 G–277 G.

that in Canticles i:[1] *We will be glad and rejoice in Thee with glory,* that is, in Thee, the Holy One and Blessed One. For here it is like to a certain queen whose husband, sons, and sons-in-law past over the sea; a great while afterwards it was said to her, 'Thy sons-in-law have come.' She answered: 'What is that to me? Let my daughters rejoice.' It was said to her, 'Thy sons are come.' She answered, 'What is that to me? Let my daughters-in-law rejoice.' But when it was said to her, 'Thy husband is come', she said, 'Now is my joy made perfect.'

"So[2] it was that there were prophets in Jerusalem saying to Jerusalem, 'Thy sons from afar are come.' She answered, 'What is that to me? Let the daughters of Judah be glad.' But when that in Zech. ix was said to her, *Behold thy King cometh,* then was there perfect joy for her.

"Whence it is there sufficiently premised: *Rejoice greatly, O daughter of Zion; shout, O daughter of Jerusalem,* etc. From this gloss it appears that the prophet Zechariah is speaking of the coming of God to the sons of Israel. If, therefore, according to them that authority speaks of the Messiah who also in the same authority is said to come in poverty, the conclusion is that He is God and man; so that He is poor in relation to humanity, and potent to save in relation to Divinity."

Lyra then begins to show that the Time of this Incarnation is past. He quotes many passages besides Gen. xlix. 10, but none that are new to us, or of special interest.[3] He then mentions various Jewish tales of the locality where the Messiah now actually is; after, as the Jews say, being born on the day of the destruction of the Temple.[4]

At this point[5] he speaks of a Book of "Judicum ordinariorum" handed down by the House of Elijah, i.e. by his disciples. A little lower down[6] he adds: "R. Moses in the Book of Judicum ordi-

---

[1] *Midrash Cant. R.* i. 4, end.

[2] The Midrash says: "So in the time to come the Prophets come and say to Jerusalem, *Thy sons come from afar* (Isa. lx. 4). But she answers them, 'What is that to me?' [They say] *And thy daughters are nursed at thy side.* She says, 'What is that to me?' But when, etc."

[3] Pp. 277 G-278 F.   [4] T. J. *Berakoth,* II. 4 (p. 5 a).

[5] P. 278 G; 1634 edition, col. 1710: "In quodam libro, qui apud eos vocatur liber Judicum ordinariorum, traditur a domo Elia, id est, a discipulis ejus."

[6] "R. Moyses in libro Judicum ordinariorum Jesus Nazarenus visus est esse Messias, et interfectus est per domum judicii, et ipse fuit causa et promeruit ut destruerit (destrueretur, 1664 edition) Israel in gladio" (p. 278 H; 1664 edition, col. 171)

nariorum says: Jesus of Nazareth appeared to be the Messiah, and was killed by the Beth Din, and was himself the cause, and so much deserved (his punishment) that he destroyed Israel by the sword."[1]

After quoting the famous passage in Josephus,[2] and Isaiah liii, Lyra claims that all these things were plainly fulfilled in Jesus of Nazareth, and "it is reasonably concluded that He is the very Christ".[3]

The Jew, however, adduces four objections taken from the prediction in Isa. ii. (1) Jesus did not come "in novissimis temporibus"—"*in the last days*". (2) Mount Sion still stands where it was, and has not been moved to *the top of the mountains*. (3) *All nations shall flow*; yet all nations do not believe in Jesus of Nazareth. (4) Their swords have not been beaten into plowshares. Similarly, (5) The wolf and the lamb do not lie down together (Isa. xi. 6), so that Christ has not yet come.[4]

Again, (6) Deut. xxx. 3 says that God will restore Israel. As this has not taken place, Messiah has not come. (7) Zech. vi. 12: Messiah is to build the Temple, but Jesus built no temple, so that He is not the Messiah. To this Lyra replies that "their doctor, Rabbi Solomon" (Rashi), says that Zechariah refers to the Second Temple, so that objection does not hold good. (8) Jer. xxiii. 6: *Judah is to be saved*, etc. Answer: This refers to the true sons of Israel. (9) Dan. vii. 13: Jesus did not come in *clouds*! Answer: There is a Second Coming. (10) Isa. xxx. 26: *The light of the sun* was to be sevenfold, and this has not yet happened! (11) Isa. liii. 10: *He shall see his seed, he shall prolong his days*; and Ps. lxxxix. 29: *His seed also shall endure for ever.* But we are not told that Jesus had

---

[1] The origin of these two quotations is uncertain, but I venture to suggest the following explanation: (*a*) "R. Moses" is Maimonides, and the second quotation is a summary of the famous uncensored passage in his *Hilkoth Melakim*, Pereq xi, at the very end of the fourteenth and last book of his *Mishneh Torah*. (*b*) This last book is entitled "The fourteenth book, which is the Book of Judges" (*Shophetim*), of which *Liber Judicum ordinariorum* is a fair paraphrase. It may be noticed that the first treatise in this book is called *Sanhedrin*, i.e. the (legal) Court. One difficulty, however, remains. It does not seem that Maimonides speaks of "the house of Elijah". But in T.B. *Sanhedrin*, 97 a the *Tanna de Be Elijahu* (Pereq 2) is quoted as speaking of the days of Messiah, and it is possible that the MS. of Maimonides used by de Lyra had some such reference. T.B. *Aboda Zara*, 9 a has the same quotation from the *Tanna de Be Elijahu*. See M. Friedmann's edition of this, entitled *Seder Elijahu Rabba*, 1902, p. 7.

[2] Antt. xviii. iii. 3 (§ 63).

[3] "Rationabiliter concluditur quod ipse sit verus Christus" (p. 279 A, B).

[4] P. 279 B–D.

any children! Answer: He has had spiritual children. (12) Ezek. xl–xliv: The Temple was to be rebuilt in the Land of Israel. Answer: This refers to the heavenly House, as Ezekiel says at the very end: *The name of the city from that day shall be, The LORD is there.*

The treatise ends with a few remarks by Nicolas on the subject in general. Three causes hinder the Jews from becoming Christians. (*a*) Fear of poverty. (*b*) The prejudices that have been instilled into them. (*c*) The difficulty of the Christian doctrines, and the mistakes they make about them.[1]

II. AGAINST A CERTAIN JEW
WHO DENOUNCED THE GOSPEL ACCORDING TO ST MATTHEW[2]

The second treatise by Nicolas de Lyra is entitled *Against a certain Jew who denounced the Gospel according to St Matthew.*[3] It begins: After I had written about each Testament (presumably meaning after he had finished his *Postillae*) "a certain Treatise composed by a certain Jew came into my hands, in which he endeavours to denounce from the very words of the Gospel our Lord Jesus Christ, the Author of the Gospel".[4] Nicolas says that he will consider the objections one by one. In fact, however, he combines more than one objection under one head.[5]

(1) In the Genealogy no good woman is included; only four women are there, and they all are bad. The Genealogy therefore tends to promote sins of the flesh, and therefore Jesus cannot have been the Messiah. Again, Christians break the Law, by eating pork, etc. And, in particular, they are idolators because they

---

[1] P. 279 H.

[2] The edition used is the *Biblia* with Lyra's commentary in six volumes, Basle, 1506–1508. The two treatises are in vol. vi. pp. 275 b–279 b, and pp. 280 a–285 a. Use has also been made of the *Biblia Sacra*, Antwerp, 1634, vi. coll. 1695–1716 and 1716–1736. At the end of this last volume is added Paul of Burgos' *Scrutinium* (coll. 1793–2070). The Latin titles are: I. *C. Judaeos probatio temporis incarnationis Christi*. F. Vernet, however, thinks it was *Questio de divinitate Christi* (see his very full article on Nicolas de Lyra in the *Dictionnaire de Théologie Catholique*, 1926, ix. coll. 1410–1422). II. *C. quendam Judaeum impugnatorem evangelii secundum Matthaeum.*

[3] So far I have failed to identify the author of this attack.

[4] "In quo ex verbis evangelicis auctorem evangelii Dominum nostrum Jesum Christum nititur impugnare" (p. 280 A).

[5] The following pages state only the more important arguments on either side, particularly on the Jewish side, and do not pretend to do more than whet the reader's palate for the varied food that Nicolas supplies.

worship Jesus, a mere man. And, even worse, they "worship the Host as God, though they have made it out of corn, and have baked it—and this is ludicrous! And afterwards they eat it, and this is dreadful." Nicolas, of course, replies that the Messiah is God as well as man, and, among other arguments, quotes the famous passage in Josephus.[1] He does not say much about the Host, but adds a good deal about the Divinity and the Incarnation.

One of Lyra's arguments is taken from Isa. ix. 7 (Heb. 6), where, in the middle of the Hebrew word for *of-the-increase-of*, a form of the letter M occurs which is properly found only at the end of a word. The usual form of the M in the middle of a word is partly opened, but the final form has no such opening, and is called "closed". "By this the Prophet wished to hint to students that the Boy of whom he was speaking would be born of a Mother who remained still a virgin."[2] After other passages proving the Divinity and Incarnation of Messiah, he quotes Lam. v. 3: *We have been made orphans without a father*,[3] and says that Rabbi Barachias expounds this as meaning: "The Redeemer whom I will raise up from you will be without father, viz. on the earth, even as He is without mother in heaven."[4] He also quotes Bonaventura (A.D. 1221–1274) as saying: "There was this wonderful thing about the Virgin Mary, that although she was very beautiful, yet she had never had intercourse with a man. Nor may that testimony of unbelievers be despised, for one ought to receive witness from them that are without."[5]

(2) The second passage is an attack on our Lord's Baptism. So He too had some sins to be washed away! And, further, He had not the Holy Spirit before He was baptised!

(3) The third is the Temptation. How can we praise a God for fasting? Anyhow, Jesus was inferior to Moses, who fasted for forty days and forty nights yet was not hungry. Again, when Jesus

[1] *Vide supra*, p. 193.
[2] "Ex matre clausa virginitate" (p. 281 c).
[3] "Pupilli sumus facti sumus absque patre."
[4] Evidently from Raymund Martini, *Pugio Fidei*, p. 594, where the quotation is taken from the *Breshith Rabba* according to Moses ha Darshan (cent. xi), which has not come down to us. On Moses ha Darshan see the *Jew. Enc.* ix. 4.
[5] Bonaventura, *Sententiarum*, III. iii. 1, Art. ii. Q. 3 (1887, 77 b), writes: "Quidam Judaei asserunt, hoc mirum fuisse in Virgine Maria, quod cum esset pulcherrima, tamen a nullo unquam viro fuerit concupita. Nec vilipendendum est illud infidelium testimonium: *oportet enim testimonium habere ab his qui foris sunt* (1 Tim. iii. 7)." Nicolas adds that he does not know Bonaventura's authority for saying this, but he would not have said it carelessly.

says, *In every word that proceedeth out of the mouth of God,* He ought to have said "in every *thing,* etc." because God can make any thing give man food. And He should also have said "out of *My* mouth", if He was God.

(4) The fourth argument is an attack on the Sermon on the Mount. Jesus has destroyed the Law even in morals, though Christians deny this. Not to resist evil would destroy all justice. Christians disobey the Law of Jesus who bid them not insist on eye for eye. Love your enemies! This is contrary to God's own order to destroy the Canaanites.

(5) Fifthly, the Jew takes exception to Matt. viii 4. Jesus says in ix. 13, *I will have mercy and not sacrifice,* and yet here he bids the leper offer sacrifices. Jesus is inconsistent in word and will. And, again, though in Luke viii. 39 He bids the demoniac declare what great things God has done to thee, He here tells the leper to tell no one.

(6) Sixthly, the Prayer in Matt. xi. 25–27 contradicts the doctrine of the Trinity in Unity. If the Father and the Son are One, how can Jesus confess to His Father? And if He received all things He must previously have been deficient in them.

(7) The seventh objection is against Matt. xii. 1–4. God ordered the Sabbath, yet Jesus, though God, relaxes it! David was in much more need than were the Disciples.

(8) Matt. xii. 31, 32. How can blasphemy against one Person in the Trinity be more serious than against one of the other two?

(9) Matt. xviii. 14: *Not the will of your Father who is in heaven that one of these little ones should perish.* And yet Jesus says in xiii. 13 that He speaks in parables because they do not understand! Jesus contradicts Himself, and the second passage is in flat contradiction to Ezek. xviii. 23.

(10) Matt. xxi. 19: Why curse the Fig-tree? Had Jesus been God He would have known the facts. And why curse a tree that had done Him no harm? He was in a passion.[1]

(11) Matt. xxvi. 31–46: Gethsemane. How should God pray? He ought to be the object of prayer. And here is a God afraid! One too who had no power to save His own life!

(12) Matt. xxviii. 18: The same objection as the sixth. If all power was given to Jesus, He was not God.

It is not possible (as has been said above) to give Lyra's detailed answers to these objections, and indeed where no answer has been

[1] "Ex perturbatione" (p. 284 F). *Vide supra,* p. 88.

given none is required, for the Jew's statements are often ludicrous. But on p. 285[1] Lyra adds three "arguments of a Jew taken from the words of Christians".[2]

First. Were the Father and the Holy Ghost separated from the Son in the Incarnation? Nicolas replies: "The descent of the Son into the Virgin's womb is not to be understood of local motion, but of a new effect in the Virgin. This effect is the union of the Divine and the Human nature in one Person."

Second. Did Christ "send" or was He "sent"? If the latter, who ever heard of God being "sent" to another person? If the former, Christians make Jesus a liar, for He says: *Lo, I am not alone, but I and the Father who sent Me.* Answer: He is both Sender and Sent.

Third. "In the Book of Simon Cephas Jesus says: Lo, Satan endeavours to kill Me, (taking Me) out of the hand of the Lord, and He will not give me (up) into the hand of Satan.[3] From this the Jew argues, saying, Why are you Christians not ashamed of yourselves to say that this God of yours speaks thus?"

Answer. Your objector takes falsehood for truth. For neither in the Epistles of Peter nor elsewhere is this saying of Jesus to be found. But, if it were, there would be no difficulty. For as God He allowed Himself to be tempted as far as He was man.

Here the second treatise ends, rather abruptly. Perhaps Lyra meant to make some concluding remarks, and became too old, or too ill, to do so.

[1] 1634 edition, col. 1734.
[2] "Argumenta Judaei ex verbis Christianorum."
[3] This quotation seems not to be in any apocryphal book that has come down to us. But cf. *The Acts of Peter*, vii (M. R. James, *Apocryphal N.T.* p. 311). Nor is it (as it seems) in the Hebrew Haggadoth about St Peter (see Eisenstein, *Ozar Midrashim*, 1915, pp. 557–559).

EPILOGUE

The treatises which we have considered show a sincere desire on the part of the writers to use the evidence of the Old Testament as well as they knew how, according to the light of their time Their weakness lies in estimating the Jewish use of Scripture wrongly. They never understood the mind of the Jews. For, in spite of a verbal theory of inspiration, so minute as to include each letter, by which anything that could possibly be got out of the Hebrew words and letters might well be of spiritual value, Jews never attributed to such Midrashic and Haggadic methods the force of proof in the strictest sense. Interpretations derived by Midrash and Haggada had, no doubt, their own benefit for devout souls, but could not possibly serve as proofs to establish any doctrine.

Christian writers, in their zeal for God and for the inspiration of His word, forgot this all-important fact, and expected Jews to receive Haggada as direct evidence for the truth of Christian doctrines which were "proved" by its means. They blamed the obstinate Jews for not accepting the evidence which seemed to them so strong. But, in reality, this was only because they themselves misconceived the case. A passage in the Old Testament may be a very valuable illustration, and may even bring out the principle underlying some important Christian truth, and yet be quite worthless if it is used as a definite proof in the usual and strict meaning of the term. Even to-day the distinction is not always clearly perceived. It is quite legitimate, and indeed desirable, to try to discover in the Old Testament latent principles which are fully exposed in the New, for so we are led to deeper meditation on the ways and words of God, and into closer touch with Him. But we may not, and must not, go further, and say either that the writers of the Old Testament themselves were consciously predicting the facts and doctrines of the New, or, at least, that God in inspiring them intended their words to constitute proof.

We cannot then refuse to give credit to the writers of these treatises for being, in the large majority of cases (though there are, alas, a few unworthy exceptions), devout and honest men, who, according to the knowledge of their day, earnestly desired to win Jews to accept the beauty and glory of the full Christian Faith.

INDICES

N.B. *These Indices are not intended to be complete. Only items of special importance or interest are included.*

I. GENERAL

Abel and Seth, meaning of names, 307

Abner of Burgos, 259

Adam, his skull at Golgotha, 157, 160

Adam, Apocalypse of, 21; *the Mystery of,* 321

Ad Quirinum, 56; summary, 57

Ad Vigilium episcopum (Celsus "Afer"), 64

Adversus Judaeos (Tertullian), 43; its relation to *Adv. Marc.* iii, 44; summary, 45

Adversus Judaeos (Ps.-Cyprian), 65

Adversus Quinque Haereses, etc. (Ps.-Augustine), 319

Against Jews, with reference to the Brazen Serpent (Ps.-Chrysostom), 140

Against the Jews (Stephen of Bostra), 167

Against Jews and Greeks and Heretics (Ps.-Chrysostom), 139

Against the Jews, concerning the Sabbath (St John of Damascus), 167

Agobard, 348; why hateful to Jews, 356

Alphabet, Jews say its letters are eternal, 351

Alphonso of Valladolid, *see* Abner of Burgos

Alphonso de Spina, 277

Altercatio Legis inter Simonem Judaeum et Theophilum Christianum (Evagrius), 298

Alvaro and Bodo, 224

"Ambrosiaster", 318

Amulo, 358

Amulonis Epistola, etc., 358

Anacephalosis (of Geronimo de Santa Fé), 265

"Anastasius", 175

Andronicus of Constantinople, 181

Anonymous Treatise against the Jews, An, 395

Another Enquiry (second addition to "Anastasius"), 179

Antichrist, born in Babylon of Dan, 280; of basilisks' eggs, 392; will be accepted at first by Jews, then rejected for Christ, 280

Antilogus contra Judaeos (Peter Damiani), 367

Aphrahat, 95

Apostasy from Christianity to Judaism, 224; a danger in Chrysostom's time, 132; by baptized Jews, 216; Bodo, 224; Leontius, 157

Aqiba, R., 396; his holiness foretold to Moses, 238; imprisoned because he had sold a Jew (i.e. Jesus), 239

Aquila's version, 128

Arian, An, writer against the Jews, 306

Ark, Jews have none now, 135

"Ark" in synagogue, 97

Asellinus, Bishop, Letter to (Augustine), 318

Atkinson, B. F. C., 178, 329

Atonement, Day of, perhaps on Friday, 23; not on Friday or Sunday, 239; satisfying the Devil, 378

Augustine, 312; urges love to the Jews, 317

Badge, 241

Baptism, sermon after midnight service in preparation for, 322

Baptisms, Jews think sins forgiven by baptisms in cold water, 405

Barachias, R., 413

Barcelona, Disputation at in 1263, 245

Barnabas, Epistle of, 14; author, 18; date, 17 *sq.*; does it use N.T.?, 15; no bitterness against the Jews, 19; non-biblical details in, 22–26; summary, 20 *sq.*

Old Testament, belongs to Christians more than to Jews, 313; Canon of, 72; predictions why not plainer?, 143, cf. 59; principles of interpretation, 63; sayings interpreted by later events, by Jews and Christians, 11, 108

"Odollami" explained, 221

Oral Law, the absurdities of, 250

Origen, 79; answers Celsus' *True Account*, 80; his mother of Jewish origin, 81; the most "modern" of the early writers, 90

Panther(a), 82, 156, 363

Papiscus and Philo, Dialogue of, 169; sources used, 171; two recensions of, 170; Longer Recension quotes the *Quaestio* freely, 171; used by "Anastasius", 171

Paradise, its nature, 197

Passover, not to be observed on Monday, Wednesday or Friday, 239

Paul of Burgos, Life, 267

Paulus Christiani, 244

Pearl, the, a picture of the Incarnation, 75; of Christ, 304

"*Perfidia*", 359, 400

Peter Alphonsi, 233

Peter of Blois, 400

Peter de Bruis, 385

Peter Damiani, 366

Peter the Venerable, of Cluny, 384

Pharez, Son of, *i.e.* Messiah, 274

Philo, 193, 203, 361, 371, 404

Philosopher, who?. 186; some philosophers recognised God, 165

Philosophy, 235

Pilate, The Letter of, 341, 404

Plato, *Timaeus*, 35 A, 36 B, 296

Pletho, 196

Pomegranate, a figure of the Church, 302

Porging, 354

Pork, 165 *sq.*, 179; = pig-like actions, 303

Poverty, the real test of Messiahship, 398

"Power", The, 119

Prayer, by a convert, 304

Prayer against Christians, Jews forbidden to use it, 260

Predictions of O.T., why not clearer?, 49, 143, 165, 173, 176, 179, 192

Prophets, Books of, brought from synagogue, 172

Prudentius, 209; knew Tertullian's *Adv. Judaeos*, 213

Pugio Fidei (Raymund Martini), its aim and method, 249; its history, 248; summary, 251

Quaestiones ad Antiochum ducem, 160; used by *Dialogue of Papiscus and Philo*, 162

Quotations, from unknown sources, 22, 25, 126, 301, 342; source doubtful, 54; wrongly assigned, 9, 34, 46, 285

Rabanus Maurus, 365

"R. Rachmon", 249, 273

Raymund de Peñaforte, 242

Raymund Lull, 256; his earlier and later attitudes to missions, 257 *sq.*; three books on Jews attributed to him, 256

Raymund Martini, 248; a Gentile, *ibid.*; called a Jewish Rabbi by Paul of Burgos, 273

Red Heifer, 24

Refutation of the errors of the Jews etc., A (Gennadius), 188

Resurrection of Christ, 88; of the body, 406

Revelation, development of, 387

Rhythm against the Jews on Palm Sunday (Ps.-Ephraim), 104

Roman Empire, Messiah to come while it is standing, 156

Sabbath, 46, 97, 154, 167, 272, 291, 303, 396

"*Sabbatum sabbatorum*", 303

Sacrifices, a concession to moral weakness, 164; appointed for a disobedient people, 371; not meant to be of heart only, 316

Samuel, R., The Letter of, 228

Sargis D'Aberga, 151; meaning of title, 153

Unicorn, figure of Christ, 397; horns of, 39
"*Ussum Hamizri*", 362

Veil, put over the Heptateuch, 226
Vergil, 4th Eclogue, 397, 406
Vicente Ferrer, 261
Virgin Birth, cf. Adam of virgin earth, 343

Waldensians, 7
Wisdom, 37, 60, 117 *sqq.*

Zacchaeus and Apollonius, Discussions of, 295
Zohar, material used by Peter Alphonsi, 235

II. HOLY SCRIPTURE AND OTHER EARLY LITERATURE

(a) OLD TESTAMENT

Gen. i. 1	29, 297, 300, 307, 395 *sq.*	Josh. v. 2	38, 291
i. 2	310	v. 15	62
i. 26	37, 119	2 Sam. vii. 4, 5, 12–14, 16	59
ii. 2	396	vii. 12	226
iii. 15	396	xii. 25	74
iii. 22	164	Job xl. 25 (Theod.)	54
xiv. 14	24	Ps. xix. 3 *sq.*	289
xvii. 5	98	xxii, title	362
xvii. 9	187	xxii. 16	368
xviii. 3	179	xxiv. 8	230
xix. 18	320	xxxiii. 6	119, 125
xxv. 23	328	xlv, title	313
xxxiv. 26	327	xlv. 16	137
xxxvii. 25	184	lvii, title	287
xxxviii. 12	221	lvii. 8	332
xlix. 6	50	lxviii. 26	186
xlix. 17	187	lxviii. 35	185
Ex. xvii. 12	62	lxix	53
xxiii. 21	218	lxxii. 1	236
xxv. 19	379	lxxii. 6–19	123
xxxii. 24	45	lxxii. 8	236
xxxiii. 1	22	lxxxii. 1	299
xxxiv. 14	111	lxxxii. 6	147
Num. xxiii. 19	63, 297	xc. 4	220
xxiii. 22	397	xcv. 8–11	178
Deut. iv. 2	107	xcvi. 2	315
iv. 26	145	xcvi. 10	287
x. 16 (Aquila)	128	xcvii. 4	177
xxi. 22 *sq.*	362	cx	37, 172
xxi. 23	39, 49, 225	cx. 1	27, 246
xxviii. 65 *sq.*	50, 123, 127, 177, 290, 331	civ. 29 *sq.*	130
		cvii. 20	110
xxx. 11–14	316	cxxxii. 17 *sq.*	308
xxxii. 32–34	304	Prov. i. 20	296
xxxii. 39	168	viii. 22	300
xxxiii. 13–17	39	viii. 22–36	37

(b) Apocrypha and Pseudepigrapha

(c) New Testament

(d) Rabbinic Literature

CAMBRIDGE: PRINTED BY WALTER LEWIS, M.A., AT THE UNIVERSITY PRESS